PRINCIPALS OF MODERN PSYCHOLOGICAL MEASUREMENT

A Festschrift for Frederic M. Lord

PRINCIPALS OF MODERN PSYCHOLOGICAL MEASUREMENT

A Festschrift for Frederic M. Lord

Edited by
Howard Wainer and Samuel Messick
Educational Testing Service

LEA LAWRENCE ERLBAUM ASSOCIATES, PUBLISHERS
1983 Hillsdale, New Jersey   London

Copyright © 1983 by Lawrence Erlbaum Associates, Inc.
All rights reserved. No part of this book may be reproduced in
any form, by photostat, microform, retrieval system, or any other
means, without the prior written permission of the publisher.

Lawrence Erlbaum Associates, Inc., Publishers
365 Broadway
Hillsdale, New Jersey 07642

Library of Congress Catalogue number   83-81933

ISBN 0-89859-277-1

Printed in the United States of America
10 9 8 7 6 5 4 3 2 1

to Fred

Contents

Preface — xiii

Frederic M. Lord: A Biographical Sketch
Howard Wainer — xv

Publications of Frederic M. Lord — xix

To Fred Lord: An Appreciation
William W. Turnbull — xxvii

PART I: STATISTICS AND ITS APPLICATIONS

1. **On Lord's Paradox**
   Paul W. Holland and Donald B. Rubin — 3
   Introduction   3
   A Model for Causal Inference   4
   Lord's Examples   9
   Discussion   18

2. **Predictive Bias as an Artifact of Selection Procedures**
   Robert L. Linn — 27
   The Model   28
   Implications for Bias Studies   33
   Empirical Results   35
   Modeling the Selection Process   37

3. **The Centrality of Lord's Paradox and Exchangeability for All Statistical Inference**
   Melvin R. Novick   41
   Frederic Lord, An Appreciation   41
   Lord's Paradox   42
   Simpson's Reversal Paradox   43
   Exchangeability   46
   Non-orthogonal Univariate and Multivariate Analysis of Variance and Covariance   47
   A Prevision for Behavioral Statistics (2012)   48

4. **Multiple Comparisons Through Orderly Partitions: The Maximum Subrange Procedure**
   Henry I. Braun and John W. Tukey   55
   Introduction   55
   More Complex Procedures   57
   The Maximum Subrange Procedure   58
   Simulations   60
   Conclusions   64
   Appendix   64

PART II: ITEM RESPONSE THEORY AND ITS APPLICATIONS

5. **The Promise of Tailored Tests**
   Bert F. Green   69
   Feasibility   70
   Efficiency   71
   Summary   79

6. **Ability Measures and Theories of Cognitive Development**
   John A. Keats   81
   The Process of Cognitive Development   82
   Formalizations of Cognitive Development   83
   Theoretical Comparisons of the Exponential and the Hyperbolic Forms of the Cognitive Growth Curve   89
   Relationships Between Parameters of Growth Curves and Traditional Measures   94
   Summary and Discussion   96

7. **The Discrete Bayesian**
   R. Darrell Bock **103**
   A Personal Linear Trend Model 104
   Estimation of Σ_ϵ, μ and Σ. 107
   More General Assumptions 108
   Marginal Maximum Likelihood Estimation
   of Σ_ϵ, μ, and Σ. 109
   Applications 111
   Conclusion 113

8. **A General Latent Structure Model for Contigency Table Data**
   Erling B. Andersen **117**
   Contigency Tables and Latent Structure Models 117
   A General Latent Structure Model 119
   Estimation of Item Parameters 123
   The Population Density of the Latent
   Parameter 125
   Check of the Category Weights 127
   Examples 129

9. **Notes on the Exponential Latency Model and an Empirical Application**
   Gerhard H. Fischer and Rupert Kisser **139**
   Parameterization of the Psychometric Model 140
   Consequences of the Sufficiency
   of the Total Time 142
   Parameter Estimation in the Exponential
   Latency Model 145
   A Simulation Study 147
   An Empirical Application of the LEM 152
   Discussion 155

10. **Some Methods and Approaches of Estimating the Operating Characteristics of Discrete Item Responses**
    Fumiko Samejima **159**
    Introduction 159
    Information Functions 161

x CONTENTS

    Asymptotic Normality of the Conditional
        Distribution of the Maximum Likelihood
        Estimate, Given Latent Trait   165
    Constant Standard Error of Estimation   167
    Normal Approximation Method   169
    Conditional Moments of Latent Trait, Given
        Its Maximum Likelihood Estimate   173
    Bivariate P.D.F. Approach   175
    Conditional P.D.F. Approach   177
    Discussion and Conclusions   180

PART III: FACTOR ANALYSIS

11. Factor Analysis as an Errors-in-Variables Model
Karl G. Jöreskog   **185**
    Introduction and Summary   185
    The Factor Analysis Model as an
        Errors-in-Variables Model   186
    The Instrumental Variables Estimator   188
    The Two-Stage Least Squares Estimator   189
    Least Squares and Maximum Likelihood
        Estimators   189
    Conclusion   195

12. Exploratory and Confirmatory Nonlinear Common Factor Analysis
Roderick P. McDonald   **197**
    Introduction   197
    General Theory   198
    Exploratory Methods   203
    Confirmatory Methods   206
    Conclusion   211

13. Searching for Structure in Binary Data
Ledyard R Tucker   **215**
    Item Characteristic Function Approaches   216
    Notes on Analysis Techniques   225

Examples of Data Generated With Two
  Common Factors   227
Summary and Discussion   232

14. **The Greatest Lower Bound to Reliability**
    Peter M. Bentler and J. Arthur Woodward   **237**
    Introduction   237
    The Greatest Lower Bound to
      Reliability   239
    Basic Theory   242
    Computational Methods   244
    Statistical Issues   246
    Examples   249

PART IV: OTHER MODELS FOR PSYCHOLOGICAL MEASUREMENT

15. **The Difficulty of a Test and Its Factor Composition Revisited**
    John B. Carroll   **257**
    Theoretical Development   259
    Application to the Seashore Sense of
      Pitch Test   268

16. **Evaluating Guttman Scales: Some Old and New Thoughts**
    Norman Cliff   **283**
    Consistency of Dichotomous Manifest Data   285
    Average Tau Coefficients   287
    Other Approaches   294
    Conclusion   299

17. **Some Problems in Estimating Response Time Distributions**
    Bruce Bloxom   **303**
    Discussion and Summary   322
    Appendix: Estimating Density Functions   323

18. **The Ideal Type Model**
    Warren S. Torgerson — 329
    Summary Comments on Ideal Type Structures   340

PART V: COMMENTS ON THE MEASUREMENT OF TRAITS

19. **Traits, States, and Situations: A Comprehensive View**
    Anne Anastasi — 345
    Traits and Situations   345
    Traits and States   348
    Trait Concepts Reexamined   351

20. **How Can We Practice What We Preach?**
    Robert L. Thorndike — 357

    Author Index — 365

    Subject Index — 371

Preface

With the approach of Frederic Lord's seventieth birthday November 12, 1982, Educational Testing Service decided in late 1981 that the time had come to honor Fred Lord formally and to celebrate his contributions to psychometrics and to ETS. Following time-honored custom, a Festschrift volume was planned so that a broad cross-section of Lord's colleagues in the field could join in the tribute.

In addition, a conference was organized at which the Festschrift papers could be presented to a still larger audience of well-wishers. The conference was conceived to serve two specific purposes: First, it would provide a festive occasion at which both ETS and the field of psychometrics could pay their respects to Lord; second, it would provide a hard and fast deadline for the contributors to this volume to complete their work. The idea of a party was irresistible and, with the caveat that it was more for the second reason than the first, ETS was pleased to provide the resources necessary to complete the project.

The ETS Invitational Conference Commemorating the Seventieth Birthday of Frederic M. Lord was held on May 21–23, 1982 at the Henry Chauncey Conference Center at Educational Testing Service, with attendees coming from as far away as Australia and South Africa. All but three of the papers in this Festschrift were presented at the ETS conference. The remaining three essays (by John B. Carroll, Karl Jöreskog, and Melvin Novick) would have been presented had not the authors been prevented from attending either by illness or distance.

The lion's share of the work involved in organizing and running the conference was done by Vera House, ably assisted by Dorothy Birch, Linda De-Lauro, and Kathy Fairall. Additionally, we are grateful to Elaine Guennel, Ruth Myernick, Ann Jungeblut, and Lawrence Erlbaum for their roles in completing the work on this volume. Special thanks go to Educational Testing Service and, in particular, to Ernest Anastasio, Gregory Anrig, Winton Manning, Robert Solomon, and William Turnbull for their personal enthusiasm and support for this enterprise. Finally, the editors wish to thank Fred Lord personally for his many generous contributions of time, example, insight, and wisdom to our own intellectual development.

Howard Wainer
Samuel Messick

Frederic M. Lord:
A Biographical Sketch

Howard Wainer
Educational Testing Service

Frederic Mather Lord was born on November 12, 1912, in Hanover, New Hampshire, where his father taught anatomy at the Dartmouth Medical School. He subsequently attended Dartmouth College, graduating with a degree in Sociology in 1936. Two years later he enrolled in graduate school at the University of Minnesota and was awarded a masters degree in Educational Psychology in 1943. In 1941 he joined the U.S. Civil Service Commission where his duties primarily involved writing test items. He worked under Marion Richardson; among his co-workers was B. J. Winer. At the end of this time (1944) he published his first three papers; one examined the effect on the reliability of a multiple-choice item of varying the number of response alternatives, the second was a nomograph to aid in calculating correlations, and the third was an applied paper reporting the results of a test given in Latin America. In 1944 he began his long association with what was to become the Educational Testing Service, first with the Graduate Record Office of the Carnegie Foundation, rising from the position of Research Assistant (1944) to Assistant Director (1946). In March of 1949 he joined the newly formed Educational Testing Service as the Head of Statistical Analysis (in the Test Programs Statistical Service Division). Eight months later he began his work in the Research Division, where he has remained until the present day. He is currently the Chairman of ETS's Psychometric Research Group with the rank of Distinguished Research Scientist. He has been a Visiting Professor at Princeton University (1959–1971), the University of Wisconsin (1963–1964), and the University of Pennsylvania (1969).

After joining ETS he began in earnest what was to be his life's work, the study of mental tests. Between 1949 and 1952 he published seven papers on a variety of topics ranging from the very applied (how to prepare profile charts on the IBM tabulator) to the theoretical. In 1951 he was awarded a Ph.D. in Psychology from Princeton University. His thesis, *A Theory of Test Scores,* was developed from work he began in 1941 on what is now called item response theory (IRT). This constitutes a new set of models, whose origins were found in Thurstone's work in the 20's as well as pieces by Lawley and Guttman in the 40's. The simple model that George Rasch developed in 1960 is a special case of this broad class of IRT models.

Lord's thesis was published as a *Psychometrika Monograph* in 1952, and in conjunction with Gulliksen's *Theory of Mental Tests,*[1] formed the basis of much of ETS's methodology for the subsequent 30 years. In those next 30 years he continued to work on problems, theoretical and applied, which surfaced during the operation of the world's largest independent testing organization. In 1968 he coauthored with M. R. Novick what chroniclers (Bock & Wood, 1971)[2] called "the signal event of the decade" in mental test theory, *Statistical Theories of Mental Test Scores.* This book reflected 16 years of research in mental test theory since the publication of Lord's 1952 monograph. In addition to putting the capstone on true score theory, it also provided an introduction to several rich new approaches to mental test theory. The book contained four chapters by Allan Birnbaum on "latent trait models," more recently renamed "Item Response Theory," which have formed the basis of much of Lord's work. Twelve years after *Statistical Theories of Mental Test Scores,* Lord published a detailed view of the theory and methods for using the IRT models in *Applications of Item Response Theory to Practical Testing Problems.* IRT, when appropriate, provides graceful answers to thorny questions, equating becomes a matter of test linking, standard errors are easy to determine, test updating can be done on samples of differing ability, and of great importance, comparable ability estimates can be obtained from individuals who take completely different tests. This last characteristic is of paramount importance as the theoretical underpinning of computerized adaptive testing.

In addition to the three important monographs, Lord has authored more than 100 other papers and chapters on a variety of topics allied to psychometrics. His treatise on the statistical analysis of football numbers has been reprinted often and is familiar to many students who are trying to understand the relationship of scale-type to allowable arithmetic operations. His 1967 paper on group comparisons introduced to the literature the puzzling "Lord's Paradox," which has only just been convincingly unraveled (see Holland and Rubin's chapter in this volume).

While these publications provide us with a full view of the psychometric research that Lord engaged in, they do not show the full extent of his involvement in the field and his position of leadership within it. He has served on the

---

[1] Gulliksen, H. (1950). *Theory of mental tests.* New York: Wiley.
[2] Bock, D. R. & Wood, R. (1971). Test Theory, *Annual Review of Psychology,* 193–224.

editorial council of the Psychometric Society continuously since 1953 and was the Chairman for 8 of those 30 years. For the past 10 years he has been serving on the editorial board of *Psychometrika*. He has been honored as a Fellow of the American Psychological Association, the American Statistical Association, and the Institute of Mathematical Statistics. He was elected President of the Division of Evaluation and Measurement of the American Psychological Association and the Psychometric Society.

Another of Lord's major contributions was as the driving force behind the formation and maintenance of the Psychometric Research Group at ETS. This group was kept vital through the continuous infusion of new ideas and people that Lord recruited. He convinced both Henry Chauncey and William Turnbull to provide the resources to bring talented scholars to ETS on either a temporary or long-term basis. Lord identified these scholars with uncanny accuracy through his careful scrutiny of the field. From Karl Jöreskog's preliminary work in factor analysis, Lord identified him as having great potential and brought him from Sweden to ETS as a visiting scholar and then as a staff member; Michael Browne came from South Africa; Erling Andersen from Denmark; Fumiko Samejima from Japan; Walter Kristof from Germany; and Melvin Novick from North Carolina. Among the others who were lured to spend time at ETS were: Murray Aitken, Allan Birnbaum, R. Darrell Bock, Leon Gleser, Robert Jennrich, John Keats, Michael Levine, Jon Kettenring, William Meredith, Roderick McDonald, Ingram Olkin, J. Philip Sutcliffe, and Joseph L. Zinnes.

These individuals, under Lord's quiet leadership, provided a critical mass of researchers who did much of the path-breaking research that began the explosion of results characterizing Psychometrics in the 1960s. This work and these individuals have provided an important core of the field until the present day.

Publications of Frederic M. Lord

Psychological testing theory. In S. Kotz & N. L. Johnson (Eds.), *Encyclopedia of statistical sciences.* New York: Wiley, in press.

The standard error of equipercentile equating. *Journal of Educational Statistics,* 1982, *7,* 165–174.

Standard error of an equating by item response theory. *Applied Psychological Measurement,* 1982, *6,* 463–472.

Item response theory and equating—A technical summary. In P. W. Holland & D. B. Rubin (Eds.), *Test equating.* New York: Academic Press, 1982, 141–148.

A prediction interval for a score on a parallel test form. *Educational and Psychological Measurement,* 1981, *41,* 359–364.

Applications of item response theory to practical testing problems. Hillsdale, N.J.: Lawrence Erlbaum Associates, 1980.

Some how and which for practical tailored testing. In L. J. Th. van der Kamp, W. F. Langerak, & D. N. M. de Gruijter (Eds.), *Psychometrics for educational debates.* New York: Wiley, 1980.

Small N justifies Rasch methods. In D. J. Weiss (Ed.), *Proceedings of the 1979 Computerized Adaptive Testing Conference.* Minneapolis, Minn.: Psychometric Methods Program, Department of Psychology, University of Minnesota, 1980. Also in W. J. Weiss (Ed.), *New horizons in testing: Latent trait test theory and computerized adaptive testing.* New York: Academic Press, in press.

A broad-range tailored test of verbal ability. *Applied Psychological Measurement,* 1977, *1,* 95–100.

A study of item bias, using item characteristic curve theory. In Y. H. Poortinga (Ed.), *Basic problems in cross-cultural psychology.* Amsterdam: Swets and Zeitlinger B. V., 1977.

Optimal number of choices per item—A comparison of four approaches. *Journal of Educational Measurement,* 1977, *14,* 33–38.

Practical applications of item characteristic curve theory. *Journal of Educational Measurement,* 1977, *14,* 117–138.

Some item analysis and test theory for a system of computer-assisted test construction for individualized instruction. *Applied Psychological Measurement,* 1977, *1,* 447–456.

Statistical problems in mental testing. In P. R. Krishnaiah (Ed.), *Applications in statistics.* New York: North-Holland, 1977.

Test theory and the public interest. In *Proceedings of the 1976 ETS Invitational Conference—Testing and the Public Interest.* Princeton, N.J.: Educational Testing Service, 1977.

An interval estimate for making statistical inferences about true scores. (with M. Stocking) *Psychometrika,* 1976, *41,* 79–87.

Some likelihood functions found in tailored testing. In C. L. Clark (Ed.), *Proceedings of the First Conference on Computerized Adaptive Testing.* Washington, D.C.: United States Civil Service Commission, 1976.

An empirical Bayes procedure for finding an interval estimate. (With N. Cressie) *Sankhya, Series B,* 1975, *37,* 1–9.

Automated hypothesis tests and standard errors for nonstandard problems. *The American Statistician,* 1975, *29,* 56–59.

Formula scoring and number-right scoring. *Journal of Educational Measurement,* 1975, *12,* 7–11.

Lord's paradox. In S. B. Anderson, S. Ball, R. T. Murphy, and Associates, *Encyclopedia of educational evaluation.* San Francisco: Jossey-Bass, 1975, 232–236.

Relative efficiency of number-right and formula scores. *British Journal of Mathematical and Statistical Psychology,* 1975, *28,* 46–50.

The 'ability' scale in item characteristic curve theory. *Psychometrika,* 1975, *40,* 205–217.

Estimation of latent ability and item parameters when there are omitted responses. *Psychometrika,* 1974, *39,* 247–264.

Individualized testing and item characteristic curve theory. In D. H. Krantz, R. C. Atkinson, R. D. Luce, and P. Suppes (Eds.), *Contemporary developments in mathematical psychology* (Vol. II). San Francisco: Freeman, 1974.

Quick estimates of the relative efficiency of two tests as a function of ability level. *Journal of Educational Measurement,* 1974, *11,* 247–254.

Significance test for a partial correlation corrected for attenuation. *Educational and Psychological Measurement,* 1974, *34,* 211–220.

The relative efficiency of two tests as a function of ability level. *Psychometrika,* 1974, *39,* 351–358.

Variance stabilizing transformation of the stepped-up reliability coefficient. *Journal of Educational Measurement,* 1974, *11,* 55–57.

Power scores estimated by item characteristic curves. *Educational and Psychological Measurement*, 1973, *33*, 219–224.

Testing if two measuring procedures measure the same dimension. *Psychological Bulletin*, 1973, *79*, 71–72.

A theoretical study of two-stage testing. *Psychometrika*, 1971, *36*, 227–242.

Comment on 'Statistical treatment of nominal numbers.' *Psychological Reports*, 1971, *29*, 372.

Efficiency of estimation when there is only one common factor. (with Marilyn S. Wingersky) *British Journal of Mathematical and Statistical Psychology*, 1971, *24*, 169–173.

Robbins–Monro procedures for tailored testing. *Educational and Psychological Measurement*, 1971, *31*, 3–31.

Tailored testing, an application of stochastic approximation. *Journal of the American Statistical Association*, 1971, *66*, 707–711.

The self-scoring flexilevel test. *Journal of Educational Measurement*, 1971, *8*, 147–151.

The theoretical study of the measurement effectiveness of flexilevel tests. *Educational and Psychological Measurement*, 1971, *31*, 805–813.

Binomial error models in mental testing. In G. P. Patil (Ed.), *Random counts in scientific work* (Vol. 2). *Random counts in biomedical and social sciences*. University Park, Pa.: The Pennsylvania State University Press, 1970.

Item characteristic curves estimated without knowledge of their mathematical form: A confrontation of Birnbaum's logistic model. *Psychometrika*, 1970, *35*, 43–50.

Problems arising from the unreliability of the measuring instrument. In P. H. Dubois & G. D. Mayo (Eds.), *Research strategies for evaluating training*. Chicago: Rand McNally, 1970.

Some test theory for tailored testing. In W. H. Holtzman (Ed.), *Computer-assisted instruction, testing, and guidance*. New York: Harper and Row, 1970.

A computer program for estimating true-score distributions and graduating observed-score distributions. (with M. S. Wingersky, D. M. Lees, and V. Lennon), *Educational and Psychological Measurement*, 1969, *29*, 689–692.

Estimating true-score distributions in psychological testing (An empirical Bayes estimation problem). *Psychometrika*, 1969, *34*, 259–299.

Statistical adjustments when comparing preexisting groups. *Psychological Bulletin*, 1969, *72*, 336–337.

An analysis of the Verbal Scholastic Aptitude Test using Birnbaum's three-parameter logistic model. *Educational and Psychological Measurement*, 1968, *28*, 989–1020.

Statistical theories of mental test scores. (with M. R. Novick), Reading, Mass.: Addison-Wesley, 1968, 1974.

A paradox in the interpretation of group comparisons. *Psychological Bulletin*, 1967, *68*, 304–305.
A note on the normal ogive or logistic curve in item analysis. *Psychometrika*, 1965, *30*, 371–372.
A strong true-score theory, with applications. *Psychometrika*, 1965, *30*, 239–270.
An empirical study of item-test regression. *Psychometrika*, 1965, *30*, 373–376.
An empirical comparison of the validity of certain formula-scores. *Journal of Educational Measurement*, 1964, *1*, 29–30.
Human judgments considered as fallible measures. In M. W. Shelly, II, & G. L. Bryan (Eds.), *Human judgments and optimality*. New York: Wiley, 1964.
Nominally and rigorously parallel test forms. *Psychometrika*, 1964, *29*, 335–345.
The effect of random guessing on test validity. *Educational and Psychological Measurement*, 1964, *24*, 745–747.
Biserial estimate of correlation. *Psychometrika*, 1963, *28*, 81–85.
Cutting scores and errors of measurement—A second case. *Educational and Psychological Measurement*, 1963, *23*, 63–68.
Elementary models for measuring change. In C. W. Harris (Ed.), *Problems in measuring change*. Madison: University of Wisconsin Press, 1963.
Formula scoring and validity. *Educational and Psychological Measurement*, 1963, *23*, 663–672.
A theoretical distribution for mental test scores. (with J. A. Keats), *Psychometrika*, 1962, *27*, 59–72.
Cutting scores and errors of measurement. *Psychometrika*, 1962, *27*, 19–30.
Estimating norms by item sampling. *Educational and Psychological Measurement*, 1962, *22*, 259–267. Reprinted in W. A. Mehrens & R. L. Ebel (Eds.), *Principles of educational and psychological measurement*. Chicago: Rand McNally, 1967.
Review of *Studies in item analysis and prediction* by Herbert Solomon (Ed.), *Psychometrika*, 1962, *27*, 207–213.
Test reliability: A correction. *Educational and Psychological Measurement*, 1962, *22*, 511–512.
A nomograph for computing partial correlation coefficients. (with R. W. Lees) *Journal of the American Statistical Association*, 1961, *56*, 995–997.
An empirical study of the normality and independence of errors of measurement in test scores. *Psychometrika*, 1960, *25*, 91–104.
Inferring the examinee's true score. In H. Gulliksen & S. Messick (Eds.), *Psychological scaling: Theory and applications*. New York: Wiley, 1960.
Large-sample covariance analysis when the control variable is fallible. *Journal of the American Statistical Association*, 1960, *55*, 307–321.
Use of true-score theory to predict moments of univariate and bivariate observed-score distributions. *Psychometrika*, 1960, *25*, 325–342.

An approach to mental test theory. *Psychometrika,* 1959, *24,* 283–302.
An index of the discriminating power of a test at different parts of the score range. (with R. Levine), *Educational and Psychological Measurement,* 1959, *19,* 497–503.
Inferences about true scores from parallel test forms. *Educational and Psychological Measurement,* 1959, *19,* 331–336.
Problems in mental test theory arising from errors of measurement. *Journal of the American Statistical Association,* 1959, *54,* 472–479. Reprinted in W. A. Mehrens & R. L. Ebel (Eds.), *Principles of educational and psychological measurement.* Chicago: Rand McNally, 1967.
Randomly parallel tests and Lyerly's assumption for the Kuder-Richardson formula (21). *Psychometrika,* 1959, *24,* 175–177.
Statistical inferences about true scores. *Psychometrika,* 1959, *24,* 1–17.
Test norms and sampling theory. *Journal of Experimental Education,* 1959, *27,* 247–263.
Tests of the same length do have the same standard error of measurement. *Educational and Psychological Measurement,* 1959, *19,* 233–239. Reprinted in D. A. Payne and R. F. McMorris (Eds.), *Educational and psychological measurement—Contributions to theory and practice.* Waltham, Mass.: Blaisdell, 1967.
The joint cumulants of true values and errors of measurement. *Annals of Mathematical Statistics,* 1959, *30,* 1000–1004.
Problems in mathematical education. (with H. S. Dyer and R. Kalin). Princeton, N.J.: Educational Testing Service, 1959.
An empirical study of the stability of a group mean in relation to the distribution of test items among students. (with M. C. Johnson) *Educational and Psychological Measurement,* 1958, *18,* 325–329.
Further problems in the measurement of growth. *Educational and Psychological Measurement,* 1958, *18,* 437–451. Reprinted in D. N. Jackson & S. Messick (Eds.), *Problems in human assessment.* New York: McGraw-Hill, 1967.
Some relations between Guttman's principal components of scale analysis and other psychometric theory. *Psychometrika,* 1958, *23,* 291–296.
The utilization of unreliable difference scores. *Journal of Educational Psychology,* 1958, *49,* 150–152.
A significance test for the hypothesis that two variables measure the same trait except for errors of measurement. *Psychometrika,* 1957, *22,* 207–220.
Do tests of the same length have the same standard errors of measurement? *Educational and Psychological Measurement,* 1957, *17,* 510–521. Reprinted in W. A. Mehrens & R. L. Ebel (Eds.), *Principles of educational and psychological measurement.* Chicago: Rand McNally, 1967.
A study of speed factors in tests and academic grades. *Psychometrika,* 1956, *21,* 31–50.
Sampling error due to choice of split-half reliability coefficients. *Journal of Experimental Education,* 1956, *24,* 245–249.

The measurement of growth. *Educational and Psychological Measurement*, 1956, *16*, 421–437.//
The most reliable composite with a specific true score. (with M. A. Woodbury), *British Journal of Statistical Psychology*, 1956, *9*, 21–28.
A survey of observed test-score distributions with respect to skewness and kurtosis. *Educational and Psychological Measurement*, 1955, *15*, 383–389.
Estimating test reliability. *Educational and Psychological Measurement*, 1955, *15*, 325–336.
Estimation of parameters from incomplete data. *Journal of the American Statistical Association*, 1955, *50*, 870–876.
Equating test scores: A maximum likelihood solution. *Psychometrika*, 1955, *20*, 193–200.
Nomograph for computing multiple correlation coefficients. *Journal of the American Statistical Association*, 1955, *50*, 1073–1077.
Sampling fluctuations resulting from the sampling of test items. *Psychometrika*, 1955, *20*, 1–22.
Some perspectives on 'The attenuation paradox in test theory.' *Psychological Bulletin*, 1955, *52*, 505–510.
Further comments on 'football numbers.' *American Psychologist*, 1954, *9*, 264–265. Reprinted in J. M. Vanderplas (Ed.), *Controversial issues in psychology*. Boston: Houghton Mifflin, 1966.
Problems and procedures in profile analysis. *Proceedings of the Invitational Conference on Testing Problems*. Princeton, N.J.: Educational Testing Service, 1954.
Scaling. *Review of Educational Research*, 1954, *24*, 357–392.
An application of confidence intervals and of maximum likelihood to the estimation of an examinee's ability. *Psychometrika*, 1953, *18*, 57–76.
On the statistical treatment of football numbers. *American Psychologist*, 1953, *8*, 750–751. Reprinted in R. O. Mason & E. B. Swanson (Eds.), *Measurement for management decision*. Reading, Mass.: Addison-Wesley, 1981. Also in G. M. Maranell (Ed.), *Scaling: A sourcebook for behavioral scientists*. Chicago: Aldine, 1974. Also in A. Haber, R. P. Runyon, & P. Badia (Eds.), *Readings in statistics*. Reading, Mass.: Addison-Wesley, 1970, 30–33. Also in J. M. Vanderplas (Ed.), *Controversial issues in psychology*. Boston: Houghton Mifflin, 1966.
Review of *Statistics in psychology and education* by H. E. Garrett. *Journal of the American Statistical Association*, 1953, *48*, 913–915.
The relation of test score to the trait underlying the test. *Educational and Psychological Measurement*, 1953, *13*, 517–549. Reprinted in P. F. Lazarsfeld and N. W. Henry (Eds.), *Readings in mathematical social sciences*. Chicago: Science Research Associates, 1966.
A theory of test scores. *Psychometric Monograph No. 7*. Psychometric Society, 1952.

Notes on a problem of multiple classification. *Psychometrika,* 1952, *17,* 297–304.

The relation of the reliability of multiple-choice tests to the distribution of item difficulties. *Psychometrika,* 1952, *17,* 181–194.

The Pre-Engineering Inventory as a predictor of success in engineering colleges. (with J. T. Cowles and M. Cynamon), *Journal of Applied Psychology,* 1950, *34,* 30–39.

Preparation of profile charts on the IBM tabulator. *Educational and Psychological Measurement,* 1949, *9,* 781–785.

A report on scholarship examinations given in Latin American countries for the selection of students to be trained in meteorology. (with A. V. Carlin), *Educational and Psychological Measurement,* 1944, *4,* 69–74.

Alignment chart for calculating the fourfold point correlation coefficient. *Psychometrika,* 1944, *9,* 41–42.

Reliability of multiple-choice tests as a function of number of choices per item. *Journal of Educational Psychology,* 1944, *35,* 175–180.

To Fred Lord:
An Appreciation

William W. Turnbull
Center for Advanced Study in the Behavioral Sciences, Stanford, Calif.
Educational Testing Service, Princeton, N.J.

Webster's Dictionary says that to celebrate is "to observe a notable occasion with festivities" and "to demonstrate satisfaction in (as an anniversary) by festivities or other deviations from routine; to hold up for public acclaim."

The events and discussions of the day have been anything but routine and tonight's banquet is indeed festive. What I have been invited to do tonight is, in effect, to render Fred Lord acutely uncomfortable by adding to that last bit of the definition of the word "celebrate"—holding him up for public acclaim. Causing Fred discomfort on an occasion in his honor seems grossly unjust. Maybe he will endure the ordeal with less embarrassment if I am brief and occasionally a bit irreverent.

I've known Fred since the mid-forties when he was involved in research and technical operations at the offices of the Graduate Record Examinations and the Cooperative Test Service in New York. When ETS was formed in 1948, Fred came to Princeton to work with Ledyard Tucker in Statistical Analysis while working on his doctorate with Harold Gulliksen at Princeton. That trio was quite a team, by the way; and having people like John Tukey and Sam Wilks in the wings made the early ETS an even livelier center of discussion.

After a year or so, Fred transferred to the Research Division where—to the great good fortune of many people—he has been ever since.

Research in education and in the social and behavioral sciences broadly has been a basic goal of ETS since its earliest days, and research in measurement theory has been a cornerstone of the research program. Although I am anything but an impartial observer, I like to believe that through its sustained commitment to research of high quality—which simply means commitment to people of extraordinary talent—ETS has made deep and lasting contributions to the quality of its own work and to the field. (End of commercial.)

Although many important research studies are of course not designed especially to advance measurement theory, an overarching belief has always been that *all* studies should be sound in the quantitative methods used. This respect for appropriate design and analytic techniques has been communicated instantly and insistently to newcomers to the ETS research enterprise, as well as to others of us, no longer freshly minted, who may be short on technical knowledge or simply charter members of the murky-minded majority.

Given this institutional imperative, people at ETS who *are* truly expert in quantitative methods have sometimes led a harried life. Their colleagues poach unmercifully on their time.

Now, to the outside observer it might well seem that Fred Lord must have been more than fully occupied over the last several decades in developing a sweepingly comprehensive general theory of latent traits and reformulating much of psychometrics. Let me point out that he has done those things despite the best efforts of many of us to distract him. But don't judge us too harshly. In the first place, for well over 30 years having Fred within hailing distance has been a remarkable resource for anybody at ETS who was wrestling with a problem in measurement theory. In the second place, Fred has a wonderful knack for turning naive questions into good ones and incorporating the answers neatly into the main body of his work, crediting the *questioner* with having had a shrewd insight.

Certainly I count myself as a prime beneficiary of Fred's willingness to untangle my thinking. For me, in fact, preparing this piece has been a great nostalgia trip through past perplexities revisited. As I've reviewed my own memory bank of conceptual skeins Fred has unsnarled for me and ideational traps he has carefully led me around, I have realized how much I have been the gainer. I suspect that my own memory chain in this regard could be paralleled or exceeded by many people here who have worked with Fred.

Usually when I have confronted Fred with a puzzle that I think is as complicated as Rubik's Cube, he has listened carefully and then solved it with humiliating speed—one twist of his mental wrist. Sometimes I have wished he would take a little longer and sometimes he has obliged. The best example that comes to mind relates to a theoretical base for tailored or adaptive testing. I can recall a conversation with Fred that must go back to the early 1950s in which I asked him if a good theoretical base had been developed for tailored testing. He said, "Not to my knowledge." Then he wrinkled his brow as he often does when a problem has got to him and added, "Let me think about it." Several years later—in the cafeteria line, I recall—he said, in effect, "I think I'm getting somewhere." That was about 1968. In the next year or so he set out in five articles published in 1970 and 1971 most of the basic theory that has guided the development of tailored testing through the seventies and embodied those principles in what he has called the flexilevel test. Subsequently he devised a further embodiment in his computer-based broad-range tailored test of verbal ability. That's what I call following through to dignify a naive question.

As a long-time Lord-watcher I have tried to analyze how he approaches the problems that people bring him—not the kind entailed in developing a whole new theory but the merely intricate kind having to do with questions that can be solved more or less on the spot if you happen to be or know Fred Lord. Essentially, he seems to proceed by asking just enough questions to allow him to pare away the erroneous and the extraneous. He is a practitioner par excellence of the technique of excluding false assumptions and blind alleys of deductive illogic until he has left a nugget of truth. You can almost see him shaving your fuzzy ideas with Occam's Razor.

Incidentally, for a man who is sparing in his verbal communications, Fred has a remarkably rich and clear body language, when his mind is in its processing mode. Not when he's in his input mode. While you are presenting your problem, Fred rivets his attention on you and what you want to say for as long as you want to keep on saying it. This he does without moving a muscle. But while he processes, he becomes silently expressive. A lifted eyebrow. Perhaps a smile and nod as if complimenting the problem on its complexity. Sometimes a shake of the head in apparent despair—or to shake away cobwebs of confusion with which the stated problem is festooned. Possibly standing for a while in his favorite pose of contemplation, which sometimes involves looking out a window while assuming his best problem-solving configuration—a stance in which he achieves, from the waist up, a backward slant of alarming proportions, as if he is keeping his head clear of the intellectual underbrush he sees before him while he fixes his gaze on the higher planes of logic. Then sitting down and producing the answer in a few sentences. It's quite a procedure.

Now I should tell you that there's some part of this recipe for instant insight that Fred is holding back, because I've tried going through every bit of the ritual as revealed to me over the years to no noticeable effect except an occipital lump from leaning over backward too far. I intend to take this up with Fred sometime.

With true scores and latent traits on his mind *and* with colleagues on his doorstep, *then* you might think that Fred would be more than fully occupied; but he has found time over the years to vary his regimen with other pursuits. Many people in this room have discovered that Fred is formidable not only behind his desk but also over the bridge table. Characteristically, once he got into the game he was drawn farther and farther into theory—but as a man with proper respect for data he arranged frequent empirical tests of his conceptual scheme over the years, with enough success that a good many years ago he attained the rank of Life Master, which is the highest rating awarded by the American Contract Bridge League. Mighty impressive to us old Whist players. I haven't dared confront Fred in the bridge arena for 20 years.

Perhaps fewer of you know of his greenhouse experiments with exotic flora—especially orchids and other tropical plants. A very early memory is of recuperating at home after a minor illness in the 1950s and receiving a marvelous Bird of Paradise plant which Fred had grown.

Fred is indeed a man of parts. Of course, as soon as a few people heard that I was to speak about him tonight, many of them came forward with their own contributions to the apocrypha. Some time I must ask Fred if it's true, for example, that as alleged by a friend he would like to do petit-point, "but only of Bavarian castles." Petit-point, sure, but Bavarian castles?

But back to psychometrics. Fred's theoretical work over the years has led directly or indirectly to a wide variety of applications at ETS and elsewhere that are of fundamental importance to present practice. Since the influence of basic ideas is pervasive, it would be impossible to trace the innumerable lines of influence that have in effect radiated outward from Fred and into procedures, often through second, third, and fourth parties who have added their own insights and refinements along the way. But some paths are clearer and more direct than others.

In the 1950s, Fred developed the techniques of cluster sampling that were applied at the time to the norming of SCAT and STEP and, because of their exceptional efficiency in producing better norms with fewer students, have been used broadly since that time. His method for deriving the standard error of measurement of a test directly from raw scores has similarly been a boon to practice.

Early in his career, Fred prepared a Research Bulletin laying out and explaining carefully virtually the whole à la carte menu of available equating methods—in effect, all the techniques we had used to that time and have used over the ensuing years. More recently, he has had a major hand in a massive re-examination of equating methods, nudging us toward the adoption of procedures built on Item Response Theory—procedures used now in one major program (the Test of English as a Foreign Language) and likely soon to be adopted in others.

Fred Lord is best known, of course, for his steady flow of basic contributions to the theoretical literature. His professional productivity over the years is legendary. His bibliography runs to some 140 titles, including, of course, many landmark entries. All of his articles are addressed to important topics and all make original contributions in a rigorous way. That is not to say they are devoid of humor. Russell Baker distinguishes between the serious, which deals honestly with genuine problems, in any style however humorous, and the solemn, which deals with any problem in stuffy style. Fred is serious by that definition but certainly not solemn. He has a little of Lewis Carroll in him and it comes out in subtle ways. I think of his much republished 1953 fable "On the statistical treatment of football numbers."[1] Recall this excerpt:

---

[1] *American Psychologist,* 1953, *8,* 750–751.

So, when the problem had been explained to him, the statistician chose not to use the elegant nonparametric methods of modern statistical analysis. Instead, he took the professor's list of the 100 quadrillion "football number," that had been put into the machine. He added them all together and divided by 100 quadrillion.

"The population mean," he said, "is 54.3."

"But these numbers are not cardinal numbers," the professor expostulated. "You can't add them."

"Oh, can't I?" said the statistician. "I just did. Furthermore, after squaring each number, adding the squares, and proceeding in the usual fashion, I find the population standard deviation to be exactly 16.0."

"But you can't multiply 'football numbers'," the professor wailed. "Why, they aren't even ordinal numbers, like test scores."

"The numbers don't know that," said the statistician. "Since the numbers don't remember where they came from, they always behave just the same way, regardless."

The professor gasped.

That little piece, I submit, is a direct lineal descendant of Alice's conversation with the Red Queen.

Fred's titles in fact sometimes exhibit a certain playfulness which creeps out despite his best efforts to keep it sternly under control—as in his "Some How and Which for Practical Tailored Testing."[2] Then there are sequences: for example, his article published in *Educational and Psychological Measurement* in 1957 entitled "Do Tests of the Same Length Have the Same Standard Error of Measurement?"[3] followed two years later in the same journal by one entitled, "Tests of the Same Length Do Have the Same Standard Error of Measurement." Some of the same zest shows up in his zippy name for a non-computer-based tailored testing system—"The Self-Scoring Flexilevel Test."[4] His pithy observations are treasured by his friends like Ben Schrader, who quotes Fred to the effect that "Equating is either impossible or unnecessary" and "If you can equate a less reliable test to a more reliable one, you don't need the latter." Fred is, in fact, simply a superb communicator. He puts even his most technically sophisticated ideas forward not only in mathematical form but also in verbal forms that are intuitively compelling. He is a good editor as well as a good writer. For example, he would never speak as I just did of verbal forms that are intuitively compelling: more likely he would say "clear prose." For me, Fred's writing has always had a directness and a laconic elegance that makes it look easy and even convinces me I understand it. Moreover, his writing convinces me that the logical progression of each article is inevitable and that I probably understood it all along if I had had the wit to realize it. The only people who can convey that impression are

---

[2]In L. J. Th. van der Kamp, W. F. Langerak, and D. N. M. de Gruijter (Eds.), *Psychometrics for Educational Debates*. New York: Wiley, 1980, pp. 189–205.

[3]*Educational and Psychological Measurement*, 1957, *17*, 510–521.

[4]*Journal of Educational Measurement*, 1971, *8*, 147–151.

excellent writers and/or con artists. In Fred's line of work, con artists don't last and he's been around for some time.

The heart of Fred Lord's contribution, of course, is neither in the admirable scope and quantity of his output nor in the felicity of his prose. Rather, it is in the power of his reconceptualization of much of test theory, a reconceptualization expanded and deepened over some 40 years. Fred's interest was engaged at least by the early forties when he was Principal Assistant in Personnel Research with the U. S. Civil Service Commission, spending part of his time writing test items. He wondered—fatefully, we now know—about the relationship between the characteristics of items in a test and the characteristics of the test as a whole.

There is, I think, a marvelous continuity in Fred's most basic contributions since those early years. His first recorded publication, in 1944, treated the "Reliability of Multiple-Choice Tests as a Function of the Number of Choices per Item."[5] In 1952 he put together his thinking on test items, reliability error, true scores, and underlying abilities in the comprehensive "A Theory of Test Scores."[6] And of course these themes have been brilliantly expanded since then in Fred's work, reaching encompassing scope in his *Statistical Theories of Mental Test Scores*[7] written with Mel Novick in 1968 and deepened in his *Applications of Item Response Theory to Practical Testing Problems*[8] which despite its title is an innovative and integrative formulation of theory as well as a guide to practice.

What is rare in any discipline is the emergence of an encompassing and unifying theory—the twist of the kaleidoscope of facts and hypotheses that shows a new ordering which carries explanatory power, provides a consistent framework for understanding. The disparate pieces fall into place, the relationships between elements are made evident. The appearance of such a new ordering based on an underlying logic is always a giant step in science, and that is what Fred's work gives us. He has provided and continues to deepen the foundations of a broad synthesizing structure. Much of existing theory is seen in new perspective to have built on special cases which can now be placed in broad logical context. As his work increases our understanding, it will set new research agendas and drive advances in practice for many years to come.

In 1958 James Thurber wrote to E. B. White: "We might as well face the truth that to researchers of the future, poking about among the ruins of time, we shall all be tiny glitters. But then, so are diamonds."

Fred Lord's glitter won't be tiny, and it will be special.

---

[5]*Journal of Educational Psychology*, 1944, *35*, 175–180.
[6]*Psychometric Monograph No. 7*, Psychometric Society, 1952.
[7]Addison-Wesley, Reading, Mass.
[8]Hillsdale, N.J.: Lawrence Erlbaum Associates, 1980.

STATISTICS AND ITS APPLICATIONS

In addition to his path-breaking work on mental test theory, Fred Lord has done a number of important papers on various aspects of statistical theory and practice. His fable about the statistical theory of football numbers has been reprinted many times (see Turnbull's *Appreciation* in this volume for more details of this). He has worked on various innovative methods for hypothesis testing in nonstandard situations; he has also clearly presented one very confusing problem—what has become known as *Lord's Paradox*.

Twenty-five years have elapsed since Lord first put forth his perplexing paradox. Since that time there have been a number of discussions of it attempting to unravel the mystery. **Paul Holland** and **Donald Rubin** here provide the first full solution; done from the perspective of a formal model for causal inference. Viewed in this way the apparent contradictions disappear, leaving behind a clear resolution of this problem, as well as pointing the way toward a general solution for many derivitive problems.

Robert Linn examines one important such problem in his paper on predictive bias. He points out that Lord's conclusion about what may and what may not be inferred in his cafeteria situation applies directly when one is trying to estimate the predictive validity of an admissions procedure.

Melvin Novick amplifies these remarks, drawing a parallel between Lord's and Simpson's paradoxes. He suggests that the implication of these paradoxes and the methods devised for resolving them will remain central to future work in statistical inference.

The last paper in this section, by **Henry Braun** and **John Tukey,** provides a new method for making inferences about the means of several sub-populations. They discuss the general problem of pair-wise comparisons and show the area of preference for their new maximum subrange procedure.

1 On Lord's Paradox

Paul W. Holland
Donald B. Rubin
Educational Testing Service

ABSTRACT

Lord's Paradox is analyzed in terms of a simple mathematical model for causal inference. The resolution of Lord's Paradox from this perspective has two aspects. First, the descriptive, non-causal conclusions of the two hypothetical statisticians are both correct. They appear contradictory only because they describe quite different aspects of the data. Second, the causal inferences of the statisticians are neither correct nor incorrect since they are based on different assumptions that our mathematical model makes explicit, but neither assumption can be tested using the data set that is described in the example. We identify these differing assumptions and show how each may be used to justify the differing causal conclusions of the two statisticians. In addition to analyzing the classic "diet" example which Lord used to introduce his paradox, we also examine three other examples that appear in the three papers where Lord discusses the paradox and related matters.

1. INTRODUCTION

Lord's Paradox first appeared in a short, two-page article (Lord, 1967) in *Psychological Bulletin*. This article presents a remarkable contrast between two statisticians who draw widely different conclusions from the same set of data. The culprit appears to be that the analysis of covariance cannot be counted on to make a proper allowance for uncontrolled preexisting differences between natural groups. Much to the dismay of the editor of *Psychological Bulletin*, Lord did not resolve his paradox. This fact increases the interest in the questions it raises. The impact of the paper has been an extensive analysis and criticism of the use of the analysis of covariance that still continues (e.g., Games, 1976; Lindley & Novick, 1981). Lord wrote two additional short pieces on the paradox—a second article in *Psychological Bulletin* (Lord, 1969) and an entry in the *Encyclopedia of Educational Evaluation* (Lord, 1973 in Anderson, Ball and Murphy, 1973, page 233). We base our discussions on these three articles by Lord.

Lord uses examples to illustrate his points, and there are four examples discussed in the three papers. Our approach differs from Lord's in that we first present a mathematical framework that is complex enough to accommodate what we regard to be the important features of the examples treated by Lord, and we then apply this framework to each of his examples. As will become evident, we believe that there are several different issues that arise in these examples, and we feel that our mathematical framework provides the structure for a precise analysis.

Our paper is organized as follows. In section 2 we describe the general mathematical framework or model for causal inference. In section 3 we apply this general framework to each of the examples appearing in Lord's three papers. Section 4 gives our general conclusions regarding the nature of Lord's Paradox. We include an Appendix which indicates various related results that follow from our model.

2. A MODEL FOR CAUSAL INFERENCE

In this section we describe our model for causal inference and derive the results from it that we need for the examples that Lord discussed. More technical consequences of the model are derived in the Appendix.

2.1 The Elements of the Model

The chief issue that is of concern in Lord's Paradox is the attribution of cause. Much has been written about causation but our point of departure is the analysis of causal effects given in Rubin (1974, 1977, 1978, 1980). However, it will be sufficient for our purposes to deal with a simplified, population-level, version of Rubin's model. We have used this simplified model elsewhere (Holland & Rubin, 1980) to analyze causal inference in retrospective, case-control studies often used in medical research.

Our model is similar to those used to describe many simple statistical problems. However, we are absolutely explicit about certain distinctions and elements that are usually left implicit in other discussions. We believe that it is impossible to give a coherent analysis of causal inference without being at least as explicit as we are here.

The basic elements of our model are:

1. A population of units, P
2. An "experimental manipulation," with levels t or c and its associated indicator variable, S
3. A subpopulation indicator variable, G
4. An outcome variable, Y
5. A concomitant variable, X

Each of these components to the model needs further specification and we do this in the next subsection. Figure 1.1 summarizes this framework.

2.2 Discussion of the Elements of the Model

The population P of units underlies the rest of the model. Typical examples of "units" are human subjects or rats or households or corn seeds. All *variables* are assumed to be functions that are defined on every unit in P. All probabilities, distributions and expected values are computed over P. A probability will mean nothing more nor less than a proportion of units in P. The expected value of a variable is merely its average value over all of P. Conditional expected values are subgroup averages where the subgroups are defined by the conditioning statement. In Fig. 1.1 there are N units in P.

The "experimental manipulation" is the focus of all causal inference in our model. It is important to realize that by using the term "experimental manipulation" we do not mean to limit our discussion to the activities within a controlled randomized laboratory study. We do mean to include any sort of well-defined experience to which each of the units in P *may or may not* be exposed. The key notion is the potential for exposing each unit to any one of the experimental

	S	G	Y_t	Y_c	X_t	X_c
1	t or c	1 or 2				
2						
.						
.						
.						
N						

Population P of Units

FIG. 1.1 A framework for causal inference.

conditions in the study. For causal inference, it is critical that each unit be *potentially exposable* to any one of the experimental conditions. As an example, the schooling a student receives is an experimental manipulation in our sense, whereas the student's race or gender is not.

For simplicity, in this chapter we assume that there are just two different experimental conditions or levels of treatment, denoted t (treatment) and c (control). We will let S be a variable that indicates the experimental condition to which each unit in P is exposed, that is, $S = t$ indicates the unit is exposed to t, while $S = c$ indicates exposure to c. In a controlled study, S is constructed by the experimenter. In an uncontrolled study S is determined to some extent by factors beyond the experimenter's control. In either case, the critical feature of the "experimental manipulation" is that the value of S for each unit could have been different.

We make the simplifying assumption that S is defined on all of P so that for each unit either $S = t$ or $S = c$. In two of the examples in section 3, S is a constant over P (i.e., there is only one treatment to which units are actually exposed). In one example, there is no S since there is no identified treatment. Our model is at the "population level" because we do not consider the inference problems associated with the sampling of units in P for study. The model described by Rubin (1974, 1977, 1978, 1980) deals with the added complexity of the sampling of units.

The term "independent variable" is often used to refer to a treatment indicator variable like S, but it is also applied more loosely to include an entirely different type of variable. In our model this second type of variable is the subpopulation indicator variable G. Evans and Anastasio (1968), among others, distinguish clearly between "genuine independent variables, treatments that can be manipulated" and "classifications or other variables which describe the intact groups." Lord is quite aware of the distinction and, in fact, describes his paradox as "a problem that arises in interpreting data on preexisting groups." He also refers to the impossibility of random assignment in the "comparison of the educational achievements of different racial groups." In our model we have two different variables, S and G, in order to represent both cases. The variable G indicates the subpopulation membership of each unit, such as race or gender of students, "varieties" of corn, and so forth. Unlike S, it is not possible for the value of G for each unit to have been other than what it is. For the purposes of this chapter, we have a single subpopulation indicator variable G which has only two possible values ($G = 1,2$) indicating, for example, male and female students, as shown in Fig. 1.1.

By the "outcome variable" Y, we mean to convey the usual notion of dependent or criterion variable, with one important extension. When there is an experimental manipulation, there are multiple versions of Y, one for each treatment condition. In our case, these are denoted by Y_t and Y_c. The interpretation of these two values of Y for a given unit is that Y_t is the value of Y that would be observed if the unit were exposed to t while Y_c is the value of Y that would be observed *on the same unit* if it were exposed to c. The basic notion that a treatment *influences* the dependent variable is formalized in the model by the two values, Y_t and Y_c. If t influences Y, then the effect of the experimental manipulation is to make the value Y_t different from the value Y_c for each unit. The null hypothesis of "no treatment effect" (in its strongest form) corresponds to $Y_t = Y_c$ for all units in P. In studies where there is no experimental manipulation, there is only one version of Y. In such cases, we do not put a subscript on Y, nor do we subscript Y when we are referring to it without reference to the treatment conditions.

Central to Lord's Paradox is the availability of a variable X that is auxiliary to the outcome variable Y. We will call X a *concomitant variable* to distinguish it from Y. However, in Lord's examples there are two distinct types of concomitant variables that arise—those that *are* and those that *are not* potentially influenced by the experimental manipulation. This state of affairs can be expressed as follows. Let X_t and X_c denote the value of X that would be observed if the unit were exposed to t or to c, respectively. If $X_t = X_c$ for all units, then X is not influenced by the treatment, and in this special case we shall call X a *covariate*. If $X_t \neq X_c$ for some units, then it is not a covariate, but we will still use the more general term *concomitant variable* to describe X in this case. By definition, the subpopulation indicator variable G is an example of a covariate. In real-life research designs, the question of whether or not $X_t = X_c$ can be quite serious and difficult to answer. Under the usual circumstances of educational research, pretests *are* covariates because they are recorded prior to the exposure of units to the treatment conditions, and they are, hence, not affected by exposure to one treatment or another.

2.3 Three Kinds of Studies

The primary purpose of our model is to allow an explicit description of the quantities that arise in three types of studies that we shall refer to as:

1. Descriptive studies
2. Uncontrolled causal studies
3. Controlled causal studies

Although this is an oversimplified categorization of research studies, we believe that it captures important distinctions that are germane to our analysis of Lord's Paradox.

A *descriptive study* has no experimental manipulation so that there is only one version of Y and X and no treatment indicator variable S.

Controlled and *uncontrolled causal studies* both have an experimental manipulation and differ only in the degree of control that the experimenter has over the treatment indicator, S. In a controlled causal study, the values of S are determined by the experimenter and can depend on numerous aspects of each unit, for example, subpopulation membership, values of covariates, but not on the value of Y_t or Y_c since the value of the outcome variable is observed after the values of S are determined by the experimenter. In an uncontrolled causal study the values of S are determined by factors that are beyond the experimenter's control. Of critical importance is the fact that, in a controlled causal study S can be *made* to be statistically independent of Y_c and Y_t whereas in an uncontrolled causal study this is not true. All of Lord's examples concern either descriptive studies or uncontrolled causal studies; these are the types of studies that commonly arise in the behavioral sciences and involve "preexisting groups."

2.4 Causal Effects and Related Quantities in Causal Studies

The *causal effect* of t on Y (relative to c) for each unit in P is given by the difference,[1] $Y_t - Y_c$. This is the amount that t has increased (or decreased) the value of Y (relative to c) on each unit. The expected value $E(Y_t - Y_c)$ is the average causal effect of t versus c on Y in P. Since the expected value of a difference is the difference in expected values, that is

$$E(Y_t - Y_c) = E(Y_t) - E(Y_c), \tag{2.1}$$

we see that the unconditional means of Y_t and Y_c over P have direct causal interpretations.

In a causal study, whether controlled or uncontrolled, the value of Y that is observed on each unit is Y_S, so that when $S = t$, Y_t is observed and when $S = c$, Y_c is observed. Hence the expected value of Y for the "treatment group" is the following conditional expectation:

$$\text{treatment group mean} = E(Y_t | S = t). \tag{2.2}$$

The mean of Y for the "control group" is

$$\text{control group mean} = E(Y_c | S = c). \tag{2.3}$$

In general, there is no reason why $E(Y_t)$ and $E(Y_t | S = t)$ should be equal. Similarly for $E(Y_c)$ and $E(Y_c | S = c)$. Hence, in general, neither $E(Y_t | S = t)$ nor $E(Y_c | S = c)$ has a direct causal interpretation.

However, $E(Y_t)$ and $E(Y_t | S = t)$ are always related through this basic equation:

$$E(Y_t) = E(Y_t | S = t) P(S = t) + E(Y_t | S = c) P(S = c). \tag{2.4}$$

---

[1] In a more general setting the definition of a causal effect at the unit level would not require that the subtraction, $Y_t - Y_c$, be meaningful. This is beyond the scope of this chapter but is discussed in Holland and Rubin (1980).

Similarly,

$$E(Y_c) = E(Y_c|S = c) P(S = c) + E(Y_c|S = t) P(S = t). \quad (2.5)$$

Note that equation (2.4) involves the average value of Y_t among those units exposed to c. Similarly, equation (2.5) involves the average value of Y_c among those units exposed to t. But, $E(Y_t|S = c)$ and its companion $E(Y_c|S = t)$ can never be *directly measured* except when Y_t and Y_c can *both* be observed on all units. This is the fundamental problem of causal inference. In the Appendix we show how experimental randomization resolves this problem by making (2.1) equal to the difference between (2.2) and (2.3).

3. LORD'S EXAMPLES

Lord uses four principal examples over the course of his discussion in Lord (1967, 1969, 1973). Each example is a fictitious research study that could describe a real-life investigation. Example 1 is usually referred to as Lord's Paradox. The other three examples amplify the issues that arise there. In this section, we analyze each example in terms of the model given in section 2.

3.1 Example 1: Two Subpopulations Receiving One Treatment

Lord's famous paradox is the centerpiece of both Lord (1967) and Lord (1973) and a variant of it is mentioned briefly in Lord (1969). It is introduced in Lord (1967) with this short paragraph:

> A large university is interested in investigating the effects on the students of the diet provided in the university dining halls and any sex differences in these effects. Various types of data are gathered. In particular, the weight of each student at the time of his arrival in September and his weight the following June are recorded. (p. 304)

There is no other information describing this hypothetical study in the three papers; but other information is given describing the observed data values. Nevertheless, from this short description we can identify all of the relevant elements of the model. Table 1.1 summarizes this identification.

The question mark (?) in Table 1.1 is due to the fact that although the dining hall diet is clearly the treatment, t, whose effect on student weight is sought by the study, there is no control diet, c, even hinted at in the three papers. In our model the influence of t on Y is always relative to some other condition c. The fact that, in this example, Y_c is vaguely defined and not observed directly plays a crucial role in our analysis of the paradox. It should be remembered that Y_c

TABLE 1.1
Identification of the Elements of the Model in Example 1

Study Design

P : The students at the university in the specified school year,
t : The dining hall diet,
c : ?
S : $S = t$ for all units.

Variables Measured

G : Student gender (1 = male, 2 = female),
X : The weight of a student in September.
Y : The weight of a student in June.

represents the weight in June of a student exposed to the control diet. Since no one is exposed to c, anyone analyzing the data will be forced to make untestable assumptions about the value of Y_c in order to obtain numerical answers to causal questions.

There is only one version of X in this example since it is measured in September, prior to the onset of the treatment; hence, X is a covariate. Finally, since all students are exposed to t and none to c we have $S = t$ for all students.

Lord frames his paradox in terms of the analyses of two hypothetical statisticians who come to quite different conclusions from the data in this example. The samples are all assumed to be large so that the focus is on the interpretation of the values of parameters that have been estimated with high precision. We shall summarize all statistical analyses in terms of the parameters that are estimated. The effect of the dining hall diet on a student's weight is given by the difference $Y_t - Y_c$, so that the average causal effect of the diet on student weight is the expected value of this difference. However, one of the features of this study is an expressed interest in ". . . any sex differences in these effects." Thus, the average causal effects for males and for females need to be separately estimated. The parameters of interest are the average causal effects for males and for females

$$\Delta_i = E(Y_t - Y_c | G = i), \quad i = 1, 2, \tag{3.1}$$

and the difference of average causal effects,

$$\Delta = \Delta_1 - \Delta_2. \tag{3.2}$$

In terms of the individual subpopulation averages, Δ may be expressed either as

$$\Delta = [E(Y_t | G = 1) - E(Y_c | G = 1)] - [E(Y_t | G = 2) - E(Y_c | G = 2)], \tag{3.3}$$

or as

$$\Delta = [E(Y_t|G = 1) - E(Y_t|G = 2)] - [E(Y_c|G = 1) - E(Y_c|G = 2)].$$
(3.4)

Equation (3.4) is especially useful in this example since it separates the observed Y_t from the unobserved Y_c.

Statistician 1 bases his conclusion about the effect of the diet on the difference between the distributions of Y_t and of X in each subpopulation—that is, males and females. In terms of the means of these distributions, the corresponding parameters are the average differences

$$D_i = E(Y_t - X|G = i), \quad i = 1,2. \tag{3.5}$$

The quantity D_i is the mean weight gain in subpopulation i. The difference of the gains is

$$D = D_1 - D_2. \tag{3.6}$$

From the description of the pattern of data values given by Lord in this example Statistician 1 *observes* that there are no differences between the beginning and ending weight distributions for either males or females. Thus the D_i in (3.5) are both zero. From this observation, Statistician 1 *concludes* that

> ... as far as these data are concerned, there is no evidence of any interesting effect of diet (or of anything else) on student weight. In particular, there is no evidence of any differential effect on the two sexes, since neither group shows any systematic change. (p. 305)

This causal inference is not true without making additional assumptions. The D_i in (3.5) are *not* average causal effect parameters. In drawing his conclusion, Statistician 1 is making an assumption about the numerical values of the unobserved variable Y_c. There are several possible assumptions he could make to justify his conclusion. One of the simplest is to assume that the response to the control diet, whatever it might be, is given by the student's weight in September, that is

$$Y_c = X. \tag{3.7}$$

Under this entirely untestable assumption, the D_i in (3.5) are equal to the average causal effects parameters Δ_i in (3.1).

In Lord (1969), Lord makes a brief reference that is related to the assumption (3.7). He refers to critics of Lord (1967) who suggest that "the obvious procedure to use" is the "gain score," $Y_t - X$. We would interpret such critics as attempting to obtain an estimate of the causal effect of the dining hall diet on each student by making assumption (3.7). Since assumption (3.7) cannot be tested with the available data, acceptance or criticism of it must be based on intuition and/or subject-matter experience.

Statistician 2 computes a covariance adjusted difference of the two subpopulation means. This corresponds to computing the following two conditional expectations (i.e., within-group regression functions):

$$E(Y_t|X, G = i), \quad i = 1,2. \tag{3.8}$$

The mean, conditional, weight gain in group i at X is

$$D_i(X) = E(Y_t - X|X, G = i), \quad i = 1,2. \tag{3.9}$$

The difference in these conditional weight gains at X is

$$D(X) = D_1(X) - D_2(X). \tag{3.10}$$

For simplicity, Lord assumes that the conditional expectations in (3.8) are both linear and parallel. Thus we can write

$$E(Y_t|X, G = i) = a_i + bX, \quad i = 1,2. \tag{3.11}$$

Hence, $D_i(X)$ simplifies to

$$D_i(X) = a_i + (b-1)X, \quad i = 1,2, \tag{3.12}$$

and $D(X)$ simplifies to

$$D(X) = a_1 - a_2. \tag{3.13}$$

Thus, $D(X)$ is independent of the value of X. Statistician 2 correctly interprets $D(X)$ as the average amount more that a male ($G = 1$) will weigh in June than will a female ($G = 2$) of equal initial weight, X. Although correct, this statement about $D(X)$ bears no direct relevance to the differential causal effect of the dining hall diet on the June weights of male and female students. This is because $D(X)$ in (3.10) is not directly related to the causal effect parameters Δ_1, Δ_2 and Δ given in (3.1) and (3.2).

However, under an untestable assumption that is akin to but different from (3.7), $D(X)$ equals Δ and consequently does measure the differential causal effect of interest. To see this we generalize the assumption (3.7) to

$$Y_c = \alpha + \beta X. \tag{3.14}$$

Assumption (3.14) asserts that a student's weight in June under the control diet, Y_c, is a deterministic linear function of the value of the student's weight in September, X. Furthermore, the same linear function applies to all students regardless of gender. The assumption of Statistician 1 is that of no weight change under the control diet: that is, $\alpha = 0$, $\beta = 1$. If Statistician 2 makes the alternative assumption that $\beta = b$ where b is the common slope of the two within-groups regression lines in (3.11), then he may interpret $D(X)$ in (3.10) as the difference in causal effects, Δ defined in (3.2). We omit the straightforward algebra that shows this. These results are summarized in Table 1.2:

TABLE 1.2
A Summary of Two Sets of Assumptions That Lead to the
Conclusion of Each Hypothetical Statistician in Lord's Paradox

	Statistician 1	Statistician 2
Testable Assumptions		$E(Y_t \mid X, G = i) = a_i + bX$
Untestable Assumptions	$\alpha = 0$ $\beta = 1$	$\beta = b$
Formula for Causal Effects Δ_i	$\Delta_i = E(Y_t - X \mid G = i)$	$\Delta_i = E(Y_t - \alpha - bX \mid G = i)$
Formula for Differential Causal Effect Δ	$\Delta = E(Y_t \mid G = 1)$ $- E(Y_t \mid G = 2)$ $- [E(X \mid G = 1)$ $- E(X \mid G = 2)]$ = difference in mean weight gains	$\Delta = E(Y_t \mid G = 1) - E(Y_t \mid G = 2)$ $- b[E(X \mid G = 1) - E(X \mid G = 2)]$ = covariance adjusted mean difference in June weights

Both assume $Y_c = \alpha + \beta X$ for all units in P.

We wish to emphasize that the assumptions that lead to the formulas used by the two statisticians in Table 1.2 are not the only ones, nor are they the most general ones. For example, Statistician 1 could make the weaker assumption that $E(Y_c \mid G = i) = E(X \mid G = i)$ instead of (3.7). Any assumption about Y_c *must be untestable* in this example and yet will lead to a formula for Δ. The plausibility of any particular assumption about Y_c must be argued from considerations external to the data, and in many cases particular assumptions may be perfectly reasonable. There are statements in Lord (1967) and Lord (1973) that suggest that Lord would be willing to accept the assumption that justifies Statistician 1 rather than the one that justifies Statistician 2. Our view is slightly different. To paraphrase Lord, there is no statistical procedure that can be counted on to make untestable assumptions that are correct. In the case of the diet example, neither assumption seems obviously appropriate.

In summary, we believe that the following views resolve Lord's Paradox. If both statisticians made only descriptive statements, they would both be correct. Statistician 1 makes the unconditional descriptive statement that the average weight gains for males and females are equal; Statistician 2 makes the conditional (on X) statement that for males and females of equal September weight, the males gain more than the females. In contrast, if the statisticians turned these descriptive statements into causal statements, neither would be correct or incorrect because untestable assumptions determine the correctness of the causal statements. These sets of assumptions are outlined in Table 1.2. In a sense then,

Statistician 1 is wrong because he makes a causal statement without specifying the assumption needed to make it true. Statistician 2 is more cautious, since he makes only a descriptive statement. However, unless he too makes further assumptions, his descriptive statement is completely irrelevant to the campus dietician's interest in the effect of the dining hall diet.

3.2 Example 2: A Descriptive Study

This example is given at the beginning of Lord (1969) as an illustration of a type of situation in which the analysis of covariance is often applied. Lord gives only the following discussion of Example 2.

> ... a group of underprivileged students is to be compared with a control group on freshman grade-point average (y). The underprivileged group has a considerably lower mean grade-point average than the control group. However, the underprivileged group started with a considerably lower mean aptitude score (x) than did the control group. Is the observed difference between groups on y attributable to initial differences on x? Or shall we conclude that the two groups achieve differently even after allowing for initial differences in measured aptitude? (p. 336)

In attempting to identify the various elements of the model of section 2 for this example we must decide whether this study is intended to be descriptive or causal. This decision hinges on the interpretation given to the "control group." "Underprivileged" refers to a vague mixture of social, nutritional, economic, and educational circumstances and sometimes even to racial differences. In some unusual circumstances, such as with twins separated shortly after birth, it can be reasonable to consider "underprivileged" as an experimental manipulation; in such cases, both the mean aptitude score X and the freshman grade-point average Y would be affected by exposure to this experimental manipulation, and both would be represented in our model by two versions, that is, X_t, X_c, Y_t, Y_c. Although it is conceptually possible to regard "control" and "underprivileged" as two levels of an experimental manipulation, in practice it is often unreasonable to do so since the exposure essentially begins at birth. Hence we shall interpret this example simply as a descriptive study in which there are two subpopulations (i.e., "underprivileged" and the "control group") being compared. Table 1.3 identifies the elements of the model with the interpretation of Example 2 as a descriptive study.

The concomitant variable X defines a subpopulation of P for each of its values, that is, the subpopulation of P for which $X = 75$. In terms of our model, it is not possible to ask if the value of Y for a unit would be different had the value of X for that unit been different. This fact renders meaningless the question of whether or not an observed difference between two groups on Y is attributable to differences in the values of X for the two groups. In order to attribute cause to the values of a variable (i.e., to estimate a causal effect in our model), it is necessary

TABLE 1.3
Identification of the Elements of the Model in Example 2

Study Design
P: The freshman class at the university in a given year.
Variables Measured
G: Underprivileged status (1 = underprivileged, 2 = control).
X: Score on an aptitude test taken prior to college entrance.
Y: Freshman grade-point average.

for these values to indicate the levels of a treatment. Hence, causal statements involving the influence of a concomitant variable on a dependent variable are generally not meaningful. However, there are useful descriptive parameters that can be estimated in this type of study. The mean difference between the grade-point average of students in the two subpopulations with the same value of X is given by the difference between the two regression functions

$$E(Y|G = 1, X) - E(Y|G = 2, X). \tag{3.15}$$

This difference may be useful for predictive purposes, but it cannot be given a causal interpretation in our model.

3.3 Example 3: Contemplating New Treatments

Lord gives this example in Lord (1969). His description is as follows:

> ... Suppose an agronomist is studying the yield of various varieties of corn. He plants 20 flower pots with seeds of a "black" variety and 20 more pots with seeds of a "white" variety. For simplicity of illustration, suppose that he treats all 40 plants equally for several months, after which he finds that the white variety has yielded considerably more marketable grain than the black variety. However, it is a fact that black variety plants average only 6 feet high at flowering time, whereas white variety plants average 7 feet. He now asks the question, would the black variety produce as much salable grain if conditions were adjusted so that it averaged 7 feet in height at flowering time? (p. 336)

Table 1.4 identifies the elements of the model in this example.

This example is like the first one in that only one level of the experimental manipulation occurs in the study. However, Lord is quite clear in this example as to the problems created by not having an explicitly defined alternative experimental condition. In fact, the question he raises in this example concerns the choice of t. In his words:

> In practice, the answer depends on what we do to secure black-variety plants averaging 7 feet in height. This could be done by destroying the shorter plants, by

TABLE 1.4
Identification of the Elements of the Model in Example 3

Study Design

    P: Corn seeds.
    t : ?
    c : The "standard" treatment applied by the agronomist.
    S: $S = c$ for all units.

Variables Measured

    G: Corn variety (1 = "black," 2 = "white").
    X: Height at flowering time.
    Y: Amount of marketable grain produced.

applying more fertilizer, or by stretching the plants at night while they are young, or by other means. *The answer depends on the means used.* (p. 337)

The role of the concomitant variable in this example is quite different from the previous ones. It is evident that the measured value of X will be affected by t since that would be the stated purpose of the treatment. Thus, there are two versions of X, X_t and X_c, and only X_c is measured in this study. Not only must one make untestable assumptions as to the value of Y_t, it is also necessary to make assumptions about the value of X_t. The parameter of interest in this example is the average causal effect on yield for the "black" variety, that is

$$E(Y_t - Y_c | G = 1) = E(Y_t | G = 1) - E(Y_c | G = 1). \qquad (3.16)$$

The value of $E(Y_c | G = 1)$ can be computed from the data, but the value of $E(Y_t | G = 1)$ is determined by whatever untestable assumptions we make.

Let $\mu_t(x)$ and $\mu_c(x)$ be defined by

$$\mu_t(x) = E(Y_t | G = 1, X_t = x) \qquad (3.17)$$

$$\mu_c(x) = E(Y_c | G = 1, X_c = x),$$

so that $\mu_t(x)$ is the regression of Y on X under treatment t for the "black" variety, and $\mu_c(x)$ is this regression under treatment c. To obtain an "analysis of covariance" solution we may assume that these two regression functions are equal, that is

$$\mu_t(x) = \mu_c(x). \qquad (3.18)$$

Let us also suppose that this regression is linear, that is

$$\mu_c(x) = a_c + b_c x. \qquad (3.19)$$

Assumption (3.18) is untestable, but assumption (3.19) can be tested with the data. We may then compute the unknown quantity in (3.16), $E(Y_t | G = 1)$, by the formula

$$E(Y_t|G = 1) = E(\mu_c(X_t)|G = 1) = a_c + b_c E(X_t|G = 1). \tag{3.20}$$

Since the mean of Y_c for $G = 1$ can be expressed as

$$E(Y_c|G = 1) = E(\mu_c(X_c)|G = 1) = a_c + b_c E(X_c|G = 1), \tag{3.21}$$

the average increase in yield for the "black" variety is:

$$E(Y_t - Y_c|G = 1) = b_c[E(X_t|G = 1) - E(X_c|G = 1)] \tag{3.22}$$

which is an "analysis of covariance" solution. However, we agree with Lord that the plausibility of the untestable assumption (3.18) depends on the choice of t. For example, it might be a plausible assumption if "additional fertilizer" is the new treatment, but "stretching the young plants at night" might only lengthen them with no corresponding change in yield or might kill them, and in either case (3.18) would not be appropriate.

3.4 Example 4: Two Explicit Treatments

Although the first three examples are intended to illustrate certain points and are not considered by Lord as indicative of real research studies, the final example, in Lord (1973), illustrates that "the paradox is not just an amusing statistical puzzle." Lord's statement of the example is as follows.

> ... consider the problem of evaluating federally funded special education programs. A group of disadvantaged children are pretested in September, then enrolled in a special program, and finally posttested in June. A control group of children are similarly pretested and posttested but not enrolled in the special program. Since the most disadvantaged children are selected for the special program, the control group ... will typically have higher pretest scores than the disadvantaged group. (p. 235)

This is the first of these examples in which *two* levels of an experimental manipulation are explicitly present. Table 1.5 identifies the elements of the model in this example.

Even though two treatments are explicitly defined, there is ambiguity as to how they are assigned and what the relationship between S and G is. The remark "Since the most disadvantaged children are selected for the special program" might be read as meaning that the selection of a unit into a treatment group is made on the basis of the pretest score, with the lower scoring children more likely to be enrolled in the special program. On the other hand, the description might be interpreted as implying that $S = G$ and that G indicates a classification of children into "disadvantaged" and "control", not determined by X. The differences between these two possibilities are of fundamental importance.

First, suppose that assignment to t or c was based on the value of X, and that the values of G are just labels determined by the covariate X. If the regressions of

TABLE 1.5
Identification of the Elements of the Model in Example 4

Study Design

P: The students in the specific schools in the given school year.
t: The special education program.
c: The standard educational program.
S: Treatment indicator.

Variables Measured

G: Disadvantaged indicator (1 = disadvantaged, 2 = control).
X: Pretest in September.
Y: Posttest in June.

Y_c and Y_t on X are linear and parallel, then, as we show in the Appendix, the usual covariance adjusted estimator estimates the causal effect, $E(Y_t - Y_c)$.

In contrast, suppose that $S = G$ and that there are two existing subpopulations indicated by G, and that G is not a function of X alone. Now S and G are completely confounded, so that in order to estimate the effect of t versus c on Y for each subpopulation, we must make assumptions about the values of Y_t and Y_c for the groups exposed to c and t respectively. These assumptions will be untestable and similar to those made in Example 1.

4. DISCUSSION

We believe that Lord touched upon a number of important issues in the examples that surround his paradox. The blind use of complicated statistical procedures, like the analysis of covariance, is doomed to lead to absurd conclusions. On the other hand, the analysis of covariance is a useful tool that can often render an apparently intractable problem manageable. We think that the value of the model described in section 2 is that it forces one to think carefully about the attribution of cause. Causal statements made in natural language are often vague and potentially misleading. The role of mathematics is to give precision to natural language statements, and we believe that this is an important aspect of our analysis of Lord's Paradox.

We believe that the appropriate way to resolve Lord's Paradox is to be absolutely explicit about the untestable assumptions that need to be made to draw causal inferences. These assumptions all involve the responses of units to a treatment to which they are unexposed and thereby turn observations about data (i.e., descriptive conclusions) into causal inferences. We only disagree with the tone of Lord's three articles that suggests the analysis of covariance cannot be trusted except under special experimental designs. We feel that our model shows that in most complex studies in which causal inferences are of concern, there are always both testable and untestable assumptions that must be made in order to draw causal conclusions. We believe that it is both scientifically necessary and pragmatically helpful to make these assumptions explicit.

The distinction between causal inference and descriptive inference is essential in many contexts, and this distinction is clarified by our framework. For example, questions such as "Is the new diet more effective for males or females?" are causal and imply a comparison of an outcome for the new diet with an outcome for the control diet. Similar sounding questions may not be causal and involve no attribution of cause. For example, "Who gained more under the new diet, males or females?" is not a causal question, but a purely descriptive one, and, as such, it can be answered without making the assumptions necessary for causal inferences. Descriptive questions differ from causal questions in that there is no implied comparison of the values of an outcome variable under different levels of an experimental manipulation.

As illustrated in the Appendix, the calculations required to answer descriptive questions may, in some cases, be identical to the calculations that are required to answer causal questions under specific assumptions. The scientific and practical interpretations of the results of the calculations are, however, dramatically different for descriptive and causal questions. The Appendix shows how experimental randomization can alleviate the problem of having to make untestable assumptions to draw causal inferences. This should not be interpreted as meaning that randomization is necessary for drawing causal inferences. In many cases, appropriate untestable assumptions will be well supported by intuition, theory, or past evidence. In such cases, we should not avoid drawing causal inferences and hide behind the cover of uninteresting descriptive statements. Rather we should make causal statements that explicate the underlying assumptions and justify them as well as possible.

Appendix: Randomization and Inference for Causal Effects

We now shall show how randomization and related topics can be brought into the model and how they allow causal inferences to be drawn using standard statistical methods.

A.1 The Completely Randomized Experiment

Randomization has a powerful effect and a special place in our model. In a completely randomized study, great effort is made to insure that S is statistically independent of all other variables in the study. In particular S is made to be independent of Y_t and Y_c. Hence we have

$$E(Y_t) = E(Y_t|S = t) = E(Y_t|S = c) \qquad (A.1)$$

and

$$E(Y_c) = E(Y_c|S = c) = E(Y_c|S = t). \quad (A.2)$$

The crucial consequence of randomization in our model is that it forces the equality of the average causal effect and the treatment-control-group mean difference:

$$E(Y_t - Y_c) = E(Y_t|S = t) - E(Y_c|S = c). \quad (A.3)$$

A.2 Causal Effects in Subpopulations

When subpopulations have been defined using G, it is natural to want to estimate a causal effect in each subpopulation. By analogy with equation (4.3), the average causal effect in subpopulation i is:

$$E(Y_t - Y_c|G = i) = E(Y_t|G = i) - E(Y_c|G = i). \quad (A.4)$$

Thus, the unconditional means of Y_t and Y_c for the units with $G = i$ have direct causal interpretations. However, the expected values of Y for treated and control units with $G = i$ is given by, in analogy with (2.2) and (2.3),

$$\text{treatment group mean for } G = i \text{ units} = E(Y_t|S = t, G = i) \quad (A.5)$$

and

$$\text{control group mean for } G = i \text{ units} = E(Y_c|S = c, G = i). \quad (A.6)$$

The quantities in (A.4) are related to the quantities in (A.5) and (A.6) by the following equations which are analogous to equations (2.4) and (2.5):

$$E(Y_t|G = i) = E(Y_t|S = t, G = i) P(S = t|G = i)$$
$$+ E(Y_t|S = c, G = i) P(S = c|G = i), \quad (A.7)$$

$$E(Y_c|G = i) = E(Y_c|S = c, G = i) P(S = c|G = i)$$
$$+ E(Y_c|S = t, G = i) P(S = t|G = i). \quad (A.8)$$

Note that equation (A.7) involves the mean of Y_t for units exposed to c with $G = i$ and equation (A.8) involves the mean of Y_c for units exposed to t with $G = i$, $i = 1,2$. But $E(Y_t|S = c, G = i)$ and $E(Y_c|S = t, G = i)$ can never be directly measured. As with causal effects in the population, randomization plays a special role when estimating causal effects in subpopulations.

A.3 Randomization Within Subpopulations

Suppose that within each subpopulation, S is independent of (Y_t, Y_c). This will hold, for example, in completely randomized experiments and in "randomized block" experiments, where different randomization rules might be used within each subpopulation. For example, when $G = 1$, the probability of being treated is .4 whereas when $G = 2$, the probability of being treated is .6. If S is conditionally independent of (Y_t, Y_c) given G, then

and $E(Y_t|G = i) = E(Y_t|S = t, G = i) = E(Y_t|S = c, G = i),$

$E(Y_c|G = i) = E(Y_c|S = c, G = i) = E(Y_c|S = t, G = i).$

Thus randomization within subpopulations forces the within subpopulation equality of the average causal effect and the treatment-control-group mean difference, that is

$E(Y_t - Y_c|G = i) = E(Y_t|S = t, G = i) - E(Y_c|S = c, G = i).$

A.4 Randomization Based on a Covariate

Suppose the concomitant X is a covariate so that $X = X_t = X_c$. When a covariate is observed before treatment conditions are selected, it can be used to select units into treatment conditions. For example, let X be a pretest, and suppose students with low scores of X are assigned with high probability to take a special educational program, those with middle scores are assigned with equal probability to the special and regular programs, and those with high scores are assigned with high probability to the regular program.

In such a situation, the randomization is a function of the observed value of X, and it follows that S and Y_1, Y_2 are conditionally independent given X. Hence,

$$E(Y_t|X) = E(Y_t|S = t, X) = E(Y_t|S = c, X) \tag{A.9}$$

and

$$E(Y_c|X) = E(Y_c|S = c, X) = E(Y_c|S = t, X). \tag{A.10}$$

The importance of equations (A.9) and (A.10) is that from the observed data (Y_S, S, X) we may estimate these regressions:

$E(Y_t|S = t, X)$ and $E(Y_c|S = c, X).$

From (A.9) and (A.10) it follows that these regressions equal $E(Y_t|X)$ and $E(Y_c|X)$, respectively. Now suppose that $E(Y_t|X)$ and $E(Y_c|X)$ are linear, say

$$E(Y_t|X) = \alpha_t + \beta_t X \tag{A.11}$$

and

$$E(Y_c|X) = \alpha_c + \beta_c X. \tag{A.12}$$

Then the least squares regression of Y_t on X for the treatment group units estimates equation (A.11), and the least squares regression of Y_c on X for the control group units estimates equation (A.12). Of course, there are other ways to estimate these conditional expectations when they are linear and more generally, when they are not (e.g., see Rubin, 1977).

Suppose that we have estimated $E(Y_t|X)$ and $E(Y_c|X)$; how can we estimate the average causal effect $E(Y_t - Y_c)$ in P? Let $P(X)$ represent the distribution of X in P. Then

$$E(Y_t - Y_c) = \sum_X [E(Y_t|X) - E(Y_c|X)]P(X). \tag{A.13}$$

That is, the average causal effect of t versus c on Y in P is simply the average value of the difference between the conditional expectations of Y_t and of Y_c at X, where the average over X is weighted to reflect the proportion of units at each value of X. If

$$E(Y_t|X) - E(Y_c|X) = K \text{ for all } X, \tag{A.14}$$

then the causal effect of t versus c is the same for all X, and equals the causal effect of t versus c in P. When (A.14) holds, the averaging in (A.13) is irrelevant. Assumption (A.14) (i.e., parallel regressions), when combined with the linearity assumptions (A.11) and (A.12), yields the model underlying the usual covariance adjusted estimator. That is, if

$$E(Y_t|X) = \alpha_t + \beta X$$

and

$$E(Y_c|X) = \alpha_c + \beta X$$

then

$$E(Y_t - Y_c) = \alpha_t - \alpha_c.$$

Thus, the standard analysis of covariance estimator is appropriate when (a) assignment into treatment group is based on X, and (b) the t and c regressions of Y on X are linear and parallel. Rubin (1977) discusses this case and more complicated ones.

A.5 Randomization Based on a Covariate Within Subpopulations

The argument of section A.4 can be extended to cases with subpopulations. An example of such a study would be an evaluation of the effects of a special diet ($S = t$) versus a normal diet ($S = c$) for males ($G = 1$) and females ($G = 2$), in which the probability of assignment to treatment depends on initial weight (X) with different assignment rules being used for males and females (e.g., for $X =$ weight in pounds, $P(S = 1|X, G = 1) = [1 + X/150]^{-1}$ and $P(S = 1|X, G = 2)$

$= [1 + X/120]^{-1})$. In such cases, S is conditionally independent of (Y_t, Y_c) given (G, X).

The entire argument of section A.4 can be applied separately to each subpopulation indicated by G. Having obtained estimates of the causal effect of t versus c in each subpopulation, these estimates can be averaged (weighted by the relative frequency of the subpopulation) to obtain an estimate for the entire population. Alternatively, the difference between the subpopulation estimates can be computed in order to estimate the differential causal effect of t versus c in the two subpopulations.

It is important to note that this comparison of the sizes of the causal effects relies on the assumption of the conditional independence of S and (Y_t, Y_c) given (X, G) and involves the comparison of Y_t and Y_c, only one of which can be observed on each unit; this assumption has been called "strongly ignorable treatment assignment" in Rosenbaum and Rubin (1983) and plays a central role in causal inference.

A.6 Descriptive Studies

Descriptive studies are different from causal studies in that there is no experimental manipulation involved and therefore there is only one version of Y. The treatment indicator is not even defined in this case. For example, suppose $G = 1$ for males, $G = 2$ for females, $Y =$ June weight in pounds and $X =$ previous September weight in pounds. One descriptive question is, "How much more do males weigh in June than do females?" The answer is given by the parameter:

$$E(Y|G = 1) - E(Y|G = 2).$$

Another descriptive question is, "How much more weight have males gained from September to June than have females?" It is answered by

$$E(Y - X|G = 1) - E(Y - X|G = 2)$$
$$= [E(Y|G = 1) - E(X|G = 1)] - [E(Y|G = 2) - E(X|G = 2)]$$
$$= [E(Y|G = 1) - E(Y|G = 2)] - [E(X|G = 1) - E(X|G = 2)].$$

More complicated questions can be formulated by conditioning on X. For example: "How much more do males with September weight X weigh in June than do females with the same September weight, X?" It is answered by

$$E(Y|G = 1, X) - E(Y|G = 2, X). \tag{A.15}$$

If the regressions of Y on X are linear and parallel in the subpopulations, that is

$$E(Y|G = i, X) = \alpha_i + \beta X, \ i = 1,2,$$

then (A.15) equals $\alpha_1 - \alpha_2$ for all X, which is estimated by the standard analysis of covariance estimator. It is critical to realize, however, that the analysis of covariance estimator in this case is answering a purely descriptive question and not a causal question.

If the regressions of Y on X are not parallel in the subpopulation, that is, if (A.15) is not constant for all X, then the answers to such descriptive questions as "How much more do males with September weight X weigh in June than do females with September weight X?" depend on the value of X. Sometimes, an average answer may be desired, and then the difference given by (A.15) will be averaged over the distribution of X in some standard population, say P:

$$\sum_X [E(Y|G = 1, X) - E(Y|G = 2, X)]P(X). \qquad (A.16)$$

Although (A.16) looks formally similar to (A.13), (A.13) is the answer to a causal question since it involves the comparison of Y_t and Y_c, whereas (A.16) is the answer to a descriptive question since it involves the comparison of the distribution of Y for two different values of G.

ACKNOWLEDGMENT

Prepared for the Festschrift in honor of Frederick M. Lord, May 22–23, 1982. The preparation of this paper was supported in part by the Program Statistics Research Project, Educational Testing Service, Princeton, N.J.

REFERENCES

Anderson, S. B., Ball, S. and Murphy, R. T. *Encyclopedia of Educational Evaluation*. San Francisco, Calif.: Jossey-Bass, 1973.

Evans, S. H., & Anastasio, E. J. Misuse of analysis of covariance when treatment effect and covariate are confounded. *Psychological Bulletin*, 1968, *69*, 225–234.

Games, P. A. Limitations of analysis of covariance on intact group quasi-experimental designs. *Journal of Experimental Education*, 1976, *44*, 51–54.

Holland, P. W., & Rubin, D. B. *Causal inference in case-control studies*. Jerome Cornfield Memorial Lecture, American Statistical Association Meetings, Houston, August, 1980.

Lindley, D. V., & Novick, M. R. The role of exchangeability in inference. *Annals of Statistics*, 1981, *9*, 45–58.

Lord, F. M. A paradox in the interpretation of group comparisons. *Psychological Bulletin*, 1967, *68*, 304–305.

Lord, F. M. Statistical adjustments when comparing preexisting groups. *Psychological Bulletin*, 1969, *72*, 336–337.

Lord, F. M. Lord's Paradox. In S. B. Anderson et al. *Encyclopedia of Educational Evaluation*. San Francisco, Calif.: Jossey-Bass, 1973.

Rosenbaum, P. R. & Rubin, D. B. The central role of the propensity score in observational studies. *Biometrika*, 1983.

Rubin, D. B. Estimating causal effects of treatments in randomized and non-randomized studies. *Journal of Educational Psychology*, 1974, *66*, 688–701.

Rubin, D. B. Assignment to treatment group on the basis of a covariate. *Journal of Educational Statistics*, 1977, *2*, 1–26.
Rubin, D. B. Bayesian inference for causal effects: The role of randomization. *The Annals of Statistics*, 1978, *7*, 34–58.
Rubin, D. B. Discussion of "Randomization analysis of experimental data in the Fisher randomization test," by Basu. *Journal of the American Statistical Association*, 1980, *75*, 591–593.

2 Predictive Bias as an Artifact of Selection Procedures

Robert L. Linn
University of Illinois at Urbana-Champaign

Studies of predictive validity of necessity are usually conducted in selected samples. As a consequence, validity coefficients often suffer from a substantial negative bias, and the influence of selection on correlation coefficients is widely recognized. Procedures due to Pearson (1903) for adjusting correlation coefficients for selection effects are also quite familiar. There is debate about the advisability of making the adjustments because of concern about the underlying linearity and homoscedasticity assumptions. Lord and Novick (1968), for example, concluded that caution was needed in the use of these formulas "in any applications in which the ratio of standard deviations in the unselected group to standard deviations in the selected group is more than 1.40" (p. 147). Unfortunately, many selection situations yield ratios of standard deviations much larger than this and hence the advisability of making the adjustments would be questioned using Lord and Novick's rule-of-thumb. There is little question, however, that a correlation in a highly selected sample is apt to give an unduly pessimistic indication of the predictive validity of a measure when used with an unselected group.

Of course, a correlation coefficient is a rather limited summary of the results of a predictive validity study in the first place. Regression equations, standard errors of prediction, and expectancy tables provide more valuable information for many purposes. The fact that regression equations and expectancy tables are obtained for selected samples but applied to unselected groups is generally ignored. The results are treated as if they were sample free.

If selection takes place solely on the basis of the predictor variable of interest, then it is quite reasonable to use the resulting regression equation without adjustment for selection effects. Although selection can be expected to result in less stable estimates, the selection does not bias the estimates provided the regression is linear. This is, no doubt, a major reason that selection effects are seldom considered in using regression equations and expectancy tables resulting from predictive validity studies.

Selection solely on the basis of a predictor, such as a test, however, is the exception rather than the rule. Indeed, such selection is not consistent with recommended practice. Nor is selection usually limited to several variables that are readily quantified. According to Evans (1977), for example, in addition to undergraduate grade-point averages and test scores, law schools take into account many other factors such as "quality of undergraduate institution, major field, explanations of discrepancies in the records, graduate study, work experience, extracurricular activities, significant achievements, letters of recommendation, residence, and personal statements filed by applicants" (p. 579). Selection effects are further complicated by individual decisions. That is, self-selection as well as institutional selection influences the nature of the sample available for a validity study. Finally, there is attrition from the sample that occurs after selection. Students, for example, who enroll but do not complete a semester are excluded from analyses involving first-semester grades.

Although the conclusion is hardly new, the effects of selection can result in biased and inconsistent estimates of regression parameters. As noted by Muthen and Jöreskog (in press), for example, "selectivity problems have been of considerable interest in recent economic work" (p. 1 of typescript). A number of expositions of work in economics are now available (see, for example, Berk, Ray, & Cooley, 1982; Goldberger, 1981; Heckman, 1979; Muthen & Jöreskog, in press; Olsen, 1980). This work is yet to have an impact, however, on applied test validation work or on investigations of predictive bias. It is in the latter contexts that this chapter will address the selectivity bias problem and methods for dealing with the problem.

THE MODEL

For simplicity, much of the discussion will focus on a single predictor variable, X, and a single criterion measure, Y. Generalizations to multiple predictors are straightforward, however. A linear regression of Y on X is assumed for the unselected population, that is,

$$y = \beta_0 + \beta_1 x + e, \tag{1}$$

and e is uncorrelated with x. Scores on x are assumed to be available for a random sample from the population. But, scores on y are available only for a nonrandomly selected sample. Selection is assumed to take place on the basis of a third variable, u, which typically is unobserved. The regression of u on x is given by

2. PREDICTIVE BIAS AS AN ARTIFACT OF SELECTION PROCEDURES

$$u = \alpha_0 + \alpha_1 x + d. \tag{2}$$

Following Muthen and Jöreskog (in press) and others except for some changes in notation, it is assumed that in the unselected population the joint distribution of e and d is independent of x with means of zero. For convenience, the variance of d is assumed to equal 1. The covariance between d and e is denoted by γ, and since the variance of d is 1, γ is also the slope of the regression of e on d, which is given by

$$e = \gamma d + c, \tag{3}$$

where c is uncorrelated with d. It follows that the variance of e is $\gamma^2 + \sigma_c^2$ where σ_c^2 is the variance of c.

Linear Regression in Selectable Population

Units are considered selectable if u is greater than zero. The linear regression of y on x for the selectable units is given by

$$y = \beta_0^* + \beta_1^* x + e^*. \tag{4}$$

If β_0^* and β_1^* are obtained from the usual normal equations, they will not, in general, equal β_0 and β_1. For example,

$$\beta_1 = \rho xy \frac{\sigma_y}{\sigma_x},$$

whereas

$$\beta_1^* = \frac{\rho_{xy} - w\rho_{ux}\rho_{uy}}{1 - w\rho_{ux}^2} \frac{\sigma_y}{\sigma_x}, \tag{5}$$

where ρ's and σ's represent correlations and standard deviations in the unselected population and

$$w = 1 - \frac{\sigma_u^{*2}}{\sigma_u^2},$$

where σ_u^{*2} is the variance of u for the selectable population.

There are two special cases where $\beta_1^* = \beta_1$. These are: (1) the correlation between u and x is .0 or (2) the partial regression weight of y on u given x is zero. More simply in terms of equations (2) and (3) $\beta_1^* = \beta_1$ when $\gamma = 0$, that is, d and e are uncorrelated. The first special case cannot be expected to hold in practice.

The second special case in essence would require that deviations from selection strictly on the basis of x contribute nothing to the prediction of y. For example, d might simply be random deviations independent of x and y. It seems much more likely that the unmeasured variables contributing to selection have some relationship with the criterion. And it seems especially likely that the students who drop out of school or the employees who terminate prior to the collection of criterion data would contribute to a nonzero relationship between d and y, or in other words, cause γ to be nonzero. Thus, unless $\rho ux = 1.0$, the second special case is not apt to hold in practice.

In practical selection situations, the regression of y on x will generally have a flatter slope and higher intercept in the selectable population than in the unselected population. The flatter slope will be produced whenever

$$\rho_{uy} > \rho_{ux} \rho_{xy},$$

assuming that the correlations are all positive. The correlation between u and x will often be quite high, say .9 or even higher, because x is a major determiner of selection, but it is still less than 1.0. Thus the above inequality will hold even if the correlations of u with y and of x with y are equal. Often the unobserved part of u may increase the correlation.

The reduced slope and higher intercept have implications for the use of regression results with applicants. These changes in the regression equation also have implications for studies of predictive bias. Before exploring these implications, however, the effects of selection on the conditional means and variances of y will be briefly reviewed.

Conditional Means and Variances

The regression in the unselected population is assumed to be linear and homoscedastic. However, selection on u will produce a regression of y on x that is nonlinear and heteroscedastic whenever the covariance between d and e is nonzero. Given the usual normality assumptions, that is, that e and d have a bivariate normal distribution independent of x, Muthen and Jöreskog (in press) show that the conditional means and variances of y given x in the selectable population are

$$E^* (y|x) = \beta_0 + \beta_1 x + \gamma f(\lambda), \tag{6}$$

and

$$Var^* (y|x) = \sigma_e^2 - \gamma^2 f(\lambda) [\lambda + f(\gamma)], \tag{7}$$

where $\lambda = \alpha_0 + \alpha_1 x$ and $f(\lambda)$ is the ratio of the density function to the cumulative distribution function.

A simple example may help clarify the nature of the effect that may reasonably be expected in a typical practical selection situation. Parameters in an unselected population are presented in Table 2.1 for a hypothetical example. As can be seen, the correlation between the test, x, and the criterion y is set at a reasonable level of about .5. It is assumed that selection takes place on a highly related variable u (correlation of u and x equals .89) which is a somewhat better predictor of y than x is (correlation of u and y equals .56).

2. PREDICTIVE BIAS AS AN ARTIFACT OF SELECTION PROCEDURES

TABLE 2.1
Parameters for a Hypothetical Example Illustrating the Effects of Selection on Validity Study Results

	Unselected Population				
Regressions:	$y = .6x + e$				
	$u = 2x + d$				
	$e = .3d + c$				
Distributions:	x, d & c, independent $N(0, 1)$				

		Standard	Intercorrelations		
Variable	Mean	Deviation	u	x	y
u	.0	2.236	1.0		
x	.0	1.000	.894	1.0	
y	.0	1.204	.557	.498	1.0

	Selectable Population ($u > 0$)				
Regression:	$y = .219 + .4438x + e^*$				

			Intercorrelations		
Variable	Mean	Deviation	u	x	y
u	1.784	1.348	1.0		
x	.714	.701	.770	1.0	
y	.535	1.079	.375	.289	1.0

The selectable population is limited to persons with u greater than zero. The resulting means, standard deviations, correlations and regression of y on x are given at the bottom of Table 2.1. In practice, of course, only the parameters for x and y would be estimated since u is unobserved. Compared to the unselected population, the regression in the selectable population has a flatter slope (.44 vs. .6) and a higher intercept (.22 vs. 0).

Plots of the linear regressions for the unselected and selected populations defined by this hypothetical example are shown in Fig. 2.1. Also shown in Fig. 2.1 is a plot of the conditional means of y given x for the selectable population. The plot is shown for x scores within two standard deviations of the mean for the selectable population. As can be seen, the regression equation for the selectable population yields higher predicted scores than the equation for the unselected population for x scores of about 1.4 or below. That is, the predicted scores based on the selectable population tend to be too high when used with an unselected population for all but very high predictor scores.

Compared to the conditional means, the selectable population linear regression is too high for x scores near the mean and too low for x scores that deviate from the mean by more than roughly a standard deviation. The discrepancies between the conditional means for the selectable and the unselected populations

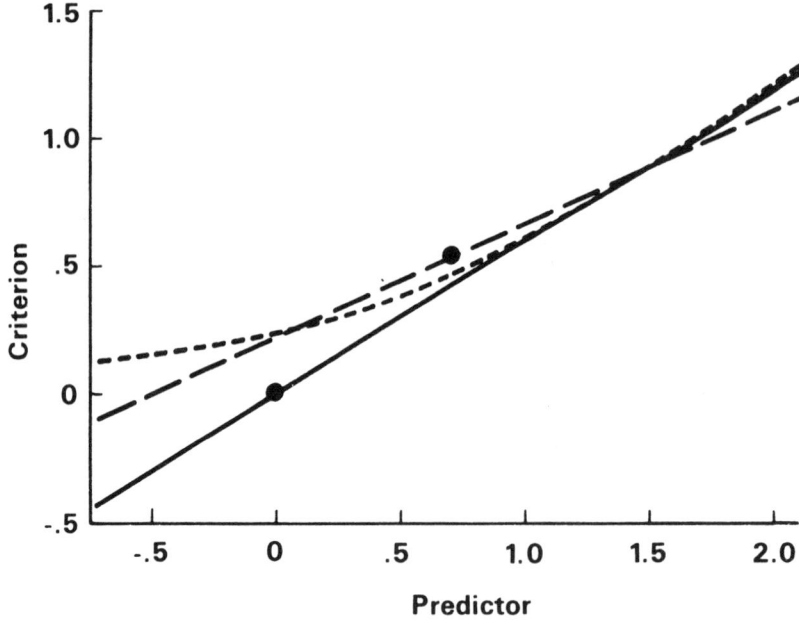

Legend:
——— linear regression in unselected population
— — linear regression in selectable population
- - - - - conditional means in selectable population
● population means

FIG. 2.1 Linear regressions in unselected and selectable populations and conditional means in selectable population.

are less than those illustrated by Muthen and Jöreskog (in press) because the magnitude of γ in the present hypothetical example is more modest than the ones that they used. The discrepancies in Fig. 2.1 are still quite substantial, especially for low predictor scores.

The variation in the conditional variance of y for different values of x is not very large for values of x that are apt to be encountered in the present hypothetical example. For x values of -2 to $+2$, the conditional variance of y given x ranges from 1.01 to 1.09. As can be seen in equation (8) this modest range of values of conditional variance is the consequence of the small value of γ. Larger values of γ such as Muthen and Jöreskog used, obviously yield quite a different picture. Within the context of predictive validity studies, however, values of γ that are much larger than the one in the hypothetical example seem unlikely.

IMPLICATIONS FOR BIAS STUDIES

Implications of the effects of selection illustrated in Fig. 2.1 are especially important for studies of predictive bias. The common approach to investigating the possibility that a test yields biased predictions for members of a minority group is to compare the minority and majority group regression equations. Numerous studies of this kind have been conducted within the last 15 years in undergraduate colleges, in graduate and professional schools, and in military and civilian employment settings (see, for example, Breland, 1978; Linn, 1982; Reynolds, in press, for reviews of that work). The most common result of predictive bias studies which have compared equations for blacks and whites is that the equation for whites tends to overpredict the actual criterion performance of blacks.

The overprediction result runs contrary to a commonly held expectation that tests are unfair to certain minority groups in the sense that they give a misleadingly low indication of the likely performance on the job or in school. The overprediction finding suggests that, if anything, just the opposite is true. The interpretation of the overprediction result is problematic, however. Difficulties in interpreting comparative results for preexisting groups were discussed by Lord (1967, 1969). He concluded that "with the data usually available for such studies, there simply is no logical or statistical procedure that can be counted on to make proper allowances for uncontrolled preexisting differences between groups" (1967, p. 305). While Lord's focus was on comparing treatment effects, his conclusion has relevance for studies of predictive bias. As shown by Linn and Werts (1971) and Reilly (1973), the direction and amount of the apparent bias in prediction can change as the result of inclusion or exclusion of a second predictor variable in the regression equations.

Interpretation of the results of predictive bias are further complicated by selection effects. The study results are, of course, based on selected samples. It is quite possible that the overprediction finding is an artifact of the selection process (Cronbach & Schaeffer, 1981; Linn, in press). That is, even if the unselected majority group prediction equation yielded predictions that were too low for the unselected group members, the process of selection could produce just the opposite finding when predictive bias is investigated in the selected groups.

The results in Fig. 2.1 can be used to illustrate how the process of selection can produce the overprediction result (1) where there is none prior to selection or even (2) where there is underprediction prior to selection. The results presented in Fig. 2.1 and Table 2.1 are assumed to apply to the majority group. Two possible corresponding cases for the unselected minority group are illustrated in Table 2.2. Each of these cases is combined with three possible selection processes for the minority group members. The latter are defined in Table 2.3. Case 1 assumes that prior to selection the regression equations of minority and majority groups are identical. Case 2 assumes that prior to selection the majority group equation underpredicts the minority group performance by one tenth of a within group standard deviation on y. The three minority group selection situations, defined in Table 2.3, are (a) no selection or random selection, (b) selection of the top half on the basis of u defined the same as in the majority group, and (c) selection of the top half on u', which places less weight on x for minority group members than for majority group members.

It should be noted that all three selection situations represent differential selection procedures for minority and majority group candidates since the selection is done within group and the groups are assumed to differ by a within group standard deviation on x. In varying ways, the three selection situations may be thought of as modeling affirmative action. Situation (a) involves no selection for minority group members. Situation (b) selects on the same variables in both groups but sets within group selection ratios equal despite between group differences on the observed predictor variable. Situation (c) also sets selection ratios equal within groups. In addition, however, less weight is placed on the predictor variable for minority group members.

TABLE 2.2
Parameters for Unselected Minority Group
(Hypothetical Examples)

Case 1:   Identical Minority & Majority Regressions Prior to Selection

Regression: $y = .6x + e$

Distributions: $x, N(-1, 1)$
$e, N(0, 1.09)$

Variable	Mean	Standard Deviation	Correlation with x
x	-1.00	1.000	
y	- .60	1.204	.498

Case 2:   Majority Regression Underpredicts for Minority Group Prior to Selection

Regression: $y = .12 + .6x + e$

Distributions: $x, N(-1, 1)$
$e, N(0, 1.09)$

Variable	Mean	Standard Deviation	Correlation with x
x	-1.00	1.000	
y	- .48	1.204	.498

2. PREDICTIVE BIAS AS AN ARTIFACT OF SELECTION PROCEDURES

TABLE 2.3
Basis of Minority Group Selection:
Three Hypothetical Situations[1]

Situation a:	No Selection or Random Selection.
Situation b:	Selectable if $u > 0$ where,
	$u = 2 + 2x + d$
	$e = .3d + c,$
Situation c:	Selectable if $u' > 0$ where,
	$u' = 1 + x + 2d$
	$e = .3d + c$

[1] c and d are defined as in Table 3.1.

The expected outcome of studies of predictive bias are summarized in Table 2.4 for the six possibilities defined by the combination of the two cases for regression equations and the three selection situations. As can be seen from the last column of Table 2.4, overprediction is to be expected as the result of the selection process in all three minority group selection situations for case 1. In other words, starting with identical regression equations in the unselected populations, the selection process modeled in these examples would produce the overprediction result that is commonly obtained. Even in case 2 where prior to selection there is an underprediction of .12, selection situations (a) and (b) result in a finding of overprediction in the selected groups. In situation (c) the underprediction is still there after selection but at a reduced level (.04 rather than .12).

EMPIRICAL RESULTS

The above analyses, while suggestive, are based on hypothetical examples. Because the actual selection process is usually unknown, direct empirical results comparable to the above hypothetical examples are not available. However, there are a number of empirical findings which are generally consistent with the conclusion based on the above analyses that overprediction may be largely a consequence of the selection process.

Studies of predictive bias often provide several comparisons of regression equations. Separate comparisons may be reported for each individual predictor and for various combinations of predictors. Cronbach and Schaeffer (1981) commented on the practice of reporting a comparison for two predictors such as previous grades and scores on a test separately for each predictor and for the two predictors together. They noted that "if the selection took place on both, the comparison across groups of unadjusted regression coefficients for separate variables is distorted. If selection took place on only one, the comparison of regression for the other variable or for the two together is distorted" (p. 42).

TABLE 2.4
Observed and Predicted Criterion Score Means Based on the
Selectable Majority Group Equation Evaluated at the
Minority Group Mean[1]

Case[2]	Selection Situation[3]	Observed Mean	Predicted Mean	Predicted Minus Observed
1	a	-.600	.225	.825
	b	-.065	.092	.157
	c	-.172	-.093	.079
2	a	-.480	.225	.705
	b	.055	.092	.037
	c	-.052	-.093	-.041

[1] Equation from Table 2.1, $\hat{y} = .219 + .4438x + e*$.
[2] Cases 1 and 2 are defined in Table 2.1.
[3] Selection situations a, b and c are defined in Table 2.3.

Cronbach and Schaeffer's conclusion is quite consistent with the above analysis, but can be carried one additional step by noting that selection is more apt to depend on both predictors than either one alone and, equally important, that selection will not be completely determined by the observed predictors. The second observation leads to the conclusion that comparisons of regressions for both variables together as well as either one alone are distorted. However, the first observation leads to the expectation that the results are apt to be less distorted when the regressions for the two variables together are compared than when those for either variable alone are compared. Furthermore, if the selection process tends to distort the results in the direction of the overprediction finding, then the amount of overprediction would be expected to be greater in comparisons of regressions involving a single predictor than in those involving both predictors.

The typical finding is consistent with the expectation based on the above reasoning. That is, there is a tendency to find a larger amount of overprediction when regressions for single predictors are compared than when regressions for multiple predictors are compared. At the undergraduate level, for example, Breland (1978) summarized results of studies in which comparisons were made for regressions of college grades on test scores alone, on high school grades alone, and on both together. Not all comparisons were available for all studies but the tendency to have greater overprediction is evident. Table 2.5 lists the number of studies showing overprediction, the number showing underprediction, and the median amount of overprediction on a 4-point scale where comparisons are based on individual predictors and on combinations of predictors. Using an equation for test scores and high school records combined, the median overprediction of minority group means is only one third as large as the median for

TABLE 2.5
Over- and Underprediction of College Grades
(Based on Breland, 1978)

Overpredictor (s)	Number of Studies Showing		Median Overprediction
	Overprediction	Underprediction	
High School Record Only	25	0	.28
Verbal Test Only	26	3	.16
Quantitative Test Only	24	3	.16
Verbal & Quantitative Tests	18	3	.16
Tests & High School Record	25	8	.05

tests alone and less than a fifth as large as the median for high school records alone.

Similar results were reported by Powers (1977) for 29 law schools. An equation based on a combined group of black and white students overpredicted the actual mean first-year grades in all 29 schools when first-year grades were regressed on LSAT scores alone or undergraduate grade-point average (UGPA) alone.

On a scale with a standard deviation of 10, the median overprediction for the 29 schools was 10.0 for the regression on UGPA alone, and 5.3 for the regression on LSAT alone. When both predictors were included in the regression, there was still some overprediction in 28 of the 29 schools. However, the median amount of overprediction was reduced to 2.2.

As was shown by Linn (in press), the amount of overprediction due to the selection process should be greater in highly selective institutions that also have a strong affirmative action program. A high degree of selectivity for the majority group on a variable, u, that is not perfectly related to the predictor variables will tend to increase the difference between the regressions for the unselected and the selectable majority group populations. Thus, the amount of overprediction would tend to be larger at the more highly selective institutions.

The above expectation is quite consistent with the results reported by Powers (1977). The LSAT standard deviation for white students is taken as an index of the degree of selectivity of the law school. As can be seen in Fig. 2.2, there is a substantial relationship between the amount of overprediction for black students based on the regression of first-year grades in law school and the standard deviation of the LSAT for white students. The more selective the law school, the smaller is the standard deviation, and the greater is the degree of overprediction.

MODELING THE SELECTION PROCESS

It is clear that selection biases can distort regressions and expectancy tables. As Berk, Ray and Cooley (1982) point out, however, "there may be a wide gap

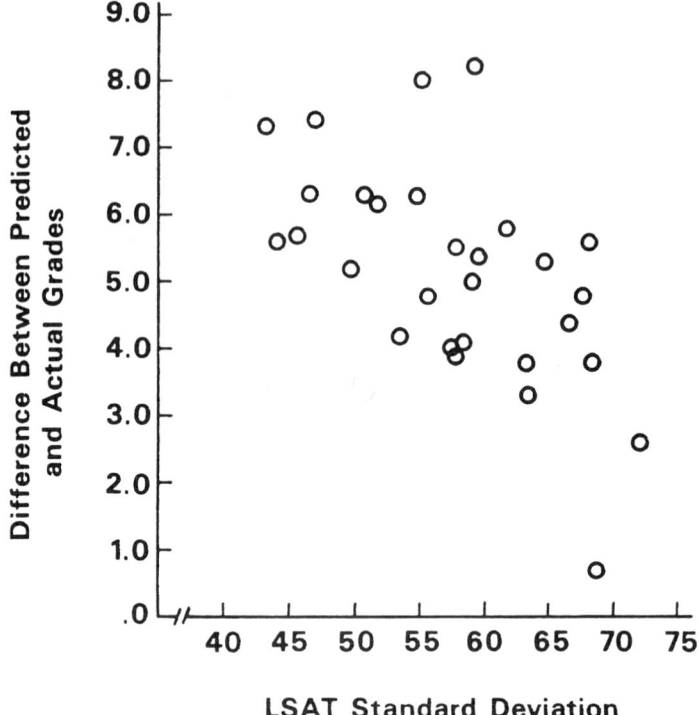

FIG. 2.2 Scatterplot of differences between predicted and actual average grade (amount of overprediction) for minority group law students against the majority group standard deviation on the LSAT (based on Powers, 1977).

between the prospect of selection biases and the reality of selection biases. The key is in the cross-correlation between the error terms which under properly specified models (or reasonably close approximations) will often turn out to be small'' (p. 59). For the applied researcher conducting validity studies or investigating possible predictive bias there are two important implications of Berk, Ray and Cooley's conclusion. First, the focus should be on regressions and expectancy tables based on the full set of available predictors rather than results for predictors considered one at a time. Between-group comparisons of regression equations involving several predictors are apt to be less subject to distortion than comparisons of individual predictors. If the x's in equations (1) and (2) are replaced by vectors of predictors, the residual error terms are apt to be less correlated.

The second implication is that more effort needs to be put into understanding and modeling the selection process itself. Several procedures are available for estimating the coefficients in equation (1) or its multiple predictor counterpart that take into account the selection process (see, for example, Heckman, 1979; Muthen & Jöreskog, in press). They all involve modeling the selection process, however. For example, Heckman's two-stage estimators start with a probit analysis to estimate the parameters of equation 2, or its multiple predictor counterpart. The probit analysis results are used to estimate $f(\lambda)$ in equation (6), and then ordinary least squares is used to estimate the regression parameters in equation (6), that is, the betas and gamma.

Information regarding the selection process is seldom considered a part of a validity study or a study of predictive bias. As demonstrated above, however, failure to consider the selection process can have unfortunate consequences. Problems caused by selection cannot ordinarily be avoided by the textbook advice to use a randomly selected sample for purposes of test validation. As desirable as randomization might be it is seldom feasible. Fortunately, randomization is not the only approach to obtaining unbiased estimates of regression. This is well stated in another context by Cain (1975) who concluded that "the critical difference for avoiding bias is not whether the assignments are random or nonrandom, but whether the investigator has *knowledge of and can model* this selection process" (p. 304). It seems clear that more attention needs to be given to the selection process in studies of predictive validity and/or bias. Gaining better knowledge of and modeling the selection process can substantially improve the interpretation of validity and predictive bias study results.

REFERENCES

Berk, R. A., Ray, S. C., & Cooley, T. F. *Selection biases in sociological data*. Project Report, National Institute of Justice (Grant No. 80-1J-CX-0037). University of California, Santa Barbara, 1982.

Breland, H. M. *Population validity and college entrance measures* (RDR 88-79, No. 2). New York: College Entrance Examination Board, 1978.

Cain, G. C. Regression and selection models to improve nonexperimental comparisons. In C. A. Bennett & A. A. Lumsdaine (Eds.), *Evaluation and experiment, some critical issues in assessing social programs*. New York: Academic Press, 1975.

Cronbach, L. J. & Schaeffer, G. A. *Extensions of Personnel Selection theory to aspects of minority hiring* (Project Report No. 81-A2). Stanford, Calif. Stanford University, Institute for Research on Educational Finance and Governance, 1981.

Evans, F. R. Applications and admissions to ABA accredited law schools: An analysis of national data for the class entering in the fall of 1976. In Law School Admission Council, *Annual Council Report*, 1977.

Goldberger, A. S. Linear regression after selection. *Journal of Econometrics*, 1981, *15*, 357–366.

Heckman, J. J. Sample selection bias as specification error. *Econometrics*, 1979, *47*, 153–161.

Linn, R. L. Ability testing: Individual differences and differential prediction. In A. K. Wigdor & W. R. Garner (Eds.), *Ability testing: Uses, consequences, and controversies, Part II*. Report of the National Academy of Sciences Committee on Ability Testing. Washington, D.C.: National Academy Press, 1982.

Linn, R. L. The Pearson selection formulas: Implications for studies of predictive bias and estimates of additional effects in selected samples. *Journal of Educational Measurement*, in press.

Linn, R. L., & Werts, C. E. Considerations for studies of predictive bias. *Journal of Educational Measurement,* 1971, *8,* 1–4.

Lord, F. M. A paradox in the interpretation of group comparisons. *Psychological Bulletin,* 1967, *68,* 304–305.

Lord, F. M. Statistical adjustments when comparing preexisting groups. *Psychological Bulletin,* 1969, *72,* 336–337.

Lord, F. M., & Novick, M. R. *Statistical theories of mental test scores.* Reading, Mass.: Addison-Wesley Publishing Co., 1968.

Muthen, B., & Jöreskog, K. G. Selectivity problems in quasi-experimental studies. *Evaluation Review,* in press.

Olsen, R. Approximating a truncated normal regression with the method of moments. *Econometrika,* 1980, *48,* 1099–1105.

Pearson, K. Mathematical contributions to the theory of evolution-XI. On the influence of natural selection on the variability and correlation of organs. *Philosophical Transactions of the Royal Society of London: Series A,* 1903, *200,* 1–66.

Powers, D. E. Comparing predictions of law school performance for black, Chicano, and white law students (Rep. LSAC-77-3). In Law School Admission Council (Ed.), *Reports of LSAC sponsored research: 1975–1977,* (Vol. 3). Princeton, N.J.: Law School Admission Council, 1977.

Reilly, R. R. A note on minority group bias studies. *Psychological Bulletin,* 1973, *80,* 130–133.

Reynolds, C. R. (Ed.) *Perspectives on bias in mental testing.* New York: Plenum Press, in press.

3 The Centrality of Lord's Paradox and Exchangeability for All Statistical Inference

Melvin R. Novick
The University of Iowa

FREDERIC LORD, AN APPRECIATION

The work of Frederic M. Lord enjoys a unique position in the development of quantitative methods in the behavioral sciences. He has, for 30 years, dominated the field of test theory. Indeed his name and the field are virtually synonymous. Certainly there were predecessors. Brown, Guttman, Gulliksen, Kelley, Kuder, Richardson, Spearman, Thurstone, Tucker and others made important contributions. But it was Lord who codified the field. It was Lord who first brought the rigors of mathematical statistics to the field and thus made it possible to resolve much of the confusion that had plagued the field for half a century. Beginning with his path-breaking monograph in 1952 and continuing until today, by his accomplishment and his example, he has fostered the development of test theory as a rigorous scientific discipline.

It is not my intention to chronicle Frederic Lord's many achievements. These are noted elsewhere in this volume. But before addressing the topic of this chapter, one further comment seems in order. In the decade of the 1960s when our society had a more enlightened understanding of the value of basic research, Frederic Lord was able to organize a Seminar in Mathematical Psychology at Educational Testing Service. Participating in that seminar from time to time were Erling Andersen, Murray Aitken, Alan Birnbaum, Michael Browne, Leon Gleser, Robert Jennrich, John Keats, Karl Joreskog, Walter Kristoff, Michael Levine, Roderic McDonald, William Meredith, Ingram Olkin, Roger Owen, Fumiko Samejima, Tom Stroud, J. P. Sutcliffe, Joseph Zinnes, and a few others in addition to Fred and myself. In my judgment, it was Fred Lord's leadership during that seminar that fostered the explosion of relevant mathematical development in test theory that continues to the present day. One product of that enterprise was the writing of what has been recognized as the definitive text in this field, *Statistical Theories of Mental Test Scores*. It was a great honor and privilege to be chosen directly from my doctoral program in mathematical statistics to assist in the writing of that important work.

LORD'S PARADOX

The paper that I now submit in honor of Lord's distinguished career does not deal with test theory, as such, but rather with a topic covered in two very brief papers published in the *Psychological Bulletin* (Lord, 1967, 1969), an earlier paper published in *The Journal of the American Statistical Association* (Lord, 1960) and a later entry in Anderson (1975). In the two two-page *Bulletin* papers Lord noted a paradoxical feature sometimes found in group comparisons. Seldom has so large a contribution been made in so few pages. Lord not only brought a fundamental paradox to our attention, he also, in the 1969 paper, gave us the key to its solution. It is true that many others had made mention of this problem, and indeed some methods had been made available, but it was Lord's paper that got to the heart of the matter and showed us what needed to be done. In 1981 my paper with D. V. Lindley developed a general methodology derived from the work of DeFinetti but which, at its core, incorporated the lessons of Lord's paradox.

It is interesting that two other chapters in this volume, those by Linn, and by Holland and Rubin, address issues related to Lord's paradox. Continuing from these two chapters, I contribute a third, writing from my own perspective, but recognizing that there are other contemporaneous perspectives. For historical purposes I note the antecedent work of Yule (1903), Cohen and Nagel (1934), Chung (1942), Ziesel (1947), Kendall and Lazersfeld (1950), Simpson (1951), Simon (1954), Meehl and Rosen (1955), Lazersfeld, Gandet and Berdsom (1956), Wold (1956) and the more recent works of Snedecor and Cochran (1967), J. Cohen (1968), Cochran (1968a, 1968b), Evans and Anastasio (1968), Kalton (1968), Elashoff (1969), Moses (1969), Meehl (1970), Linn and Werts (1971), Blyth (1972), Wiley (1973), Fleiss (1973), Reilly (1973), Solomon (1973), Rubin (1974), Willingham (1974), Bickel, Hammel, and O'Connell (1975), Cain (1975), Maxwell and Cramer (1975), Maxwell and Jones (1976), Appelbaum and Cramer (1976), Games (1976), Gardner (1976), Rubin (1977), Wolins (1978), Rubin (1978), Hand (1979), Heckman (1979), Rubin (1980), Goldberger (1981), Wolins (1982), and Wagner (1982). I have also touched on this issue in several of my own papers in recent years (Lindley & Novick, 1981; Novick, 1978, 1981). I borrow freely from these latter papers in my current presentation and hope to show a broader field of applicability of Lord's seminal contribution than was previously recognized, even in the Lindley-Novick (1981) treatment. Thus, the primary intended contributions of this chapter are expository, integrative, didactic, and bibliographic.

SIMPSON'S REVERSAL PARADOX

Table 3.1 demonstrates some fundamental difficulties that arise in data analysis whenever an attempt is made to investigate the effects of variables that cannot be controlled experimentally. This problem arises, for example, whenever the effects of demographic variables are studied, whenever an existing system is under study, as in all evaluation studies, and sometimes in experimental studies when complete randomization is not possible; or when, despite randomization, an imbalance in important factors occurs (e.g. see Novick, 1978/1981). In this table are recorded the numbers and percentages of persons hired, cross-classified by race, gender, and location.

According to the data presented in the upper left quadrant of the table, 40% of blacks and 50% of whites are hired. Under federal guidelines, this disparity is sufficient to trigger a finding of adverse impact and to require proof of the business necessity (the validity) of the selection procedure being used. However if we look at the upper right quadrant where the data are further crossclassified by gender, an opposite picture emerges. We find that for males the percentage of blacks selected is much greater than for whites and the same result holds for females. Thus it appears that for both males and females the selection procedure has adverse impact for whites, whereas for the total group the selection procedure has adverse impact for blacks. The further breakdown by location demonstrates a reversal of the original reversal, providing a paradox within a paradox.

The observed phenomenon, called Simpson's (1951) paradox, can occur only in the presence of an unbalanced design and then only with some uncontrolled but controlling variables that are naturally linked with the dependent variables, some careful data construction, or some very bad luck in observation. I demonstrate this shortly with another constructed example. However, actual examples have been found in practice to which the works of Bickel, et al., Hand, and Wagner, mentioned above, attest.

To simplify the forthcoming analysis consider Tables 3.2 and 3.3. These tables record results for 40 patients who were given or not given a treatment T for some malady and who recovered R or did not. We are not considering small-sample problems so we take the numbers in the tables to be multiplied by 10,000. It is then clear that the recovery rate for patients receiving the treatment at 50% exceeds that for the control at 40% and the treatment is apparently to be preferred. However in Table 3.3 where the results are given differentially for males and females we find the recovery rate for the control patients is 10% higher both for males and for females. Thus, what is good for men and good for women is bad for the population as a whole.

TABLE 3.1
Data for Analysis to Infer Adverse Impact, Mindful, or Intentional Discrimination
Hirings (H) and Nonhirings (NH) of Black (B) and White (W) Applicants

Total Group	NH	H	Total	Males	NH	H	Total	Gender Females	NH	H	Total
W	200	200 (50%)	400	W	120	180 (60%)	300	W	80	20 (20%)	100
B	240	160 (40%)	400	B	30	70 (70%)	100	B	210	90 (30%)	300
	440	360	800		150	250 (63%)	400		290	110 (28%)	400

Urban	Location NH	H	Total	Urban Males	NH	H	Total	Location by Gender Urban Females	NH	H	Total
W	112	99 (47%)	211	W	110	90 (45%)	200	W	2	9 (81%)	11
B	34	81 (70%)	115	B	15	10 (40%)	25	B	19	71 (79%)	90
	146	180 (55%)	326		125	100	225		21	80	101

Rural	Location NH	H	Total	Rural Males	NH	H	Total	Location by Gender Rural Females	NH	H	Total
W	88	101 (53%)	189	W	10	90 (90%)	100	W	78	11 (12%)	89
B	206	79 (28%)	285	B	15	60 (80%)	75	B	191	19 (9%)	210
	294	180 (38%)	474		25	150	175		269	30	299

Note: Sample sizes are equal to tabled values times 1000.
Copyright © by Melvin R. Novick. Permission is granted to photoreproduce this page *in full only* for noncommercial purposes, provided this notice is included in the reproduction.

3. LORD'S PARADOX AND EXCHANGEABILITY

TABLE 3.2
Recovery Rates Under Treatment and Control

	R	R		Recovery Rate
T	20	20	40	50%
T̄	16	24	40	40%
	36	44	80	

Lindley and Novick (1981) describe a mechanism that could account for this paradox. It is possible that the males have been assigned to the treatment group, the females to the control group; perhaps because the doctor distrusted the treatment and so was reluctant to give it to the females where the recovery rate is much lower than for males. Thus, in the design, treatment and gender have been confounded. The question then is, Do we use the treatment or do we not? The apparent answer is that when we know that the gender of the patient is male or when we know that it is female we do not use the treatment, but if the gender is unknown we should use the treatment! Obviously that conclusion is ridiculous, and a careful analysis of the causal relationship between the variables tells us that the treatment is not efficacious. Unfortunately, reality is not often so easily fathomed, but at least we begin to see how a solution may be found.

Lord's (1967, 1969) work deepens the enigma and yet provides the basis for a resolution. Keeping the numbers in Tables 3.2 and 3.3 the same, imagine treatment and nontreatment being replaced by black and white varieties of a pea plant and recovery and nonrecovery being replaced by high and low yields, the confounding factor being whether the plant grew tall (M) or short (F). Then the white variety is 10% worse among both tall and short plants, but 10% better overall. However, in this case, Lord's careful analysis convinces us that the white variety is to be preferred. Further details of this analysis are given in the Holland-Rubin paper.

TABLE 3.3
Recovery Rates Under Treatment and Control With Sex
as an Added Variable

Males	R	R		Recovery Rate
T	18	12	30	60%
T̄	7	3	10	70%
	25	15	40	
Females	R	R		Recovery Rate
T	2	8	10	20%
T̄	9	21	30	30%
	11	29	40	

The fundamental importance of Lord's and Simpson's paradoxes is not that there is the possibility of confusion *sometimes,* but rather that all data analysis is subject to the biases and confusion noted. The work of Campbell and his associates (e.g. Campbell & Ehrlebacher, 1970; Campbell & Stanley, 1963; Cook & Campbell, 1979) on quasiexperimentation is so important for this reason.

EXCHANGEABILITY

Lord's fundamental contribution was the realization that paradoxes such as these can only be resolved by making realistic assumptions about which variables in the analysis are fundamental and which ones are concomitant. Elashoff (1969) later treated this consideration with some care and Lindley and Novick (1981) proposed a general methodology. Developing original ideas due to De Finetti (1974) and to Meehl and Rosen (1955), they suggested that statistical inference must be based on clearly articulated assumptions of exchangeability or, in the language of Fisher (1956), the specification of the relevant subpopulation. Lindley and Novick (1981), matched the idea of relevant subpopulation with that of specifying the correct conditional probability. Thus, to determine the correct prognostication for a new individual it is necessary to determine the appropriate (conditional) subpopulation from the table from which the individual can be taken as an exchangeable member and then to select the (conditional) probability distribution that is appropriate to that population. A fully developed rationale for this process was given by Lindley and Novick (1981) though, in fact, some elements of the methodology had been employed by Zeisel (1947) and by Lazersfeld et al. (1956), and a careful consideration of this problem had been given in the context of the analysis of covariance by Elashoff (1969).

The following passage from Lord (1967) is often quoted: "with the data usually available for such studies, there simply is no logical or statistical procedure that can be counted on to make proper allowances for uncontrolled preexisting differences." Comment on this statement is given by Holland and Rubin (this volume). Yet for all of the progress made in the past 15 years there remains an essential truth to it. Methods described by Holland and Rubin, Lindley and Novick, Campbell and associates, and others are helpful. And surely Cain (1975) is correct when he states that "the critical difference in avoiding bias is not whether the assignments are random or nonrandom, but whether the investigator has knowledge of and can model his selection process." Statements in Lindley and Novick (1981) concerning exchangeability make the same point. The fundamental point, of course, is that inferences *always* depend on assumptions or, in the Bayesian language, all inferences are conditional. If you and I disagree on model assumptions, we may come up with different conclusions. It was Lord's work that taught us that humbling lesson.

From the Lindley-Novick point of view, the key to data analysis in general and to the solution of Lord's and Simpson's paradoxes in particular lies in the concept of exchangeability and relevant subpopulations. Randomization is useful, but exchangeability through modeling, blocking, and covariation is fundamental. For an extended discussion of population relevance see Novick (to appear). The ideas presented there are not entirely new, but are explicated in greater detail than previously. Gardner (1976) gives us the following enlightening quote from John Stuart Mill's *A System of Logic*. "The universe, so far as known to us, is so constituted, that whatever is true in any one case, is true in all cases of a certain description; the only difficulty is, to find what description." Perhaps due to the work of Lord and others, the "finding" is a little less difficult than it was in 1967.

It often happens that a methodological controversy exists in a field for many years generated by a multitude of papers each providing a unique solution. Then along comes a paper that organizes and integrates previous work and raises the level of discourse to a new plateau. The work of Meehl and Rosen (1955) was such a paper as were Lord's (1967, 1969). Each of these papers unraveled enigmas by looking carefully at appropriate and inappropriate (wrong) conditional probabilities. For an interesting case in which careful consideration of right and wrong conditional probabilities helped resolve an enigma, see Petersen and Novick (1976).

NON-ORTHOGONAL UNIVARIATE AND MULTIVARIATE ANALYSIS OF VARIANCE AND COVARIANCE

Another area in which there has been much controversy concerns the analysis of nonorthogonal experimental designs. The topic was one of frequent discussion for many years in the *Psychological Bulletin*. The major references are Overall and Spiegel (1969); Joe (1971); Rawlings (1972); Rawlings (1973); Overall and Spiegel (1973); Smith (1973); Gocka (1973); Appelbaum and Cramer (1974); Burdick, Herr and O'Fallon (1974); Carlson and Timm (1974); Wolf and Cartwright (1974); Overall, Spiegel, and Cohen (1975); Speed and Hocking (1976); Keren and Lewis (1976); Keren and Lewis (1977); Lewis and Keren (1977); and Herr and Gaebelein (1978). Part of the problem arose from a desire for simple solutions in the days when matrix inversion taxed computing and individual theoretical capabilities. The larger problem arose however from a failure to have a general theory that showed when particular solutions were applicable. Another problem arose and remains because of the standard Yule formulation of the analysis of variance model. Most texts write the two-way model as the sum of row effects $a(i)$, column effects $b(j)$, and interaction effects $g(i,j)$. The more natural way is to follow Fisher and write the model using only cell parameter $c(i,j)$. Effects are then obtained by linear transformation on the parameter space. The Yule model offers some greater simplicity for orthogonal designs at the expense of confusion in the nonorthogonal case. The Fisher model, however, is completely general and in the long run leads to greater clarity. The Yule model is often called the reduced rank model. The Fisher model is often called the full-rank model. It will surprise no one to learn that I have advocated for some years that all analysis of variance and multivariate analysis of variance be done by Payesian full-rank methods. Such methods were used by Box and Tiao (1973), but not precisely advocated as a general prescription. That prescription was given more recently by Woodworth (1979) whose programs are available on the CADA Monitor (Novick, Hamer, Libby, Chen, & Woodworth, 1980). Corresponding programs for the analysis of covariance are also available. Unfortunately, these methods are not yet worked out for the general case of exchangeable prior distributions, though fully exchangeable Bayesian solutions are available for one-way designs. For example, see Jackson, Novick and Thayer, 1971; Lindley and Smith, 1972; Novick, Jackson and Thayer, 1971; Novick, Jackson, Thayer and Cole, 1972; Novick, Lewis and Jackson, 1973; Novick and Jackson, 1974; Lewis, Wang and Novick, 1975, to name only a few contributors to an expanding literature. There are also some excellent empirical Bayesian (I prefer the term pseudo Bayesian) methods. While purist Bayesians, like myself, consider these methods to be unnecessarily atheoretical, it must be acknowledged that they often yield workable solutions in cases where fully Bayesian methods remain intractable. The adjective empirical is, of course, largely rhetorical. Rubin, Holland and their associates, for example, have produced work that is useful and noteworthy. However, pseudo Bayesian methods do not produce precise posterior distributions that are combinable with assessed utilities to yield fully Bayesian decision theoretic solutions, and it is less clear how the fundamental concept of exchangeability can be made operational outside a Bayesian framework.

A PREVISION FOR BEHAVIORAL STATISTICS (2012)

In my recent Psychometric Society address "Statistics as Psychometrics" (Novick, 1980), I indicated how I thought the field of behavioral statistics would develop during the next two decades. I now update my prevision with a target date of November 12, 2012. On that date I foresee that behavioral statistics will—

1. be less dependent on constricting models such as the normal and will primarily use more general classes of distributions, for example, the exponential power distribution;

2. be fully Bayesian with full emphasis on the psychometric assessment of proper prior distributions;
3. be fully decision theoretic with emphasis on the psychometric assessment of individual and institutional utilities;
4. use robust classes of prior distributions and utility functions as well as robust model distributions;
5. rely completely on full-rank Bayesian univariate and multivariate analyses of variance and covariance using fully exchangeable, informative prior distributions as appropriate;
6. emphasize exchangeability through careful modeling, blocking, and covariation with randomization playing a residual role;
7. emphasize the use of posterior predictive distributions using the lessons of Lord's paradox, exchangeability, and appropriate conditional probabilities;
8. place great emphasis on numerical solutions when exact Bayesian solutions prove intractable;
9. still use some pseudo Bayesian methods when both theoretical and computational fully Bayesian solutions remain intractable. (This prevision is subject to modification if I can convince Rubin, Holland and their associates to devote their impressive skills to the quest for fully Bayesian solutions. Should this happen, there may be no need for any pseudo Bayesian methods.)

I also foresee that on November 12, 2012, we shall all appreciate even more fully the *Centrality of Lord's Paradox and Exchangeability for all Statistical Inference*.

ACKNOWLEDGMENTS

I am indebted to Tim Ansley for bibliographic and editorial assistance and to Lloyd Bond, Charles Lewis, Shinichi Mayekawa and George Woodworth for constructive suggestions.

REFERENCES

Anderson, S. B. et al. *Encyclopedia of Educational Evaluation*. San Francisco, Calif.: Jossey-Bass, 1975.

Appelbaum, M. I., & Cramer, E. M. Some problems in the nonorthogonal analysis of variance. *Psychological Bulletin*, 1974, *81*, 335–343.

Appelbaum, M. I., & Cramer, E. M. Balancing-analysis of variance by another name. *Journal of Educational Statistics*, 1976, *1*, 233–252.

Bickel, P. I., Hammel, E. A., & O'Connell, J. W. Sex bias in graduate admissions: Data from Berkeley. *Science*, 1975, *187*, 398–404.

Blyth, C. R. On Simpson's paradox and the sure-thing principle. *Journal of the American Statistical Association,* 1972, *67,* 364–366.

Box, G. E., & Tiao, G. *Bayesian Inference in Statistical Analysis.* Reading, Mass.: Addison-Wesley, 1973.

Burdick, D. S., Herr, D. G., O'Fallon, W. M. & O'Neill, B. V. Exact methods in the unbalanced, two-way analysis of variance—A geometric approach. *Communications in Statistics,* 1974, *3,* 581–594.

Cain, G. C. Regression and selection models to improve nonexperimental comparisons. In C. A. Bennett & A. A. Lumsdaine (Eds.), *Evaluation and experiment, some critical issues in assessing social programs.* New York: Academic Press, 1975.

Campbell, D. T., & Erlebacher, A. How regression artifacts in quasi-experimental evaluations can mistakenly make compensatory education look harmful. *Disadvantaged Child,* 1970, 185–210.

Campbell, D. T., & Stanley, J. C. *Experimental and quasi-experimental designs for research.* Chicago: Rand McNally, 1963.

Carlson, J. E., & Timm, N. H. Analysis of nonorthogonal fixed-effects designs. *Psychological Bulletin,* 1974, *81,* 563–570.

Chung, Kai-Lai. "On Mutually Favorable Events." *Annals of Mathematical Statistics,* 1942, *13,* 338–349.

Cochran, W. G. Errors of measurement in statistics. *Technometrics,* 1968, *10,* 637–666. (a)

Cochran, W. G. The effectiveness of adjustment by subclassification in removing bias in observational studies. *Biometrics,* 1968, *24,* 295–313. (b)

Cohen, M. R., & Nagel, E. An *introduction to logic and scientific method.* New York: Harcourt Brace, 1934.

Cohen, J. Multiple regression as a general data-analytic system. *Psychological Bulletin,* 1968, *70,* 426–443.

Cook, T. D., & Campbell, D. T. *Quasti-experimentation design of analysis issues for field settings* Chicago: Rand McNally, 1979.

De Finetti, B. *Theory of probability* (2 vols.). London: Wiley, 1974.

Elashoff, J. D. Analysis of covariance: A delicate instrument. *American Educational Research Journal,* 1969, *6,* 383–401.

Evans, S. H., & Anastasio, E. J. Misuse of analysis of covariance when treatment effect and covariate are confounded. *Psychological Bulletin,* 1968, *69,* 225–234.

Fisher, R. A. *Statistical methods and scientific inference.* Edinburgh: Oliver and Boyd, 1956.

Fleiss, J. L. *Statistical methods for rates and proportions.* New York: Wiley, 1973.

Games, P. A. Limitations of analysis of covariance on intact group quasi-experimental designs. *Journal of Experimental Education,* 1976, *44,* 51–54.

Gardner, M. On the fabric of inductive logic and some probability paradoxes. *Scientific American,* 1976, *234,* 119–124.

Gocka, E. F. Regression analysis of proportional cell data. *Psychological Bulletin,* 1973, *80,* 25–27.

Goldberger, A. S. Linear regression after selection. *Journal of Econometrics,* 1981, *15,* 357–366.

Hand, D. J. Psychiatric examples of Simpson's paradox. *British Journal of Psychiatry,* 1979, *135,* 90–91.

Heckman, J. J. Sample selection bias as specification error. *Econometrika,* 1979, *47,* 153–161.

Herr, D. G., & Gaebelein, J. Nonorthogonal two-way analysis of variance. *Psychological Bulletin,* 1978, *85,* 207–216.

Jackson, P. H., Novick, M. R., & Thayer, D. Estimating regressions in m groups. *British Journal of Mathematical and Statistical Psychology,* 1971, *24,* 129–153.

Joe, G. W. Comment on Overall and Spiegel's "Least squares analysis of experimental data." *Psychological Bulletin,* 1971, *75,* 364–366.

Kalton, G. Standardization: A technique to control for extraneous variables. *Applied Statistics,* 1968, *17,* 118–136.

Kendall, P. L., & Lazersfeld, P. F. Problems of survey analysis. In R. K. Merton & P. F. Lazersfeld, (Eds.), *Continuities of Social Research.* Glencoe, Ill.: Free Press of Glencoe, 1950.

Keren, G., & Lewis, C. Nonorthogonal designs: Sample versus population. *Psychological Bulletin,* 1976, *83,* 817–826.

Keren, G., & Lewis, C. A comment on coding in nonorthogonal designs. *Psychological Bulletin,* 1977, *84,* 346–348.

Lazersfeld, P., Gandet, H., & Perdsom, B. *The people's choice,* New York: Columbia University Press, 1956.

Lewis, C., & Keren, G. You can't have your cake and eat it too: Some considerations of the error term. *Psychological Bulletin,* 1977, *84,* 1150–1154.

Lewis, C., Wang, M., & Novick, M. R. Marginal distributions for the estimation of proportions in *m*-groups. *Psychometrika,* 1975, *40,* 63–75.

Lindley, D. V., & Novick, M. R. The role of exchangeability in inference. *Annals of Statistics,* 1981, *9,* 45–58.

Lindley, D. V., & Smith, A. F. M. Bayes estimates for the linear model. *Journal of the Royal Statistical Society, Series B,* 1972, *34,* 1–41.

Linn, R. L. & Werts, C. E. Considerations for studies of predictive bias. *Journal of Educational Measurement,* 1971, *8,* 1–4.

Lord, F. M. Large-sample covariance analysis when the control variable is fallible. *Journal of the American Statistical Association,* 1960, *55,* 309–321.

Lord, F. M. A paradox in the interpretation of group comparisons. *Psychological Bulletin,* 1967, *68,* 304–305.

Lord, F. M. Statistical adjustments when comparing preexisting groups. *Psychological Bulletin,* 1969, *72,* 336–337.

Maxwell, S., & Cramer, E. M. A note on analysis of covariance. *Psychological Bulletin,* 1975, *82,* 187–190.

Maxwell, S. E., & Jones, L. V. Female and male admission to graduate school: An illustrative inquiry. *Journal of Educational Statistics,* 1976, *1,* 1–37.

Meehl, P. E. Nuisance variables and the ex post facto design. In M. Radner & S. Winokur (Eds.), *Minnesota studies in the philosophy of science* (Vol. 4). Minneapolis; University of Minnesota Press, 1970.

Meehl, P. E., & Rosen, A. Antecedent probability and the efficiency of psychometric signs, patterns, or cutting scores. *Psychological Bulletin,* 1955, *52,* 194–216.

Moses, L. E. Comparison of crude and standardized anesthetic death rates. In J. P. Bunker, W. H. Forrest, F. Mosteller, & L. D. Vandam (Eds.), *The national halothane study; A study of the possible association between halothane anesthesia and postoperative hepatic necrosis.* Washington: U.S. Government Printing Office, 1969.

National Assessment of Educational Progress, Report 7: Science group results B, 1971. Washington: U.S. Government Printing Office, 1973.

Novick, M. R. Statistics as psychometrics. *Psychometrika,* 1980, *45,* 411–424.

Novick, M. R. Burden of Proof/Burden of Remedy, *Public Personnel Management,* 1981, *10,* 333–341.

Novick, M. R. Data analysis in the absence of randomization. *Sozialwissenschaftliche Annalen,* B and 2, 1978, Seite 77–91. Physica-Verlag, Wien. (Reprinted with revisions in R. Boruch, Paul M. Wortman, & David S. Cordray, [Eds.], *Reanalyzing program evaluations: Policies and practices for secondary analysis of social and educational programs.* San Francisco: Jossey-Bass Publishers, 1981.)

Novick, M. R. Educational Testing: Inferences in relevant subpopulations, 1982, *11,* 4–10.

Novick, M. R., Hamer, R. M., Libby, D. L., Chen, J. J., & Woodworth, G. G. *Manual for the computer-assisted data analysis (CADA) monitor—1980,* The University of Iowa, 1980.

Novick, M. R., & Jackson, P. H. Further cross-validation analysis of the Bayesian m-group regression method. *American Educational Research Journal,* 1974, *11,* 77–85.

Novick, M. R., Jackson, P. H., & Thayer, D. T. Bayesian inference and the classical test theory model: Reliability and true scores. *Psychometrika,* 1971, *36,* 261–288.

Novick, M. R., Jackson, P. H., Thayer, D. T., & Cole, N. S. Estimating multiple regressions in m-groups: A cross-validation study. *The British Journal of Mathematical and Statistical Psychology,* 1972, *25,* 33–50.

Novick, M. R., Lewis, C., & Jackson, P. H. The estimation of proporations in m-groups. *Pychometrika,* 1973, *38,* 19–46.

Overall, J. E. and Spiegel, D. K. Concerning least squares analysis of experimental data. *Psychological Bulletin,* 1969, *72,* 311–322.

Overall, J. E., & Spiegel, D. K. Comment on "Regression analysis of proportional cell data." *Psychological Bulletin,* 1973, *80,* 28–30.

Overall, J. E., Spiegel, D. K., & Cohen, J. Equivalence of orthogonal and nonorthogonal analysis of variance. *Psychological Bulletin,* 1975, *82,* 182–186.

Petersen, N. S., & Novick, M. R. An evaluation of some models for culture-fair selection. *Journal of Educational Measurement,* 1976, *13,* 3–29.

Rawlings, R. R., Jr. Note on nonorthogonal analysis of variance. *Psychological Bulletin,* 1972, *77,* 373–374.

Rawlings, R. R., Jr. Comments on the Overall and Spiegel paper. *Psychological Bulletin,* 1973, *79,* 168–169.

Reilly, R. R. A note on minority group bias studies. *Psychological Bulletin,* 1973, *80,* 130–133.

Rubin, D. B. Estimating causal effects of treatments in randomized and non-randomized studies. Journal of Educational Psychology, 1974, *66,* 688–701.

Rubin, D. B. Assignment to treatment group on the basis of a covariate. *Journal of Educational Statistics,* 1977, *2,* 1–26.

Rubin, D. B. Bayesian inference for causal effects; The role of randomization. *Annals of Statistics,* 1978, *6,* 34–58.

Rubin, D. B. Discussion of "Randomization analysis of experimental data in the Fisher randomization test," by Basu. *The Journal of the American Statistical Association,* 1980, *75,* 591–593.

Simon, H. A. Spurious correlation; A causal interpretation. J. Amer. Statist. Assoc., 1954, *49,* 467–479.

Simpson, E. H. The interpretation of interaction contingency tables. *Journal of the Royal Statistical Society Series B,* 1951. *13,* 238–241.

Smith, I. L. Comment on Joe's "Comment on Overall and Spiegel's 'Least squares analysis of experimental data.'" *Psychological Bulletin,* 1973, *79,* 170–171.

Snedecor, G. W., & Cochran, W. G. *Statistical methods* (6th ed.). Ames, Iowa: Iowa State University Press, 1967.

Solmon, L. C. Women in doctoral education: Clues and puzzles regarding institutional discrimination. *Research in Higher Education,* 1973, *1,* 299–332.

Speed, F. M. & Hocking, R. R. The use of the R ( ) notation with unbalanced data. *American Statistician,* 1976, *30,* 30–33.

Wagner, C. H. Simpson's paradox in real life. *The American Statistician,* 1982, *36,* 46–48.

Wiley, D. E. Auf dem Wege zum "Ceteris Paribus." Datenkorrektur in der Bildungsforschung. In W. Edelstein & D. Hopf (Eds.), *Bedingungen des Bildungsprozessess: Psychologishe und Padagocische Forschung zum Lehren und Lernen in der Schule.* Stuttgart: Klett, 1973. (Also appears as: Approximations to *ceteris paribus:* Data adjustment in educational research. In W. H. Sewell, R. M. Hauser, & D. L. Featherman (Eds.), *Schooling and achievement in American society.* New York: Academic Press, 1981.

Willingham, W. W. Predicting success in graduate education. *Science*, 1974, *183*, 273–278.

Wold, H. Causal inference from observational data. *Journal of the Royal Statistical Society*, 1956, 28–60.

Wolf, G., & Cartwright, B. Rules for coding dummy variables in multiple regression. *Psychological Bulletin*, 1974, *81*, 173–179.

Wolins, L. Sex differentials in salaries: Faults in analysis of covariance. *Science*, 1978, *200*, 717.

Wolins, L. *Research mistakes in the behavioral sciences*. Ames: Iowa State University Press, 1982.

Woodworth, G. E. Bayesian full rank MANOVA/MANCOVA: An intermediate exposition with interactive computer examples, *Journal of Educational Statistics*, 1979, *4*, 357–404.

Yule, G. U. Notes on the theory of association of attributes in statistics, *Biometrika*, 1903, *2*, 121–134.

Zeisel, H. *Say it with figures* (5th ed.). New York, Harper & Row, 1968.

4 Multiple Comparisons Through Orderly Partitions: The Maximum Subrange Procedure

Henry I. Braun
Educational Testing Service

John W. Tukey
Bell Telephone Laboratories and Princeton University

1. INTRODUCTION

Simultaneous inference deals with the problem of making useful multiple inferences in a single experiment. The inferences may be in the form of a set of confidence intervals or a set of confident inequalities (confident directions). The general aim is to control the experimentwise error rate while obtaining the greatest power. The experimentwise error rate is the probability of making one or more false statements among the ensemble of statements associated with the analysis of the experiment. There are a number of different kinds of power one can consider in this area. We deal with two in what follows.

The problem we wish to consider is one of pairwise multiple comparisons. The prototypical situation arises when n observations are made on each of the k populations. It is desired to make inferences concerning the means of the k populations; in particular, which differences have confident signs and, by omission, which do not. To facilitate the analysis, it is natural to begin by assuming that the observations are normally distributed about the population means with some common (unknown) variance. Eliminating or weakening these assumptions is an important task not addressed in this chapter.

A popular confidence interval procedure is based on the use of the studentized range statistic (Miller, 1981). If $\bar{y}_i$ denotes the sample mean for population i ($i = 1, 2, \ldots, k$) and s^2 denotes the pooled estimate of the within-population variance, then the procedure constructs $\binom{k}{2}$ intervals of the form

$$(\bar{y}_i - \bar{y}_j) \pm q(k;v,\alpha) s/\sqrt{n}$$

for the differences $\mu_i - \mu_j$ of population means. The population means μ_i and μ_j are declared significantly different at level α if the corresponding confidence interval does not contain zero. The constant $q(k;v,\alpha)$ is the upper α-percent point of the studentized-range distribution for k means and an estimate of variance based on v degrees of freedom. Under the null hypothesis

$$H_0: \mu_1 = \mu_2 = \ldots = \mu_k$$

the probability that at least one pair of means is falsely declared significantly different is exactly α.

A common confident-difference procedure which does not involve setting confidence intervals is the Newman-Keuls procedure (Miller, 1981). To carry it out, the sample means are ordered, yielding:

$$y_{(1)} \leq y_{(2)} \leq \ldots \leq y_{(k)}.$$

For every pair $i < j$, $y_{(j)} - y_{(i)}$ is compared with $q(j-i+1;v,\alpha)s/\sqrt{n}$ and if it exceeds it, the corresponding difference of population means, $\mu_j - \mu_i$, is declared confidently positive, provided that a consistency condition is not violated. The consistency condition may be stated as follows: If a stretch $(y_{(i)}, y_{(j)})$ is not declared significantly different, then no stretch $(y_{(l)}, y_{(k)})$ ($i \leq l \leq j-1$; $i+1 \leq k \leq j$) contained in $(y_{(i)}, y_{(j)})$ may be declared significant. Under $H_0: \mu_1 = \ldots = \mu_k$ the experimentwise error rate is α. Since $q(k_1;v,\alpha) \leq q(k_2;v,\alpha)$ for $k_1 \leq k_2$, Newman-Keuls gains in power, in terms of confident signs, over the studentized procedure at the expense of not making confidence interval statements.

The consistency condition mentioned above may be thought of as an example of interference, in the sense that the decision about one pair of means influences the decision about other pairs. More complex forms of interference are the essence of some procedures we discuss in section 2.

As Welsch (1977) has noted, in the analysis of real data the hypothesis that all means are equal may not be plausible as, for example, when a few members of each of a number of treatment groups are being investigated. Null hypotheses in which the means are partitioned into blocks of equal means are more plausible. One example might be:

$$H_1: \mu_1 = \mu_2 \ll \mu_3 \ll \mu_4 = \mu_5 = \mu_6 \ll \mu_7 = \mu_8.$$

The two procedures we have described above may well considerably exceed their nominal error rates under such partition hypotheses. Ryan (1959, 1960) and Welsch (1977) have devised procedures which do control error rates under such hypotheses by comparing differences of sample means with suitably elevated critical values. Both are confident-direction-only procedures and invoke consistency conditions as does Newman-Keuls.

2. MORE COMPLEX PROCEDURES

Peritz (1970) devised a complex modification of the Newman-Keuls procedure which successfully controlled the experimentwise error rate. Both Begun and Gabriel (1981) and Ramsey (1981) provide simplified descriptions of the Peritz procedure. Ramsey's description is most appropriate for our purposes. Define the null hypothesis corresponding to each partition of the k means to be that means in the same element of the partition are equal. If a partition contains only one element with more than one mean, then the test for the partition consists of carrying out the Newman-Keuls procedure for the means in that element. If the partition contains two or more elements with more than one mean in each, then each element i is tested according to Ryan's procedure. This is similar to Newman-Keuls except that the critical value used to test a p-stretch is $q(p; v, \alpha_p)$ where $\alpha_p = 1 - (1-\alpha)^{p/k}$. The partition hypothesis is rejected if the means in any of the components are declared significantly different by Ryan's test.

A partition hypothesis is said to be relevant to a pair of means if they are contained in the same element of the corresponding partition.

A pair of means is declared significantly different (according to Peritz) if and only if every relevent partition hypothesis has been rejected. Thus, a pair of means are Peritz significant if they are Ryan significant or if they are Newman-Keuls significant and if every subset of the remaining $(k-2)$ means is Ryan significant. Begun and Gabriel prove that Peritz's procedure does have an experimentwise error rate $\leq \alpha$.

The interesting feature of the Peritz procedure is that the configuration of all the other means is allowed to interfere with the decision about a pair of means rendered by Newman-Keuls. If the remaining means are sufficiently distant, the rejection of equality by Newman-Keuls is allowed to stand; otherwise, the hypothesis of equality is not rejected. In this manner, the excessive rejections of Newman-Keuls are brought under control.

Ramsey (1981) introduced a competitor to Peritz called the model-testing procedure (M-T). Like Peritz, the hypothesis $\mu_i = \mu_j$ is rejected only if every relevant hypothesis is rejected. The difference is that the rejection of a partition hypothesis is based on an F-statistic criterion. Specifically, suppose a partition had p elements with m_i means ($m_i \geq 2$) in the ith element ($i = 1, 2, \ldots, p$). Let SS_i denote the sum of squares between sample means in the ith element and s^2 the pooled estimate of within population variance based on v degrees of freedom. Then the calculated statistic is $T = \dfrac{\Sigma SS_i}{m_+ - k} / s^2$, where $m_+ = \sum_i m_i$. The corresponding partition hypothesis is rejected if T exceeds $F(m_+ - k, v; \alpha)$.

Ramsey carried out a small sampling experiment to investigate the power of several pairwise multiple comparison procedures. The Peritz and M-T procedures performed well, though neither completely dominated the other. Presumably the virtue of these procedures lies in their judging the significance of a difference in the light of both the error term and any other difference of means that happen to be small (although this effect is indirect). The motivation for the maximum subrange procedure (MSR) was to capture this advantage with less computation.

3. THE MAXIMUM SUBRANGE PROCEDURE

The MSR procedure compares $y_{(i)} < y_{(j)}$ in the following steps:

(i) Determine $d = y_{(j)} - y_{(i)}$ and the length of the stretch $(j-i+1)$.
(ii) How many stretches outside $[y_i, y_j]$ of maximum span can be put down disjointly with length less than or equal to d?
(iii) Is $d \sqrt{n}/s$ greater than the corresponding critical value, Q, where the value of Q is a function of the number and span of the stretches identified in (ii)?

An example best illustrates the procedure. Consider the following ordered sequence of sample means:

$$d_3 = 1.20$$

2.54 3.69 7.71 8.19 8.92 9.39 14.21 16.18 16.82 17.04 21.02 22.10

$d_2 < 1.20$ $\qquad\qquad\qquad\qquad\qquad d_3 < 1.20 \qquad d_2 < 1.20$

Inference concerning the population means μ_α and μ_β corresponding to sample means 8.19 and 9.39 proceeds as follows:

(i) $d = 9.39 - 8.19 = 1.20$
  $j-i+1 = 6-4+1 = 3$
(ii) (a) Among the sample means less than 8.19, the stretch of maximum span < 1.20 is the gap between 2.54 and 3.68.
  (b) Among the sample means greater than 9.39, the stretch of maximum span < 1.20 is the three-stretch from 16.18 to 17.04.
  In this case, among the remaining means there is another stretch less than 1.20—namely the gap between 21.02 and 22.10.
(iii) Denote the configuration of means relevant to testing $\mu_\alpha = \mu_\beta$ by (3,3,2,2), reflecting the fact that the ordered sample means corresponding to μ_α and μ_β have span 3 and that there are 3 other disjoint stretches

4. THE MAXIMUM SUBRANGE PROCEDURE

with spans 3, 2 and 2 of smaller length. The statistic is denoted as $T(3,3,2,2)$ and equals 1.20. To carry out the test, $T(3,3,2,2)\sqrt{n}/s$ is compared with $Q(3,3,2,2;v,\alpha)$. For example, $Q(3,3,2,2;\infty,.05) = 3.83$. If $n = 5$ and $s = 1$, the hypothesis $\mu_\alpha = \mu_\beta$ would not be rejected.

The computation of the critical values Q is described in the Appendix. They are derived from the distribution of the studentized range. Note that 3.83 exceeds $3.31 = q(3;\infty,.05)$, the appropriate critical value for the N-K procedure. Thus like Peritz and M-T, the MSR procedure controls the excessive rejections of N-K by employing more extreme critical values. The critical value is determined for each pair by the configuration of the sample means relevant to the test, as described above.

The MSR requires far less computation than does Peritz or M-T. Instead of looking at all partitions, it considers only those conforming to the ordering of the sample means. Moreover, because it looks for disjoint stretches of maximal span, it generally does not search through all "orderly" partitions. Nonetheless, limited experimental sampling suggests its performance is comparable to Peritz or M-T.

Although the experimentwise error rate for the MSR remained below the nominal level in all the simulations, we can identify configurations of means for which the error rate will slightly exceed the nominal level. An example follows. Suppose the true state of nature is

$$\mu_1 = \mu_2 \ll \mu_3 = \mu_4 \ll \mu_5 = \mu_6$$

where the distance between the equally spaced pairs is very large in comparison to the within group variance. Thus, with near certainty, the sample means will appear in corresponding groups. Let

$$d_1 = |\bar{y}_1 - \bar{y}_2|, d_2 = |\bar{y}_3 - \bar{y}_4| \text{ and } d_3 = |\bar{y}_5 - \bar{y}_6|.$$

Denote the reordered absolute gaps by $f_{(1)} \leq f_{(2)} \leq f_{(3)}$. For a test of nominal level .05 (and assuming $v = \infty$), a Type I error occurs if any of the following events occur:

$$\sqrt{n} f_{(1)}/s > 2.77$$

or

$$\sqrt{n} f_{(2)}/s > 3.19$$

or

$$\sqrt{n} f_{(3)}/s > 3.38$$

Now 3.38 is the upper 95% point of the distribution of the maximum of three studentized gaps. Consequently, $Pr\{\sqrt{n}f_{(3)}/s > 3.38\} = .05$ and so $Pr\{$Type I error } > .05. In the present instance, it can be shown that the Type I error ≤ .053. More thorough investigations of the error rate properties of the procedure are planned.

4. SIMULATIONS

A small-scale simulation was carried out so that the power of the procedure could be compared to that of Peritz and M-T. We will report on one set of simulations involving an experimental setup with the following parameters:

Number of populations $(k) = 6$
Number of observations per population $(n) = 5$
Significance level $(\alpha) = .05$
Degrees of freedom for variance estimation $(\nu) = 24$.

The ratio of between-means variance to within-means variance was allowed to vary systematically. If the latter variance is denoted by σ^2 and the former by $\tau^2 = k^{-1} \sum_{i=1}^{k} (\mu_i - \bar{\mu})^2$, then the effect size, f, is defined by $f = \tau/\sigma$.

For each fixed value of f many configurations of means are still possible. We considered four such configurations, as did Ramsey (1981):

(i) Equally spaced means: Adjacent means are equally distant.
(ii) Equally spaced null pairs: Adjacent pairs of equal means are equally distant.
(iii) Maximal configuration: Means are arranged to have the maximum range. For k even, the two extreme means are placed on either side of, and equidistant from, a central cluster of $(k-2)$ equal means.
(iv) Minimal configuration: Means are arranged to have the minimum range. For k even, two clusters of $(k/2)$ equal means each are created.

For each value of f, 1,000 simulations for each configuration were run. Each set of 1,000 simulations was begun with the same seed for the random number generator. Pseudo-random uniform deviates were obtained from a Tausworthe generator written in Assembler. Gaussian deviates were derived using the Box-Muller method. A simulation consisted of generating n independent $N(\mu_i, 1)$ observations $(i = 1, 2, \ldots, k)$ and carrying out the MSR and Peritz procedures. The M-T procedure has not been implemented by us as of this writing and we have had to use Ramsey's experimental results (also based on 1,000 simulations) to make any comparisons with MSR. These comparisons are thus necessarily less precise than those between MSR and Peritz based on our simulations.

4. THE MAXIMUM SUBRANGE PROCEDURE   61

Ramsey has suggested that the configuration of equally spaced null pairs provides a stringent test of the Type I error characteristics of a multiple comparisons procedure. In approximately ten sets of 1,000 simulations, with values of f varying from .5 to 10.0, the empirical error rate of the MSR never exceeded the nominal error rate of .05. The same holds true for the corresponding simulations for the other configurations.

Following Ramsey, two kinds of power were considered. Any-pair power is the probability of detecting at least one true difference between pairs of means. It measures sensitivity to the largest difference in a configuration of means. All-pairs power is the probability of detecting all true differences between pairs of means. It measures sensitivity to the smallest true difference in a configuration of means. Any-pair power is of interest for small values of f while all-pairs power is of interest for large values of f ($f > 1$).

Table 4.1 presents the results for a comparative study of any-pair power. Only the MSR and M-T procedures are shown because the Peritz procedure was nearly equivalent (though very slightly worse) to the MSR in the range of f values studied. Except for one instance ($f = .7$, maximal configuration), the MSR is uniformly more powerful than M-T. That one instance seems somewhat anomalous in view of Fig. 4.1 which presents plots of the Gaussian Equivalent Deviate expressed (GED-expressed) power against f^2. In classical notation, power is denoted by 1-β where β is the Type II error. The GED-expressed power is simply $\Phi^{-1}(1-\beta)$, where $\Phi(\cdot)$ is the unit Gaussian cumulative, and is a useful linearizing transformation for power curves, as the figure attests.

Table 4.2 presents the results for a comparative study of all-pairs power. Here again the MSR is uniformly more powerful than M-T. Peritz is slightly more powerful than MSR for maximal configurations and slightly less powerful for minimal configurations.

TABLE 4.1
Any-Pair Power

Effect Size	Maximum Configuration		Minimum Configuration	
	MSR	M-T	MSR	M-T
.4	.31	.23	.27	.20
.5	.47	.37	.40	.33
.6	.62	.58	.55	.53
.7	.78	.87	.68	.64
.8	.90		.79	

[1] Experimental setup: $k = 6$; $n = 5$; $\alpha = .05$; $\nu = 24$.
[2] Based on simulations of 1000 experiments.
[3] M-T power taken from Ramsey (1981).

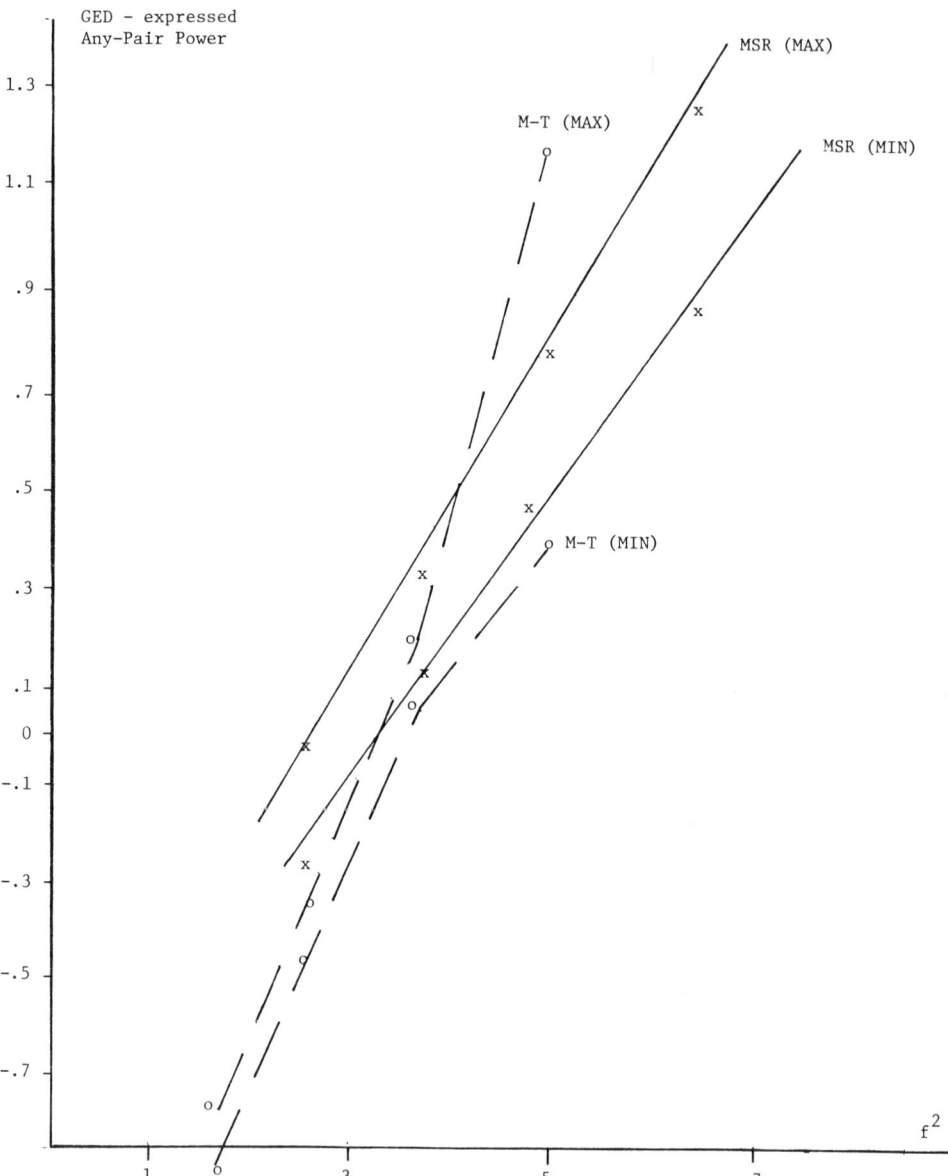

FIG. 4.1 Power of MSR and M-T procedures for maximal and minimal configurations.

4. THE MAXIMUM SUBRANGE PROCEDURE

TABLE 4.2
All-Pairs Power

Effect Size (f)	Maximum Configuration			Minimum Configuration		
	M-T	MSR	Peritz	M-T	MSR	Peritz
1.00	–	.08	.09	–	.22	.20
1.15	–	–	–	.37	–	–
1.20	.18	.22	.23	.43	.48	.44
1.25	–	–	–	.49	–	–
1.30	.27	.33	.35	.57	.62	.60
1.40	.40	.48	.50	–	.75	.74
1.50	.53	.64	.65	–	.87	.85

[1] Experimental setup: k = 6; n = 5; α = .05; ν = 24.
[2] Based on simulations of 1000 experiments.
[3] M-T power taken from Ramsey (1981).

Table 4.3 shows the behavior of:

$$\frac{\text{GED-expressed power} + C}{f^2}$$

where C is chosen to keep the resulting numbers nearly constant over a broad range of effect sizes. The actual and relative sizes of the medians over f are shown. In relative terms, M-T is at 90.5 and 94.5, MSR is at 98 and 100, while Peritz is at 100 and 98. Clearly the differences in performance between MSR and

TABLE 4.3
All-Pairs Power
(GED-Expressed and Converted)

Effect Size (f)	Maximum Configuration $(GED + 2.770)/f^2$			Minimum Configuration $(GED + 2.120)/f^2$		
	M-T	MSR	Peritz	M-T	MSR	Peritz
1.00	–	1.39	1.40	–	1.35	1.27
1.15	–	–	–	1.36	–	–
1.20	1.29	1.38	1.41	1.35	1.43	1.37
1.25	–	–	–	1.33	–	–
1.30	1.28	1.38	1.41	1.36	1.43	1.40
1.40	1.28	1.39	1.41	–	1.43	1.41
1.50	1.27	1.39	1.40	–	1.50	1.40
Median	1.28	1.39	1.41	1.36	1.43	1.40
Relative Size	91	98	100	95	100	98

[1] Experimental setup: k = 6; n = 5; α = .05; ν = 24.
[2] Based on simulations of 1000 experiments.
[3] M-T power taken from Ramsey (1981).
[4] Ratio of median power to maximum median power.

Peritz (except for maximum configuration and $f = 1.5$) are not of practical importance.

5. CONCLUSIONS

The maximum subrange procedure appears to be a plausible competitor to the Peritz and model-testing procedures while maintaining a substantial edge in simplicity and computational speed.

Its experimentwise error rate and power characteristics need to be evaluated more thoroughly and its properties analyzed analytically. It does seem to hold substantial promise.

APPENDIX

The critical values for the MSR procedure are obtained by integration and interpolation. Let $F_p(\cdot)$ denote the cumulative distribution function of the range of p independent unit Gaussian random variables.

$$F_p(u) = p \int_{-\infty}^{\infty} \phi(y) [\Phi(y) - \Phi(y - u)]^{k-1} dy,$$

where $\phi(\cdot)$ and $\Phi(\cdot)$ are the density function and distribution function of the unit Gaussian. When the range is studentized by division by the square root of the ratio of an independent chi-square random variable on ν degrees-of-freedom to its degrees-of-freedom, the distribution function, denoted by H_p, may be represented as

$$H_p(u) = \int_0^{\infty} F_p(ux) \frac{\nu^{\nu/2} x^{\nu-1} e^{-\nu x^2/2} dx}{\Gamma(\nu/2) 2^{(\nu/2)-1}}.$$

For a fixed value of α and a configuration $(\ell_1, \ell_2, \ldots, \ell_m)$ we seek a value u_0 such that $J(u_0) = 1 - \prod_{j=1}^{m} H_{\ell_j}(u_0)$ is equal to α.

The desired value of u_o was obtained by evaluating $J(\cdot)$ at some 30 points and carrying out Aitken's scheme of polynomial interpolation by ascending degrees, using the DALI subroutine of SSP. The integrals $H_p(u)$ were evaluated with a 16-point Gauss-Hermite quadrature using the DQH16 subroutine of SSP. For certain choices of p and u, the values of the integral were checked against those tabulated in Harter (1960). Table 4.A1 displays the critical values for a test of level .05 for all configurations arising from ten means when the estimate of variance is based on 24 or ∞ degrees of freedom.

TABLE 4.A1
Critical Values for Maximum Subrange Procedure

Configuration	$v = \infty$	$v = 24$	Configuration	$v = \infty$	$v = 24$
10	4.47	4.92	4,4,2	4.02	4.40
9	4.39	4.81	4,4,3	3.99	4.37
8,2	4.31	4.72	4,4	3.98	4.34
8	4.29	4.68	4,3,2	3.91	4.26
7,3	4.25	4.66	4,2,2,2	3.86	4.21
7,2	4.20	4.59	4,3	3.85	4.18
7	4.17	4.54	4,2,2	3.80	4.13
6,4	4.21	4.62	4,2	3.73	4.02
6,3	4.13	4.52	4	3.63	3.90
6,2,2	4.11	4.49	3,3,3	3.87	4.22
6,2	4.07	4.43	3,3,2,2	3.83	4.17
6	4.03	4.37	3,3,2	3.76	4.08
5,5	4.19	4.60	3,2,2,2	3.70	4.02
5,4	4.10	4.48	3,3	3.67	3.97
5,3,2	4.04	4.42	3,2,2	3.60	3.90
5,3	4.00	4.36	3,2	3.48	3.74
5,2,2	3.97	4.32	3	3.31	3.53
5,2	3.91	4.25	2,2,2,2,2	3.64	3.94
5	3.86	4.17	2,2,2,2	3.52	3.81
			2,2,2	3.38	3.63
			2,2	3.17	3.37
			2	2.77	2.92

REFERENCES

Begun, J., & Gabriel, R. Closure of the Newman-Keul's multiple comparisons procedure. *Journal of the American Statistical Association,* 1981, *76,* 241–245.

Harter, H. L. Tables of range and studentized range. *Annals of Mathematical Statistics,* 1960, *31,* 1122–1147.

Miller, R. G. *Simultaneous statistical inference* (2nd ed.). New York: Springer-Verlag, 1981.

Peritz, E. A Note on Multiple Comparisons (unpublished manuscript) Jerusalem: Hebrew University, 1970.

Ramsey, P. H. Power of univariate pairwise multiple comparison procedures. *Psychological Bulletin,* 1981, *90,* 352–366.

Ryan, T. A. Multiple comparisons in psychological research. *Psychological Bulletin,* 1959, *56,* 26–47.

Ryan, T. A. Significance tests for multiple comparison of proportions, variance, and other statistics. *Psychological Bulletin,* 1960, *57,* 318–328.

Welsch, R. E. Stepwise multiple comparison procedures. *Journal of the American Statistical Association,* 1977, *72,* 566–575.

II ITEM RESPONSE THEORY AND ITS APPLICATIONS

Much of Lord's work over the past twenty years has been on the development, refinement, and testing of item response theory. In this section are six essays that describe various aspects of modern latent trait models that extend Lord's results theoretically, or expand them into new areas of application.

Bert Green notes that one of the most important applications of item response theory is for use as a theoretical basis for computerized adaptive testing (CAT). He describes the potential that CAT has toward providing us with increased efficiency of testing when tests are of high quality. His engineering approach yields numerical benchmarks required for a viable CAT program. These include such characteristics as item pool size and item quality.

John Keats and **Darrell Bock** both agree that it is sensible to view a behavioral relationship, not as a fixed law, but as a family of laws, the parameters of which describe the individual behavioral tendencies of the subjects in the population. Keats examines the extent to which this formulation can be used to characterize long-term human cognitive growth (see Anastasi's chapter in this volume for a further discussion of this point). He explores two models that may be appropriate, but indicates the theoretical and practical limitations. These considerations impel him inexorably toward a latent ability formulation, as being crucial to a satisfactory solution to this problem.

Bock continues this development, but with a more general view noting that this formulation leads inevitably to Bayesian methods of data analysis. This conclusion is derived from the implied two stage sampling of the problem definition—responses are sampled within subjects and subjects within populations. He develops and discusses a new and more general method of analysis that provides a rigorous structure for examining longitudinal change.

Erling Andersen connects the models of item response theory associated with the analysis of categorical data to those for the analysis of contingency tables. He shows how this approach allows each method to borrow strength from the other and so provide a more powerful tool for the analysis of categorical data. He demonstrates the method's versatility with analyses of two different data sets.

Gerhard Fischer and Rupert Kisser demonstrate how item response theory can be applied to the analysis of latencies (see Bruce Bloxom's chapter in this volume for more on this topic). They describe a model and the estimation procedures it requires. In their analysis of latency data from a test of driving ability they provide supporting evidence for making "stop" signals red.

Finally, **Fumiko Samejima** provides a thorough justification of the importance and usefulness of the operating characteristic function as a descriptor of performance. She then provides us with a variety of methods for estimating it.

5 The Promise of Tailored Tests

Bert F. Green
The Johns Hopkins University

Adaptive testing, or tailored testing as it is sometimes called, is the process of adjusting the difficulty level of successive items presented to a test-taker in an attempt to make the difficulty of the item appropriate for the test-taker. Binet (1909) did this in the first intelligence tests, and the process has continued to this day on the Stanford Binet IQ test. The procedure requires individualized testing, with a test administrator for each test-taker, and is impractical for large-scale testing. The paper and pencil test was invented to provide the needed administrative efficiency. With interactive computers readily available the computer can replace the human as test administrator, so individualized testing is again attractive.

The past decade has seen vigorous developments of the methods of computerized adaptive testing (CAT). Lord (1970, 1971a, 1971b, 1971c, 1977) has played a leading role in this development, but so have many others, especially Samejima (1969, 1977a, 1977b), Bock and Lieberman (1970), Urry (1977), Weiss (1974, 1978, 1979, 1980), as well as Rasch (1960), Fischer (1980), and Wright (1977). Adaptive testing requires the new test theory that Birnbaum (1968) discussed as latent trait theory, but that Lord now calls item response theory (IRT). In a sense, whoever helped develop IRT helped develop tailored testing. In fact, adaptive testing is one of the most important applications of IRT. Much of the impetus for the development of IRT and CAT came from the Office of Naval Research (ONR), under Marshall Farr, Charles Davis, and others. They deserve great credit for supporting these developments, which have culminated in the current efforts to develop a CAT version of the Armed Services Vocational Aptitude Battery (ASVAB). This pioneering work, being led by James McBride, Malcolm Ree, and Michael Patrow, among others, deserves our support, encouragement, and gratitude.

ADVANTAGES OF COMPUTER PRESENTATION

Quite apart from the apparent efficiency of asking questions of appropriate difficulty, computer presentation of tests has many other advantages, both administrative and psychometric. One of the most attractive administrative advantages is improved test security. Although computers are not larceny proof, surely a test is more secure in a computer system than in a desk drawer.

Also with a computer there are no more messy answer sheets, no more ambiguity about students' responses, and no chance that the student will mark the wrong item on the answer sheet. The test can be scored immediately and a computer record is automatically available for item analysis.

Perhaps the most intriguing psychometric advantage of individualized tests is that an examinee can work at his/her own pace, which yields an ideal power test. Present testing programs have time limits chosen to balance the time that the very able student must sit and wait, with the opportunity for slow students to finish most of the test. In a computerized adaptive test, each examinee stays busy, productively. Moreover, everyone is challenged but not too discouraged, since with multiple choice questions, the best choice of difficulty is such that each person gets about three out of five items correct. Another psychometric plus is that items can be unobtrusively slipped into the sequence for pretests, assuming sophisticated software. Finally, if the item pool is big enough (and the bigger the better) then the entire pool can be published without compromising the test.

The most important benefit of computer presentation is the potential for new items. First there is the real possibility of constructed responses. Certainly, numerical answers to arithmetic problems can be typed; probably responses to word fluency tests can be typed. Memory can be tested by use of successive frames. The use of pictures and even video clips, using video disk technology, can replace long-winded explanations of situations, for example, on police or fire fighter exams. Tests of diagnostic skill or problem-solving skill can require the examinee to seek the information actively. The possibilities are vast.

All of these advantages, however, can be realized only if CAT is adopted. Before embracing CAT enthusiastically, we must answer two hard questions. Is computerized adaptive testing really feasible and is it really efficient?

FEASIBILITY

Feasibility seems imminent. The rapid development of computer terminals and microcomputers is driving the price down to a manageable level. The U.S. Armed Services now have under development a terminal that will be especially designed for computerized adaptive testing, in connection with their intent to computerize the ASVAB. These terminals can be expected to be available commercially for little more than the cost of a television set. Notice that CAT is especially suited to a situation, as in the military or the government or a personnel office generally, where applicants come in more or less continuously. Large-scale testing programs like the Graduate Record Examination or the College Board, which offer a limited number of national administrations each year, would require a complete logistic transformation to adopt such a procedure, but that will happen some day.

Given the equipment, there remains the need for a large pool of items, of widely varying difficulty. Further, the items have to be of high quality. Specifically, they have to have high values of a, the discrimination parameter of the three-parameter Item Response Curve. Now, there are two ways to get highly discriminating items. One is to select the cream of a very, very large pool of items. Another, often easier way, is to test a heterogeneous population. IRT is commonly said to be independent of the population of test takers, and so it is, largely. But the parameters must refer to some scale. And the reference scale is defined in terms of the mean and variance of some reference group. Thus a set of items with a's of .5 with respect to one reference group become items with a's of 1.0 by changing to a new reference group with twice the standard deviation.

This seems an elementary point, but it deserves emphasis. The ASVAB population is essentially the high-school population; the civil service system (which almost installed CAT), has a heterogeneous clientele, and Fred Lord's major effort at test construction has been a broad-range tailored test of verbal ability. There is plainly more to be gained with a variable group than with a homogeneous group.

I make a point of this partly because I failed to understand it a decade ago when I produced a discouraging comment (Green, 1970) on Lord's (1970) "Some Test Theory for Tailored Tests." Both Fred and I focused on a test with a values of .5, and discovered that the gains are only substantial for the most extreme abilities, beyond two standard deviations. As a fan of tailored testing, I have been feeling guilty about those old comments ever since I made them, but it wasn't until I met the ASVAB, where a values are almost all above 1, and have an average of about 1.4 (Bock & Mislevy, 1981) that I realized how unnecessarily pessimistic I had been.

EFFICIENCY

Let us look at some engineering calculations concerning the efficiency of tailored tests. Throughout, the three-parameter logistic model will be used; this paper examines properties of that model (see Birnbaum, 1968; Lord, 1980). Three levels of the a parameter are used, .8, 1.2, and 1.6. The c parameter is fixed at .2, and the b parameter is as needed, as we shall see. The corresponding item response curves (IRC) are shown in Fig. 5.1, and the corresponding item information (I) functions are in Fig. 5.2. Note that a small change in the slope of the IRC makes a large difference in the information curve.

The first problem is to select the proper foil—the proper conventional group test against which to compare the tailored test. The main value of the tailored test is to permit testing all candidates to the same level of precision. Item response theory permits calculating the test information function, which is the sum of the item information functions, and shows for each ability value, θ, the amount of information supplied by those items about that θ value. The variance of measurement errors is the reciprocal of the test information function. Ordinary paper and pencil tests usually have an information function that is peaked in the middle, whereas the ideal CAT has a perfectly flat information function, since testing is continued until information reaches some criterion value.

A reasonable group test to use for comparison would have a flat information function over a considerable range. I chose a range of $-1.5 < \theta < 1.5$, and found, by trial and error, a selection of b values to yield a flat function (defined

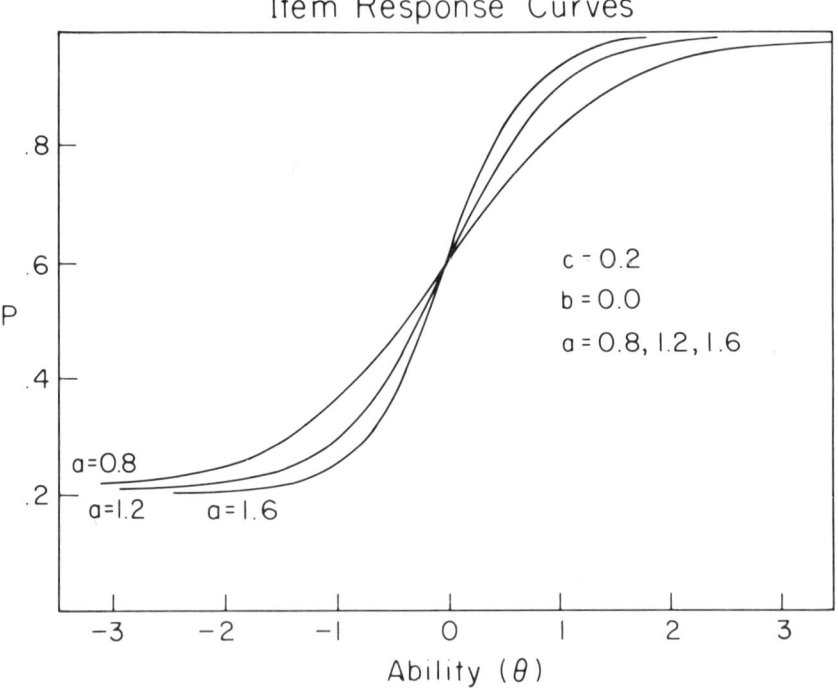

FIG. 5.1. Item response functions for three values of a: .8, 1.2, and 1.6. All curves have $b = 0$, $c = .2$. These curves give the probability of a correct response to this item, as a function of ability, θ.

Item Information Functions

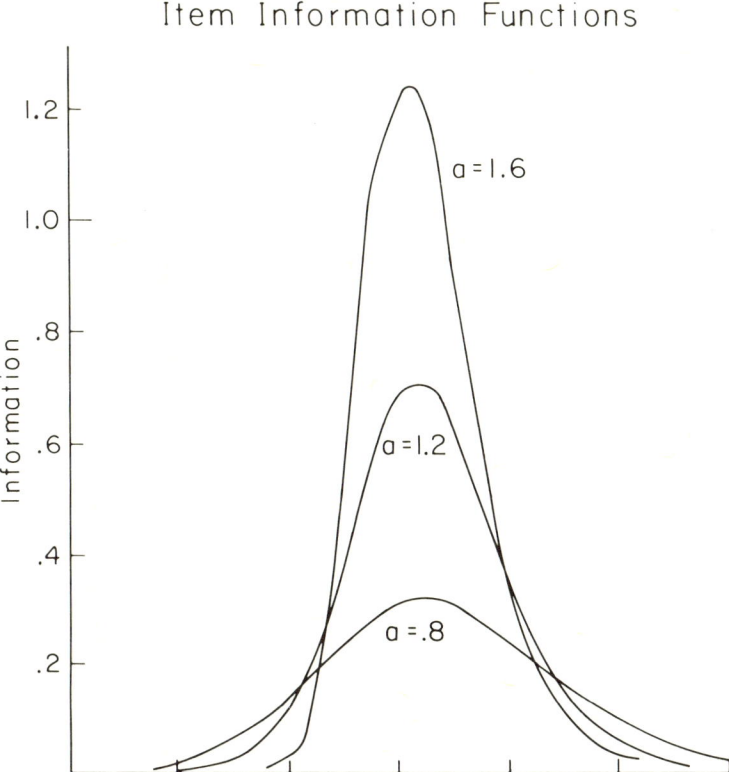

FIG. 5.2. Item information function for three values of a: .8, 1.2 and 1.6. All curves have $b = 0$, $c = .2$. The curves give the information contained in an item response, as a function of ability, θ.

by the selection with the highest minimum in that range). Many possible selections of b-values yield essentially the same curve; requiring a wider interval of flatness would require a few more items to reach a given information level. The selection was made for $I = 10$, the number of items needed for other values of I were calculated by assuming proportionality of n and I. Table 5.1 shows the number of items needed for each of five levels of Information, 5, 7, 10, 14, and 20, for both a broad-range conventional test and an ideal test. To obtain corresponding reliabilities, we note that reliability can be defined as the ratio of true variance to true variance plus error variance, which leads to the following index of reliability:

TABLE 5.1
Number of Items to Achieve Various Levels of Test Information

(a) Broad Range Group Test

a-value	Information				
	5	7	10	14	20
.8	32	43	64	86	128
1.2	20	28	40	56	80
1.6	14	20	28	40	56

(b) Ideal Test

a-value	5	7	10	14	20
.8	16	23	32	44	64
1.2	8	10	15	20	29
1.6	4	6	8	12	16

$$r_{\theta\theta} = \frac{1}{1 + \frac{1}{I}} = \frac{I}{I+1}.$$

(This formula is appropriate as a marginal reliability only if I is approximately constant, which it is here.) The reliabilities corresponding to the levels of I are .833, .875, .909, .933, and .952, respectively.

This is how well we can do with a broad-range group test. How well could we do with any test at all? According to IRT, the best we could possibly do is administer items exactly appropriate to each person's ability, θ. That, of course, is what tailored testing tries to do; it is, however, hampered by not knowing θ. To obtain a lower bound on the number of items necessary, let us assume that we know θ, and further than we have all of the items that we might possibly need. Then the number of items needed to achieve the given levels of information can be readily calculated. They are shown in Table 5.1. Tailored tests will be somewhere between the broad-range group test and the optimum.

Consider next an adaptive test in the realistic situation that the candidate's ability, θ, is unknown, but in the somewhat idealistic case that we have access to all the items we might possibly need, that is, to an infinite item pool. Since nothing is known initially about the ability of the candidate, θ is initially set at zero for everyone. Then, after every item, a maximum likelihood estimate is made of the person's score, based on the item responses and the characteristics of the items presented. That estimate, θ, is used to select the next item.[1] Here we assume that there is an item with a as specified (a = .8, 1.2, or 1.6, with c = .2; and with b ideal for every θ). We assume that the pool contains such an item, and we administer it. We stop when the information, I, at the estimated ability, θ, reaches the specified value (5, 10, or 20), and note the number of items needed to achieve that level. The median numbers of items needed are shown in Table 5.2, for one simulation, using 100 cases at each of nine values of theta: $-2(.5)2$. The results are very consistent. Table 5.2 shows average values for $I = 10$. Basically the tailored test turns out to be very nearly as good as the ideal test.

Although the item pool was assumed to be infinite, the computer actually tallied how many items it used in each interval of b-values. Assuming intervals .2 θ wide, the maximum number of items used in any category is shown in Table 5.3. On the average, when $I = 10$, each category needs about 30, 15, or 8 items, for the three item qualities examined. That translates to a need for about 25 sets of items, each of that size, which means item pools of size 750, 350, or 225, respectively. It seems likely that very little harm would be done by smaller item pools.

The simulation results shown in Table 5.3 are only a part of the total results. Intermediate values were used, and intermediate results obtained. There is nothing exceptional about any of the intermediate values, which are therefore not depicted here. Technical experts will recognize that no estimate of ability is possible until the examinee has made at least one correct and one incorrect response. The present algorithm starts θ at .0, and increases it by 1.0 (-1.0) for every correct (incorrect) response initially until the simulated examinee makes one incorrect (correct) response, at which point a proper estimate can be made.

The simulations show that the actual error variance corresponds quite well with $1/I$, as it should. In theory, the error variance approaches $1/I$ as the number of items increases, but for small numbers of items there can readily be a discrepancy, since the theoretical error variance is the variance for fixed θ. The corre-

TABLE 5.2
Median Number of Items Needed to Achieve Information = 10
(Reliability = .91) for an Ideal CAT

	Item Quality (a)		
	.8	1.2	1.6
Broad-range group test	64	40	28
Ideal test	32	15	8
Ideal CAT			
$\theta = -2.0$	35.9	19.2	12.9
$\theta = -1.5$	36.0	17.8	11.4
$\theta = -1.0$	35.0	17.5	10.9
$\theta = -0.5$	35.3	16.9	10.5
$\theta = 0$	35.6	17.2	10.4
$\theta = 0.5$	35.3	17.4	10.9
$\theta = 1.0$	35.4	17.4	11.4
$\theta = 1.5$	35.5	17.7	11.5
$\theta = 2.0$	36.3	18.5	12.2

TABLE 5.3
Monte Carlo Estimates of Number of Items of Various Quality to Achieve Various Levels of Information. The Resultant Number of Items Used Are Shown for the Most Frequent b Category of Width .20. The Average Squared Bias, and Actual and Theoretical Error Variance are Also Shown. N = 100 Cases for Each Value of True Ability (θ)

Nominal I	θ	No. of Items Median	No. of Items Range	Items per Category	Squared Bias$\times 10^3$	Error Var. $\times 10^3$ Actual	Error Var. $\times 10^3$ Theory
Item discrimination parameter $a = 1.6$							
5	-2.0	7.2	5-19	4	150	603	200
	-1.0	6.3	5-16	4	11	204	200
	0	6.2	5-15	3	0	233	200
	1.0	6.9	5-16	3	23	417	200
	2.0	7.8	6-12	4	63	281	200
10	-2.0	12.9	10-29	9	8	184	100
	-1.0	10.9	10-25	9	1	96	100
	0	10.4	10-22	8	0	107	100
	1.0	11.4	10-28	8	3	111	100
	2.0	12.4	10-24	8	16	139	100
20	-2.0	21.4	19-42	20	0	62	50
	-1.0	19.4	18-32	21	0	50	50
	0	19.2	18-34	20	3	46	50
	2.0	19.5	18-36	19	1	51	50
	2.0	21.0	19-41	21	1	54	50
Item discrimination parameter $a = 1.2$							
5	-2.0	11.4	9-22	6	8	275	200
	-1.0	7.8	8-21	6	15	315	200
	0	9.5	8-20	6	0	219	200
	1.0	9.6	8-17	6	3	240	200
	2.0	10.5	9-23	6	7	171	200
10	-2.0	19.2	16-43	13	6	120	100
	-1.0	17.5	15-30	15	19	178	100
	0	17.2	15-30	13	0	126	100
	1.0	17.4	16-27	14	4	132	100
	2.0	18.5	17-29	14	3	107	100
20	-2.0	34.2	31-60	30	1	46	50
	-1.0	32.5	30-74	34	3	46	50
	0	31.7	30-43	34	0	54	50
	1.0	32.1	30-42	34	1	64	50
	2.0	33.1	31-47	32	1	53	50
Item discrimination parameter $a = 0.8$							
5	-2.0	19.7	17-31	11	1	164	200
	-1.0	18.5	17-26	12	0	209	200
	0	18.9	17-29	12	0	205	200

(*continued*)

5. THE PROMISE OF TAILORED TESTS   77

TABLE 5.3 (Continued)

Nominal I	θ	No. of Items Median	Range	Items per Category	Squared Bias×10³	Error Var. × 10³ Actual	Theory
	1.0	18.7	17-29	14	16	197	200
	2.0	19.7	18-30	12	6	248	200
10	-2.0	35.9	35-48	28	0	81	100
	-1.0	35.0	33-71	28	0	111	100
	0	35.6	33-56	28	0	96	100
	1.0	35.4	33-55	30	2	90	100
	2.0	36.3	34-57	30	1	100	100
20	-2.0	68.9	66-68	73	0	45	
	-1.0	67.4	65-100	73	0	50	50
	0	68.1	65-100	66	0	55	50
	1.0	67.8	65-100	72	1	51	50
	2.0	69.3	66-100	74	0	52	50

sponding information should be $I(\theta)$, but is instead $\hat{I}(\theta)$. This discrepancy seems to matter at extreme values of θ.

A more disturbing problem is the extreme skew on the distributions of number of items used. A few such distributions are shown in Figure 5.3. All of the distributions are like those depicted, as can be seen in Table 5.3 by comparing the medians with the ranges. The occasional need for many more items than the median number is the result of an occasional individual who experiences a consecutive series of lucky hits, or a series of unlucky choices. When that happens, the estimate of θ becomes quite wrong, so the items given are not very appropriate, yet for a time the system is satisfied, until the weight of numbers finally begins to take effect. Eventually the estimate begins to home in on the true value. As this happens, the system finds that all those seemingly informative items weren't informative at all, $I(\theta)$ goes down, and recovery is a long process. Note carefully that these cases are unusual but not abnormal—they are to be expected from time to time as a normal part of the stochastic process. Perhaps we need some modification of the process to guard against these results, but probably there will always be such unusual, normal cases.

From an engineering viewpoint, it would be convenient to limit the number of items presented to an individual, cutting off a few persons before they reached the specified criterion. We need to know how the use of such a limit will affect the error level in the system. Also, in any real CAT, the item pool is not ideal. An item of exactly the best b-value may not be available, so the system may have to choose a less than optimum item. This will especially be the case at the extremes of the ability scale, since items with extreme b-values (e.g., +3.5) may not be available at all. To test these realities, a series of runs was made in which b was limited as follows. All b's were between −2.5 and +2.5. Further, it was

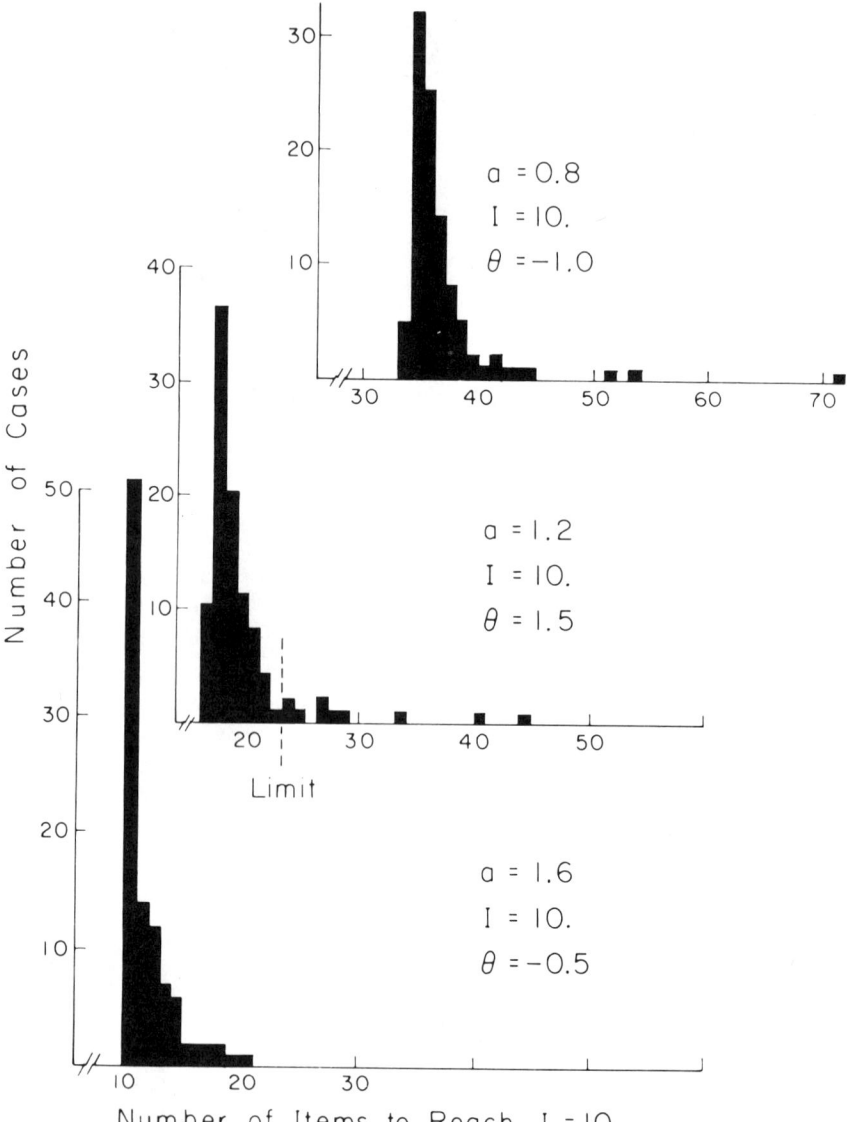

Fig. 5.3. Examples of distributions of the number of items needed in an adaptive test to attain an information level of 10, for various item qualities and various values of true ability, θ. Each distribution represents 100 similar examinees.

assumed that items were grouped by *b*-value, in .2 θ intervals, and that within each group, the *b*-values varied uniformly and randomly. When the system needed a certain *b* value, the nearest group was determined, and a *b* value selected at random from that group. For example, if the system wanted an item with $b = .76$, it went to the .70–.90 interval, and got a *b* somewhere in that interval. The difference will usually be small, since item information doesn't change drastically in a small interval; further, the system's notion of an optimum *b* is generally not really optimum anyway, because θ is only estimated. For these reasons, a small amount of fuzziness in *b* was not expected to have an appreciable effect. However, restricting the *b*'s to the range $-2.5 < b < 2.5$ might effect the extreme θ's noticeably.

Table 5.4 shows the results of a series of simulations with imperfect item pools, a restricted range of *b*'s, and a limit on the number of items presented. When these results are compared with Table 6.2, it can be seen that actuarially there is no difference in average bias, square bias, or error variance.

SUMMARY

Computerized adaptive testing is remarkably efficient, in theory, although some fine tuning is still needed. The procedure is feasible now on a small scale, and will soon be feasible for large groups. If large item pools can be found or created, computerized adaptive testing is definitely worthwhile. It has been made possible by item response theory, and represents the culmination of a lot of work by a lot of people, but Fred Lord is certainly one of its principal progenitors.

TABLE 5.4
Effects of Limiting the Number of Items and of Using Simulated Item Pools of Width 0.2 θ, for Information = 10, for $a = 1.2$, for Various Levels of True θ, N = 100 Cases at Each Level of Theta

	Unlimited				Limited				
θ	N of items (range)	Bias $\hat{\theta} - \theta$	Sq. bias x 10^3	Error var x 10^3	N of items (range)	Bias $\hat{\theta} - \theta$	Sq. bias x 10^3	Error var x 10^3	Proportion of cases limited
-2.0	17-41	.01	0	146	17-22	.22	46	102	.22
-1.5	16-29	.00	0	103	16-22	.06	4	98	.11
-1.0	16-31	.08	6	160	16-22	.11	12	166	.04
-.5	16-45	.05	3	101	16-22	.08	7	124	.08
0	15-37	-.02	0	80	15-22	-.01	0	81	.10
.5	15-40	-.03	1	96	15-22	-.04	1	99	.06
1.0	16-41	.00	0	84	16-22	-.03	1	82	.05
1.5	16-38	.08	7	131	16-22	-.03	1	123	.12
2.0	16-33	-.02	0	80	16-22	-.07	1	73	.10

REFERENCES

Binet, A. *Les idees modernes sur les enfants*. Paris: Ernest Flamorion, 1909.
Birnbaum, A. Some latent trait models and their uses in inferring an examinee's ability. In Lord, F. M. & Novick, M. R. *Statistical theories of mental test scores*. Reading, Mass.: Addision, Wesley, 1968.
Bock, R. D., & Lieberman, M. Fitting a response model for n dichotomously scored items. *Psychometrika*, 1970, 35, 179–197.
Bock, R. D., & Mislevy, R. J. *Data quality analysis of the Armed Services Vocational Aptitude Battery*. Chicago: National Opinion Research Center, August, 1981.
Fischer, G. H. Individual testing on the basis of the dichotomous Rasch model. In L. J. T. Van der Kamp, W. F. Langerak, & D. M. N. de Gruijter (Eds.), *Psychometrics for educational debates*. Chichester: Wiley, 1980.
Green, B. F. Comments on tailored testing. In W. Holtzman, (Ed.), *Computer assisted instruction, testing, and guidance*. New York: Harper & Row, 1970.
Lord, F. M. Some test theory for tailored testing. In W. Holtzman, (Ed.), *Computer assisted instruction, testing and guidance*. New York: Harper & Row, 1970.
Lord, F. M. Robbins-Monro procedures for tailored testing. *Educational and psychological measurement*. 1971, 31, 3–31. (a)
Lord, F. M. The self-scoring flexilevel test. *Journal of Educational Measurement*, 1971, 8, 147–151. (b)
Lord, F. M. A theoretical study of two-stage testing. Psychometrika, 1971, 36, 227–242. (c)
Lord, F. M. A broad-range tailored test of verbal ability. *Applied Psychological Measurement*, 1977, 1, 95–100.
Lord, F. M. *Applications of item response theory to practical testing problems*. Hillsdale, N.J.: Lawrence Erlbaum Associates, 1980.
Rasch, G. *Probabilistic models for some intelligence and attainment tests*. Copenhagen, Denmark: Dansmark Paedogogiske Institute, 1960.
Samejima, F. Estimation of latent ability using a response pattern of graded scores. *Psychometric Monograph Supplement*, No. 17, 1969.
Samejima, F. The use of the information function in tailored testing. *Applied Psychological Measurement*. 1977, 1, 233–247. (a)
Samejima, F. A method of estimating item characteristic functions using the maximum likelihood estimate of ability. *Psychometrika*, 42, 1977, 163–191. (b)
Urry, V. W. Tailored testing: A successful application of latent trait theory. *Journal of Educational Measurement*, 1977, 14, 181–196.
Weiss, D. J. *Strategies of adaptive ability measurement*. (Research Report 74–5). Psychometric Methods Program, Dept. of Psychology, University of Minnesota, Minneapolis, Minn., 1974.
Weiss, D. J., (Ed.) *Proceedings of the 1977 computerized adaptive testing conference*. Dept. of Psychology, University of Minnesota, Minn., 1978.
Weiss, D. J. *Efficiency of an adaptive inter-subtest branching strategy in the measurement of classroom achievement* (Research Report 79–6). Minneapolis, Minn.: Psychometric Methods Program, Dept. of Psychology, University of Minnesota, 1979.
Weiss, D. J., (Ed.) *Proceedings of the 1979 computerized adaptive testing conference*. Dept. of Psychology, University of Minnesota, Minneapolis, Minn., 1980.
Wright, B. D. Solving measurement problems with the Rasch model. *Journal of Educational Measurement*, 1977, 38, 97–116.

6 Ability Measures and Theories of Cognitive Development

J. A. Keats
*The University of Newcastle
Australia*

Ability measures defined in terms of latent traits were first theoretically investigated systematically by F. M. Lord (1952). During the 30 years to date there has been an increasing literature in this field, much of it acknowledging his original and continuing contribution (Lord, 1980; Lord & Novick, 1968). In the same 30 years there has also been an interest in cognitive development and the need to have an appropriate ability measure with which to describe this development (see for example Bayley, 1955). More recently Nesselroade and Baltes (1979) and others have reviewed methods of analyzing longitudinal data from various points of view. It is surprising that none of these reviews emphasizes the use of ability measures in longitudinal studies and indeed two of the more recent studies (those reported by Hindley & Owen, 1979; McCall, Appelbaum & Hogarty, 1973) continue to use deviation, IQ measures.

Theory construction in psychology is much more difficult than it is in other scientific disciplines because it involves an attempt to describe a phenomenon which cannot be precisely controlled. Random factors enter into the records of individual behavior and averaging these records over different individuals can grossly distort the relationships between variables which the theory is attempting to describe. Furthermore many of the phenomena which psychologists are most interested in describing relate to cortical functioning which is very imperfectly understood. However any psychological theory must be at least not inconsistent with physiological findings. Apart from these major problems there is the usual scientific one of finding an appropriate mathematical language in which to describe the observed relationship.

Before proceeding further with the present problem of accounting for and representing cognitive growth in a quantitative way, it is appropriate to deal with two objections that have been made to this enterprise. The first objection is that individuals differ not only in the extent of their cognitive growth but also in the ways in which they develop, so that this growth can be studied only on an individual basis and attempts to identify a general mathematical form to represent this growth let alone a group representation must prove futile. This argument advocates the ideographic as opposed to the nomothetic approach. As Marx (1976) points out, the scientific question is, to what extent can a particular mathematical form represent each of the individual sets of data by allowing one or more parameters to vary across individuals? It is the scientific question to which this chapter is addressed.

The second objection argues that any attempt to quantify cognitive growth involves the measurement of differences which is known to involve considerable unreliability. Taking this objection to its logical extreme would imply either that time is a special variable or that it is not possible to study the functional relationship between variables when at least one of them can only be measured with some not inconsiderable error. The emphasis in this chapter is on representing cognitive growth measured at a number of points over a larger age span and not on measuring the differences between performances at two age levels.

THE PROCESS OF COGNITIVE DEVELOPMENT

Very few psychologists have attempted to describe cognitive development in a way which leads to a quantitative description of this development. Piaget (1947) attributes cognitive development to the internalization of the products of the interactions of the individual with his environment and attempts to show how these internalized products lead to the creation of structures which affect future interactions. These structures may simply assimilate new products or accommodate to them. Piaget did not attempt a quantitative representation of these processes nor did he indicate any way in which systematic individual differences affected them.

Anderson (1940) proposed what might be called a minimal process which he used to account for the observed phenomenon of simplex structure in longitudinal correlation data. Anderson's process consisted of random samplings from a fixed population which added together to produce the person's ability at a given age. This model has been studied by Guttman (1955), Humphreys (1960), Jöreskog (1970), and Jensen (1973) among others. Jensen points out that this model makes no provision for individual differences and proposes a constant multiplier, the consolidation factor, varying from person to person to take care of this. He also suggests a logarithmic transformation to give the growth curve the negative acceleration we usually find.

Jensen's suggestions are not particularly acceptable because he does not show how they lead to further predictions of relationships. The inclusion of a consol-

6. ABILITY MEASURES AND THEORIES OF COGNITIVE DEVELOPMENT

idation factor does allow for the possibility of individual differences but still leaves the process unbounded. The individual goes on acquiring contributions to his ability for his whole life and never loses any through interference or decay. As will be shown, the inclusion of an interference or decay factor bounds the process and can account for individual differences.

Perhaps the biggest objection to Anderson's proposal and all developments stemming from it is that it makes no provision for the obvious fact that the human organism (and most subhuman) uses the products of interactions with the environment to monitor the input or proximal stimulus. This kind of feedback process has been recognized as an important aspect of the description of the behavior of living organisms by Powers (1978 and elsewhere) but has not been widely adopted by other psychologists. In developing his model as a time-dependent process Powers also arrives at an unbounded formulation and proceeds to restrain his model by assuming that the development of output over any time period is only a fraction of the greatest possible development. There are several ways in which individual differences can be taken into account in a feedback system of the kind suggested by Powers.

These descriptions of the process of cognitive development are obviously grossly inadequate but neither appears to be inconsistent with what is known of the nervous system. There is still the question discussed by Wickelgren (1976) in the context of his learning model of whether the process occurs at the single fiber level and is then aggregated or whether some structuring of the fibers is possible. If the former, what are the parameters of the fibers which can vary while still producing the same relationship between variables at the observed molar level as can be assumed to be operating at the individual fiber level? Wickelgren's principle of dynamic consistency can be used in other contexts.

FORMALIZATIONS OF COGNITIVE DEVELOPMENT

Formalization Based on the Anderson (1940) Model

In its simplest form the Anderson model implies that the ability (A) of individual (i) at time t_k will be:

$$A_{ik} = D_k + D_{k-1} + \cdots\cdots + D_3 + D_2 + D_1$$

where D_k represents the random increment due to interaction with the environment in the time period t_{k-1} to t_k.

A system of this kind is unbounded and assumes that the increments are permanent, that is, there is no loss due to decay or interference. These defects can be removed by assuming that only a proportion ($0 < p_i < 1$) of the total of the increments at the end of one time period are present at the next. This proportion could well differ from person to person and so form the basis of individual differences at any age level. Thus:

$$A_{ik} = D_k + p_i D_{k-1} + \ldots + p_i^{k-3}D_3 + p_i^{k-2}D_2 + p_i^{k-1}D_1$$

The randomly selected increments may be thought of as coming from a bounded frequency distribution, with a mean m, from which individuals coming from approximately equivalent environments are drawing randomly. If one could consider a very large number of individuals of the same age (t_k) and selected as having the same p value $p_i = p_o$, then the average ability ($A_{\cdot k}$) for this large group could be written as:

$$A_{\cdot k} = m(1 + p_o + p_o^2 \cdots + p_o^{k-3} + p_o^{k-2} + p_o^{k-1}) = \frac{m}{1 - p_o}(1 - p_o^k)$$

Because $0 < p_o < 1$, $A_{\cdot k}$ approaches $\frac{m}{1 - p_o}$ as k becomes larger. Such a formalization implies a latent growth curve from which the individual will depart because of the random process. Latent growth curves will be different for individuals having a p value different from p_o and for individuals from a different environment if the distribution of the D values has a different mean value in that environment.

Since $o < p < 1$, $\log p$ will be negative and can be written as $-c$ where $c > 0$, that is

$$A_{\cdot k} = \frac{m}{1 - e^{-c}}[1 - e^{-ck}]$$

The point of writing the latent growth curve in this way is that it shows its similarity to a type of exponential growth curve referred to in the literature (see, e.g., Nesselroade & Baltes, 1979).

An alternative way of modifying the Anderson model which also leads to a bounded formula and can allow for individual differences can be obtained by assuming that as the sum of the D values gets larger with increasing k, the increment in ability for a random increment of a particular size gets smaller. One method for achieving this is to assume that $k.m$ for the latent curve can be written as:

$$k.m = \frac{A_{\cdot k}}{a - c.A_{\cdot k}}$$

or

$$A_{\cdot k} = \frac{a.k.m}{1 + c.k.m}$$

This hyperbolic relationship is an alternative form of cognitive growth curve referred to in the literature (see, e.g., Nesselroade & Baltes, 1979).

Formalization Based on the Powers (1978) Model

The Anderson model has been criticized on the grounds that it does not take into account the fact that the development of ability influences the control of subsequent increments. The Powers model does take into account feedback from earlier increments on later acquisitions. Powers (1978) develops his model in terms of time dependent processes.

Power's feedback model considers three quantities: a distal stimulus or disturbance producing a quantity q_d, a proximal stimulus quantity q_i and an output quantity q_o. The system equation relates q_o to q_i

$$q_o = f(q_i) \tag{1}$$

and the environment equation relates q_i to q_d and q_o

$$q_i = g(q_o) + h(q_d) \tag{2}$$

where f, g and h are unspecified functional forms and f and g are capable of expansion in terms of Taylor series. Powers proceeds with this expansion of equation (1) about an undefined value of $q_i = q_i^*$. By factoring out $(q_i - q_i^*)$, the quotient polynomial is represented by U and

$$q_o = f(q_i^*) + U(q_i - q_i^*) \tag{3}$$

Similarly, from (2)

$$q_i = g(q_o^*) + V(q_o - q_o^*) + h(q_d) \tag{4}$$

Powers then assumes that $q_i = q_i^*$ when $h(q_d) = 0$, that is when the effect of the distal stimulus on q_i is zero and deduces from (1) and (2) that $q_i^* = g(q_o^*)$ and $q_o^* = f(q_i^*)$. Then from (3) and (4)

$$q_o - q_o^* = U(q_i - q_i^*) \tag{5}$$

and

$$q_i - q_i^* = V(q_o - q_o^*) + h(q_d) \tag{6}$$

From which it may be shown, assuming UV is not unity for any q_i or q_o:

$$g(q_o) = q_i^* + \frac{UV}{1 - UV} \cdot h(q_d) \tag{7}$$

and

$$q_i = q_i^* + \frac{1}{1 - UV} \cdot h(q_d) \tag{8}$$

Powers proceeds to show that UV is a dimensionless constant which is referred to as loop gain and distinguishes four possibilities

$UV = 0$ because $U = 0$, that is, $f = 0$ always, and there is no behaving system

$UV = 0$ because $V = 0$, that is, $g = 0$ always, and there is no feedback and the system is termed a Z system

$0 < UV < 1$ a stable positive feedback system or P system

$UV < 0$ a negative feedback or N system

As $UV < 0$ decreases in value then $\frac{UV}{1 - UV}$ approaches -1 and

$$g(q_o) = q_i^* - h(q_d) \tag{9}$$

and

$$q_i = q_i^* = g(q_o^*) = g(q_o) + h(q_d) \tag{10}$$

This is a perfect negative feedback system in that the output is such that proximal input is kept constant irrespective of changes in the distal stimulus. Compensation within the system produces invariance. The conservations described by Piaget (1947) can be regarded as invariances of quantities such as weight, volume, length, and so forth, despite disturbances. At a later stage, the invariance becomes one of relationships between quantities, for example, moments.

Formalization Based on a Sequential State Model

Powers refers to the above representation as a quasi-static analysis assuming that the negative feedback effects are instantaneous. He shows that a sequential state analysis can be carried out in the case of simple linear relationships and implies that it can be extended to nonlinear cases. From the point of view of a cognitive development model this is more interesting. The general functions f, g and h are replaced by constant coefficients F, G and H and subscripts are used to indicate time. The environment equation becomes:

$$q_{i(t)} = Gq_{o(t)} + Hq_d \tag{11}$$

and the system equation will become

$$q_{o(t+1)} = F(q_i - q_i^*)_{(t)} \tag{12}$$

which from equation (11) becomes

$$q_{o(t+1)} = FGq_{o(t)} + FHq_d - Fq_i^* \tag{13}$$

which can be solved to give

$$q_{ot} = \left(q_{o1} - \frac{F(Hq_d - q_i^*)}{1 - FG}\right)(FG)^{(t-1)} + \frac{F(Hq_d - q_i^*)}{1 - FG} \tag{14}$$

6. ABILITY MEASURES AND THEORIES OF COGNITIVE DEVELOPMENT

This series converges only if $-1 < FG < 1$ which places considerable restriction on loop gain FG (cf UV above). Powers proposes a dynamic constraint which allows $q_{o(t)}$ to increase by only a fraction ($0 < K < 1$) towards the next value of $F(q_i - q_i^*)_{(t)}$ during the interval from t to $t + 1$. Then equation 12 is modified to read:

$$q_{o(t+1)} = q_{o(t)} + k[F(q_{i(t)} - q_i^*) - q_{o(t)}]$$

and from equation (11)

$$q_{o(t+1)} = q_{o(t)} + K[FGq_{ot} + FHq_d - Fq_i^* - q_{o(t)}]$$

or

$$q_{o(t+1)} = q_{o(t)}(1 + KFG - K) + KF(Hq_d - q_i^*) \quad (15)$$

The solution to equation (15) leads to

$$q_{o(t)} = \left(q_{o1} - \frac{F(Hq_d - q_i^*)}{1 - FG}\right)(1 + KFG - K)^{t-1} + \frac{F(Hq_d - q_i^*)}{(1 - FG)} \quad (16)$$

which approaches a limit if $-1 < (1 + KFG - K) < 1$ and since $0 < K < 1$ then $FG < 1$ will meet this requirement. Thus the dynamic constraint has increased the possible range of FG, the loop gain.

It should be noted that $K = \dfrac{1}{1 - FG}$ implies a stagewise development. Equation 16 is of the same form as one variation of the Anderson model since if $0 < (1 + KFG - K) < 1$, that is, $K < \dfrac{1}{1 - FG}$, $1 + KFG - K$ may be written as e^{-c} with $c > 0$. This is the negative exponential version of this model and (16) becomes:

$$q_{o(t)} = M - (M - q_{o1}) \cdot e^{-c(t-1)} \quad (17)$$

The maximum value (M) approached by q_{ot} as t becomes large is

$$M = \frac{F(Hq_d - q_i^*)}{1 - FG} \quad (18)$$

in both formulations and Powers notes that M approaches $\dfrac{1}{G}(q_i^* - Hq_d)$ if there is very large negative feedback, that is, the output is determined by the difference between a standard input and the effect of the proximal stimulus.

It may be noted that the two formulations may be simply written in terms of M. Equations (13) and (15) become:

$$q_{o(t+1)} - q_{o(t)} = (1 - FG)(M - q_{ot}) \quad \text{with } -1 < FG < 1 \quad (19)$$

and

$$q_{o(t+1)} - q_{o(t)} = K(1 - FG)(M - q_{ot}) \text{ with } 0 < K < \frac{1}{1 - FG} < 1 \quad (20)$$

that is, $FG < 0$.

Thus the effect of the dynamic constraint is to allow for a larger negative feedback. However this result can be achieved in other ways. In particular, the increment $q_{o(t+1)} - q_{o(t)}$ may be made more dependent on time, t, by setting

$$K = \frac{1}{DFG + (1 - FG)(t + 1)}$$

that is,

$$q_{o(t+1)} - q_{o(t)} = \frac{(1 - FG)}{DFG + (1 - FG)(t + 1)} (M - q_{o(t)})$$

which may be solved to give

$$q_{o(t)} = \frac{Mt}{t + \dfrac{DFG}{1 - FG}} \quad \text{with } DFG > 0 \text{ and } FG < 1 \quad (21)$$

This is the hyperbolic version of the model.

If the output q_o is measured in certain situations by a latent trait, then Powers' feedback theory leads to either a negative exponential or a hyperbolic latent cognitive growth curve depending on the dynamic constraint applied. It has been noted that elaborations of Anderson's theory also lead to these two alternatives. It seems unlikely that the alternative formulations of either theory could be directly tested experimentally. However there may be theoretical grounds for preferring one or other of these formulations.

The Anderson and Powers models are complementary rather than competitive. Drösler (1978) has carried out a more detailed analysis of the simplex model using time series analysis. He shows that the pattern of decreasing correlation as time interval increases can be used to distinguish the Markovian process implied by the Anderson model from one which is more stable, for example, the Powers model. His examination of the data from the Berkeley Growth Study indicates that up to the age of approximately 4 years cognitive development is not inconsistent with the Anderson model, but that beyond that age a combination of the Anderson and Powers models would be required. The Anderson model leads to the notion of a latent growth curve with an increment m obtained from sampling from the environment. The remainder of that explication is concerned with providing one or more individual differences parameters to contain the process. Since the increment m is related to the effects of variations in the environment it may be equated to Hq_d in the Powers model:

6. ABILITY MEASURES AND THEORIES OF COGNITIVE DEVELOPMENT 89

$$\text{i.e. } M = \frac{F(Hq_d - q_i^*)}{(1 - FG)} = \frac{F(m - q_i^*)}{1 - FG}$$

in both the negative exponential and hyperbolic representations of the cognitive growth curve. Thus the latent curve is for subjects with the same environmental effect, m, the same q_i^*, the same loop gain, FG, and the same rate parameter, c, for the negative exponential curve and D for the hyperbolic. A question to be raised is, which of these parameters must be assumed to be varying across individuals subject to essentially the same environment?

THEORETICAL COMPARISONS OF THE EXPONENTIAL AND THE HYPERBOLIC FORMS OF THE COGNITIVE GROWTH CURVE

Dimensional Analysis

Powers has observed that the loop gain, FG, is a dimensionless constant and it is clear that if q_{ot} is measured in ability units then M must be. However the exponential term e^{-ct}, obviously involves the dimension of time to an unspecifiable degree. Thus there is a lack of dimensional balance in this formulation unless c has dimensionality (time)$^{-1}$ in which case the exponent of e is dimensionless. However, from the derivations it is not clear how c could have this dimensionality in either model.

In the case of the hyperbolic form, equation 21, the parameter D must have the dimensions of time since FG is dimensionless and $DFG/(1-FG)$ must be added to t in the denominator. The time dimension in the numerator cancels that in the denominator leaving both q_{ot} and M in the dimension of ability. Thus the hyperbolic formulation is balanced dimensionally and assigned dimensionalities are not inconsistent with either derivation.

Both formulations are dimensionally balanced with a parameter, M, in ability units, and parameters c^{-1} and D both of which have the dimension of time. However, in the case of the negative exponential the necessary interpretation of the dimensionalization of c^{-1} is not consistent with either theoretical derivation.

Dynamic Consistency

The principle of dynamic consistency appealed to by Wickelgren (1976) in the context of his neural model of learning can also be applied to other theoretical representations. In discussing outstanding problems in psychological theory Marx (1976) discusses the problem of interpreting group curves as if they applied to individual cases. However he does not press the point that mathematical formulations should be such that they can be averaged in some sense over parameters of individual differences in a way that preserves the functional form expressed in terms of averages of these parameters. This is the principle of dynamic consistency applied to individual differences. Wickelgren (1976) gives a number of examples of how this can be done with his formulation using geometric as well as arithmetic means. Stevens (1966) recommended the use of geometric means when averaging individual psychophysical curves of the power law form. He does not comment on the fact that this procedure preserves the power law relationship at the group as well as the individual level.

In the case of the negative exponential representation of cognitive growth,

$$A_{it} = M - (M - A_{i1})e^{-c(t-1)}$$

Let us assume that $t = 1$ is the largest t value at which $A_{it} = 0$. It may be assumed that the maximum value, M, varies from person to person so that

$$A_{it} = M_i[1 - e^{-c(t-1)}]$$

and averaging across individuals, i at the same age level produces

$$\bar{A}.t = \bar{M}[1 - e^{-c(t-1)}]$$

Thus the exponential growth curve is dynamically consistent when the maximum value (M) varies across individuals. However if the rate parameter, c, is also allowed to vary over subjects, dynamic consistency in this sense is lost. In the case where c varies but M does not, dynamic consistency can be achieved by defining the group curve in terms of the geometric mean of $(M - A_{it})$, that is, an inverted growth curve. This may not be acceptable.

In his discussion of the concept of mental age, Thurstone (1926) argues that the term is ambiguous because the appropriate regression could be of time on ability rather than ability on time which is the usual approach. He thus draws attention to a further way of defining a group cognitive growth curve by averaging the ages at which a certain ability is reached. If the arithmetic mean is used, the practical difficulty arises that there are probably ability levels which some subjects never achieve so that this regression will be undefined. In the case of the exponential growth curve, dynamic consistency is also preserved with growth curves obtained by using the harmonic mean of ages for a given ability when only c is allowed to vary across subjects. However, if M is also allowed to vary, dynamic consistency is not maintained. It would seem to be important to consider the two ways of forming a group growth curve, that is, by averaging in some way ability at each age level as well as by using some mean value of age at each ability level. In either case the condition of dynamic consistency should be met.

In summary the negative exponential growth curve shows dynamic consistency in the following cases:

6. ABILITY MEASURES AND THEORIES OF COGNITIVE DEVELOPMENT

1. Defining the group curve in terms of the average of ability on time. If M is allowed to vary across individuals

    Individual Curve $\quad A_{ik} = M_i[1 - e^{-c(t_k-1)}]$

    Group Curve $\quad \bar{A}_{.k} = \bar{M}[1 - e^{-c(t_k-1)}]$.

    However if c is allowed to vary across individuals the form of the relationship must be changed by averaging.

2. Defining the group curve in terms of some average of the times at which subjects reach a certain ability (A_o).
    If M is allowed to vary across individuals dynamic consistency is not achieved. If c is allowed to vary across individuals:

    Individual Curve $\quad A_o = M[1 - e^{-c_i(t_i - 1)}]$

    Group Curve $\quad A_o = M[1 - e^{-\bar{c}.H(t.-1)}]$

    where $H(t.-1)$ is the harmonic mean of $t_i - 1$ across individuals.

It should be noted that allowing M to vary but not c implies that individuals approach different maximum values but at the same rate in the sense that they reach half their individual maximum values at the same age $\left(\text{equal to}\left[1 + \dfrac{\log 2}{c}\right]\right)$. Physical height very nearly follows this pattern with individuals reaching half their adult height at approximately 2 years of age. Allowing c to vary but not M implies that subjects approach the same maximum values but at different rates.

The hyperbolic growth curve has been noted by many writers, for example Nesselroade and Baltes (1979), Keats (1978, 1981, 1982), without either of the two derivations given here being noted. Keats (1982) explored the hyperbolic curve with two parameters allowing either or both to vary across individuals. Further study using three parameters reveals that different results are obtained when each of these is allowed to vary separately across individuals. The form to be considered here is:

$$A_{ik} = \frac{at_k}{ct_k + d}$$

or

$$\frac{1}{A_{ik}} = \frac{c}{a} + \frac{d}{a} \cdot \frac{1}{t_k} \quad \text{with } a, c \text{ and } d \text{ all} > 0.$$

It should be noted that allowing the parameter a to vary but not c or d implies that the maximum value varies for each individual but the rate of approaching that maximum does not, in the sense that each subject will achieve half his particular maximum value at the same age. However allowing the parameter d to vary, but not a or c, implies that all subjects have the same maximum value which they approach at different rates and allowing c to vary implies that each subject has a different maximum which is approached at a rate depending on that maximum.

These different special cases can be clearly distinguished by considering the graphs of maximum value against age at which half this maximum is attained. Figure 6.1 displays the three possible relationships.

The results of defining the group growth curve in the two possible ways with possible variations in a, c, and d are summarized below for cases in which the principle of dynamic consistency applies:

1. Averaging ability at each value of t_k

   a. Individual curve $A_{ik} = \dfrac{a_i t_k}{c t_k + d}$

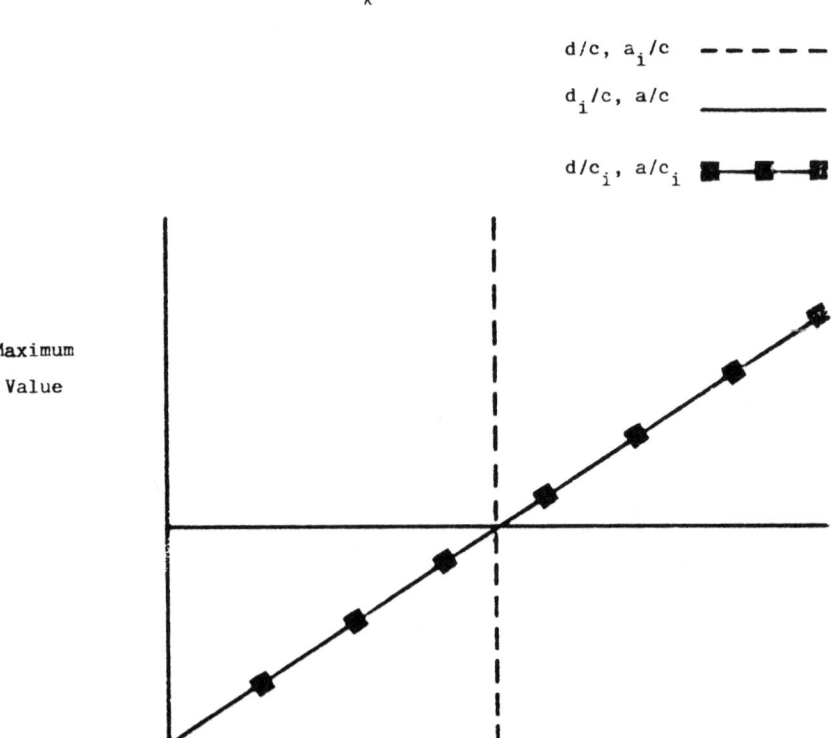

FIG. 6.1. The graph of Maximum Value plotted against Age of attaining half this value.

6. ABILITY MEASURES AND THEORIES OF COGNITIVE DEVELOPMENT

Group curve (a) $\bar{A}_{\cdot k} = \dfrac{\bar{a}t_k}{ct_k + d}$ or (b) $H(A_{\cdot k}) = \dfrac{H(a).t_k}{ct_k + d}$

b. Individual curve $A_{ik} = \dfrac{at_k}{c_i t_k + d}$

Group curve $H(A_{\cdot k}) = \dfrac{at_k}{\bar{c}t_k + d}$

c. Individual curve $A_{ik} = \dfrac{at_k}{ct_k + d_i}$

Group curve $H(A_{\cdot k}) = \dfrac{at_k}{ct_k + \bar{d}}$

d. Individual curve $A_{ik} = \dfrac{at_k}{c_i t_k + d_i}$

Group curve $H(A_{\cdot k}) = \dfrac{at_k}{\bar{c}t_k + \bar{d}}$

2. Averaging time, t_i, at each possible value of ability A_o.

a. Individual curve $t_i = \dfrac{A_o d_i}{a - A_o c}$

Group curve (a) $H(t_\cdot) = \dfrac{A_o H(d)}{a - A_o c}$

Group curve (b) $t = \dfrac{A_o \bar{d}}{a - A_o c}$

Note: In this case all subjects would have the same maximum adult value which they approached at different rates and so t_i would be finite for all values of A less than a/c; thus the arithmetic mean of these values would also be finite. In all other cases, A_o would be above the individual maximum for at least some subjects so that age at reaching A_o is not defined. It should also be noted that possible cases not listed above do not show dynamic consistency as defined in this chapter.

In the case of the hyperbolic curve when ability is averaged for a particular age, it is the harmonic mean of ability which preserves dynamic consistency in all four cases, whereas the arithmetic mean does so in only one of these cases. If age is averaged for particular ability values, d is the only parameter which can vary if dynamic consistency is to be preserved. In this particular case either the arithmetic mean or the harmonic mean satisfies this condition but the arithmetic mean has the advantage that it involves the arithmetic mean of the d_i values and is identical to the curve obtained by taking the harmonic mean of ability. Thurstone's (1926) suggestion of defining mental age as the average age for a given ability could only apply if all subjects approached the same ultimate level but at quite different rates.

It can be seen that the number of possible forms and variations is much greater for the hyperbolic than for the negative exponential form. This is due partly to the larger number of parameters considered (three instead of two) and partly to the fact that dynamic consistency is more often achieved in the hyperbolic form.

In his discussion of statistical methods for comparing growth curves Rao (1958) introduces a condition which is consistent with the principle of dynamic consistency but is more restrictive. He assumes that growth curves can be written in the form

$$Y_i = V_i + W_i \cdot r(t)$$

where Y is the variable measured, V_i and W_i are parameters which vary across individuals and $r(t)$ is a function of time which is constant across individuals. Rao shows that certain forms of comparisons between groups can be made without knowing the precise form of $r(t)$. He acknowledges a suggestion by Rasch that, given this form, $r(t)$ can be estimated by averaging Y values over individuals at the same age and that individual and subgroup curves will be linear when plotted against this estimate of $r(t)$. It should be noted that if $r(t)$ has an asymptotic value then individuals will differ in their asymptotic value but that rate of development will be determined only by this asymptotic value.

RELATIONSHIPS BETWEEN PARAMETERS OF GROWTH CURVES AND TRADITIONAL MEASURES

The principle of dynamic consistency is not only aesthetically pleasing but is also, in the case of cognitive curves, a sufficient condition for relating individual differences in the curve parameters to some traditional measures of individual differences. In the case of the exponential curve with the parameter M only varying across subjects

$$A_{it} - \bar{A}_{\cdot t} = [M_i - \bar{M}][1 - e^{-c(t-1)}]$$

and

$$\sigma_{A_{\cdot t}} = [1 - e^{-c(t-1)}] \cdot \sigma_M$$

from which

$$S_{A_{it}} = S_{M_i},$$

where S denotes standard score, for all subjects and at all age levels.

Notice also that essentially the same result is obtained in the hyperbolic case if parameter a, only, is allowed to vary, that is, $S_{A_{ik}} = S_{a_i}$ for all subjects and at all

6. ABILITY MEASURES AND THEORIES OF COGNITIVE DEVELOPMENT

age levels. In both cases the implication is that if *ability* is measured at some age level and related to that of subjects at that age level in terms of the standard score, the result is the standard score of the parameter which determines the adult value towards which the subject is approaching. The result is independent of the mathematical form of the growth curve in at least these two cases.

With the hyperbolic growth curve, the group curve is defined in terms of the harmonic mean when either or both of the parameters c and d vary. The reciprocal of the harmonic mean is the arithmetic mean of the reciprocal of A_{ik}. Using this fact one can show that $S_{(1/A_{ik})} = S_{c_i}$ or S_{d_i} depending on whether c or d is the only parameter allowed to vary. The value of $S_{(1/A_{ik})}$ would in practice not be markedly different from that of $-S_{(A_{ik})}$.

The alternative to the standard score at a particular age level sometimes used in practice is the mental age or reading age, and so forth. In the case of the hyperbolic curve with only the parameter d varying, one may define mental age either as the age at which the typical ability (defined in terms of the harmonic mean) is that of the subject *or* as the arithmetic mean of ages of subjects who have the same ability level as the subject. In either case

$$\text{Mental age} = \frac{\bar{d}}{d_i} \cdot t_{ik}$$

and

$$\text{Binet or ratio IQ, IQ}_R, = \frac{100 \cdot \bar{d}}{d_i}$$

Essentially the same result is obtained if the group curve is defined in terms of the harmonic mean of the ages of subjects at a particular ability level with $H(d.)$ replacing $\bar{d}$.

In the case of the exponential curve, if only the parameter c varies then

$$\text{IQ}_R = \frac{100 c_i}{\bar{c}}.$$

In the cases considered so far in this section there is a simple relationship between a derived score based on ability measured at a particular age and the corresponding derived score from the individual and group value of the parameter which is allowed to vary. These results imply a constancy of the derived score for the same individual at different ages because age has been eliminated from the equation. The use of a particular derived score would imply an underlying assumption about variations in the growth curve across individuals. Thus the use of a Binet or ratio IQ implies that individuals do not differ in the value they approach as adults but only in the rate at which they approach it. This implication holds for both the exponential and the hyperbolic growth curve. The use of the standard score in the case of the exponential curve implies that the maximum value, M, varies across individuals but not the rate of development as measured by the parameter c. With the hyperbolic curve the standard score could be used when any one of its three parameters varied and so the maximum varies or the rate varies as shown in Fig. 6.1.

The use of the IQ_R in situations in which the maximum value differs from person to person implies that the definition being used is the one dependent on averaging ability at each age level. The alternative is not clearly defined at *any* ability level because there will always be subjects whose maximum value is below that level, that is, will not reach it at any age. With this only possible definition one can define mental age up to, but not including, the maximum value approached by the group curve. With this restriction one may show that:

1. For the hyperbolic curve, with parameter a varying across persons

$$\frac{100}{IQ_R} = \frac{\bar{a}}{a_i} + \frac{ct_k}{d}\left(\frac{\bar{a}}{a_i} - 1\right) \text{ for } A_{ik} < \frac{\bar{a}}{c}$$

2. For the hyperbolic curve with parameter c varying across persons and the group curve defined in terms of the harmonic mean of ability at each age level

$$\frac{100}{IQ_R} = 1 + \frac{t_k}{d}(c_i - \bar{c}) \text{ for } A_{ik} < \frac{a}{\bar{c}}$$

3. For the hyperbolic curve with parameters c and d varying across persons and the group curve defined in terms of the harmonic mean of ability at each age level

$$\frac{100}{IQ_R} = \frac{d_i}{\bar{d}} + \frac{t_k}{d}(c_i - \bar{c}) \text{ for } A_{ik} < \frac{a}{\bar{c}}$$

SUMMARY AND DISCUSSION

In summary, this analysis has shown that for both the exponential and the hyperbolic growth curves, individual differences in the rate of growth parameter only imply constancy of the ratio *IQ*. To this extent they are consistent with Binet's approach to measuring cognitive ability. When the maximum value is allowed to vary across individuals then IQ_R is not constant at different age levels for subjects whose maximum value is markedly different from that of the group curve. In three of the four cases studied here $100/IQ_R$ is linear on age with negative slope for subjects whose maximum value is considerably greater than that of the group curve, and positive slope for those with a maximum value considerably less than that of the group curve. However the predicted intercept is different in the three cases. In the fourth case ratio *IQ* would also vary with age, but no simple explicit formula could be found relating IQ_R to age. Some of these predictions are displayed in Fig. 6.2.

6. ABILITY MEASURES AND THEORIES OF COGNITIVE DEVELOPMENT

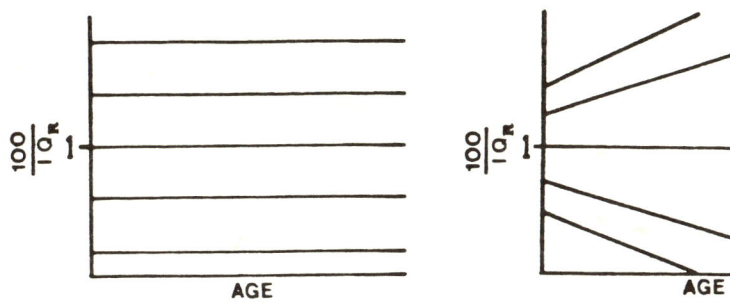

a. Constant ratio IQ.—only rate of growth varying.

b. Changing IQ_R—only parameter a varying.

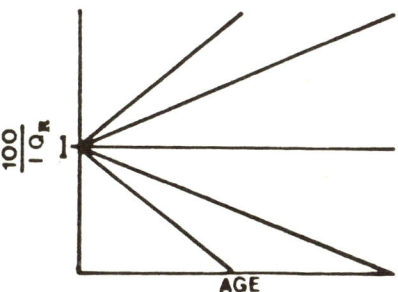

c. Changing IQ_R—only parameter c varying.

FIG. 6.2 Predicted variations in $100/IQ_R$.

Some of these results were reported in Keats (1982) and the data from Skodak and Skeels (1949) were used in that publication to test the alternatives. These data are ideal in that not only are the IQ_R values available at four well-separated age levels, but the adult IQ of the mother is also published. Two groups of subjects were identified, group A with mothers with very low IQs and group B with mothers with above average IQs. The averages for the two groups separately were plotted and the graph is reproduced here in Fig. 6.3. The data are consistent with the hyperbolic growth curve with individual differences in both c and d parameters.

In the case of variation in the parameter c only a further result may be derived. It has been shown that in this case

$$\frac{100}{IQ_R} = 1 + \frac{t_k}{d}(c_i - \bar{c})$$

and

$$IQ_D = \frac{\bar{c} - c_i}{\sigma_c} \times 15 + 100$$

If parameter c is scaled so that its standard deviation is 15, then

$$\frac{100}{IQ_R} = 1 - \frac{t_k}{d}(IQ_D - 100)$$

Keats (1982) verified this formula using data from the manual of ACER Intermediate D Test of Intelligence (1947–1951) and the graph is reproduced here as Fig. 6.4. The relationship could be explored for any test for which adequate norms are available at each of a number of age levels.

The purpose of this chapter has been to draw attention to the kinds of analysis which seem to be important in the formulation of a representation of cognitive development based on certain theoretical approaches to the nature of this development. It is not argued that either of the theoretical approaches in any of their forms is in some sense correct. The analysis does however seem to show that the choice of one form has implications for the kind of quantification that is appropriate given certain types of individual differences. Conversely the choice of a

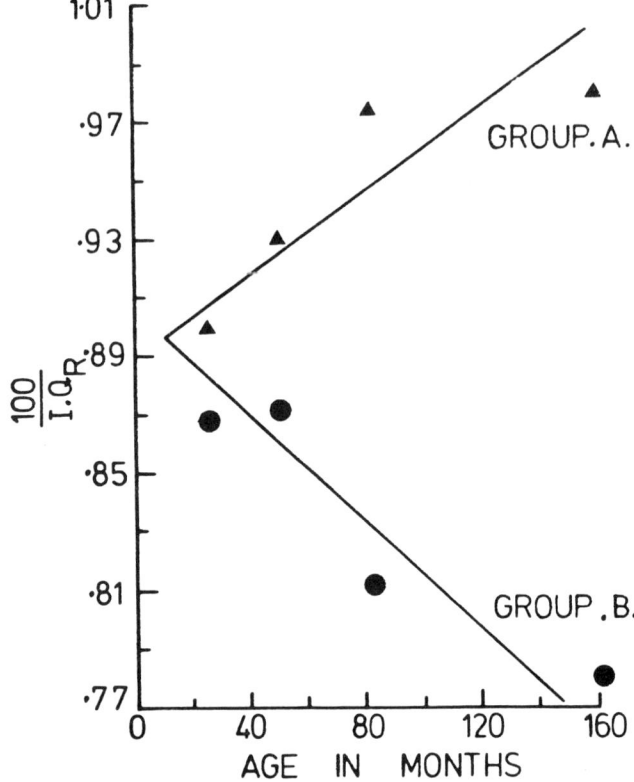

FIG. 6.3 Changes in ratio IQ with age in two groups of subjects.

6. ABILITY MEASURES AND THEORIES OF COGNITIVE DEVELOPMENT   99

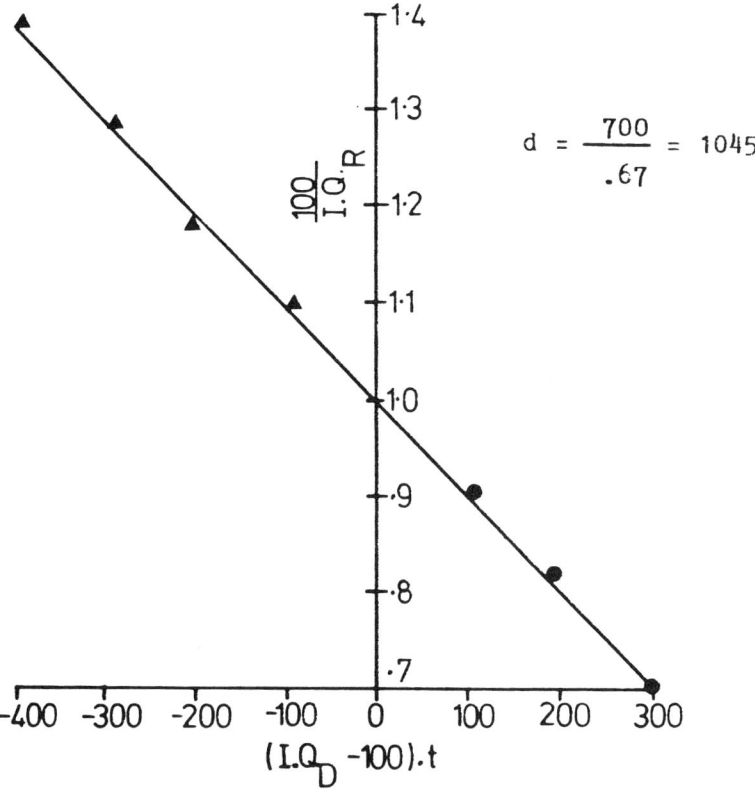

FIG. 6.4 Relationship between deviation and ratio IQ on the ACER intermediate D test of intelligence.

particular index or measure also implies characteristics of the developmental process.

A clear example of this latter conclusion is the choice of an age measure of the mental age, reading age, and so forth, variety. If this is defined in the way recommended by Thurstone (1926) there is a clear implication that individuals are developing towards the same level at maturity. If this were not so, the measure is not strictly definable at almost any level. This restriction would seem to be inappropriate in the case of mental age but may be appropriate in the case of reading simple material for which the attainment of a specified high level of performance could be expected of almost all individuals who experience the usual educational programs. The only question that arises in relation to individual differences in such a case is the age at which individuals reach this level or possibly some fraction of it. However the more usual definition of age scores makes them definable for most subjects for almost all of their development. It has been shown that different models make different predictions about the stability of this measure.

In the case of the more commonly used measures based on standard scores, stability is more often predicted by the models and seems to be more often achieved in practice. Such measures seem to imply that individuals are approaching different values at maturity but are doing so at a rate which is *either* the same for all in the sense that they reach half of their mature value at approximately the same age *or* linearly dependent on the value at maturity. Neither of these conditions appears to be strictly met in practice as shown by the work of McCall et al. (1973) and by Hindley and Owen (1979). On the basis of these two reports together with the reanalysis of the Skodak and Skeels (1949) data there seems to be a case for arguing that cognitive development should be described in terms of two parameters, one related to the asymptotic value approached at maturity and the other related to rate of development. The question of obtaining reliable estimates of these two parameters of the person is a topic for further study. Given reliable estimates of these two parameters the individual's latent cognitive development curve could be derived. Actual measures of ability at different ages could depart from this latent curve because of the random sampling of interactions with the environment referred to in the Anderson model.

As noted at the beginning of this chapter, the systematic study of cognitive growth could only be carried out satisfactorily by using estimates of latent ability. The current question of the best way to estimate this latent ability should not distract research workers from the use of estimates in some sense. Possibly the investigation of the problem of estimating parameters of the latent cognitive growth curve will throw some light on the current problem of estimating latent ability. Whether or not this is the way to proceed is for the future to decide. It is not surprising that the study of psychological tests quantifying individual differences has led to the most intensive study of the mensurational characteristics of observations of behavior. It is, however, surprising to note how little the progress made has influenced other areas of psychology. For example, it recently came to my attention that in studies of conditioned suppression, the standard index, the suppression ratio has been defined in at least five different ways, none of which has been justified in either theoretical or mensurational terms. It will probably not be until after experimental psychologists take a greater interest in the study of individual differences in the phenomena they observe that other important measurement aspects of their data will be investigated. The contribution of F. M. Lord to so many aspects of these problems in the study of individual differences for more than 30 years has been outstanding and is appropriately recognized throughout the world.

REFERENCES

ACER Intermediate Test D. Australian Council for Educational Research, 1947–51.
Anderson, J. E. The prediction of terminal intelligence from infant and pre-school tests. *Thirty-ninth*

6. ABILITY MEASURES AND THEORIES OF COGNITIVE DEVELOPMENT

Yearbook, National Society for the Study of Education, 1940, Part I, 385–403.
Bayley, N. On the growth of intelligence. *American Psychologist*, 1955, *10*, 805–818.
Drösler, J. Extending the temporal range of psychometric prediction by optimal linear filtering of mental test scores. *Psychometrika*, 1978, *43*, 533–549.
Guttman, L. A generalized simplex for factor analysis. *Psychometrika*, 1955, *20*, 173–192.
Hindley, C. B., & Owen, C. F. An analysis of individual patterns of D.Q. and I.Q. curves from 6 months to 17 years. *British Journal of Psychology*, 1979, *70*(2), 273–294.
Humphreys, L. Investigations of the simplex. *Psychometrika*, 1960, *25*, 313–323.
Jensen, A. R. *Educability and group differences*. London: Methuen Co. Limited, 1973.
Jöreskog, K. G. Estimation and testing of simplex models. *British Journal of Mathematical and Statistical Psychology*, 1970, *23*(2), 121–145.
Keats, J. A. A proposed form for a developmental function. In J. A. Keats, K. F. Collis & G. S. Halford (Eds.) *Cognitive development: Research based on a neo-Piagetian approach*. Chichester: John Wiley & Sons, 1978.
Keats, J. A. A model of cognitive development. In M. P. Friedman, J. P. Das & N. O'Connor (Eds.), *Intelligence and learning*. New York and London: Plenum Press, 1981.
Keats, J. A. Comparing latent trait with classical measurement models in the practice of educational and psychological measurement. In D. S. Spearritt (Ed.), *The improvement of measurement in education and psychology: Contributions of latent trait theorists*. Melbourne: ACER, 1982, 61–72.
Lord, F. M. A theory of test scores. *Psychometric Monograph*, 1952, 7.
Lord, F. M. *Applications of item response theory to practical testing problems*. London: Lawrence Erlbaum & Associates, 1980.
Lord, F. M., & Novick, M. R. *Statistical theories of mental test scores*. Reading, Massachusetts: Addison-Wesley, 1968.
McCall, R. B., Appelbaum, M. I., & Hogarty, P. S. Developmental changes in mental performance. *Monographs of the Society for Research in Child Development*, 1973, *38*(3, Serial No. 150).
Marx, M. H. Formal theory. In M. H. Marx and F. E. Goodson (Eds.), *Theories in contemporary psychology*. New York: Macmillan, 1976.
Nesselroade, J. R., & Baltes, P. B. (Eds.) *Longitudinal research in the study of behavior and development*. New York: Academic Press, 1979.
Piaget, J. *The psychology of intelligence*. London: Routledge & Kegan Paul, 1947.
Powers, W. T. Quantitative analysis of purposive systems: Some spadework at the foundations of scientific psychology. *Psychological Review*, 1978, *85*(5), 417–435.
Rao, C. R. Some statistical methods for comparison of growth curves. *Biometrics*, 1958, *14*, 1–17.
Skodak, M., & Skeels, H. M. A final follow-up study of one hundred adopted children. *The Journal of Genetic Psychology*, 1949, *75*, 85–125.
Stevens, S. S. Dimension luminance and the brightness exponent. *Perception and Psychophysics*, 1966, *1*, 96–100.
Thurstone, L. L. The mental age concept. *Psychological Review*, 1926, *33*, 268–278.
Wickelgren, W. A. Network strength theory of storage and retrieval dynamics. *Psychological Review*, 1976, *83*(6), 466–478.

7 The Discrete Bayesian

R. Darrell Bock
University of Chicago

Their many advantages in behavioral and educational research have encouraged the use of longitudinal designs in large-scale sample surveys. In the context of surveys they are referred to as "panel" designs, implying that each subject has made a commitment to participate in a number of future data collections. Such designs not only make possible true prospective studies and measurement of change, but they may actually be less expensive than a comparable series of cross-sectional studies. The initial cost of locating the subjects is so large in a national probability sample survey that it is more economical to call again on the same subjects than to interview new ones. For this reason, most commercial market research is based on panels of consumers, even when the data are used only cross-sectionally.

Despite recent advances in statistical methods for longitudinal research (see Nesselroade & Baltes, 1979), the analyses reported for large-scale panel studies are not always at a level commensurate with the costs of such studies. Often they consist of little more than correlational analyses of variables measured at earlier and later times, or of plots of group means at successive time points, possibly accompanied by fitted trend lines and statistical tests of the hypothesis of no trend or no difference in group mean trends.

As a purely hypothetical example illustrating some of the issues in the analysis of longitudinal data, consider the following: Suppose that a panel study has been carried out to assess, among other things, the TV viewing habits of children from their 10th to 14th birthdays. Perhaps once a year near his or her birthday, each child responds to an interviewer's questions concerning TV viewing during the previous week. At the end of the 5-year study, the data comprise a file of number of hours of TV viewing by each child at each age level.

We can then readily imagine that some data analyst might compute means for each age group and perhaps fit a linear or curvilinear trend line showing the average number of viewing hours over the age range. If the analyst is a little more sophisticated, he might even fit the line efficiently using some variant of the Potthoff-Roy procedure, although this would require the data for all subjects to be complete and similarly time structured (see Bock, 1979).

Apart from the obvious confounding of developmental and secular trend in these types of analyses, what we should object to most is the use of a mean trend in the population to represent a behavioral relationship taken to be acting within individual subjects. The report might have us believe, for example, that as *any* child matures in this age range, he or she will watch more TV. This grossly oversimplifies the actual situation. The account is only somewhat improved by the analyst's reporting of mean trends for important subgroups—boys and girls, urban and rural children, and so on. Even then the fact remains that within such groups some children are watching increasing amounts of TV, others are watching less, and still others are not changing. Like all behavioral characteristics, age trends in behavior exhibit individual differences. We should be interested in not just the mean trend, but in the distribution of these trends in the population of children. Then we can speak of the number or proportion of children who are increasing at such and such a rate, or are decreasing, or whatever. We can describe the behavioral relationship, not as a fixed law, but as a family of laws, the parameters of which describe the individual behavioral tendencies of the subjects in the population.

This view of behavioral research leads inevitably to Bayesian methods of data analysis, where the term is used broadly to mean the analysis of two-stage sampling models—sampling of responses within subjects and subjects within populations. The relevant distributions exist objectively and can be investigated empirically. The present chapter reviews some recent proposals for this type of analysis and discusses a new and more general method.

1. A PERSONAL LINEAR TREND MODEL

To begin with the simplest case, suppose in the present example that the within-subject trend in TV viewing time is linear with age in the 10- to 14-year range. Then the viewing hours, y_{it}, of subject i at age x_t may be described by

$$y_{it} = \beta_{0i} + \beta_{1i} x_t + \epsilon_{it}, \tag{1}$$

where β_{0i} and β_{1i} are the intercept and slope parameters of subject i, and ϵ_{it} is a random residual. In matrix notation, the vector of viewing hours over n years may be written,

$$\mathbf{y}_i = \mathbf{X}\boldsymbol{\beta}_i + \boldsymbol{\varepsilon}_i. \tag{2}$$

That **X** does not carry the subscript i implies that TV viewing is assessed in all subjects at the same ages (different time-structuring of the observations in different subjects can be accomodated in what follows but is not discussed in this chapter.)

Analysis of this type of data under the assumptions that $\boldsymbol{\beta}$ has a distribution in the population of subjects, and $\boldsymbol{\varepsilon}$ has a distribution both in the population of responses within subjects and in the population of subjects, belongs to the class of statistical problems called variously "mixed-model" (Elston & Grizzle, 1962), "regression with randomly dispersed parameters" (Rosenberg, 1973), "exchangeability between multiple regressions" (Lindley & Smith, 1972), "two-stage stochastic regression" (Fearn, 1975), "James-Stein estimation" (James & Stein, 1961), and "covariance component models" (Harville, 1977). For the most part, these treatments are based on the assumption that the residuals, $\boldsymbol{\varepsilon}$, are similarly distributed as $N(\mathbf{0}, \boldsymbol{\Sigma}_\epsilon)$ in all subjects and the personal trend parameters, $\boldsymbol{\beta}$, are $N(\boldsymbol{\mu}, \boldsymbol{\Sigma})$ independent of $\boldsymbol{\varepsilon}$.

For a given $\boldsymbol{\Sigma}_\epsilon$, standard results give

$$\hat{\boldsymbol{\beta}}_i = (\mathbf{X}'\boldsymbol{\Sigma}_\epsilon^{-1}\mathbf{X})^{-1}\mathbf{X}\boldsymbol{\Sigma}_\epsilon^{-1}\mathbf{y}_i \tag{3}$$

as the least squares estimator of $\boldsymbol{\beta}_i$. With respect to the sampling of responses within the subject, $\hat{\boldsymbol{\beta}}_i$ is distributed

$$N(\boldsymbol{\beta}_i, [\mathbf{X}'\boldsymbol{\Sigma}_\epsilon^{-1}\mathbf{X}]^{-1}). \tag{4}$$

These results ignore, however, the fact that $\boldsymbol{\beta}_i$ is drawn randomly from the population $N(\boldsymbol{\mu}, \boldsymbol{\Sigma})$—that the problem can be viewed not so much as one of minimizing estimated residuals but as a best choice of $\boldsymbol{\beta}$ from among its possible population values. From the latter, or Bayesian point of view, a best choice is one that minimizes the expected squared residuals over the distribution of $\boldsymbol{\beta}$. This so-called minimum squared error loss criterion leads uniquely to the mean of the conditional distribution of $\boldsymbol{\beta}$, given $\mathbf{y}_i$, as the best estimator of $\boldsymbol{\beta}_i$.

To obtain this estimator, we observe that under the stated assumptions, $\mathbf{y}$ and $\boldsymbol{\beta}$ are multivariate normal,

$$\begin{matrix} n \\ m \end{matrix} \begin{bmatrix} \mathbf{y} \\ \boldsymbol{\beta} \end{bmatrix} \sim N\left(\begin{bmatrix} \mathbf{X}\boldsymbol{\mu} \\ \boldsymbol{\mu} \end{bmatrix}, \begin{bmatrix} \mathbf{X}\boldsymbol{\Sigma}\mathbf{X}' + \boldsymbol{\Sigma}_\epsilon & \mathbf{X}\boldsymbol{\Sigma} \\ \boldsymbol{\Sigma}\mathbf{X}' & \boldsymbol{\Sigma} \end{bmatrix} \right); \tag{5}$$

(in the present example, $m = 2$.) The conditional distribution of $(\boldsymbol{\beta} - \boldsymbol{\mu})$, given $\mathbf{y}$, is therefore

$$(\boldsymbol{\beta} - \boldsymbol{\mu})|\mathbf{y} \sim N[\boldsymbol{\Sigma}\mathbf{X}'(\mathbf{X}\boldsymbol{\Sigma}\mathbf{X}' + \boldsymbol{\Sigma}_\epsilon)^{-1}(\mathbf{y} - \mathbf{X}\boldsymbol{\mu}),$$

$$\boldsymbol{\Sigma} - \boldsymbol{\Sigma}\mathbf{X}'(\mathbf{X}\boldsymbol{\Sigma}\mathbf{X}' + \boldsymbol{\Sigma}_\epsilon)^{-1}\mathbf{X}\boldsymbol{\Sigma}]; \tag{6}$$

(see Bock, 1975, p. 133). It is instructive here to follow the lead of Dempster, Rubin and Tsutakawa (1981) and write

$$(X'\Sigma_\epsilon^{-1}X + \Sigma^{-1})\Sigma X' = X'\Sigma_\epsilon^{-1}X\Sigma X' + \Sigma^{-1}\Sigma X'$$
$$= X'\Sigma_\epsilon^{-1}(X\Sigma X' + \Sigma_\epsilon),$$

or

$$\Sigma X'(X\Sigma X' + \Sigma_\epsilon)^{-1} = (X'\Sigma_\epsilon^{-1}X + \Sigma^{-1})^{-1}X'\Sigma_\epsilon^{-1}. \tag{7}$$

The mean of the conditional distribution may then be expressed as

$$\tilde{\beta}_i = E(\beta|y_i) = (X'\Sigma_\epsilon^{-1}X + \Sigma^{-1})^{-1}X'\Sigma_\epsilon^{-1}(y_i - X\mu) + \mu. \tag{8}$$

Taking (8) as an estimator of β_i is thus the same as using a least squares estimator in which the matrix of cross-products is conditioned by the addition of the positive-definite matrix Σ^{-1}. As others have pointed out, this has the same effect as ridge regression, but is better motivated (Zellner, 1971).

As might be expected, the inverse of the conditioned cross-product matrix in (8) is another version of the covariance matrix of the conditional distribution. From (7),

$$\Sigma_{\tilde{\beta}} = V(\beta|y) = \Sigma - \Sigma X'(X\Sigma X' + \Sigma_\epsilon)^{-1}X\Sigma$$
$$= \Sigma - (X'\Sigma_\epsilon^{-1}X + \Sigma^{-1})^{-1}X'\Sigma_\epsilon^{-1}X\Sigma$$
$$= (X'\Sigma_\epsilon^{-1}X + \Sigma^{-1})^{-1}(X'\Sigma_\epsilon^{-1}X + \Sigma^{-1})\Sigma$$
$$- (X'\Sigma_\epsilon^{-1}X + \Sigma^{-1})^{-1}X'\Sigma_\epsilon^{-1}X\Sigma$$
$$= (X'\Sigma_\epsilon^{-1}X + \Sigma^{-1})^{-1}. \tag{9}$$

Psychometricians will recognize (8) as the multivariate generalization of Kelley's (1947) formula for estimating a subject's true score, τ, from a fallible test score, y; that is,

$$\tilde{\tau} = \rho y + (1 - \rho)\mu, \tag{10}$$

where ρ is the reliability of the test and μ is the population mean of τ. Similarly, the conditional variance of τ, given y, is

$$(1 - \rho)\sigma^2, \tag{11}$$

where σ^2 is the population variance of τ. To see the relationship of these formulas to (8), write

$$(X'\Sigma_\epsilon^{-1}X + \Sigma^{-1})^{-1}X'\Sigma_\epsilon^{-1}$$
$$= \Sigma\Sigma^{-1}(X'\Sigma_\epsilon^{-1}X + \Sigma^{-1})^{-1}X'\Sigma_\epsilon^{-1}X(X'\Sigma_\epsilon^{-1}X)^{-1}X'\Sigma_\epsilon^{-1}$$
$$= \Sigma[\Sigma + (X'\Sigma_\epsilon^{-1}X)^{-1}]^{-1}(X'\Sigma_\epsilon^{-1}X)^{-1}X'\Sigma_\epsilon^{-1},$$

and let the $m \times m$ matrix $R = \Sigma[\Sigma + (X\Sigma_\epsilon^{-1}X)^{-1}]^{-1}$ be the "multivariate analogue of reliability" (Bock, 1966) in the context of a linear regression model such as (1). Then the mean of the conditional distribution is

$$\beta_i = R(X'\Sigma_\epsilon^{-1}X)^{-1}X'\Sigma_\epsilon^{-1}(y_i - X\mu) + \mu$$
$$= R\hat{\beta}_i + (I - R)\mu. \tag{12}$$

Similarly, the covariance matrix of the conditional distribution is

$$\Sigma_{\tilde{\beta}} = \Sigma - \Sigma X'(X\Sigma X' + \Sigma_\epsilon)^{-1} X\Sigma$$
$$= \Sigma - (X'\Sigma_\epsilon^{-1}X + \Sigma^{-1})^{-1} X'\Sigma_\epsilon^{-1} X\Sigma$$
$$= \Sigma - \Sigma[\Sigma + (X'\Sigma_\epsilon^{-1}X)^{-1}]^{-1} (X'\Sigma_\epsilon^{-1}X)^{-1} X'\Sigma_\epsilon^{-1} X\Sigma$$
$$= (I - R)\Sigma. \tag{13}$$

To the extent that y is fallible as an indicator of the true trend, $X\beta$, the generalized Kelley estimator of β regresses the least squares estimator, $\hat{\beta}$, toward the population mean. Although this estimator yields minimum average squared error for the population as a whole, it is not in general an unbiased estimator of β. Nevertheless it is a consistent estimator with increasing n; that is, the bias goes to zero as the number of observations on the subject becomes large, at which point R approaches I and (12) becomes the least squares estimator.

Despite prevailing use of the term "Bayes estimator" for the mean of the conditional distribution of β, given y_i, a case can be made for calling it the "Expected A Posteriori," or EAP estimator. This distinguishes it from the often useful *mode* of the conditional distribution, or "Maximum A Posteriori" (MAP) estimator.

EAP and MAP estimators have important advantages as descriptors of behavioral relationships within individual subjects. Because the number of repeated observations that can be obtained from the same subject may be limited, the data may determine the parameters of the model very poorly. If so, the least squares estimator may not exist or may give wildly implausible values. In particular, if the number of free parameters in the model exceeds the number of within-subject observations, the least squares estimator will not exist. EAP and MAP estimators, on the other hand, always exist and always give plausible values.

2. ESTIMATION OF Σ_ϵ, μ AND Σ.

Practical applications of (8) or (12) obviously require some method of estimating the structural parameter Σ_ϵ, and the population parameters μ and Σ, none of which are typically known a priori. It is usually possible to obtain a so-called "calibration" sample in which these parameters may be estimated. In survey research there is almost always ample data for this purpose within the main study.

If the model is linear and the distribution and independence assumptions of section 1 apply, the estimation problem may be solved by methods closely related to variance component analysis for unbalanced designs (see Harville, 1977). Laird (1982) shows how the calculations for these analyses can be carried out iteratively by the EM algorithm. Dempster, Rubin and Tsutakawa (1981) have applied such methods to the random regressions problem in the special case where $\Sigma_\epsilon = \sigma^2 I$. With the advent of the EM algorithm, and possibly with computational tricks to increase the speed of convergence, no insurmountable barrier now exists to trend analysis of longitudinal data from a linear random regressions point of view.

3. MORE GENERAL ASSUMPTIONS

Linear models such as (1) are appealing statistically because, under multivariate normal assumptions, the relevant joint, conditional, and marginal distributions are all normal. As a result, the structural and population parameters have simple sufficient statistics for which the conditional expectations required in the EM algorithm are easily obtained. Moreover, the model belongs to the exponential family in which the likelihood surface is concave and convergence of the EM algorithm can be guaranteed (see Dempster, Laird & Rubin, 1977; Pratt, 1981).

Statistical considerations aside, however, linear models are far from ideal representations of development. No organic growth, human or otherwise, can be linear in the long run. Where a wide range of growth is to be described, logistic models or mixtures of such models are much more satisfactory (see section 5), but these models present more difficult problems of estimation. Even when errors and random effects are assumed independent multivariate normal as in section 1, the marginal and conditional distributions are not normal, and some or all of the parameters to be estimated may not enjoy simple sufficient statistics. When the developmental model is nonlinear, the approach used by Dempster, Rubin and Tsutakawa (1981) in the linear random regressions problem would not, strictly speaking, apply.

Nevertheless, the general approach, that of maximum likelihood estimation of the fixed parameters after integrating over the distribution of the randomly dispersed parameters, remains valid. Dempster, Laird and Rubin (1977) propose a generalized EM algorithm (GEM) to cover this case, but it is more difficult to apply, and convergence cannot be guaranteed (Wu, 1981). A more straightforward approach, applied in a similar situation by Bock and Lieberman (1970), is to integrate *numerically* within the marginal maximum likelihood equations. This approach is greatly facilitated by a representation of the distribution of the random effect (prior distribution in this context) as a discrete distribution on a finite number of points (i.e., a histogram). Provided a sufficient number of points are taken in the range of the random effect, the marginal maximum likelihood estimates of the fixed parameters are, in general, little affected by the approximation entailed. Handled in this way, the estimation problem posed in section 2 has a straightforward solution even when the developmental model is nonlinear.

4. MARGINAL MAXIMUM LIKELIHOOD ESTIMATION OF Σ_ϵ, μ, AND Σ.

Suppose in the present example that $f(\theta)$ is some nonlinear function describing personal developmental trend over the range of ages at which the behavior in question is observed. Let all other aspects of the model remain the same. In particular, let the residuals, $\epsilon = y - f(\theta)$, be distributed $N(0, \Sigma_\epsilon)$, and the personal parameters, θ, be distributed $N(\mu, \Sigma)$, independent of ϵ. Then, the marginal density of y_i in the population may be expressed as the following m-fold definite integral of the likelihood, $\ell(\cdot)$, weighted by the prior density, $g(\cdot)$:

$$h(y_i) = \int_{-\infty}^{\infty} \ell(y_i|\theta) g(\theta) d\theta, \tag{14}$$

where

$$\ell(y_i|\theta) = (2\pi)^{-n/2} |\Sigma_\epsilon|^{-1/2} \exp(-\tfrac{1}{2} \epsilon' \Sigma_\epsilon^{-1} \epsilon)$$

and

$$g(\theta) = (2\pi)^{-m/2} |\Sigma|^{-1/2} \exp[-\tfrac{1}{2} (\theta - \mu)' \Sigma^{-1} (\theta - \mu)].$$

For a sample of N independently responding subjects,

$$\log L = \sum_i^N \log h(y_i). \tag{15}$$

Differentiating (15) with respect to μ, we obtain

$$\frac{\partial \log L}{\partial \mu} = \sum_i^N \frac{1}{h(y_i)} \int_{-\infty}^{\infty} \ell(y_i|\theta) g(\theta) (\theta - \mu) \Sigma^{-1} d\theta.$$

Equating to zero,

$$\sum_i^N \frac{\hat{\mu}}{h(y_i)} \int_{-\infty}^{\infty} \ell(y_i|\theta) g(\theta) d\theta = \sum_i^N \frac{1}{h(y_i)} \int_{-\infty}^{\infty} \theta \ell(y_i|\theta) g(\theta) d\theta,$$

or

$$\hat{\mu} = \frac{1}{N} \int_{-\infty}^{\infty} \theta \sum_i^N \frac{\ell(y_i|\theta)}{h(y_i)} g(\theta) d\theta \tag{16}$$

By a similar calculation,

$$\hat{\Sigma} = \frac{1}{N}\int_{-\infty}^{\infty} (\theta - \mu)(\theta - \mu)' \sum_{i}^{N} \frac{\ell(y_i|\theta)}{h(y_i)} g(\theta) d\theta, \qquad (17)$$

and

$$\hat{\Sigma}_\varepsilon = \frac{1}{N}\int_{-\infty}^{\infty} \sum_{i}^{N} [y_i - f(\theta)][y_i - f(\theta)]' \frac{\ell(y_i|\theta)}{h(y_i)} g(\theta) d\theta. \qquad (18)$$

Again, the solution of these equations proceeds iteratively. Provisional values of Σ_ε, μ and Σ are assigned in order to compute the prior and likelihood, improved values are obtained, and another cycle of calculations carried out. If m is not greater than 4 or 5, practical evaluation of these integrals may be performed by nested Gauss-Hermite quadratures after centering the variables of integration and transforming to orthogonality. To this end, let $\xi = T^{-1}(\theta - \mu)$, or $\theta = T\xi + \mu$, where $TT' = \Sigma$ is the Cholesky decomposition of Σ (see Bock, 1975, p. 85). Then $E(\xi) = 0$, and $V(\xi) = T^{-1}\Sigma(T^{-1})' = I$. Now, let X_{kj} and $A(X_{kj})$ be a node and corresponding coefficient of a q-point Gauss-Hermite quadrature, and, for a provisional μ and Σ, let $Z_k = TX_k + \mu$ be a transform of a vector of m nodes. Then,

$$\hat{v}_j = \frac{1}{N}\sum_{k_1}^{q}\sum_{k_2}^{q}\cdots\sum_{k_m}^{q} X_{kj} \sum_{i}^{N} \frac{\ell(y_i|Z_k)}{h(y_i)} A(X_{k_1})A(X_{k_2})\cdots A(X_{k_m}), \qquad (19)$$

$$\hat{\phi}_{jj'} \simeq \frac{1}{N}\sum_{k_1}^{q}\sum_{k_2}^{q}\cdots\sum_{k_m}^{q} (X_{kj} - \hat{v}_j)(X_{kj'} - \hat{v}_{j'}) \sum_{i}^{N} \frac{\ell(y_i|Z_k)}{h(y_i)} A(X_{k_1})A(X_{k_2})\cdots A(X_{k_m}), \qquad (20)$$

and

$$\sigma_{\varepsilon jj'} \simeq \frac{1}{N}\sum_{k_1}^{q}\sum_{k_2}^{q}\cdots\sum_{k_m}^{q}\sum_{i}^{N}[(y_{kj} - f_j(Z_k)][y_{ij'} - f_{j'}(Z_k)]\frac{\ell(y_i|Z_k)}{h(y_i)} A(X_{k_1})A(X_{k_2})\cdots A(X \qquad (21)$$

where

$$h(\mathbf{y}_i) \simeq \sum_{k_1}^{q} \sum_{k_2}^{q} \cdots \sum_{k_m}^{q} \ell(\mathbf{y}_i|\mathbf{Z}_k)A(X_{k_1})A(X_{k_2}) \cdots A(X_{k_m}). \tag{22}$$

At the end of cycle ι, the improved estimates of $\boldsymbol{\mu}$ and $\boldsymbol{\Sigma}$ may be recovered by the inverse transformation $\boldsymbol{\mu}^{(\iota + 1)} = \mathbf{T}^{(\iota)}\mathbf{v}^{(\iota)} + \boldsymbol{\mu}^{(\iota)}$ and $\boldsymbol{\Sigma}^{(\iota + 1)} = \mathbf{T}^{(\iota)}\boldsymbol{\Phi}^{(\iota)}(\mathbf{T}^{(\iota)})'$. At convergence, $\mathbf{v}$ will approach $\mathbf{0}$, $\boldsymbol{\Phi}$ will approach $\mathbf{I}$, and the transformation will cease to change. At present there is no guarantee that the procedure will converge, and any tendency of $\boldsymbol{\Sigma}$ or $\boldsymbol{\Sigma}_e$ to approach singularity will certainly cause difficulties. But a number of applications of closely related models have been successful in this respect, so there is perhaps reason for optimism (see Section 5).

These are *EM*-like iterations. The accumulating of posterior densities over the sample is an *E* step, and the calculations for the moment estimates is an *M* step.

5. APPLICATIONS

The Triple Logistic Growth Model. Bock and Thissen (1976, 1980) use two-stage sampling concepts in their study of the so-called "triple-logistic" model for a child's growth in stature between one year and maturity. The model is the sum of three logistic components, each containing three parameters to be determined. The nine parameters are under one linear constraint, however, leaving eight free parameters to be chosen in order to describe the growth of a given child.

Because of the nonlinearity and high dimensionality of this model, it is not computationally feasible to obtain the Bayes (EAP) estimate of a child's individual growth parameters. The mode (MAP estimate) of the posterior distribution, on the other hand, is easy to compute and the covariance matrix of the posterior can be approximated by the inverse of the matrix of second derivatives of the log likelihood in the region of the mode.

In this application, the MAP estimate has the admirable property of existing for any number of height measurements that may be available for the child in question. In particular, it may be calculated from a single measurement of the child's height at an age prior to maturity. The estimate then has the effect of selecting the growth curve in the population that is most probable for this child, given the measurement. The curve in turn predicts the child's height at any age from one year onwards, including mature stature, say at age 21. In this way, MAP estimation provides a method of predicting stature at maturity from height measurements in childhood. It can also incorporate other information to improve prediction by conditioning the prior distribution on, for example, mid-parent stature. Applications of this method of prediction to cases from the Berkeley and Fels samples appear in Bock (1982a, 1982b), and an evaluation of the method appears in Bock (1982b).

The high dimensionality of the triple-logistic model makes impractical, however, the quadratures in equations (19) through (22). Fortunately, these forms of likelihood equations lend themselves to Monte Carlo integration. It is necessary only to draw random normal deviates from the prior distribution and to compute moments for the latent variables weighted by the average posterior density over the sample of subjects. The contribution of the prior is automatically incorporated in the random number generation. Although the computational burden is fairly heavy (the Monte Carlo integrations must be repeated in each cycle of the EM like steps), it is well within the capacity of a modern computer. Estimation of the population mean and covariance matrix of the growth parameters based on a sample of boys from the Fels study by this method is reported in Bock (1982a).

Trends in Correlated Proportions. Gibbons (1981) has used a discrete, finite representation of a distribution of random effects to solve the hitherto intractable problem of testing and estimating trends in correlated proportions—that is, sample proportions arising from repeated classifications of the same subjects. (The case of two such classifications is handled by McNemar's test.) Gibbons assumes a latent random regression model in which each subject is following a personal straight-line trend. Assuming that the intercepts and slopes of these lines are bivariate normally distributed in the population of subjects, he expresses the unconditional probability of each possible pattern of binary responses as an integral over this distribution. This result reduces the problem to that of a confirmatory factor analysis of dichotomous variables, to which the full-information solution given by Bock and Aitkin (1981) applies. But Gibbons extends the model further, introducing a first-order (Markov) autocorrelation structure for deviations from the latent trend lines. Using the so-called "Clark algorithm" to approximate orthant probabilities for n-variate normal deviates with this correlation structure, he is able to estimate the correlation parameter in a second stage of the marginal maximum likelihood procedure.

Gibbons and Bock (1982) generalize this method to provide tests and estimates of differences in average trend between treatment groups. They apply their procedure to dichotomous psychiatric ratings of the clinical status (improved vs. not improved) of patients on two antidepressant drugs.

Characterizing Population Distributions. Mislevy (submitted for publication) proposes marginal maximum likelihood methods for estimating parameters in three different characterizations of population latent distributions. Each of these methods employs a finite discrete representation of a provisional prior distribution.

The simplest characterization is a discrete distribution on the same points as the prior, but with average posterior probability densities at these points, given the data, replacing the prior densities. These posterior densities, averaged over the subjects in the sample, are the marginal maximum likelihood estimates of the population densities. In the estimation of other fixed parameters, this empirically determined distribution can then replace the provisional discrete prior in the quadrature formulas employing these points. If both these steps are carried out iteratively in the same data, the procedure is empirical Bayes in the sense of Robbins (1955).

When a parametric family of population distributions, such as the normal or lognormal, is assumed, the parameters that index a particular distribution can be estimated by marginal maximum likelihood beginning from an assumed or empirical discrete prior. Using a similar procedure but with a different method of numerical integration, Andersen and Madsen (1977), for example, have estimated the mean and variance of an assumed normal distribution of latent ability, given a sample of item response data to which a Rasch model had been fitted. The finite discrete prior method applied to these data by Mislevy (1982) reproduces their results almost exactly.

The third type of parametric representation of population latent distributions, one that is especially appropriate for behavioral and educational research, is a mixture of Gaussian components with different proportions and means, but common variance. For any assumed number of components, the mixing proportions, means, and common variance can be estimated by marginal maximum likelihood, given a sample from the population and assuming a provisional discrete prior. The procedure is similar to the iterative method for fitting normal mixtures proposed by Day (1969), except that posterior densities on the points of the discrete distribution play the role of weighted data in Day's method.

These Gaussian mixture distributions are capable of representing the wide variety of platykurtic and skewed distributions that arise when heterogeneous human populations are sampled. They can readily be extended to the multivariate case, and likelihood ratio tests of the number and dimensionality of the components are available. Many results of statistical inference based on the normal distribution generalize straightforwardly to the mixtures when the proportions and means are specified. Examples may be found in Mislevy (submitted for publication).

6. CONCLUSION

The purpose of psychometrics is to describe persisting characteristics of individual subjects as dependably as possible. Inevitably, the exigencies of large-scale research leaves some subjects for whom the data are too meager or unreliable for accurate description. In the past, investigators have typically set such cases aside and carried out their analyses on the possibly unrepresentative complete cases that remained. But a more rational approach is to make use of the fact that the subjects are drawn from a population in which the characteristics in question have a distribution. If this distribution can be specified, it is more efficient to take a Bayesian approach and to assign all subjects the population value that is expected or most probable given whatever data is available for each. The mean square error for the sample as a whole will then be smaller than that of any other estimator. In effect, the procedure will attribute to subjects for whom the data are unreliable a value that is optimal by the criterion of least mean-square error.

The main obstacle to the Bayesian approach has always been uncertainties about the specification of the population distribution, for it is precisely when the data for a subject are most limited that the prior distribution most influences the result. The burden of the present chapter is to argue that the problem of specification can be solved empirically, using data from large-sample studies and taking advantage of the computational convenience of finite discrete representations of the population distribution. In the types of Bayes methods described here, only a rough characterization of the prior is required. The resulting estimates are sufficiently insensitive to minor variation in the prior that more elaborate and precise representations are not warranted. If enough points are assigned in the relevant range, the finite discrete priors are quite adequate, and they have the great advantage of fitting neatly into the quadrature formulas by which the marginal maximum likelihood equations can be solved.

It is curious that statistical workers have made so little use of this type of numerical integration, which is widely applied in engineering fields. Apparently, the Fisherian emphasis on sufficient statistics and derived distributions has deflected attention from the possibilities of direct representations of likelihoods and posterior densities and numerical methods of exploiting them. Only recently has interest begun to shift in the latter direction (see Kalbfleisch, 1979; Brillinger and Preisler, 1982).

REFERENCES

Andersen, E. B., & Madsen, M. Estimating parameters of the latent population distribution. *Psychometrika*, 1977, *42*, 357–374.

Bock, R. D. Contributions of multivariate experimental designs to educational research. In R. B. Cattell (Ed.). *Handbook of multivariate experimental psychology*. Chicago: Rand-McNally, 1966.

Bock, R. D. *Multivariate statistical methods in behavioral research*. New York: McGraw-Hill, 1975.

Bock, R. D. Univariate and multivariate analysis of time-structured data. In J. R. Nesselroade & P. B. Baltes (Eds.). *Longitudinal research in the study of behavior and development*. New York: Academic Press, 1979.

Bock, R. D. Prediction of mature stature. *Proceedings of the Golden Jubilee Celebration of the Indian Statistical Institute*, Calcutta, 1982.

Bock, R. D. Predicting the mature stature of preadolescent children. *NATO Advanced Study Workshop*, Brussels, 1982.

Bock, R. D. & Aitkin, M. Marginal maximum likelihood estimation of item parameters: Application of an EM algorithm. *Psychometrika*, 1981, *46*, 443–459.

Bock, R. D. & Lieberman, M. Fitting a response model for *n* dichotomously scored items. *Psychometrika*, 1970, *35*, 179–197.

Bock, R. D., & Thissen, D. Fitting multi-component models for growth in stature. *Proceedings of the 9th International Biometric Conference*, 1976, *1*, 431–442.

Bock, R. D. & Thissen, D. Statistical problems of fitting individual growth curves. In F. E. Johnston, A. F. Roche & C. Susanne (Eds.). *Human physical growth and maturation: Methodologies and factors*. New York: Plenum, 1980.

Brillinger, D. R. & Preisler, H. K. Maximum likelihood estimation in a latent variable problem. Technical Report No. 15, 1982. Department of Statistics, University of California at Berkeley.

Day, N. E. Estimating the components of a mixture of normal distributions. *Biometrika*, 1969, *56*, 463–474.

Dempster, A. P., Laird, N. M. & Rubin, D. B. Maximum likelihood from incomplete data via the *EM* algorithm (with Discussion). *Journal of the Royal Statistical Society, Series B*, 1977, *39*, 1–38.

Dempster, A. P., Rubin, D. B., & Tsutakawa, R. K. Estimation in variance component models. *Journal of the American Statistical Association*, 1981, *76*, 341–353.

Elston, R. C., & Grizzle, J. E. Estimation of time-response curves and their confidence bands. *Biometrics*, 1962, *18*, 148–159.

Fearn, T. A Bayesian approach to growth curves. *Biometrika*, 1975, *62*, 89–100.

Gibbons, R. *Analysis of discrete time-structured data*. Unpublished Ph.D. dissertation, Department of Behavioral Sciences, University of Chicago, 1981.

Gibbons, R. D., & Bock, R. D. Trend in correlated proportions. (submitted for publication).

Harville, D. A. Maximum likelihood approaches to variance component estimation and to related problems. *Journal of the American Statistical Association*, 1977, *72*, 320–340.

James, W., & Stein, C. Estimation with quadratic loss. *Proceedings of the Berkeley Symposium on Mathematical Statistics and Probability*, 1961, 361–379.

Kalbfleisch, J. D. *Probability and statistical inference*. New York: Springer-Verlag, 1979.

Kelley, T. L. *Fundamentals of statistics*. Cambridge: Harvard University Press, 1947.

Laird, N. M. Computation of variance components using the *EM* algorithm. *Journal of Statistical Computation and Simulation*, 1982, *14*, 295–303.

Lindley, D. V., & Smith, A. F. M. Bayes estimation for linear models (with Discussion). *Journal of the Royal Statistical Society, Series B*, 1972, *34*, 1–41.

Mislevy, R. J. Characterizing latent distributions. (submitted for publication).

Nesselroade, J. R., & Baltes, P. B. (Eds.) *Longitudinal research in the study of behavior and development*. New York: Academic Press, 1979.

Pratt, J. W. Concavity of the log likelihood. *Journal of the American Statistical Association*, 1981, *76*, 103–106.

Robbins, H. An empirical Bayes approach to statistics. In J. Neyman (Ed.). *Proceedings of the Third Berkeley Symposium on Mathematical Statistics and Probability*. Berkeley: University of California Press, 1955.

Rosenberg, B. Linear regression with randomly dispersed parameters. *Biometrika*, 1973, *60*, 65–72.

Wu, C. *On the convergence of the EM algorithm*. (Technical Report No. 642). Department of Statistics, University of Wisconsin, Madison, 1981.

Zellner, A. *Introduction to Bayesian inference in econometrics*. New York: Wiley, 1971.

8 A General Latent Structure Model for Contingency Table Data

Erling B. Andersen
University of Copenhagen

ABSTRACT

A general model is suggested for latent structure analysis of categorical data. The data is viewed as a contingency table and the connection to other approaches in contingency table analysis is briefly discussed. The suggested model assumes that category weights, needed to estimate a one-dimensional latent variable, are known, although some suggestions are made for tentative estimates of the weights. It is then shown that all the elements of well-known inference methods for the Rasch model applies, for example, population free estimates of item parameters and estimation in and check of the latent population distribution based on the observed score distribution. The theory is applied to one set of data from depression rating and one set from consumer complaint behavior.

1. CONTINGENCY TABLES AND LATENT STRUCTURE MODELS

Latent structure analysis is a method for analyzing multivariate categorical or continuous data, where knowledge of extra unobservable variables simplify the description of the structure of the data. For continuous data such an analysis usually takes the form of a structural analysis of the variance–covariance matrix. For a survey and further references the reader is referred to Bentler and Weeks (1980), Jöreskog (1978), or Jöreskog and Sörbom (1977). In this chapter we discuss the discrete case. Multi-variate categorical data are often thought of as a contingency table and we start our discussion by considering a k- dimensional contingency table. Let $x_{ij\ldots r}$ be the observed numbers in cell $(i,j,\ldots,r)$ and

$p_{ij\ldots r}$ the corresponding cell probability that a randomly chosen individual from the population falls in cell $(i,j, \ldots, r)$. Dependent on the observation design and other assumptions, several models are possible for a contingency table. A common model is to assume independency between the N observed individuals and constant cell probabilities over the population. If in the sample design only N is given beforehand, the model is then multinomial with number parameter

$$N = \sum_{i=1}^{m_1} \sum_{j=1}^{m_2} \cdots \sum_{r=1}^{m_k} x_{ij\ldots r}$$

and the $p_{ij\ldots r}$'s as probability parameters. For further reference we have denoted the number of categories for variable q by m_q.

In ordinary contingency table analysis, the aim is to describe dependencies among the variables by parametric expressions, so-called interactions. It is important to note that cases with dependencies are cases, where we reject the simple model

$$p_{ij\ldots r} = p_{i\ldots} \times p_{.j\ldots} \times \ldots \times p_{\ldots r} \qquad (1)$$

of independence between the variables.

In latent structure analysis, the dependencies, and thus the deviations from independency, are ascribed to a common dependency on unobservable latent variables. Latent structure models have been studied by many authors. It was introduced as a concept by Lazarsfeld (1950). His original idea and further developments are surveyed in the monograph by Lazarsfeld and Henry (1968). The first effective statistical methods were developed by Andersson (1954). New and more efficient statistical methods were developed by Goodman (1974). For further references the reader is referred to Goodman (1978, chapters 8–10), Haberman (1979, chapters 9 and 10), Madansky (1978), or Andersen (1982).

In a parallel development, latent structure models have been treated for many years in psychology and education in the form of latent trait models. Statistical models which gave a precise description of the probability of observed binary data in terms of a latent trait or latent individual parameter were formulated by Lawley (1943), Lord (1952), Birnbaum (1957) and Rasch (1960). Since 1960, there has been a rich literature on various latent trait models. Recent survey papers, which update the hitherto most authoritative textbook, Lord and Novick (1968), are Baker (1977), and Hambleton, Swaminathan, Cook, Eigner and Gilford (1978).

In this chapter, we search for a general latent structure model. By introducing a few (not very restrictive) assumptions we formulate a latent structure model, which covers the general case with an arbitrary number of variables, k, having an arbitrary (though finite) number of categories $m_1, \ldots, m_k$. A survey of the literature indicates that the models treated so far only rarely cover cases with m_q

> 2 and then only the special case $m_1 = m_2 = \cdots = m_k$. In addition, the earlier methods usually required k to be moderate, often not larger than 4.

2. A GENERAL LATENT STRUCTURE MODEL

As indicated above, we now relax the assumption of constant cell probabilities and let them vary with the individuals. Thus instead of the common cell probability $p_{ij\ldots r}$, we consider the individual cell probabilities

$$p_{ij\ldots r}^{(v)} = P\{\text{individual no. } v \text{ belongs to cell } (i,j,\ldots,r)\}; \qquad (2)$$
$$v = 1, \ldots, N.$$

It is convenient to think of the k dimensions of the contingency tables as k variables, or items. Then $m_1, \ldots, m_k$ are the number of categories for items $1, 2, \ldots, k$ and if we introduce $U_1^{(v)}, \ldots, U_k^{(v)}$ as the responses for individual v on the k items, we can write (2) as

$$p_{ij\ldots r}^{(v)} = P\{U_1^{(v)} = i, U_2^{(v)} = j, \ldots, U_k^{(v)} = r\}. \qquad (3)$$

In order to establish a workable model we make two essential assumptions:

(A1) For each v, $U_1^{(v)}, \ldots, U_k^{(v)}$ are independent random variables.
(A2) The individual cell probabilities (3) can be parametrized as regards the dependency on v through a finite number of individuals' parameters $\theta_{v1}, \ldots, \theta_{vM}$.

Assumption (A1) is often termed *local independence* and means that we have independence in the contingency table at the individual level. It thus implies independence in the observed table if all individuals have the same parameters $(\theta_{v1}, \ldots, \theta_{vM}) = (\theta_1, \ldots, \theta_M)$ and approximate independency if the θ_v's do not vary much.

(A2) is a necessary assumption if we want the statistical inference concerning the individuals to take the form of classical statistical parametric inference.

With the introduction of the $U_q^{(v)}$'s of (3), we can write the complete set of observed categorical variables on the matrix form

$$\{U_q^{(v)}\}, v = 1, \ldots, N; q = 1, \ldots, k.$$

With assumptions (A1) and (A2) we can write (3) as

$$p_{ij\ldots r}^{(v)} = p_{1i}(\theta_v) \cdots p_{kr}(\theta_v) \qquad (4)$$

where $\theta_v = (\theta_{v1}, \ldots, \theta_{vM})$.

The full likelihood function is of course rather complicated for such a general setup, and we shall not write it down here.

Instead we shall try to simplify it by making one more assumption as follows.

(A3) For each individual there must exist a vector-valued sufficient statistic $t = (t_{\nu 1}, \ldots, t_{\nu M})$ for the individual parameter vector $\theta = (\theta_{\nu 1}, \ldots, \theta_{\nu M})$.

Assumption (A3) does not directly and in any unique way lead to one class of models. This has to do with the general problem in mathematical statistics of finding a unique class of models which admit sufficient statistics for the parameters. For continuous random variables some relatively strong results are available (cf., for example, Brown, 1964). This is not the case for discrete and, in particular, categorical variables. A few papers deal with the problem, for example, Denny (1972) and Andersen (1970b). On the other hand, almost all manageable models which admit sufficient statistics belong to the exponential family of distributions. Log-linear models for contingency tables are important examples.

If we restrict attention to exponential family type distributions, we can formulate a rather general class of latent structure models. For convenience we consider only models for one-dimensional latent variables, that is, for $M = 1$. It is not difficult to write the corresponding expressions for $M > 1$, but they become more complicated, at least typographically.

Thus let θ_ν be a one-dimensional individual parameter and let $(U_1^{(\nu)}, \ldots, U_k^{(\nu)})$ as before, be the response of individual ν on the k items. Then in order to belong to an exponential family and thus admit a sufficient statistic for θ_ν, the response probabilities must have the form

$$P\{U_q^{(\nu)} = u_q^{(\nu)}\} = C_q(\theta_\nu) exp(\theta_\nu a_q(u_q^{(\nu)})) \cdot h_q(u_q^{(\nu)}). \tag{5}$$

The possible values of $u_q^{(\nu)}$ are $1, \ldots, m_q$, where m_q may vary with q. Consider now formula (5) for $u_q^{(\nu)} = i$, $i = 1, \ldots, m_q$ and put

$$a_q(i) = a_{qi}, i = 1, \ldots, m_q$$

and

$$h_q(i) = exp(b_{qi}), i = 1, \ldots, m_q$$

Then

$$P\{U_q^{(\nu)} = i\} = C_q(\theta_\nu) \, exp(\theta_\nu a_{qi} + b_{qi}) \tag{6}$$

with

$$C_q(\theta_\nu) = \left[\sum_{i=1}^{m_q} exp(\theta_\nu a_{qi} + b_{qi})\right]^{-1} \tag{7}$$

From ordinary exponential family theory now follows that

$$t_\nu = a_{1i} + a_{2j} + \cdots + a_{kr}, \tag{8}$$

8. GENERAL LATENT STRUCTURE MODEL

is minimal sufficient for θ_ν, when $i, j, \ldots, r$ are the observed responses of individual ν.

The existence of the sufficient statistic t_ν for θ_ν is essential for all the inference procedures we develop in subsequent sections. We note, however, that t_ν is only observable, and thus a statistic in the true sense, if the a's are known quantities. We, therefore, make the somewhat restrictive assumption that the a's are known.

Note that the a's form a matrix of weights such that response i on item 1 enters the estimation of θ_ν with the weight a_{1i}.

We return to a further discussion of the role of the a's in subsequent sections.

It is instructive, however, to consider a few special cases. First, we consider the case $m_1 = m_2 = \ldots = m_k = 2$. The model (6) then reduces to

$$P\{U_q^{(\nu)} = 1\} = \exp\{a_q(\theta_\nu - b_q)\}/(1 + \exp\{a_q(\theta_\nu - b_q)\})$$

with

$$a_q = a_{q1} - a_{q2} \text{ and } b_q = (b_{q1} - b_{q2})/a_q$$

or the two-parameter logistic model by Birnbaum (1957). We note that $a_1, \ldots, a_k$ are the item-discriminating powers and b_q the item difficulties. The Rasch model is a special case with all a's equal to 1. As remarked above, we assume in this chapter that the a's are known. We thus avoid an estimation of the item-discriminating powers. A maximum likelihood estimation of the parameters of a two-parameter and three-parameter logistic model was first reported by Lord (1968). Recently Bock and Aitkin (1981) have suggested a method, which seems to be reliable. We show later that several of the important steps of a statistical analysis are relatively insensitive to the choice of the a's, which indicates that even rather crude estimates of the item-discriminating powers may serve well for practical purposes. In addition there are presumably many situations where model considerations, prior to the statistical analysis, point to specific choices of the a's.

Second, we consider the case $m_1 = m_2 = \cdots = m_k = m > 2$.

If for this case the category weights a_{qi} are the same for all items, that is, $a_{qi} = a_i$ for all q, then (6) is identical with the polychotomous model suggested by Rasch (1961) and discussed by Bock (1972) and Andersen (1973b). For unknown a's the model is usually treated as a model with vector-valued latent variables. Thus for the latent variable θ_ν redefined as the vector

$$\theta_{\nu i} = \theta_\nu a_i, \, i = 1, \ldots, m,$$

we have the form

$$p_{ij\ldots r}^{(\nu)} = P\{U_1^{(\nu)} = i, U_2^{(\nu)} = j, \ldots, U_k^{(\nu)} = r\}$$

$$= \prod_{q=1}^{k} C_q(\theta_\nu)\exp\{\theta_\nu t_\nu + b_{1i} + \cdots + b_{kr}\} \quad (9)$$

The marginal cell probability for a randomly drawn individual then becomes

$$p_{ij\ldots r} = \exp\{b_{1i} + \cdots + b_{kr}\} \int \left[\prod_{q=1}^{k} C_q(\theta) \right] e^{\theta' v} g(\theta) d\theta, \quad (10)$$

where $g(\theta)$ is the population density of θ.

A third important quantity is the conditional probability of $U_1^{(v)}, \ldots, U_k^{(v)}$ given t_v, which by sufficiency of t_v is independent of θ_v. It takes the form

$$p_{ij\ldots r}(t_v) = P\{U_1^{(v)} = i, \ldots, U_q^{(v)} = r | a_{1i} + \cdots + a_{kr} = t_v\} \quad (11)$$
$$= \exp\{b_{1i} + \cdots + b_{kr}\}/S(t_v; b_1, \ldots, b_k),$$

with $b_q = (b_{q1}, \ldots, b_{qm_q})$ and

$$S(t_v; b_1, \ldots, b_k) = \sum_{a_{1i} + \cdots + a_{kr} = t_v} \exp\{b_{i1} + \cdots + b_{kr}\}$$

The summation in $S(t_v; b_1, \ldots, b_k)$ is over all responses $(i, j, \ldots, r)$ for which $a_{i1} + \cdots + a_{kr} = t_v$.

A likelihood function for the observations can be derived from (9), (10), or (11). Which one to choose will depend on the parameters to be estimated and the preferred estimation method.

The density $g(\theta)$ in (10) may depend on certain parameters. In this chapter we consider only the two parameter case and assume that $g(\theta)$ is a normal density. We can then write $g(\theta)$ as

$$g(\theta) = \varphi(\theta | \mu, \sigma^2)$$

But other densities can also be used, for example, a logistic density with a location parameter and a scale parameter as the population parameters, or a gamma density with a shape parameter and a scale parameter.

Fur further reference, we call $\theta_1, \ldots, \theta_N$ *individual parameters*, $b_1, \ldots, b_k$ *item parameters* and μ and σ^2 *population parameters*. The a's, which in this chapter are known constants, are called *category weights*.

3. ESTIMATION OF ITEM PARAMETERS

The item parameters can be estimated based on (9), (10), or (11). Based on (9) we can derive $b_1, \ldots, b_k$ as maximum likelihood (*ML*) estimates jointly with the θ's. Based on (10) we get *ML*-estimates for b's jointly with the population parameters (μ, σ^2). This is essentially the method of Bock and Lieberman (1970), Bock (1972), and Bock and Aitkin (1981). However, we prefer to derive the b-estimates as *conditional maximum likelihood* (CML) estimates based on (11). This method is traditionally used for the Rasch model and has attractive asymptotic properties as described by Andersen (1970a, 1973a, 1973b). Unlike a

8. GENERAL LATENT STRUCTURE MODEL   123

direct *ML*-estimation based on (10), it is independent of the choice of the population density $g(\theta)$. Compared with (9), the CML method is consistent for $N \to \infty$, which a direct *ML* estimation based on (9) is not. Earlier the CML-method was considered to be too complicated and time consuming. Now these problems are manageable when modern high-speed computers are used for the computations.

The conditional likelihood is obtained by (11) as

$$L_c = \exp\left\{\sum_{q=1}^{k}\sum_{i=1}^{m_q} b_{qi}u_{qi}\right\} \Big/ \prod_{v=1}^{N} S(t_v; b_1, \ldots, b_k), \quad (12)$$

where

u_{qi} = number of individuals who have used category i on item q

The denominator in (12) can be written in a more compact form, when we note that t_v, being a discrete random variable, has only a limited number of possible values $\underline{t}, \ldots, \bar{t}$.

Let n_t, $t = \underline{t}, \ldots, \bar{t}$, be the number of individuals with score $t_v = t$. Then (12) can be written as

$$L_c = \exp\left(\sum_{q=1}^{k}\sum_{i=1}^{m_q} b_{qi}u_{qi}\right) \Big/ \prod_{t=\underline{t}}^{\bar{t}} [S(t; b_1, \ldots, b_k)]^{n_t} \quad (13)$$

The conditional distribution of $u_{11}, \ldots, u_{km_k}$ given $n_{\underline{t}}, \ldots, n_{\bar{t}}$, expressed through (13), is again an exponential family. Hence CML-estimates for the b_{qi}'s are obtained by solving the equations

$$u_{qi} = E[U_{qi}|n_{\underline{t}}, \ldots, n_{\bar{t}}], \quad \begin{array}{l} i = 1, \ldots, m_q, \\ q = 1, \ldots, k. \end{array} \quad (14)$$

Note that we take *conditional mean values* on the right-hand sides. These conditional mean values are simple versions of the *S*-functions. Thus (14) has the form

$$u_{qi} = \exp(b_{qi}) \sum_{t=\underline{t}}^{\bar{t}} n_t \sum_{\ell=1}^{m_q} \frac{S(t - a_{i\ell}; b_1, \ldots, b_{q-1}, b_{q+1}, \ldots, b_k)}{S(t; b_1, \ldots, b_k)}$$

The *S*-functions are polychotomous generalizations of the elementary symmetric functions, which are well known from the theory of the Rasch model, and recursive formulas for their compilation are easily established (cf. Andersen, 1972 or Fischer, 1974, chap. 21). Hence (14) can be solved by direct marginal fitting or by a Newton-Raphson procedure. In the examples shown later a Newton-Raphson procedure is used as it also provides estimates of the standard errors of the *b*-estimates.

Also the goodness of fit test by Andersen (1973a) applies. If we divide the range $(\underline{t}, \bar{t})$ in G intervals by the cutting points $s_0 = \underline{t}, s_1, \ldots, s_G = \bar{t}$, we can estimate the item parameters within each such score group.

Let $b_{11}^{(r)}, \ldots, b_{km_k}^{(r)}$ be the CML-estimates obtained by maximizing

$$L_c^{(r)} = \exp\left\{\sum_{q=1}^{k} \sum_{i=1}^{m_q} b_{qi} u_{qi}^{(r)}\right\} \prod_{s_{r-1} < t \leq s_r} [S(t; b_1, \ldots, b_k)]^{n_t}$$

where $u_{qi}^{(r)}$ are the item totals based only on individuals in score group r. The within-score-group CML-estimates can then be compared to the overall CML-estimates $(b_1, \ldots, b_k)$ obtained from (14). The model gives a good fit when the score group estimates do not exhibit significant differences from the overall estimates. This can be checked graphically by plotting the score group estimates against the overall estimates, or by a conditional likelihood ratio (CLR) test defined as

$$z = -2\ln[L_c(\hat{b}_1, \ldots, \hat{b}_k)/\prod_r L_c^{(r)}(\hat{b}_1^{(r)}, \ldots, \hat{b}_k^{(r)})] \tag{15}$$

which is asymptotically χ^2-distributed with $(G - 1)M$ degrees of freedom, where M is the number of unconstrainted b's to be estimated.

In order to determine M, we return to the models (6) and (7). We note first that a parameter change from b_{qi} to $b_{qi}^* = b_{qi} - b_{qm_q}$ does not change the model structure. Hence we can put

$$b_{qm_q} = 0, q = 1, \ldots, k. \tag{16}$$

Second, a change of the origin of the θ_v axes by $\theta_v^* = \theta_v + c$, can be compensated by changing b_{qi} to $b_{qi}^{**} = b_{qi} - ca_{qi}$. Since c is arbitrary we can accordingly introduce the constraint

$$\sum_q \sum_i b_{qi} = 0. \tag{17}$$

From (16) and (17) we conclude that

$$M = \sum_q m_q - k - 1.$$

The theory of this chapter runs parallel to the theory of the Rasch model treated earlier by the author and others (cf. Andersen, 1980; Fischer, 1974; Wright & Masters, 1982; Wright & Stone, 1979). We have thus omitted much theoretical background in this account. The model presented in this chapter is on the other hand much more general than the earlier treated models. In the dichotomous case it includes the two-parameter logistic model with known item-discriminating powers, and in the polychotomous case it allows for a varying number of response categories for the different items.

One slightly surprising result is that the theory for the Rasch model applies to the two-parameter logistic model, when the item-discriminating powers are known.

The requirement of *known category weights* seems to be indispensable for an application of the powerful and well-documented methods described above. We discuss whether this is a reasonable assumption, whether it can be checked, and the consequences of it not being fulfilled, in later sections.

4. THE POPULATION DENSITY OF THE LATENT PARAMETER

As noted above it is a powerful property of the model that inference about the item parameters and a first check of the model structure is independent of our choice of the latent density $g(\theta)$. We also note that the first factor on the right-hand side of (10) is independent of θ and is thus of no consequence for likelihood considerations concerning θ and $g(\theta)$. This means that likelihood inference concerning $g(\theta)$ can be based on the joint distribution of $n_t, t = \underline{t}, \ldots, \bar{t}$, given by the multinomial probability

$$f(n_{\underline{t}}, \ldots, n_{\bar{t}}) = \binom{n}{n_{\underline{t}} \ldots n_{\bar{t}}} \prod_{t=\underline{t}}^{\bar{t}} \pi_t^{n_t}, \tag{18}$$

where

$$\pi_t = h(t) \int \left[\prod_q C_q(\theta) \right] e^{\theta t} g(\theta) d\theta.$$

and $h(t)$ is a normalizing factor defined by $\Sigma \pi_t = 1$.

If we assume that $g(\theta)$ is the normal distribution density $\varphi(\theta | \mu, \sigma^2)$ we thus have a *parametric multinomial* distribution (18) with

$$\pi_t = \pi_t(\mu, \sigma^2) = h(t) \int \left[\prod_q C_q(\theta) \right] e^{\theta t} \varphi(\theta | \mu, \sigma^2) d\theta. \tag{19}$$

We note from (7) that $C_q(\theta)$ depends on the b's. Hence we need values for the item parameters in order to use (18) as a likelihood function. In this chapter, we use the CML-estimates from section 3 as known values. Unfortunately we do not know yet exactly what the consequences are of using estimates based on the same data for the item parameters. But presumable inference based on (18) concerning the form of φ and the value of μ and σ^2 is little affected by the actual values of the b-estimates, if these are based on a reasonably large sample. One advantage of using a Newton-Raphson procedure to obtain estimates of the b's is that we get approximations of their standard errors and thus have the possibility of judging the accuracy of the estimates.

Based on these considerations we now take as likelihood for inference about $g(\theta)$, μ and σ^2 the function

$$L_g = \binom{n}{n_{\underline{t}} \ldots n_{\bar{t}}} \left[\prod_{t=\underline{t}}^{\bar{t}} \pi_t(\mu,\sigma^2) \right]^{n_t} \tag{20}$$

derived from (18) and (19).

As (20) is a parametric multinomial distribution we can apply well-known theory from, for example, Rao (1973, chapters 5 and 6). A recent discussion of these methods applied to (20) is due to Tjur (1982).

The latent distribution parameters μ and σ^2 can be estimated as ML-estimates either by a Newton-Raphson procedure along the lines described in Andersen and Madsen (1977) or by the EM-algorithm as described by Sanathanan and Blumenthal (1978). The estimates in the examples of this chapter were obtained by a Newton-Raphson procedure, which also provides standard errors of the estimates.

In the following, let $\hat{\mu}$ and $\hat{\sigma}^2$ be the ML-estimates obtained by maximizing (20).

Still referring to general theory for the parametric multinomial distribution, we can check the fit to observed data of a normal latent density by a Pearson χ^2-test or by a transformed LR test. We choose the latter, where the test quantity takes the form

$$z = 2 \sum_{t=\underline{t}}^{\bar{t}} n_t \{\ln(n_t) - \ln(n\pi_t(\hat{\mu},\hat{\sigma}^2))\}, \tag{21}$$

with

$$n = \sum_t n_t.$$

A table of n_t compared with a table of

$$\hat{n}_t = n\pi_t(\hat{\mu},\hat{\sigma}^2)$$

may also be helpful to determine if the deviations are systematic.

It is important to note that sections 3 and 4 of this chapter represent two very distinct parts of the analysis of a given set of data. The analysis based on the conditional likelihood (13) is primarily a check of *the structure of the model*. Since the analysis is conditional upon sufficient statistics for the individual parameters, we investigate those characteristic structures of the data which cannot be attributed to variations among individuals. This is essentially the idea behind the formulation of the one-parameter logistic model by Georg Rasch in 1960 (cf. the reprinting of his book as Rasch, 1980). But in this chapter the idea is extended to the two-parameter model and to the more general contingency table situation.

The analysis based on the likelihood (20) is, on the other hand, a direct analysis of the variation between individuals, assuming that we have a latent structure with an estimation of the individual parameters of the form

$$t_v = a_{1i} + a_{2j} + \cdots + a_{kr} \approx \theta_v$$

for an observed response pattern $(i, j, \ldots, r)$ and known category weights a_{qi}, $q = 1, \ldots, k$, $i = 1, \ldots, m_q$.

5. CHECK OF THE CATEGORY WEIGHTS

As a correct set of category weights is critical for a correct analysis of the data, we need some kind of a check on the chosen a's.

The computer program we apply to the examples of this chapter can for practical reasons only handle integer valued scores t. In addition we require a_{qm_q} to be 0 and also usually assume that

$$a_{q1} > a_{q2} > \cdots > a_{qm_q}.$$

Hence $\underline{t} = 0$ and $\bar{t} = a_{11} + \cdots + a_{k1}$. There is, however, no requirement of all values between $\underline{t}$ and $\bar{t}$ being attainable and $\bar{t}$ can be as large as 300. Also any multiplicative change of the a's can be compensated in the θ's. Hence we can work with rather general weights. In case $k = 4$ and $m_q = 3$, $q = 1, \ldots, 4$, we can, for example, apply weights like

$$[a_{qi}] = \begin{bmatrix} 1 & 1/2 & 0 \\ 1 & 1/3 & 0 \\ 1 & 1/4 & 0 \\ 2 & 1 & 0 \end{bmatrix}$$

by using the equivalent weights

$$[a_{qi}] = \begin{bmatrix} 12 & 6 & 0 \\ 12 & 4 & 0 \\ 12 & 3 & 0 \\ 24 & 12 & 0 \end{bmatrix}$$

The most obvious way to check a given set of weights is simply to analyze the data with alternative sets of weights to see which set gives a better fit. A somewhat more satisfactory possibility is available if $m_q = m$ and $a_{qi} = a_i$, $q = 1, \ldots, k$. The original likelihood of the observations can then be written as

$$L = \prod_v \prod_q C_q(\theta_v) \exp \left\{ \sum_q \sum_i b_{qi} u_{qi} + \sum_v \sum_i \theta_v a_i t_{vi} \right\}, \qquad (22)$$

when u_{qi} as before are the item totals, while

t_{vi} = number of times individual v had used response category i,

such that $(t_{v1}, \ldots, t_{vm})$ is the score vector of individual v. If $a_1, \ldots, a_m$ are unknown, we may then estimate the auxiliary parameters

$$\theta_{vi} = \theta_v a_i, \quad v = 1, \ldots N, \quad i = 1, \ldots, m, \tag{23}$$

as ML-estimates from (22). The distribution (22) is an exponential family, so that the likelihood equations become

$$t_{vi} = E[T_{vi}].$$

These are easily solved by a Newton-Raphson procedure, if $t_{vi} \neq 0$ for all i. Hence we can for all score vectors $v = (v_1, \ldots, v_m)$ with $v_i > 0$ obtain the ML-estimate $\hat{\theta}_1(v), \ldots, \hat{\theta}_m(v)$. Since all individuals with the same score vector will get the same estimate (in the original model), this means that the estimates $\hat{\theta}_1(v), \ldots, \hat{\theta}_m(v)$ must exhibit the same multiplicative structure as (23). If we let $\hat{\theta}(v)$ be a common estimate for $\hat{\theta}_v$ within the group of $n(v)$ individuals with score vector v, we thus must have

$$\hat{\theta}_i(v) \approx \hat{\theta}(v) a_i. \tag{24}$$

A tentative way of estimating a_i and $\hat{\theta}(v)$ from this relation would be to minimize

$$Q = \sum_v \sum_i n(v)[\hat{\theta}_i(v) - \hat{\theta}(v) a_i]^2, \tag{25}$$

where the first summation runs over all v, for which we have estimates of $\hat{\theta}_i(v)$, that is, for $v_i > 0$, $i = 1, \ldots, m$ and $n(v) > 0$.

Minimization of (25) is equivalent to finding the largest eigenvalue λ and the corresponding eigenvector a of

$$\hat{\boldsymbol{\theta}}' \hat{\boldsymbol{\theta}},$$

where

$$\hat{\boldsymbol{\theta}} = \{\hat{\theta}_i(v)\}$$

with $i = 1, \ldots, m$ corresponding to columns and the v's corresponding to rows. Then the eigenvector $(a_1, \ldots, a_m)$ will estimate the category weights.

We can, in addition, obtain expressions for the $\hat{\theta}(v)$'s as

$$\hat{\theta}(v) = \sqrt{\lambda} \sum_{i=1}^{m} \hat{\theta}_i(v) a_i,$$

and we can check the structure (24) by comparing $\hat{\theta}_i(v)$ with

$$\hat{\theta}(v) a_i.$$

We must emphasize of course that this technique is a rather crude way of checking a given choice of response category weights. But so far we know of nothing better.

In section 6 we show an application of the technique.

In addition, one of the examples shows the effect of different choices of response category weights on the analyses of both section 3 and section 4.

6. EXAMPLES

We shall first discuss a set of depression-rating data. As the data were first presented to the author they were 10 items of a depression test, on which a depression rating of 452 patients was based. Six of the items had three response categories, while the remaining four items had four response categories. When we analyzed these data by the methods of sections 3 to 5, we discovered a number of peculiarities which forced us to go back to the data source to make further inquiries. At this point we discovered that there were some errors in our understanding of the structure and the source of the data. As this process is illustrative of the potential of the methodology, we present our first analysis rather than the final (correct) analysis of the data.

The first step of the data analysis was to estimate the item parameters and check the model. With the notations of section 3 we have $k = 10$, $m_1 = \ldots = m_6 = 3$ and $m_7 = \ldots = m_{10} = 4$. We started by assuming an equidistant scoring, that is

$$a_{q1} = 2, a_{q2} = 1, a_{q3} = 0, q = 1, \ldots, 6$$
$$a_{q1} = 3, a_{q2} = 2, a_{q3} = 1, a_{q4} = 0, q = 7, \ldots, 10.$$

With these specifications we got the estimates shown in Table 8.1.

We checked the model by the CLR-test (15) of section 3. With possible scores ranging from 0 to 24 with the given weights, we divided the range into intervals 0–11, 12–13, 14–15 and 16–24. In Fig. 8.1 we have plotted the score-group

TABLE 8.1

$\hat{b}_{iq}$	$i = 1$	2	3	4
q = 1	-.32	-.43	.00	—
2	+.35	-.23	.00	—
3	+.70	+.19	.00	—
4	+1.36	+.23	.00	—
5	+1.22	+.16	.00	—
6	+1.09	+.38	.00	—
7	-.64	-.34	-.03	.00
8	-.81	-.49	-.33	.00
9	-.60	-.18	+.00	.00
10	-.66	-.37	-.27	.00

130 ANDERSEN

estimates $\hat{b}_{qi}^{(r)}$ against the overall estimates $\hat{b}_{qi}$ in such a way that there is one plot for each score group. A score group is identified by its score interval.

The CLR-test statistic (15) takes the value

$$z = 165.3, \; df = 69$$

The degrees of freedom are obtained from $M = 23$ and $G = 4$.

Both Fig. 8.1 and the test statistic clearly indicate that the model does not fit the data. We could also conclude from Fig. 8.1 that points which originate from

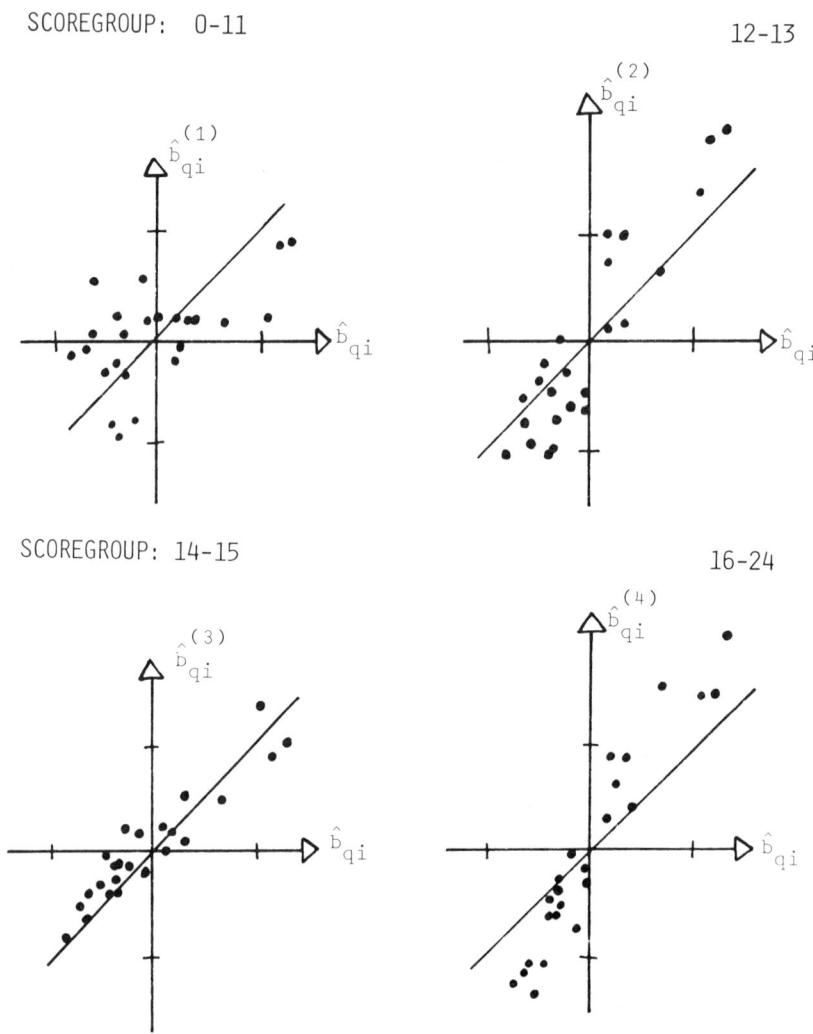

FIG. 8.1.

8. GENERAL LATENT STRUCTURE MODEL

items 1–6 and those which originate from items 7–10 fall in different clusters and that a better fit could be expected if we treat items 1–6 and items 7–10 separately.

Before we decided to separate the two sets of items, we tried, however, to repair the lack of fit by choosing other category weights. We tried two sets of alternative weights

$$(i) \begin{cases} (6, 3, 0) \text{ for items 1 to 6} \\ (6, 4, 2, 0) \text{ for items 7 to 10.} \end{cases}$$

The idea was here to have the same numerical distance from a_{q1} to a_{qmq} for all items.

$$(ii) \begin{cases} (4, 1, 0) \text{ for items 1 to 6} \\ (6, 4, 2, 0) \text{ for items 7 to 10.} \end{cases}$$

This second set was chosen just to see what happened.

In Fig. 8.2 we have plotted the estimated item parameters with weights (i) and (ii), respectively, against the estimates of Table 8.1.

The figure clearly shows that changes in the weights have very little effect on the values of the estimates.

The CLR-test (15) was computed to

(i) $z = 141.6$, $df = 69$

and

(ii) $z = 153.4$, $df = 69$

for the two cases. So the numerical model check was also only slightly affected by changes in the category weights.

Since nothing was gained in the fit by changing the weights we finally decided to separate the two sets of items.

For items 1 to 6 we applied the equidistant weights (2, 1, 0) and the score grouping 0–6, 7, 8, 9–12. The graphical check corresponding to Fig. 8.1 is shown in Fig. 8.3, and the z-test (15) was computed to

$$z = 38.3, df = 33.$$

Thus a satisfactory fit was obtained.

For items 7–10 we used the category weights (3, 2, 1, 0) and the score grouping 0–4, 5, 6, 7, 8–12. The graphical check is not shown as the b_{qi}'s are close to zero and the graph is not informative. The z-test was computed to

$$z = 44.1, df = 44.$$

Hence we also found a satisfactory data fit for the last four items. We became, however, a bit suspicious of these four items as all item parameters were very

132 ANDERSEN

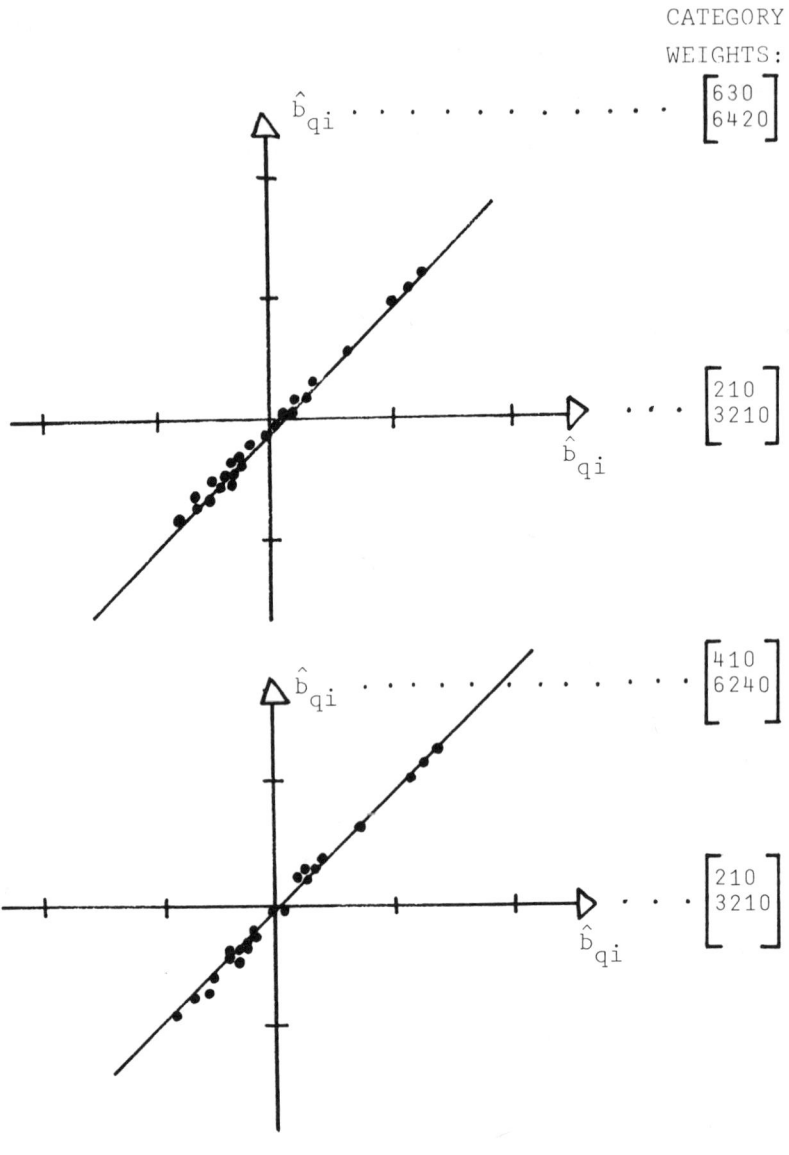

FIG. 8.2.

close to zero, a suspicion, which was to be confirmed by the last part of the data analysis to be described below.

Finally the theory of section 4 was applied to the original set of 10 items as well as to the two sets of 6 and 4 items. For the 10 items, we got

$\hat{\mu} = .24$

$\hat{\sigma}^2 = .04$

and a goodness of fit test (21) of

$z = 11.8$, $df = 12$.

Hence, in spite of the fact that the first model check showed an unsatisfactory fit, we still seem to be able to fit the observed score distribution by a normal density. We should, however, be very careful using this fit, as we have no guarantee that the scores estimate a meaningful latent variable, when a model for which the score is a sufficient statistic for the latent variable is not accepted.

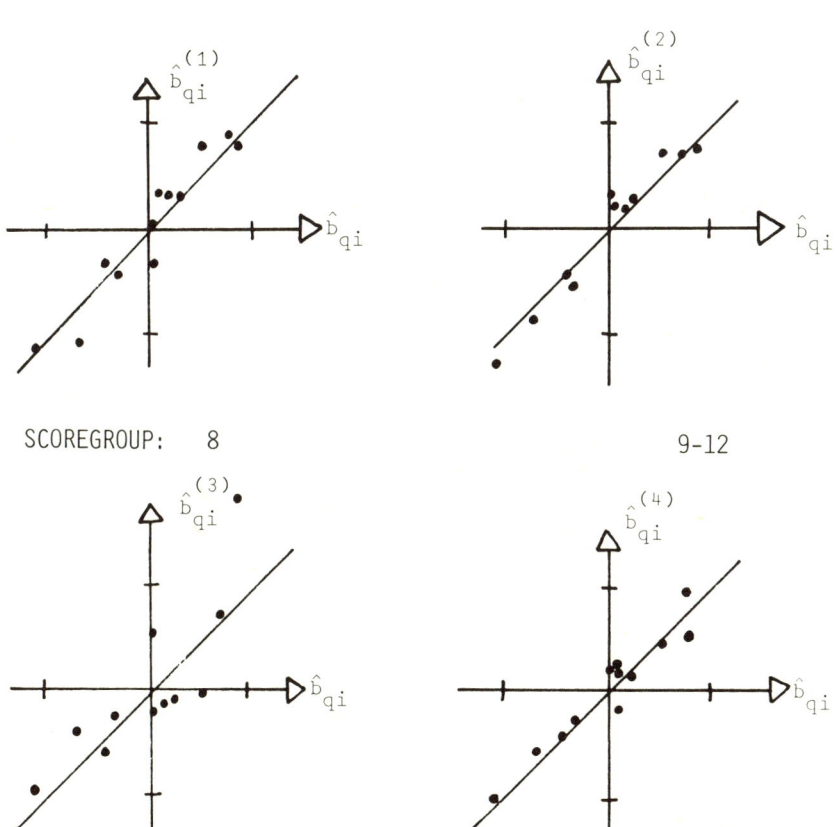

FIG. 8.3.

For the first six items we got

$$\hat{\mu} = .65$$
$$\hat{\sigma}^2 = .42$$

with a goodness of fit test of

$$z = 10.5, \, df = 8,$$

which again is a very good fit.

For the last four items the computer program gave no convergence to the ML-estimate of σ^2, and it was clear that the fit became better the closer σ^2 was chosen to 0. If we go back to (19), we note, however, that $\sigma^2 = 0$ is meaningful and corresponds to

$$\pi_t(\mu_0, 0) = h(t) \left[\prod_q C_q(\mu_0) \right] e^{\mu_0 t},$$

for $\theta = \mu_0$ with probability one. Hence we can compute (21) with

$$\pi_t(\hat{\mu}, \hat{\sigma}^2) = \pi_t(\hat{\mu}, 0).$$

This gave a test quantity of

$$z = 10.6, \, df = 9,$$

with

$$\hat{\mu} = -.004.$$

Although we thus had a fit at both stages of the analysis for items 6–10, we had confirmed our suspicion that something was wrong with these items. Obviously a set of items with $b_{qi} \simeq 0$, $\sigma^2 \simeq 0$ and $\mu \simeq 0$ is of no informative value. At this stage we asked the data collector, who confessed that items 1 to 6 were real items applied to 452 depressive patients, whereas the remaining four items represented artificially generated data.

We have shown above that the estimation of item parameters and the first model check is very insensitive to the choice of category weights. But it is still of interest to get an empirical estimate of the weights. For the first six items of the depression data, we applied the method of section 5.

The estimated weights $\hat{a}_1$ and $\hat{a}_2$ derived from (25) were found to

$$\hat{a}_1 = 0.854$$
$$\hat{a}_2 = 0.520$$

with $\hat{a}_3 = 0$. This is not far from the chosen weights (2,1,0), which under the eigenvector constraint

$$\sum_{i=1}^{3} a_i^2 = 1$$

become

$$a_1 = 0.89$$
$$a_2 = 0.45$$

so that the choice of equidistant weights is empirically justified.

As our second data set we consider a set of six items on consumer complaint behavior. The six items correspond to six consumer situations, where each respondent expresses his or her intention to complain or not. We use this data set to show an application of the general computer program to the binary situation with and without item-discriminating powers.

The item parameters were estimated by the CML-method to

$$\hat{b} = (+2.47, +.64, +.48, -.66, -.96, -1.97).$$

with category weights $a_{q1} = 1$, $a_{q2} = 0$.

The graphical check based on the grouping 0–1,3,4–6 of the score is shown in Fig. 8.4. The numerical test based on this grouping gave a test quantity of

$$z = 17.4, \, df = 10.$$

Weinreich (1982) tried to fit a two-parameter logistic model with item parameters b_q as well as item-discriminating powers a_q, that is

$$P\{\text{complain on item } q|\theta_v\} = e^{a_q\theta_v + b_q}[1 + e^{a_q\theta_v + b_q}]$$

He estimated the a's to

(1.01, 1.04, .91, .74, 1.44, .98).

This would correspond roughly to the category weights

$$[a_{qi}] = \begin{bmatrix} 2 & 0 \\ 2 & 0 \\ 2 & 0 \\ 1 & 0 \\ 3 & 0 \\ 2 & 0 \end{bmatrix}$$

in model (6). With these weights the b_q's were estimated to

$$\hat{b} = (2.50, .66, .49, -.16, -1.50, -1.99),$$

or very similar to the estimates of the b_q's with equal item-discriminating powers. The numerical test for goodness of fit is only possible for the score grouping 0–6, 7–12 and we get

136 ANDERSEN

SCOREGROUP

0-2

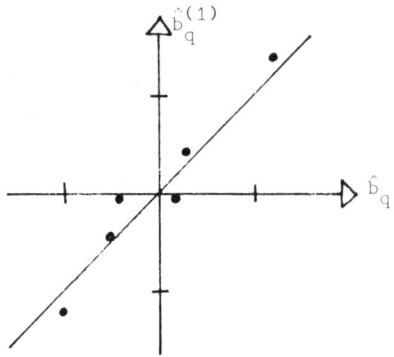

3

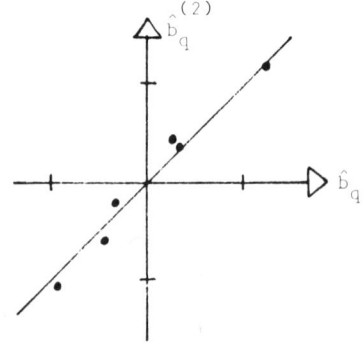

4-6

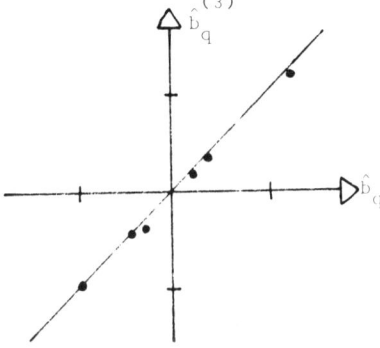

FIG. 8.4.

$$z = 1.7, df = 5. \tag{26}$$

In comparison, a corresponding test with only two score groups and equal item-discriminating powers would be based on the score groups 0–3, 4–6. Here we get

$$z = 9.0, df = 5. \tag{27}$$

We can accordingly increase the goodness of fit by adding estimated item-discriminating powers. But we must be a bit careful about the significance of the increased goodness of fit. Actually the test quantity (26) is based on more estimated parameters than (27), and the value 1.7 cannot be compared directly to the five degrees of freedom. We would have been on safer ground if the category weights for the calculation of (26) were chosen without any data-based calculations.

REFERENCES

Andersen, E. B. Asymptotic properties of conditional maximum likelihood estimators. *Journal of the Royal Statistical Society,* B., 1970, *32,* 283–301. (a)

Andersen, E. B. Sufficiency and exponential families for discrete sample spaces. *Journal of the American Statistical Association,* 1970, *65,* 1248–1255. (b)

Andersen, E. B. The numerical solution to a set of conditional estimation equations. *Journal of the Royal Statistical Society,* 1972, *34,* 42–54.

Andersen, E. B. A goodness of fit test for the Rasch model. *Psychometrika,* 1973, *38,* 123–140. (a)

Andersen, E. B. Conditional inference and multiple-choice questionnaires. *British Journal of Mathematical and Statistical Psychology,* 1973, *26,* 31–44. (b)

Andersen, E. B. *Discrete statistical models with social science applications.* Amsterdam: North Holland Publishing Co., 1980.

Andersen, E. B. Latent structure analysis. A review. *Scandinavian Journal of Statistics,* 1982, *9,* 1–12.

Andersen, E. B., and Madsen, M. Estimating the parameters of the latent population distribution. *Psychometrika.* 1977, *42,* 457–374.

Anderson, T. W. On estimation of parameters in latent structure analysis. *Psychometrika,* 1954, *19,* 1–10.

Baker, F. B. Advances in item analysis. *Review of Educational Research,* 1977, *47,* 151–178.

Bentler, P. M., & Weeks, D. G. Linear structural equation with latent variables. *Psychometrika,* 1980, *45,* 289–308.

Birnbaum, A. *On the estimation of mental ability.* (Report No. 15). Randolph Air Force Base USAF School of Aviation Medicine, San Antonio, Texas, 1957.

Bock, R. D. Estimating the parameters and latent ability when responses are scored in two or more nominal categories. *Psychometrika,* 1972, *37,* 1320–1322.

Bock, R. D., & Aitkin, M. Marginal maximum likelihood estimation of item parameters: Application of an EM algorithm. *Psychometrika,* 1981, *46,* 443–459.

Bock, R. D., and Lieberman, M. Fitting a response model for n dichotomously scored items. *Psychometrika,* 1970, *35,* 179–197.

Brown, L. Sufficient statistics in the case of independent random variables. *Annals Mathematical Statistics,* 1964, *35,* 1456–1474.

Denny, J. L. Sufficient statistics and discrete exponential families. *Annals of Mathematical Statistics*, 1972, *43*, 1320–1322.
Fischer, G. H. *Einfuhrung in die Theorie Psychologischer Tests*. Bern: Verlag Hans Huber, 1974.
Goodman, L. A. Exploratory latent structure analysis using both identifiable and unidentifiable models. *Biometrika*, 1974, *61*, 215–231.
Goodman, L. A. *Analayzing qualitative/categorical data. Log-linear models and latent structure analysis*. London: Addison & Wesley, 1978.
Haberman, S. J. *Analysis of qualitative data* (Vol. 2). New York: Academic Press, 1979.
Hambleton, R. K., Swaminathan, H., Cock, L. L., Eigner, D. R., & Gilford, J. A. Developments in latent trait theory: Models, technical issues and applications. *Review of Educational Research*, 1978, *48*, 467–510.
Jöreskog, K. G. Structural analysis of covariance and correlation matrices. *Psychometrika*, 1978, *43*, 443–477.
Jöreskog, K. G., & Sörbom, D. Statistical methods for analysis of longitudinal data. In D. J. Aigner & A. S. Goldberger (Eds.), *Latent variables in socio-economics*. Amsterdam: North Holland Publ. Co., 1977.
Lawley, D. N. On problems connected with item selection and test construction. *Proceedings of the Royal Society of Edinburgh*, 1943, *61*, 273–287.
Lazarsfeld, P. F. The logical and mathematical function of latent structure analysis. In Stouffer et al., *Measurement and prediction*. Princeton: Princeton University Press, 1950.
Lazarsfeld, P. F., & Henry, N. W. *Latent structure analysis*. Boston: Houghton-Mifflin, 1968.
Lord, F. M. A theory of test scores. *Psychometric Monographs*, 1952 (*No. 7*).
Lord, F. M. An analysis of the verbal scholastic aptitude test using Birnbaum's three parameter logistic model. *Educational and Psychological Measurement*, 1968, *28*, 989–1020.
Lord, F. M., & Novick, M. R. *Statistical theories of mental test scores*. Reading: Addison & Wesley, 1968.
Madansky, A. Latent structure. In *International encyclopedia of statistics*. New York: The Free Press, 1978.
Rao, C. R. *Linear statistical inference and its applications*. (2nd Ed.). New York: John Wiley & Sons, 1973.
Rasch, G. *Probabilistic models for some intelligence and attainment tests*. Copenhagen: Danmarks Pædagogiske Institut, 1960.
Rasch, G. On general laws and the meaning of measurement in psychology. *Proceedings of the Fourth Berkeley Symposium on Mathematical Statistics and Probability Theory*. 1961, *5*, 321–333.
Rasch, G. *Probabilistic models for some intelligence and attainment tests*. Chicago: University of Chicago Press, 1980.
Sanathanan, L., & Blumenthal, S. The logistic model and estimation of latent structure. *Journal of the American statistical Association*, 1978, *73*, 794–799.
Tjur, T. A connection between Rasch's item analysis model and a multiplicative Poisson model. *Scandinavian Journal of Statistics*, 1982, *9*, 23–30.
Weinreich, M. *The 2-parameter logit model* (Research Report No. 81). Copenhagen: Department of Statistics, University of Copenhagen, 1982.
Wright, B. D., & Masters, G. N. *Rating scale analysis*. Chicago: MESA Press, 1982.
Wright, B. D., & Stone, M. H. *Best test design*. Chicago: MESA Press, 1979.

9 Notes on the Exponential Latency Model and an Empirical Application

Gerhard H. Fischer
University of Vienna

Rupert Kisser
Austrian Road Safety Board

During the last decade, the availability of electronic computers for the administration of tests and for on-line analysis of responses has increased enormously. This has spurred the further theoretical development and the practical application of probabilistic item response theories. First, the often quite involved numerical computations can now be done quickly and inexpensively. Second, computerized test administration allows for new testing technologies, such as adaptive strategies, which efficiently utilize the power of item response models: Testing time is reduced, and a maximum gain of information meets with a high level of testee-motivation. The work of Lord (1980) impressively demonstrates the profusion of these developments in the area of item response theory and its applications.

The use of computers for test administration and the development of relatively inexpensive micro-computer test devices moreover invites studying new types of observations that were not available in paper and pencil tests, as, for example, the response time of each reaction to an item. While analyzing these response latencies, one encounters the old unresolved problem of speed and power confoundation in test achievement. However, diagnostically relevant types of achievement tests do exist where the speed factor is of primary concern, for instance, in complex reaction tasks as are used in industrial, clinical, or traffic psychology.

In the following, some new results on an exponential latency model for speed tests, which is due to Scheiblechner (1979), are derived, and an empirical application is presented.

The "negative exponential distribution" seems especially appropriate for describing response latencies. A random response latency T with realization t is said to follow the negative exponential distribution if its density $f(t)$ is defined by

$$f(t|\lambda) = \lambda exp(-\lambda t), \quad \lambda > 0, t \geq 0, \qquad (1)$$

with $f(t|\lambda) = 0$ for $t < 0$. This distribution, which in the following shall be called "exponential distribution" for short, is well-known in physics and in mathematical statistics; its expectancy and variance are given by

$$E(T) = \lambda^{-1} \quad \text{and} \quad \sigma^2(T) = \lambda^{-2}, \qquad (2)$$

respectively (cf. Feller, 1966, p. 8, or Johnson & Kotz, 1970, pp. 207–211).

The exponential distribution can be generated by different kinds of processes, each of which may be considered a plausible explanation for the indeterminateness in the individual latencies: In a series of independent successive trials, each with identical duration Δt and probability p of success, the number of trials up to the success, that is, the waiting time, has a geometric distribution. This approaches an exponential distribution in the limit, if $p/\Delta t$ tends to a constant $\lambda > 0$ while the duration Δt tends to zero (see Feller, 1966, p. 1; McGill, 1963). In addition, within a series of parallel search processes, the waiting time up to the first success may have an approximate exponential distribution if the number of these processes and the expected duration of each of them is great. Even more complex and, therefore, psychologically more interesting processes result in exponentially distributed latencies, like, for example, mechanisms with intervening latent subresponses of random exponential duration when the number of subresponses is geometrically distributed (McGill, 1963). In plain language, if the correct response requires a sequence of cognitive operations or steps, whereby the durations as well as the number of these steps are certain random variables, the total latency up to the first success will have an exponential distribution.

All this helps to justify the assumption of the exponential distribution as the basis for psychometric models for response latencies. However, because the exponential distribution leaves ample play for different processes, the fit of the model eventually obtained is insufficient for making inferences about the underlying mechanism.

PARAMETERIZATION OF THE PSYCHOMETRIC MODEL

Suppose that n items of a speed test, $i = 1, \ldots, n$, are given to a sample of N testees, $a = 1, \ldots, N$, and that one response latency t_{ia} is observed for each testee on each item. Let these latencies have exponential distributions with parameters λ_{ia}. Furthermore, suppose one wants to assign one speed parameter θ_a to each testee and one easiness parameter ϵ_i to each item, in order to carry out quantitative comparisons between testees and between items. Then each parameter λ_{ia} must be decomposed into ϵ_i and θ_a in a suitable way. How this should be done remains as yet undetermined.

In the context of measuring reading speed in children, Rasch (1960) chose the multiplicative concatenation $\lambda_{ia} = \epsilon_i \theta_a$. The advantage of this assumption lies in the readiness of its psychological interpretation: The average reading speed of a child for any text is proportional to his/her parameter θ_a, and hence the ratio of the average reading speeds of two children a and a' is the quotient of their parameters $\theta_a/\theta_{a'}$. In other words, the parameter θ_a is a direct measure of the speed of the latent cognitive processes. Furthermore, the ratio of the expected reading times needed for two different texts is the same for all children, independent of their speed parameters.

The drawback of this intuitively appealing multiplicative model is that no simple sufficient statistics for the parameters exist. The likelihood of the data matrix $((t_{ia}))$ is

$$L = \left\{\prod_i \epsilon_i\right\}^N \left\{\prod_a \theta_a\right\}^n \exp\left(-\sum_a \theta_a \sum_i \epsilon_i t_{ia}\right).$$

Joint maximum likelihood (JML) estimates $\hat{\epsilon}_i$ and $\hat{\theta}_a$ are obtained by differentiating $\ln L$ with respect to the parameters and setting the derivatives equal to zero. This yields the following estimation equations ("hats" are dropped for simplicity):

$$\epsilon_i^{-1} = \frac{1}{N} \sum_a \theta_a t_{ia} \quad \text{for } i = 1, \ldots, n, \qquad (3)$$

$$\theta_a^{-1} = \frac{1}{n} \sum_i \epsilon_i t_{ia} \quad \text{for } a = 1, \ldots, N. \qquad (4)$$

These equations reveal that no sufficient statistics for the ϵ_i's independent of the θ_a's, and vice versa, exist. In other words, it is not feasible to separate the two types of parameters. It is possible to insert equations (3) into (4) and thus to obtain a set of equations for the θ_a's alone, and similarly another set of equations for the ϵ_i's. However, this yields no advantage over solving (3) and (4) simultaneously for all the parameters.

Reventlow (1970) used a generalized multifactorial version of this model for analyzing experimental data on the nesting behavior of male sticklebacks. The time span of males remaining at the nest was described as a function of several experimental conditions, such as presentation of a female in heat or experimental spoiling of the nest, and of an individual parameter of each fish. Wottawa (1971) used the same model for describing practice effects in a test of manual dexterity, and Fellner (1976) applied it to the effects of various external conditions on playgrounds in regard to the time children spend on a game they are engaged in.

For practical applications of such models to psychodiagnostic tests, it would be advantageous if the total time a testee needs for a given set of items were a meaningful measure of his/her speed, that is, if the total time were a sufficient statistic for θ_a. Then it would not be necessary to record the latencies of the subject on each item, but only the total time required for the task.

Scheiblechner (1979) introduced a parameterization of the exponential model which includes this property. His model is

$$f_{ia}(t) = (\epsilon_i + \theta_a)exp\{-(\epsilon_i + \theta_a)t\}, \epsilon_i \geq 0, \theta_a > 0. \tag{5}$$

He showed that the marginal sums

$$t_{i.} = \sum_a t_{ia} \quad \text{and} \quad t_{.a} = \sum_i t_{ia}$$

are sufficient statistics for ϵ_i and θ_a, respectively, and he derived conditional maximum likelihood (CML) estimation equations for the ϵ_i's by maximizing the likelihood for the observed response latencies given the marginals $t_{.a}$.

He furthermore introduced the "linear exponential model" (LEM) as a generalization of (5). Its central assumption is that the item parameters ϵ_i can be explained as weighted sums of certain "basic parameters" η_j which correspond to hypothetical constructs or experimental factors determining the latency mechanism. The specification equation of the LEM is

$$\epsilon_i = \sum_{j=1}^{m} q_{ij}\eta_j + c, \tag{6}$$

where $Q = ((q_{ij}))$ is a (n,m)-matrix of given constants with $m < n$ and rank $(Q) = m$, and c is a normalization constant. Q is called the structural or design matrix of the model. Scheiblechner (1979) showed that all the essential properties of the exponential model (5) also hold for the LEM.

CONSEQUENCES OF THE SUFFICIENCY OF THE TOTAL TIME

Scheiblechner's detailed discussion of the properties of the model did not, however, advance any substantial justification for the choice of the parameterization. "The dependence of a latency on two (or more) parameters is compelling in many situations, but their additivity merely plays the role of a simple hypothesis without substantial justification" (Scheiblechner, 1979, p. 20). Nevertheless, since the sufficiency of the total time $t_{.a}$, as a consequence of the parameterization, is an interesting property, we shall investigate whether the model (5) is uniquely characterized by the sufficiency of $t_{.a}$, or whether other exponential latency models with one parameter per subject and per item share this property as well.

If $t_{.a}$ is sufficient, then this must also hold for $n = 2$ items. We therefore begin by considering $n = 2$ observed response latencies $t_{1a} =: t_1 > 0$ and $t_{2a} =: t_2 > 0$ of one subject a on two items which are realizations of exponential random variates with $\lambda_{1a} =: \lambda_1$ and $\lambda_{2a} =: \lambda_2$. (The limiting case $t = 0$ can be excluded). Under the assumption of local stochastic independence, the joint likelihood of the two latencies is

$$L(t_1, t_2) = \lambda_1 \lambda_2 \exp(-\lambda_1 t_1 - \lambda_2 t_2). \tag{7}$$

In the special case $\lambda_1 = \lambda_2 =: \lambda$, (7) becomes

$$L(t_1, t_2) = \lambda^2 \exp(-\lambda t_{.a}),$$

where $t_{.a}$ is evidently sufficient for the parameter λ. However, λ can no longer be decomposed into item and person parameters, because the model would then be overparameterized. Therefore, $\lambda_1 \neq \lambda_2$ is assumed for the following.

The likelihood for the total time $t_{.a} = t_1 + t_2$ is

$$L(t_{.a}) = \int_0^{t_{.a}} \lambda_1 \lambda_2 \exp\{-\lambda_1 t_1 - \lambda_2(t_{.a} - t_1)\} dt_1,$$

which, after integration, yields

$$\frac{\lambda_1 \lambda_2}{\lambda_2 - \lambda_1} \{\exp(-\lambda_1 t_{.a}) - \exp(-\lambda_2 t_{.a})\}. \tag{8}$$

As regards the dependence of the latency distributions on the speed of the person and on the easiness of the items, the following additional assumptions are made:

1. $\lambda_1 = \lambda_1(\theta_a, \epsilon_1)$ and $\lambda_2 = \lambda_2(\theta_a, \epsilon_2)$ are strictly monotone increasing in θ_a and ϵ_1 or in θ_a and ϵ_2, respectively. Any change of θ_a, therefore, entails an inverse change of the expected latency of subject a on both items, and the same holds for ϵ_1 or ϵ_2, respectively.
2. The functions λ_1 and λ_2 are assumed to be differentiable.

If the total time needed for both items is to be a sufficient statistic for θ_a, then

$$L(t_1, t_2 | t_{.a}) = \frac{L(t_1, t_2)}{L(t_{.a})} =: c(t_1, t_2, \epsilon_1, \epsilon_2) \tag{9}$$

must be independent of θ_a. Inserting (7) and (8) into (9) gives

$$\frac{(\lambda_2 - \lambda_1) \exp(-\lambda_1 t_1 - \lambda_2 t_2)}{\exp(-\lambda_1 t_{.a}) - \exp(-\lambda_2 t_{.a})} = c, \tag{10}$$

where $\lambda_1 \neq \lambda_2$ and $t_{.a} > 0$ must be assumed as above. For simplicity, let $\lambda_2 - \lambda_1 =: \delta(\theta_a, \epsilon_1, \epsilon_2)$, $\delta \neq 0$, let $t_1 = 1$ be the time unit, and let $t_2 =: t$; then it follows from (10) that

$$\delta/(exp(\delta t) - exp(-\delta)) = c,$$

or equivalently

$$exp(\delta t) - exp(-\delta) = \delta/c. \qquad (11)$$

Differentiating (11) partially with respect to θ_a yields

$$exp(\delta t)\delta' t + exp(-\delta)\delta' = \delta'/c, \qquad (12)$$

with δ' for $\partial \delta/\partial \theta_a$. It will now be shown that from (12) follows $\delta' = 0$ everywhere, which, assuming appropriate monotone parameter transformations, yields an additive concatenation of the person and item parameters.

Suppose that a point $(\bar{\theta}_a, \bar{\epsilon}_1, \bar{\epsilon}_2)$ exists with $\delta'(\bar{\theta}_a, \bar{\epsilon}_1, \bar{\epsilon}_2) \neq 0$; for this point it then follows from (12) that

$$exp(\delta t)t + exp(-\delta) = 1/c.$$

Differentiating partially with respect to θ_a once again, one obtains

$$exp(\delta t)t^2\delta' - exp(-\delta)\delta' = 0,$$

and because $\delta' \neq 0$ it follows that

$$exp(\delta t)t^2 - exp(-\delta) = 0,$$

which has the solution $\delta = -2\ln t/(t + 1)$. However, this implies $\delta' = 0$, which contradicts the assumption $\delta' \neq 0$. Therefore, $\delta' = 0$ everywhere, that is, $\lambda_2 - \lambda_1 = \delta$ must be independent of θ_a.

Now consider the strictly monotone transformations

$$\bar{\epsilon}_1 = \lambda_1(\theta^*, \epsilon_1), \ \bar{\epsilon}_2 = \lambda_2(\theta^*, \epsilon_2), \qquad (13)$$

$$\bar{\theta}_a = \lambda_1(\theta_a, \epsilon_1^*) - \lambda_1(\theta^*, \epsilon_1^*),$$

where the λ's are > 0 according to (1), and $\theta^* > 0$ and $\epsilon_1^* \geq 0$ are arbitrary but fixed constants. Because $\lambda_2 - \lambda_1$ is independent of θ_a, $\lambda_2(\theta_a, \epsilon_2) - \lambda_1(\theta_a, \epsilon_1) = \lambda_2(\theta^*, \epsilon_2) - \lambda_1(\theta^*, \epsilon_1) = \bar{\epsilon}_2 - \bar{\epsilon}_1$ holds true. Hence, with $\epsilon_1 = \epsilon_1^*$ it follows that

$$\lambda_2(\theta_a, \epsilon_2) = \lambda_1(\theta_a, \epsilon_1^*) + \bar{\epsilon}_2 - \lambda_1(\theta^*, \epsilon_1^*) = \bar{\theta}_a + \bar{\epsilon}_2, \qquad (14)$$

$$\lambda_1(\theta_a, \epsilon_1) = \lambda_2(\theta_a, \epsilon_2) - \bar{\epsilon}_2 + \bar{\epsilon}_1 = \bar{\theta}_a + \bar{\epsilon}_1.$$

If $\bar{\theta}_a > 0$, (14) is equivalent to the structure (5). If $\bar{\theta}_a \leq 0$, let $\lambda_2 \geq \lambda_1$ without loss of generality, which implies $\bar{\epsilon}_2 \geq \bar{\epsilon}_1$. Then the further transformations $\bar{\theta}_a \to \bar{\theta}_a + d$, $\bar{\epsilon}_1 \to \bar{\epsilon}_1 - d$, $\bar{\epsilon}_2 \to \bar{\epsilon}_2 - d$ with $d = (\bar{\epsilon}_1 - \bar{\theta}_a)/2$ make all the parameters $\bar{\theta}_a$, $\bar{\epsilon}_1$, $\bar{\epsilon}_2$ positive, so that the model again attains structure (5).

These results can be summarized as follows: Under assumptions 1 and 2, model (5) is the only exponential latency model in which $t_{.a}$ is sufficient for θ_a. For the following reasons, our result also holds for $n > 2$: We have shown that model (5) is the only admissible model if $t_{.a}$ is to be sufficient. Scheiblechner has shown that the model actually maintains the required property for $n > 2$. Hence, our result immediately generalizes to $n > 2$.

PARAMETER ESTIMATION IN THE EXPONENTIAL LATENCY MODEL

Scheiblechner (1978, 1979) presented a conditional maximum likelihood (CML) procedure for estimating the item parameters. It is based on maximizing the likelihood of the latencies given the marginal sums $t_{.a}$, which is independent of the parameters θ_a, cf. our equations (9) and (10). The estimates $\hat{\epsilon}_i$ so obtained are therefore "sample free" with respect to the sample of subjects.

The disadvantage of this approach to computing the $\hat{\epsilon}_i$'s is their numerical instability. Often the procedure breaks down even when n is small, and it is also sensitive to increases in the sample size N.

To make the model applicable for a range from moderate to large sizes of item and person samples, respectively, a joint estimation procedure (JML) for the item and person parameters is derived here. In order to allow for incomplete data (i.e. when no response times have been observed for some subjects on some items), we first define a matrix $V = ((v_{ia}))$ with elements $v_{ia} = 1$ if a latency of subject a on item i has been recorded, and $v_{ia} = 0$ otherwise. The missing observations are replaced by some dummy constant $t_{ia} = c > 0$ to render algebraic operations possible. Now the likelihood function of the latencies t_{ia} becomes

$$L = \prod_i \prod_a (\epsilon_i + \theta_a)^{v_{ia}} \exp\{-(\epsilon_i + \theta_a) t_{ia} v_{ia}\}. \qquad (15)$$

Taking logarithms, differentiating partially with respect to the parameters and setting the derivatives equal to zero, yields the two mutually dependent systems (16) and (17),

$$\frac{\partial \ln L}{\partial \epsilon_i} = \sum_a \frac{v_{ia}}{\epsilon_i + \theta_a} - \sum_a t_{ia} v_{ia} = 0 \qquad \text{for } i = 1, \ldots, n, \qquad (16)$$

$$\frac{\partial \ln L}{\partial \theta_a} = \sum_i \frac{v_{ia}}{\epsilon_i + \theta_a} - \sum_i t_{ia} v_{ia} = 0 \qquad \text{for } a = 1, \ldots, N. \qquad (17)$$

Obviously (16) are estimation equations for one item parameter ϵ_i each, and (17), for one person parameter θ_a each. The sum of the expected latencies of all the testees on an item i is equated to the respective marginal sum $t_{i.}$, and the sum of expected response latencies of testee a is equated to the observed total time $t_{.a}$ of that person,

$$t_{i.} = \sum_a t_{ia} v_{ia} \quad \text{and} \quad t_{.a} = \sum_i t_{ia} v_{ia}.$$

This is in accordance with a general principle of maximum likelihood estimation in exponential families of distributions (cf. Andersen, 1980, p. 56). The equations (17), by the way, are identical with those given by Scheiblechner (1979, formula 14) for the person parameters.

The easiest way to solve these sets of equations is to insert some approximate values for the person parameters θ_a and to solve each equation (16) separately for one item parameter ϵ_i by means of the simple iterative Newton method. Let θ_a^* be the chosen approximate values and let $\epsilon_i^{(k)}$ be the kth iterated value for the item parameter ϵ_i; then an improved value is obtained from

$$\epsilon_i^{(k+1)} = \epsilon_i^{(k)} + \left\{ \sum_a \frac{v_{ia}}{\epsilon_i^{(k)} + \theta_a^*} - t_{i.} \right\} \bigg/ \left\{ \sum_a \frac{v_{ia}}{(\epsilon_i^{(k)} + \theta_a^*)^2} \right\}.$$

After the equations (16) have been solved, the item parameters obtained are inserted as approximate values ϵ_i^* into (17) and each of these equations is solved by means of the Newton method with respect to one person parameter. Let $\theta_a^{(k)}$ be the kth iterated value for θ_a, then an improved value is given by

$$\theta_a^{(k+1)} = \theta_a^{(k)} + \left\{ \sum_i \frac{v_{ia}}{\epsilon_i^* + \theta_a^{(k)}} - t_{.a} \right\} \bigg/ \left\{ \sum_i \frac{v_{ia}}{(\epsilon_i^* + \theta_a^{(k)})^2} \right\}.$$

The solutions of the equations (17) are then again inserted into (16) as approximate values θ_a^*, and so forth. This simple algorithm allows one to estimate the parameters for all sample sizes n and N occurring in practice.

In a similar manner, one can set up a simple procedure for JML estimation of the parameters η_j and θ_a in the LEM. Differentiating the likelihood (15) under the restrictions (6) yields

$$\frac{\partial \ln L}{\partial \eta_j} = \sum_i q_{ij} \left\{ \sum_a \frac{v_{ia}}{\epsilon_i + \theta_a} - t_{i.} \right\} = 0 \quad \text{for } j = 1, \ldots, m \quad (18)$$

as estimation equations for the basic parameters η_j. These equations replace (16), whereas (17) remains unchanged.

Rather than a separate equation for each parameter, there is instead a simultaneous system of equations for the basic parameters η_j. They can be solved by means of the Newton-Raphson algorithm. Let again θ_a^* be approximate values for the person parameters θ_a which are inserted into (18). Then the elements $h_{j\ell}$ of the matrix $\mathbf{H}$ of second-order partial derivatives are given by

$$\frac{\partial^2 \ln L}{\partial \eta_j \partial \eta_\ell} = -\sum_i q_{ij} q_{i\ell} \sum_a \frac{v_{ia}}{(\epsilon_i + \theta_a^*)^2} = h_{j\ell}. \quad (19)$$

Furthermore, let $\mathbf{\eta}^{(k)}$ be a column vector containing the kth iterated values $\eta_j^{(k)}$ and let $\mathbf{f}^{(k)}$ be a column vector with elements $f_j^{(k)} = \partial \ln L / \partial \eta_j$ taken at the point

$(\theta_1^*, \ldots, \theta_N^*, \eta_1^{(k)}, \ldots, \eta_m^{(k)})$, that is, $f_j^{(k)}$ be the residuals of (18). A vector of improved values $\eta_j^{(k+1)}$ is then obtained from the equation

$$\boldsymbol{\eta}^{(k+1)} = \boldsymbol{\eta}^{(k)} - \mathbf{H}^{-1}\mathbf{f}^{(k)}.$$

As soon as the system (18) has been solved by this iterative method, the solutions obtained are inserted as approximate values ϵ_i^* into equations (17) which are then solved with respect to the person parameters as above. These are again inserted into (18), and so forth. This simple procedure turned out to be quite effective in practical applications of the LEM.

Another possibility of estimating the item parameters (or basic parameters, respectively) would be the "marginal maximum likelihood" (MML) method (cf. Bock & Aitkin, 1981; Dempster, Laird, & Rubin, 1977) where some latent distribution of the parameters θ_a is assumed; this approach has not been developed for the exponential latency model so far.

A SIMULATION STUDY

For the dichotomous Rasch model (Rasch, 1960) it is well known that the JML estimates are biased. The bias of the item parameters even for large N is due to the fact that the person parameter estimates entering into the estimation equations of the item parameters become inaccurate when n is small, and that furthermore any increase of N increases the number of unknown parameters. A proof of the consistency of the item parameter estimates exists for the case when both n and N tend to infinity (Haberman, 1977). However, the bias seems to become negligible as, say, n approaches or exceeds 50 (cf. Andersen, 1980, p. 244).

A similar bias of the JML estimates is also to be expected in the exponential latency model. In order to obtain some preliminary information about the bias, a small simulation study was made. From the item parameters ϵ_i given in Table 9.1, sets of $n = 2, 4, 8, 16$, and 32 values were chosen, whereby the smallest of them always was $\epsilon_1 = 0$ as a normalization condition. For each set of item parameters, $N = 100, 250$, and 500 person parameters θ_a were sampled out of a normal distribution with $E(\theta) = 50$ and $\sigma(\theta) = 25$, however, with the restriction $\theta_a > 0$. For each of the parameters $\lambda_{ia} = \epsilon_i + \theta_a$, one response latency was generated by means of a subroutine for exponential random deviates taken from the IMSLIB (1980) program library. These data were analyzed by means of the JML method and, as far as possible, also by the CML method, that is, item and person parameters were estimated and compared with the corresponding true values. The CML algorithm turned out to be applicable only in the following cases: $n = 2$ with $N = 100$ and 250, $n = 4$ with $N = 100$ and 250, $n = 8$ with $N = 100$ and 250, $n = 16$ with $N = 100$. In the remaining cases, no sufficient numerical accuracy could be achieved; this was due to the fact that the conditional estimation equations involve the terms

TABLE 9.1
True Parameters ϵ_i and Residuals $\epsilon_i - \hat{\epsilon}_i$ Obtained in the Simulation Study. Of Each Pair of Residuals, the First One Refers to the JML and the Second One to the CML Method

ϵ_i	n=2			n=4			n=8			n=16			n=32		
	N=100	N=250	N=500	N=100	N=250	N=500	N=100	N=250	N=500	N=100	N=250	N=500	N=100	N=250	N=500
00	—, —	—, —	—, —	—, —	—, —	—, —	—, —	—, —	—, —	—, —	—, —	—, —	—, —	—, —	—, —
05	—, —	—, —	—, —	—, —	—, —	—, —	—, —	—, —	—, —	—, —	—, —	—, —	4, —	0, —	2, —
10	—, —	—, —	—, —	—, —	—, —	—, —	—, —	—, —	—, —	7, 6	2, —	3, —	-1, —	0, —	1, —
15	—, —	—, —	—, —	—, —	—, —	—, —	—, —	—, —	—, —	—, —	—, —	—, —	2, —	5, —	4, —
20	—, —	—, —	—, —	—, —	—, —	—, —	3, -1	8, 6	3, —	8, 6	2, —	4, —	-1, —	0, —	4, —
25	—, —	—, —	—, —	—, —	—, —	—, —	—, —	—, —	—, —	9, 6	7, —	6, —	-8, —	-2, —	-3, —
30	—, —	—, —	—, —	—, —	—, —	—, —	—, —	—, —	—, —	—, —	—, —	—, —	-8, —	-5, —	-2, —
35	—, —	—, —	—, —	—, —	—, —	—, —	—, —	—, —	—, —	—, —	—, —	—, —	1, —	0, —	0, —
40	—, —	—, —	—, —	2, -6	6, -2	12, —	18, 14	10, 5	4, —	11, 7	11, —	1, —	14, —	5, —	0, —
45	—, —	—, —	—, —	—, —	—, —	—, —	—, —	—, —	—, —	—, —	—, —	—, —	6, —	4, —	-2, —
50	—, —	—, —	—, —	—, —	—, —	—, —	—, —	—, —	—, —	-5, -10	-2, —	-4, —	7, —	3, —	7, —
55	—, —	—, —	—, —	—, —	—, —	—, —	—, —	—, —	—, —	—, —	—, —	—, —	6, —	8, —	6, —
60	—, —	—, —	—, —	—, —	—, —	—, —	7, 0	3, -4	8, —	-6, -10	-13, —	-2, —	12, —	15, —	4, —

```
 65
 70
 75
 80   12  -4  17   0  16  —  27  17  21  10  11  —   -5  -14  11   3  12  —  25  21  15  —   9  —  10  —   6  —  -4
 85                                                                                          -10 -15   5  —   3  —  -11 —  -2  —  10
 90                                                                                            4  -1  -3  —   5  —   11 —   9  —   2
 95                                                                              -12 -21   9   0   6  —  15  10   7  —   3  —  29  —   9  —   9  —   3
100                                                                                                                                  -28 —  -11 —   6  —  15
105                                                                                         -22 -29  -4  —   9  —  -52 —   3  —  11
110
115                                                                35  23  29  15  14  —   -5 -15  -3 -13  -1  —   1  -5  12  — 17  —  18  —  16  —   7
120                                                                                                                                   -3 —  -6  —   4
125                                                                                            5  -1  15  —   3  —  -16 —   3  —   9
130                                                                                                                                    6 —   5  —  -4
135                                                                                           43  34  15   4  12  —  15   9  11  — 14  — -36 —  -1  —   4
140                                                                                                                                    4 —   4  —  -4
145                                                                                            2  -4 -12  —  -6  —   5  —  -4  —  19
150                                                                                                                                   17 —  15  —  -14
155                                                                                                                                  -17 — -15
```

$$X_i = \left\{ \prod_{\ell \neq i} (\hat{\epsilon}_\ell - \hat{\epsilon}_i) \right\}^{-1},$$

which become infinitely large whenever at least two parameter estimates $\hat{\epsilon}_\ell$ and $\hat{\epsilon}_i$ attain the same value.

Table 9.1 gives the true parameter values ϵ_i and the residuals $\epsilon_i - \hat{\epsilon}_i$. Because the smallest parameter estimate was always set equal to 0 as a normalization condition, the respective residual necessarily had to be 0 as well; these meaningless residuals were omitted from Table 9.1. In the case $n = 2$ with $N = 100$, for example, the two true parameters were $\epsilon_1 = 0$ (=normalization) and $\epsilon_2 = 80$, the JML estimate of ϵ_2 resulted to be 68, and the CML estimate, 84; hence the respective pair of entries in Table 9.1 are $80 - 68 = 12$ and $80 - 84 = -4$. Each such pair of residuals stems from the same set of simulated data; hence the difference between two such residuals is essentially independent of sampling errors and, therefore, is due to the estimation methods.

As descriptive statistics, the correlations $r_{\hat{\epsilon}\epsilon}$, the regression coefficients $b_{\hat{\epsilon}\epsilon}$, the correlations $r_{\hat{\theta}\theta}$, and the regression coefficients $b_{\hat{\theta}\theta}$ were computed. They are given in Table 9.2. Again, all the entries in one column stem from the same set of simulated data, so that the differences between the JML and the CML values are essentially due to the difference in the estimation methods. For $n = 2$, the correlations $r_{\hat{\epsilon}\epsilon}$ were omitted since they would have to be 1 in any case.

The results, though based solely on this very limited simulation, seem to draw quite a clear picture. For small item samples ($n = 2, 4$, and 8) the JML estimates are markedly biased, that is, the variance of the item parameters is underestimated. The CML method does not share this bias. Both methods, however, show a like bias of the person parameter estimates θ_a, the variance of the true parameters being strongly overestimated. The correspondence of this bias of the person parameter estimates in both methods is due to the fact that they use the same equations (17) for calculating the $\hat{\theta}_a$'s, the only difference being caused by the estimates $\hat{\epsilon}_i$ which enter these equations. The correlations $r_{\hat{\epsilon}\epsilon}$ and $r_{\hat{\theta}\theta}$ are almost the same in both methods. The main difference, therefore, appears to be an approximately linear scale transformation of the parameters in the JML method. From the behavior of the bias in the cases $n = 2, 4$, and 8 it can be hypothesized that already from $n = 16$ upwards the results of both methods should be fairly equivalent. Since the CML method sacrifices part of the statistical information of the data (cf. Andersen, 1980, p. 86), the JML method might even be superior to the CML method in cases where n is moderate or large. For the time being, this remains mere speculation, because the CML procedure yielded no results for $n = 8$ with $N = 500$, $n = 16$ with $N = 250$ and 500, and for $n = 32$ in all three cases. More thorough investigations will be needed for clarifying the merits of both methods.

TABLE 9.2

Correlations $r_{\hat{\varepsilon}\varepsilon}$ and $r_{\hat{\theta}\theta}$ Between Parameter Estimates and True Values, and Regression Coefficients $b_{\hat{\varepsilon}\varepsilon}$ and $b_{\hat{\theta}\theta}$ of Estimates on True Values, Obtained in the Simulation Study

		2				4				8				16				32		
		n																		
	N	100	250	500	100	250	500	100	250	500	100	250	500	100	250	500			
JML	$r_{\hat{\varepsilon}\varepsilon}$	—	—	—	.99	1.00	1.00	.94	.99	1.00	.97	.98	.99	.95	.99	.99			
	$b_{\hat{\varepsilon}\varepsilon}$	.85	.78	.80	.68	.74	.90	.91	.97	.95	1.01	.99	.95	1.05	1.00	.99			
	$r_{\hat{\theta}\theta}$	.36	.38	.37	.61	.52	.51	.69	.62	.59	.78	.79	.77	.85	.83	.85			
	$b_{\hat{\theta}\theta}$	2.11	2.35	2.39	2.06	1.44	1.34	1.44	1.15	1.14	1.01	1.15	1.17	1.07	1.09	1.08			
CML	$r_{\hat{\varepsilon}\varepsilon}$	—	—	—	.99	1.00	—	.94	.99	—	.98	—	—	—	—	—			
	$b_{\hat{\varepsilon}\varepsilon}$	1.05	.99	—	.77	.86	—	.97	1.04	—	1.05	—	—	—	—	—			
	$r_{\hat{\theta}\theta}$	.36	.38	—	.61	.51	—	.68	.62	—	.78	—	—	—	—	—			
	$b_{\hat{\theta}\theta}$	2.07	2.31	—	2.02	1.40	—	1.41	1.12	—	.99	—	—	—	—	—			

AN EMPIRICAL APPLICATION OF THE LEM

The statement of the problem and the data for this application were taken from a research project of the Department of Traffic Psychology of the Austrian Road Safety Board. The aim of that study was to investigate the effects of certain experimental conditions and of test instructions on the testees' achievement in a complex reaction test. As test device, the "Vienna Determination Apparatus" (Schuhfried, 1981; see also Klebelsberg, 1960) was employed, controlled by a newly developed micro-processor testing system (Schuhfried, 1982). It allows the presentation of any sequences of signals out of a set of optical and acoustical stimuli which must be answered by activating the corresponding keys or pedals. The apparatus is programmable and therefore suited for testing performance on different levels of task complexity. In several European countries it is a standard test device for the assessment of driving ability (Zuschlag & Winkler, 1980), but it is also used in industrial, clinical, forensic, and rehabilitation psychology.

The signals chosen for this study were the following 14 stimuli: optical stimuli—two lights each in white, yellow, green, blue, and red—which had to be answered by pressing key buttons in the corresponding colors, two other white lights (separated from the other lamps by a mask) which required pressing a left or a right foot pedal, and two acoustical stimuli of different pitch which had to be answered by pressing the respective sound keys. Each signal was presented until the testee gave the correct response; false reactions were ignored. As soon as the correct response was made, that signal ceased and the next signal was presented without delay. Response latencies were measured in units of 1/100 second.

The test comprised 4 presentations of the series of 14 stimuli, albeit, in different orders, that is, the test consisted of a total of 56 signals. Testing was preceded by a standardized instructional and training phase which familiarized the testees with the task. After this, the test was given once with "power" instructions to make as few mistakes as possible and once with "speed" instructions to complete the test as fast as possible. Hence each subject responded to 8 series of the 14 stimuli, that is, to a total of 112 signals. Half the sample worked first under power and then under speed instructions (P-S group), the other half in reverse order (S-P group).

The subjects were a random sample ($N = 153$) from the clientele of the Department of Traffic Psychology, varying considerably in age and level of performance. About one-third of the sample were young, healthy persons with good performance capacity, tested on the occasion of their application for a driver's license for bus or for special-license vehicles. One-third, on the other hand, had a significant degree of impairment due to advanced age, neurological diseases, or the abuse of alcohol.

The 112 response latencies recorded per testee refer to 14 different signals only, which were, however, presented after a varying number of previous trials and under different instructional conditions. It was expected that the average

9. EXPOTENTIAL LATENCY MODEL   153

response times would decrease with practice and that the responses would be faster under speed than under power instructions. Therefore, the number of previous presentations of a signal as well as the effect of the instructional condition were included in the analysis.

Two simple hypotheses concerning the dependence of the latency distributions on the signals, on practice, and on the instructions, were formulated by means of the LEM. Formally, it was necessary to model a total of 224 "technical" item (T-item) parameters because the testees in the P-S group gave their reactions under different conditions than the testees in the S-P group. The following basic parameters were assumed to be effective:

α_j . . . . the easiness parameter of the jth stimulus, $j = 1, \ldots, 14$;
β_ℓ . . . . the effect of the first ℓ trials on a stimulus with respect to the $\ell + 1^{\text{st}}$ trial on the same stimulus, $\ell = 1, \ldots, 7$; β_0 was introduced as a dummy parameter;
γ . . . . the relative effect of "speed" as compared to "power" instructions.

For writing down the linear constraints (6) for these 224 T-item parameters, 4 subgroups of T-items are distinguished for convenience: The parameters for the first 56 reactions of each person in the P-S group were assumed to be

$$\epsilon_{14(k-1)+j} = \alpha_j + \beta_{k-1}, \; j = 1, \ldots, 14; \, k = 1, \ldots, 4. \quad (20)$$

For the second set of 56 reactions of persons in the P-S group, that is, for T-items 57 through 112, the parameters were assumed to be

$$\epsilon_{14(k-1)+j} = \alpha_j + \beta_{k-1} + \gamma, \, j = 1, \ldots, 14; \, k = 5, \ldots, 8. \quad (21)$$

Similarly, for the persons in the S-P group, the parameters of the first 56 reactions, that is, for T-items 113 through 168, were

$$\epsilon_{14(k+7)+j} = \alpha_j + \beta_{k-1} + \gamma, \, j = 1, \ldots, 14; \, k = 1, \ldots, 4. \quad (22)$$

Finally, for the second set of 56 reactions of persons in the S-P-group, that is for the T-items 169 through 224, the parameters were defined by (23),

$$\epsilon_{14(k+7)+j} = \alpha_j + \beta_{k-1}, \; j = 1, \ldots, 14; \, k = 5, \ldots, 8. \quad (23)$$

The linear constraints (20) through (23) expressed the assumption that the practice effect that occurred when the testee reacted to a signal, making the next reaction to the same stimulus easier, was of the same magnitude for all stimuli, but could vary between trials. In this manner provision was made for a nonlinear learning curve. The effect of speed instructions, relative to power instructions, was assumed to be constant over all stimuli and trials. The model contained 14 stimulus parameters α_j, however, subject to one normalization condition, namely $\Sigma\alpha_j = 0$; furthermore, 8 practice effects β_ℓ with the normalizing restriction $\Sigma\beta_\ell = 0$; finally, 1 instruction parameter γ. Altogether, there were $23 - 2 = 21$

independent parameters. This parameterization of the model is denoted by H_1 for short.

In addition to this, one special case of (20) through (23) was considered, namely the assumption that practice was a linear function of the number of trials,

$$\beta_{k-1} = \beta_0 + (k-1)\beta, \qquad k = 1, \ldots, 8. \tag{24}$$

This reduced model contained only one practice effect parameter β (besides β_0) and, therefore, a total of 15 independent parameters. Hypothesis (24) is denoted by H_0.

The empirical estimates of the basic parameters are given in Table 9.3. In order to obtain some rough assessment of the accuracy of these estimates, asymptotic confidence intervals were derived from the inverse of **H** defined in (19). Unfortunately, there is no rigorous justification for such confidence intervals since the matrix **H** depends on the parameters θ_a which are unknown and must be replaced by their estimates $\hat{\theta}_a$. Nevertheless, the obtained confidence intervals, which average $\hat{\alpha}_j \pm 10$ for the stimulus parameters and $\hat{\beta}_\ell \pm 9$ for the practice effects, may be used as a guideline for interpreting the results; cf. Lord (1980, p. 181) for a similar argument in connection with the logistic latent trait model. Accordingly the parameter estimates in Table 9.3 are given without decimal places, except for the values $\hat{\beta}_\ell$ computed under H_0 which include one decimal place such that the linear learning process is adequately described.

TABLE 9.3
Parameter Estimates for the 14 Stimuli ($\hat{\alpha}_j$), Practice Effects ($\hat{\beta}_\ell$), and Effect of Instruction ($\hat{\gamma}$). The Normalization Conditions are
$\Sigma \alpha_j = \Sigma \beta_\ell = 0$

Stimuli	Parameters	Estimates	Practice Effects	Estimates Under H_0	Estimates Under H_1
Upper Red Light	α_1	46	β_0	-8.8	-12
Upper Green Light	α_2	-15	β_1	-6.3	-4
Upper Blue Light	α_3	10	β_2	-3.8	-5
Upper Yellow Light	α_4	27	β_3	-1.2	4
Upper White Light	α_5	-23	β_4	1.3	3
Lower Red Light	α_6	39	β_5	3.8	2
Lower Green Light	α_7	-10	β_6	6.3	4
Lower Blue Light	α_8	-9	β_7	8.8	8
Lower Yellow Light	α_9	24			
Lower White Light	α_{10}	-48			
White Light for Left Pedal	α_{11}	16		Instructional Effect	Estimate
White Light for Right Pedal	α_{12}	1			
Low Pitched Tone	α_{13}	-31		γ	15
High Pitched Tone	α_{14}	-27			

On this basis, the H_0 of a linear learning curve cannot be rejected, see also Fig. 9.1. It shows that there is a slow but steady increase in skill (that is, of the parameters β_ℓ) during test taking. The relative modesty of the practice effects may be due to the instructional and training phase that preceded the test. As an aside it should be mentioned that the deviations of the learning curve from the straight line, though not strictly significant, are easily interpretable: Between the fourth and the fifth trial on the entire series of 14 stimuli, the test was interrupted, and instructions were changed. Apparently, this effected a temporary decrease of the capacity of the testees and entailed a corresponding temporary drop of the learning curve.

The estimates of the α_j's and of γ are exactly the same under H_1 and under H_0, because the present experimental design is orthogonal with respect to the factors "stimuli", "practice effects", and "instructions". The relative magnitude of the $\hat{\alpha}_j$'s conforms to practical experiences with the test apparatus, for example, the two red lights are rather conspicuous and the respective reactions are easy to learn, whereas, for example, the "Lower White Light" is sometimes confounded with one of the two other white stimuli which ought to be answered by pressing the respective pedals; accordingly, all the reactions to white stimuli are relatively slower. The most difficult reactions are those to the acoustical stimuli which require discriminating between two tones of different pitch. Finally, it is obvious that the subjects generally accelerate their reactions under speed instructions ($\hat{\gamma} = 15$, with an approximate confidence interval of $\hat{\gamma} \pm 5$, is positive).

DISCUSSION

The exponential latency model with additively concatenated item and person parameters has the remarkable feature that the total time $t_{.a}$ the testee needs for taking the test is sufficient for his/her ability parameter θ_a. This is a convenient property because, once the item parameters have been calibrated, in principle it would suffice to record the total time as a raw score. Another resultant implication deserves note. If the test is given with a time limit and if some testees cannot finish the test within that limit, then the number of items solved becomes a sufficient statistic for θ_a (instead of $t_{.a}$), so that the parameter estimates $\hat{\theta}_a$ for such testees still remain comparable to those of the persons who completed the test (Scheiblechner, 1979, p. 30). Hence the model is of great interest for many areas of application.

However, these model properties are not always really an advantage. It might happen that some testees with a high ability level react slowly to some of the items due to periods of distraction. If only the total time $t_{.a}$ is used as a statistic for θ_a, even one exceptionally long latency may then cover up all the fast

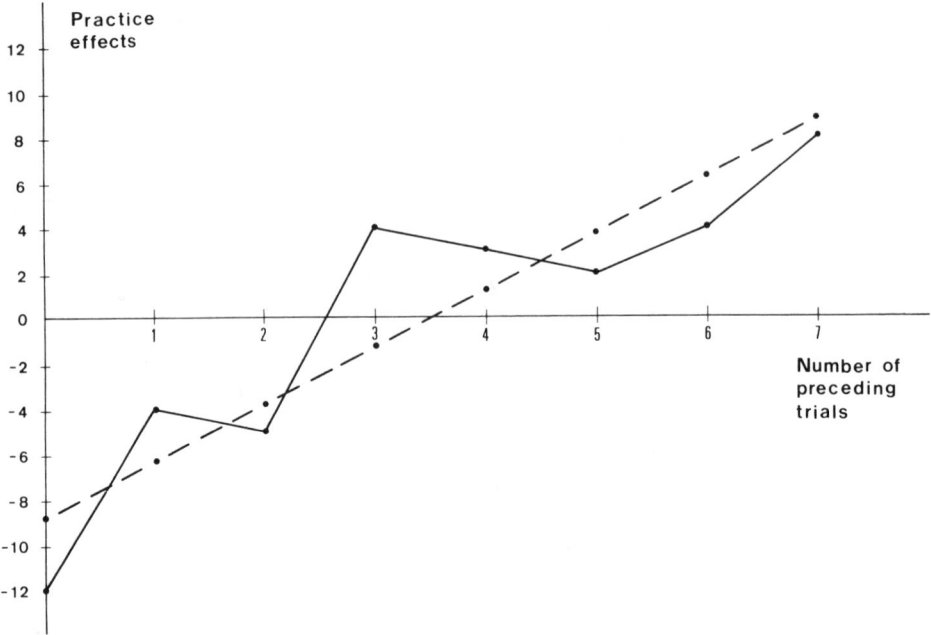

FIG. 9.1 Linear vs. non-linear learning. One "trial" consists of a series of 14 stimuli.

reactions. If, on the other hand, all the latencies were recorded and used for assessing the testee's performance, the testee's high ability level would be recognized in spite of some delayed reaction(s). It could be argued that the occurrence of periods of distraction are no fault of the model but rather of the data, but this is what happens in practice. Hence, it still remains necessary to record and to analyze all reaction latencies.

If one accepts the assumption of the sufficiency of $t_{.a}$ in addition to the exponential distribution of the latencies, then, as proven in the present chapter, the additive concatenation of item and person parameters is a necessary consequence (except for tautological parameter transformations). Furthermore, it follows from the structure of the model that the parameters can be efficiently estimated by means of the JML method, even in large samples of items. This was demonstrated here by means of an empirical example with 114 real and 224 "technical" items. The disadvantage of the JML approach, in contrast to the CML method, consists in a bias of the estimates in cases of few items, and, more aggravating, the lack of rigorously founded test statistics. The CML method, on the other hand, has all the desirable theoretical properties, but it is impractical even for moderate numbers of items, at least at the present state of development.

But because it is likely that the CML method can still be considerably improved, further studies of the virtues of both estimation approaches are indicated.

REFERENCES

Andersen, E. B. *Discrete statistical models with social science applications*. Amsterdam: North-Holland Publishing Company, 1980.

Bock, R. D., & Aitkin, M. Marginal maximum likelihood estimation of item parameters: Application of an EM algorithm. *Psychometrika*, 1981, *46*, 443–459.

Dempster, A. P., Laird, N. M., & Rubin, D. B. Maximum likelihood from incomplete data via the EM algorithm. *Journal of the Royal Statistical Society, Series B*, 1977, *39*, 1–38.

Feller, W. *An introduction to probability theory and its applications* (Vol. 2). New York: J. Wiley, 1966.

Fellner, H. *Die Problemsituation des schulpflichtig gewordenen Kindes hinsichtlich seines Spiels im Freien*. Vienna: Philosophical Dissertation at the University of Vienna, 1976.

Haberman, S. J. Maximum likelihood estimates in exponential response models. *The Annals of Statistics*, 1977, *5*, 815–841.

IMSLIB (IMS Library), Edition 8. Houston: International Mathematical and Statistical Libraries Inc., 1980.

Johnson, N. L., & Kotz, S. *Distributions in statistics. Continuous univariate distributions-1*. Boston: Houghton Mifflin, 1970.

Klebelsberg, D. Zwei neue Reaktionstestgeräte. Beck-Apparat/Wiener Determinationsgerät. *Diagnostica*, 1960, *6*, 164–166.

Lord, F. M. *Applications of item response theory to practical testing problems*. Hillsdale, N.J.: Lawrence Erlbaum Associates, 1980.

McGill, W. J. Stochastic latency mechanisms. In R. D. Luce, R. R. Bush, & E. Galanter (Eds.), *Handbook of mathematical psychology* (Vol. 1). New York: J. Wiley, 1963.

Rasch, G. *Probabilistic models for some intelligence and attainment tests*. Copenhagen: Denmarks Paedagogiske Institut, 1960.

Reventlow, I. *Studier af komplicerede psykobiologiske faenomener*. Copenhagen: Munksgaard, 1970.

Scheiblechner, H. *Computer routines for conditional inference for the linear exponential model*. Marburg/Lahn: Reports from the Institute of Psychology, Philipps Universität, 1978.

Scheiblechner, H. Specifically objective stochastic latency mechanisms. *Journal of Mathematical Psychology*, 1979, *19*, 18–38.

Schuhfried, G. *Vienna determination apparatus*. Mödling, N.Ö.: Dr. G. Schuhfried GmbH., 1981.

Schuhfried, G. *Vienna testing system*. Mödling, N.Ö.: Dr. G. Schuhfried GmbH., 1982.

Wottawa, H. *Das "Kompensationsgerät" als Instrument zur diagnostischen Untersuchung der Psychomotorik*. Vienna: Philosophical Dissertation at the University of Vienna, 1971.

Zuschlag, B., & Winkler, W. Verkehrspsychologie in Deutschland. *Psychologische Rundschau*, 1980, *31*, 145–162, 229–249.

10 Some Methods and Approaches of Estimating the Operating Characteristics of Discrete Item Responses

Fumiko Samejima
University of Tennessee

I. INTRODUCTION

Psychology deals with hypothetical constructs such as ability, achievement, attitude, motivation, and so forth, which can only be observed indirectly, through an individual's reactions to concrete stimuli. Yet these constructs prove to be useful in explaining human behavior. Latent Trait Theory is a family of theories and models which have been developed to measure hypothetical construct, or constructs, from individuals' reactions to particular stimuli. As a logical consequence of this objective, it is important to create a rationale which relates the individual's reaction to the stimulus with his or her hypothetical construct. There may be an enormous number of factors eliciting his or her specific overt reactions to a stimulus, and, therefore, it is suitable, even necessary, to handle the situation in terms of the probabilistic relationship between the two. The smallest unit of such a stimulus is called an item in Latent Trait Theory, and the selected set of the individual's reactions to an item is called a response.

"Trait" in the context of Latent Trait Theory simply indicates a hypothetical construct, which is assumed to exist behind the individual's observed behavior. This by no means suggests that it is inherited. Take achievement, for example. It is a hypothetical construct which is subject to change, or improvement, as an individual learns the content better, perhaps through some training process. In an effort to avoid possible misinterpretation of "trait," some researchers use the term, Item Response Theory, in preference to Latent Trait Theory. In this chapter, the terminology of Latent Trait Theory is used to maintain consonance with prior work.

In Latent Trait Theory, the latent space, or space of the hypothetical construct, is usually represented by some uni- or multi-dimensional continuum of real numbers (Samejima, 1974a, 1974b); and the item response can be treated as a discrete or a continuous variable (Samejima, 1973a, 1974a). Latent Trait Theory relates the item response to the latent trait in terms of the operating density characteristic when the item response is continuous, and of the operating characteristic when the item response is discrete.

The operating density characteristic of the continuous item response is the conditional density function of a particular item response, given the latent trait. The operating characteristic of the item response on the discrete response level is the conditional probability function of the item response, given the latent trait.

In a special case of the discrete response level where the item response is binary, (e.g., correct or incorrect in ability or achievement measurement, positive or negative in attitude measurement, etc.) the operating characteristic of the positive response is called the item characteristic function (Lord & Novick, 1968, chap. 16). On the dichotomous response level, in the unidimensional latent space, mathematical models such as the Rasch model (Rasch, 1960), the normal ogive model (Lord, 1952; Tucker, 1951), the logistic model (Birnbaum, chaps. 17–20, 1968), and so forth, have been proposed and used. When an item is scored into more than two graded response categories, the operating characteristic must be specified for each item score category. This graded response level is further categorized into the homogenous and heterogenous cases. The former has the property that any recategorization of the item score provides us with a binary item that yields an identical item characteristic function (except for the location) on the latent space. Samejima has proposed the normal ogive model and the logistic model developed for the homogenous case of the graded response level (Samejima, 1969, 1972). The discrete response level also includes the nominal response level, in which response categories are not explicitly ordered. The set of wrong answers used as the alternatives in the multiple-choice test item in addition to the correct answer provides us with a good example of this nominal response level. It should be noted that the multiple-choice test item can be treated either as a binary item by categorizing all the wrong answers into one category, that is, "incorrect," or, using the nominal response model, we can also make use of the information contained in separate incorrect answers. In the latter case, the multiple-choice test item is no longer a "blurred" image of the free-response test item, to which the examinee may respond freely without being forced to choose one of the given alternative answers, but it provides us with the information which the free-response test item does not. The three-parameter logistic model (Birnbaum, 1968), has been widely used as a model for the multiple-choice test item. The item is treated as a binary item and the rationale is based upon the knowledge or random-guessing principle. Bock proposed a multinomial response model (Bock, 1972) which is applicable for the multiple-choice test item when the effect of random guessing is negligibly small. Bock's model can also be considered as a model for the heterogenous case of the graded response level (Samejima, 1972). Samejima proposed a family of models for the multiple-choice test item (Samejima, 1979b), which accounts both for the information provided by the wrong answers and for the effect of random guessing.

When a mathematical model is assumed, the problem of estimating the operating characteristics is converted to the problem of estimating item parameters. This simplifies the problem, for one does not have to challenge the direct estimation of the operating characteristics without assuming any mathematical form. When some specific mathematical model is assumed, model validation becomes one of the most important processes of conscientious research. We can see a fine example of this in one of Lord's works (Lord, 1970), where he validated the three-parameter logistic model for several SAT Verbal test items.

The direct estimation of the operating characteristics of discrete item responses has been attempted by Lord (1969). In this approach, the estimation of the true test score distribution of each subgroup of examinees, who share the same item score for the target test item, plays an essential role. The estimated density function of each subgroup is divided by the estimated density function of the total group of examinees to provide us with the estimated conditional probability of the item response, given the true test score. The true score is transformed to the latent trait by virtue of the one-to-one correspondence between the two. Samejima has developed a series of methods and approaches of estimating the operating characteristics of discrete item responses without assuming any mathematical form (Samejima, 1977c, 1977e, 1978a, 1978b, 1978c, 1978d, 1978e, 1978f, 1980a, 1980b). These methods are outlined in the present chapter. Levine (1980) has also developed a method for a similar purpose, in which he utilizes eigenfunctions effectively. Lord's method is basically oriented towards a large set of data, such as those available from large-scale testing programs. Samejima's and Levine's are oriented towards smaller sets of data, of the sort usually collected on university campuses.

2. INFORMATION FUNCTIONS

Let k_g denote a discrete item response to item denoted g. Let θ be the unidimensional latent trait, which may assume any real number. Let $P_{k_g}(\theta)$ denote the operating characteristic of the discrete item response k_g. The response pattern, V, for the set of n items is defined as a set of n item responses, such that

$$V = (k_1, k_2, \ldots, k_g, \ldots, k_n)'. \tag{2.1}$$

The operating characteristic of the response pattern V, which is denoted by $P_V(\theta)$, is the conditional probability of V, given the latent trait θ. When local independence holds (Lord & Novick, 1968, chap. 16), this operating characteristic of the response pattern V is given as the product of the n operating characteristics of the item responses, that is

$$P_V(\theta) = \prod_{k_g \in V} P_{k_g}(\theta). \tag{2.2}$$

This operating characteristic, $P_V(\theta)$, is also the likelihood function used in estimating the latent trait for the examinee with the particular response pattern V. We can write for the likelihood equation

$$\frac{\partial}{\partial \theta} \log L_V(\theta) = \frac{\partial}{\partial \theta} \log P_V(\theta) = \sum_{k_g \in V} A_{k_g}(\theta) = 0, \tag{2.3}$$

where $A_{k_g}(\theta)$ is the basic function for the item response k_g, defined by

$$A_{k_g}(\theta) = \frac{\partial}{\partial \theta} \log P_{k_g}(\theta). \tag{2.4}$$

When a simple sufficient statistic does not exist for the response pattern V, as in the case of the normal ogive model, this basic function plays an important role in obtaining the maximum likelihood estimate θ_V with the aid of a computer. It has been shown (Samejima, 1969, 1972) that in such models as the normal ogive model and the logistic model on the graded response level and Bock's multinomial model, the basic function satisfies the unique maximum condition. This assures the existence of a unique maximum likelihood estimate for every possible response pattern, whereas in the three-parameter logistic or normal ogive model this condition is not satisfied, and the unique maximum likelihood estimate is not assured for every response pattern (Samejima, 1972, 1973b).

The item response information function, $I_{k_g}(\theta)$, is defined by

$$I_{k_g}(\theta) = -\frac{\partial}{\partial \theta} A_{k_g}(\theta), \tag{2.5}$$

and the item information function, $I_g(\theta)$, is given as the conditional expectation of the item response information function, given θ, so that

$$I_g(\theta) = E[I_{k_g}(\theta)|\theta] = \sum_{k_g} I_{k_g}(\theta) P_{k_g}(\theta) = \sum_{k_g} \left[\frac{\partial}{\partial \theta} P_{k_g}(\theta) \right]^2 [P_{k_g}(\theta)]^{-1}. \tag{2.6}$$

It can be seen from (2.6) that the item information function, $I_g(\theta)$, is nonnegative in nature, even if the item response information function assumes negative values for some range of θ.

The response pattern information function, $I_V(\theta)$, is defined by

$$I_V(\theta) = -\frac{\partial^2}{\partial \theta^2} \log P_V(\theta) = \sum_{k_g \in V} I_{k_g}(\theta). \tag{2.7}$$

The test information function, $I(\theta)$, is the conditional expectation of the response pattern information function, given the latent trait θ, so that

$$I(\theta) = E[I_V(\theta)|\theta] = \sum_V I_V(\theta) P_V(\theta). \qquad (2.8)$$

It can be shown from (2.6), (2.7) and (2.8) that this test information function is the sum of the n item information functions, yielding

$$I(\theta) = \sum_{g=1}^{n} I_g(\theta). \qquad (2.9)$$

Let τ be a strictly increasing function of θ, such that

$$\tau = \tau(\theta). \qquad (2.10)$$

From the definition of the operating characteristic, it is obvious that

$$P^*_{k_g}[\tau(\theta)] = P_{k_g}(\theta) \qquad (2.11)$$

and

$$P^*_V[\tau(\theta)] = P_V(\theta), \qquad (2.12)$$

where $P^*_{k_g}(\tau)$ and $P^*_V(\tau)$ are the operating characteristics of the item response k_g and of the response pattern V, respectively, in τ. We can write for the four types of information functions, $I^*_{k_g}(\tau)$, $I^*_g(\tau)$, $I^*_V(\tau)$ and $I^*(\tau)$, in τ, and the counterparts of the four information functions defined by (2.5) through (2.8) become

$$I^*_{k_g}(\tau) = I_{k_g}(\theta) \left[\frac{d\theta}{d\tau}\right]^2 - \frac{\partial}{\partial \theta} \log P_{k_g}(\theta) \cdot \frac{d^2\theta}{d\tau^2}, \qquad (2.13)$$

$$I^*_g(\tau) = I_g(\theta) \left[\frac{d\theta}{d\tau}\right]^2, \qquad (2.14)$$

$$I^*_V(\tau) = I_V(\theta) \left[\frac{d\theta}{d\tau}\right]^2 - \frac{\partial}{\partial \theta} \log P_V(\theta) \cdot \frac{d^2\theta}{d\tau^2}, \qquad (2.15)$$

$$I^*(\tau) = I(\theta) \left[\frac{d\theta}{d\tau}\right]^2. \qquad (2.16)$$

It is apparent from these formulae that the information functions are subject to change over the transformation of the latent trait. However, there exists a certain constancy. Let $\underline{\theta}$ and $\bar{\theta}$ denote the lower and upper endpoints of an arbitrarily chosen subinterval of the original latent trait θ, and $\underline{\tau}$ and $\bar{\tau}$ be the corresponding endpoints under the transformations, that is,

$$\begin{cases} \underline{\tau} = \tau(\underline{\theta}) \\ \bar{\tau} = \tau(\bar{\theta}). \end{cases} \qquad (2.17)$$

From (2.14) and (2.16) we obtain

$$\int_{\underline{\tau}}^{\bar{\tau}} [I_g^*(\tau)]^{1/2} d\tau = \int_{\underline{\theta}}^{\bar{\theta}} [I_g(\theta)]^{1/2} d\theta, \qquad (2.18)$$

and

$$\int_{\underline{\tau}}^{\bar{\tau}} [I^*(\tau)]^{1/2} d\tau = \int_{\underline{\theta}}^{\bar{\theta}} [I(\theta)]^{1/2} d\theta. \qquad (2.19)$$

Thus it is clear that the areas under the curves of the square root of the item information function, and of the square root of the test information function, are unchanged by any strictly increasing transformation of the original latent trait, for an arbitrarily chosen subinterval of the latent trait. Although the amount of information, which is defined locally, can be radically changed in the transformation, the amount of information is constant under the transformation for an arbitrary subinterval. This does not hold for the item or the test information function; only for their square roots.

The above fact implies that we can always find a transformed latent trait τ which provides us with a constant amount of information for the test of our interest, for any subinterval of the latent trait. Let C be the desired constant value of the square root of the test information functioin for the interval, $[\underline{\tau}, \bar{\tau}]$. Then the transformation of θ to τ is given by

$$\tau(\theta) = C^{-1} \int_{-\infty}^{\theta} [I(u)]^{1/2} du + \tau_0, \qquad (2.20)$$

where τ_0 is an arbitrary constant, or the value of τ which corresponds to the origin of θ. This fact is extremely useful in the estimation of the operating characteristics of discrete item responses, which will be introduced in later sections.

It has been shown (Samejima, 1979a) that the above constancy leads to the fact that the area under the curve of the square root of the item information funtion is constant over different models that belong to the same type. Consider, for example, the family of models on the dichotomous response level, each of whose item characteristic functions, $P_g(\theta)$, is strictly increasing in θ, and its two asymptotes satisfy

$$\begin{array}{c} \lim_{\theta \to \underline{\theta}} P_g(\theta) = 0 \\ \lim_{\theta \to \bar{\theta}} P_g(\theta) = 1, \end{array} \qquad (2.21)$$

where $\underline{\theta}$ and $\bar{\theta}$ are the lower and upper endpoints of the interval of θ. This family includes the normal ogive model, the logistic model, the linear model, and so forth, and $\underline{\theta}$ and $\bar{\theta}$ are negative and positive infinities, respectively, in the first two models, and assume finite values in the third model. The area under the curve of the square root of the item information function equals π for any model of this type (Samejima, 1979a).

3. ASYMPTOTIC NORMALITY OF THE CONDITIONAL DISTRIBUTION OF THE MAXIMUM LIKELIHOOD ESTIMATE, GIVEN LATENT TRAIT

It is well known that the maximum likelihood estimate asymptotically distributes normally with the true parameter and the inverse of the square root of the amount of information as the first and second parameters, respectively, when the observations are taken from identical distributions (e.g., Kendall & Stuart, 1961). The situation corresponds to the case where all the test items are equivalent, that is, when they have an identical set of operating characteristics of the item responses. The proof for this theorem is expanded to the general case when the test items are not equivalent (Samejima, 1975).

Let ϵ be the error in estimating in the maximum likelihood estimation of the latent trait θ, such that

$$\hat{\theta}_V = \theta + \epsilon. \tag{3.1}$$

Then $\hat{\theta}_V$ is asymptotically and conditionally unbiased, and normally distributed with $\sigma(\theta)$ as the second parameter, such that

$$E(\hat{\theta}_V|\theta) \simeq \theta, \tag{3.2}$$

and

$$\sigma(\hat{\theta}_V|\theta) \simeq [I(\theta)]^{-1/2}. \tag{3.3}$$

We can rephrase the statement that the asympototic conditional distribution of the error ϵ, given θ, is normal, with

$$E(\epsilon|\theta) \simeq 0 \tag{3.4}$$

and (3.3) as the two parameters.

This asymptotic property of the maximum likelihood estimate is useful if the speed of convergence to the normality is high. In such a case, we can approximate the conditional distribution of $\hat{\theta}_V$, given θ, by the normal distribution when both the number of test items and the amount of test information are relatively small. Some Monte Carlo studies have been made (Samejima, 1975, 1977a, 1977b, 1977c) to observe the speed of convergence of the conditional distribution of the maximum likelihood estimate, $\hat{\theta}_V$, given θ, to normality. Figure 10.1 illustrates some of the results of such studies. In this example, θ is set equal to $-.3$, and, by the Monte Carlo method, 100 response patterns were produced for

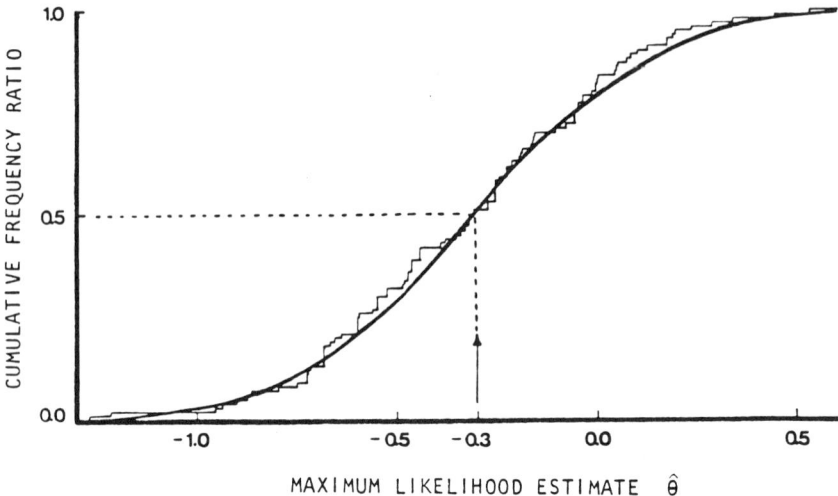

FIG. 10.1 Cumulative frequency ratios of maximum likelihood estimates, which are based upon the response patterns of twenty-four binary test items produced by the monte carlo method at $\theta = -0.3$, in comparison with the normal distribution function, $N(-.3,.3685)$.

the 24 hypothetical binary test items, each of which follows the normal ogive model on the dichotomous response level whose item characteristic function is given by

$$P_g(\theta) = [2\pi]^{-1/2} \int_{-\infty}^{a_g(\theta - b_g)} e^{-u^2/2} du. \tag{3.5}$$

The discrimination parameter a_g (> 0) and the difficulty parameter b_g of each item g of the 24 hypothetical test items are shown in Table 10.1. The maximum likelihood estimate for each of these 100 response patterns was obtained by using the basic function, $A_{k_g}(\theta)$, which was introduced in section 1. The value of $\sigma(\hat{\theta}_V|\theta)$, which is obtained from equations (3.3), (3.5), (2.5), and (2.8), turned out to be .3685. The smooth curve in Fig. 10.1 indicates the normal distribution function, $N(-.3, .3685)$, and the jagged curve indicates the cumulative frequency ratios of the 100 maximum likelihood estimates. We can see in this example that the approximation by the normal distribution, $N(-.3, .3685)$, of the conditional distribution of the maximum likelihood estimate, $\hat{\theta}_V$, given θ, works well even when the number of binary test items as small as 24 and the inverse of the square root of the test information is as large as .3685. Similar results have been obtained for the other examples, some of which include graded test items. Note that, if we use graded test items instead of binary test items, we will need fewer test items, since the amount of item information is larger for each item.

TABLE 10.1
Item Discrimination Parameter a_g and Item Difficulty Parameter b_g of Each of the 24 Binary Test Items

Item g	a_g	b_g
1	0.5	0.2
2	0.5	-2.0
3	0.6	2.1
4	0.6	1.3
5	0.7	-1.3
6	0.7	2.0
7	0.8	1.9
8	0.8	-1.1
9	0.9	0.6
10	0.9	-1.6
11	1.0	-1.8
12	1.0	1.6
13	1.1	1.1
14	1.1	-1.0
15	1.2	0.8
16	1.2	-1.7
17	1.3	1.4
18	1.3	0.8
19	1.4	1.1
20	1.4	0.6
21	1.5	-1.9
22	1.5	0.9
23	1.6	0.8
24	1.6	-1.4

4. CONSTANT STANDARD ERROR OF ESTIMATION

It has been observed in section 2 that when the amount of test information is not constant for the interval of θ of interest, we can always transform θ to τ to provide us with a constant test information function. Note, however, that in order to approximate the conditional distribution of the maximum likelihood estimate $\hat{\tau}_V$, given the latent trait τ, it is necessary, in spite of its irregularity, that the amount of test information defined for the original latent trait θ be substantially large throughout the interval of θ of interest. The transformation of θ to τ is made by (2.20), in which the test information function defined for the original latent trait θ plays an important role. It should be noted that we can write for the relationship between the density function of the transformed latent trait τ and that of the original latent trait θ,

$$f^*(\tau) = f(\theta)\frac{d\theta}{d\tau}. \tag{4.1}$$

where $f^*(\tau)$ and $f(\theta)$ denote the respective density functions.

By virtue of the transformation-free character of the maximum likelihood estimate, the new maximum likelihood estimate, $\hat{\tau}_V$, can be obtained through the same transformation, namely,

$$\hat{\tau}_V = \tau(\hat{\theta}_V). \tag{4.2}$$

This is convenient, for it means that we do not need to directly obtain the maximum likelihood estimate $\hat{\tau}_V$ by redefining the basic functions of the item responses for the transformed latent trait τ and proceed through the numerical process of obtaining $\hat{\tau}_V$.

We notice that the transformation of θ to τ, which is given by (2.20), may be rather complicated, requiring the integration of the square root of the test information function, $I(\theta)$, given by (2.9). This is simplified by the polynomial approximation of the square root of the test information function. Samejima and Livingston (1979) showed that the polynomial of a specified degree which is obtained by the method of moments (Elderton & Johnson, 1969) provides us with the least square solution. The method of moments also reduces rounding error because it does not require the inversion of an ill-conditioned matrix. With such a polynomial, say, of degree m, we can write for the square root of the test information function

$$[I(\theta)]^{1/2} \doteq \sum_{k=0}^{m} \alpha_k \theta^k. \tag{4.3}$$

Substituting (4.3) into (2.20), we obtain

$$\tau(\theta) \doteq C^{-1} \sum_{k=0}^{m} \alpha_k (k+1)^{-1} \theta^{k+1} + \tau_0 = \sum_{k=0}^{m+1} \alpha_k^* \theta^k, \tag{4.4}$$

where

$$\alpha_k^* \begin{cases} = \tau_0 & k = 0 \\ = (Ck)^{-1} \alpha_{k-1} & k = 1, 2, \ldots, m+1, \end{cases} \tag{4.5}$$

(cf. Samejima, 1980a) and where C is defined in section 2. Thus we can transform the original latent trait θ to τ more straightforwardly using the polynomial of degree $(m+1)$ given by (4.4).

In tailored testing, or computerized adaptive testing, the constant standard error of estimation can easily be obtained for the interval of θ of interest (Samejima, 1977b). This is accomplished by using a set amount of test information as the criterion for terminating the presentation of new test items from our item pool, for each examinee. In so doing, therefore, we can make the accuracy of estimation for the total group of examinees equal. This can be repeated as many times as we wish, and the resultant sessions can be considered as weakly parallel tests (Samejima, 1977d), even though, within each session, each examinee has taken a set of test items tailored specifically for him or her.

5. NORMAL APPROXIMATION METHOD

Suppose we have a set of test items whose operating characteristics are known. For simplicity, hereafter, we shall call this set of test items the "Old Test." When the operating characteristics of the test items of the Old Test satisfy the unique maximum condition (Samejima, 1969, 1972), we can obtain the maximum likelihood estimate of the latent trait θ for each of those examinees to whom the Old Test was administered. Suppose, further, that there is another set of test items whose operating characteristics are yet to be discovered. For convenience, herein, we shall call each item of this second set an "unknown test item." If these unknown test items are administered to the same group of examinees, then we can estimate the operating characteristics of the discrete item responses for each unknown test item by using the maximum likelihood estimates of the latent trait obtained on the Old Test.

When the maximum likelihood estimate, $\hat{\theta}_V$, is obtained for each examinee, the simple ratio of the frequency of the examinees who share a specified item response to the total frequency, which are observed for each of the appropriately set small subintervals of $\hat{\theta}_V$, provides us with the estimated operating characteristic of the item response. Although this approach is legitimate, there are several considerations. First of all, this method can safely be applied only when the size of the sample, or the number of examinees, is as large as, say, ten thousand, in order to ensure an accurate estimate of the operating characteristic. In practice, however, most researchers, who collect their data on university campuses, for example, must satisfy themselves with no more than a thousand examinees. Second, even if we have collected data for ten thousand examinees, the computing time involved in obtaining the maximum likelihood estimates for all the examinees will be enormously large, and, therefore, the method is of little practical usefulness. Third, since there is no one-to-one correspondence between θ and $\hat{\theta}_V$ and, in general, the regression of θ on $\hat{\theta}_V$ is not linear, even when the maximum likelihood estimate $\hat{\theta}_V$ is approximately conditionally unbiased, given the latent trait θ, and the standard error of estimation is constant for the interval of θ of interest, the resultant estimated operating characteristic will be stretched unevenly. We find that, although we have for the expectation of $\hat{\theta}_V$

$$E(\hat{\theta}_V) \simeq E(\theta), \tag{5.1}$$

when the maximum likelihood estimate $\hat{\theta}_V$ is approximately conditionally unbiased, given θ, we obtain for the variance of $\hat{\theta}_V$

$$Var.(\hat{\theta}_V) \simeq Var.(\theta) + E[Var.(\hat{\theta}_V|\theta)] \geq Var.(\theta). \tag{5.2}$$

This result comes from the general formula for the m-th conditional moment of $\hat{\theta}_V$, given θ,

$$E[\hat{\theta}_V - E(\hat{\theta}_V)]^m = \sum_{r=0}^{m} \binom{m}{r} E[\{\theta - E(\theta)\}^{m-r} E(\hat{\theta}_V - \theta)^r | \theta\}], \quad (5.3)$$

(cf. Samejima, 1977c). For these reasons, it is desirable to discover methods which ameliorate these deficiencies.

Let h denote an unknown test item and k_h be its discrete item response. We can categorize the group of examinees of our sample into subgroups depending upon their item scores, k_h. If the density function, $f_{k_h}(\theta)$, of each discrete item score k_h is estimated, then the estimated operating characteristic, $\tilde{P}_{k_h}(\theta)$, can be represented by

$$\tilde{P}_{k_h}(\theta) = N_{k_h} \cdot \tilde{f}_{k_h}(\theta) [\Sigma N_j \cdot f_j(\theta)]^{-1}, \quad (5.4)$$

where N_{k_h} is the number of examinees belonging to the item response category k_h, and $\tilde{f}_{k_h}(\theta)$ is the estimation of the density $f_{k_h}(\theta)$. Thus our objective is to estimate $f_{k_h}(\theta)$ from the set of maximum likelihood estimates, $\hat{\theta}_V$, of our sample of examinees.

Let us assume that: (1) our Old Test has a sufficiently large amount of test information at any point in the interval of θ of interest, and (2) θ is transformed to τ which has a constant test information throughout the corresponding interval of τ. Then

$$\hat{\tau}_V = \tau + \epsilon, \quad (5.5)$$

where the same symbol ϵ denotes the error in estimating $\hat{\tau}_V$, for convenience. In the Normal Approximation Method, we assume a bivariate normal distribution for the joint distribution of $\hat{\tau}_V$ and ϵ, for each subpopulation of examinees who share the same discrete item response k_h to the unknown item h. For simplicity, we drop the subscript from $\hat{\tau}_V$. The sample linear regression, $\dot{\epsilon}(\hat{\tau})$, of the error ϵ on the maximum likelihood estimate $\hat{\tau}$ is given by

$$\dot{\epsilon}(\hat{\tau}) = \alpha + \beta \hat{\tau}, \quad (5.6)$$

where

$$\alpha = -C^{-2} E(\hat{\tau}) [Var.(\hat{\tau})]^{-1} \quad (5.7)$$

and

$$\beta = C^{-2} [Var.(\hat{\tau})]^{-1}. \quad (5.8)$$

We can write for the conditional variance of ϵ, given $\hat{\tau}$,

$$Var.(\epsilon | \hat{\tau}) \doteq C^{-2}[1 - C^{-2}[Var.(\hat{\tau})]^{-1}]. \quad (5.9)$$

Thus the approximate joint distribution of ϵ and $\hat{\tau}$ are completely specified through equations (5.6) through (5.9) for each subpopulation of examinees.

Using the Monte Carlo method, we can produce as many error scores as we wish for each value of $\hat{\tau}$, and subsequently obtain values of τ, which we shall denote by $\tilde{\tau}$. The resulting set of $\tilde{\tau}$ for each item response subgroup k_h will be appropriately categorized into small subintervals to provide us with the approximate product of the interval width of θ and the frequency $N_{k_h} \cdot \tilde{f}_{k_h}(\theta)$ in (5.4), by virtue of the one-to-one correspondence between θ and τ, and, therefore, it can be used in both the numerator and denominator of (5.4).

Figure 10.2 presents an example of the results (Samejima, 1977c) obtained by the Normal Approximation Method. In this example, a hypothetical test, Test A, which consists of 35 graded items, was used as the Old Test.

Let x_g be the graded item score of item g, which assumes integers, 0 through m_g. Each item of Test A follows the normal ogive model on the graded response level, whose operating characteristic, $P_{x_g}(\theta)$, is given by

$$P_{x_g}(\theta) = [2\pi]^{-1/2} \int_{a_g(\theta - b_{x_g+1})}^{a_g(\theta - b_{x_g})} e^{-u^2/2} du, \qquad (5.10)$$

where

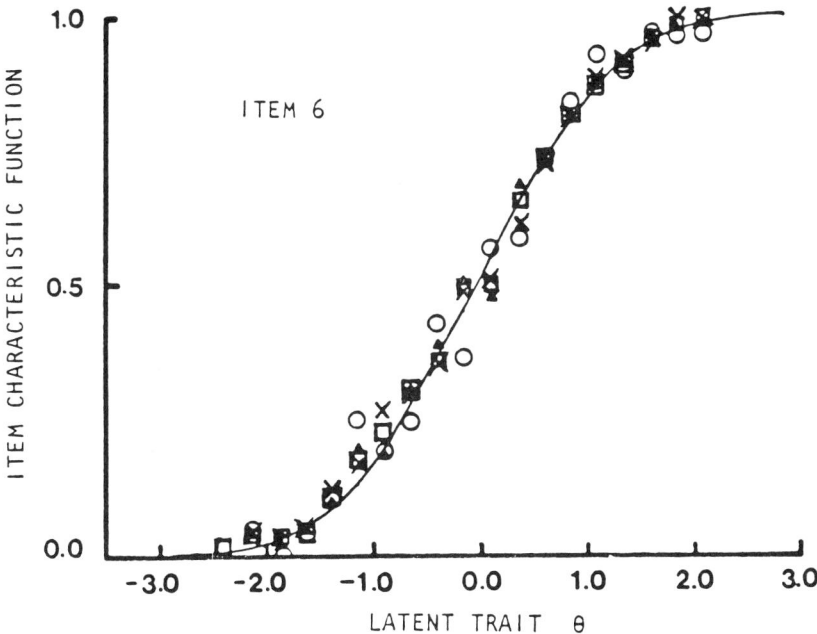

FIG. 10.2 Estimated item characteristic functions of item 6 based upon 500 $\tilde{\theta}$'s (hollow circles), upon 2,500 $\tilde{\theta}$'s (solid triangles), upon 2,500 $\tilde{\theta}$'s (crosses) and upon 5,000 $\tilde{\theta}$'s (hollow squares), obtained by the normal approximation method, using test A as the old test.

$$-\infty = b_0 < b_1 < \ldots < b_{m_g} < b_{m_g+1} = \infty. \quad (5.11)$$

The item discrimination parameter, a_g (>0), and the set of m_g ($=2$) item difficulty parameters, b_{x_g}, of each of the 35 test items of Test A are presented in Table 10.2. The amount of test information of Test A is approximately 21.63 throughout the interval of θ, $(-3.0, 3.0)$, and, therefore, the standard error of estimate is approximately .215 for this interval of θ (cf. Samejima, 1977c). Five

TABLE 10.2
Item Discrimination Parameter a_g and Two Item Difficulty Parameters b_{x_g} for $x_g = 1$ and $x_g = 2$ of Each of the 35 Graded Items of Test A

Item g	a_g	b_1	b_2
1	1.8	-4.75	-3.75
2	1.9	-4.50	-3.50
3	2.0	-4.25	-3.25
4	1.5	-4.00	-3.00
5	1.6	-3.75	-2.75
6	1.4	-3.50	-2.50
7	1.9	-3.00	-2.00
8	1.8	-3.00	-2.00
9	1.6	-2.75	-1.75
10	2.0	-2.50	-1.50
11	1.5	-2.25	-1.25
12	1.7	-2.00	-1.00
13	1.5	-1.75	-.75
14	1.4	-1.50	-.50
15	2.0	-1.25	-.25
16	1.6	-1.00	.00
17	1.8	-.75	.25
18	1.7	-.50	.50
19	1.9	-.25	.75
20	1.7	.00	1.00
21	1.5	.25	1.25
22	1.8	.50	1.50
23	1.4	.75	1.75
24	1.9	1.00	2.00
25	2.0	1.25	2.25
26	1.6	1.50	2.50
27	1.7	1.75	2.75
28	1.4	2.00	3.00
29	1.9	2.25	3.25
30	1.6	2.50	3.50
31	1.5	2.75	3.75
32	1.7	3.00	4.00
33	1.8	3.25	4.25
34	2.0	3.50	4.50
35	1.4	3.75	4.75

hundred hypothetical examinees whose positions on the latent trait θ are at 100 equally spaced points of θ which start with −2.475 and end with 2.475, with five examinees placed at each position, were used. For Test A, we can set $\tau = \theta$, and the transformation of the latent trait is not necessary. The unknown test item, which is given as item 6, is one of the 10 binary items, each of which follows the normal ogive model on the dichotomous response level whose item characteristic function is given by (3.5), and its two item parameters, a_g and b_g, are presented in Table 10.3. In this figure, the result obtained by producing only one value of $\hat{\tilde{\tau}}$ for each τ_V plotted by hollow circles, the two sets of results obtained by producing five values of $\hat{\tilde{\tau}}$ for each $\hat{\tau}$ are plotted by solid triangles and crosses, respectively, and the result obtained by combining these two sets of five values of $\hat{\tilde{\tau}}$ for each $\hat{\tau}$ is plotted by hollow squares. From these results, we can see that, as we produce a larger number of $\hat{\tilde{\tau}}$, the accuracy of the estimation of the operating characteristic becomes higher. We can further improve the results if we produce more $\hat{\tilde{\tau}}$'s for each $\hat{\tau}$, and make the subinterval width of θ smaller. Similar results were also obtained for the other nine unknown test items.

6. CONDITIONAL MOMENTS OF LATENT TRAIT, GIVEN ITS MAXIMUM LIKELIHOOD ESTIMATE

It has been shown (Samejima, 1977e) that, if an estimate of the latent trait is conditionally unbiased and its conditional distribution is normal with a constant second parameter, the conditional moments of the latent trait, given its estimate, will be obtained solely from the density function of the estimate and the constant second parameter of the normal distribution. When the conditional distribution of the maximum likelihood estimate $\hat{\tau}$, given τ, is approximated by $N(\tau, C^{-1})$,

TABLE 10.3
Item Discrimination Parameter a_h and Item Difficulty Parameter b_h of Each "Unknown" Test Item h

Item h	a_h	b_h
1	1.5	-2.5
2	1.0	-2.0
3	2.5	-1.5
4	1.0	-1.0
5	1.5	-.5
6	1.0	.0
7	2.0	.5
8	1.0	1.0
9	2.0	1.5
10	1.0	2.0

where C is the constant square root of the test information function of our test defined for the transformed latent trait τ, we can obtain approximate values for these conditional moments. Let $g(\hat{\tau})$ be the density function of $\hat{\tau}$ and assume that $g(\hat{\tau})$ is four-times differentiable. Then the conditional expectation of τ, given $\hat{\tau}$, and the second through fourth conditional moments of τ, given $\hat{\tau}$, are:

$$E(\tau|\hat{\tau}) = \hat{\tau} + C^{-2} \frac{d}{d\hat{\tau}} \log g(\tau). \quad (6.1)$$

$$\mathrm{Var.}(\tau|\hat{\tau}) = C^{-2} \left[1 + C^{-2} \frac{d^2}{d\tau^2} \log g(\hat{\tau}) \right]. \quad (6.2)$$

$$E[\{\tau - E(\tau|\hat{\tau})\}^3 | \hat{\tau}] = C^{-6} \left[\frac{d^3}{d\hat{\tau}^3} \log g(\hat{\tau}) \right]. \quad (6.3)$$

$$E[\{\tau - E(\tau|\hat{\tau})\}^4 | \hat{\tau}] = C^{-4} \left[3 + 6C^{-2} \left\{ \frac{d^2}{d\tau^2} \log g(\hat{\tau}) \right\} \right. \quad (6.4)$$
$$\left. + 3C^{-4} \left\{ \frac{d^2}{d\tau^2} \log g(\hat{\tau}) \right\}^2 + C^{-4} \left\{ \frac{d^4}{d\hat{\tau}^4} \log g(\hat{\tau}) \right\} \right]$$

This enables us to estimate the (unobservable) distributions of the latent trait τ from the set of the maximum likelihood estimates, which is directly observable. In so doing, the density function, $g(\hat{\tau})$, must be estimated from observable maximum likelihood estimates. This can be done by fitting a polynomial of an appropriate degree to the set of maximum likelihood estimates $\hat{\tau}$ (cf. Samejima & Livingston, 1979).

These conditional moments can be used to estimate the conditional distribution of τ, given $\hat{\tau}$, especially if we assume a Pearson Type distribution for the conditional distribution. Let κ denote Pearson's criterion. We can write

$$\kappa = \beta_1(\beta_2+3)^2[4(2\beta_2-3\beta_1-6)(4\beta_2-3\beta_1)]^{-1}, \quad (6.5)$$

where

$$\beta_1 = (E[\{\tau-E(\tau|\hat{\tau})\}^3 | \hat{\tau}])^2 \, (Var.[\tau|\hat{\tau}])^{-3}, \quad (6.6)$$

and

$$\beta_2 = (E[\{\tau-E(\tau|\hat{\tau})\}^4|\hat{\tau}]) \, (Var.[\tau|\hat{\tau}])^{-2}. \quad (6.7)$$

The value of this criterion obtained by substituting (6.2), (6.3), and (6.4) into (6.6) and (6.7) for any specified value of $\hat{\tau}$ points to a unique Pearson Type distribution (Elderton & Johnson, 1969). This can be used to approximate conditional distribution of $\hat{\tau}$, given τ. We shall call this method the Pearson System Method (Samejima, 1978b).

The Pearson System Method can produce varieties of different shapes for the estimated conditional density functions in accordance with their sets of estimated conditional moments. In this sense, the approximation is expected to be accurate.

It has its share of problems, however. In the first place, the parameter estimations of some of the Pearson Type distributions are rather difficult. Second, the estimated fourth conditional moment of τ, given $\hat{\tau}$, sometimes turns out to be negative for some values of $\hat{\tau}$. (With less frequency the same thing happens for the estimated second moment also.) To avoid the increased inaccuracies of estimation of conditional moments of higher orders, it is sometimes suitable to use only the first and second conditional moments. If we do, and approximate the conditional distribution by a normal distribution, we call this process the Normal Approach Method (Samejima, 1978b). In this method, although each estimated conditional density function is forced to be symmetric, we can avoid the error caused by estimating higher conditional moments. For added flexibility, we can also use a Beta distribution, whose two parameters, the lower and the upper endpoints of the interval for which the density is positive, are given a priori. Thus, as in the Normal Approach Method, we need only the first two conditional moments to estimate the remaining two parameters of the Beta distribution. It has the advantage of allowing the estimated conditional density functions to be asymmetric. We call this method the Two-Parameter Beta Method (Samejima, 1977e, 1978a). The biggest problem with this method is finding a suitable set of two a priori set parameters for each $\hat{\tau}$. Our experience shows, however, that there is a certain degree of robustness, so that fairly arbitrarily chosen sets of endpoints provide accurate estimated operating characteristics (Samejima, 1978c).

We can conceive of other varieties of distributions using certain numbers of estimated conditional moments of τ, given $\hat{\tau}$, and further studies are desired adopting varieties of different types of data. Which method should be chosen in a specific situation depends upon the nature of the data.

7. BIVARIATE P.D.F. APPROACH

Normal Approximation Method which was introduced in section 5, can be considered as a bivariate p.d.f. approach. A similar approach is possible with somewhat different rationale (Samejima, 1978f). Let $g_{k_h}(\hat{\tau})$ denote the density function of the maximum likelihood estimate $\hat{\tau}$, and $\phi_{k_h}(\tau|\hat{\tau})$ be the conditional density function of τ, given $\hat{\tau}$, for each subpopulation of examinees who share the same discrete item response k_h. We can write for the joint density function, $\xi_{k_h}(\tau,\hat{\tau})$, of τ and $\hat{\tau}$

$$\xi_{k_h}(\tau,\hat{\tau}) = \phi_{k_h}(\tau|\hat{\tau}) g_{k_h}(\hat{\tau}). \qquad (7.1)$$

This estimated joint density function can be obtained by using one of the three approximations to the conditional density function of τ, given $\hat{\tau}$, and the estimated density function of τ, which were introduced and discussed in section 6. From the resultant estimated joint density functions for the separate item response subpopulations and the frequencies of examinees for the corresponding item response subgroups, we can write for the estimated operating characteristic

$$\tilde{P}_{k_h}[\theta(\tau)] = N_{k_h} \int_{-\infty}^{\infty} \tilde{\xi}_{k_h}(\tau,\hat{\tau})d\hat{\tau} \left[\sum_j N_j \int_{-\infty}^{\infty} \tilde{\xi}_j(\tau,\hat{\tau})d\hat{\tau} \right]^{-1}. \quad (7.2)$$

Figure 10.3 illustrates the results obtained by using the Bivariate P.D.F. Approach which is combined with the Normal Approach Method, with the same set of simulated data that was introduced in section 5. The unknown test item illustrated here is, again, item 6, whose item parameters are shown in Table 10.3. In these three cases, three different degrees, that is, degrees 3, 4, and 5, respectively, were used for the polynomials which were obtained using the method of moments, to provide us with the estimated density function, $\tilde{g}_{k_h}(\hat{\tau})$, of each discrete item response k_h. In the same figure are the frequency ratios of the item response subgroup k_h to the total frequency for each small subinterval of θ, whose common width is .25.

We can see in this example that the result of Degree 3 Case does not fit the theoretical item characteristic function as well as those of Degree 4 and 5 Cases, although it is still fairly close to the theoretical curve. This is not a general

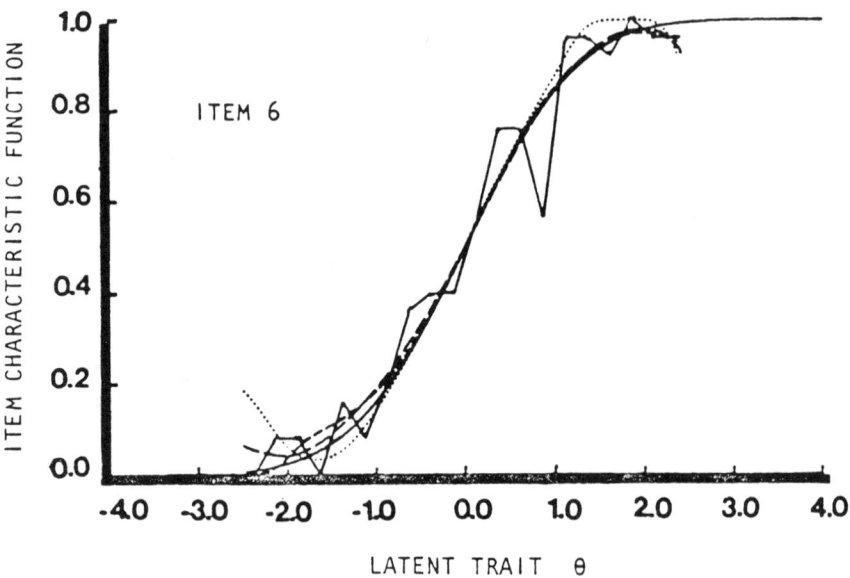

FIG. 10.3 Estimated item characteristic functions of item 6 for Degree 3 (dotted curve), Degree 4 (short, dashed curve) and Degree 5 (long, dashed curve) Cases of the Bivariate P.D.F. Approach with the Normal Approach Method, which were obtained by using Test A as the Old Test, together with the theoretical item characteristic function (smooth solid curve) and the frequency ratios of latent trait θ (jagged solid curve).

10. ESTIMATING OPERATING CHARACTERISTICS

tendency, however, and those curves of Degree 3 Case fit just as closely to the corresponding theoretical item characteristic functions as those of Degree 4 and 5 Cases for most of the other nine unknown test items. In fact, for item 7, it provides us with the best fit among the three estimated item characteristic functions.

Comparison of these three resultant estimated item characteristic functions to the frequency ratios of θ of the subgroup of examinees who answered item 6 correctly for each subinterval, to the total subgroup, indicates that all three results are much closer to the theoretical item characteristic function than the frequency ratios, which are based upon the true positions of the 500 hypothetical examinees on the latent trait θ. This is the case with all the other nine unknown test items, which indicates the success of the present approach.

The Bivariate P.D.F. Approach is an orthodox approach in the sense that we estimate the joint distributions of the latent trait τ and its maximum likelihood estimate $\hat{\tau}$. If we have a large number of unknown test items, however, the computing time will be substantially large, since we must approximate the joint density function for *each* discrete item response to *each* unknown test item. The cost of the research will be relatively high, therefore, and researchers may wish to turn to a simplified approach, which is called the Conditional P.D.F. Approach.

8. CONDITIONAL P.D.F. APPROACH

This approach is further categorized into three procedures, the Simple Sum Procedure (Samejima, 1978a), the Weighted Sum Procedure (Samejima, 1978d), and the Proportioned Sum Procedure (Samejima, 1978e). Let $\hat{\tau}_s$ be the maximum likelihood estimate of the latent trait τ assigned to the examinee denoted s, and $w(\hat{\tau}_s)$ denote an appropriately chosen weight for $\hat{\tau}_s$. In the Weighted Sum Procedure, the estimated operating characteristic of the discrete item response k_h to the unknown test item h is given by

$$\tilde{P}_{k_h}[\theta(\tau)] = \sum_{s \in k_h} w(\hat{\tau}_s) \tilde{\phi}(\tau|\hat{\tau}_s) \left[\sum_{s=1}^{N} w(\hat{\tau}_s) \tilde{\phi}(\tau|\hat{\tau}_s) \right]^{-1}. \quad (8.1)$$

where $\tilde{\phi}(\tau|\hat{\tau}_s)$ is the estimated conditional density function of τ, given $\hat{\tau} = \hat{\tau}_s$, which was discussed in section 6.

In a special case where $w(\hat{\tau}_s) = 1$ for all $\hat{\tau}_s$'s, (8.1) can be reduced to

$$\tilde{P}_{k_h}[\theta(\tau)] = \sum_{s \in k_h} \tilde{\phi}(\tau|\hat{\tau}_s) \left[\sum_{s=1}^{N} \tilde{\phi}(\tau|\hat{\tau}_s) \right]^{-1}. \quad (8.2)$$

The procedure which adopts (8.2) instead of (8.1) is called Simple Sum Procedure.

Let $p(s \epsilon k_h)$ be the probability with which the examinee s belongs to the item response subgroup k_h. This can be estimated by the proportion of examinees who belong to a specified discrete item response k_h. In the Proportioned Sum Procedure, the estimated operating characteristic of the discrete item response k_h to the unknown test item h is given by

$$\tilde{P}_{k_h}[\theta(\tau)] = \sum_{s \epsilon k_h} \tilde{p}(s \epsilon k_h) \tilde{\phi}(\tau | \hat{\tau}_s) \left[\sum_{s=1}^{N} \tilde{\phi}(\tau | \hat{\tau}_s) \right]^{-1} \tag{8.3}$$

where $\tilde{p}(s \epsilon k_h)$ is the proportion thus obtained as the estimate of the probability $p(s \epsilon k_h)$.

Figures 10.4 through 10.6 illustrate three examples obtained by the Simple Sum Procedure of the Conditional P.D.F. Approach, which is combined with the Normal Approach Method (section 6). The simulated data used in these examples are the same as those introduced in sections 5 and 7. These results are for Degree 4 Case, and similar results were also obtained for Degree 3 Case. We can see that, again, the estimated item characteristic function is fairly close to the theoretical item characteristic function, and much more so in comparison to the corresponding frequency ratios, for each of the three unknown test items.

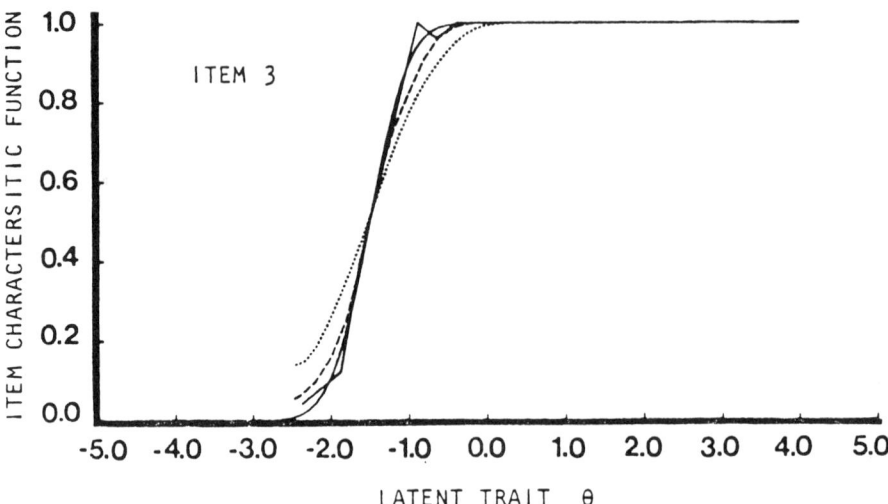

FIG. 10.4 Estimated item characteristic functions of item 3 obtained by the Simple Sum Procedure of the Conditional P.D.F. Approach with the Normal Approach Method, Degree 4 Case, using Test A (dashed curve) and its subtest of 11 test items (dotted curve) as the Old Test, respectively, in comparison with the theoretical item characteristic function (smooth solid curve) and the frequency ratios of latent trait θ (jagged solid curve).

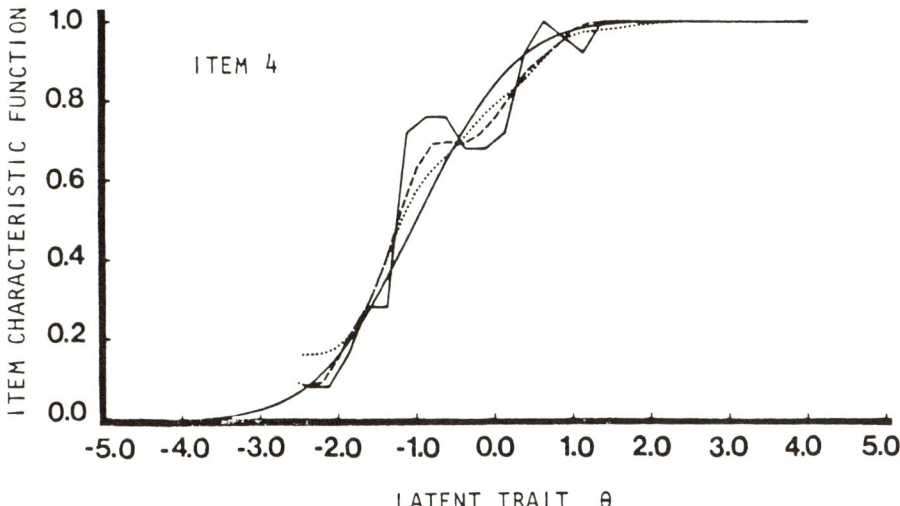

FIG. 10.5 Estimated item characteristic functions of item 4 obtained by the Simple Sum Procedure of the Conditional P.D.F. Approach with the Normal Approach Method, Degree 4 Case, using Test A (dashed curve) and its subtest of 11 test items (dotted curve) as the Old Test, respectively, in comparison with the theoretical item characteristic function (smooth solid curve) and the frequency ratios of latent trait θ (jagged solid curve).

In each of the three figures, also presented is the resultant estimated item characteristic function of the Degree 4 Case obtained by using a subtest of our original Old Test as the Old Test. The subtest consists of 11 items of the original Old Test. Specifically, out of the 35 items every third item was chosen, starting with the third and ending with the 33rd item (Samejima & Changas, 1981). Note that, in this second situation, the original latent trait θ was transformed to τ, since the amount of test information function is not constant for the interval of θ, in which all the 500 hypothetical examinees are located. The resultant estimated item characteristic functions for the three unknown test items are fairly close to the corresponding theoretical item characteristic functions. For item 4, the fit is even better than the one obtained upon the original Old Test, although it is slightly worse for item 3 and approximately the same for item 5. For each of the other seven unknown test items, the two sets of results turned out to be just as close to each other. The fact that we can obtain a reasonably good result by using only 11 items in our Old Test indicates the robustness of the procedure.

Similar studies have been made (Samejima, 1980b, 1981) using a subtest of the original Old Test as the Old Test, and for any subtest whose test items number between 11 and 25 the results turned out to be just as good as those obtained upon the original Old Test.

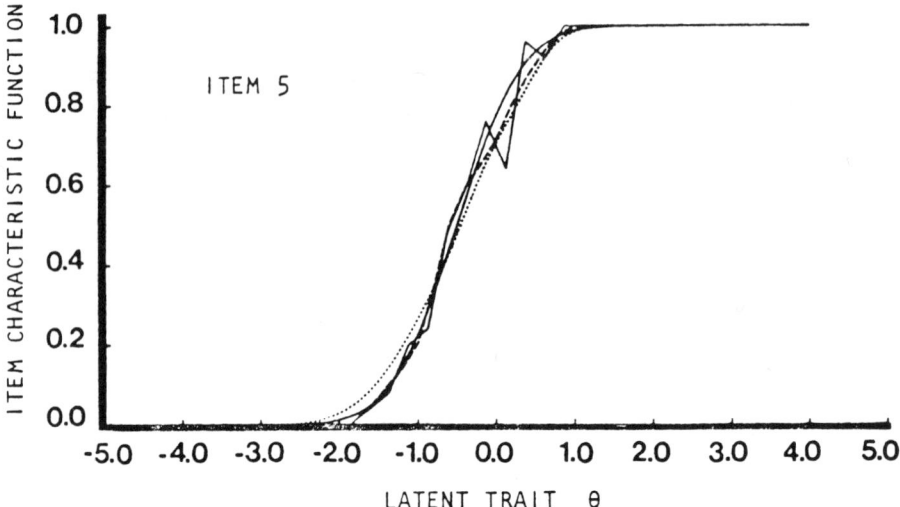

FIG. 10.6 Estimated item characteristic functions of item 5 obtained by the Simple Sum Procedure of the Conditional P.D.F. Approach with the Normal Approach Method, Degree 4 Case, using Test A (dashed curve) and its subtest of 11 test items (dotted curve) as the Old Test, respectively, in comparison with the theoretical item characteristic function (smooth solid curve) and the frequency ratios of latent trait θ (jagged solid curve).

9. DISCUSSION AND CONCLUSIONS

Several methods and approaches for estimating the operating characteristics of discrete item responses without assuming any mathematical form have been introduced and discussed. They have been tested with simulated data consisting of 500 hypothetical examinees, whose latent trait distributes uniformly in the interval of θ, (−2.5, 2.5), and with 10 binary test items whose item characteristic functions are to be estimated. There are indications that these methods are promising and have certain degrees of robustness, both with respect to the numbers of items and the amount of test information of the Old Test and to the polynomial approximation to the density function, $g(\hat{\tau})$, of the maximum likelihood estimate $\hat{\tau}$.

We notice that the same methods and approaches for estimating the operating characteristics of the discrete item responses of unknown test items can also be used for model validation for items of our Old Test. If the adopted model, or models, is appropriate, then the estimated operating characteristics of the discrete item responses of each of the Old Test should be close to those which are assumed by the model. This comparison can be performed by deleting a test item and using the remaining $(n-1)$ test items as the Old Test, and estimating the operating characteristics of the discrete item responses of the deleted test item.

There is no straightforward answer to the question of which method, or combination of a method and an approach, is the best one. It depends on the specific situation and the nature of the data. Further studies are necessary to find out and clarify in detail which method, or combination of a method and an approach, is most suitable for which specific situation and nature of the data. The author hopes that other researchers will use these methods and approaches in various different situations and further this research.

ACKNOWLEDGMENT

Research is partly supported by the Office of Naval Research under Contract N00014-77-C-0360, NR. 150-402.

REFERENCES

Birnbaum, A. Some latent trait models and their use in inferring an examinee's ability. In F. M. Lord & M. R. Novick, *Statistical theories of mental test scores*. Reading, Mass.: Addison-Wesley, 1968.

Bock, R. D. Estimating item parameters and latent ability when responses are scored in two or more nominal categories. *Psychometrika*, 1972, *37*, 29-51.

Elderton, W. P., & Johnson, N. L. *Systems of frequency curves*. Cambridge: Cambridge University Press, 1969.

Kendall, M. G., & Stuart, A. *The advanced theory of statistics* (Vol. 2). New York: Hafner, 1961.

Levine, M. *Appropriateness measurement and the formula-score method: overview, intercorrelations and interpretations*. Paper presented at the ONR Conference on Model-Based Psychological Measurement, Iowa City, Iowa, 1980.

Lord, F. M. A theory of test scores. *Psychometric Monograph*, No. 7, 1952.

Lord, F. M. Estimating true-score distributions in psychological testing (an empirical Bayes estimation problem). *Psychometrika*, 1969, *34*, 259-299.

Lord, F. M. Item characteristic curves estimated without knowledge of their mathematical form—a confrontation of Birnbaum's logistic model. *Psychometrika*, 1970, *35*, 43-50.

Lord, F. M., & Novick, M. R. *Statistical theories of mental test scores*. Reading, Mass.: Addison-Wesley, 1968.

Rasch, G. *Probabilistic models for some intelligence and attainment tests*. Copenhagen: Nielson & Lydiche, 1960.

Samejima, F. Estimation of ability using a response pattern of graded scores. *Psychometrika Monograph*, No. 17, 1969.

Samejima, F. A general model for free-response data. *Psychometrika Monograph*, No. 18, 1972.

Samejima, F. Homogeneous case of the continuous response level. *Psychometrika*, 1973, *38*, 203-219. (a)

Samejima, F. A comment on Birnbaum's three-parameter logistic model in the latent trait theory. *Psychometrika*, 1973, *38*, 221-233. (b)

Samejima, F. Normal ogive model on the continuous response level in the multidimensional latent space. *Psychometrika*, 1974, *39*, 111-121. (a)

Samejima, F. *Normal ogive model on the graded response level in the multidimensional latent space*. Paper presented at the Psychometric Society spring meeting, Stanford University, Stanford, California, 1974. (b)

Samejima, F. Graded response model of the latent trait theory and tailored testing. *Proceedings of the Conference on Computerized Adaptive Testing,* U.S. Civil Service Commission, 1975.

Samejima, F. Effects of individual optimization in setting the boundaries of dichotomous items on the accuracy of estimation. *Applied Psychological Measurement,* 1977, *1,* 77–94. (a)

Samejima, F. A use of the information function in tailored testing. *Applied Psychological Measurement,* 1977, *1,* 233–247. (b)

Samejima, F. A method of estimating item characteristic functions using the maximum likelihood estimate of ability. *Psychometrika, 42,* 1977, 163–191. (c)

Samejima, F. Weakly parallel tests in latent trait theory with some criticisms on classical test theory. *Psychometrika,* 1977, *42,* 193–198. (d)

Samejima, F. *Estimation of the operating characteristics of item response categories I; Introduction to the Two-Parameter Beta Method*. ONR Research Report 77-1, 1977. (e)

Samejima, F. *Estimation of the operating characteristics of item response categories II: Further development of the Two-Parameter Beta Method*. ONR Research Report 78-1, 1978. (a)

Samejima, F. *Estimation of the operating characteristics of item response categories III: The Normal Approach Method and the Pearson System Method*. ONR Research Report 78-2, 1978. (b)

Samejima, F. *Estimation of the operating characteristics of item response categories IV: Comparison of the different methods*. ONR Research Report 78-3 1978. (c)

Samejima, F. *Estimation of the operating characteristics of item response categories V: Weighted Sum Procedure in the Conditional P.D.F. Approach*. ONR Research Report 78-4, 1978. (d)

Samejima, F. *Estimation of the operating characteristics of item response categories VI: Proportioned Sum Procedure in the Conditional P.D.F. Approach*. ONR Research Report 78-5, 1978. (e)

Samejima, F. *Estimation of the operating characteristics of item response categories VII: Bivariate P.D.F. Approach with Normal Approach Method*. ONR Research Report 78-6, 1978. (f)

Samejima, F. *Constant Information Model: A new, promising item characteristic function*. ONR Research Report 79-1, 1979. (a)

Samejima, F. *A new family of models for the multiple-choice item*. ONR Research Report 79-4, 1979. (b)

Samejima, F. *Estimation of the operating characteristics when the test information of the Old Test is not constant I: Rationale*. ONR Research Report 80-2, 1980. (a)

Samejima, F. Latent trait theory and its applications. In Krishnaiah, P. R. (Ed.), *Multivariate Analysis V*. Amsterdam, Netherlands: North-Holland, 1980. (b) Also paper presented at *the Fifth International Symposium on Multivariate Analysis,* University of Pittsburgh, Pittsburgh, Pennsylvania, 1978. (g)

Samejima, F. *Estimation of the operating characteristics when the test information of the Old Test is not constant II: Simple Sum Procedure of the Conditional P.D.F. Approach/Normal Approach Method using three subtests of the Old Test*. ONR Research Report 80-4, 1980. (b)

Samejima, F. *Estimation of the operating characteristics when the test information of the Old Test is not constant II: Simple Sum Procedure of the Conditional P.D.F. Approach/Normal Approach Method using three subtests of the Old Test. No. 2*. ONR Research Report 81-2, 1981.

Samejima, F., & Changas, P. S. *How small the number of the test items can be for the basis of estimating the operating characteristics of the discrete responses to unknown test items*. ONR Research Report 81-3, 1981.

Samejima, F., & Livingston, P. S. *Method of moments as the least squares solution for fitting a polynomial*. ONR Research Report 79-2, 1979.

Tucker, L. R. *Academic ability test*. (ETS RM 51–17). Princeton, New Jersey: Educational Testing Service, 1951.

FACTOR ANALYSIS

Since factor analytic models and item characteristic curve models are both special cases of general latent trait theory, there is a natural affinity between the work of modern factor analytic theorists and the work of Fred Lord. Testimony to this affinity appears in the following chapters.

Karl Jöreskog formulates the factor analytic model as an errors-in-variables model, deriving two simple estimators of factor loadings based on instrumental variable techniques. These new estimators yield slightly larger standard errors than the usual unweighted least squares and maximum likelihood procedures, but their ease of rapid computation without iteration supports their practical use for most applied purposes.

Roderick McDonald points out that since strictly linear and alternative nonlinear common factor models can give rise to the same covariance structure, it follows that linear and non linear factor models cannot be distinguished on the basis of their covariance structure alone. Conventional applications of linear factor analysis may therefore lead to misinterpretations of data, as witness the longstanding psychometric problem of "difficulty factors." To clarify this situation, McDonald distinguishes among three classes of models: "strictly linear" models where the regressions are linear both in the coefficients describing the observed variables and in the latent trait scores characterizing examinees;

"wide-sense" linear models where the regressions are linear functions of the factor coefficients but nonlinear functions of the latent trait scores; and, "strictly nonlinear" models where the regressions are nonlinear functions of both the factor coefficients and the latent traits. Normal ogive and logistic item characteristic curve models are examples of the latter strictly nonlinear case. McDonald demonstrates, however, that such strictly nonlinear models can be closely approximated by a wide-sense linear model with a finite number of components.

Ledyard Tucker also emphasizes that the problem of difficulty factors or Guttman-type scalability components in linear factor analysis of binary item intercorrelations very likely stems from curvilinear relations of the item responses to the underlying latent trait. As an alternative approach to resolving this problem, he attempts to fit a multiple common factor model with unique factors directly to binary response data.

In the last chapter of this section, **Peter Bentler** and **Arthur Woodward** review the major development in reliability theory in terms of factor analytic formulations. They highlight the concept of "greatest lower bound to reliability," which was originally defined by superimposing the factor analytic model on a traditional true- plus error-score model. Noting the close connection between this greatest lower bound and minimum trace factor analysis, they then review basic theory and computational methods for minimum trace approaches.

11 Factor Analysis as an Errors-in-Variables Model

Karl G. Jöreskog
University of Uppsala
Department of Statistics

1. INTRODUCTION AND SUMMARY

The estimation problem in factor analysis has been considered by many researchers during the last 50 years. Before the mid-sixties the predominant method for estimating factor loadings was based on some form of iterative principal components of the correlation matrix with communalities in the diagonal, which we now understand as unweighted least squares (ULS). After the mid-sixties, the maximum likelihood (ML) method due to Lawley (1940) has attracted considerable attention. For both ULS and ML several alternative algorithms exist.

The first successful real application of the maximum likelihood method to a large set of variables was by Lord (1956). This was long before efficient computational algorithms for ML had been developed, see, for example, Jöreskog (1967) or Jennrich and Robinson (1969). Nowadays the ML method is generally regarded as the preferred method, being most efficient in large samples.

In this chapter we draw on work by Madansky (1964) and Hägglund (1982) and formulate the factor analysis model as an errors-in-variables model. This formulation of the model leads to two simple consistent estimators of factor loadings which may be computed very rapidly without iteration. These estimators, which are both based on instrumental variables techniques, are called the instrumental variables (IV) estimator and the two-stage least squares (TSLS) estimator. They are presented in sections 3 and 4 of the chapter, respectively. Formulas for their asymptotic covariance matrices are also given. The asymptotic covariance matrices of the ULS and ML estimators are given in section 5. A comparison of the asymptotic standard errors of the four estimators is given in section 6. This is based on one set of artificial data and one set of real data. The results indicate that ULS and ML are more efficient in the sense of having smaller asymptotic standard errors. But the differences in standard errors between methods are in general small and can be ignored for most practical purposes. Hence the IV and TSLS estimators may be preferred because they are easy to compute. Of these two, the TSLS estimator is preferred since it is scale free.

2. THE FACTOR ANALYSIS MODEL AS AN ERRORS-IN-VARIABLES MODEL

The factor analysis model is usually defined by the equation

$$\mathbf{x} = \mathbf{\Lambda}\boldsymbol{\xi} + \boldsymbol{\delta} \tag{1}$$

where $\mathbf{x}(p \times 1)$ is a vector of observed variates, $\boldsymbol{\xi}(k \times 1)$ is a vector of unobserved variates, the common factors, $\mathbf{\Lambda}(p \times k)$ is a matrix of factor loadings assumed to be of rank $k < p$ and $\boldsymbol{\delta}(p \times 1)$ is a vector of residual variates, the unique parts of $\mathbf{x}$. For convenience, and without loss of generality, the means of all variates are taken to be zero. The variates of $\boldsymbol{\delta}$ are assumed to be uncorrelated with $\boldsymbol{\xi}$ and uncorrelated among themselves. It follows that the covariance matrix $\mathbf{\Sigma} = E(\mathbf{xx'})$ of $\mathbf{x}$ has the form

$$\mathbf{\Sigma} = \mathbf{\Lambda}\mathbf{\Phi}\mathbf{\Lambda}' + \mathbf{\Theta} \tag{2}$$

where $\mathbf{\Phi} = E(\boldsymbol{\xi}\boldsymbol{\xi}')$ is the covariance matrix of $\boldsymbol{\xi}$ and $\mathbf{\Theta} = E(\boldsymbol{\delta}\boldsymbol{\delta}')$ is the diagonal matrix whose diagonal elements are the residual variances.

It is well known that, when $k > 1$, the factors $\boldsymbol{\xi}$ in (1) are only determined up to an arbitrary nonsingular transformation (see, e.g., Jöreskog, 1969). Traditional factor analysis is usually performed in two steps: First one estimates an arbitrary matrix $\mathbf{\Lambda}$ and then this is transformed according to external criteria (simple structure) to facilitate interpretation of the data. In this chapter we assume that the model is identified by a priori specified elements in $\mathbf{\Lambda}$, usually zeros and ones. More precisely, it is assumed that $\mathbf{\Lambda}$ contains k rows with elements which are all known and that these rows form a matrix of rank k. Without loss of generality, we may assume that this matrix is an identity matrix and that the variates in $\mathbf{x}$ have been ordered so that this corresponds to the first k rows of $\mathbf{\Lambda}$ (see, e.g., Madansky, 1964). Partitioning $\mathbf{x}$ into two parts $\mathbf{x}_1(k \times 1)$ and $\mathbf{x}_2(q \times 1)$, where $q = p - k$, and $\boldsymbol{\delta}$ similarly into $\boldsymbol{\delta}_1(k \times 1)$ and $\boldsymbol{\delta}_2(q \times 1)$, (1) can be written

$$\mathbf{x}_1 = \boldsymbol{\xi} + \boldsymbol{\delta}_1, \tag{3}$$

$$\mathbf{x}_2 = \mathbf{\Lambda}_2\boldsymbol{\xi} + \boldsymbol{\delta}_2, \tag{4}$$

where $\mathbf{\Lambda}_2(q \times k)$ consists of the last $p - k$ rows of $\mathbf{\Lambda}$. The matrix $\mathbf{\Lambda}_2$ may, but need not, contain a priori specified elements. Following Jöreskog (1969), we

11. FACTOR ANALYSIS AS AN ERROR IN VARIABLES MODEL

shall say that the model is *unrestricted* when Λ_2 is entirely unspecified and that the model is *restricted* when Λ_2 contains a priori specified elements.

Solving (3) for ξ and substituting into (4) gives

$$x_2 - \delta_2 = \Lambda_2(x_1 - \delta_1), \tag{5}$$

which shows that there is an exact linear relationship between the error-free variables $x_2 - \delta_2$ and $x_1 - \delta_1$. Equation (5) can also be written

$$x_2 = \Lambda_2 \xi + \delta_2 \tag{6}$$

or

$$x_2 = \Lambda_2 x_2 + u \tag{7}$$

where $u = \delta_2 - \Lambda_2 \delta_1$. Equation (6) may be interpreted as the multivariate regression of x_2 on ξ. However, the explanatory variables are only observed by means of x_1 which contain measurement errors δ_1, hence the name errors-in-variables model. Equation (7), on the other hand, is not the regression of x_2 on x_1, because u is generally correlated with x_1, since δ_1 is correlated with x_1.

In this chapter we consider the estimation of Λ_2 by four different methods:

1. The instrumental variables method (IV)
2. The two-stage least squares method (TSLS)
3. The unweighted least squares method (ULS)
4. The maximum likelihood method (ML)

The relative advantages and disadvantages of these methods from computational and statistical points of view are discussed.

In terms of the parameters of the errors-in-variables model, the covariance matrix Σ, partitioned according to x_1 and x_2, is

$$\Sigma = \begin{pmatrix} \Sigma_{11} & \Sigma_{12} \\ \Sigma_{21} & \Sigma_{22} \end{pmatrix} = \begin{pmatrix} \Phi + \Theta_1 & \Phi \Lambda_2' \\ \Lambda_2 \Phi & \Lambda_2 \Phi \Lambda_2' + \Theta_2 \end{pmatrix} \tag{8}$$

It should be noted that since $\Sigma_{12} = \Phi \Lambda_2'$, then

$$\Sigma_{22} = \Lambda_2 \Sigma_{12} + \Theta_2, \tag{9}$$

an equation which was used by Hägglund and Jöreskog (1980) to derive compact expressions for the IV and TSLS estimators discussed in this chapter.

It should be emphasized that if Λ_2 is unconstrained, then the errors-in-variables model is just another parametrization of the traditional factor analysis model in which $\Phi = I$ and Λ is unconstrained. To obtain such a factor solution from an errors-in-variables model, let $\Phi = TT'$ be an arbitrary complete factorization of Φ and take $\Lambda' = (T', T\Lambda_2')$. Then $\Sigma = \Lambda\Lambda' + \Theta$ and this Λ may be rotated according to any external criteria.

3. THE INSTRUMENTAL VARIABLES ESTIMATOR

Hägglund (1982) showed that a very simple consistent estimate of Λ_2 may be obtained by instrumental variables methods. Let

$$x_i = \lambda_i' \mathbf{x}_1 + u_i, \tag{10}$$

where λ_i' is the i:th row of Λ_2, be the i:th equation in (7) and let $\mathbf{x}_{(i)}(q - 1 \times 1)$ be a vector of the remaining variables in $\mathbf{x}_2$. Then u_i is uncorrelated with $\mathbf{x}_{(i)}$ so that $\mathbf{x}_{(i)}$ may be used as instrumental variables for estimating (9). The instrumental variables estimator given by Hägglund (1982) is

$$\hat{\lambda}_i = (\mathbf{S}_{(i)1}' \mathbf{S}_{(i)1})^{-1} \mathbf{S}_{(i)1}' \mathbf{s}_{(i)i}, \tag{11}$$

where

$$\mathbf{S}_{(i)1} = \frac{1}{n} \sum_{\alpha=1}^{N} (\mathbf{x}_{(i)\alpha} - \bar{\mathbf{x}}_{(i)})(\mathbf{x}_{1\alpha} - \bar{\mathbf{x}}_1)'$$

and

$$\mathbf{s}_{(i)i} = \frac{1}{n} \sum_{\alpha=1}^{N} (\mathbf{x}_{(i)\alpha} - \bar{\mathbf{x}}_{(i)})(x_{i\alpha} - \bar{x}_i)'$$

where N is the sample size, $n = N - 1$ and quantities with bars on top are sample means. It may easily be verified that if plim $\mathbf{S} = \mathbf{\Sigma}$, then $\hat{\lambda}_i$ is a consistent estimator of λ_i. If λ_i contains fixed zero elements one need only omit those variables in $\mathbf{S}_{(i)1}$ which are excluded from $\mathbf{x}_1$ in (10), so the same general formula may be used to obtain estimates even when Λ_2 contains fixed zero elements.

Hägglund (1982) suggested that the whole matrix Λ_2 may be estimated by repeated application of (11) for $i = 1, 2, \ldots, q$. However, when Λ_2 is unconstrained, this requires the repeated inversion of the matrix $\mathbf{S}_{(i)1}' \mathbf{S}_{(i)1}$, which is somewhat uneconomical since only one row of $\mathbf{S}_{(i)1}$ is changed each time. In another paper (Hägglund and Jöreskog, 1980), we have shown that the repeated formation and inversion of $\mathbf{S}_{(i)1}' \mathbf{S}_{(i)1}$ can be avoided and that the whole matrix $\hat{\Lambda}_2$ can be computed in a single step.

Although very simple to compute, this estimator has the disadvantage that it is not scale free. If $\mathbf{D}_1(k \times k)$ and $\mathbf{D}_2(q \times q)$ are diagonal matrices of positive scale factors and $\mathbf{x}_1$ is replaced by $\mathbf{D}_1 \mathbf{x}_1$ and $\mathbf{x}_2$ is replaced by $\mathbf{D}_2 \mathbf{x}_2$, the property of scalefreeness requires that $\hat{\Lambda}_2$ is changed to $\mathbf{D}_2 \hat{\Lambda}_2 \mathbf{D}_1^{-1}$. However, as is easily verified, this is not the case.

An advantage of the IV estimator (11) is that asymptotic standard errors of the estimated factor loadings may be obtained easily using quantities already included in (11). Hägglund demonstrates that the asymptotic covariance matrix of $\hat{\lambda}_i$ is given by

$$n \, \text{Cov}(\hat{\boldsymbol{\lambda}}_i) = \sigma_{ii}(\boldsymbol{\Sigma}'_{(i)1}\boldsymbol{\Sigma}_{(i)1})^{-1}(\boldsymbol{\Sigma}'_{(i)1}\boldsymbol{\Sigma}_{(i)(i)}\boldsymbol{\Sigma}_{(i)1})(\boldsymbol{\Sigma}'_{(i)1}\boldsymbol{\Sigma}_{(i)1})^{-1}, \qquad (12)$$

where $\sigma_{ii} = E(u_i^2)$, $\boldsymbol{\Sigma}_{(i)1} = E(\mathbf{x}_{(i)}\mathbf{x}'_1)$ and $\boldsymbol{\Sigma}_{(i)(i)} = E(\mathbf{x}_{(i)}\mathbf{x}'_{(i)})$. A consistent estimate of $\text{Cov}(\hat{\boldsymbol{\lambda}}_i)$ may be obtained by substituting into (12) sample quantities $\mathbf{S}$ for $\boldsymbol{\Sigma}$ and a consistent estimate of σ_{ii} for σ_{ii}. The condition under which (12) is valid is given in section 5.

4. THE TWO-STAGE LEAST SQUARES ESTIMATOR

Hägglund (1982) also derived another consistent estimator of $\boldsymbol{\Lambda}_2$. Returning to the problem of estimating $\boldsymbol{\lambda}_i$ in (9), this estimator is

$$\hat{\boldsymbol{\lambda}}_i = (\mathbf{S}'_{(i)1}\mathbf{S}^{-1}_{(i)(i)}\mathbf{S}_{(i)1})^{-1}\mathbf{S}'_{(i)1}\mathbf{S}^{-1}_{(i)(i)}\mathbf{s}_{(i)i} \qquad (13)$$

where $\mathbf{S}_{(i)1}$ and $\mathbf{s}_{(i)i}$ are as before and

$$\mathbf{S}_{(i)(i)} = \frac{1}{n}\sum_{\alpha=1}^{N}(\mathbf{x}_{(i)\alpha} - \bar{\mathbf{x}}_{(i)})(\mathbf{x}_{(i)\alpha} - \bar{\mathbf{x}}_{(i)})'.$$

Hägglund suggested estimating $\boldsymbol{\Lambda}_2$ by repeated application of (13) for $i = 1, 2, \ldots, q$, but also in this case a more compact formulation exists, see Hägglund and Jöreskog (1980). The estimator (13) is called the TSLS estimator since it may be obtained from (10) by first replacing $\mathbf{x}_1$ by its regression on $\mathbf{x}_{(i)}$ and then estimating $\boldsymbol{\lambda}_i$ by ordinary least squares. Contrary to the IV estimator, the TSLS estimator is scale free as may easily be verified.

The asymptotic covariance matrix of $\boldsymbol{\lambda}_i$ in (13) is given by

$$n \, \text{Cov}(\boldsymbol{\lambda}_i) = \sigma_{ii}(\boldsymbol{\Sigma}'_{(i)1}\boldsymbol{\Sigma}^{-1}_{(i)(i)}\boldsymbol{\Sigma}_{(i)1})^{-1} \qquad (14)$$

which may be used to compute large-sample approximate standard errors of the factor loadings in the same way as for the IV-estimator. A theorem of Rao (1967, p. 358) may be used to demonstrate that the difference matrix (12) minus (14) is positive semidefinite. A consequence of this is that TSLS estimates are superior to IV estimates in the sense that standard errors of TSLS estimates are not larger than those of the corresponding IV estimates. This is examined further in section 6.

5. LEAST SQUARES AND MAXIMUM LIKELIHOOD ESTIMATORS

The IV estimator (11) and the TSLS estimator (13) appear to be the only existing noniterative consistent estimators of factor loadings. These estimators are limited information estimators in the sense that they do not use all the information provided by the full sample covariance matrix **S** of **x** and that they do not minimize any fitting function of **S** and **Σ**. Also, obviously, these methods do not provide estimators of the other parameters **Φ** and **Θ** of the model, although simple consistent estimators of **Φ** and **Θ** can easily be derived conditional on **Λ** being given.

Traditional statistical methods for factor analysis estimation are based on fitting functions which minimize some "distance" between **S** and **Σ**. The most common fitting functions are the unweighted least squares (ULS) which minimize

$$Q = tr(\mathbf{S} - \mathbf{\Sigma})^2 \tag{15}$$

and the maximum likelihood method (ML) which minimizes

$$F = tr(\mathbf{\Sigma}^{-1}\mathbf{S}) - log|\mathbf{\Sigma}^{-1}\mathbf{S}| \tag{16}$$

Let $\mathbf{\Theta}(t \times 1)$ be a vector of all free parameters in **Λ**, **Φ** and **Θ** to be estimated. Then **Σ** is a function $\mathbf{\Sigma}(\mathbf{\Theta})$ and Q and F are to be minimized with respect to **Θ**. Both functions are minimized numerically using an iterative algorithm. For practical purposes the computer program LISREL V of Jöreskog and Sörbom (1981) may be used. This program also gives asymptotic standard errors for ML estimators but does not currently give standard errors for ULS estimators. Asymptotic standard errors for ULS estimators may be obtained from results first derived by Browne (1974). Let $\dot{\mathbf{\Theta}}_{ML}$ and $\dot{\mathbf{\Theta}}_{ULS}$ be the ML and ULS estimator respectively. Then Browne's general result (Browne 1974, Proposition 2) may be used to obtain the formulas

$$nCov(\dot{\mathbf{\Theta}}_{ML}) = 2[\mathbf{\Delta}'(\mathbf{\Sigma}^{-1} \otimes \mathbf{\Sigma}^{-1})\mathbf{\Delta}]^{-1} \tag{17}$$

$$nCov(\dot{\mathbf{\Theta}}_{ULS}) = 2(\mathbf{\Delta}'\mathbf{\Delta})^{-1}\mathbf{\Delta}'(\mathbf{\Sigma} \otimes \mathbf{\Sigma})\mathbf{\Delta}(\mathbf{\Delta}'\mathbf{\Delta})^{-1} \tag{18}$$

where $\otimes$ denotes a Kronecker product and $\mathbf{\Delta}(p^2 \times t)$ is the matrix $\partial vec\mathbf{\Sigma}/\partial\mathbf{\Theta}$. The theorem of Rao (1967, p. 358) may be used again to show that the difference matrix (18) minus (17) is positive semidefinite. This means that ML estimates are superior to ULS estimates in the sense that standard errors of ML estimators are never larger than those of ULS estimators. This is examined further in the next section.

The condition under which (17) and (18) are valid have been stated by Browne (1974, p. 2) as follows. The distribution of **S**, as n increases indefinitely, is to be multivariate normal with mean **Σ** and covariances given by

$$nCov(s_{gh}, s_{ij}) = \sigma_{gi}\sigma_{hj} + \sigma_{gj}\sigma_{hi} \tag{19}$$

This requires only that all fourth-order cumulants of the distribution of **x** are zero. The same condition was used by Hägglund to derive the formulas (12) and (14). Thus the four formulas (12), (14), (17), and (18) are all valid under the same condition.

6. COMPARISON OF ASYMPTOTIC STANDARD ERRORS

In this section the four different estimators are compared with respect to their asymptotic standard errors. The comparisons are based on one set of artificial data and one set of real data.

The artificial data was constructed earlier for the purpose of explicating the factor analysis model (see Jöreskog, 1979) but may be used ideally for testing computer programs and other comparisons such as this one. The artificial data consists of six variates constructed to have the following oblique simple structure solution.

$$\Lambda = \begin{bmatrix} .9 & 0 \\ .8 & 0 \\ 0 & .7 \\ 0 & .6 \\ 0 & .5 \\ .3 & 0 \end{bmatrix} \quad \Phi = \begin{bmatrix} 1 & \\ .6 & 1 \end{bmatrix}$$

$$\Theta = \text{diag}(.19, .36, .51, .64, .75, .91)$$

To be consistent with the notation in section 1 we interchange variables 2 and 3 and scale the factors by scale factors .9 and .7, respectively. This gives

$$\Lambda = \begin{bmatrix} 1 & 0 \\ 0 & 1 \\ .889 & .000 \\ .000 & .857 \\ .000 & .714 \\ .333 & .000 \end{bmatrix} \quad \Phi = \begin{bmatrix} .810 & \\ .378 & .490 \end{bmatrix}$$

The matrix Σ according to (2) becomes

$$\Sigma = \begin{bmatrix} 1.000 & & & & & \\ .378 & 1.000 & & & & \\ .720 & .336 & 1.000 & & & \\ .324 & .420 & .288 & 1.000 & & \\ .270 & .350 & .240 & .300 & 1.000 & \\ .270 & .126 & .240 & .108 & .090 & 1.000 \end{bmatrix}$$

Any method for factor analysis that claims to provide consistent estimates must be able to analyze this Σ and reproduce exactly the elements of Λ, Φ and Θ. This holds for all four methods of this chapter.

We analyze both the unrestricted model Λ_u and the restricted model Λ_R:

$$\Lambda_u = \begin{bmatrix} 1 & 0 \\ 0 & 1 \\ x & x \\ x & x \\ x & x \\ x & x \end{bmatrix} \quad \Lambda_R = \begin{bmatrix} 1 & 0 \\ 0 & 1 \\ x & 0 \\ 0 & x \\ 0 & x \\ x & 0 \end{bmatrix}$$

where x stands for a free parameter to be estimated. The results for the asymptotic standard errors are shown in Table 11.1.

It has generally been assumed that the ML estimator is greatly superior to other estimators. However, Table 11.1 shows that the differences in standard errors are generally small. For example, in a sample of 400, say, the standard error of λ_{31} is $4.14/20 = .207$ for IV and $4.11/20 = .206$ for ML, a difference which is negligible for all practical purposes. A 95% prediction interval for λ_{31} is $.89 \pm .40$ in future samples of size 400. Although the differences between standard errors are small, there is a strict order among the different methods from left to right in Table 11.1. The largest difference between estimators is between TSLS and ULS, the differences between IV and TSLS and those between ULS and ML being generally somewhat smaller.

The striking feature of Table 11.1 is the large differences in standard errors for the same factor loadings in the unrestricted model compared with the restricted model. The standard errors for the restricted model are generally much smaller than those of the unrestricted model. Thus, adding zero restrictions in the

TABLE 11.1
Artificial Data

Parameter	Parameter Value	IV	TSLS	ULS	ML
Unrestricted Model					
λ_{31}	.89	4.14	4.14	4.11	4.11
λ_{32}	.00	3.71	3.70	3.51	3.50
λ_{41}	.00	2.66	2.62	2.42	2.40
λ_{42}	.86	4.41	4.40	4.33	4.33
λ_{51}	.00	2.38	2.35	2.12	2.10
λ_{52}	.71	3.64	3.62	3.54	3.53
λ_{61}	.33	2.12	2.12	1.98	1.98
λ_{62}	.00	3.02	3.01	2.54	2.53
Restricted Model					
λ_{31}	.89	1.65	1.64	1.49	1.47
λ_{42}	.86	2.32	2.30	2.22	2.16
λ_{52}	.71	2.13	2.11	2.05	1.98
λ_{61}	.33	1.37	1.32	1.26	1.20

Note: $\sqrt{n}$ times asymptotic standard error

TABLE 11.2
Nine Psychological Variables

Correlation Matrix (N = 73)

	1	2	3	4	5	6	7	8	9
1. Visual Perception	1.000								
2. Paragraph Comprehension	.401	1.000							
3. Addition	-.078	.215	1.000						
4. Cubes	.411	.223	-.042	1.000					
5. Lozenges	.479	.231	-.126	.463	1.000				
6. Sentence Completion	.370	.659	.293	.198	.272	1.000			
7. Word Meaning	.393	.688	.226	.244	.357	.649	1.000		
8. Counting Dots	.389	.221	.602	.169	.153	.279	.298	1.000	
9. Straight-curved Capitals	.411	.256	.446	.324	.307	.324	.294	.630	1.000

factor matrix can greatly increase precision in the remaining factor loadings to be estimated.

The second set of data consists of nine psychological variables, a subset of 26 tests collected by Holzinger and Swineford (1939). The variables and the correlations are given in Table 11.2. The correlations are based on a subsample of 73 eighth-grade school children, the exploration sample (see Lawley & Maxwell, 1971, p. 96). This correlation matrix is known to have a three-factor solution where the factors represent visual perception, verbal ability, and speed. Also this data is analyzed under an unrestricted and a restricted factor model with the following factor patterns

$$\Lambda_u = \begin{bmatrix} 1 & 0 & 0 \\ 0 & 1 & 0 \\ 0 & 0 & 1 \\ x & x & x \\ x & x & x \\ x & x & x \\ x & x & x \\ x & x & x \\ x & x & x \end{bmatrix} \quad \Lambda_R = \begin{bmatrix} 1 & 0 & 0 \\ 0 & 1 & 0 \\ 0 & 0 & 1 \\ x & 0 & 0 \\ x & 0 & 0 \\ 0 & x & 0 \\ 0 & x & 0 \\ 0 & 0 & x \\ x & 0 & x \end{bmatrix}$$

The unrestricted ML solution has a goodness-of-fit measure $\chi^2 = 5.59$ with 12 degrees of freedom. The restricted ML solution has a goodness-of-fit measure $\chi^2 = 25.84$ with 23 degrees of freedom. The estimates as well as the standard errors of the estimates are given in Table 11.3 for the unrestricted model and in Table 11.4 for the restricted model.

Inspecting first the parameter estimates in Table 11.3, it is seen that the differences between methods are fairly small. For the restricted model in Table 11.4, these differences are somewhat larger, probably reflecting the fact that the

TABLE 11.3
Nine Psychological Variables (N = 73)

	Unrestricted Model							
	Parameter estimates				$\sqrt{n}$ · standard error[a]			
Parameter	IV	TSLS	ULS	ML	IV	TSLS	ULS	ML
λ_{41}	1.00	.96	.99	.96	2.49	2.49	2.35	2.34
λ_{51}	1.11	1.10	1.11	1.09	2.83	2.81	2.54	2.50
λ_{61}	.13	.14	.10	.10	1.79	1.78	1.68	1.67
λ_{71}	.25	.29	.20	.21	1.72	1.71	1.63	1.62
λ_{81}	.72	.71	.78	.78	2.13	2.12	2.07	2.05
λ_{91}	.95	.94	.99	.96	2.38	2.37	2.28	2.26
λ_{42}	-.14	-.11	-.17	-.15	2.10	2.10	1.93	1.93
λ_{52}	.21	.17	-.09	-.09	2.12	2.12	1.95	1.93
λ_{62}	.84	.83	.84	.84	1.67	1.67	1.61	1.61
λ_{72}	.84	.82	.86	.85	1.65	1.65	1.60	1.59
λ_{82}	-.34	-.33	-.37	-.36	1.92	1.92	1.79	1.79
λ_{92}	-.29	-.28	-.35	-.34	2.09	2.08	1.90	1.89
λ_{43}	-.24	-.26	-.18	-.19	1.71	1.70	1.53	1.53
λ_{53}	-.42	-.44	-.34	-.34	1.89	1.87	1.60	1.58
λ_{63}	.09	.08	.12	.12	1.23	1.22	1.11	1.11
λ_{73}	-.01	-.01	.02	.03	1.20	1.19	1.08	1.08
λ_{83}	.93	.93	.90	.89	1.84	1.84	1.72	1.72
λ_{93}	.54	.54	.61	.61	1.65	1.65	1.53	1.53

[a] All standard errors computed at the ML-solution.

TABLE 11.4
Nine Psychological Variables (N = 73)

	Restricted Model							
	Parameter estimates				n · standard error[a]			
Parameter	IV	TSLS	ULS	ML	IV	TSLS	ULS	ML
λ_{41}	.70	.74	0.67	.82	1.82	1.72	1.71	1.70
λ_{51}	.79	.83	0.75	.92	1.88	1.79	1.78	1.77
λ_{91}	.71	.75	0.41	.42	1.87	1.85	1.47	1.40
λ_{62}	1.01	0.94	1.02	.96	1.30	1.17	1.17	1.17
λ_{72}	1.08	1.00	1.07	1.02	1.30	1.19	1.19	1.19
λ_{83}	1.14	.96	1.60	1.34	2.65	2.31	2.31	2.30
λ_{93}	.46	.49	.90	.87	1.80	1.79	1.73	1.66

[a] All standard errors computed at the ML-solution.

restricted model does not fit quite as well as the unrestricted model. In particular, the spread among the estimates is relatively large for parameters λ_{83} and λ_{93} in the restricted solution compared with the same parameters in the unrestricted solution.

Next, inspecting the standard errors, much the same conclusions as in the previous example are reached. The differences between methods are generally small and the largest differences are between models rather than between methods. The standard errors in Table 11.4 are mostly smaller than for the corresponding parameters in Table 11.3 but again the parameters λ_{83} and λ_{93} are exceptions. For these parameters the puzzling result is that their standard errors in the restricted solution are larger than their standard errors in the unrestricted solution. The most plausible explanation for this is that the speed factor is not sufficiently well represented in the battery of tests. It was originally hypothesized that variable 9 (straight-curved capitals) measures only speed but previous analyses have established that this variable has a large perceptional component.

In computing the asymptotic standard errors by any one of the formulas (12), (14), (17), or (18) one must have a consistent estimate of Σ but in principle any such estimate will do. In practice one would normally use the respective solution for Θ and compute $\dot{\Sigma} = \Sigma(\Theta)$. This will result in a different $\dot{\Sigma}$ for different methods. For comparative purposes we have used the same $\dot{\Sigma}$ for all methods in Table 11.3 namely that obtained from the ML solution. The estimate of $\dot{\Sigma}$ is different, however, for the unrestricted model and the restricted model, and this may be one explanation for the different standard errors for λ_{83} and λ_{93}.

7. CONCLUSION

Four different consistent estimators of factor loadings have been considered. Two of these, the ULS and ML estimators, require fairly heavy iterative computations. The other two estimators, the IV and TSLS estimators, can be computed much more rapidly without iteration. The TSLS and ML estimators are scale free but the IV and ULS estimators are scale dependent. A comparison of the asymptotic standard errors, based on two small data sets, shows that the ULS and ML methods are more efficient than the IV and TSLS estimators in the sense of having smaller standard errors. But the differences in standard errors among all four methods are in general small and may be negligible for most practical purposes.

ACKNOWLEDGMENT

The research reported in this paper has been supported by the Swedish Research Council in Humanistic and Social Sciences under project *Research in Psychometrics*.

REFERENCES

Browne, M. W. Generalized least squares estimators in the analysis of covariance structures. *South African Statistical Journal.*, 1974, *8*, 1–24.

Holzinger, K., & Swinford, F. A study in factor analysis: The stability of a bifactor solution. *Supplementary Educational Monograph no. 48.* Chicago: University of Chicago Press, 1939.

Hägglund, G. Factor analysis by instrumental variable methods. *Psychometrika*, 1982, *47*, 209–222.

Hägglund, G., & Jöreskog, K. G. *Factor analysis by instrumental variables methods.* Unpublished paper presented at The Ledyard Tucker Symposium on Psychometric Theory at the University of Illinois at Urbana-Champaign April, 24–25, 1980.

Jennrich, R. I., & Robinson S. M. A Newton-Raphson algorithm for maximum likelihood factor analysis. *Psychometrika*, 1969, *34*, 111–123.

Jöreskog, K. G. Some contributions to maximum likelihood factor analysis. *Psychometrika*, 1967, *32*, 443–482.

Jöreskog, K. G. A general approach to confirmatory maximum likelihood factor analysis. *Psychometrika*, 1969, *34*, 183–202.

Jöreskog, K. G. Basic ideas of factor and component analysis. In K. G. Jöreskog & D. Sörbom: *Advances in factor analysis and structural equation models.* Cambridge, Mass.: Abt Books, 1979.

Jöreskog, K. G., & Sörbom, D. *LISREL V:Analysis of linear structural relationships by maximum likelihood and least squares methods.* Chicago: International Educational Services, 1981.

Lawley, D. N. The estimation of factor loadings by the method of maximum likelihood. *Proceedings of the Royal Society of Edinburgh*, 1940, *60*, 64–82.

Lawley, D. N., & Maxwell, A. E. *Factor analysis as a statistical method* (2nd ed.). London: Butterworths, 1971.

Lord, F. M. A study of speed factors and academic grades. *Psychometrika*, 1956, *21*, 31–50.

Madansky, A. Instrumental variables in factor analysis. *Psychometrika*, 1964, *29*, 105–113.

Rao, C. R. Least square theory using an estimated dispersion matrix and its application to the measurement of signals. *Proceedings of the 5th Berkeley Symposium on Probability and Mathematical Statistics*, 1967, 355–372.

12 Exploratory and Confirmatory Nonlinear Common Factor Analysis

Roderick P. McDonald
Macquarie University

ABSTRACT

A distinction is made between models that are linear in both their coefficients and the latent traits, models that are linear in their coefficients but not in the latent traits, and models that are nonlinear in both. Exploratory devices for distinguishing between alternative models, linear in their coefficients, for data with a given covariance structure, are described. General theory is given for the fitting of a prescribed nonlinear hypothesis, linear or nonlinear in its coefficients, by least squares or maximum likelihood-ratio criteria.

1. INTRODUCTION

The object of the following is to review developments in the theory of nonlinear factor analysis. These developments fall into two phases, widely separated in time. The first phase (McDonald, 1962, 1965, 1967a, 1967b, 1967c, 1967d) provided theory and computer programs for fitting polynomial models by what must be described as crude exploratory devices. The second phase (McDonald, 1979; Etezadi-Amoli & McDonald, in press) yields a general approach to the fitting of a prescribed nonlinear factor model. It can reasonably be characterized as confirmatory analysis.

In section 2, it is shown that we may distinguish in theory between models that are linear in their coefficients but not in the latent traits, and models that are nonlinear in both. At the same time it is shown that we cannot distinguish between the three types of model on the basis of the covariance structures that they imply.

Section 3 gives a concise review of methods for distinguishing between alternative models, linear in their coefficients, for a data-set with a given covariance structure. A simple device that should be suitable for interactive computer systems is recommended for the purpose of generating a specific nonlinear hypothesis.

Section 4 gives an account of general theory for the fitting of a prescribed nonlinear hypothesis by least squares or maximum likelihood-ratio criteria.

2. GENERAL THEORY

The general nonlinear common factor model (McDonald, 1967b) may be expressed as the nonlinear multivariate regression equation

$$\gamma = \varepsilon\{y|x\} = \phi(x) \tag{2.1}$$

where y is a $n \times 1$ vector of observed random variables, ϕ is a $n \times 1$ vector of functions, in general nonlinear, and x is a $t \times 1$ vector of *latent traits* (common factors) defined by the principle of local independence. This may be adopted either in its strong form, which states that for fixed x the observed variables $y_1, \ldots, y_n$ are mutually statistically independent, or in the implied weaker form, which states that

$$Cov\{j, y_k|x\} = 0, j \neq k. \tag{2.2}$$

From the definition of the vector of *residuals*

$$e = y - \varepsilon\{y|x\} = y - \gamma, \tag{2.3}$$

we have

$$\varepsilon\{e|x\} = 0, \tag{2.4}$$

$$\varepsilon\{e\gamma'|x\} = 0, \tag{2.5}$$

and hence

$$\varepsilon\{e\} = 0, \tag{2.6}$$

$$\varepsilon\{e\gamma'\} = 0. \tag{2.7}$$

Also by (2.2),

$$\varepsilon\{ee'|x\} \text{ is diagonal}, \tag{2.8}$$

hence the residual covariance matrix

$$\varepsilon\{\mathbf{ee}'\} = \mathbf{U}^2, \tag{2.9}$$

diagonal, at least nonnegative definite. (We do not in general require the residual variance to be homoscedastic.)

From (2.1), (2.6), (2.7), and (2.9), we have

$$\mathbf{C} = Cov\{\mathbf{y}\} = Cov\{\boldsymbol{\phi}(\mathbf{x})\} + \mathbf{U}^2 = Cov\{\boldsymbol{\gamma}\} + \mathbf{U}^2 \tag{2.10}$$

(under mild regularity conditions requiring the existence of $Cov\{\boldsymbol{\gamma}\}$). In the tautology

$$\mathbf{y} = \boldsymbol{\gamma} + \mathbf{e} \tag{2.11}$$

we may refer to $\boldsymbol{\gamma}$ as the *common part* of $\mathbf{y}$ and to $\mathbf{e}$ as the *unique* part of $\mathbf{y}$. Equations (2.7) and (2.9) suffice to define a (linear or nonlinear) common factor model (McDonald, 1975). (McDonald, 1975, adds a condition on the rank of $Cov\{\boldsymbol{\gamma}\}$ which in retrospect is clearly unnecessary.)

If we choose functions $\phi_j(\mathbf{x})$ in (2.1), possibly together with an assumed distribution of $\mathbf{x}$, in such a way that we may write

$$Cov\{\phi_j(\mathbf{x})\} = g_{jk}(\boldsymbol{\beta}) \tag{2.12}$$

where g_{jk} is a known function of p parameters $\beta_1, \ldots, \beta_p$, it should be possible to fit the covariance structure

$$Cov\{\mathbf{y}\} = \mathbf{G}(\boldsymbol{\beta}) + \mathbf{U}^2, \tag{2.13}$$

where $\mathbf{G} = [g_{jk}]$, to a sample covariance matrix by methods described in McDonald (1980). However, for some reasonable choices of the regression functions $f_j(\mathbf{x})$ it may prove difficult to obtain expressions for the covariances of the common parts as functions of a set of fundamental model-parameters. Perhaps more important, it may also be impossible, as we shall see shortly, to discriminate between alternative nonlinear models on the basis of the covariance structure alone.

We distinguish three classes of model contained in (2.1), namely, *strictly linear* models, *wide-sense linear* models, and *strictly nonlinear* models. In a strictly linear model, the functions $\boldsymbol{\phi}(\mathbf{x})$ are linear both in the regression coefficients of the model (the parameters describing the observed variables, usually test scores or item scores), and linear in the latent traits (usually characterizing examinees). In such a case we have

$$E\{y_j|\mathbf{x}\} = \sum_{s=1}^{t} f_{js}x_s, \quad j = 1, \ldots, n$$

or (2.14)

$$E\{\mathbf{y}|\mathbf{x}\} = \mathbf{F}\mathbf{x}$$

where $\mathbf{F}$ is $n \times t$, the very well-known linear common factor model. Equation

(2.14) with (2.9) readily yields the well-known covariance structure

$$Cov\{\mathbf{y}\} = \mathbf{FPF'} + \mathbf{U}^2, \tag{2.15}$$

where

$$\mathbf{P} = Cov\{\mathbf{x}\},$$

which is a special case of (2.13). In restricted applications of the model the elements of $\mathbf{F}$, $\mathbf{P}$, and $\mathbf{U}^2$ can be written as functions (commonly the constant-function or the identity-function) of p parameters $\beta_1, \ldots, \beta_p$. In unrestricted applications of the model (2.15), the $n \times t$ elements of $\mathbf{F}$ are independently estimated, the latent traits are assumed uncorrelated, yielding

$$\mathbf{C} = \mathbf{FF'} + \mathbf{U}^2, \tag{2.16}$$

and the underidentifiability of $\mathbf{F}$ is usually treated by finding a $t \times t$ orthogonal transformation that carries $\mathbf{F}$ into a matrix that approximates Thurstone simple structure.

In a *wide-sense linear* model, the regression functions $\phi_j(\mathbf{x})$ may be written in the form

$$E\{y_j|\mathbf{x}\} = \sum_{s=1}^{r} a_{js} \phi_s(x_1, \ldots, x_t)$$

or (2.17)

$$E\{\mathbf{y}|\mathbf{x}\} = \mathbf{A}\boldsymbol{\phi}(\mathbf{x})$$

where $A = [a_{js}]$ is $n \times r$, and $\phi_1(\mathbf{x}), \ldots, \phi_r(\mathbf{x})$ are a set of r functions in $x_1, \ldots, x_t$ whose parameters are independent of j. We will refer to the quantities $\phi_p(x_1, \ldots, x_t)$ as the *components* of the model. The regressions are linear functions of the coefficients a_{js} and nonlinear functions of the latent traits x_s.

Substituting (2.17) in (2.10) yields

$$\mathbf{C} = \mathbf{A}\, Cov\{\boldsymbol{\phi}(\mathbf{x})\}\mathbf{A'} + \mathbf{U}^2 = \mathbf{AQA'} + \mathbf{U}^2, \text{ say.} \tag{2.18}$$

If the elements of $\mathbf{A}$ are unrestricted, we may always orthonormalize the functions $\boldsymbol{\phi}(\mathbf{x})$, defining

$$\boldsymbol{\psi}(\mathbf{x}) = \mathbf{T}^{-1}\boldsymbol{\phi}(\mathbf{x}) \tag{2.19}$$

where $\mathbf{T}$ is any Gram-factor of $\mathbf{Q}$ (commonly chosen to be triangular), and thence writing

$$E\{\mathbf{y}|\mathbf{x}\} = \mathbf{AT}\boldsymbol{\psi}(\mathbf{x}) = \mathbf{B}\boldsymbol{\psi}(\mathbf{x}) \tag{2.20}$$

where $\mathbf{B} = \mathbf{AT}$. The resulting functions $\boldsymbol{\psi}(\mathbf{x})$ are orthonormal, that is,

$$Cov\{\boldsymbol{\psi}(\mathbf{x})\} = \mathbf{I}_r, \tag{2.21}$$

and the resulting covariance structure is

$$\mathbf{C} = \mathbf{BB'} + \mathbf{U}^2. \tag{2.22}$$

For example, McDonald (1967a, 1967b) showed that if x is normally distributed, a single-factor cubic model may be written in the form

$$E\{y_j|x\} = b_{j1}\psi_1(x) + b_{j2}\psi_2(x) + b_{j3}\psi_3(x) \tag{2.23}$$

where

$$y_1 = x\,;\ y_2 = (x^2 - 1)/\sqrt{2};\ y_3 = (x^3 - 3x)/\sqrt{6}, \tag{2.24}$$

the first three terms of the Hermite-Tchebycheff orthonormal polynomial series, yielding

$$Cov\{y_j, y_k\} = b_{j1}b_{k1} + b_{j2}b_{k2} + b_{j3}b_{k3},\ j \neq k. \tag{2.25}$$

However, in such a model $\mathbf{y}$ is in general not normally distributed.

It follows that we cannot distinguish between strictly linear models and wide-sense linear models on the basis of their covariance structure alone. For example, we cannot distinguish on this basis between the single-factor cubic model (2.23) with (2.24) and the three-factor linear model. The distinction is important, as McDonald (1965, 1967a, 1981) and McDonald and Ahlawat (1974) have shown, since failure to distinguish between a single-factor nonlinear model and a multiple-factor linear model gives rise to the long-standing psychometric problem of "difficulty factors" with its attendant ambiguities of substantive interpretation.

In a strictly nonlinear model the regression functions $f_j(\mathbf{x})$ cannot be written in the form (2.17), with the functions $f(\mathbf{x})$ independent of j, with a finite number of terms. Loosely speaking, the regressions are nonlinear functions of both the coefficients and the latent traits. A well-known example is the normal ogive model for binary data in item response theory,

$$E\{y_j|x\} = N\left(\frac{x - \mu_j}{\sigma_j}\right) \tag{2.26}$$

where $N\,(\cdot)$ is the (unit) cumulative normal distribution function. These, like other cumulative-distribution-function models such as the logistic model, do not readily yield expressions for the covariances of the common parts in (2.10) as functions of the parameters μ_j, σ_j, $j = 1, \ldots, n$, and hence are not directly amenable to fitting by the analysis of covariance structures. Direct treatments of such models have been thoroughly developed by Lord (see Lord, 1980).

In principle, any strictly nonlinear model may be approximated as closely as we please by a wide-sense linear model. Using classical results from harmonic analysis, McDonald (1967a) showed that if x has a normal distribution (with a choice of metric such that its mean is zero and its variance unity) then the normal ogive model (2.26) may be represented by the infinite series

$$E\{y_j/x\} = \sum_{s=0} b_{js} h_p(x) \tag{2.27}$$

where

$$h_p(x) = \frac{1}{\sqrt{p!}} \sum_{v=0}^{q} (-)^v \frac{x^{p-2v}}{2^v v! p - 2v!} \tag{2.28}$$

where $q = s$ if $p = 2s$ and if $p = 2s + 1$, the normalized Hermite-Tchebycheff polynomial series, and

$$b_{jo} = N\{-\mu_j/(1 + \sigma_j^2)^{1/2}\}, \tag{2.29}$$

$$b_{jp} = \frac{1}{\sqrt{p}} (1 + \sigma_j^2)^{-p/2} h_{p-1}\{\mu_j/(1 + \sigma_j^2)^{1/2}\}. \tag{2.30}$$

If we terminate the series (2.27) at r components, the resulting (finite) wide-sense linear model is a best approximation to the normal ogive model in a weighted least squares sense. That is, the quantity

$$I = \int_{-\infty}^{\infty} \left[N\left(\frac{x - \mu_j}{\sigma_j}\right) - \sum_{p=0}^{r} b_{jp}^* h_p^*(x) \right]^2 n(x) dx$$

(where $n(\cdot)$ is the unit normal density function and $h_p^*(x)$ is a polynomial of degree p) is a minimum when $h_p^*(x)$ is chosen to be $h_p(x)$ given by (2.28) and b_{jp}^* is chosen to be b_{jp} given by (2.29) and (2.30). That is, the squared distance between the normal ogive and a polynomial of degree r, weighted by density of x, is a minimum with this choice of a polynomial series. More generally, for any strictly nonlinear model, unidimensional or multidimensional, there will exist a wide-sense linear model in the form of a polynomial series giving a least-squares best approximation to it, weighted by an appropriate density function, for any number of components in the series, and approximating the model as closely as we please by the retention of enough components. In addition to the results for the normal ogive, McDonald (1967a) gave an infinite polynomial-series representation of Lazarsfeld's latent distance model, which includes Guttman's perfect scale as a limiting case, but the theory of such representations does not seem to have been carried further.

To sum up this section, we have seen that three main cases of the general nonlinear common factor model may be distinguished in theory, namely: strictly linear models which are linear in the regression coefficients and in the latent traits, wide-sense linear models which are linear in the regression coefficients and nonlinear in the latent traits, and strictly nonlinear models which are nonlinear in both, and cannot be represented by a wide-sense linear model containing a finite number of components. We have also seen that strictly linear and wide-sense linear models yield equivalent covariance structures, and that a strictly nonlinear model can be approximated as closely as we please by a wide-sense linear model with a finite number of components.

3. EXPLORATORY METHODS

Polynomial models have a number of advantages in exploratory nonlinear common-factor analysis. First, as we have already noted, harmonic analysis provides the necessary theory for approximating strictly nonlinear models by wide-sense linear models, taking account of the density function of the latent traits. Second, as we shall see, wide-sense linear models can employ the classical covariance-structure analysis methods of common-factor theory to determine the number and distribution of the components. Third, the use of polynomial components enables us to examine the distribution of the t latent traits in the r-space spanned by the r components, using methods described by McDonald (1967a, 1967b, 1967c, 1967d). To fit the model (2.20) we use the data first to determine how many components are needed, second to identify each component as an orthonormal component of precise degree in one or more latent traits, and third to estimate the regression coefficients of the components.

First we note that (2.20) implies that $\mathbf{y}$ has the covariance structure (2.22) in which $\mathbf{B}$ is determined only up to an orthogonal $r \times r$ transformation. Suppose we have the representation

$$\mathbf{C} = \mathbf{FF}' + \mathbf{U}^2 \tag{3.1}$$

for (2.22), with $\mathbf{F}$ and $\mathbf{U}^2$ known, and

$$\mathbf{B} = \mathbf{FL}, \tag{3.2}$$

where $\mathbf{L}$ is an as-yet-unknown orthogonal matrix. Then

$$\mathbf{y} = \mathbf{Fw} + \mathbf{e} \tag{3.3}$$

where

$$\mathbf{F} = \mathbf{BL}' \tag{3.4}$$

and

$$\mathbf{w} = \mathbf{L}\psi(\mathbf{x}). \tag{3.5}$$

If $\mathbf{y}^*$ is any observation of $\mathbf{y}$, the weighted least squares estimate of corresponding $\mathbf{w} = \mathbf{w}^*$ is given by the expression, due to Bartlett,

$$\hat{\mathbf{w}}^* = (\mathbf{F}'\mathbf{U}^{-2}\mathbf{F})^{-1}\mathbf{F}'\mathbf{U}^{-2}\mathbf{y}^* \tag{3.6}$$

(see McDonald & Burr, 1967). If $\mathbf{e}$ is assumed multivariate normal, this is also the maximum likelihood estimate. We define the random vector

$$\mathbf{v} = (\mathbf{F}'\mathbf{U}^{-2}\mathbf{F})^{-1}\mathbf{F}'\mathbf{U}^{-2}\mathbf{y} \tag{3.7}$$

and note that by (3.2) and (3.6)

$$\mathbf{v} = \mathbf{w} + \mathbf{d} \tag{3.8}$$

where

$$\mathbf{d} = (\mathbf{F}'\mathbf{U}^{-2}\mathbf{F})^{-1}\mathbf{F}'\mathbf{U}^{-2}\mathbf{e}, \tag{3.9}$$

and also that

$$E\{\mathbf{v}|\mathbf{x}\} = \mathbf{w} \tag{3.10}$$

and

$$Cov\{\mathbf{v}\} = \mathbf{I}_r + Cov\{\mathbf{d}\} \tag{3.11}$$

where

$$Cov\{\mathbf{d}\} = (\mathbf{F}'\mathbf{U}^{-2}\mathbf{F})^{-1}. \tag{3.12}$$

In geometric terms, specific hypotheses as to the form of the r orthonormal functions $\psi_1(\mathbf{x}), \ldots, \psi_r(\mathbf{x})$ are assertions that these r components span the space by lying on a curvilinear manifold of dimension t. Corresponding to certain specific hypotheses we may write a set of $r - t$ equations to the curvilinear manifold of the type

$$\theta_k[\psi(\mathbf{x})] = \theta_k[\mathbf{L}'\mathbf{w}] = 0, \quad k = 1, \ldots, r - t. \tag{3.13}$$

These equations are satisfied if and only if

$$\eta = \sum_{k=1}^{r-t} E\{\theta_k^2[\mathbf{L}'\mathbf{w}]\} = 0. \tag{3.14}$$

If such hypotheses hold, then, there will exist an orthogonal transformation $\mathbf{L}$ such that the corresponding equations (3.13) hold, and the quantity η attains a minimum value of zero.

Since, by theory due to Kestelman (1952) and Guttman (1955), the components $\mathbf{w}$ are indeterminate if the number of variables is finite, the investigation of their distribution must be indirect. The moments of the distribution of $\mathbf{v}$, which is a weighted combination of $\mathbf{y}$, are obtainable from the distribution of $\mathbf{y}$. Since the components of $\mathbf{d}$ are linear functions of n unique variables $e_1, \ldots, e_n$, the joint density function of $d_1, \ldots, d_r$ should approximate the normal density function, if n is sufficiently large, by the multivariate central limit theorem. The higher joint moments of $\mathbf{d}$ are then determined by $Cov\{\mathbf{d}\}$, and the higher joint moments of $\mathbf{w}$ are determinable from the moments of $\mathbf{v}$ and $\mathbf{d}$. If the components $\psi(\mathbf{x})$ are orthonormal polynomials, then the quantity η in (3.14) reduces to an expression in the moments of $\mathbf{w}$, and we may choose $\mathbf{L}$ to minimize η. The coefficients of the orthonormal polynomials are themselves given by the moments of **x**, which also become known on determining **L**, so the application of **L** to **F** in (3.2) completes the determination of the parameters of the model. In practice, these results are applied to sample analogues.

McDonald (1962, 1967a, 1967b, 1967c, 1967d) gives a detailed account of this method for fitting polynomial models, together with computer programs, for the central tasks of estimating the moments of **w** from a sample of observations of **y** and estimating the required rotation **L**. The method has been shown to recover known nonlinear structures from constructed data-sets, and to give plausible results from quite large empirical data-sets. It has the advantage of being free of prior assumptions and the attendant disadvantage that it depends for its results on a series of data-analytic devices for determining and fitting the components and discriminating between nonlinear models, with the result that the final parameter values are not optimally estimated in any clearly defined way. In a sense, the method is too crude (in comparison with those described in the next section) to be used as the final method of estimation of a nonlinear model, and at the same time it is perhaps unnecessarily refined if considered merely as a device for discriminating between the alternative models in t latent traits that yield r components.

An exploratory device was suggested by McDonald (1967d) that should yield a rotation of the distribution of the estimates of the components which allows us to discriminate between models on the basis of a visual display of graphical plots of pairwise bivariate marginals. It is easy though a little tedious to show that if x has a unit normal distribution, the fourth moments of the orthonormal polynomials in x (the Hermite series) increase rapidly with the degree of the polynomial. Similarly, if $x_1, x_2, \ldots, x_t$ are independent normal variables, then the fourth moment of a product of them (i.e. an interaction term in the sense of McDonald, 1967c) increases rapidly with the order of the product. This suggests a general procedure in which we choose a rotation of the distribution of the factor score estimates **v** in (3.7) to maximize the fourth moment of each component in turn. This option in program PROTEAN (McDonald, 1967d) has been found effective in revealing known structures, and should suffice to suggest a hypothesis, by inspection of the resulting marginal bivariate distributions. The method would be very suitable for use on the visual display units of interactive computer systems. A variant on the well-known quartimax method of Neuhaus and Wrigley for rotating factor loadings to approximate simple structure could be employed. (Program PROTEAN uses numerical methods which do not take advantage of the trigonometry of the fourth-moment problem, since this does not apply to the corresponding minimization problems for prescribed polynomials.) While the methods of the next section are recommended for fitting a chosen nonlinear model, it seems that the theory of this section may continue to be useful as a basis for choosing an appropriate model.

4. CONFIRMATORY METHODS

We return to the general nonlinear common factor model (2.1), which, by (2.3) and (2.9), may be rewritten as

$$y_j = \phi_j(x_1, \ldots, x_t; \beta_{j1}, \ldots, \beta_{js}) + e_j, \tag{4.1}$$

with

$$\text{Cov}\{e_j, e_k\} = \delta_{jk} u_j^2 \tag{4.2}$$

where $\beta_{j1}, \ldots, \beta_{js}$ is a set of parameters determining the jth regression function, and δ_{jk} is Kronecker's delta. We suppose that the number of latent traits is specified, and the form of the functions $\phi_j(x_1, \ldots, x_t)$ is prescribed, so that it remains only to estimate the parameters $\beta_{j1}, \ldots, \beta_{js}$, and u_j^2, $j = 1, \ldots, n$. We may estimate these parameters and also the latent trait values of a sample of observations simultaneously by a straightforward generalization on results given by McDonald (1979) for linear and polynomial models.

We let the columns of $\mathbf{Y} = [y_{ji}]$ contain m independent observations of y_j, $j = 1, \ldots, n$, and corresponding to (4.1) we write

$$\mathbf{Y} = \mathbf{\Phi}(\mathbf{X};\boldsymbol{\beta}) + \mathbf{E}, \tag{4.3}$$

where $\mathbf{\Phi} = [\phi(x_{1i}, \ldots, x_{ti}; \beta_{j1}, \ldots, \beta_{js})]$, $\mathbf{X} = [x_{pi}]$, $\boldsymbol{\beta} = [\beta_{jq}]$, and $\mathbf{E} = [e_{ji}]$.

We define also

$$\mathbf{Q} = \frac{1}{m} \mathbf{E}\mathbf{E}'. \tag{4.4}$$

By definition of $\mathbf{E}$,

$$E\{\mathbf{E}\} = \mathbf{0}, \tag{4.5}$$

and by the hypothesis (4.2) of (weak) local independence

$$\mathbf{Q} = \mathbf{U}^2, \text{ diagonal.} \tag{4.6}$$

McDonald (1979) gave theory for the linear case, in which

$$\mathbf{\Phi} = \mathbf{F}\mathbf{X} + \mathbf{m}\mathbf{1}', \tag{4.7}$$

(where in an obvious sense $\mathbf{F}$ is a $n \times t$ matrix of common factor loadings and $\mathbf{m}$ is a vector of means) and also for the case of polynomial regressions. The theory generalizes without further work to yield the following results, which may be stated without proof.

We may fit the model (4.3), estimating both the $n \times s$ matrix $\boldsymbol{\beta}$ of regression coefficients and the $t \times m$ matrix $\mathbf{X}$ of latent trait values, as well as the matrix of residual variances $\mathbf{U}^2$, by minimizing the ordinary least squares loss-function

$$\omega = \tfrac{1}{2}\mathrm{Tr}\{(\mathbf{Q} - \mathbf{U}^2)^2\} \tag{4.8}$$

with respect to $\boldsymbol{\beta}$, $\mathbf{X}$, and $\mathbf{U}^2$. This function will be recognized as the well-known MINRES loss-function due to Harman. We seek to minimize the sum of squares of the residual covariances of distinct variables.

If we may assume that the m columns of $\mathbf{E}$ are normally distributed, with covariance matrix $\mathbf{U}^2$, then minimizing the loss-function

$$\ell = -\tfrac{1}{2} \log|\mathbf{R}_e| \tag{4.9}$$

where

$$\mathbf{R}_e = (\mathrm{Diag}\ \mathbf{Q})^{-1/2}\mathbf{Q}(\mathrm{Diag}\ \mathbf{Q})^{-1/2},$$

is equivalent to maximizing the ratio of the likelihood under the hypothesis (4.6) to the likelihood under the hypothesis that $E\{\mathbf{Q}\}$ is any positive definite matrix. In the linear case, and more generally, minimizing ℓ circumvents a problem noted by Anderson and Rubin (1956), namely that, in general, maximum likelihood estimators do not exist in this model. Minimizing the likelihood ratio criterion ℓ also maximizes the determinant of the residual correlation matrix $\mathbf{R}_e$, and makes it as close as possible, in that sense, to a diagonal matrix. Thus the use of this criterion does not rest critically on the assumption that the residuals are jointly normal, and (like the least squares criterion ω in (4.8)) it could reasonably be applied even if they are not homoscedastic.

Both loss-functions yield, as we would expect, the estimate of $\mathbf{U}^2$,

$$\hat{\mathbf{U}}^2 = \mathrm{Diag}\ \{\mathbf{Q}\}, \tag{4.10}$$

for any choice of $\boldsymbol{\beta}$ and $\mathbf{X}$, as the minimum point with respect to $\mathbf{U}^2$. Let σ represent either loss-function. Then their derivatives with respect to x_{pi} and β_{jq} are given by

$$\frac{\partial \sigma}{\partial x_{pi}} = \mathbf{r}'_{pi}\mathbf{G}\mathbf{e}_i, \tag{4.11}$$

and

$$\frac{\partial \sigma}{\partial \beta_{jq}} = \mathbf{g}'_j\mathbf{E}\mathbf{c}_{jq}, \tag{4.12}$$

where

$$\mathbf{G} = -\frac{2}{m}(\mathbf{Q} - \mathrm{Diag}\ \mathbf{Q}) \tag{4.13}$$

if $\sigma = \omega$, and

$$\mathbf{G} = \frac{1}{m}(\mathbf{Q}^{-1} - [\text{Diag } \mathbf{Q}]^{-1}) \qquad (4.14)$$

if $\sigma = \ell$; $\mathbf{e}_i$ is the ith column of $\mathbf{E}$, $\mathbf{g}_j$ is the jth column of $\mathbf{G}$, and

$$\mathbf{r}'_{pi} = \left[\frac{\partial \phi_{1i}}{\partial x_{pi}} \cdots \frac{\partial \phi_{ni}}{\partial x_{pi}}\right]$$

and

$$\mathbf{c}'_{jq} = \left[\frac{\partial \phi_{j1}}{\partial \beta_{jq}} \cdots \frac{\partial \phi_{jm}}{\partial \beta_{jq}}\right].$$

The estimators of x_{pi} and b_{jq} are found among the solutions of the equations obtained by setting these derivatives equal to zero. In principle, a computer program could be written for the general purpose of fitting any prescribed nonlinear model, with the user supplying subroutines to define and evaluate the functions $\mathbf{\Phi}$ and the vectors of derivatives $\mathbf{r}_{pi}$ and $\mathbf{c}_{jq}$. It is likely, however, that any proposed model will require careful study, possibly yielding a specialized computer program.

The case of polynomial models with pairwise interactions has been studied by Etezadi-Amoli and McDonald (in press). It proves possible to fit this type of model by minimizing the loss-function with respect to x_{pi} using a numerical algorithm, such as the method of conjugate directions, and, for each set of values of x_{pi} obtained in the course of this process, fitting the regressions in closed form using the normal equations of general (wide-sense) linear regression theory. That is, for every iteration of an algorithm intended to minimize these loss-functions with respect to x_{pi}, we minimize the loss-function

$$\tau = Tr\{Q\} \qquad (4.15)$$

with respect to β_{jq}, instead of the loss-functions ω or ℓ. This is not only possible, but necessary for the attainment of satisfactory estimates. From (4.13) and (4.14) it may be seen that $\mathbf{G}$ is null, for either loss-function, if and only if $\mathbf{Q}$ is diagonal, a condition which obtains if the fit of the model is perfect. In such a case, the conditions (4.11) and (4.12) for a minimum are satisfied for many values of $\mathbf{X}$ and $\boldsymbol{\beta}$. If $\mathbf{Q}$ is approximately diagonal, in the desirable case in practice where the model fits well, simultaneously minimizing ω or ℓ with respect to $\mathbf{X}$ and $\boldsymbol{\beta}$ yields poor estimates because the conditions (4.11) and (4.12) are satisfied approximately over wide ranges of $\mathbf{X}$ and $\boldsymbol{\beta}$.

If, instead, we minimize the function τ in (4.15) with respect to $\boldsymbol{\beta}$, quite generally this yields a minimum of the loss-functions ω and ℓ. This may be seen from the fact that

$$\frac{\partial \tau}{\partial \beta_{jp}} = \mathbf{E}\mathbf{c}_{jq} \qquad (4.16)$$

where c_{jq} is defined as before. Hence if this derivative vanishes, so does the derivative of ω or ℓ, given by (4.12). Thus, in any specification of the model (4.1), whether wide-sense linear or strictly nonlinear, we should fit the model by alternating the minimization of the loss function ω or ℓ with respect to $\mathbf{X}$ and the minimization of the loss-function τ with respect to $\boldsymbol{\beta}$.

Two special cases are described, to indicate the scope of the theory. The first is the linear common factor model. In the linear case (4.7), treated by McDonald (1979), we obtain

$$\frac{\partial \sigma}{\partial x_{pi}} = \mathbf{r}'_{pi}\mathbf{G}\mathbf{e}_i, \tag{4.17}$$

where

$$\mathbf{r}'_{pi} = [f_{1p}, \ldots, f_{np}], \tag{4.18}$$

independent of x_{pi}. It is then easy to see that (4.17) may be rewritten as

$$\frac{\partial \sigma}{\partial \mathbf{X}} = \mathbf{F}'\mathbf{G}\mathbf{E}. \tag{4.19}$$

Similarly,

$$\frac{\partial \sigma}{\partial f_{jq}} = \mathbf{g}'_j\mathbf{E}\mathbf{c}_{jq} \tag{4.20}$$

where

$$\mathbf{c}'_{jq} = [x_{j1}, \ldots, x_{jm}] \tag{4.21}$$

Again, (4.20) may be rewritten as

$$\frac{\partial \sigma}{\partial \mathbf{F}} = \mathbf{G}\mathbf{E}\mathbf{X}'. \tag{4.22}$$

Further,

$$\frac{\partial \sigma}{\partial m_j} = \mathbf{g}'_j\mathbf{E}\mathbf{c}_j \tag{4.23}$$

where, by (4.7), we have

$$\mathbf{c}_j = [11 \ldots 1], \tag{4.24}$$

an $n \times 1$ vector. We may rewrite (4.23) as

$$\frac{\partial \sigma}{\partial \mathbf{m}} = \mathbf{G}\mathbf{E}\mathbf{1}_n. \tag{4.25}$$

The derivatives (4.19), (4.22), (4.25), which were obtained by McDonald (1979) from the equations of the linear case, have thus been obtained as specializations of the general results (4.11) and (4.12).

As a second special case we take a strictly nonlinear model, namely a cumulative-distribution-function model of the type considered in item response theory. In item response theory for dichotomous data the two best known regression functions (item characteristic functions), the normal ogive and the logistic functions, take the form of a cumulative distribution function. We write $P(z)$ for any such function, and $p(z)$ for its first derivative (which is the corresponding density function). In the unidimensional case ($t = 1$) the model becomes

$$y_{ji} = P(z_{ji}) + e_{ji} \tag{4.26}$$

where

$$z_{ji} = f_j x_i + m_j. \tag{4.27}$$

The conditional distribution of y_{ji}, given x_i, is binomial, with heteroscedastic variances given by

$$E\{e_{ji}^2 | x_i\} = P(z_{ji})[1 - P(z_{ji})], \tag{4.28}$$

and certainly not normal. Some investigators would then prefer the least squares loss-function to the maximum-determinant loss-function. Allowing both options, we obtain the required derivatives for this case on substituting

$$\mathbf{r}_i' = [f_1 p(z_{1i}), \ldots, f_n p(z_{ni})] \tag{4.29}$$

in (4.11) to obtain the derivative with respect to x_i, and, successively,

$$\mathbf{c}_j' = [x_1 p(z_{j1}), \ldots, x_m p(z_{jm})] \tag{4.30}$$

and

$$\mathbf{c}_j' = [p(z_{j1}), \ldots, p(z_{jm})] \tag{4.31}$$

to obtain the derivative with respect to f_j and the derivative with respect to m_j. Inspection of these derivatives suggests that a minimization algorithm for this problem may behave badly. By choosing x_i negative and sufficiently large, we can make the vectors (4.29), (4.30), (4.31) as small as we please while the other terms in the derivatives of the loss-functions remain finite, so the derivatives themselves will tend to vanish. This observation is not encouraging, yet it may be worthwhile to test the method by programming it, since other methods for fitting such models may also be somewhat problematic. For the present purpose, it suffices to show how the general theory given here may allow us in principle to fit any prescribed nonlinear model, whether wide-sense linear or strictly nonlinear.

The wide-sense linear approximation (2.23) to the normal ogive model, obtained by truncating the series (2.27) at $p = 3$, has been shown to give reasonable estimates of the item-parameters (McDonald, 1980, 1982) and to provide a criterion for determining if the fit is acceptable.

Generally, given estimates of the parameters of a nonlinear common factor model by the methods described, we would wish to determine whether the fit to the model is in some well-defined sense satisfactory. In two clear senses, the loss-functions ω and ℓ measure the departure of the residual covariance matrix from a diagonal matrix. On some experiential basis we should be able to agree to regard the fit of the model as acceptable if the residual covariances are sufficiently small.

It follows from theory given by McDonald (1979) that in the linear case (4.7), the quantity $m\ell$, where m is the sample-size and ℓ is given by (4.9), is asymptotically distributed as chi-square, with df the same as in the corresponding random model treated by the analysis of covariance structures, that is,

$$df = \tfrac{1}{2}[(n - t)^2 - (n + t)],$$

if the factor loadings are unrestricted. Monte Carlo studies by Etezadi-Amoli and McDonald (in press) have provided confirmation for a conjecture that this result generalizes to a wide-sense linear model in $r > t$ components, with

$$df = \tfrac{1}{2}[(n - r)^2 - (n + r)].$$

(Note that this depends on the number of orthogonal components, not on the number of latent traits.) The conjecture requires further study. One may question whether a test of significance is of much value in this context. Structural models of the type considered here do not fit into the framework of Neyman-Pearson decision theory, since we wish to affirm restrictive hypotheses which must be false and will be rejected on the basis of a sufficiently large sample.

5. CONCLUSION

It has been pointed out that alternative nonlinear common factor models can give rise to the same covariance structure. Linear factor analysis as conventionally employed may therefore lead an investigator to misinterpret his data, possibly with consequences of substantive significance.

Exploratory devices given by McDonald (1967a, 1967b, 1967c, 1967d) may be used to distinguish between alternative nonlinear common factor models explaining a given covariance structure. Of these, the simplest device, rotating the estimated factor score distribution to maximize the fourth moment of one or more marginal univariate distributions, seems readily adaptable to present-day visual display units on interactive computer systems. These exploratory devices have been shown to be capable of recovering known structures from simulated data-sets, and of yielding plausible results from quite large empirical data-sets. For example, the analysis by McDonald (1967b) of 65 measures of aphasic dysfunction on 157 cases gave a plausible account of the data in terms of two latent traits, replacing a five-factor analysis using the linear model.

The methods have not been widely used. It is, of course, always possible to obtain, and usually possible to interpret, an analysis in terms of the linear model. Therefore, unless an investigator feels a particular need for caution because of a clear suggestion in his data of departure from multivariate normality, or unless he has been convinced by the literature on difficulty factors and related problems that caution is always necessary, it is to be expected that he might accept the linear model and consequently will never discover whether it was wrong to do so. Yet the work needed for a graphical display of the factor score distribution is a negligible component in the total cost of a factor analytic investigation, so failure to carry it out may be questioned in cost benefit terms.

The general theory given in section 4 enables research to be carried out on numerical methods for fitting any member of the class of nonlinear common factor models. The case of a polynomial model with pairwise interactions has been programmed by Etezadi-Amoli (see Etezadi-Amoli & McDonald, in press). The program recovers known structures from simulated data-sets, and can be recommended for use in empirical research, given a prescribed polynomial hypothesis. Such a hypothesis can be derived from an exploratory study of the factor score distribution from a linear factor analysis. The evidence suggests that the nonlinear model is not subject to worse problems of identifiability than is the linear model. On the contrary, certain prescribed nonlinear models are not subject to rotational indeterminacy. Further research should cover the use of spline functions and monotone regression functions, as a basis for a nonparametric common factor analysis, and such strictly nonlinear functions as the logistic and normal ogive functions commonly used in item response theory.

REFERENCES

Anderson, T. W., & Rubin, J. Statistical inference in factor analysis. *Proceedings of the third Berkeley Symposium on Mathematical Statistics and Probability*, 1956, *5*, 111–150.

Etezadi-Amoli, J., & McDonald, R. P. A second-generation nonlinear factor analysis. In press.

Guttman, L. The determinacy of factor score matrices with implications for five other basic problems of common factor theory. *British Journal of Statistical Psychology*, 1955, *8*, 65–82.

Kestelman, H. The fundamental equation of factor analysis. *British Journal of Psychology*, Statistics Section, 1952, *5*, 1–6.

Lord, F. M. *Applications of item response theory to practical testing problems*. New Jersey: Lawrence Erlbaum Associates, 1980.

McDonald, R. P. A general approach to nonlinear factor analysis. *Psychometrika*, 1962, *27*, 397–415.

McDonald, R. P. Difficulty factors and nonlinear factor analysis. *British Journal of Mathematical and Statistical Psychology*, 1965, *18*, 11–23.

McDonald, R. P. Nonlinear factor analysis. *Psychometric Monograph*, 1967, *No. 15*. (a)

McDonald, R. P. Numerical methods for polynomial models in nonlinear factor analysis. *Psychometrika*, 1967, *32*, 77–112. (b)

McDonald, R. P. Factor interaction in nonlinear factor analysis. *British Journal of Mathematical and Statistical Psychology*, 1967, *20*, 205–215. (c)

McDonald, R. P. *PROTEAN - a comprehensive CD3200/3600 program for nonlinear factor analysis* (ETS RM-67-26). Princeton, N.J.: Educational Testing Service, 1967. (d)

McDonald, R. P. Descriptive axioms for common factor theory, image theory, and component theory. *Psychometrika,* 1975, *40,* 137–152.

McDonald, R. P. The simultaneous estimation of factor loadings and scores. *British Journal of Mathematical and Statistical Psychology,* 1979, *32,* 212–228.

McDonald, R. P. A simple comprehensive model for the analysis of covariance structures: some remarks on applications, *British Journal of Mathematical and Statistical Psychology,* 1980, *33,* 161–183.

McDonald, R. P. The dimensionality of tests and items. *British Journal of Mathematical and Statistical Psychology,* 1981, *34,* 100–117.

McDonald, R. P. Fitting latent trait models In D. Spearritt (ed.), *The improvement of measurement in education and psychology.* Australian Council for Educational Research, 1982.

McDonald, R. P., & Ahlawat, K. S. Difficulty factors in binary data. *British Journal of Mathematical and Statistical Psychology,* 1974, *27,* 82–99.

McDonald, R. P., & Burr, E. J. A comparison of four methods of constructing factor scores. *Psychometrika,* 1967, *32,* 381–401.

13 Searching for Structure in Binary Data

Ledyard R Tucker
University of Illinois at Urbana-Champaign

This chapter is a tale of a purpose, some ideas, some successes, some disappointments, and a need for further workable ideas. The search for factor analytic type structures in dichotomously scored items has presented nasty, exasperating problems for many years. Three publications in 1941 provide early indications as to the nature of these problems. Guilford (1941) published an analysis of Seashore's test of musical talent in which there were factors related to the difficulty of the items. Ferguson's (1941) article on the factorial interpretation of test difficulty gave a theoretic basis for factors related to item difficulty. Guttman (1941) presented his theory for the quantification of a class of attributes which included his components of scalability. Wherry and Gaylord (1944) followed the Guilford and Ferguson articles with a publication relating content, difficulty, and constant error factors to the type of correlation coefficients used. Guilford used tetrachoric correlation coefficients while Ferguson's development was based on the phi coefficient. Carroll (1945) pointed out the need to correct the fourfold tables for the effects of guessing before obtaining tetrachoric correlations and removed much of the effects of item difficulty from the Guilford analysis. Gourlay (1951) published on the difficulty factors arising from the use of tetrachoric correlations. Dingman (1958) also commented on the relation between coefficients of correlation and difficulty factors. Carroll (1961) discussed the nature of data with a relation as to how to choose a correlation coefficient. Carroll (1983) returned to consideration of effects of the probabilities examinees know the answer to an item as well as the effects of chance guessing on the product moment correlations and the tetrachoric correlations between items. He did not consider how to correct the correlations for these influences.

Lord (1958) pointed out relations between Guttman's principal components of scale analysis and other psychometric theory. A point that should appear obvious for items that form a perfect Guttman scale is that there should be a single, underlying trait which is dichotomized at different points by the various items. In this author's opinion, the components obtained by Guttman from use of product moment or phi correlations represent power series type functions produced by curvilinear relations of the item responses to such an underlying trait. For a group of items which form a perfect Guttman scale, the tetrachoric correlations between the items are all unity (some items may have to be reversed) and the matrix of tetrachoric correlations will yield a single factor. When the items are less than perfect and when some guessing might have occurred, a matrix of tetrachoric correlations may yield difficulty factors as has been pointed out previously. In many cases a matrix of tetrachoric correlations may not be Gramian.

The preceding disucssion is not intended to be a complete review, but to touch on some of the highlights. To this author, many of these efforts represent an adventitious wedding of correlation-like techniques to factor analytic-like techniques. Carroll stressed the study of the type of data in the choice of the type of correlation coefficient; this went more deeply in theory than an arbitrary decision in the choice of type of correlation.

ITEM CHARACTERISTIC FUNCTION APPROACHES

A different approach was initiated by Bock and Lieberman (1970) in their publication of fitting a response model for n dichotomously scored items. In this development they referred back to work of Lawley (1944), Tucker (1948), and Lord (1952) who used item characteristic functions in relating item responses to traits. Bock and Lieberman developed a technique for fitting a single trait to responses of a sample of individuals to a group of items. In their development they assumed that the population was distributed normally on this trait. Christoffersson (1975), Muthen (1978), and Muthen and Christoffersson (1981) have extended this approach to multidimensional cases, still with an assumption of a multidimensional normal distribution in the population.

An Approach for Representation of Binary Data

The purpose of the present project may be simply stated as a desire to develop a technique to fit a multiple common factor analytic type model with unique factors directly to binary data using as few strong distributional assumptions as possible. In this purpose is a desire to avoid adventitious wedding of correlation type coefficients to the factor analytic model.

For an introduction to the technique, consider Table 13.1 for a "know" or "guess" simulated situation. The upper section gives the generation parameters.

13. SEARCHING FOR STRUCTURE IN BINARY DATA 217

TABLE 13.1
Example 1: A Know or Guess Situation

| | Data Generation Parameters | | | | | | | | | |
| | | | | | Item | | | | | |
Probability	1	2	3	4	5	6	7	8	9	10
Knowing	.95	.85	.75	.65	.55	.45	.35	.25	.15	.05
Guessing	.25	.25	.25	.25	.25	.25	.25	.25	.25	.25
Correct	.9625	.8875	.8125	.7375	.6625	.5875	.5125	.4375	.3625	.2875

Population Distribution on Trait: Rectilinear in the Range 0 - 1. Sample Size: 500.

Results

| | | Factor Loadings | | | Data Fitting Function | |
Item	Proportion Correct	Common Factor	Unique Factor	Slope	Additive Constant	Log Likelihood
1	.958	.85	.53	46.5	1.69	-.00013
2	.890	.93	.37	61.3	1.22	-.00026
3	.824	.90	.43	117.6	1.04	-.00008
4	.714	.93	.37	59.2	.66	-.00047
5	.682	.88	.47	51.3	.55	-.00061
6	.606	.86	.52	73.2	.30	-.00028
7	.544	.85	.52	151.1	.08	-.00004
8	.482	.70	.71	46.5	-.12	-.00038
9	.396	.61	.79	132.2	-.39	-.00000
10	.326	.45	.89	40.2	-.55	-.00084

Total Log Likelihood = -.00310

For each individual in a sample of 500 simulated individuals a random number was drawn from a rectilinear distribution in the range of zero to unity. The upper 5% of the individuals knew all items, the upper 15% knew items 1 through 9, and so forth. The lowest 5% did not know even item 1. Thus, knowing the items formed a perfect scale running from item 1 through item 10. When an individual did not know an item, that individual guessed (randomly among four choices) with a probability of guessing right equal to 25%. This simulation yielded a series of ten 0 or 1 scores for each of the 500 individuals. Now consider Fig. 13.1. Scores were developed for each individual on a common factor and ten unique factors by a procedure to be described later. Figure 13.1 presents a scatter plot of the scores on the common factor and unique factor 5. Notice the diagonal gap running from upper left to lower right. Figure 13.2 presents this scatter plot with a dashed line drawn through the gap. Perpendicular to the dashed line is a solid line with an arrowhead, labeled "Model Score." Measurements on the model score are taken in the direction of the arrow.

The observed binary response for individual $i(i = 1,N)$ on item $j(j = 1,n)$ is

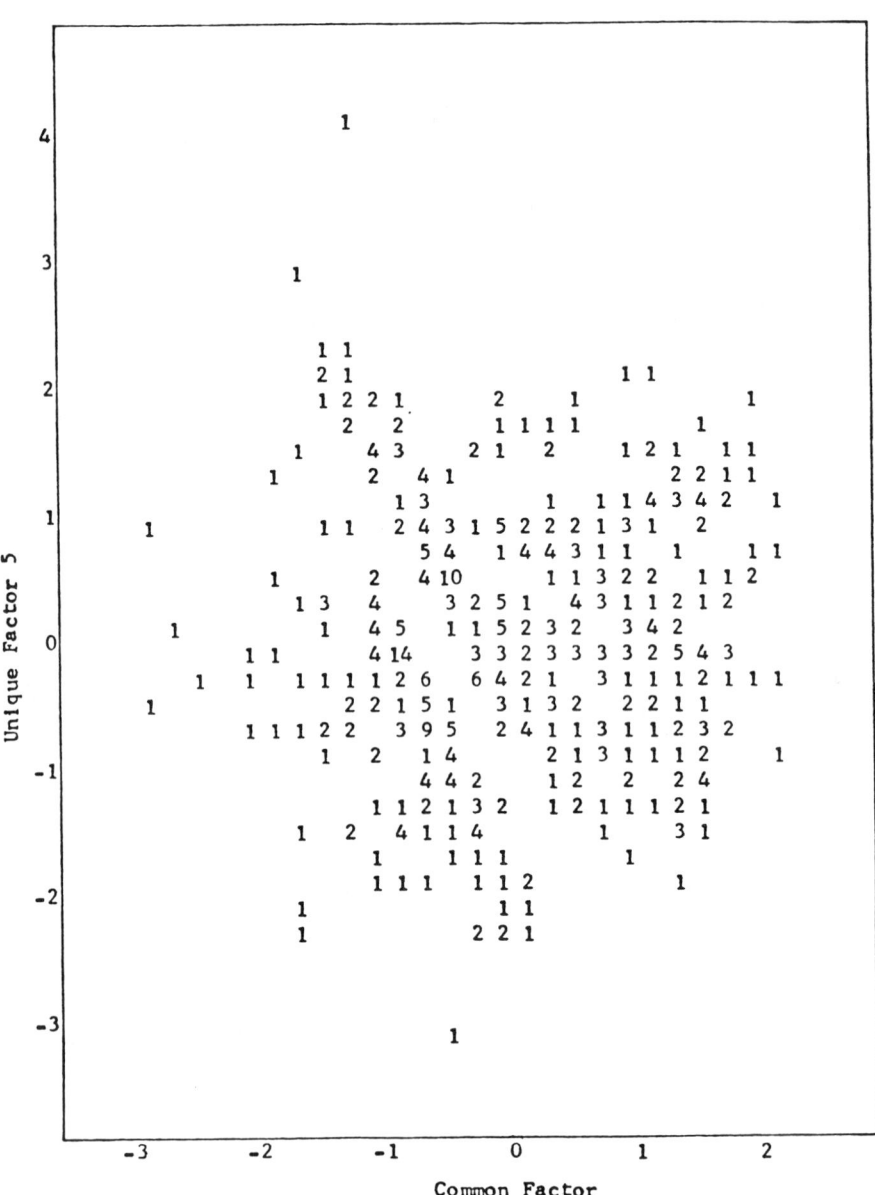

FIG. 13.1 Factor score scatter plot, Example 1: common factor with unique factor 5.

13. SEARCHING FOR STRUCTURE IN BINARY DATA   219

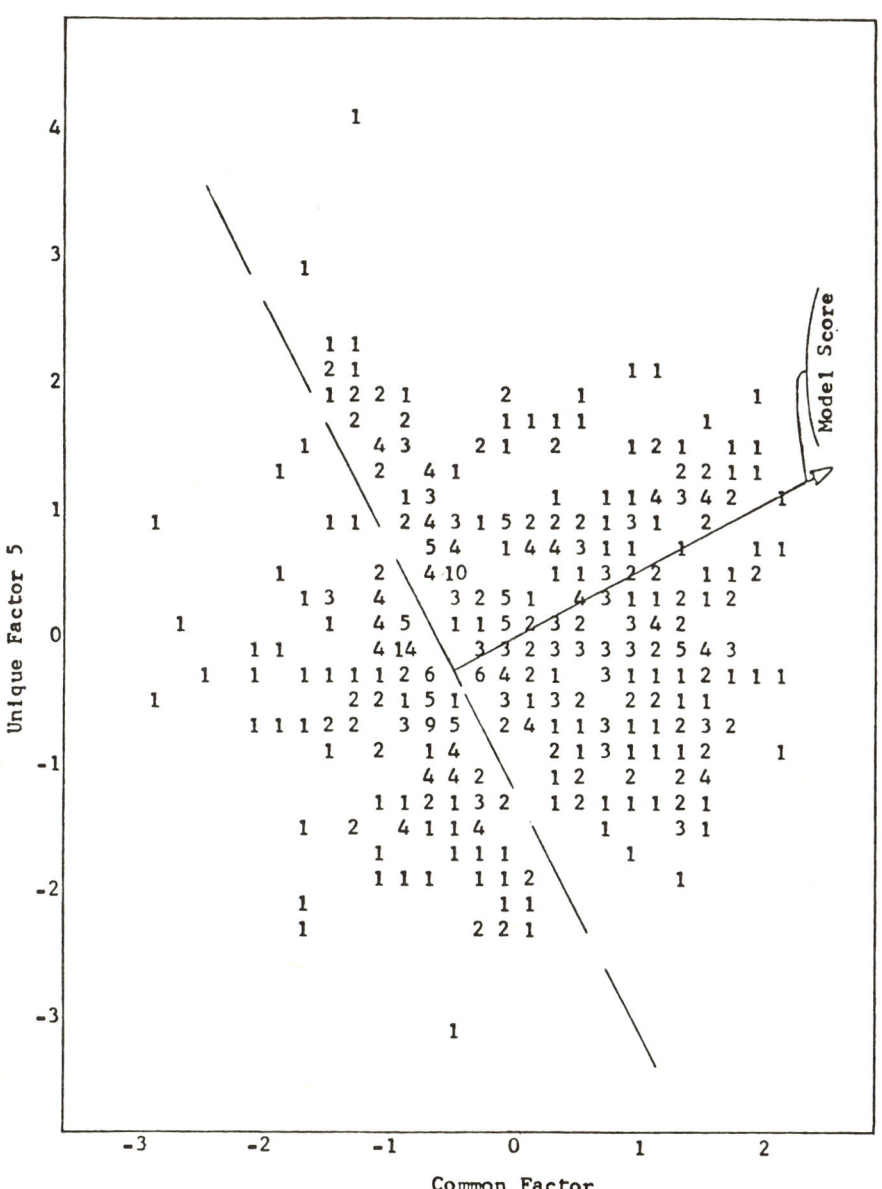

FIG. 13.2   Factor score scatter plot, Example 1: item 5 model score indicated.

designated by b_{ij} which has values of 0 or 1. Corresponding to each b_{ij} is a model score z_{ij} derived from a factor analytic model as given by equation (1) for m common factors.

$$z_{ij} = \sum_{f=1}^{m} x_{aif} a_{jf} + x_{uij} u_j. \tag{1}$$

The coefficients in this equation are:

x_{aif} is the score of individual i on common factor f;
a_{jf} is the loading of item j on common factor f;
x_{uij} is the score of individual i on unique factor j;
u_j is the factor loading of item j on unique factor j.

The factor scores are taken to be standardized, uncorrelated. However, the common factors may be transformed to a simple structure (if such a structure exists) with correlated factors.

Now, return to Table 13.1 and the "know" or "guess" example. A one-factor model with uniquenesses was developed for this body of data. On the left of the lower section of Table 13.1 are the proportions of the individuals who got each item correct and the developed factor loadings. Note that the model scores for item 5 are a combination of the individuals' common factor scores and their unique factor 5 scores. The direction of the arrow in Fig. 13.2 represents the two-factor loadings for item 5.

Consider each level of common factor score shown in Fig. 13.2. Individuals having 0 responses to item 5 are below the dashed line and individuals having 1 responses are above the dashed line. The proportion of individuals at given levels of common factor scores increases from lower common factor score levels to higher levels of common factor scores. This effect can be seen in Fig. 13.3, upper graph, which presents the relation of responses of 0 or 1 on item 5 to the common factor scores. A three-parameter logistic item characteristic function has been fitted to the data of the upper plot relating probability of a response of 1 on item 5 to the common factor score. Figures 13.2 and 13.3 provide a manner for generation of an item characteristic function against a trait score when the responses are dichotomized on a model score. Tucker (1946, 1948) used this method for conceiving item characteristic functions. He generated the two parameter normal ogive function from a bivariate, normal distribution.

The lower plot of Fig. 13.3 presents the relation of item 5 responses to the model score. A two-parameter logistic function has been fitted to the observations. Note that this function is very steep and could be a vertical line producing a step function between the 0 responses and the 1 responses. (The computing procedure stopped at the function given, there being no power to force it to a steeper function.) While this function is similar to an item characteristic function, a different interpretation is possible. A measure derived from this function

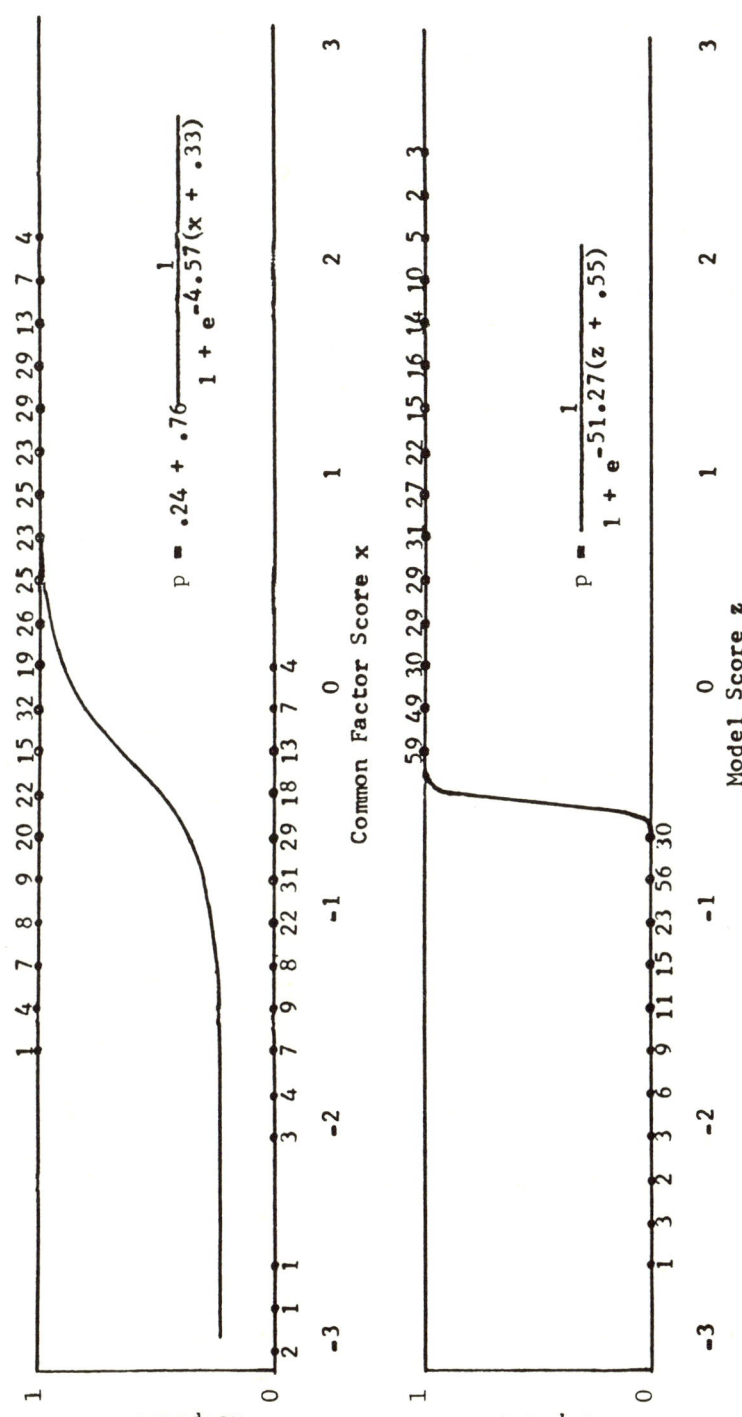

FIG. 13.3 Characteristic curves for Example 1, item 5 responses.

in relation to the binary data may be used as an index of goodness of fit of the model to the data. This function is termed a binary fit function and is presented as such by equations (2) and (3).

p_{ij} be the conditional probability, given the model score, that $b_{ij} = 1$;

q_{ij} be the conditional probability, given the model score, that $b_{ij} = 0$.

$$q_{ij} = 1 - p_{ij}. \tag{2}$$

The logistic fit function is defined to be:

$$p_{ij} = \frac{1}{[1 - e^{-s_j(z_{ij} + a_{j0})}]} \tag{3}$$

where s_j is a slope parameter and a_{j0} is an additive constant parameter.

Before progressing to the technique for fitting the model to the binary data, consider Fig. 13.4 which presents the scatter plot of scores on the common factor with scores on unique factor 6. Again there is a gap running from upper left to lower right which separates the 0 responses on item 6 from the 1 responses. Figure 13.5 presents the scatter plot for scores on unique factor 5 and unique factor 6. In this plot the points are quite scattered. Note that the scores on all factors, common and unique, are standardized and uncorrelated.

A point to note is that these factor scores are not unique given the factor matrix and the model scores as has been shown by Guttman (1955). No claim is made here as to the uniqueness of the factor scores. Rather, at least one matrix of factor scores is determined so as to be able to fit the model to the binary data. A major objective is to determine a factor matrix which will indicate the nature of underlying, latent traits.

A Binary Fit Function with a Maximum Likelihood Criterion

Use of a maximum likelihood criterion in fitting the model to the binary data appears to this author to be quite natural. Equations (2) and (3) give a priori statements of probability which are converted in equations (4) and (5) to likelihoods for the observed data. For a given body of binary data, the probabilities of equation (3) may be converted to likelihoods of the observed b_{ij}; these likelihoods will be designated as L_{ij}.

$$L_{ij} = p_{ij} \quad \text{for } b_{ij} = 1; \tag{4}$$

$$L_{ij} = q_{ij} \quad \text{for } b_{ij} = 0. \tag{5}$$

13. SEARCHING FOR STRUCTURE IN BINARY DATA 223

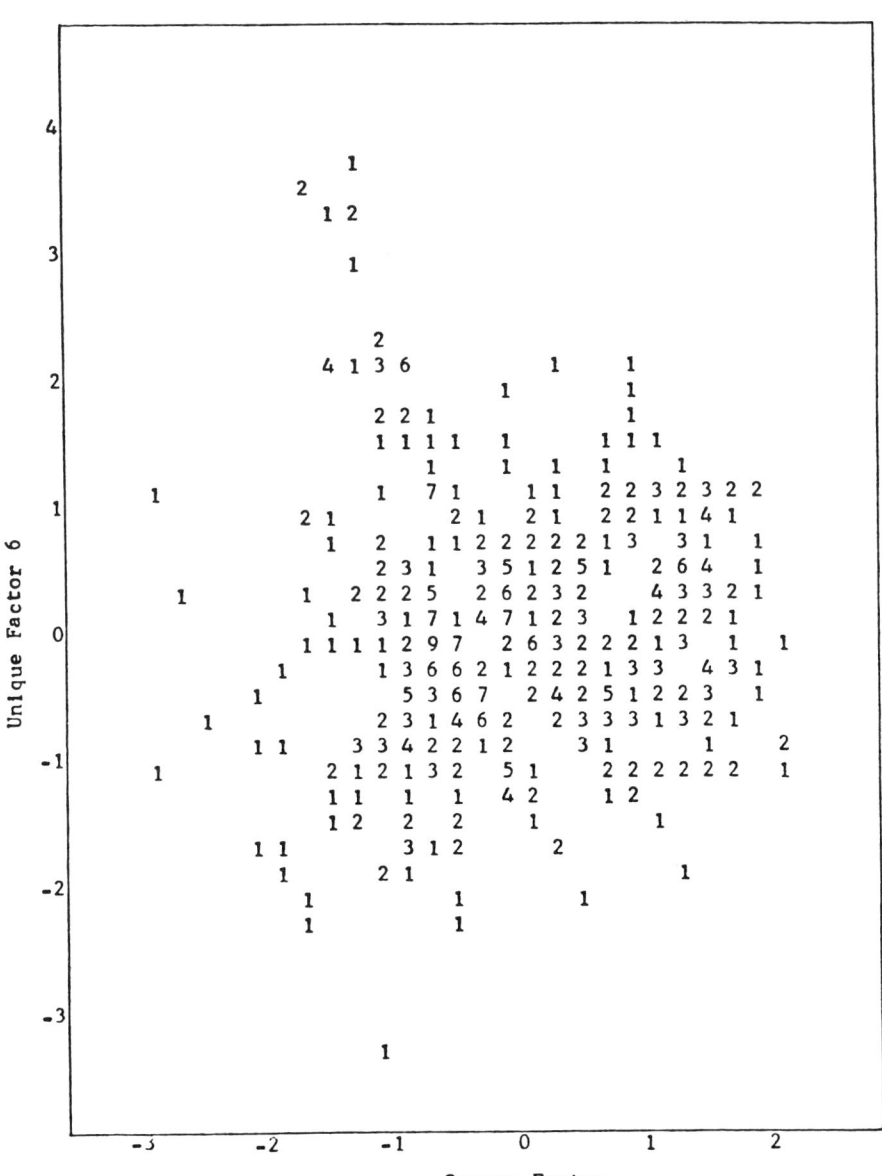

FIG. 13.4 Factor score scatter plot, Example 1: common factor with unique factor 6.

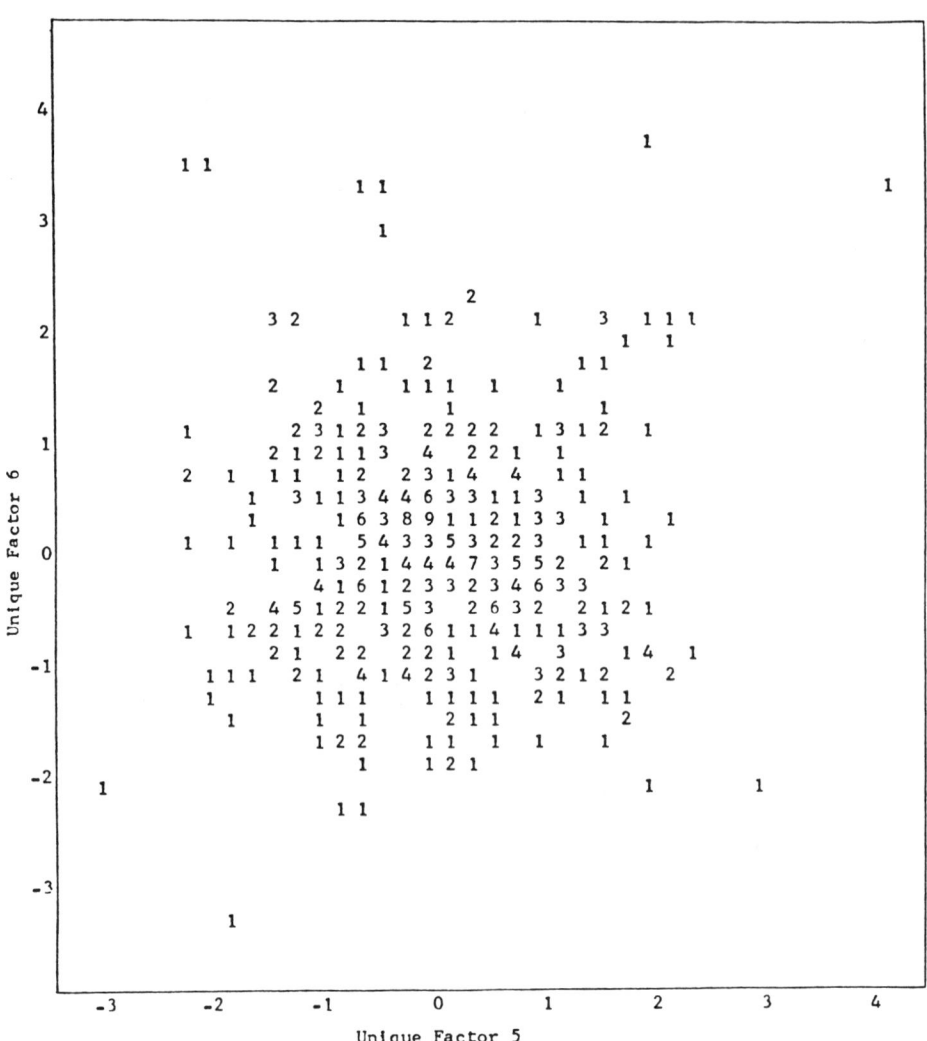

FIG. 13.5 Factor score scatter plot, Example 1: unique factor 5 with unique factor 6.

The observed data are taken to be experimentally independent, being linked only through elements of the model. Consequently, general likelihoods may be obtained as products of the likelihoods of the single observations. $L_{\cdot j}$ is the likelihood of vector b_{ij} for a given item j:

$$L_{\cdot j} = \prod_{i=1}^{N} L_{ij}. \tag{6}$$

13. SEARCHING FOR STRUCTURE IN BINARY DATA 225

L_T is the overall likelihood of the body of data.

$$L_T = \prod_{j=1}^{n} L_{.j}. \tag{7}$$

Parameters in the maximization of the overall likelihood are the two parameters of the binary fit function (slope and additive constant), the factor loadings and the factor scores. Several constraints on these parameters exist from factor analytic theory. The factor scores are to be standardized and uncorrelated. The factor weight vector for each item is to be of unit length. Several additional constraints appear to be needed on the factor scores. The number of these parameters is quite large so that propositions as to efficient statistics of the maximum likelihood do not hold. The combination of the binary fit function with the likelihood technique has the desirable property of approaching a maximum when model scores are developed which may be dichotomized so as to represent the observed 0 and 1 responses. In Table 13.1 for the know or guess situation, results for the data-fitting function are presented at the lower right. The slopes for the item functions are quite high. The additive constants are in order of easiness of the items; to obtain an index of item difficulty, the signs of the additive constants would have to be changed. The log likelihoods are tiny, negative values (natural logarithms are used throughout) so that no likelihood can be less than .999. We conclude: for this body of simulated data, a one common factor model with unique factors has been computed which represents the binary responses.

In order to present a partial contrast with the preceding results, two matrices of correlation were computed for the know or guess situation. Table 13.2 presents the matrix of phi correlations between the items in the upper section. This table shows the typical simplex type structure with high correlations near the diagonal and lower correlations away from the diagonal. Analysis of this matrix with unities in the diagonal results in the usual components of scalability. Analysis of the phi correlation matrix with SMC's in the diagonal does not eliminate the components of scalability factors which may be interpreted as difficulty factors. In the lower section of Table 13.2 is the matrix of tetrachoric correlations uncorrected for guessing. The simplex structure has not disappeared. In fact, this matrix is non-Gramian, having a negative eigenvalue. A matrix of tetrachoric correlations with correction for guessing was not computed.

NOTES ON ANALYSIS TECHNIQUES

Some notes on analysis techniques is in order at this point. An alternating scheme was followed attending to the item parameters first followed by adjustments of the factor scores. An initial matrix of factor scores was obtained from analysis of the phi coefficients matrix with SMC's in the diagonal to the desired number of

TABLE 13.2
Correlation Matrices for Example 1

Phi Coefficients

	1	2	3	4	5	6	7	8	9	10
1	100	47	30	22	16	12	15	08	05	04
2	47	100	44	48	31	21	18	16	08	08
3	30	44	100	53	34	30	33	13	10	11
4	22	48	53	100	54	43	45	19	10	08
5	16	31	34	54	100	52	40	27	11	02
6	12	21	30	43	52	100	48	33	17	11
7	15	18	33	45	40	48	100	39	23	03
8	08	16	13	19	27	33	39	100	30	10
9	05	08	10	10	11	17	23	30	100	13
10	04	08	11	08	02	11	03	10	13	100

Tetrachoric Correlations

	1	2	3	4	5	6	7	8	9	10
1	100	83	65	55	41	32	43	24	14	12
2	83	100	72	83	58	43	37	34	16	19
3	65	72	100	80	57	53	58	24	18	22
4	55	83	80	100	76	65	69	32	16	14
5	41	58	57	76	100	75	61	44	18	03
6	32	43	53	65	75	100	69	50	27	18
7	43	37	58	69	61	69	100	58	36	05
8	24	34	24	32	44	50	58	100	46	16
9	14	16	18	16	18	27	36	46	100	22
10	12	19	22	14	03	18	05	16	22	100

factors. Factor score estimates were obtained for the common factors and a small random value, rectilinearly distributed in the range of $-.1$ to $+.1$, was added to each factor score estimate. Unique factor scores were obtained by adding a small random value to the observed binary scores. This matrix was transformed to a standardized, uncorrelated form by a minimal transformation related to Green's (1969) development on best linear composites with a specified structure. A further transformation was applied to the unique factor scores so that each unique factor had a zero product moment correlation with the binary observations on every item except the corresponding item to the unique factor. The reason for this step is presented shortly. Having a matrix of factor scores, the item parameters were determined to maximize the likelihoods of the binary responses on the items by a Newton-Raphson technique. Having obtained the item parameters, the factor scores were adjusted by a gradient technique which included the adjustments described previously. Computations were continued until only tiny improvements in the likelihoods were obtained.

In an experiment preceding the ones presented here a group of items which scaled perfectly by a Guttman scale was used. The present technique fit a single common factor model to the data without unique scores. A result that was expected. However, without the constraint that the unique scores had to have zero correlations with noncorresponding item responses, a model with no common factor plus unique factors fit the data perfectly. The fact that a common factor was not necessary to fit items which scaled perfectly was disturbing. A switch had occurred from having to have too many factors to requiring too few factors. Inserting the constraint that each unique factor should be correlated with responses on only the corresponding item corrected this situation.

For the know or guess example a computer run was performed under the condition of no common factor, only unique factors. This run reached the time limit set for the computations without reaching the criterion for convergence. However, the last permissible gradient step for the factor scores involved only a tiny step size, and the likelihood criterion improvement was very small. The overall log likelihood at this termination of computation was $-.234$ which may be compared with the value of $-.0031$ for the one common factor solution. A conclusion appears to be justified that a no common factor model will not be fitted satisfactorily to the data.

EXAMPLES OF DATA GENERATED WITH TWO COMMON FACTORS

Two simulated data examples were generated and run for two factor structures. The distributions of the factor scores in the population were controlled to be nonnormal. Table 13.3 presents the population skewness and kurtosis of the factor scores for these examples. Only unique factors 3 and 7 had score distributions in the population approaching normal distributions by these measures. For each simulated individual a vector of factor scores was drawn with the separate scores being drawn independently. These scores were converted to model scores using a data generation factor matrix. For Example A this matrix is given in Table 13.4 along with a cutting score for each item. When a model score was greater than the cutting score for an item, the individual response to the item was taken to be a 1; otherwise, the individual response was taken to be a 0. A sample of 500 cases was drawn.

Table 13.5 presents the results for a two-common factor solution for Example A. The fit to the data is excellent as judged by the log likelihoods. When the signs of the additive constants are changed to obtain a measure of item difficulty, these additive constants are quite similar to the cutting scores given in Table 13.4. Figure 13.6 presents the factor plots for factor 1 and 2 for the data generation parameters on the left and for the obtained two-factor solution on the

TABLE 13.3
Generating Factor Score Skewness and Kurtosis
Two Factor Examples A and B

Factor		Skewness	Kurtosis
Common	1	.00	-1.20
"	2	1.74	5.23
Unique	1	.00	-1.20
"	2	1.74	5.23
"	3	.00	- .01
"	4	1.74	5.23
"	5	-1.74	5.23
"	6	1.74	5.23
"	7	.00	- .01
"	8	-1.74	5.23
"	9	.00	-1.20
"	10	.00	-1.20
"	11	1.74	5.23
"	12	-1.74	5.23
"	13	-1.74	5.23
"	14	1.74	5.23
"	15	1.74	5.23

TABLE 13.4
Data Generation Parameters for Two Factor Example A

	Factor Loadings			
	Common			
Item	1	2	Unique Factors	Cutting Score
1	.60	.00	.80	-1.28
2	.60	.00	.80	1.28
3	.45	.00	.89	.00
4	.30	.00	.95	- .84
5	.30	.00	.95	.84
6	.40	.20	.89	- .52
7	.40	.20	.89	.52
8	.30	.30	.91	.00
9	.20	.50	.84	- .84
10	.20	.50	.84	.84
11	.00	.35	.94	-1.04
12	.00	.35	.94	1.04
13	.00	.50	.87	.00
14	.00	.65	.76	- .84
15	.00	.65	.76	.84

Note. Number of Cases = 500.

TABLE 13.5
Two Factor Solution for Example A

	Factor Loadings			Data Fitting Function		
	Common		Unique		Additive	Log
Item	1	2	Factors	Slope	Constant	Likelihood
1	.60	-.52	.60	51.1	1.31	-.00003
2	.42	-.30	.86	68.9	-1.42	-.00008
3	.46	-.65	.61	46.5	.01	-.00027
4	.34	-.61	.71	64.5	1.10	-.00005
5	.31	-.72	.62	86.4	-1.12	-.00007
6	.75	-.38	.54	134.2	.48	-.00005
7	.72	-.36	.59	81.3	- .57	-.00007
8	.79	.22	.58	56.4	.09	-.00016
9	.73	.29	.63	346.6	1.02	-.00003
10	.75	.17	.64	52.5	- .84	-.00008
11	.37	.62	.69	46.6	1.44	-.00007
12	.56	.47	.68	73.9	-1.23	-.00005
13	.46	.73	.50	122.4	.11	-.00008
14	.68	.59	.44	53.7	1.19	-.00003
15	.54	.57	.61	101.0	-1.16	-.00001

Note. Total Log Likelihood = -.00113.

right. A rotation of axes of approximately 45 degrees is indicated for the obtained factor matrix. However, the spread of the points about the rotated factor planes appear somewhat large. A further comparison is of the unique factor loadings. One may conclude that a sloppy recovery of the generating factor matrix and cutting scores has been obtained for this example.

A greater disappointment is presented in Table 13.6. A computer run was made for a single common factor with the result that a satisfactory solution could be obtained as judged by the log likelihoods. Since the data were generated with two common factors, the hope was that a one-factor solution could not be found. This is not the case.

Results from Example A lead to a speculation that the structure had been made too weak to define a two-common factor structure and not a one-factor solution. Two alternatives were considered: one to employ more items and a larger sample and a second to use better items. In order to maintain lower costs the second alternative was chosen. Table 13.7 presents the data generation parameters for Example B. Again, there were 15 items; however, the factor loadings of these items are considerably larger than for Example A. Table 13.8 presents the results for a two-factor solution. The fit of this solution to the input data is excellent. Figure 13.7 presents the factor plot for the generating factor loadings on the left and the plot for the two-factor solution on the right. Increasing the quality of the items by using higher common factor generating loadings has improved the quality of the solution over that which was obtained for Exam-

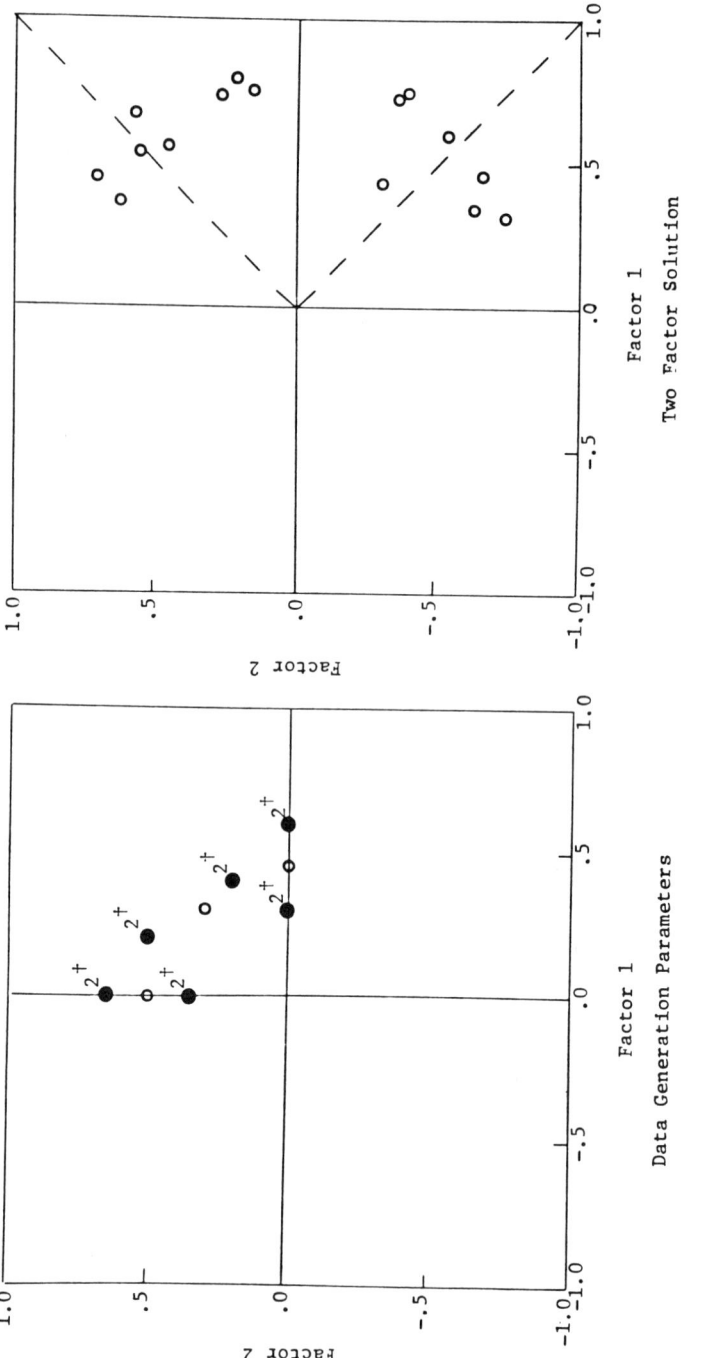

FIG. 13.6 Factor plots for two factor Example A.

13. SEARCHING FOR STRUCTURE IN BINARY DATA 231

TABLE 13.6
One Factor Solution for Example A

Item	Factor Loadings		Slope	Data Fitting Function	
	Common	Unique		Additive Constant	Log Likelihood
1	.53	.85	64.6	1.16	-.00008
2	.40	.92	31.9	-1.49	-.00043
3	.61	.79	60.8	.02	-.00035
4	.41	.91	34.3	.97	-.00051
5	.57	.82	72.0	-1.10	-.00019
6	.73	.68	47.5	.47	-.00068
7	.68	.74	54.3	- .49	-.00051
8	.69	.72	101.2	.15	-.00032
9	.66	.75	63.1	.82	-.00035
10	.62	.78	71.6	- .70	-.00041
11	.52	.85	41.0	1.18	-.00040
12	.57	.82	76.8	-1.15	-.00014
13	.63	.78	58.1	.30	-.00044
14	.77	.64	34.2	1.12	-.00054
15	.45	.90	66.0	- .97	-.00023

Note. Total Log Likelihood = -.00556.

TABLE 13.7
Data Generation Parameters for Two Factor Example B

Item	Factor Loadings		Unique Factors	Cutting Score
	Common			
	1	2		
1	.80	.00	.60	-1.25
2	.80	.00	.60	- .75
3	.80	.00	.60	- .25
4	.80	.00	.60	.25
5	.80	.00	.60	.75
6	.80	.00	.60	1.25
7	.70	.50	.51	- .50
8	.70	.50	.51	.50
9	.60	.60	.53	.00
10	.00	.80	.60	-1.25
11	.00	.80	.60	- .75
12	.00	.80	.60	- .25
13	.00	.80	.60	.25
14	.00	.80	.60	.75
15	.00	.80	.60	1.25

Note. Number of Cases = 500.

TABLE 13.8
Two Factor Solution for Example B

Item	Factor Loadings			Data Fitting Function		
	Common		Unique		Additive	Log
	1	2	Factors	Slope	Constant	Likelihood
1	.85	-.39	.35	155.4	1.30	-.00011
2	.90	-.32	.29	189.4	.82	-.00036
3	.83	-.43	.36	122.1	.38	-.00043
4	.80	-.41	.44	153.0	-.35	-.00035
5	.84	-.49	.26	279.8	-.72	-.00013
6	.79	-.40	.46	174.4	-1.46	-.00028
7	.94	.14	.32	256.1	.64	-.00016
8	.94	.11	.31	276.0	-.52	-.00010
9	.84	.35	.42	268.6	.01	-.00022
10	.51	.81	.29	100.5	1.62	-.00021
11	.35	.84	.40	303.4	1.08	-.00011
12	.25	.91	.32	566.2	.41	-.00010
13	.33	.88	.35	200.4	-.28	-.00038
14	.42	.79	.45	147.2	-1.00	-.00040
15	.33	.69	.64	68.0	-1.41	-.00027

Note. Total Log Likelihood = -.00361.

ple A. Table 13.9 presents the results for a one-factor solution. Again, a one-factor solution can be found. This continues the disappointing results from Example A.

SUMMARY AND DISCUSSION

A purpose was stated to develop for binary data a method of analysis which would lead to a common factor plus unique factor structure solution revealing a structure underlying the data. Further, the weakest of distributional assumptions should be employed. The ideas of using a logistic fit function with a likelihood function criterion were developed and utilized in a computer program. A moderate degree of success was obtained with simulated data for which the structure was known when the correct number of common factors was used. However, an area of disappointments was uncovered; the binary data could be represented by a model having fewer common factors than the generating structure. A satisfactory method should not indicate fewer common factors than the number in the generating structure. Some further ideas are needed to constrain the solution so as to eliminate the fitting of solutions having too few factors. These constraints should not involve overly stringent assumptions such as the population distribution being multidimensional normal. A possible direction of constraint is toward further definition of statistical independence of the factor scores. A moments

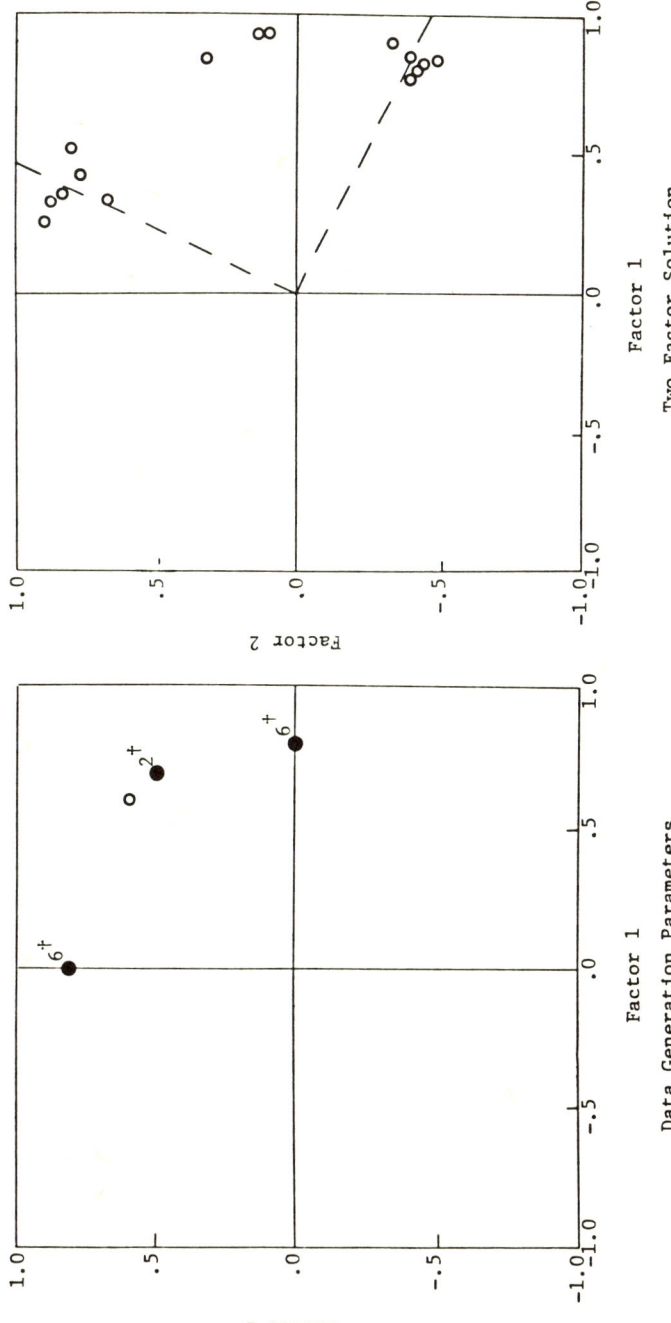

FIG. 13.7 Factor plots for two factor Example B.

TABLE 13.9
One Factor Solution for Example B

	Factor Loadings			Data Fitting Function	
				Additive	Log
Item	Common	Unique	Slope	Constant	Likelihood
1	.76	.65	168.5	1.29	-.00004
2	.81	.59	73.2	.73	-.00062
3	.75	.66	61.7	.30	-.00044
4	.72	.70	167.3	- .25	-.00009
5	.82	.58	404.4	- .60	-.00006
6	.67	.74	146.0	-1.41	-.00010
7	.89	.46	140.3	.59	-.00020
8	.90	.43	80.3	- .47	-.00041
9	.84	.54	252.2	.02	-.00001
10	.84	.54	212.3	1.34	-.00003
11	.78	.63	169.7	1.06	-.00002
12	.63	.77	67.7	.50	-.00036
13	.53	.85	42.1	- .08	-.00224
14	.64	.77	81.2	-1.09	-.00013
15	.48	.88	122.0	-1.52	-.00004

Note. Total Log Likelihood = -.00480.

type approach beyond the product moment correlations between factors may be workable and is to be explored.

REFERENCES

Bock, R. D., & Lieberman, M. Fitting a response model for *n* dichotomously scored items. *Psychometrika*, 1970, *35*, 179–197.

Carroll, J. B. The effect of difficulty and chance success on correlations between items or between tests. *Psychometrika*, 1945, *10*, 1–20.

Carroll, J. B. The nature of data, or how to choose a correlation coefficient. *Psychometrika*, 1961, *26*, 347–372.

Christoffersson, A. Factor analysis of dichotomized variables. *Psychometrika*, 1975, *40*, 5–32.

Dingman, H. F. The relation between coefficients of correlation and difficulty factors. *British Journal of Statistical Psychology*, 1958, *11*, 13–17.

Ferguson, G. A. The factorial interpretation of test difficulty. *Psychometrika*, 1941, *6*, 323–329.

Gourlay, N. Difficulty factors arising from the use of tetrachoric correlations in factor analysis. *British Journal of Psychology* (Statistical Section), 1951, 65–76.

Green, B. F. Best linear composites with a specified structure. *Psychometrika*, 1969, *34*, 301–318.

Guilford, J. P. The difficulty of a test and its factor composition. *Psychometrika*, 1941, *6*, 67–77.

Guttman, L. The quantification of a class of attributess: A theory and method of scale construction. In Paul Horst et al., *The prediction of personal adjustment*. New York: Social Science Research Council, 1941, 321–348.

Guttman, L. The determinacy of factor score matrices with implications for five other basic problems in common factor theory. *British Journal of Statistical Psychology*, 1955, *8*, 65–81.

Lawley, D. N. The factorial analysis of multiple item tests. *Proceedings of the Royal Society of Edinburgh,* 1944, 62-A, 74–82.

Lord, F. M. A theory of test scores. *Psychometric Monograph,* No. 7, 1952.

Lord, F. M. Some relations between Guttman's principal components of scale analysis and other psychometric theory. *Psychometrika,* 1958, *23,* 291–296.

Muthen, B. Contributions to factor analysis of dichotomous variables. *Psychometrika,* 1978, *43,* 551–560.

Muthen, B., & Christoffersson, A. Simultaneous factor analysis of dichotomous variables in several groups. *Psychometrika,* 1981, *46,* 407–419.

Tucker, L. R. Maximum validity of a test with equivalent items. *Psychometrika,* 1946, *11,* 1–13.

Tucker, L. R. A method for scaling ability test items taking item unreliability into account. *American Psychologist,* 1948, *3,* 309–310.

Wherry, R. J., & Gaylord, R. H. Factor pattern of test items and tests as a function of the correlation coefficient: Content, difficulty, and constant error factors. *Psychometrika,* 1944, *9,* 237–248.

14 The Greatest Lower Bound to Reliability

P. M. Bentler
J. Arthur Woodward
University of California, Los Angeles

ABSTRACT

Reliability coefficients for composites of variables traditionally are derived on the basis of an assumed decomposition of the component variables into unobserved additive true and error parts obeying strong assumptions about the dimensionality of the latent variables as well as possible homogeneities of their variances. A reliability coefficient can be defined for this classic linear latent variable model under the minimal assumptions that the true and error scores are independent, that error scores are mutually independent, and that their covariance matrices are Gramian. The greatest lower bound to this minimal assumption reliability coefficient is introduced, and its history is traced. The relation of the greatest lower bound to other reliability coefficients is established. Computational theory and practice are reviewed, and some new results are developed. Sampling characteristics of the coefficient, and especially its asymptotic variance and bias, are discussed, and some new results are described. The concept of the greatest statistical lower bound to reliability is introduced. Some examples are provided to illustrate the approach.

INTRODUCTION

A major focus of the past 80 years of research on reliability theory has been the measurement of population reliability of a composite formed from unit weighted component parts. The practical use in assessment instruments of this simple sum score always has been widespread, and during the early years of reliability research, the study of composite reliability provided one of the only tractable avenues for development of the field. In recent years, of course, the field has advanced into many new exciting domains (e.g., Lord, 1980; Lord & Novick, 1968), aided by increasingly sophisticated mathematical models and stimulated by the advent of computers. Still, the study of composite reliability based on a linear model of true and error latent variables remains as one viable research area having both practical and theoretical importance. In this chapter we briefly review several major themes in this most traditional topic of reliability theory, and then provide a detailed account of one currently developing approach, the greatest lower bound to reliability.

Three major approaches to the study of composite reliability can be identified in the literature. These may be called the strong-assumption, assumption-testing, and weak-assumption approaches. In the strong-assumption approach, it is assumed a priori that the component measurements conform to some specific common factor analysis model $\Sigma = \Lambda\Phi\Lambda' + \Omega^2 + E^2$, where Σ is the $n \times n$ population covariance matrix of the measured variables, Λ is the $n \times r$ common factor loading matrix, Φ is the factor covariance matrix, Ω^2 is the positive semidefinite diagonal matrix of specific variances, and E^2 is the positive semidefinite diagonal matrix of error variances. Historically, very restrictive assumptions were made about the above model in order to define a function of Σ that would exactly equal the population reliability of the sum score, here defined as $\rho_{xx} = 1 - 1'E^2 1/1'\Sigma 1$. For example, if one can make the strong assumption that the component parts conform to an essentially tau-equivalent model where Λ is $n \times 1$, the true score variances [Diag $(\Lambda\Phi\Lambda')$] are equal, and $\Omega^2 = 0$, then coefficient α, a simple function of the covariance matrix $\alpha = [n/(n - 1)][1 - 1'D_\Sigma 1/1'\Sigma 1]$, equals the population reliability (Bentler, 1968; Novick & Lewis, 1967). Most recently, the required assumptions have been relaxed some, so that a function of the population matrix can be formed that will exactly equal ρ_{xx} under the assumption of congeneric component measures where Λ is $n \times 1$ and Ω^2 is null (e.g., Kristof, 1974). The coefficients that result from the a priori covariance structure approach typically are simple to compute (e.g. coefficient α), but since they are tailored to the a priori form of the model, they may have undesirable properties when the model assumptions are not met. Thus, a second approach has emerged in which the covariance structure is not accepted a priori, but is accepted or rejected on the basis of a statistical test of a hypothesized structure.

In the assumption-testing approach (e.g., Bentler & Browne, 1980; Jöreskog, 1971; Jöreskog, 1974) a variety of specific hypotheses about $\Sigma = \Lambda\Phi\Lambda' + E^2$ (assuming Ω^2 to be null) can be tested statistically using a generalized least squares or maximum likelihood approach (e.g. Bentler, 1982; Jöreskog & Sörbom, 1978). Following parameter estimation, if the model is accepted as plausible on the basis of the accompanying goodness of fit test, then the reliability of the sum of the components is given by

$$\hat{\rho}_{xx} = 1 - '\hat{\Lambda}\hat{\Phi}\hat{\Lambda}'1/1'(\hat{\Lambda}\hat{\Phi}\hat{\Lambda}' + \hat{E}^2)1,$$

where $\hat{\Lambda}$, $\hat{\Phi}$, and $\hat{E}^2$ are the estimators of the parameters of the model. The value of this approach is that the specific assumptions about the model are testable; and second, that one is not restricted to the limited class of parallel, tau-equivalent, or congeneric models typically studied in the strong-assumption approach. A major disadvantage is that the procedure requires a relatively small set of component variables in order to be manageable. And, if a large set of measures is being studied, rejection of a specific hypothesized model could leave the investigator with the expensive and difficult task of discovering the appropriate model, possibly without any a priori theory as a guide. But this problem may be nothing other than the difficult and unresolved problem of exploratory factor analysis if the restrictions imposed on the model are only rank related (e.g. see Hakstian, Rogers, & Cattell, 1982, for a recent study). The point estimators of reliability under this approach are not necessarily lower bounds to reliability. Hence, in order to obtain a lower bound to reliability and to obviate estimation problems associated with large data sets, one may also consider lower bound approaches originally developed under strong assumption models. That is, in addition to the point estimator $\hat{\rho}_{xx}$, one may compute some simple function of Σ such as coefficient alpha, since alpha is a lower bound to reliability under the general conditions specified by the common factor model, that is, $\alpha \leq \rho_{xx}$ (Novick & Lewis, 1967). Unfortunately, while it is important to measure composite reliability under these general conditions, it is known that alpha can *grossly* underestimate the population reliability.

The weak-assumption approach to reliability attempts to impose few a priori conditions for an estimator. As we point out in the next section, the minimal assumptions that may be invoked are simply the independence of true and error variables, the mutual independence of the various error components, and possibly the nonimaginary nature of these scores. Among weak-assumption estimators are several that were proposed by Guttman (1945), Jackson and Agunwamba (1977), and Bentler and Woodward (1980), including the maximal split-half coefficient obtainable by methods described by Bentler and Woodward (1980), and Callender and Osburn (1977). Since there are many possible lower bound estimators available under the minimal assumption approach, the logical one to consider is that which yields the greatest lower bound to reliability, as is shown next.

THE GREATEST LOWER BOUND TO RELIABILITY

The basic idea of the greatest lower bound to reliability originated with Bentler (1972). Three ideas fundamental to the development of the greatest lower bound were introduced in that paper. First is that the a priori restriction of a single factor model, as well as other restrictions typically associated with the strong assumption approach to reliability, were relaxed in measuring composite reliability—

thus yielding a dimension-free approach in the terminology of Bentler (1972). Second, a specific approach to the lower bound measurement of reliability was defined by using the factor analytic model superimposed on a traditional true and error score model. That is, a new lower bound to reliability was defined in terms of factor analytic variates that allow one to combine specific aspects of true scores with random error variates into a vector of unique scores. Finally, Bentler's third major contribution was to develop a computational theory that led to an efficient computer algorithm for calculating the new coefficient that he proposed. This algorithm still provides the foundation for today's only effective algorithm for computing the greatest lower bound. Bentler also showed that his coefficient is always an improvement over coefficient α.

Before explicitly defining Bentler's lower bound coefficient for the dimension-free measurement of internal consistency, the conceptual basis of the approach is reviewed. Let us consider a rank-free decomposition of the $n \times 1$ observed score vector x as

$$x = \mu + \tau + \omega + e,$$

where μ is a mean vector, τ is a vector of common true scores, ω is a vector of specific true scores, and e is an error vector. The covariance matrix of the observed scores x is $\Sigma = cov(x - \mu)(x - \mu)'$, and, on the assumption that the random vectors τ, ω, and e are mutually independent,

$$\Sigma = \Sigma_\tau + \Omega^2 + E^2,$$

where Σ_τ is the covariance matrix of the true scores, and Ω^2 and E^2 are the diagonal covariance matrices of ω and e respectively. On the basis of internal consistency information alone, factor analytic specificity ω and error e cannot be separated, so that the decomposition of x can be simplified to

$$x = \mu + \tau + \epsilon,$$

where ϵ represents a vector of unique scores. It follows that

$$\Sigma = \Sigma_\tau + \psi^2,$$

where $\psi^2 = \Omega^2 + E^2$. Upon defining reliability and internal consistency coefficients of the unit weighted composite $1'x$ as

$$\rho_{xx} = 1 - var(1'e)/var(1'x) \text{ and}$$
$$\rho_I = 1 - var(1'\epsilon)/var(1'x),$$

it is apparent that

$$\rho_I \leq \rho_{xx}.$$

That is, all coefficients based on ψ^2 and Σ rather than E^2 and Σ are lower bounds to reliability.

14. THE GREATEST LOWER BOUND TO RELIABILITY

Assuming that Σ is a fixed population covariance matrix, we can define a general scalar function $\rho = f(\psi^2) = 1 - 1'\psi^2 1/1'\Sigma 1$, the domain of which is the set of ψ^2 matrices consistent with the tautology

$$\Sigma = (\Sigma - \psi^2) + \psi^2,$$

where $\Sigma_\tau = \Sigma - \psi^2$. Note that ψ^2 defines Σ_τ via Σ. Under certain restrictions on the domain of the function ρ, minima can be identified with a useful lower bound property. Specifically, Bentler (1972) defined ρ_ℓ as the smallest possible $f(\psi^2)$ subject to the constraint that underlying common factors are nonimaginary. Thus

$$\rho_\ell = \min f(\psi^2) = 1 - 1'\psi_\ell^2 1/1'\Sigma 1 \qquad ((\Sigma - \psi_\ell^2) \geq 0),$$

where the inequality indicates that the true score covariance matrix is Gramian. It follows immediately that

$$\rho_\ell \leq \rho_I.$$

In comparison to the assumption-testing approach to reliability, no specific factor structure is assumed to underlie the covariance matrix, and thus no such structural hypothesis is tested.

From the above, it is apparent that ψ^2 should be a Gramian matrix as well, if the residual or error vector ϵ is real valued. This consequence was realized by Bentler, but he did not have any procedure to impose the constraint. This natural constraint, however, provides the important conceptual leap in going from *a* lower bound to the dimension-free measurement of interval consistency to *the* greatest lower bound to reliability, as was done by Jackson and Agunwamba (1977) and independently by Bentler and Woodward (1980). Specifically, the greatest lower bound to the reliability of the sum is

$$\rho_+ = \min f(\psi^2) = 1 - 1'\psi_+^2 1/1'\Sigma 1 \qquad ((\Sigma - \psi_+^2) \geq 0, \; \psi_+^2 \geq 0). \quad (1)$$

The additional restriction that the diagonal matrix ψ^2 must be nonnegative definite has practical importance in the sense that the solution to ρ_ℓ could lead to unique variances in ψ_ℓ^2 being negative (i.e., a Heywood case). Theoretically, the importance is as follows. Since ρ_+ is based on more restrictions than ρ_ℓ, it follows that

$$\rho_\ell \leq \rho_+ \leq \rho_I \leq \rho_{xx}.$$

In fact, the coefficient ρ_+ is the greatest lower bound to reliability (Bentler & Woodward, 1980). The notation $\rho_+ = \text{glb}(\rho)$ or $\inf(\rho)$ may be used, where the greatest lower bound or infimum has the standard definition (see, e.g., Clark, 1978, p. 93).

It should be noted explicitly that the greatest lower bound is an obvious consequence of the minimal assumption approach to reliability. The only assumption being made is that there exists a Gramian diagonal matrix ψ^2 such that

$\Sigma - \psi^2$ also is Gramian. No further assumptions about homogeneity of variances or dimensionality of true and error scores needs to be made. It is possible, of course, that traditional assumptions about the rank of $\Sigma - \psi^2$, or equal diagonal elements in ψ^2 and/or $\Sigma - \psi^2$, may be correct, but these need not be assumed. Although the linearity assumption in the decomposition $x = \mu + \tau + \epsilon$ is made, no further assumptions are made about the distribution of the continuous variables involved. Statistical distribution assumptions need only be added as necessary to obtain statistical statements about the resulting coefficients computed from sample data.

Minimum Trace Factor Analysis. The above relationships can be reformulated in the following way to yield a perhaps more familiar form. Selecting ψ^2 to minimize $(1 - 1'\psi^2 1/1'\Sigma 1)$ is the same as selecting ψ^2 (subject to restrictions) so that trace (ψ^2) is maximized, since Σ is fixed. But from the basic tautology $\Sigma = (\Sigma - \psi^2) + \psi^2$ it can be shown that this is tantamount to selecting ψ^2 to minimize the trace of $(\Sigma - \psi^2)$. Thus, the problem reduces to finding new diagonal elements for Σ such that the sum of the diagonal values is as small as possible (subject to constraints). This is just one formulation of the communality problem in traditional exploratory factor analysis. Selection of ψ_ℓ^2 so as to minimize trace $(\Sigma - \psi^2)$ subject to the constraints that $(\Sigma - \psi_\ell^2) \geq 0$ was referred to as minimum trace factor analysis (MTFA) (Bentler, 1972). The concept of MTFA had earlier been discussed by Ledermann (1939), but he provided no computational approach for actually finding the minimum trace solution.

Recently, Shapiro (1982), ten Berge, Snijders, and Zegers (1981), Della Riccia and Shapiro (1980), have discussed minimum trace factor analysis where the trace $(\Sigma - \psi^2)$ is minimized subject to the constraints that $(\Sigma - \psi_+^2) \geq 0$ and $\psi_+^2 \geq 0$. This, they refer to as constrained minimum trace factor analysis (CMTFA). Using this factor analysis formulation, they established necessary and sufficient conditions for MTFA and CMTFA, as well as a uniqueness proof for CMTFA (or MTFA) solutions. These uniqueness proofs are directly relevant to establishing the uniqueness of the greatest lower bound to reliability. In addition, Della Riccia and Shapiro (1980) provide insight, beyond that provided by Ledermann (1937, 1939), into the relation between minimum trace and minimum rank factor analysis (MRFA). Their work relating MTFA and MRFA provides a theoretical explanation to the empirical observation (e.g. Bentler & Woodward, 1980) that MTFA and MRFA approaches usually lead to very similar numerical results.

BASIC THEORY

Consider the set Π of matrices N such that $N = TT'$ with diag(N) = I. Under the tautology $\Sigma = (\Sigma - \psi^2) + \psi^2$,

14. THE GREATEST LOWER BOUND TO RELIABILITY

$$T'\Sigma T = T'(\Sigma - \psi^2)T + T'\psi^2 T.$$

Under MTFA, $(\Sigma - \psi^2) \geq 0$, so that the sum of diagonal elements are related by

$$tr T'\Sigma T \geq tr T'\psi^2 T = tr\psi^2 TT' = 1'\psi^2 1.$$

Dividing both sides by the constant $1'\Sigma 1$, and subtracting from 1, yields

$$\rho_T = 1 - tr T'\Sigma T/1'\Sigma 1 \leq 1 - 1'\psi^2 1/1'\Sigma 1 = \rho.$$

In particular,

$$\max_T \rho_T \leq \min_{\psi^2} \rho.$$

The largest ρ_T is obtained by a minimization of $tr T'\Sigma T$. Let T_ℓ be the minimizating T. Bentler and Woodward (1980) show that T_ℓ defines a matrix ψ_ℓ^2 such that when $(\Sigma - \psi_\ell^2)T_\ell = 0$, $\rho_{T_\ell} = \rho_\ell$, the lower bound coefficient introduced by Bentler (1972). Della Riccia and Shapiro (1980), ten Berge, Snijders and Zegers (1981), and Shapiro (1982) show that $(\Sigma - \psi_\ell^2)$ is Gramian, and that the solution is unique.

Bentler and Woodward (1980) also investigated reliability coefficients ρ_T where T can vary in rank. They established that $\rho_{T_1} \leq \rho_{T_2} \leq \cdots \rho_\ell$, where ρ_{T_1} is Guttman's (1945) λ_4 coefficient. As noted above, Bentler (1972) showed that $\alpha \leq \rho_\ell$. Those coefficients, however, are not necessarily associated with Gramian true or error covariance matrices.

The above theory, relevant to defining Bentler's (1972) ρ_ℓ is modified trivially to yield the greatest lower bound. This extension was explicitly noted in Bentler and Woodward's (1980) optimization theory and more recently by ten Berge et al. (1981). That is, let Π^* be the set of matrices N^* such that $N^* = TT'$ with diag(N^*) $\geq I$. Let T_+ be the minimizing T under Π^* and T_ℓ be the minimizing T under Π of $tr T'\Sigma T$. Since T_+ is based on fewer restrictions than T_ℓ, $tr T'_+ \Sigma T_+ \leq tr T'_\ell \Sigma T_\ell$. Thus, for all choices ψ^2 for ρ, $\rho_\ell \leq \rho_+ \leq \rho$. Equality is attained, again, when $(\Sigma - \psi_+^2)T_+ = 0$. Then, both $(\Sigma - \psi_+^2)$ and ψ_+^2 are Gramian and unique, and $\rho_{T_+} = \rho_+$ with ρ_+ being the greatest lower bound to reliability. It is based on a unique CMTFA solution (Della Riccia & Shapiro, 1980; Shapiro, 1982; ten Berge et al., 1981).

Any other matrix ψ^{2*} that allows $(\Sigma - \psi^{2*})$ and ψ^{2*} to be Gramian will lead to a coefficient ρ^* that is larger than ρ_+. However, since ρ^* has no natural upper bound other than 1.0, it cannot be taken to be a lower bound to reliability. For example, it is always possible to choose a Gramian diagonal matrix D such that $\psi^{2*} = \psi_+^2 - D$ is Gramian (e.g., let D contain a single nonzero element that is smaller than a corresponding positive element of ψ_+^2). It follows that $\Sigma - \psi^{2*} = (\Sigma - \psi_+^2) + D$ is Gramian as well, and that the corresponding $\rho^* > \rho_+$. But ρ^* cannot be shown to be smaller than the true internal consistency reliability ρ_I

which might in principle be defined on a structural decomposition of Σ. Since D may be chosen to be larger and larger, arbitrarily, (until $D = \psi_+^2$, in which case $\psi^{2*} = 0$ and $\Sigma - \psi^{2*} = \Sigma$), ρ^* can take on any arbitrary value between ρ_+ and 1.0. On the other hand, ρ_+ is the unique smallest possible coefficient consistent with the minimal Gramian CMTFA assumptions. It cannot, therefore, exceed the "true" internal consistency ρ_I or the true reliability ρ_{xx}. Clearly, ρ_+ is the greatest lower bound.

COMPUTATIONAL METHODS

The basic theory outlined above has transformed the problem of finding the matrix ψ_+^2 that yields the greatest lower bound into the problem of finding the matrix T_+ that minimizes the function $tr T'\Sigma T$ subject to $\text{diag}(TT') \geq I$. The minimization problem under the equality restriction $\text{diag}(TT') = I$ was first introduced and solved by Bentler (1972). Bentler and Woodward (1980) extended the solution to the inequality constraint $\text{diag}(TT') \geq I$, and developed two published algorithms to yield the solution. In the widely circulated draft of their published paper, they also proposed an algorithm that is a slight modification of their finally published algorithm. This algorithm provides the basis for a further technical development, made below, based on the Kuhn-Tucker theory for inequality constrained problems. We shall prove convergence for the faster modified algorithm, thus eliminating an incompleteness in published proofs.

Woodhouse and Jackson (1977) provided algorithms having a totally different conceptual basis for reaching the greatest lower bound to reliability. According to ten Berge et al. (1981), these methods have computational pitfalls that can make them fail. Consequently, they are not described here.

In the Bentler and Woodward (1980) algorithm, the reliability estimator is based on minimizing the function $f = \sigma^2 t't + 2\sigma_o'Tt + tr\, T^{o'}\Sigma^o T^{o'} - \Delta(t't - 1) - tr\, \Delta^o(T^oT^{o'} - I)$, where σ^2 is the pth diagonal element of the known $(n \times n)$ symmetric nonnegative definite matrix Σ, t' is the pth row of the unknown $(n \times i)$ matrix T, σ_o' is the pth row of $(\Sigma\text{-diag }\Sigma)$, T^o is a matrix of the $m = n - 1$ rows that remain after removing t' from T, Σ^o and Δ^o are the $(m \times m)$ matrices resulting when the pth row and column are eliminated from Σ and an unknown diagonal matrix Δ_i, and Δ is the pth diagonal element of Δ_i. It was shown that the estimation of t and Δ is separable from T^o and Δ^o, and they proposed to update t and Δ as $p = 1, \ldots, n$. Thus for a given p, the function $g = \sigma^2 t't + 2\sigma_o'Tt - \Delta(t't - 1)$ is minimized. In practice, T may be in echelon form; in that case, T and t are replaced in f and g by $T.$ and $t.$, where $T = [T., T..]$, $t' = [t.', t..']$, and $t..'$ contains known zero elements. The order of $t..'$ is given by the number of fixed zeros; $t' = t.'$ if there are none. Consequently, $g = \sigma^2 t.'t. + 2\sigma_o'T.t. - \Delta(t.'t. - 1)$.

It is apparent from the discussion surrounding this form of the algorithm

14. THE GREATEST LOWER BOUND TO RELIABILITY   245

(Bentler & Woodward, 1980, pp. 258–9) that the problem requires the imposition of the additional constraint $\Delta \geq 0$. This constraint was effectively dealt with in the algorithm, but a unifying optimization theory was not presented. We employ the elegant Kuhn-Tucker (1951) theory for optimization subject to inequality constraints, which then provides the relevant theory and suggests a minor algorithmic modification. We also show that certain function evaluations proposed in the original Bentler-Woodward algorithm can be eliminated, thus speeding up convergence.

Let $h = \Delta$ be the constrained function, and consider g as an unconstrained function of $\theta' = (t.', \Delta)$, a vector of unknown parameters. The problem is to minimize g under the constraint $h \geq 0$. The Kuhn-Tucker first-order necessary condition guarantees the existence of a Lagrangian multiplier λ such that (i) $\partial g/\partial \theta + \lambda(\partial h/\partial \theta) = 0$, (ii) $\lambda h = 0$, and (iii) $\lambda \geq 0$. Condition (i) implies $T.'\sigma_o + (\sigma^2 - \Delta)t. = 0$ as noted by Bentler and Woodward, but also that $\lambda = (t.'t. - 1)$; with λ so defined, conditions (ii) and (iii) were also known (e.g., $t.'t. \geq 1$). It can easily be verified that these conditions are met by an estimator that takes one of the following three forms: if $\sigma_o'T.T.'\sigma_o = 0$, $\Delta = \sigma^2$, $t.$ is an arbitrary normal vector, and $\lambda = 0$; if $0 < (\sigma_o'T.T.'\sigma_o)^{1/2} < \sigma^2$, $\Delta = \sigma^2 - (\sigma_o'T.T.'\sigma_o)^{1/2}$, $t. = -T.'\sigma_o(\sigma_o'T.T.'\sigma_o)^{-1/2}$ and $\lambda = 0$ (only positive squareroots are taken); or, if $(\sigma_o'T.T.'\sigma_o)^{1/2} \geq \sigma^2$, $\Delta = 0$, $t. = -T.'\sigma_o/\sigma^2$, and $\lambda = t.'t. - 1 > 0$. (Note that if $\sigma_o'T.T.'\sigma_o = 0$ and $\sigma^2 = 0$, $\Delta = 0$ with $\lambda > 0$ and $t.$ an arbitrary nonnormal vector also meets conditions (i)–(iii); if one also requires (ii) to be satisfied by $\lambda \neq h$, the nonnormal replacement is required. This condition is not necessary to an algorithm, however.)

An algorithm consistent with these Kuhn-Tucker results is the following. Let $T.$ be a feasible current matrix, $t.^{(i)}$ be current $t.$ vector, $v.$ be an arbitrary normal vector (e.g., a vector with a single unit and all zeros otherwise), and δ be a predetermined small number. It follows that $g^{(i)} = \sigma^2 t.^{(i)}{}'t.^{(i)} + 2\sigma_o'T.t.^{(i)}$, that is, that $\Delta^{(i)}(t.^{(i)}{}'t.^{(i)} - 1) = 0$. It is desired to minimize $g^{(i+1)}$ subject to $h \geq 0$ for a given p; to cycle through $p = 1, \ldots, n$; and to iterate cycles until no further decreases in any g are possible. Then, for a given p, a step of the algorithm consists of either (a), (b), or (c), where

(a) $t.^{(i+1)} = v.$ if $(\sigma_0'T.T.'\sigma_0)^{1/2} \leq \delta$

(b) $t.^{(i+1)} = -T.'\sigma_0(\sigma_0'T.T.'\sigma_0)^{-1/2}$ if $\delta < (\sigma_0'T.T.'\sigma_0)^{1/2} < \sigma^2$ (2)

(c) $t.^{(i+1)} = -T.'\sigma_0/\sigma^2$ otherwise.

In (2), $\Delta^{(i+1)}$ takes on the value σ^2, $\sigma^2 - (\sigma_o'T.T.'\sigma_o)^{1/2}$ or 0 under (a), (b), and (c) respectively, and $(\sigma_o'T.T.'\sigma_o)^{1/2} = |(\sigma_o'T.T.'\sigma_o)^{1/2}|$. It follows that $g^{(i+1)} = \sigma^2 t.^{(i+1)}{}'t.^{(i+1)} + 2\sigma_o'T.t.^{(i+1)}$, that is, the constraint $\Delta^{(i+1)}(t.^{(i+1)}{}'t.^{(i+1)} - 1) = 0$ continues to be met.

Step (a) stems from $\sigma_o'T.T.'\sigma_o = 0$, with δ replacing zero to allow for computational inaccuracy. Ignoring $\sigma_o'T.t. \cong 0$, it yields $g^{(i)} - g^{(i+1)} =$

$\sigma^2(t.^{(i)\prime}t.^{(i)} - 1) \geq 0$, with $g^{(i+1)} < g^{(i)}$ when $\sigma^2 > 0$ and $t.^{(i)\prime}t.^{(i)} > 1$. Step (b) cannot increase the function. Since $\sigma_o'T.t.^{(i)} = -(\sigma_o'T.T.'\sigma_o)^{1/2} t.^{(i+1)\prime}t.^{(i)}$ and $\sigma_o'T.t.^{(i+1)} = -(\sigma_o'T.T.\sigma_o)^{1/2}$, it follows that $g^{(i)} - g^{(i+1)} = \sigma^2 t.^{(i)\prime}t.^{(i)} - 2(\sigma_o'T.T.'\sigma_o)^{1/2}t.^{(i+1)\prime}t.^{(i)} - \sigma^2 + 2(\sigma_o'T.T.'\sigma_o)^{1/2}$. Simplification yields $g^{(i)} - g^{(i+1)} = (\sigma_o'T.T.'\sigma_o)^{1/2} (t.^{(i)} - t.^{(i+1)})'(t.^{(i)} - t.^{(i+1)}) + [\sigma^2 - (\sigma_o'T.T.'\sigma_o)^{1/2}] (t.^{(i)\prime}t.^{(i)} - 1)$. It follows that $g^{(i+1)} < g^{(i)}$ if $t.^{(i+1)} \neq t.^{(i)}$. Under step (c), $g^{(i)} = \sigma^2 t.^{(i)\prime}t.^{(i)} - 2\sigma^2 t.^{(i+1)\prime}t.^{(i)}$, so that $g^{(i)} - g^{(i+1)} = \sigma^2(t.^{(i)} - t.^{(i+1)})' (t.^{(i)} - t.^{(i+1)}) > 0$, with $g^{(i+1)} < g^{(i)}$ if $t.^{(i+1)} \neq t.^{(i)}$. Consequently, g decreases monotonically to a minimum as cycles and iterations are taken with algorithm (2).

Except for step (a), algorithm (2) is identical to an algorithm described in a widely circulated draft version of the Bentler-Woodward (1980) paper, and to one more recently proposed by ten Berge, Snijders, and Zegers (1981). Step (a) in (2) differs from the Bentler-Woodward draft and the published (3.26a) in that $t^{(i+1)}$ is necessarily an inexpensive normalized step here. The theory for this step stems from the Kuhn-Tucker conditions developed above; a similar step was proposed by ten Berge et al. based on another rationale. However, the computational consequences of steps (2a) and (3.26a) are identical. Steps (b) and (c) in (2) are equivalent to the unpublished algorithm, but (b) differs from (3.26b) in that no expensive function evaluation is undertaken here. A proof for convergence under (b) was not previously available anywhere. Step (c) is equivalent to (3.26c). Finally, the discussion surrounding (3.26) (pp. 258–9) implies that a boundary constraint $\Delta^{(i+1)} = 0$ may be inappropriately imposed on a temporary basis. The above proofs clarify that such a step cannot be taken in either algorithm; this result was also noted by ten Berge et al. (1981).

Our imposition of echelon form of T is inexpensive and effective for establishing its uniqueness and for evaluating whether its rank is adequate. For the greatest lower bound, we take as the number of columns of T a number i such that $i(i + 1)/2$ equals or exceeds n, so that Shapiro's (1982) theory for the minimal rank of T is exceeded. As noted by ten Berge et al. (1981) and Shapiro (1982), the greatest lower bound will have been reached computationally only if Δ_i and $\Sigma - \Delta_i$ are Gramian. Then, we may take $\Delta_i = \psi_+^2$. The algorithm guarantees that $\Delta_i \geq 0$, so that one may wish to check whether $\Sigma - \Delta_i \geq 0$. In our experience such a check is not necessary if at the solution T is not of full column rank, which is easily seen when T is in echelon form. As noted by Bentler (1972), the rank of T corresponds to the degree of rank reduction in $\Sigma - \Delta_i$.

STATISTICAL ISSUES

It was assumed above that the population covariance matrix Σ is known and the discussion centered on the population coefficient $\rho_+ = f(\Sigma)$, where $f(\Sigma)$ is

14. THE GREATEST LOWER BOUND TO RELIABILITY   247

defined by (1) and obtained by the algorithm in (2). Typically, a sample of N entities is available and arrayed in the $N \times n$ matrix X where it is assumed that the rows of X are independently and identically distributed with mean μ and covariance matrix Σ. Estimation of Σ is through $S = (1/N\text{-}1) [X'(I - 1N^{-1}1')X]$ and a consistent estimator of the population greatest lower bound is $\hat{\rho}_+ = f(S)$. The function $f(S)$ is given by (1) and computationally evaluated by (2), given that sample statistics replace population counterparts.

At present, only the asymptotic sampling theory of $\hat{\rho}_+$ has been developed. Woodward, Browne, and Bentler (1980) developed asymptotic normal estimators of the variance of $\hat{\rho}_+$ ($var(\hat{\rho}_+)$) as well as the asymptotic distribution free variance of $\hat{\rho}_+$ ($var_{adf}(\hat{\rho}_+)$). Shapiro (1982) developed an estimator for $var(\hat{\rho}_+)$.

Asymptotic Normal Variance of $\hat{\rho}_+$. The approach of Woodward, Browne, and Bentler (1980) uses the delta method (e.g., Kendall & Stuart, 1977, p. 246) to derive an expression for the variance of $\hat{\rho}_+$. Let s be the $n^* \times 1$ vector of $n^* = (n(n + 1)/2)$ nonduplicated elements of S, and s_o be the $n^* \times 1$ vector of nonduplicated elements of Σ. Then since $\hat{\rho}_+ = f(s)$ and $\rho_+ = f(s_o)$,

$$\hat{\rho}_+ = f(s_o) + h'(s - s_o),$$

where $h = \partial f(s)/\partial s$, evaluated at s_o. The variance of $\hat{\rho}_+$ is asymptotically equal to

$$var(\hat{\rho}_+) \approx h'cov(s,s')h, \qquad (3)$$

where $\approx$ means that the difference between the left hand side and the right hand side is $o(N^{-1})$. Under normality assumptions, using the standard estimator for $cov(s,s')$ (Anderson, 1958), expression (3) can be simplified to yield

$$var(\hat{\rho}_+) \approx \tfrac{1}{2}N^{-1}tr[M^*\Sigma M^*\Sigma], \qquad (4)$$

where the $n \times n$ matrix M has typical element $[M^*]_{ij} = [M^*]_{ji} = (1 + \delta_{ij})\partial\rho_+/\partial[\Sigma]_{ij}$, and δ_{ij} is the Kronecker delta function. A consistent estimator of $var(\hat{\rho}_+)$ is

$$var(\hat{\rho}_+) = \tfrac{1}{2}N^{-1}tr[\hat{M}^*S\hat{M}^*S],$$

where $[\hat{M}^*]_{ij} = [\hat{M}^*]_{ji} = (1 + \delta_{ij})\partial\hat{\rho}_+/\partial[S]_{ij}$.

Since $\hat{\rho}_+$ is not a closed form expression, but is obtained by an iterative procedure represented in equation (2), an exact analytic expression for h has not been found. In our initial work, the derivatives are calculated numerically using a secant approximation developed by Lord (1975). The numerical derivatives are calculated using a slight modification of Lord's computer program AUTEST (Lord, 1973). Using AUTEST, this procedure is surprisingly efficient, even with moderately large matrices of 30 variables or more. A simulation, reported elsewhere (Woodward, Browne, & Bentler, 1980), indicates that the variance of $\hat{\rho}_+$

when calculated according to (4) was highly similar to the observed variance of $\hat{\rho}_+$ calculated empirically across 1000 random samples of size $N = 100$.

Recently, Shapiro (1982) provided a quasi-analytic expression for var ($\hat{\rho}_+$) under the assumption of normality. It is quasi-analytical in the sense that it provides an analytical expression involving ψ^2 and T; however, T is unknown and it must be solved by an algorithm such as (2). Shapiro's estimator for var($\hat{\rho}_+$) is based upon the Taylor approximation as is the method presented above; however, the computations required by the Shapiro estimator are simpler. Currently we are working on the extension of the Shapiro estimator to the asymptotic distribution free case.

Asymptotic Distribution Free Variance of $\hat{\rho}_+$. The assumption of normality can be relaxed by using a distribution free estimator for $cov(s,s')$ in (3). Woodward, Browne, and Bentler (1980) used the asymptotic distribution free (*a.d.f.*) covariance matrix with typical element

$$\text{a.d.f. } [\text{cov}(s,s')]_{ij,k\ell} = w_{ijk\ell} - w_{ij}w_{k\ell}, \tag{5}$$

where

$$w_{ijk\ell} = N^{-1} \sum_{r=1}^{N} (x_{ri} - \bar{x}_i)(x_{rj} - \bar{x}_j)(x_{rk} - \bar{x}_k)(x_{r\ell} - \bar{x}_\ell)$$

and

$$w_{ij} = N^{-1} \sum_{r=1}^{N} (x_{ri} - \bar{x}_i)(x_{rj} - \bar{x}_j)$$

which is found in Browne (1982) and Dijkstra (1981); see also Muirhead (1982). As before, a modified AUTEST computer program of Lord was used to approximate the derivatives, but the modification was more extreme in that Lord's program was based on the assumption of normal covariance matrices. The simulation study revealed that for normal data, the normal and *a.d.f.* estimates of the variance of $\hat{\rho}_+$ were numerically close.

Several important tasks remain for future research on the sampling theory of $\hat{\rho}_+$. Shapiro's results, as well as our own, require that $\hat{\rho}_+$ be a differentiable function of s. This differentiability is guaranteed under certain conditions of regularity as described by Shapiro, but it appears to be possible for $\hat{\rho}_+$ not to be a differentiable function of S under some conditions. Whether the delta method can be used in practice in such situations is not known, but it cannot be justified theoretically, and alternative approaches remain to be developed. Further, no small sample approaches to statistical variation in $\hat{\rho}_+$ have been attempted. And, finally, it is known that $\hat{\rho}_+$ is upwardly biased (Zegers & Knol, 1980) unless the population Σ is used. No expression for the bias term has yet been developed. It is not known how large samples must be for the bias to be negligible, but one can assume that national testing associations often have samples that are so large (say, 2000 or more) that bias will likely be a third-decimal phenomenon. For more ordinary situations, when an expression for the bias term has been found, it will be possible to develop a statistical lower bound for $\hat{\rho}_+$ in parallel to that developed for coefficient α (Woodward & Bentler, 1978). That is, the statistical lower bound coefficient will lie below the population value ρ_+ with a given probability selected by the researcher. As it stands, no known relation exists to express how $\hat{\rho}_+$ and ρ_+ are related. (Note that, contrary to common belief, $\hat{\alpha}$ is not necessarily a lower bound to α).

EXAMPLES

The first example is from Lord and Novick (1968, p. 91) and represents four sections of the Educational Testing Service *Test of English as a Foreign Language*. The covariance matrix, presented in Table 14.1, was computed from $N = 1416$ foreign students seeking admission to U.S. colleges in 1965. For this covariance matrix coefficient $\hat{\alpha}$ is .891, and assuming normality, the estimated standard error (SE) of $\hat{\alpha}$ is $SE(\hat{\alpha}) = .0043$ (the standard error of $\hat{\alpha}$ was computed with the same delta method algorithm used for the standard error of $\hat{\rho}_+$). The solution for $\hat{\rho}_+$ yielded a $\hat{T}_+$ matrix with two columns, which is reproduced in the right hand part of Table 14.1. Since all unique variances $\hat{\psi}^2_+$ were positive, $\hat{\rho}_\ell = \hat{\rho}_+ = .920$, as reported in Bentler (1972) and Bentler and Woodward (1980). Assuming normality, the standard error of $\hat{\rho}_+$ was calculated via (4) as $SE(\hat{\rho}_+) = .0037$. Note that because the normality assumption is made, the standard errors were computed from the covariance matrix. These computations do not require the raw data as do the asymptotic distribution-free standard errors.

The second example is taken from the Comrey Personality Scales (Comrey, 1970) and deals with five measures of social conformity versus rebelliousness. Each of the five parts is based on four self-report questionnaire items. The items are law enforcement, acceptance of social order, intolerance of nonconformity,

TABLE 14.1
ETS Test of English as a Foreign Language
for a Sample of N = 1416

	Covariance Matrix				$\hat{T}_+$	
	1	2	3	4	1	2
1	94.7				1.000	0
2	87.3	212.0			-.996	.092
3	63.9	138.7	160.5		.262	-.965
4	58.4	128.2	109.8	115.4	.395	.919

$\hat{\alpha} = .891$ $\hat{\rho}_\ell = \hat{\rho}_+ = .920$
$SE(\hat{\alpha}) = .0043$ $SE(\hat{\rho}_+) = .0037$

TABLE 14.2
Social Conformity Versus Rebelliousness for a Sample of N = 746

	Covariance Matrix					$\hat{T}_+$	
	1	2	3	4	5		
1	21.44					-1.000	.000
2	13.39	22.47				.857	.514
3	14.28	11.42	23.23			.929	.368
4	14.29	13.11	14.36	28.30		-.101	-.994
5	7.54	7.49	9.24	9.17	22.94	-.961	.274

$\hat{\alpha} = .823$ $\hat{\rho}_\ell = \hat{\rho}_+ = .851$

$SE(\hat{\alpha}) = .0102$ $SE(\hat{\rho}_+) = .0098$

respect for law, and need for approval. The covariance matrix, presented in Table 14.2, is based on a sample of $N = 746$. This covariance matrix yields an $\hat{\alpha} = .823$, with normal standard error $SE(\hat{\alpha}) = .0102$. The greatest lower bound algorithm yielded a $\hat{T}_+$ matrix of two columns, which is shown in the right-hand side of Table 14.2. The unique variances are positive and $\hat{\rho}_\ell = \hat{\rho}_+ = .851$. The normal standard error for $\hat{\rho}_+$ is $SE(\hat{\rho}_+) = .0098$. As in the previous example, the estimate of the standard error for $\hat{\rho}_+$ numerically is almost equal to that of $\hat{\alpha}$.

The third example is based on the intercorrelations among social class indicators obtained by Warner, Meeker, and Eels (1960). The intercorrelation matrix is presented in Table 14.3. Since the data are not based on a single sample size N, but rather represent correlations obtained from various sources, and since variances are not available, no statistical statements are made. However, it is noted that in this example $\hat{\rho}_\ell$ is not the greatest lower bound. The greatest lower bound exceeds $\hat{\rho}_\ell$ by a small amount, since $\hat{\rho}_\ell$ is based on a solution containing negative variance estimates. In our experience, when $\hat{\rho}_+$ is larger than $\hat{\rho}_\ell$, it is only larger by a very small amount.

TABLE 14.3
Social Class Data from Warner, Meeker and Eels

	Covariance Matrix						$\hat{T}_+$
	1	2	3	4	5	6	
1	1.00						1.230
2	.87	1.00					-2.730
3	.76	.82	1.00				1.000
4	.71	.81	.71	1.00			1.000
5	.70	.81	.69	.74	1.00		1.000
6	.77	.59	.64	.70	.65	1.000	-1.320

$\hat{\alpha} = .942$ $\hat{\rho}_\ell = .969$ $\hat{\rho}_+ = .976$

TABLE 14.4
Six Verbal Intelligence Subtests of the Wechsler Adult Intelligence Scale for a Sample of N = 96

| | Covariance Matrix | | | | | | $\hat{T}_+$ | |
	1	2	3	4	5	6		
1	6.073						1.000	.000
2	4.554	10.103					.040	.999
3	4.685	4.029	8.234				-.811	-.584
4	3.427	4.320	3.616	5.988			.784	-.621
5	3.558	2.398	3.809	3.220	8.725		-.082	.997
6	5.144	6.084	3.965	4.606	3.541	7.238	-.778	-.628

$\hat{\alpha} = .869$ $\hat{\rho}_\ell = \hat{\rho}_+ = .916$
$SE(\hat{\alpha}) = .0212$ $SE(\hat{\rho}_+) = .0156$
$SE_{adf}(\hat{\alpha}) = .0243$ $SE_{adf}(\hat{\rho}_+) = .0175$

Our final example concerns the measurement of verbal intelligence using the six verbal subscales of the Wechsler Adult Intelligence Scale (Wechsler, 1955), namely, information, comprehension, arithmetic, similarities, digit span, and vocabulary. The data are taken from a study of sources of individual differences in verbal memory performance, where the sum of the six subscales was used as a measure of verbal intelligence (Woodward, Geiselman, Beatty, 1982). Although it is reasonable to assume the data are normally distributed, we analyze the raw data in order to compute, for illustration, the asymptotic distribution-free standard errors of $\hat{\alpha}$ and $\hat{\rho}_+$ using the *a.d.f.* covariance matrix in (5). The covariance matrix, computed from a sample of 96 UCLA undergraduate students, appears in Table 14.4. The solution for $\hat{\rho}_+$ yielded a $\hat{T}_+$ matrix with two columns, presented on the right-hand side of Table 14.3. The unique variance estimates are all positive and thus $\hat{\rho}_\ell = \hat{\rho}_+ = .916$. In contrast, $\hat{\alpha} = .869$. As with the previous examples, the normal standard errors in $\hat{\alpha}$ and $\hat{\rho}_+$ are quite similar in value. The *a.d.f.* standard errors are quite similar in value to the normal standard errors, though slightly larger, as we would expect from theory and from previous simulation (Woodward, Browne, & Bentler, 1980). Surprisingly, however, the *a.d.f.* estimated standard error for $\hat{\rho}_+$ is smaller than for that $\hat{\alpha}$. This result may be a sampling fluctuation rather than something to be regularly anticipated.

ACKNOWLEDGEMENTS

This research was supported in part by U.S. Public Health Service grants DA00017 and DA01070.
   Address reprints to P.M. Bentler or J. A. Woodward, Department of Psychology, University of California, Los Angeles, CA 90024.

REFERENCES

Anderson, T. W. *An introduction to multivariate analysis.* New York: Wiley, 1958.
Bentler, P. M. Alpha-maximized factor analysis (alphamax): Its relation to alpha and canonical factor analysis. *Psychometrika,* 1968, *33,* 335–345.
Bentler, P. M. A lower-bound method for the dimension-free measurement of internal consistency. *Social Science Research,* 1972, *1,* 343–357.
Bentler, P. M. *Theory and implementation of EQS, a structural equations program.* Department of Psychology, University of California, Los Angeles, California, 1982.
Bentler, P. M., & Browne, M. W. *P+1 parameter test theory models.* Paper presented at European meetings of the Psychometric Society, Groningen, June 1980.
Bentler, P. M., & Woodward, J. A. Inequalities among lower bounds to reliability: With applications to test construction and factor analysis. *Psychometrika,* 1980, *45,* 249–267.
Browne, M. W. Covariance structures. In D. M. Hawkins (Ed.), *Applied multivariate analysis.* London: Cambridge, 1982.
Callender, J. C., & Osburn, H. G. A method for maximizing split-half reliability coefficients. *Educational and Psychological Measurement,* 1977, *37,* 819–825.
Clark, C. *The theoretical side of calculus.* Huntington, N.Y.: Krieger, 1978.
Comrey, A. L. *EITS manual for the Comrey Personality Scales.* San Diego, Calif.: Educational & Industrial Testing Service, 1970.
Della Riccia, G., & Shapiro L. *Minimum rank and minimum trace of covariance matrices.* Department of Mathematics, Ben Gurion University of the Negev, Beer-Sheva, Israel, 1980.
Dijkstra, T. K. *Latent variables in linear stochastic models.* Ph.D. dissertation, Groningen, 1981.
Guttman, L. A basis for analyzing test-retest reliability. *Psychometrika,* 1945, *10,* 255–282.
Hakstian, A. R., Rogers, W. T., & Cattell, R. B. The behavior of number-of-factors rules with simulated data. *Multivariate Behavioral Research,* 1982, *17,* 193–219.
Jackson P. H., & Agunwamba, C. C. Lower bounds for the reliability of the total score on a test composed of non-homogeneous items: I: Algebraic lower bounds. *Psychometrika,* 1977, *42,* 567–578.
Jöreskog, K. G. Statistical analysis of sets of congeneric tests. *Psychometrika,* 1971, *36,* 109–133.
Jöreskog, K. G. Analyzing psychological data by structural analysis of covariance matrices. In R. C. Atkinson, D. H. Krantz, R. D. Luce, & P. Suppes (Eds.), *Contemporary developments in mathematical psychology (Vol. II.)* San Francisco: Freeman, 1974.
Jöreskog, K. G., & Sörbom, D. *LISREL IV user's guide.* Chicago: National Educational Resources, 1978.
Kendall, M. G., & Stuart, A. *The advanced theory of statistics* (Vol. I). London: Griffin, 1977.
Kristof, W. Estimation of reliability and true score variance from a split of a test into three arbitrary parts. *Psychometrika,* 1974, *39,* 491–499.
Kuhn, H. W., & Tucker, A. W. Nonlinear programming. In J. Neyman (Ed.), *Proceedings of the second Berkeley symposium on mathematical statistics and probability.* Berkeley: University of California Press, 1951.
Ledermann, W. On the rank of the reduced correlation matrix in multiple-factor analysis. *Psychometrika,* 1937, *2,* 85–93.
Ledermann, W. On a problem concerning matrices with variable diagonal elements. *Proceedings of the Royal Society of Edinburgh,* 1939, *60,* 1–17.
Lord, F. M. *Automated hypothesis tests and standard errors for nonstandard problems.* Research Bulletin 72-42 (rev. ed.). Princeton, New Jersey: Educational Testing Service, 1973.
Lord, F. M. Automated hypothesis tests and standard errors for non standard problems. *The American Statistician,* 1975, *29,* 56–59.
Lord, F. M. *Applications of item response theory to practical testing problems.* Hillsdale, N.J.: Lawrence Erlbaum Associates, 1980.

Lord, F. M., & Novick, M. R. *Statistical theories of mental test scores*. Reading, Mass.: Addison-Wesley, 1968.

Muirhead, R. J. *Aspects of multivariate statistical theory*. New York: Wiley, 1982.

Novick, M. R., & Lewis, C. Coefficient alpha and the reliability of composite measurements. *Psychometrika*, 1967, *32*, 1–13.

Shapiro, A. Rank-reducibility of a symmetric matrix and sampling theory of minimum trace factor analysis. *Psychometrika*, 1982, *47*, 187–199.

ten Berge, J. M. F., Snijders, T. A. B., & Zegers, F. E. Computational aspects of the greatest lower bound to reliability and constrained minimum trace factor analysis. *Psychometrika*, 1981, *46*, 201–213.

Warner, W. L., Meeker, M., & Eels, K. *Social class in America*. New York: Harper & Row, 1960.

Wechsler, D. *Manual for the Wechsler adult intelligence scale*. New York: Psychological Corporation, 1955.

Woodhouse, B., & Jackson, P. H. Lower bounds for the reliability of the total score on a test composed of non-homogeneous items: II: A search procedure to locate the greatest lower bound. *Psychometrika*, 1977, *42*, 579–591.

Woodward, J. A., & Bentler, P. M. A statistical lower bound to population reliability. *Psychological Bulletin*, 1978, *85*, 1323–1326.

Woodward, J. A., Browne, M. W., & Bentler, P. M. *Asymptotic standard errors of reliability estimators*. Paper presented at the annual meeting of the Society for Multivariate Experimental Psychology, Ft. Worth Texas, 1980.

Woodward, J. A., Geiselman, R. E., & Beatty, J. *Sources of individual differences in verbal memory performance*. Department of Psychology, University of California, Los Angeles, California, 1982.

Zegers F. E., & Knol D. L. *Chance capitalization in the greatest lower bound to the reliability of a test*. Paper presented at the European meeting of the Psychometric Society, Groningen, June 1980.

IV. OTHER MODELS FOR PSYCHOLOGICAL MEASUREMENT

Whenever a powerful measurement model such as Lord's Item Response Theory is developed and refined, it often provides a convenient backdrop for viewing other models. For example, sometimes another measurement model might be usefully characterized as a transposition of IRT entailing person characteristic curves rather than item characteristic curves. Or in another case, an alternative procedure might be seen as an attempt to deal with essentially the same kind of item response data but invoking less underlying structure and statistical machinery; or as an estimation procedure for error-free aspects of performance, such as response time, that are not amenable to IRT-type models based on probability of success; or as a scaling model more concerned with latent types than latent dimensions. Although such characterizations of measurement models in terms of their differences from a standard at best only help us understand what these models are *not*, for what it is worth, each of the instances just mentioned is crudely applicable in turn to the four chapters in this section, respectively. We must look to those chapters to understand what these other measurement models *are*.

John Carroll proposes a measurement model based on person characteristic functions corrected for the effects of scedastic and topastic variance as a general solution to the problem of "difficulty factors." These corrections adjust the latent trait distributions for two of the major distortions that led to difficulty factors in the first place—namely, the influence on the magnitude of correlation coefficients of disparities in the distributions of variables differing in difficulty level, and of disparities among the variables in the effects of chance success by guessing. This procedure thus provides an alternative to the factor analytic approaches to the problem offered by McDonald and Tucker in Section III.

Norman Cliff reviews a number of efforts, including his own, to describe binary response data in terms of ordinal and dominance concepts and methods that stay close to the actual form of the manifest data. In the process, he documents a remarkable convergence in the variety of attempts to measure consistency in binary data without recourse to assumptions about underlying continuous true scores or populations of items.

Bruce Bloxom, noting the increasing importance of response time in cognitive psychology, assays the difficult task of estimating response time distributions without making strong assumptions about functional form. In seeking a flexible function for mapping a continuous random variable such as response time onto a density estimate, he explores quadratic spline functions because of their attractive features in this regard. The spline function's main attraction is its visual smoothness in that it has the flexibility to approximate a variety of types of functions without numerous unwanted inflections.

In the final chapter in this section, **Warren Torgerson** formulates a multidimensional scaling model applicable to ideal types. The basic notion of the ideal type model is that the spatial location of a particular stimulus is given by its distance from each of a number of ideal stimulus types. Hence, the degree of dissimilarity or distance between two stimuli depends on how close each is to the various ideals. This leads to parsimonious representation of the stimuli as points in a multidimensional hyperspherical space.

15 The Difficulty of a Test and Its Factor Composition Revisited

John B. Carroll
The L. L. Thurstone Psychometric Laboratory
University of North Carolina at Chapel Hill

ABSTRACT

Effects of scedastic and topastic variance on Pearsonian and tetrachoric correlation coefficients are investigated with two models of a person characteristic function relating performance to task difficulty. Scedastic variance is the variance around true probabilities in a series of Bernoulli trials; topastic variance is that resulting from the effects of chance success by guessing. Even when it is assumed that sets of n equivalent items at different difficulty levels measure a single unitary trait, effects of scedastic and topastic variance can cause severe constraints on correlations between their scores and can lead to misleading results in factor analysis, making it appear that such sets of equivalent items measure different abilities. This is demonstrated with new data ($N = 1082$) from the Seashore Sense of Pitch Test that Guilford (1941) reported as measuring three distinct abilities. Except for certain perturbations arising from defects in the original phonograph recording, it appears that the Sense of Pitch Test measures only one trait of pitch discrimination ability. Implications for test theory and factor analysis are discussed.

In R-technique factor analysis, the objective is to determine the minimum number of latent traits underlying a set of variables. If the variables analyzed are measures of abilities, the latent traits represent underlying abilities.

The fundamental equations of factor analysis require that any correlation coefficient between two variables be an informative and unbiased index of the degree to which those variables measure, in common, one or more underlying traits or abilities. Various conditions, however, can prevent correlation coefficients from having this desired property, and when such conditions are present, a factor analysis is in danger of yielding artifactual results. This can occur when the magnitudes of correlations are influenced by disparities in the distributions of the variables, as when Pearsonian correlation coefficients are used with items or tests that vary widely in difficulty. A more serious case occurs when the effects of chance success by "guessing" are unequal between the variables being correlated. Both these cases were treated by Carroll (1945, 1961).

These propositions about correlation coefficients used in factor analysis are apparently not widely known or accepted. Examination of a number of standard texts on factor analysis discloses that they are only infrequently mentioned or well discussed. Most texts consider only what type of correlation coefficient should be used with dichotomous variables. Guertin and Bailey (1970), for example, favor use of tetrachoric r, but do not adequately explain why it should be used, or whether it has any limitations. Comrey (1973) recommends use of the φ coefficient with dichotomous variables; in more general cases, he urges that studies be designed in such a way that Pearson coefficients are appropriate, with routine checks of the assumption of rectilinearity. Gorsuch (1974) discusses the use of a so-called G-coefficient with dichotomous variables, but makes no mention of distributional disparity or the effects of chance success. Kim and Mueller (1978) warn against use of the φ coefficient but do not enter into any full discussion of the problems. A brief discussion is presented by Harman (1976, p. 24), with a reference to Carroll (1961). A somewhat fuller discussion is provided by Cattell (1978, pp. 467–475) with references to Carroll (1961), Gourlay (1951), and other special treatments, but a reader is not adequately warned about distributional disparities and effects of chance success. Rummel (1970) treats distributional disparities but not the effects of chance success.

Guilford (1941) factor-analyzed tetrachoric correlations among the ten subtests of the Seashore Sense of Pitch Test (Seashore, 1919). After considering and rejecting the notion that "some arbitrary characteristic of the data may have induced the factor pattern" (p. 74), he came to "accept the hypothesis that [the three factors identified in his study] represent three distinct human abilities involved in the comparison and judgment of tones as to pitch" (p. 75). Gourlay (1951) pointed out that Guilford's results were probably artifactual, resulting from the operation of chance success effects on tetrachoric correlations as earlier described by Carroll (1945). John and Burt (1951), however, expressed doubt about Gourlay's conclusion. Guilford's result has frequently been cited as valid and trustworthy. Jensen (1980, p. 214) cites Guilford's study as showing that "pitch discrimination ability is not a unitary factor." Mulaik (1972, p. 359) states that Guilford presented "evidence to show that tests measuring a single dimension but representing different difficulty levels produce more than one factor in a factor analysis of their intercorrelations, with the resulting 'extra' factors being possibly artifacts of scaling." (Actually, this statement seems not to represent Guilford's conclusion accurately.) McDonald and Ahlawat (1974), in a detailed study of the problem of "difficulty factors" in binary data, contend that "it is still possible that in Guilford's original study different (linear) content factors underlie the easy and the difficult pitch discriminations" (p. 85), but because their analysis does not cover the case of n equivalent items affected by guessing effects, this judgment does not seem well supported.

From this evidence, it appears not to be widely accepted that the use of inappropriate correlation coefficients can yield artifactual "difficulty factors" or, specifically, that Guilford's (1941) study yielded such difficulty factors, as claimed by Gourlay (1951) and Carroll (1961). Unfortunately, neither of these claims was adequately worked out. Gourlay failed to show how the claim applied to correlations between tests with n items, and Carroll did not present the details of his claim. In the present chapter, I intend to do this, with the deeper theoretical analysis of the problem that is necessary to support its full treatment.

This treatment is of interest in the theory of mental tests because it utilizes the "person characteristic function" (PCF) introduced by Mosier (1940, 1941; see also Weiss, 1980, and Carroll, 1980). PCF theory presents an interesting contrast to Lord's (1980) item response theory in that it focuses on the responses of single individuals to items of different difficulties rather than the responses of individuals of different ability levels to single items. Also, this treatment makes available alternatives to the types of bivariate distribution analysis given by Lord (1980, section 17.4).

After presentation of the basic theoretical development, I intend to show: (a) that the Seashore (1919) Sense of Pitch Test is essentially unidimensional, and that Guilford's (1941) finding of three ability factors in this test was at least misleading if not in error; and (b) that in general, erroneous results in factor analysis can arise from the failure to take into account the effects of scedastic and topastic variance when there is disparity among variables in the latent distributions of ability.

The demonstration that Guilford's (1941) findings were artifactual is based on new but long delayed analyses of data collected more than 30 years ago. Only the present availability of computing facilities adequate to the task, particularly interactive microcomputer facilities, has made it possible to complete these analyses.

THEORETICAL DEVELOPMENT

Models of Function Operating Characteristics in PCF Theory

This development is concerned with the properties of sets of items or tasks that are assumed to be homogeneous in the sense that they all measure a single ability. Such tasks are assumed to vary in "difficulty" because of stimulus or task characteristics.

Assume that we have a series of tasks, measuring a single ability, that can be ordered on a scale of difficulty, however defined. *For a single individual,* the latent relation between task difficulty and the probability of success, defined as the *person characteristic function,* could take any of many forms. These functions would be monotonic because it is reasonable to suppose that the probability of success would tend to decrease as task difficulty increases. Here, we consider the three possible forms illustrated in Fig. 15.1.

Figure 15.1a represents what may be called the Walker-Guttman function (Guttman, 1941; Walker, 1931, 1936, 1940) that implies that individual i will "pass" all tasks that have difficulties less than a certain value $\beta(i)$, and "fail" all tasks with difficulties greater than $\beta(i)$. (To make notation parallel with that of item response theory, we use β as the analog to the item position parameter b of that theory.) The Walker-Guttman function is an ideal that is rarely if ever attained in practice. It may, however, be regarded as the limiting case of the function represented in Fig. 15.1b, which may be taken to be either the familiar normal ogive function or the logistic approximation to it. This function has two parameters for any individual i, the position parameter $\beta(i)$ and the slope parameter $\alpha(i)$ (analogous to the slope parameter a of item response theory). The position parameter $\beta(i)$ is defined as the value of a quantity β at which the true probability of success, $p(i,j)$, of individual i on task j is .5. β (without subscript) is thus a general measure of task difficulty.

Figure 15.1c represents the function assumed by the so-called *quantal hypothesis* of psychophysics proposed by von Békésy (1930; see Engen, 1971, pp. 33–34). While the underlying theory of the neural quantum may be only rarely applicable in mental test theory, this function appears to be useful either on its own merits or as a simplification of the more complex normal ogive and logistic functions. It has two parameters, the position parameter $\beta(i)$, similar to that of the normal ogive or logistic function, and the slope parameter $\alpha(i)$, defined as the difference $(\beta(0) - \beta(1))$, that is, the distance measured by β from the intersection with $p(i,j) = 0$ to the intersection with $p(i,j) = 1$. (Note that $\alpha(i)$ defined for this function is oriented opposite to the $\alpha(i)$ defined for the normal ogive or logistic function.)

Score Distributions for *n* Equivalent Items

1. Distributions of Latent Trait Measurements. We define latent trait measurements as those that would be obtained were there no effects of scedastic or topastic variance (as defined below). In the case of the Walker-Guttman function (Fig. 15.1a), it is obvious that the latent trait measurements would be two-point distributions: At a given level of difficulty β, a certain proportion of individuals would have $p(i,j) = 1$, and thus scores of n, and the complement of this proportion would have $p(i,j) = 0$, and thus scores of 0. This case is unlikely and will not be further considered.

In the case of the normal ogive and logistic functions, latent trait distributions on n equivalent items would be a function of the distribution of parameters $\beta(i)$

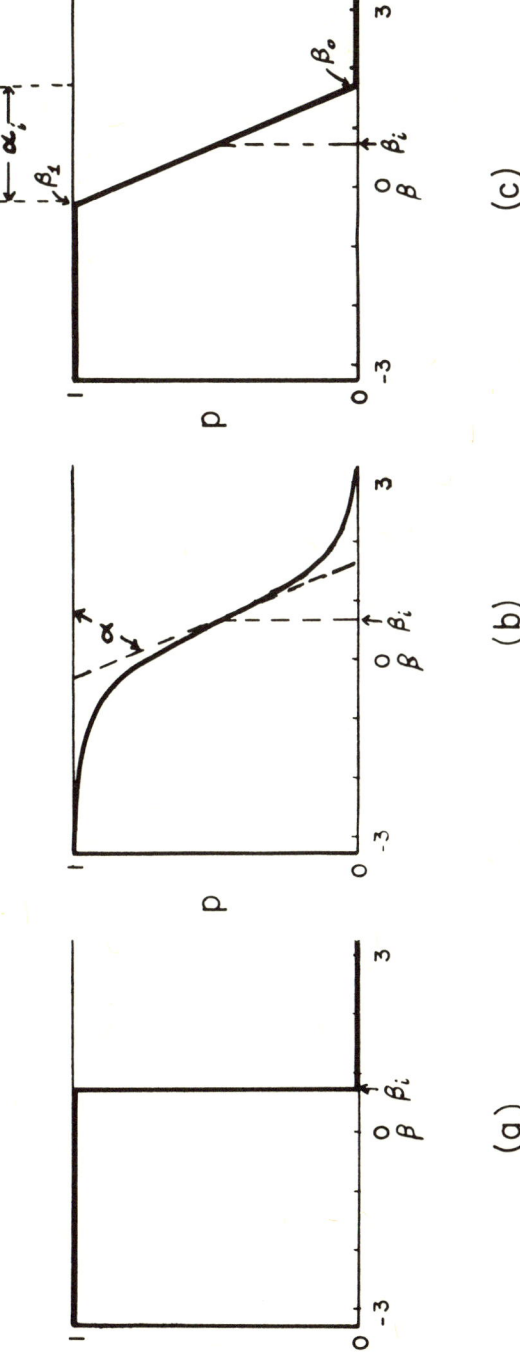

FIG. 15.1. Three possible forms of the person characteristic function relating probability of success (p) to task difficulty expressed as β: (a) the Walker-Guttman function; (b) the normal or logistic ogive function; (c) the quantal model function. α is the slope parameter.

over the range of the difficulty continuum β, as well as the distribution of the slope parameters $\alpha(i)$, for the intersections of the functions at the particular value of β for the n equivalent items or tasks. For convenience, assume that all $\alpha(i)$ are equal, and that the parameters $\beta(i)$ are distributed normally or logistically. The latent trait distribution would arise as shown in Fig. 15.2; in this figure, it is assumed that there are 10 equivalent items; because scores are discrete ($L = 0, 1, 2, \ldots, n - 1, n$), frequencies are determined only for class intervals with corresponding upper bounds $p = .05, .15, .25, \ldots, .95, 1.0$. Given the difficulty of the n equivalent items in terms of β, and the assumed value of α (constant over individuals), one may compute the expected frequencies in these intervals, using normal or logistic distribution functions. It is interesting to note that for $\alpha < 1$, the resulting distributions are concave downward; for $\alpha = 1$, the distribution is uniform over the range $L = 1$ to $n - 1$, and for $\alpha > 1$ the distributions tend to be concave upward (i.e., U-shaped).

In the case of the quantal model implied in Fig. 15.1c, the latent trait distribution arises as depicted in Fig. 15.3. This figure assumes that the distribution of $\beta(i)$ is normal or logistic and that all values of $\alpha(i)$ are equal; as previously, frequencies are for discrete class intervals. It is convenient, however, to assume two "extra" class intervals, denoted $L = 0^*$ and $L = n^*$, the first containing the scores of those individuals for whom $p(i,j)$ = exactly zero, the latter containing the scores of those for whom $p(i,j)$ = exactly 1. These individuals exist in the tails of the distribution implied by the quantal hypothesis. The score interval $L = 0$ is reserved for those with $0 < p(i,j) \leq \frac{1}{2}n$, and the score interval $L = n$ for those with $(1 - \frac{1}{2}n) \leq p(i,j) < 1$. As before, given appropriate parametric values, it is possible to compute the expected latent trait distribution. The Walker-Guttman model is the limiting value of this function when $\alpha = 0$; with $\alpha > 0$, the distributions over the range $L = 0$ to $L = n$ are sections of the logistic density function, and the frequencies for $L = 0^*$ and $L = n^*$ are the areas of the tails of the distribution. As α increases, the sum of the frequencies in these tails becomes smaller.

2. Scedastic Variance and its Effects on Distributions. In any latent trait distribution in which the theoretical probability that individual i will pass item j, $p(i,j)$, is greater than 0 and less than 1, scedastic variance will be present, in the sense that on any given trial or occasion the scedastic score S on n items is a random variable with variance $np(i,j)q(i,j)$, where $q(i,j)$ is the complement of $p(i,j)$. The scedastic score is the score attained exclusive of, or as it were, "prior" to the effect of any topastic variance as described subsequently. It may be noted that scedastic variance is here described more precisely than it was in a previous article by the writer, Carroll (1961). Also, note that scedastic variance is analogous to that occurring in the distribution of test scores for given ability as described by Lord (1980, section 4.1).

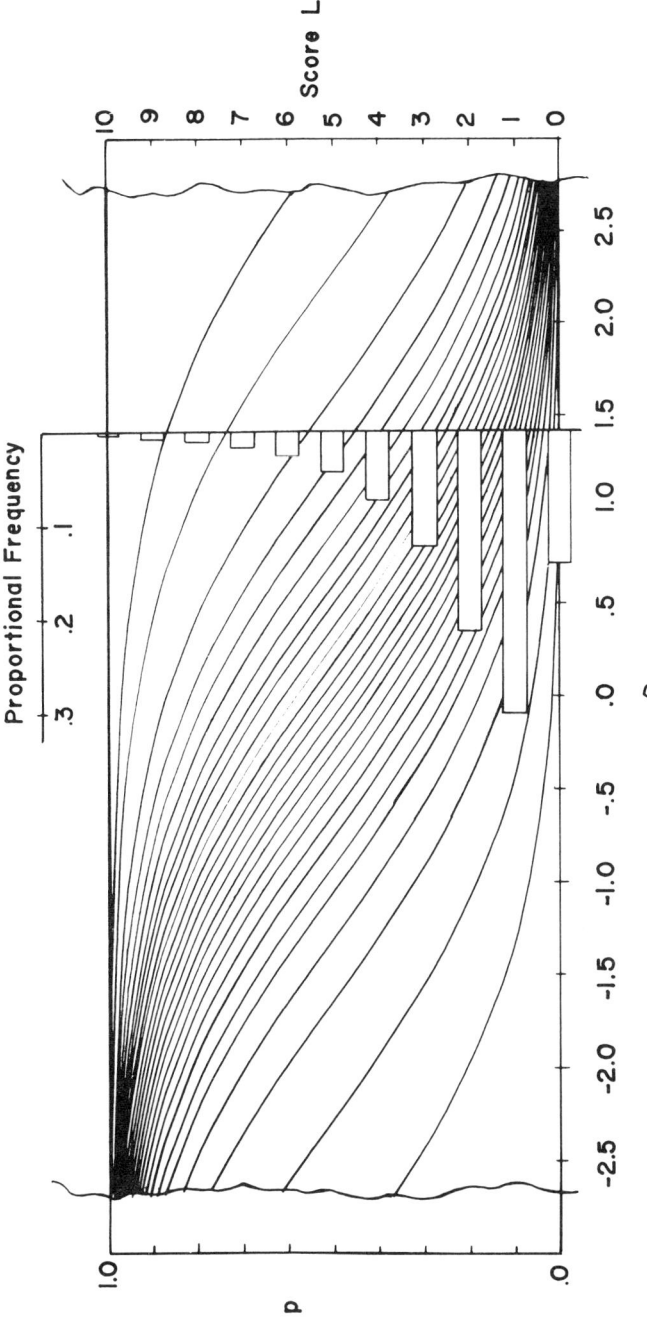

FIG. 15.2. Illustration of the generation of a latent trait distribution by a population of person characteristic functions following the logistic model, for a test of 10 equivalent items at $\beta = 1.415$; $\alpha_i = .702$ for all i. (These are the parameters for subtest H; see Table 15.1.)

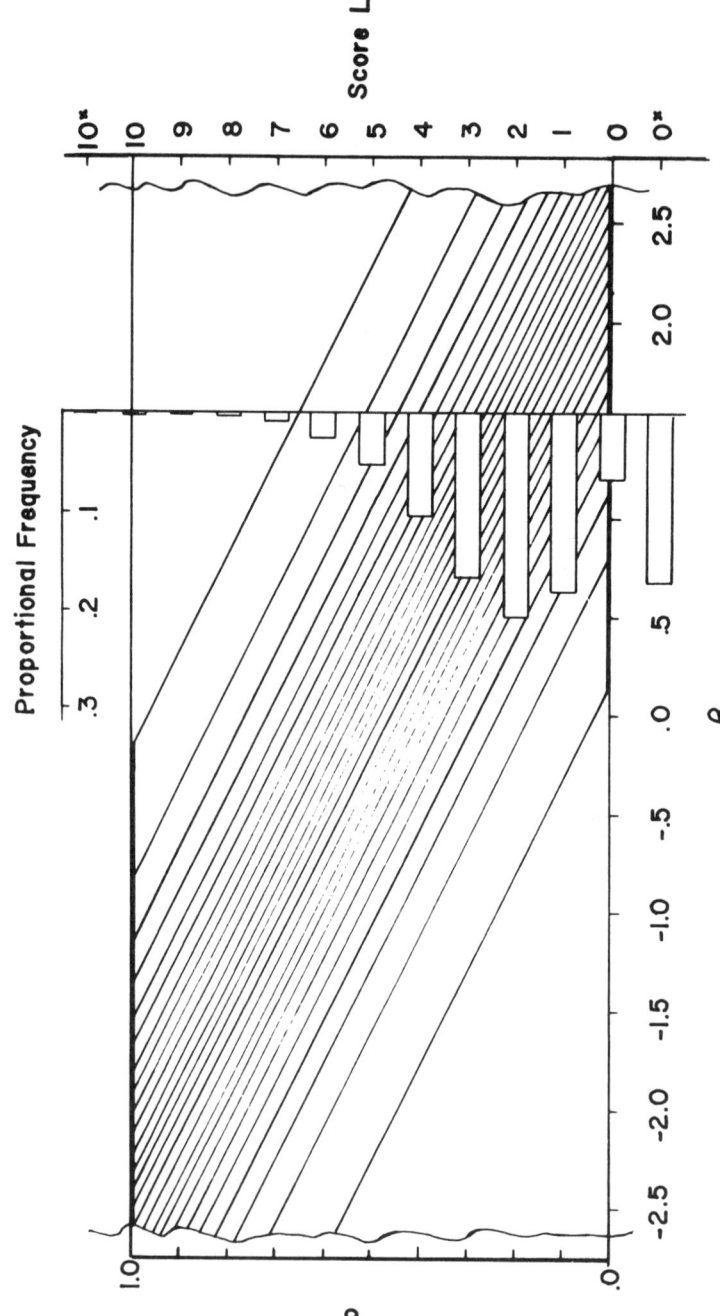

FIG. 15.3. Illustration of the generation of a latent trait distribution by a population of person characteristic functions following the quantal model, for a test of 10 equivalent items at $\beta = 1.53$; $\alpha_i = 4.93$ for all i. (These are the parameters for subtest H; see Table 15.2.)

It is useful to determine the frequency distribution of scedastic scores $S = 0, 1, \ldots, n$, given the frequency distribution of latent trait scores $L = 0, 1, \ldots, n$. Let $\pi(L)$ be the proportional frequency of score L in the latent trait distribution. This proportional frequency arises for the range of values $np(i,j)$ in the class interval represented by L. From the definition of scedastic variance, the distribution of S-scores arising from a particular class interval of the L-distribution can be expressed in terms of the binomial expansion of the values of $p(i,j)$ within the range of the interval, say from p' to p'' (for convenience, subscripts are dropped here). Thus, the proportional frequency of such a score S arising from a particular score L is:

$$f(S(L)) = \pi(L) \left[\frac{\binom{n}{S}}{p'' - p'} \int_{p'}^{p''} q^{n-S} p^S dp \right] \quad (1)$$

More generally, the effect of scedastic variance can be expressed as a matrix product

$$\mathbf{D}(L)\mathbf{S}(n) = \mathbf{D}(S), \quad (2)$$

where $\mathbf{D}(L)$ is a row vector containing the proportional frequencies $\pi(L)$ of scores $L = 0, 1, \ldots, n$; $\mathbf{S}(n)$ is the $(n + 1)$ by $(n + 1)$ scedastic transformation matrix containing the multipliers of $\pi(L)$ bracketed in equation (1), and $\mathbf{D}(S)$ is the corresponding row vector of proportional frequencies of scedastic scores.

In case the quantal model is used, the row vector $\mathbf{D}(L^*)$ contains two additional entries, one for $L = 0^*$ and one for $L = n^*$, as described previously. In this case the scedastic transformation matrix is expanded to a matrix $\mathbf{S}^*$ of order $(n + 3)$; in the first and last rows and columns, all entries are zeros except the diagonals, which are unities. This is because scores of 0^* and n^* are not subject to scedastic variance. The second to the $(n - 2)$th rows and columns contain entries from the scedastic transformation matrix before expansion. Equation (2) is then modified to

$$\mathbf{D}(L^*)\mathbf{S}^*(n) = \mathbf{D}(S^*). \quad (2a)$$

After use of equation (2a) the vector $\mathbf{D}(S^*)$ can be reduced to $\mathbf{D}(S)$ by summing frequencies for $S = 0^*$ and $S = 0$ and for $S = n$ and $S = n^*$.

Following are the exact theoretical relations between the means and variances, respectively, of the score distributions $\mathbf{D}(L)$ and $\mathbf{D}(S)$:

$$\mu(S) = \mu(L) \quad (3)$$

$$\sigma^2(S) = \sigma^2(L) + (\mu(L)(n - \mu(L)) - \sigma^2(L))/n \quad (4)$$

These relations, however, will be confirmed only approximately if computations are based on the above matrix formulations, because of approximations arising from discrete class intervals.

3. Topastic Variance and its Effects on Distributions. Topastic variance is variance that arises from the possibility of chance success by guessing. Various formulas for its operation were given by Carroll (1945). A matrix formulation of its effects on a distribution of scores was given by Carroll (1961, Appendix B); with some change of notation, that formulation is repeated here. If **D**(S) is the row vector containing the $(n + 1)$ proportional frequencies of non-topastically affected (but possibly scedastically affected) scores $S = 0, 1, 2, \ldots, n$, and **D**(X) is the corresponding row vector of topastically affected scores $X = 0, 1, 2, \ldots, n$, the relation between **D**(S) and **D**(X) is expressed by the matrix product

$$\mathbf{D}(S)\mathbf{T}(n,c) = \mathbf{D}(X), \tag{5}$$

where $\mathbf{T}(n,c)$ is a matrix of order $(n + 1)$ with the general form

		|	0	1	2	$\cdots$	$(n-1)$	n
	0	|	d^n	$nd^{n-1}c$	$\frac{1}{2}n(n-1)d^{n-2}c^2$	$\cdots$	ndc^{n-1}	c^n
	1	|	—	d^{n-1}	$nd^{n-2}c$	$\cdots$	ndc^{n-2}	c^{n-1}
	2	|	—	—	d^{n-2}	$\cdots$	ndc^{n-3}	c^{n-2}
	3	|	—	—	—	$\cdots$	ndc^{n-4}	c^{n-3}
S	.	|	.	.	.	$\cdots$	.	.
	.	|	.	.	.	$\cdots$	.	.
	.	|	.	.	.	$\cdots$	.	.
	$n-1$	|	—	—	—	$\cdots$	d	c
	n	|	—	—	—	$\cdots$	—	1

with the column header X over the table. (6)

It is assumed that c, the probability of chance success (however defined or determined) is constant for all items; $d = 1 - c$. (Equation (5) is applicable even when the n items generating **D**(S) are nonequivalent, but the interest here is in the case of n equivalent items.)

These formulations imply the following exact relations, from equations (35) and (36) in Carroll (1945), between the means and variances, respectively, of the distributions **D**(S) and **D**(X):

$$\mu(X) = n - d(n - \mu(S)) \tag{7}$$

$$\sigma^2(X) = d^2\sigma^2(S) + cd(n - \mu(S)) \tag{8}$$

4. Estimation of Latent Trait Distributions From Observed Score Distributions. A method of estimating latent trait distributions is to—

1. generate such distributions from trial values of β and α, given either a logistic or a quantal model of the person characteristic function;

2. carry such distributions through appropriate scedastic and topastic transformations by Equations (2) or (2a) and (5);
3. compute the mean and standard deviation of the resulting distributions;
4. iterate this process (using a two-dimensional linear interpolation method within successively smaller intervals) until the means and standard deviations of the expected distributions are as close as desired to those of the observed distributions.

In this way one finds, if they exist, the values of β and α, and the implied latent trait distributions, that generate distributions of scedastically and topastically affected scores that have the same means and variances as those of observed distributions. The fit between expected and observed distributions can be evaluated by the usual chi-square tests, with appropriate combinations of frequencies in adjacent class intervals to insure expected frequencies of sufficient magnitude (say, > 10). A computer program that accomplishes this is given in an expanded version of the present chapter (Carroll, 1982).

Joint Distributions of Two Sets of Equivalent Items Measuring a Single Function at Different Levels of Difficulty

1. Joint Distributions of Latent Trait Measurements. The basic theory is to be found in Carroll (1961, pp. 350–352). Essentially, given two latent trait distributions, one constructs the joint distribution whereby the maximum positive relation is found. The resulting joint distribution can be represented as a matrix $\mathbf{J}(L:n,m)$ of order $n + 1$ by $m + 1$, where n and m are, respectively, the numbers of items in the two sets. For the quantal model the resulting joint distribution is denoted $\mathbf{J}(L^*:n,m)$ and is of order $n + 3$ by $m + 3$. For present purposes we consider only the case where $n = m$.

2. Joint Distributions of Scedastic Measurements. For the general case of two sets of items, the effect of scedastic variance is given by a formula for the joint distribution matrix $J(S:n,m)$ of scedastically affected scores:

$$\mathbf{J}(S:n,m) = \mathbf{S}'(n)\mathbf{J}(L:n,m)\mathbf{S}(m), \tag{9}$$

where $\mathbf{S}(n)$ and $\mathbf{S}(m)$ are scedastic transformation matrices for n and m items, respectively. For the quantal model this becomes

$$\mathbf{J}(S^*:n,m) = \mathbf{S}^{*'}(n)\mathbf{J}(L^*:n,m)\mathbf{S}^*(m) \tag{9a}$$

3. Joint Distributions of Topastic Scores. Similarly, the effect of topastic variance is given as

$$\mathbf{J}(X:n,m,c) = \mathbf{T}'(n,c)\mathbf{J}(S:n,m)\mathbf{T}(m,c). \tag{10}$$

In the case of the quantal model, it is necessary to reduce the matrix $\mathbf{J}(S^*:n,m)$ of order $n + 3$ by $m + 3$ to the matrix $\mathbf{J}(S:n,m)$ of order $n + 1$ by $m + 1$ by combining frequencies in the first two, and the last two, rows and columns.

4. Fit of Expected and Observed Joint Distributions. If frequencies (summing to unity) in the expected joint distribution $\mathbf{J}(X:n,m,c)$ are multiplied by N, the number of cases in an observed joint distribution, the fit to that distribution can be evaluated by chi-square techniques, with appropriate combinations of frequencies in adjacent class intervals to insure expected frequencies of sufficient magnitude (say, > 10).

APPLICATION TO THE SEASHORE SENSE OF PITCH TEST

Characteristics of the Test

The test analyzed by Guilford (1941) is a subtest, the Sense of Pitch Test, from the original edition of the Seashore Measures of Musical Talent (Seashore, 1919). The basis of this test is a phonograph record, Columbia Record 53004-D (51651). The test consists of 100 items, each of which presents a pair of tones, the second of which is to be judged whether it is "higher" or "lower" than the first. The test is thus designed as a measure of pitch discrimination ability (not "sense of pitch"). There are approximately equal numbers of items keyed "higher" and "lower." The 100 items are divided into sets of 10 items each, designated A through J; these are hereafter termed subtests. The pitch differences in the successive subtests are, respectively, 30, 23, 17, 12, 8, .5, 1, 2, 3, and 5 Hz. The subtests are scored in terms of the number correct. No correction for chance success is made because it is assumed that subjects respond to every item. From the nature of the task, for any item the probability of chance success by guessing may be taken to be .5.

An unfortunate defect was discovered during use of this original version of the test, namely, the fact that systematic relations tend to exist between the keying of an item as "higher" or "lower" and the relative loudness of the tones. In subtests A through E, when the second tone is keyed as "higher," it tends also to be softer, and when keyed as "lower," it tends to be louder. An opposite relation obtains in subtests F through J (presented on the second side of the record). If individuals respond to some items on the basis of loudness rather than pitch (as some apparently do)—marking "higher" when the second tone is louder and "lower" when the second tone is softer—they will tend to make low scores on the easier subtests A through E and higher scores on the harder subtests F through J.

The study was continued, after this defect was discovered, because of interest in comparing the results with those obtained by Guilford (1941). It was found that after appropriate screening of cases the theoretical analysis was not unduly affected. Nevertheless, it would be desirable to repeat the study using a series of stimuli in which perceptible loudness differences are not present—possibly the pitch discrimination test in the revised edition of *Measures of Musical Talents* (Seashore, Lewis, & Saetveit, 1939). If such an analysis were done, it is believed that conclusions similar to those of the present study would emerge with even greater clarity than they do here.

Procedures

Arrangements were made, about 1948, to test students in introductory or applied psychology at the University of Maryland and at George Washington University. In administering the test, emphasis was laid upon the necessity for making a judgment on each item. Answer sheets that gave evidence that the subject had not understood the instructions, had failed to answer all items, or had lost place during the test were eliminated. Usable answer sheets were obtained for a total of 1204 students, but only 1082 of these were used in the analysis, in an attempt to minimize the effects of the defect in the test noted above. The 122 discarded cases were those of 115 students whose total scores on subtests A through E were lower than their total scores on subtests F through J, and an additional 7 cases whose scores on the total test, or on subtests A through E or subtests F through J, were at or below -3σ on the theoretical distribution of scores for a population of pure guesses.

Results

The data analyzed here can be considered closely comparable with those analyzed by Guilford (1941) because the (Pearsonian) correlation between the tetrachoric correlations presented by him and those for the present data is .891. (For reasons mentioned below, data for subtest F are not included in this calculation.)

The demonstration to be presented here, that these tetrachoric correlations are spurious and that the tests in reality measure (essentially) a single factor of ability, is based on (1) hypothesizing that they do indeed measure a single factor of ability, despite the effects of scedastic and topastic variance, and then (2) showing that the joint distributions among the subtests are approximately those that would be expected on the basis of this hypothesis, and different from those expected on the basis of an alternative hypothesis that they measure different factors of ability.

Estimation of Latent Trait Distributions for Each Subtest

In accordance with the formulations developed above, latent trait distributions were estimated for each subtest using both the logistic and the quantal model for the person characteristic function. It proved impossible to fit either model to the data for the most difficult subtest, test F. Even the hypothesis that the distribution of scores for this subtest arose from sheer random guessing was rejected ($\chi^2(6) = 42.3$, $p < .001$). Data from this subtest were therefore eliminated from further consideration.

Table 15.1 shows the estimated latent trait distributions and their parameters, the distributions expected from these latent trait distributions after application of scedastic and topastic transformations, and the observed distributions for each of the nine subtests for which it was possible to make these estimations on the basis of the logistic model of the person characteristic function. It also shows chi-square tests of the fit between the expected topastic distributions and the observed distributions, all performed with class intervals combined so that expected frequencies were equal to at least 10. Numbers of degrees of freedom were specified to take account of the fact that N's, means, and variances of the distributions compared were identical.

Table 15.2 presents data similar to those of Table 15.1, but for the quantal model of the person characteristic function. For subtests A, B, C, D, and H, the fit for the quantal model was clearly superior to that for the logistic model, and yielded chi-square probabilities generally much greater than .05, suggesting that one could not reject the hypothesis that a quantal model generated the distributions. The logistic model provided superior fits for subtests E and J, except that if scores of 9 and 10 were combined, the fit of the quantal model was satisfactory for subtest E, and even for subtest J the fit for the quantal model was not too far from being satisfactory. Neither model provided truly satisfactory fits for subtests I and G, but the quantal model was slightly better. On the whole the results using the quantal model appeared more satisfactory as a basis for further analyses, and in any case the results appeared to support the theory of scedastic and topastic variance effects that was a basis for many of the calculations.

Estimation of Expected Joint Distributions

Joint distributions of latent trait scores assuming the quantal model were constructed for all 36 pairs of the 9 subtests for which it was possible to estimate the univariate distributions. These joint distributions were constructed on the hypothesis that all latent trait distributions measured the same function.

Next, each of the joint distributions of latent trait scores was taken as a matrix $\mathbf{J}(L^*:n,n)$ and inserted in equation (9a) to produce a matrix $\mathbf{J}(S^*:n,n)$ consisting of the expected joint distribution of scedastic scores. Each of these matrices was reduced to a matrix $\mathbf{J}(S:n,n)$ by combining frequencies for scores of 0* and 0, and for scores of n and n^*.

Finally, each matrix $\mathbf{J}(S:n,n)$ was inserted in equation (10) to produce a matrix $\mathbf{J}(X:n,n,c)$, the expected joint distribution of topastic scores. Each such matrix, after multiplication of entries by $N = 1082$, was compared with the corresponding observed joint distribution in several ways—

1. by a chi-square test, usually with reduction to a 3 × 3 matrix so that expected frequencies would be of considerable magnitude.
2. by computing and comparing the corresponding tetrachoric correlations, using cuts as close to the medians as possible.
3. by computing and comparing the corresponding Pearsonian correlations.

The results are summarized in Table 15.3, which also presents Pearsonian correlations for expected latent trait and scedastic distributions. Most of the chi-square tests indicate lack of good fit between expected and observed distributions. However, nearly all of these are for comparisons involving subtests A through E, the subtests that were found to disfavor (probably a substantial minority of) subjects who responded to louder second tones as "higher." Nearly all comparisons involving *only* subtests J, I, H, and G give nonsignificant chi-square values. These are the subtests in which the relation between the key and loudness favored those who responded to louder tones as "higher" in pitch (in effect, making these subtests in a sense more consistent measures of pitch discrimination ability).

The difference between results for subtests A–E and for subtests G–J is even more strikingly apparent in Fig. 15.4 and Fig. 15.5, which show observed tetrachoric and Pearsonian correlations plotted against those expected on the hypothesis that the subtests all measure the same trait or combination of traits. Observed tetrachoric r's are very close to those expected, within subtests G–J; they are fairly close to those expected, within subtests A–E, but substantially lower than those expected when the correlation is between a subtest in set A–E and one in set G–J. Generally similar results are present in the comparisons of Pearsonian correlations, except that those for the set A–E are more deviant from those expected.

Despite these perturbations attributable to defects in the recording of the test stimuli, one cannot ignore the essential finding that the expected correlations, whether tetrachoric or Pearsonian, depart markedly from unity, mainly as a function of the difference in difficulty of the subtests. To illustrate this, Fig. 15.6 shows the expected tetrachoric correlations plotted against the absolute differences between the β parameters of the latent trait distributions. It is evident that even when it is assumed that two tests measure the same latent trait, there are severe upper limits on the coefficients when the tests differ widely in difficulty and are subject to scedastic and topastic variance. There are even more severe

TABLE 15.1
Expected Latent Trait Distributions D(L), with Their Parameters, for Nine Subtests of the Sense of Pitch Test Using the Logistic Model of the Person Characteristic Function, with Expected and Observed Topastic Distributions D(X)

Subtest	A	B	C	D	E	J	I	H	G
β	-1.872307	-1.728261	-1.233662	-.918460	-.680443	-.177048	.840892	1.415396	2.096120
α	2.019071	1.819605	2.210285	2.046278	2.153302	1.007479	.855945	.702285	.852877
L									
0	.009554	.010393	.031390	.047412	.074182	.038289	.118108	.143505	.527732
1	.007705	.009617	.021660	.035072	.049036	.078551	.236918	.340559	.294213
2	.006240	.008136	.016458	.026782	.035613	.082339	.181411	.214787	.084864
3	.006113	.008179	.015412	.024983	.032059	.086713	.133144	.122379	.037864
4	.006571	.008965	.015912	.025587	.031820	.091612	.098066	.071643	.020708
5	.007608	.010553	.017697	.028125	.033920	.097069	.073122	.043674	.012710
6	.009545	.013435	.021247	.033209	.038777	.103158	.055156	.027455	.008379
7	.013346	.019046	.028181	.042982	.048360	.109989	.041866	.017483	.005774
8	.022487	.032489	.044122	.064631	.069325	.117736	.031620	.010946	.004061
9	.062109	.090028	.105467	.140641	.139378	.126784	.022970	.006209	.002798
10	.848721	.789160	.682454	.530576	.447530	.067761	.007619	.001360	.000897
μ(L)	9.479635	9.314741	8.704414	7.995266	7.368805	5.504587	2.916923	2.086368	.881246
σ(L)	1.690936	1.860930	2.629487	3.072925	3.432623	2.909337	2.394310	1.835977	1.416943

X	Exp.	Obs.	Exp.	Obs.	Exp.	Obs.	Exp.	Obs.	Exp.	Obs.	Exp.	Obs.	Exp.	Obs.	Exp.	Obs.	Exp.	Obs.
0	.01	0			.04	0	.06	1	.09	0	.08	1	.22	1	.28	0	.56	0
1	.13	0	.16	0	.41	0	.64	2	.96	3	.91	3	2.54	4	3.29	6	6.12	6
2	.70	0	.82	1	2.13	3	3.32	4	4.91	4	5.13	5	13.76	14	17.69	16	30.22	31
3	2.26	1	2.68	2	6.72	5	10.50	5	15.36	15	17.98	13	45.59	40	57.81	61	89.38	104
4	5.04	3	6.11	2	14.63	12	22.96	15	32.99	29	44.34	35	103.32	98	127.96	120	175.97	164
5	8.52	10	10.62	11	23.80	27	37.54	38	52.53	51	82.92	93	170.15	198	202.55	201	242.24	237
6	11.97	18	15.47	16	31.50	34	49.76	59	66.85	73	125.08	136	211.71	182	236.13	245	238.45	209
7	16.33	20	21.89	35	38.68	39	60.28	76	76.07	75	161.60	147	205.49	201	206.04	199	169.03	204
8	31.36	51	40.51	59	57.06	77	81.93	99	93.95	99	190.04	199	161.10	177	135.92	134	86.53	91
9	139.88	86	150.79	100	157.83	116	174.41	113	173.51	166	214.32	210	106.58	116	68.41	83	32.91	33
10	865.81	893	832.93	856	749.20	769	640.62	670	564.77	567	239.61	240	61.54	51	25.91	17	10.59	3
Sum	1082.00	1082	1082.00	1082	1082.00	1082	1082.00	1082	1082.00	1082	1082.00	1082	1082.00	1082	1082.00	1082	1082.00	1082
$\mu(X)$	9.634917		9.560021		9.270821		8.937236		8.637733		7.748610		6.472272		6.060952		5.506477	
$\sigma(X)$	.971635		1.066918		1.454061		1.711031		1.910671		1.899928		1.883309		1.769023		1.699322	
χ^2	38.20		35.01		19.86		35.54		1.74		6.16		14.37		7.49		19.86	
df	3		3		4		5		5		5		6		6		6	
p	<.0005		<.0005		<.001		<.0005		>.80		>.20		<.05		>.20		<.005	

TABLE 15.2
Expected Latent Trait Distributions D (*L*) with Their Parameters, for Nine Subtests of the Sense of Pitch Test Using the Quantal Model of the Person Characteristic Function, with Expected and Observed Topastic Distributions D(*X*)

Subtest	A	B	C	D	E	J	I	H	G
β	-1.939377	-1.800886	-1.229071	-.913448	-.674194	-.177969	.864941	1.533545	2.416267
α	2.851900	2.866967	1.990580	1.911329	1.752951	3.074044	3.748235	4.928274	5.254471
L									
0*	.003316	.004077	.022283	.040022	.066849	.051393	.152439	.170511	.411287
0	.000906	.001119	.004000	.006730	.009916	.014338	.045854	.067592	.110694
1	.002616	.003236	.010198	.016808	.023966	.040332	.120397	.181282	.205373
2	.004218	.005223	.013950	.022307	.030385	.060662	.150699	.206009	.139624
3	.006774	.008386	.018900	.029174	.037828	.085566	.156496	.168787	.073930
4	.010805	.013353	.025278	.037433	.046042	.110368	.133955	.104997	.034029
5	.017049	.020976	.033228	.046870	.054521	.127029	.096965	.054554	.014649
6	.026446	.032265	.042701	.056921	.062499	.128375	.061999	.025710	.006124
7	.039957	.048058	.053303	.066620	.069036	.113766	.036554	.011558	.002529
8	.058034	.068255	.064178	.074681	.073200	.089666	.020530	.005086	.001039
9	.079629	.090667	.073997	.079777	.074324	.064361	.011216	.002217	.000426
10	.048105	.053127	.039915	.040593	.036567	.023878	.003486	.000580	.000106
10*	.702143	.651260	.598069	.482066	.414868	.090266	.009411	.001117	.000189
μ(*L*)	9.281641	9.133031	8.550619	7.882905	7.282099	5.499600	2.933951	2.105193	.985314
σ(*L*)	1.621623	1.758621	2.531174	2.969828	3.322333	2.882948	2.371959	1.817424	1.357926

X	Exp.	Obs.	Exp.	Obs.	Exp.	Obs.	Exp.	Obs.	Exp.	Obs.	Exp.	Obs.	Exp.	Obs.	Exp.	Obs.	Exp.	Obs.
0	.01	0	.01	0	.03	0	.06	1	.09	0	.09	1	.27	1	.34	0	.62	0
1	.07	0	.08	0	.36	0	.62	2	.99	3	1.03	3	2.95	4	3.71	6	6.55	6
2	.37	0	.46	1	1.80	3	3.09	4	4.83	4	5.42	5	14.94	14	18.86	16	31.31	31
3	1.29	1	1.59	2	5.62	5	9.53	5	14.57	15	17.94	13	46.75	40	58.86	61	90.11	104
4	3.37	3	4.16	2	12.63	12	20.90	15	30.91	29	42.86	35	101.79	98	126.29	120	174.08	164
5	7.39	10	9.10	11	22.56	27	35.98	38	50.59	51	80.45	93	165.07	198	197.75	201	238.11	237
6	14.68	18	17.98	16	35.19	34	53.22	59	69.83	73	125.84	136	208.25	182	233.31	245	236.78	209
7	27.62	20	33.51	35	51.90	39	73.02	76	88.29	75	169.38	147	209.57	201	209.83	199	172.59	204
8	49.61	51	59.35	59	73.42	77	96.45	99	107.43	99	196.68	199	168.71	177	142.11	134	91.15	91
9	84.31	86	98.83	100	100.76	116	122.16	113	126.02	166	192.59	210	105.72	116	68.94	83	33.26	33
10	893.27	893	856.94	856	778.03	769	666.98	670	588.44	567	249.71	240	57.98	51	22.01	17	7.42	3
Sum	1082.00	1082	1082.00	1082	1082.00	1082	1082.00	1082	1082.00	1082	1082.00	1082	1082.00	1082	1082.00	1082	1082.00	1082
$\mu(X)$	9.634920		9.560014		9.270819		8.937219		8.637718		7.748606		6.472271		6.060973		5.506481	
$\sigma(X)$	.971642		1.056690		1.454063		1.711028		1.910664		1.899926		1.883327		1.769057		1.699330	
χ^2	3.10		.32		6.58		3.43		16.50		9.41		13.63		6.10		12.31	
df	3		3		4		5		5		5		6		6		5	
p	>.30		>.95		>.10		>.60		<.01		>.05		<.05		>.40		<.05	

TABLE 15.3
Statistics of Joint Distributions[a]

Subtest Pairs	$\|\Delta_\beta\|$	Joint Distribution Comparisons			Tetrachoric Correlations		Pearsonian Correlations			
		χ^2	df	p	Exp.	Obs.	Expected			Obs.
							L	S	X	
A, B	.13	26.3	8	<.001	.875	.761	.981	.843	.678	.543
A, C	.70	95.5	8	<.001	.896	.721	.952	.844	.690	.439
A, D	1.02	39.4	8	<.001	.888	.715	.886	.789	.641	.436
A, E	1.26	127.7	8	<.001	.888	.710	.821	.736	.597	.375
A, J	1.75	45.5	8	<.001	.716	.460	.708	.602	.449	.298
A, I	2.79	51.9	8	<.001	.529	.342	.534	.444	.283	.185
A, H	3.46	16.2	8	<.05	.418	.235	.509	.401	.220	.187
A, G	4.35	7.1	8	n.s.	.210	.111	.321	.265	.112	.068
B, C	.57	41.6	8	<.001	.895	.783	.972	.860	.701	.545
B, D	.89	38.7	8	<.001	.888	.733	.920	.817	.663	.495
B, E	1.13	73.0	8	<.001	.888	.762	.864	.772	.624	.450
B, J	1.62	85.6	8	<.001	.710	.478	.745	.633	.471	.304
B, I	2.66	38.9	8	<.001	.542	.397	.585	.483	.307	.228
B, H	3.33	26.7	8	<.001	.426	.190	.553	.434	.237	.180
B, G	4.22	21.0	8	<.025	.166	.136	.358	.294	.124	.084
C, D	.32	32.1	8	<.001	.906	.845	.969	.885	.729	.587
C, E	.56	51.4	8	<.001	.906	.829	.930	.854	.701	.539
C, J	1.05	117.7	8	<.001	.731	.460	.813	.708	.534	.303
C, I	2.09	40.2	8	<.001	.570	.364	.655	.554	.357	.242
C, H	2.76	40.6	8	<.001	.457	.228	.626	.502	.278	.175
C, G	3.65	21.3	8	<.001	.256	.150	.416	.349	.150	.069
D, E	.24	8.1	3	<.05	.911	.866	.984	.904	.737	.636
D, J	.73	113.9	11	<.001	.732	.458	.884	.771	.578	.368
D, I	1.77	107.0	8	<.001	.589	.376	.752	.636	.408	.271
D, H	2.44	49.2	9	<.001	.474	.237	.722	.578	.318	.157
D, G	3.33	23.9	8	<.005	.299	.131	.517	.430	.183	.083
E, J	.49	100.2	8	<.001	.739	.561	.918	.804	.602	.376
E, I	1.53	84.1	8	<.001	.598	.407	.807	.685	.438	.292
E, H	2.20	49.2	8	<.001	.485	.274	.779	.626	.344	.183
E, G	3.09	52.5	8	<.001	.325	.162	.588	.486	.206	.097
J, I	1.04	7.3	8	n.s.	.483	.519	.944	.759	.446	.446
J, H	1.71	8.0	8	n.s.	.393	.400	.925	.704	.356	.332
J, G	2.60	22.2	8	<.005	.257	.180	.815	.628	.245	.165
I, H	.67	7.5	8	n.s.	.332	.362	.980	.723	.312	.356
I, G	1.56	14.8	8	n.s.	.228	.186	.922	.688	.230	.192
H, G	.89	14.2	8	n.s.	.195	.131	.925	.655	.188	.181

[a]Shown are: $|\Delta_\beta|$, the absolute difference between the β parameters of the latent trait distributions; comparisons of observed joint distributions with those expected if the subtests measure the same trait; comparisons of expected and observed tetrachoric correlations; expected Pearsonian correlations for latent trait measurements (L), scedastic scores (S), and topastic scores (X), in comparison with the observed Pearsonian correlations (N = 1082).

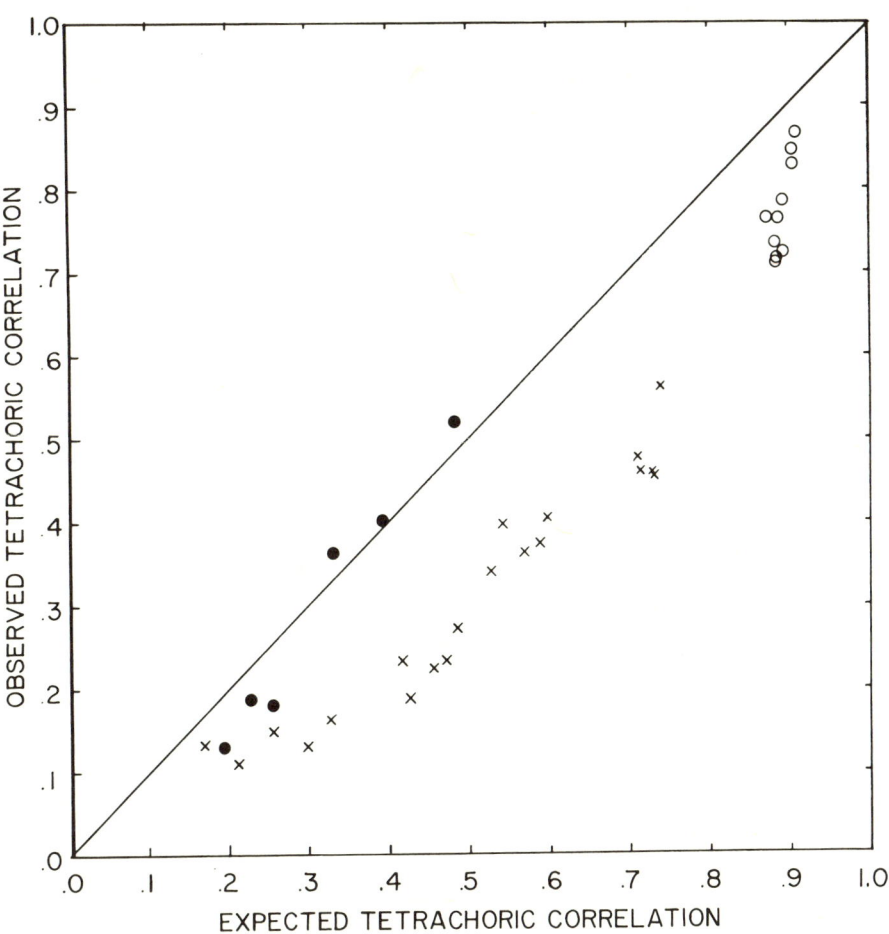

FIG. 15.4. Observed tetrachoric correlations plotted against those expected on the hypothesis that all subtests measure the same trait. Open circles are for correlations among subtests A-E; filled circles are for correlations among subtests G-J; ×'s are for correlations between any of subtests A-E and any of subtests G-J.

restrictions on the upper limits of Pearsonian coefficients, as the reader may discover by making a similar plot for these.

It can be argued that this demonstration of the essential unidimensionality of the Sense of Pitch Test would not be complete unless it is shown that the fit between an observed joint distribution and one expected on the hypothesis that the subtests measure two *independent* abilities would not be close. Accordingly, a hypothetical latent trait joint distribution for subtests J and H was constructed on the hypothesis that they measure completely independent traits, by simple multiplication of the respective marginal distributions. This matrix was then

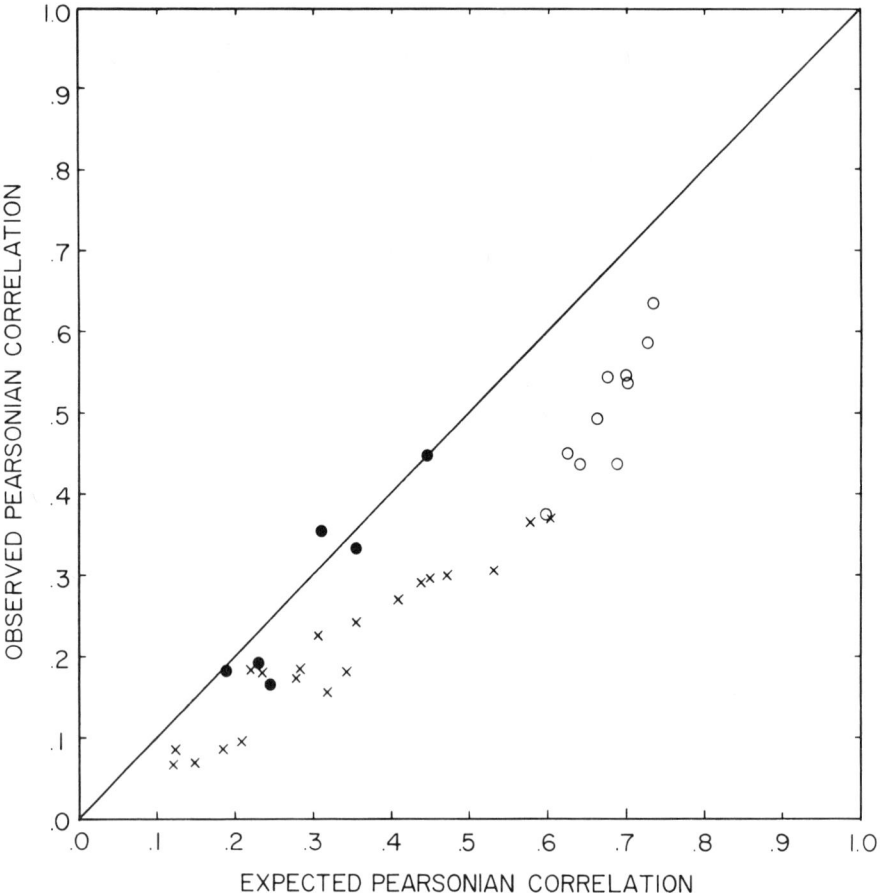

FIG. 15.5. Observed Pearsonian correlations plotted against those expected on the hypothesis that all subtests measure the same trait. Open circles are for correlations among subtests A-E; filled circles are for correlations among subtests G-J; ×'s are for correlations between any of subtests A-E and any of subtests G-J.

passed through scedastic and topastic transformations. Comparison of the expected and observed distributions indicated a serious lack of fit ($\chi^2(8) = 91.66, p < .0001$), as compared with the good fit for this pair of subtests shown in Table 15.3. Although similar calculations were not performed for all other pairs of tests, it seems reasonable to assume that these would likewise show severe failures of fit.

In an expanded version of this chapter (Carroll, 1982), fuller details of all calculations for subtests J and H are presented.

DISCUSSION

The results developed here appear to yield persuasive evidence that Guilford (1941) was misled in reporting that the Seashore Sense of Pitch Test measures three distinct factors of ability. The tetrachoric correlation coefficients on which he based his factor analysis were severely constrained by effects of scedastic and topastic variance—increasingly so when the subtests were widely different in

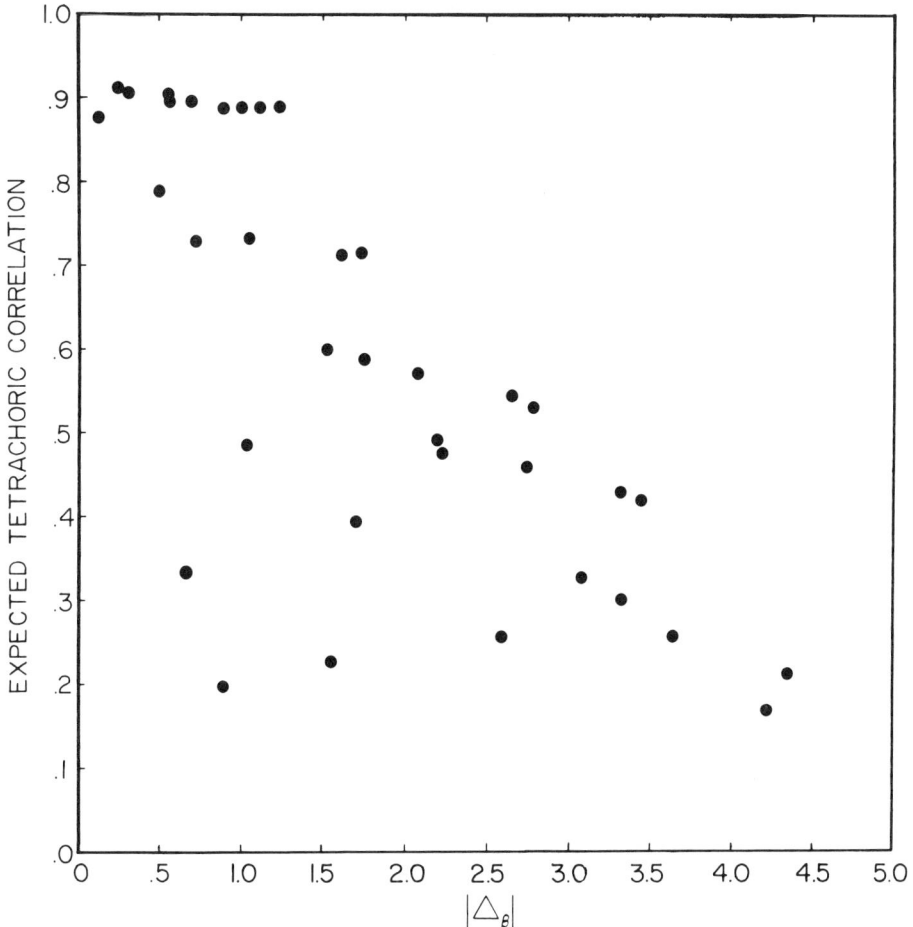

FIG. 15.6. Tetrachoric correlations among subtests expected on the hypothesis that they all measure the same trait, plotted against $|\Delta_\beta|$, the absolute difference between the β parameters of the respective subtests fitted by the quantal model, as listed in Table 15.2.

difficulty. Thus, these coefficients were not informative indices of the underlying relationships among the traits measured by the several subtests.

It is possible that Guilford's finding of three common factors in this matrix was partly a result of the defects in the original 1919 Seashore test that have been observed here. While all subtests (with the possible exception of subtest F) appear to be measures of pitch discrimination ability, subtests A through E measure, in addition, any tendency of a subject to respond "higher" to a *softer* second tone, while subtests F through J measure an opposite tendency—to respond "higher" to a *louder* second tone. The influences of these phenomena on the observed correlations are apparent in the way they deviate from those expected on the hypothesis of a single unitary dimension, and they may have influenced Guilford's factor analysis in the direction of yielding three factors rather than one. On the other hand, because of the influences of scedastic and topastic variance, the matrix was in any case a type of simplex matrix that could not have yielded a finding of a single factor in common factor analysis.

Concerning the generality of these findings to other data sets and their analysis, it can only be said at this time that there is substantial possibility that many data sets in the literature have been affected by the influences of topastic and scedastic variance demonstrated here. These effects were particularly serious in the case investigated here, where scores on sets of n equivalent items with $c = .5$ were intercorrelated. With correlations of scores from sets of items less homogeneous in difficulty and with values of c much less than .5, the effects might not be so serious, but still present if the sets of items differ substantially in average difficulty. Also, according to the mathematical developments presented by Carroll (1945, 1961), the effects should definitely be present in correlations (both Pearsonian and tetrachoric) of single items, especially when there is topastic variance and the items differ markedly in difficulty. With respect to McDonald and Ahlawat's (1974) finding that binary data do not yield "difficulty factors" when the regressions of score on ability are linear, two comments are in order: (1) such linear regressions could be expected to be highly unusual unless the items are of very low reliability or the range of ability is small, and (2) these authors do not address the effects of chance success by guessing, or topastic variance as it is termed here. I would, in fact, take exception to their contention that previous treatments of the problem of "difficulty factors" have been "misleading." If anything, McDonald and Ahlawat's treatment is misleading in focusing on item-ability regressions; according to any reasonable model, such regressions will be generally nonlinear.

It is beyond the scope of this article to consider how to "correct" for the effects of scedastic and topastic variance in order to estimate the strength of relationships among latent traits measured by items or tests of different difficulties. I have made several suggestions in this regard (Carroll, 1945, 1961), and some of these suggestions might be applied to the present data set.

The formulations developed here may be useful in the development and analysis of homogeneous tests of ability. Some evidence has been presented suggesting that use of a quantal model of the person characteristic function may be more advantageous than a normal ogive or logistic model of that function. Determination and comparison of latent trait distributions from small sets of items relatively homogeneous in difficulty might enable one to assemble a test for which one could be assured that all of the items measure a single common trait, despite the effects of scedastic and topastic variance.

REFERENCES

Carroll, J. B. The effect of difficulty and chance success on correlations between items or between tests. *Psychometrika*, 1945, *10*, 1–19.

Carroll, J. B. The nature of the data, or how to choose a correlation coefficient. *Psychometrika*, 1961, *26*, 347–372.

Carroll, J. B. Discussion. In D. J. Weiss (Ed.), *Proceedings of the 1979 Computerized Adaptive Testing Conference*. Minneapolis: University of Minnesota, Department of Psychology, Psychometric Methods Program, 1980.

Carroll, J. B. *The difficulty of a test and its factor composition revisited* (ETS RR 82-32). Princeton, N.J.: Educational Testing Service 1982.

Cattell, R. B. *The scientific use of factor analysis in behavioral and life sciences*. New York: Plenum, 1978.

Comrey, A. L. *A first course in factor analysis*. New York: Academic, 1973.

Engen, T. Psychophysics: I. Discrimination and detection. In J. W. Kling & L. A. Riggs (Eds.), *Woodworth & Schlosberg's experimental psychology* (3rd edition). New York: Holt, Rinehart & Winston, 1971.

Gorsuch, R. L. *Factor analysis*. Philadelphia: W. B. Saunders, 1974.

Gourlay, N. Difficulty factors arising from the use of tetrachoric correlations in factor analysis. *British Journal of Psychology, Statistical Section*, 1951, *4*, 65–73.

Guertin, W. H., & Bailey, J. P., Jr. *Introduction to modern factor analysis*. Ann Arbor, Mich.: Edwards Bros., 1970.

Guilford, J. P. The difficulty of a test and its factor composition. *Psychometrika*, 1941, *6*, 67–77.

Guttman, L. The quantification of a class of attributes: A theory and method for scale construction. In P. Horst et al, *The prediction of personal adjustment*. New York: Social Science Research Council, 1941.

Harman, H. H. *Modern factor analysis* (3rd ed. revised). Chicago & London: University of Chicago Press, 1976.

Jensen, A. R. *Bias in mental testing*. New York: Free Press, 1980.

John, E., & Burt, C. A reply to Mr. Gourlay's criticisms. *British Journal of Psychology, Statistical Section*, 1951, *4*, 73–76.

Kim, J-O., & Mueller, C. W. *Factor analysis: Statistical methods and practical issues*. Beverly Hills & London: Sage, 1978.

Lord, F. M. *Applications of item response theory to practical testing problems*. Hillsdale, N.J.: Lawrence Erlbaum Associates, 1980.

McDonald, R. P., & Ahlawat, K. S. Difficulty factors in binary data. *British Journal of Mathematical and Statistical Psychology*, 1974, *27*, 82–99.

Mosier, C. I. Psychophysics and mental test theory: Fundamental postulates and elementary theorems. *Psychological Review*, 1940, *47*, 355–366.

Mosier, C. I. Psychophysics and mental test theory. II. The constant process. *Psychological Review,* 1941, *48,* 235–249.
Mulaik, S. A. *The foundations of factor analysis.* New York: McGraw-Hill, 1972.
Rummel, R. J. *Applied factor analysis.* Evanston, Ill.: Northwestern University Press, 1970.
Seashore, C. E. *Manual of instructions and interpretations for Measures of Musical Talent.* Chicago: Stoelting, 1919.
Seashore, C. E., Lewis, D., & Saetveit, J. G. *Seashore Measures of Musical Talents (Revised Ed.).* New York: Psychological Corporation, 1939.
von Békésy, G. Über das Fechner'sche Gesetz und seine akustischen Beobachtungsfehler und die Theorie des Hörens. *Annalen der Physik,* 1930, *7,* 329–359.
Walker, D. A. Answer pattern and score scatter in tests and examinations. *British Journal of Psychology,* 1931, *22,* 73–86; 1936, *26,* 301–308; 1940, *30,* 248–260.
Weiss, D. J. Discussion. In D. J. Weiss (Ed.), *Proceedings of the 1979 Computerized Adaptive Testing Conference.* Minneapolis: University of Minnesota, Department of Psychology, Psychometric Methods Program, 1980.

16 Evaluating Guttman Scales: Some Old and New Thoughts

Norman Cliff
University of Southern California

For a number of years the dominant point of view in test theory has been one where there were continuous true scores measured at the interval level and stochastic models that related those true scores to the dichotomous item responses that are directly observed. This point of view culminates in what has come to be called item response theory, and there would be few who would quarrel with the statement that Fred Lord, whom this volume honors, has been the central figure in bringing to fruition that kind of test theory, and there would be equally few who would denigrate the practical achievements of that kind of theory. The recent book by Lord (1980) demonstrates the intellectual and practical achievements.

In describing test data, however, there has been a persistent, if small, minority viewpoint that attempts to stay closed to the actual form of the observed data, limiting itself to binary and ordinal concepts and methods. These methods have had some limited success at trying to describe test data, and my purpose here is to try to summarize some of the developments of this nature, developments that do not assume underlying interval-level traits.

For the most part, the references concentrate in the late 1940s and early 1950s, but there is some evidence of a revival in recent years. Fred Lord received his Ph.D. in 1952, and is reaching retirement now. The correlation between the dates seems more than a coincidence.

The current chapter, then, shows some of the results of trying to describe, and infer from, test data without recourse to the concepts and devices of item response theory. At various points the impulse of the reader is likely to be to insert the concept of a true score or an item characteristic curve. The strength of such impulses is a tribute to the amount of influence that the concepts that we associate with Fred Lord have come to have, but the impulses are not followed in this line of research.

Guttman Scales

There are always plenty of ideas. It is good ideas that are in short supply, and the Guttman scale is one of the very clearest examples of a good idea in all of psychological measurement. Even with an unsophisticated—but intelligent—consumer of psychometrics, one has only to show him a perfect scale and recognition is almost instantaneous, "Yes, that's what I want." Figure 16.1 is an example, for 10 persons and nine items. Unfortunately, that may be what one wants, but that is not what one gets. What one gets is more like Fig. 16.2, or even Fig. 16.3. One must reconcile oneself to the fact that there are no perfect scales in an imperfect world, at least none that are based on items composed by admittedly imperfect investigators and answered by decidedly imperfect respondents or examinees. I can remember Fred dismissing the relevance of Guttman scales because of their empirical implausibility. Nevertheless, given that the scale is imperfect, one may like to know just how imperfect it is. Even though

ITEMS

	1	1	1	1	1	1	1	1	1
	0	1	1	1	1	1	1	1	1
P	0	0	1	1	1	1	1	1	1
E	0	0	0	1	1	1	1	1	1
R	0	0	0	0	1	1	1	1	1
S	0	0	0	0	0	1	1	1	1
O	0	0	0	0	0	0	1	1	1
N	0	0	0	0	0	0	0	1	1
S	0	0	0	0	0	0	0	0	1
	0	0	0	0	0	0	0	0	0

FIG. 16.1 Perfect Guttman scale.

16. EVALUATING GUTTMAN SCALES: SOME OLD AND NEW THOUGHTS

ITEMS

```
            1 0 1 1 1 1 1 1
            0 1 0 1 1 1 1 1
        P   0 1 0 0 1 1 1 1
        E   0 0 1 0 1 0 1 1 1
        R   0 0 1 0 0 1 0 1 1
        S   0 0 0 1 1 0 1 1 1
        O   0 0 1 0 1 1 0 1 1
        N   0 0 0 1 1 0 1 0 1
        S   0 0 0 0 0 0 1 0 1
            0 0 0 0 0 0 1 0
```

FIG. 16.2 Imperfect Guttman scale.

some would say that there are no degrees of imperfection, this chapter is devoted to attempts to measure such imperfection.

CONSISTENCY OF DICHOTOMOUS MANIFEST DATA

Virtually all the basic data for which test theory has been developed is dichotomous, and the test consists of a single set of items. However, the dominant forms of test theory posit continuous underlying scores and assume large populations of items. There has been, however, a persistent minority viewpoint that expresses a desire to stay closer to the manifest data, describing its consistency in ways that are felt to be more direct and more natural in the sense of staying closer to its original form. The Guttman scale and the methods for evaluating it epitomize this minority tradition although several workers apparently arrived at their methods independently of Guttman (e.g., Loevinger, 1947; Sato, 1971, 1975.) These methods for evaluating the manifest data are often plausible and interesting in themselves and there are two aspects of them that are interesting from a historical point of view. One is the persistence of these efforts, the extent to

ITEMS

```
          1 0 1 0 1 1 1 1
          0 1 0 1 0 1 1 1
      P   1 0 1 0 1 0 1 1 1
      E   0 1 0 1 1 1 0 1 1
      R   0 0 1 1 0 1 1 0 1
      S   0 0 0 1 1 0 1 1 1
      O   0 0 0 0 1 0 1 1 1 0
      N   0 0 1 0 1 1 0 1 0
      S   0 1 0 0 1 0 1 0 1
          0 0 0 0 0 1 0 1 1
          1 3 3 2 3 3 2 2 2   "Errors"
```

FIG. 16.3 More imperfect scale, with number of Jackson errors.

which various people at various times have felt the need to invent such methods. The other is the extent to which the conclusions—the indices themselves—overlap in spite of the widely different directions from which these different workers began.

The first person to write on the topic was apparently Goodenough (1944). Guttman's own original paper (1941) does not deal with the topic of assessing consistency. It was not until later, particularly in the American Soldier volume (Guttman, 1950a, 1950b) that Guttman's own ideas concerning evaluation of consistency were elucidated.

Guttman's original index for measuring the quality of a Guttman scale is the one called Reproducibility. It suffers from numerous deficiencies as an ideal index and was criticized almost from the beginning (Festinger, 1947; Loevinger, 1948; Green, 1956; White & Saltz, 1957). Several workers offered improvements on it that were in the same general spirit (Goodenough, 1944; Goodman, 1959; Green, 1956; Jackson, 1949). Nonetheless it is the original form that is

16. EVALUATING GUTTMAN SCALES: SOME OLD AND NEW THOUGHTS

still widely used, being incorporated into several widely used computer programs for Guttman scaling. (See Lingoes, 1963; Proctor, 1970.) In view of the apparent validity of the criticisms, and the limited space here, reproducibility is not discussed in further detail. Its persistence, however, is an interesting datum in the sociology of science.

A Typology of Measures

Of the various measures and indices that have been used to evaluate Guttman scales, a large proportion can be put into three classes. One class notes that the dichotomous items furnish only ordinal data, and, in a number of closely related ways, they furnish numbers that are variants of Kendall's tau averaged across the items or across persons. The second type is related to these, but offers a significant refinement in correcting for chance consistency and in ensuring that the index is scaled from zero to unity. Both of these, however, are expressions of average between-item or between-person consistency. The third type is different in that it attempts to express consistency of total score and in that it uses the Pearson correlation as the measure of consistency. The three types are discussed below.

AVERAGE TAU COEFFICIENTS

Cliff's Consistency Indices

The field of evaluating person-by-item matrices was very quiet through the 1960s and early 1970s, but since then has shown signs of revival. Part of the revival came through applications to tailored tests, much of the work was detailed in an earlier paper (Cliff, 1979) starting (Cliff, 1977) from the problem of the evaluation of the internal consistency of tailored tests, where the standard methods are hard to apply due to the incompleteness of the data.

One group of indices was based on a sort of general strategy of returning to basics in test theory; trying to stay ordinal and just counting relations of various sorts, and so most of these indices can be thought of as forms of Kendall's tau. It has turned out to be related to work that was going on in Japan at the same time or earlier (e.g., Sato, 1975; Sato & Kurata, 1977) and to the work of several others both earlier and later (Harnisch & Linn, 1981; Tatsuoka & Tatsuoka, 1980; see Sato, 1981, and Kurata and Sato, 1981 for other reviews).

The basic idea that underlay that work was that the observed binary response represents a dominance relation between a person and an item; Coombs (1964) calls this two-set ordinal data, but it seems preferable to call it two-set dominance data. One can let a 1 stand for dominance, whether by person over item or vice versa, by generating both a rights matrix S and a wrongs matrix $\tilde{S}'$. (This was important in the tailored-testing context in order to distinguish between "wrong" and "not taken." Guttman (1950a, 1950b) also used the wrongs matrix in scalogram analysis, but in a different way.) Then item-item and person-person dominance data are derived indirectly. An item j dominates another item k every time a person gets k right and j wrong. A person i similarly then dominates person h every time there is an item that i gets right and h gets wrong. These counts can be made through a simple matrix multiplication:

$$N = \tilde{S}'S, \tag{1}$$

and

$$X = S\tilde{S}'. \tag{2}$$

Here, n_{jk} is the number of times (persons) on which item j dominates k, and x_{ih} is the number of times (items) on which person i dominates h. (One of the nice things about this double-matrix way of doing things is that it facilitated perception of the complete duality between persons and items.)

These matrices reflect the consistency of the relations because, if the data are perfectly consistent, that is, a Guttman scale, then the matrices will be upper triangular when items are ordered in terms of difficulty and persons in order of ability, respectively. To estimate consistency, we started from a count of the total number of relations

$$v = 1'N1; \tag{3}$$

$$g = 1'X1. \tag{4}$$

Some algebra shows that for nontailored data

$$g = \sum_j n_{j.}(n - n_{j.}) = n^2 \Sigma p_j(1 - p_j), \tag{5}$$

and

$$v = \sum_i x_{i.}(x - x_{i.}). \tag{6}$$

In (5) n is the number of persons and $n_{j.}$ is the number who fail item j; similarly, in (6) x is the number of items and $x_{i.}$ is the number correct by person i. That is, the item variances are telling us about the number of *person* relations in the data, and vice versa.

Then, we define a statistic to represent the values that g and v would have if the data were perfectly consistent, that is, were a perfect Guttman scale with the same difficulty or ability distribution. For items, assuming they are arranged in difficulty order, this is

$$v_m = \sum_j \sum_{k>j} (n_{jk} - n_{kj}) \tag{7}$$

16. EVALUATING GUTTMAN SCALES: SOME OLD AND NEW THOUGHTS

$$= \sum_j \sum_{k>j} (n_{j.} - n_{k.}) \tag{8}$$

$$= (x + 1)\Sigma n_{j.} - 2\Sigma j n_{j.} \tag{9}$$

For persons, it is

$$g_m = \sum_i \sum_{h>i} (x_{ih} - x_{hi}) \tag{10}$$

$$= \sum_i \sum_{h>i} (x_{i.} - x_{h.}) \tag{11}$$

$$= (n + 1)\Sigma x_{i.} - 2\Sigma i x_{i.} \tag{12}$$

The basic definition, given by the first versions of the two equalities, (7) and (10), is the relevant part here. The middle one, (8) and (11), is an algebraic convenience, and the last, (9) and (12), is also; these last are included partly because I recently found an equivalent expression in Carroll (1945).

The important aspect of v_m and g_m is that they reflect the difference between the number of relations that agree with difficulty order and the number that disagree with it. Then it is meaningful to define the ratios

$$c_{t1} = v_m/v \tag{13}$$

$$c_{p1} = g_m/g \tag{14}$$

The numerator of (13) is the difference between the number of difficulty relations that are consistent with the overall difficulty order and the number that disagree with it, and the denominator is the total number of relations. Equation 14 tells a similar thing about persons. These then are a kind of average Kendall's tau. (Actually, closer to Somers' 1962 asymmetric version.) Dawes (1981) was helpful in clarifying these interpretations.

These indices, or ones that use the same quantities in slightly different ways, have been developed by several other groups; we have been working apparently independently of each other. For the most part, these other indices of this family arose out of a desire to identify aberrant items or respondents. This can be done rather simply by leaving out one summation in equation 15 or 16, giving a c_{t1j} for item j or a c_{p1i} for person i:

$$c_{t1j} = \left[\sum_{k=1}^{j-1} (n_{kj} - n_{jk}) + \sum_{k=j+1}^{x} (n_{jk} - n_{kj}) \right] \bigg/ \sum_{k=1}^{x} (n_{jk} + n_{kj}) \tag{15}$$

$$c_{p1i} = \left[\sum_{h=1}^{i} (x_{hi} - x_{ih}) + \sum_{h=i+1}^{n} (x_{ih} - x_{hi}) \right] \bigg/ \sum_{h=1}^{n} (x_{ih} + x_{hi}) \tag{16}$$

Assuming that items and persons are ordered in difficulty and score order, c_{t1j} and c_{p1i} are the sum of the dominance relations involving that item or person that is above the diagonal (i.e., easier or lower scoring) minus the sum that is below, divided by the total number of relations involving that person or item. Unfortunately, the original presentation of these indices (Cliff, 1977) was done in a somewhat obscure and inconsistent fashion.

They duplicate, or are duplicated by, a number of indices for similar purposes that have been developed by others. Sato (1971) develops a person-consistency index he calls "caution index" γ, which we will subscript γ_s to distinguish it from the well-known Goodman-Kruskal coefficient (Goodman & Kruskal, 1954). This is directly related to our quantities. (He also has another person-consistency index that is mentioned later.) Sato's γ_s is

$$\gamma_s = \frac{1}{2}(1 + c_{t1j}). \qquad (17)$$

A Dutch worker, van der Flier (1977; see Tatsuoka and Tatsuoka, 1980) has an index he calls U'; it is the same as γ_s (Sato, 1981);

$$U' = \frac{1}{2}(1 + c_{t1j}) \qquad (18)$$

Tatsuoka and Tatsuoka (1980) have an index called $N.C.I.$ It is identical with c_{t1j}:

$$N.C.I. = c_{t1j}. \qquad (19)$$

(I am indebted to Maurice Tatsuoka (1981) for clarifying this relationship.)

Harnisch and Linn (1981), in addition to noting several of the relations above, point out that these indices can be interpreted as the ratio of person point-biserial to maximum person point-biserial. They also note that indices proposed by Kane and Brennan (1980) are either identical to or directly related to these although one of their coefficients is more related to those in the next section.

Thus it seems that a number of different sets of investigators have felt the need to express the same thing, and they have done so in very similar ways. The next section notes several indices that are adjustments to these consistency indices, and these, too, show a large degree of convergence.

Consistency Corrected for Chance

In several places, workers have gone about the assessment of consistency in a slightly different way. They observe that the items on a test are providing dominance relations between persons, and that the idea central to consistency is that the relations on different items be in the same direction. However, even if two items are independent, a sizable fraction of the relations will be in the same direction. They therefore "correct" the number of relations for the number to be expected if the items are independent, and convert this number into an index.

They do the conversion by constructing a "quality index." A quality index is an index based on any statistic t that is of the following form:

16. EVALUATING GUTTMAN SCALES: SOME OLD AND NEW THOUGHTS

$$q = \frac{t - t_w}{t_b - t_w}, \tag{20}$$

where t_w is the value that t takes on in a "worst case" and t_b is its value in a "best case."

Cliff (1977) defined an index of this form based on the number of relations v. Then the "worst case" is independent items and the "best case" is a Guttman scale, each with the same difficulties. Defining v_c as the number of relations that would occur if the items were independent, we can get a coefficient of the quality index types, called c_{t3} in Cliff (1977):

$$c_{t3} = \frac{v - v_c}{v_m - v_c}. \tag{21}$$

The chance expectation v_c can be gotten from the item parameters:

$$v_c = \sum_j n_{j.}(n - n_{j.})/n \tag{22}$$

Due to the duality mentioned earlier, there is a parallel index for persons:

$$c_{p3} = \frac{g - g_c}{g_m - g_c}, \tag{23}$$

with

$$g_c = \sum_i x_{i.}(x - x_{i.})/x. \tag{24}$$

A useful aspect of these indices is that they can be defined with incomplete or tailored data, including instruments like the Binet and the Bayley, although then one must use the definitional formulas, for example, (3) and (4), rather than any simplified versions, such as (5) and (6).

Interestingly enough, this index c_{t3} has been derived in two other ways. It is identical to Loevinger's H_t, her index of "homogeneity" (Loevinger, 1947, 1948), where in her definition t is the variance of the test, t_w is the variance of a test composed of independent items, and t_b is the variance of a Guttman scale, in both cases assuming the same distribution of item difficulties. That is, they not only have the same general quality index form; H_t and c_{t3} are algebraically equivalent.

Mokken (1971) also derived the same index, expressing it in terms of joint and marginal probabilities. His development is in terms of an underlying trait model, however. In view of the other, purely descriptive origins of this index, the underlying trait model is apparently not necessary for it. He (Mokken, 1971) also defines a scale that would be $1 - v/v_c$ in the present notation (Kurata & Sato, 1981).

All of these indices of consistency that are described in this and the previous section are essentially indices of inter-item agreement. That is, they are kinds of inter-item correlations. Indeed, Horst (1953) notes that the Loevinger index H_t is a kind of average inter-item phi/phi-max. It is not a literal mean because one sums the numerators of the phis and the denominators of the phi-max's and gets the ratio of these sums. More on this later. The point of the observation that these indices are indices of inter-item agreement is that, while this is a perfectly legitimate goal, it does not tell us how good the overall order provided by the total score is. One other consequence is that they are also therefore disheartingly low in numerical value. Finding that one carefully developed and dearly beloved scale has a consistency index of .14 can be discouraging.

Parallel Form Indices

It is superficially surprising that there has not been more effort devoted to parallel form indices for Guttman scales. Finding out, or estimating from internal consistency, what the correlation is between one's scale and a parallel form seems to be quite a logical way of evaluating it. Doing this means, of course, that we must assume or admit the possibility of a parallel set of items, or an item-sampling model, and so forth, departing from the goal of simply evaluating the manifest data. Nonetheless, it seems reasonable to do this.

The most obvious candidate for such a coefficient is KR-20 (Kuder & Richardson, 1937). Unfortunately, it turns out that the beautiful data of Fig. 16.1 have a KR-20 reliability of .89, due to the well-known influence of the variance of item difficulties on that coefficient. This has made KR-20 unattractive as a measure of scale consistency.

A plausible response is to reconsider the compromise made by Kuder and Richardson (1937) when they went from KR-18 to KR-20. A Pearson correlation is of course the ratio of a covariance to the product of the standard deviations, and in the case of tests the covariance term is the sum of inter-item covariances:

$$s_{xx'} = \sum_j \sum_k s_{jk}. \qquad (25)$$

If the tests are parallel in any reasonable but possibly loose item-by-item sense, then the sum may be broken down into two components:

$$s_{xx'} = \sum_j \sum_{k \neq j'} s_{jk} + \sum_j s_{jj'}, \qquad (26)$$

here j and j' are paired items. The well-known compromise of KR-20 is to assume that the average of the second sum in (26) is the same as the average of the first, but one would expect the members of the second to be on the average larger, due to the influences of differences in difficulty. Therefore, an alternative to KR-20 is to make more realistic estimates of this second term.

16. EVALUATING GUTTMAN SCALES: SOME OLD AND NEW THOUGHTS

At least three people have made workable proposals of this kind. The earliest was Horst (1953) in the paper noted earlier. He suggests that if the proportions passing j and j' are assumed to be equal, then it is possible to estimate the second sum. The Loevinger H_t ratio, or c_{t3}, is used to estimate the correlation between the equidifficult items; that is, it is assumed that the quasi-average phi/phi-max for equidifficult items is assumed to be the same as that for all the items in the present test. Then substitution in KR-18 yields the following formula:

$$\hat{r}_{xx'} = 1 - \frac{(1 - H_t)\Sigma s_j^2}{s_x^2} \tag{27}$$

Application of this seems relatively straightforward, and it seems surprising that this formula did not "catch on."

A very similar approach was taken by Cliff (1982). He suggested assuming that the average Goodman-Kruskal γ (Goodman & Kruskal, 1954) between the equidifficult items should be the same as the average between the items in the current test. This coefficient is not obviously influenced by difficulty and is virtually monotonic with the tetrachoric correlation between items. He then showed that the covariance between equidifficult items was related to their γ and their difficulty

$$c_{jj'} = p_j - p_j^2 + \tfrac{1}{2}\left(\frac{1}{\gamma} - 1\right)$$
$$- \tfrac{1}{4}\sqrt{\left(\frac{1}{\gamma} - 1\right)^2 + 8\left(\frac{1}{\gamma} - 1\right)(p_j - p_j^2)} \tag{28}$$

and then

$$\hat{r}_{xx'} = 1 - \frac{\Sigma(s_j^2 - \hat{c}_{jj'})}{s_x^2} \tag{29}$$

Mokken (1971) had a different proposal, one that rested on the assumption of unidimensionality for the test. This was that the covariance between equidifficult items could be estimated from an item's covariances with the item or items nearest to it in difficulty. There were one or two variations on this process, either picking the single item nearest in difficulty to each item and using this covariance as $c_{jj'}$, or using the items on either side of it in difficulty, and so forth. A slightly more complicated option, which Mokken does not suggest, is to plot s_{jk} as a function of p_k and fit a curve to the plot. The value of the function at p_j would be the estimated covariance between equidifficult items and used as $s_{jj'}$.

These estimates of KR-18 would seem to overcome the drawback of KR-20 as a measure of the consistency of Guttman scales. They seem likely to be greater than KR-20 as the number of items decreases and as the inter-item consistency increases, and perhaps for the typical test or scale of more than a dozen items of only moderate consistency they make too little difference to justify routine adoption. However, the slightly more complicated computations surely no longer serve as an obstacle, and they seem to deserve wider consideration.

OTHER APPROACHES

There are a number of other approaches to measuring consistency that can be mentioned. These are mainly similar in spirit to the consistency ratio mentioned first, but differ somewhat in the specific quantities that are used. It is possible that these are functionally related to the group given first, due to the many algebraic identities that exist with functions of dichotomous items, but connections have not been identified if they do exist.

Sato's Other Indices

Takahiro Sato has several other interesting indices, two of which I will mention. One with a basic idea similar to all those we have just mentioned is the "caution index" (Sato, 1975; Sato & Kurato, 1977), similar in purpose to the "appropriateness index" (Drasgow & Levine, 1981). It was developed for the purpose of identifying *individuals* who have odd response patterns, like several of the above, but like everything else can be used in the opposite way, that is, for items. It resembles a point-biserial correlation in that the sum of the difficulties of the item a person gets correct are compared to the sum of the items she gets incorrect. However, the denominator is different from r_{pb}; it is defined as the maximum that this difference could be, given the number of items the person gets correct. Sato's own original rationale is somewhat different, but this is how it can be translated (Sato & Kurata, 1977). Harnisch and Linn (1981) use essentially the same index, but reverse its direction.

If one is interested in evaluating the consistency of the whole instrument rather than a single person or item, it is simple to redefine Sato's caution index so that the sums run over both items and individuals. However, this is not what Sato uses as an overall index (Sato, 1975; Sato & Kurata, 1977). He uses what he calls the S-P index, which is very simple to apply with the small samples for which his work is designed and it has an intuitive appeal. We can illustrate it with the data from Fig. 16.3 in Fig. 16.4. What one does is rather simple; one draws a vertical line in each row between the j and $j +$ first columns, where j is the number wrong of the person in that row. Then one goes back and does the corresponding thing for columns, drawing a horizontal line between the i and $i +$ first rows, where i is the number right on the item in that column. This creates an area along from the upper left to lower right area of the matrix. Clearly, the area will be small if the data are consistent and large if they are inconsistent. One counts the number of elements that are within this area and divides by np, and the complement of that is the S-P index.

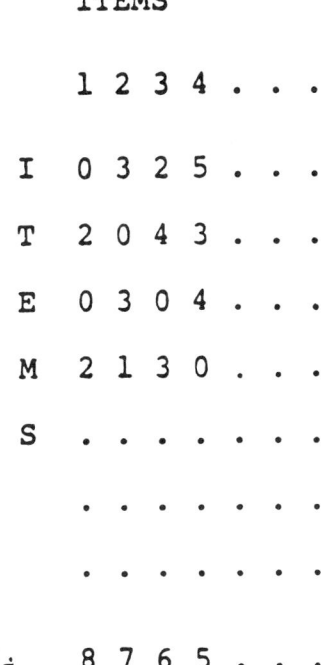

FIG. 16.4 Item dominance matrix for data of Fig. 16.3.

It is similar in spirit to Rep, and similar in approach to the modification by Jackson (1949). Therefore, it suffers from some of the same deficiencies as Rep, taking on fairly large values even when the data are random, for example. As far as I know, no one has a formal characterization of the index such as would allow theoretical investigations of it. Sato (1975) does have some theoretical work on it, but that seems to refer only to hypothetical continuous cases rather than the observed data itself. There are also simulations comparing it to KR-20 (Sato and Kurata, 1977).

Dominance, Redundancy, Contradiction, and Uniqueness

A few years ago I started pondering the reasons for the inadequacy of KR-20 for Guttman scales, also the nature of the attenuation paradox, and so forth, and concluded that the reason was that the KR formula did not take into consideration all the information in a collection of items. I am not going to try and go through all of the reasoning that this has led into, (see Cliff, 1979, for some sketches, and Cliff and Reynolds, 1980, for a detailed description) but I do want to illustrate what is meant by unique, redundant, and contradictory dominance relations, and point out some areas this has led to.

Suppose four persons respond to two items as in Fig. 16.5. Both items are assumed to tend to order persons with respect to the same dimension. Considering first item a, person 1 dominates persons 3 and 4 because she gets it right and they get it wrong (see Fig. 16.6). On item b, she dominates 2 and 4, but not 3. Thus, the relation 1-over-4 is redundant or repeated on the two items. On the other hand, the dominance of 1-over-3 is *unique* to item a, as is the dominance of 1-over-2 unique to item b. Finally, the dominance of 3-over-2 on b is *contradicted* by 2-over-3 on a. The class of each relation is noted in Fig. 16.7.

Thus, in considering the dominance relations provided by a single item in comparison to another item, some of the person dominance relations are redundant, some are contradictory, and some are unique.

The number of relations of each kind involving each pair of items can be calculated rather simply from the two-by-two contingency table for the pair of items. Given the table below

	2 +	2 −	
1 +	w	x	n_1
1 −	y	z	$n - n_1$
	n_2	$n - n_2$	

the number of redundant relations is wz, and the number of contradictory ones is xy. The number unique to item 1 is $wy + wz$. The number unique to item 2 is $wx + yz$. These may be summed across all pairs of items to form totals $r..$, $c..$, and $u..$ for the numbers of redundant, contradictory, and unique relations, and a variety of indices derived using these quantities.

Ducamp-Falmagne Consistency

One rational method of assessing score matrices that does involve counting uniquenesses follows from the theoretical work of Ducamp and Falmagne (1969). Their definition of a perfect scale was that for every pair of persons and pair of items, there must be no patterns of response like the left one in Fig. 16.8. This axiom can be restated in terms of two implication relations. These are also given in the figure. The axiom means that the existence of either of the sets of three responses in the triangles implies that the fourth response must be as indicated. This suggests that in evaluating the consistency of a set of responses, we go through and find all the times that the conditional part, within the tri-

16. EVALUATING GUTTMAN SCALES: SOME OLD AND NEW THOUGHTS

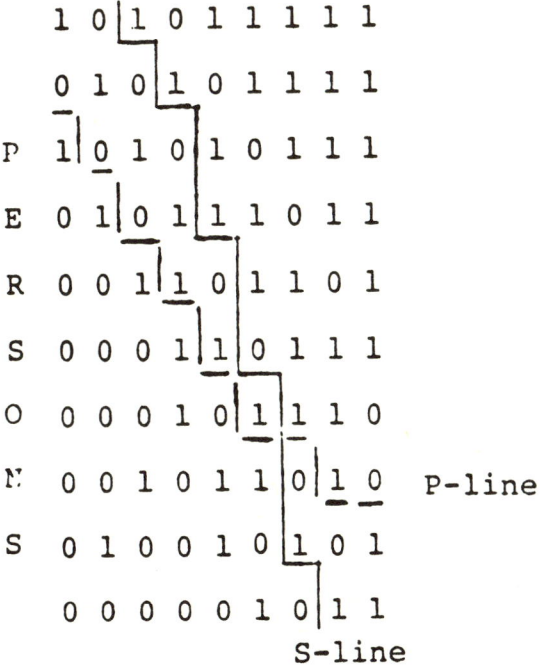

FIG. 16.5   S–P diagram for data of Fig. 16.3. There are 20 errors out of 90 responses.

FIG. 16.6   Score matrix for two items (left) and person dominance matrices for item a (middle) and b (right).

PERSONS

		1	2	3	4
P E R S O N S	1	0	u_b	u_a	r
	2	0	0	c	u_a
	3	0	c	0	u_b
	4	0	0	0	0

FIG. 16.7 Person dominance relations classified by type: r is redundant, c is contradictory, u_a is unique to a, u_b is unique to b.

angles, holds, and then observe the number of times that the implication is confirmed and the number of times it is disconfirmed.

This sounds like a horrendous job, but turns out not to be. The number of unique, redundant, and contradictory relations between a pair of items can be counted rather simply from the familiar two-by-two table involving them. Then we can count all the unique relations involving all pairs of items, u. . , and the same for the contradictory relations, c. . . The former turns out to be the number of times the Ducamp-Falmagne implication is verified, and the latter turns out to be half the number of times it is disconfirmed. This leads, to an axiomatic measurement-theory-based index of consistency:

$$c_{D-F} = \frac{u.. - 2c..}{u.. + 2c..} \tag{30}$$

That is, the numerator is the number of times the implication is confirmed minus the number of times it is disconfirmed. The denominator is the number of times the premise occurs. This quantity would be useful for implied orders tailored testing.

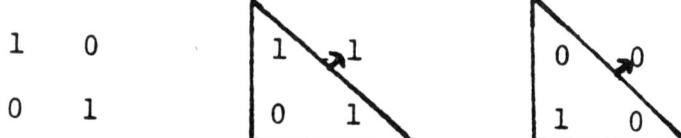

FIG. 16.8 Reformulation of the Decamp-Falmagne axiom. The D–DC axiom forbids the pattern at the left. Alternatively, one can say that the existence of the pattern in the triangle in the middle implies the 1 in the upper corner and the three responses in the triangle at the right implies the 0 in the upper right corner.

CONCLUSION

This chapter has attempted to summarize and integrate a number of attempts at assessing the consistency of test data without resort to consideration of underlying scales.

Most test data consist of a matrix of binary responses to a finite set of items. The ideal for such a set of items, from the point of view of consistent and maximal discrimination among the items, is the pattern that has come to be called a Guttman scale. Over the years there have been a number of attempts to measure the consistency of binary data matrices without resort to assumptions of underlying continuous true score or of populations of items. This chapter has been an attempt to summarize and integrate some of these indices.

A surprising number end up being quite closely related, even though the originators were often approaching from different viewpoints. This is perhaps partly a result of the algebraic simplications that occur with binary data. Many of the indices are forms of average Kendall's tau between items. Some are corrected for chance consistency, and some are not.

An alternative to assessing average inter-item consistency is estimating the correlation between total score on the present set of items and a hypothetical set of parallel items. KR-20 is the obvious candidate for such a purpose, but it cannot be unity for highly consistent items. Several attempts have been made to adapt KR-18 and thus to get more realistic estimates of the correlation.

If the past is any indication, measures of this kind, that do not assume parametric models, are likely to continue to be of interest. This will be true under a variety of circumstances, particularly where strong true score models are of dubious validity. The elegance and power of item response theory (Lord, 1980) is likely to continue, however.

REFERENCES

Carroll, J. B. The effect of difficulty and chance success on correlation between items or between tests. *Psychometrika,* 1945, *10,* 1–19.

Cliff, N. A theory of consistency of ordering generalizable to tailored testing. *Psychometrika,* 1977, *42,* 375–399.

Cliff, N. Test theory without true scores? *Psychometrika,* 1979, *44,* 373–393.

Cliff, N. *An upper bound internal consistency reliability coefficient.* Submitted for publication, 1982.

Cliff, N., & Reynolds, T. J. *Dominance, uniqueness, and nonparametric test theory* (Research Report). University of Southern California, Department of Psychology, Los Angeles, 1980.

Coombs, C. H. *A theory of data.* New York: Wiley, 1964.

Dawes, R. Personal communication, March, 1981.

Drasgow, F., & Levine, M. *Appropriateness measurement when there are omitted responses.* Paper presented at the American Psychological Convention, Los Angeles, August, 1981.

Ducamp, A., & Falmagne, J. C. Composite measurement. *Journal of Mathematical Psychology,* 1969, *6,* 359–390.
Festinger, L. The treatment of qualitative data by "Scale Analysis." *Psychological Bulletin,* 1947, *44,* 146–161.
Goodenough, W. H. A technique for scale analysis. *Educational and Psychological Measurement,* 1944, *4,* 179–190.
Goodman, L. Simple statistical methods for scalogram analysis. *Psychometrika,* 1959, *24,* 29–43.
Goodman, L., & Kruskal, W. B. Measures of association for cross-classifications. *Journal of the American Statistical Association,* 1954, *49,* 732–764.
Green, B. F. A method for scalogram analysis using summary statistics. *Psychometrika,* 1956, *21,* 79–88.
Guttman, L. The quantification of a class of attributes: A theory and method of scale construction. In P. Horst (Ed.). *The prediction of personal adjustment.* New York: Social Science Research Council, 1941.
Guttman, L. The basis for scalogram analysis. In S. A. Stouffer, et al., *Measurement and prediction.* Princeton: Princeton University Press, 1950.(a)
Guttman, L. The relation of scalogram analysis to other techniques. In S. A. Stouffer, et al., *Measurement and prediction.* Princeton: Princeton University Press, 1950. (b)
Harnisch, D. L., & Linn, R. L. Analysis of item response patterns: Questionable test data and dissimilar curriculum practices. *Journal of Educational Measurement,* 1981, *18,* 133–146.
Horst, P. Correcting the Kuder-Richardson reliability for dispersion of item difficulties. *Psychological Bulletin,* 1953, *50,* 371–374.
Jackson, J. A simple and more rigorous technique for scale analysis. In *A manual for scale analysis.* Part II. Montreal: McGill University, 1949. Mimeogram.
Kane, M. T., & Brennan, R. L. Agreement coefficients as indices of dependability for domain-referenced test. *Applied Psychological Measurement,* 1980, *4,* 105–126.
Kuder, G. F., & Richardson, M. W. The theory of estimation of test reliability. *Psychometrika,* 1937, *2,* 151–160.
Kurata, M., & Sato, T. *Similarity of some indices of item response patterns based on an S-P Chart* (Research Memorandum EI 81-4). Computer & Communication Systems Research Laboratories, Nippon Electric Co., Ltd. Tokyo, 1981.
Lingoes, J. C. Multiple scalogram analysis. A set-theoretic model for analyzing dichotomous items. *Educational and Psychological Measurement,* 1963, *23,* 501–524.
Loevinger, J. A. A systematic approach to the construction and evaluation of tests of ability. *Psychological Monographs,* 1947, *61,* (4, Whole No. 285).
Loevinger, J. A. The technique of homogeneous test compared with some aspects of "scale analysis." *Psychological Bulletin,* 1948, *45,* 507–529.
Lord, F. M. *Applications of item response theory to practical testing problems.* Hillsdale, New Jersey: Lawrence Erlbaum, Associates, 1980.
Mokken, R. J. *A theory and procedure of scale analysis.* Hawthorne, New York: Mouton, & Co., 1971.
Proctor, C. H. A probabilistic formulation and statistical analysis of Guttman scaling. *Psychometrika,* 1970, *35,* 73–78.
Sato, T. Analysis of students' performance data. In K. Hirata, & T. Sato (Eds.). *Response analyzer.* Tokyo: Kyoiku-Kogakusha, 1971. In Japanese.
Sato, T. *The construction and interpretation of S-P charts.* Tokyo: Meiji-Tosho, 1975. In Japanese.
Sato, T. *Similarity of some indices of item response patterns: van der Flier's V', Tatsuoka's NCI, and Sato's* γ (Research Memorandum EI 81-1). Computer & Communication Systems Research Laboratories, Nippon Electric Co., Ltd. Tokyo, 1981.
Sato, T., & Kurata, M. S-P score table characteristics. *NEC Research & Development,* 1977, *47,* 64–71.

Somers, R. H. A new asymmetric measure of association for ordinal variables. *American Sociological Review,* 1962, *27,* 799–811.

Tatsuoka, M. Personal Communication, May, 1981.

Tatsuoka, M., & Tatsuoka, K. *Detection of aberrant response patterns and their effects on dimensionality* (Research Report 80-4). Urbana: University of Illinois, Computer-Based Education Research Laboratory, 1980.

Van der Flier, H. Environmental factors and deviant response patterns. In Y. H. Poortigna (Ed.), *Basic problems in cross-cultural psychology.* Amsterdam: Swets & Seitlinger, 1977.

White, B. W., & Saltz, E. The measurement of reproducibility. *Psychological Bulletin,* 1957, *54,* 81–90.

17 Some Problems in Estimating Response Time Distributions

Bruce Bloxom
Vanderbilt University

A difficult task confronts the investigator who is interested in estimating a distribution of psychological response times if no strong assumptions are made about the functional form of the distribution. The primary problem is choosing a function which accurately maps the data onto an estimate of the distribution. The problem can be made more difficult by the presence of random variables such as motor reaction time which may be contaminating the response time. Furthermore, even with an a priori reasonable approach to the problem, the precision of the estimate cannot be assumed to be equivalent in all empirical contexts.

The purpose of this chapter is to discuss these difficulties which are associated with estimating response time distributions. However, before doing so, it is important to discuss the motivation for studying psychological response times, in general, and for estimating their entire distributions, in particular. Without an awareness of this motivation, the estimation of these distributions may seem to be a rather parochial exercise.

The major attraction of studying response time is found in the important position it has traditionally held in the measurement of psychological processes (e.g., see Sternberg's, 1969, discussion of Donders). Recently, response time has been quite widely employed as a measure of the efficiency or simplicity of a subject's processing of stimulus information. It has played a very important role in research on both criterion-referenced tests (Tatsuoka & Tatsuoka, 1978) and tests of pure speed (Lord & Novick, 1968), because responses on such tests are essentially error free and do not allow the straightforward application of latent trait models of the probability of correct responding. It has also played a very important role in research on cognitive processes (e.g., see Sternberg, 1969, and Townsend & Ashby, 1982) because of the close connection between response time and the number of, and the relation among, stages in component models of cognition.

The major attraction of estimating an entire distribution of response times is that such an estimate may provide diagnostic information about processes underlying response time. For example, instead of beginning a response time analysis by fitting a strong parametric model and trying to interpret discrepancies between the data and the model, one can begin by inspecting the estimated distribution for such properties as peakedness and the height of the tails to decide which of a variety of parametric models might be appropriately considered further (Tapia & Thompson, 1978).

A particularly valuable aid in this selection of a parametric model is an estimate of the distribution's hazard function (Barlow & Proschan, 1975), which is the likelihood of a response at latency t (following the item or stimulus presentation), given that the response has not yet occurred. This function can be expressed as the ratio $\hat{r}(t) = \hat{f}(t)/[1 - \hat{F}(t)]$, where $\hat{f}(t)$ is an estimate of the density function and $\hat{F}(t)$ is an estimate of the cumulative distribution function. Such a function of t is of diagnostic interest here, because it varies markedly across commonly considered types of distributions in a way that the densities of the distributions do not. Figure 17.1 illustrates differences between the hazard functions (graphed to the ninth decile) of the truncated normal and the gamma distributions, with means and variances indicated in parentheses; note that the truncated normal distribution has a hazard function which accelerates over the entire range of the random variable, but the hazard function of the gamma distribution approaches an asymptote as the random variable becomes large. Also, the log-normal and exponential distributions have hazard functions which are distinctly different from each other as well as from the hazard functions shown in Fig. 17.1 (Barlow & Proschan, 1975). Thus, if rather precise estimates of the hazard function can be obtained, that function can indicate which kind of parametric distribution might be appropriately considered.

It should be noted that the selection of a parametric model is not the only context in which a hazard function has been useful. Such a function has been employed as a descriptive tool in studies of system reliability (e.g., the likelihood of a mechanical system failing at age t, given that it has not failed yet; Barlow & Proschan, 1975), in actuarial studies (the likelihood of mortality in a cohort at age t, given survival to that age), and in studies of the effects of reinforcement schedules in operant conditioning (the likelihood of a specified inter-response latency, given that the response has not yet occurred; McGill, 1963). In such studies, the hazard function has shown departures from monotonicity which reveal subtle but important changes in the process generating the data. For example, under a fixed interval reinforcement schedule in operant conditioning, the removal of the reinforcement contingency after a fixed number of seconds reduces the hazard function associated with response latencies greater than that number of seconds; this reduction in the hazard function departs from

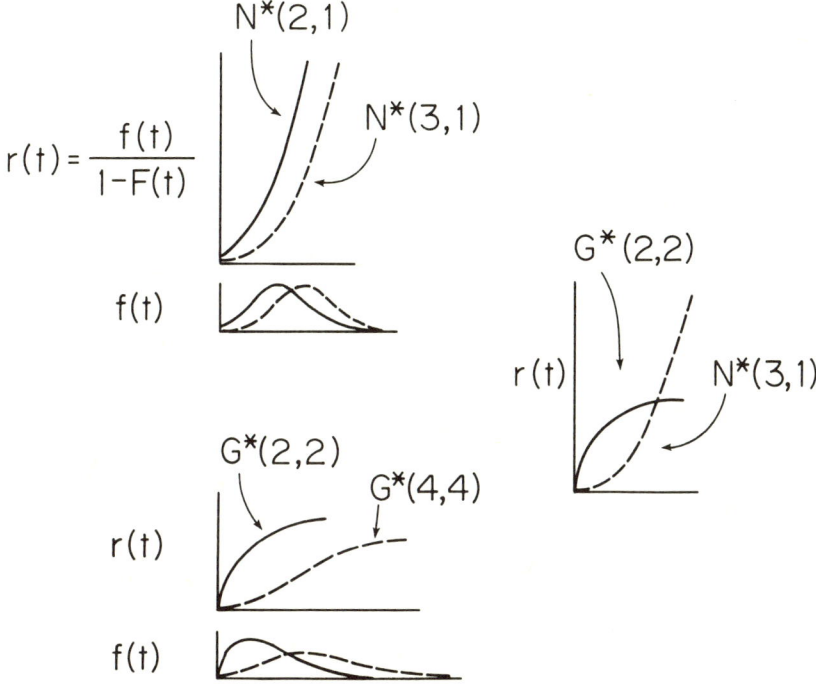

FIG. 17.1. Gamma and truncated normal density and hazard functions.

what might have been a monotonically increasing function if the reinforcement contingency had not been removed.

In summary, the primary motivation here for estimating a response time distribution is to obtain some information about the process underlying the response time without making strong a priori assumptions about the functional form of the distribution. The hazard function, expressed as a function of the distribution, can be a particularly valuable tool in this effort. However, before proceeding with a discussion of estimating distributions, it should be noted that methods exist for estimating a hazard function without the intermediate step of estimating the density and cumulative distribution functions (e.g., Rice & Rosenblatt, 1976). Such methods are not considered here because of computational difficulties which are encountered when the response time of interest is a component of a convolution, that is, is only one member of a sum of independent components contributing to the measured response time; it can be quite difficult to obtain a closed form expression for the distribution of a convolution in terms of the hazard functions of its components when the closed form expression may be obtained quite easily in terms of the density functions of the components. The usefulness of having the closed form expression is indicated in a later section of this chapter.

The following sections of this chapter suggest approaches to some problems which are associated with estimating distributions of response times and which, therefore, can be associated with estimating the hazard functions of those distributions. The first problem is choosing a type of function to map data onto a density estimate. The second problem is using that function to contend with the contamination of psychological response time by the addition of other random variables, for example, motor reaction time. The third problem is selecting a criterion to optimize when choosing parameters for the density estimate. The final section of the chapter presents the results of a small simulation study; the results suggest where one approach may, and where it may not, provide reasonably precise density estimates and hazard estimates with small samples.

The Choice of Mapping Function. A brief survey of research on nonparametric density estimation (see Appendix) indicates that numerous approaches are available for mapping a continuous random variable such as response time on to a density function without making strong assumptions about the density's functional form. Unfortunately, analytic studies of the asymptotic properties of those estimators do not indicate that any one of the methods is more precise than other methods across all true density functions. Thus, the choice among methods needs to be guided, at least in part, by a consideration of specific properties of the estimates provided by the methods.

One density estimator which has a number of particularly useful and interesting properties is a quadratic spline function. An example of such a function is shown in the middle graph of Fig. 17.2, with one possible algebraic expression of the function given directly below the graph. This is a piecewise quadratic polynomial with a continuous slope at each joint, or knot, a_k, between pieces; the expression $(t - a_k)_+$ is a function which takes on its algebraic value for values of $t > a_k$ and which is zero otherwise. Because the function has this form, its slope (in the bottom of Fig. 17.2) is a continuous piecewise linear spline, and its integral (the cumulative distribution function, $\hat{F}(t)$, in the top of Fig. 17.2) is a continuous piecewise cubic spline with continuous first and second order derivatives. The functional form of $\hat{F}(t)$ has led to the suggestion that the density be estimated by first fitting $\hat{F}(t)$ to points on the sample step function and by then taking the first derivative of $\hat{F}(t)$; the fitting procedure consists of making a rational selection of the knots and then estimating the vector of coefficients, $\hat{c}_k$, simply by solving a system of linear equations to fit $\hat{F}(t)$ to the sample step function.

A particularly attractive feature of a quadratic spline as a density estimator is the function's visual smoothness. Because it is composed of quadratic polynomials between the knots, its number of inflections is no larger than the number of knots between the upper and lower bounds on the random variable. Thus, unlike ordinary higher order polynomials, it can have the flexibility to approxi-

17. PROBLEMS IN ESTIMATING RESPONSE TIME DISTRIBUTIONS

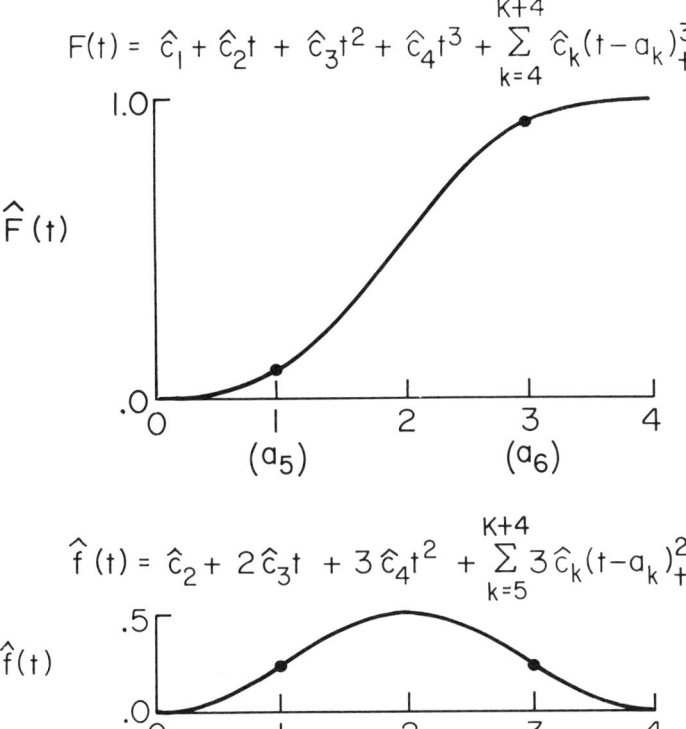

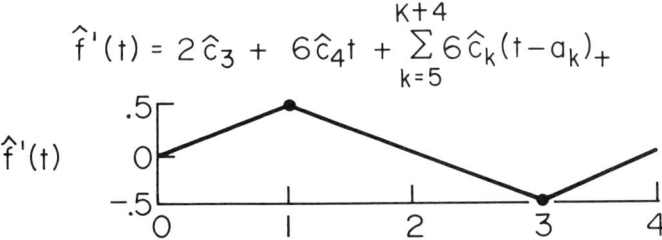

FIG. 17.2. Spline estimates of cumulative distribution, density function, and slope of density function.

mate a variety of types of functions without incurring numerous unwanted inflections.

Clearly what gives the quadratic spline such flexibility is the presence of knots, because the second and higher order derivatives are not defined at the knots. This has led to an intuitively based suggestion that the knots be concentrated where the data are most dense, so that inflections in the function will be less influenced by large sampling errors which can occur where the data are sparse. Such an intuition is supported, in part, by simulations (Lii & Rosenblatt, 1975) showing that an equal spacing of knots can result in severely inflected, seriously multimodal tails in a density estimate, particularly when the number of knots is large. Thus, it has been common to suggest that knots be no closer than every p-th order statistic, where p is at least 10 or 15. However, as the next section indicates, it is possible to have any number and spacing of knots without incurring multimodality if particular kinds of inequality constraints are placed on the spline's vector of coefficients.

In addition to its smoothness and flexibility, a quadratic spline is sometimes considered more useful than an ordinary higher order polynomial because of a lack of sampling covariance of points which are distal on the abscissa. However, such an argument is not as persuasive when the quadratic spline is being used as a density estimator and when it is constrained to have an integral equal to 1.0 between the upper and lower bounds on the abscissa. Under such a constraint, overestimating one point on the function because of sampling error can induce some amount of underestimation at any other point. Of course, this is a problem which a spline density estimator shares with any kind of estimator which is constrained to satisfy the definition of a density function.

An important technical point to be noted on the use of splines is that, once the knots have been chosen, more than one basis can be used when estimating the vector of coefficients. The basis shown in Fig. 17.2 is one which clearly reveals the linear aspect of estimating a spline function. However, other bases such as B-splines (see deBoor, 1978, or Schumaker, 1981) are better behaved when knots are in close proximity.

In summary, a quadratic spline is an attractive candidate for a density estimator, because it is flexible enough to approximate a variety of density functions without a loss of local smoothness and without incurring a large number of inflections, provided that the number of knots is small. Also, once the knots are chosen, the estimator is a linear function of a set of unknown parameters, which makes the estimation of those parameters potentially quite easy. However, in spite of the force of these arguments, it should be noted that moderately smooth, yet flexible, density estimates can be obtained by methods other than the use of splines (see Appendix). The next section describes a way in which the use of a spline estimator can have a clearer advantage over the use of those alternative methods, at least when the random variable is a measure of response time.

Response Time Contamination. An important problem in estimating the density function of response time is that contamination can occur in the measurement of the random variable. Response times of less than one second can contain an appreciable component of motor reaction time in addition to the component of time attributable to the psychological processing of stimulus information. When this contamination occurs, estimating the distribution of psychological processing time necessarily involves three distributions instead of only one, that is, the distributions of the psychological processing time, the motor response time, and the sum, or convolution, of these two times. The general problem, then, is the same as the one encountered in filtering noise from physical signals or in estimating true score distributions (Lord & Novick, 1968).

A formulation which is often used for dealing with the contamination problem (see Burbeck, 1979; Kohfeld, Santee, & Wallace, 1981; Luce & Green, 1972; Sternberg, 1969; Townsend & Ashby, 1982) is to view, say, motor reaction time as a random variable which is added to and is independent of the time required for the psychological process. Under this formulation the distribution of the total response time, u, with density $h(u)$, is the convolution of decision time, x, and motor reaction time, y, with density functions $f(x)$ and $g(y)$, respectively, as shown in Table 17.1; a sample of n_2 total response times, u_j, can be used to obtain an estimate of $h(u)$. Then, by assuming that response times obtained with

TABLE 17.1
Model of Total Response Time

Stimulus onset			*Response*
⊢	x	y	⊣
	Unobserved Component (Psychological Processing Time)	Observed Component (Motor Reaction Time)	
⊢		u	⊣
	Convolution	(Total Response Time)	

	Convolution	*Unobserved Component*	*Observed Component*
True Density	$h(u)$	$f(x)$	$g(y)$
Sample Size	n_2 of U_j	0	n_1 of Y_i
Estimated Density	$\hat{h}(u)$	$\hat{f}(x)$	$\hat{g}(y)$
Model for True Convolution	$h(u) = \int_0^u f(x) \cdot g(u\text{-}x)\, dx$		
Model for Estimated Convolution	$\hat{h}(u) = \int_0^u \hat{f}(x) \cdot \hat{g}(u\text{-}x)\, dx$		

strong stimuli minimize the contribution of psychological processing time, a sample of n_1 of those response times can be viewed as a sample of y_i and can be used to obtain an estimate of $g(y)$. Following this, the problem is to estimate the density function, $f(x)$, of the psychological processing time from estimates of the other two density functions, $h(u)$ and $g(y)$. In such a formulation, $f(x)$ and $g(y)$ can be termed the densities of the unobserved and observed components, respectively, of the convolution.

A number of approaches have been suggested for estimating the density of the unobserved component. One approach has been to capitalize on the relationship among the characteristic functions of the three distributions $v_h = v_f \cdot v_g$, where v_f, v_g, and v_h are the characteristic functions of the densities of x, y, and u, respectively. Sample characteristic functions obtained by fast Fourier transforms can be used as sample estimates of v_g and v_h, the ratio of which provides an estimate of v_f. Then an inverse Fourier transform provides a density estimate for x. If the estimates of $g(y)$ and $h(u)$ are smoothed by a kernel, that is, by a running weighted average, prior to taking their Fourier transforms, a nearly unimodal estimate of $f(x)$ may be obtained; however, negative values still can and do occasionally occur in the tail of that estimate (Burbeck, 1979; Green, 1971).

Another approach has been to use discrete Laplace series transforms of estimates of $g(y)$ and $h(u)$, smoothing these estimates by truncating each series instead of by using a kernel (Kohfeld et al., 1981). As with the Fourier transform approach, the resulting estimate of $f(x)$ can have negative values in the tail. With both approaches, these negative values can be removed by smoothing them with a kernel, but the estimate can still be multimodal. Although multiple modes can be informative, for example, of the presence of mixtures, their occurrence as a result of sampling error can produce major distortions in the form of inflections in estimates of the hazard function. This is particularly problematic in the upper tail of the distribution (Rice & Rosenblatt, 1976).

A third approach which has been developed for estimating the density of the unobserved component has been to begin by letting the density estimates of both the observed and unobserved components have a functional form such that the density estimate of the convolution can be expressed in closed form. For example, if the density estimate for the unobserved component is a quadratic spline function and if the estimated cumulative distribution of the observed component is its sample step function, then the estimate of the cumulative distribution of the convolution is the inner product of a vector of coefficients of the spline function and a vector of simple functions of the sample of the observed component (Bloxom, 1979). Following this, the coefficients of the spline function can be estimated by regressing points of the sample cumulative step function of the total response time, u, on the vectors of functions of the sample of the observed component.

A difficulty with this approach is that it can produce seriously multimodal and often negative estimates of the density of the unobserved component, even with a small number of knots in the spline. An example of such an estimate obtained in the author's early work with this approach is illustrated by the broken line in Fig. 17.3, with knots indicated by filled circles on the line; the density function that was being estimated is illustrated by the solid line in that figure. Thus, using this approach requires that additional constraints be placed on the spline estimate of $f(x)$. Even with the smoothness of the spline function, its basis appears to need more constraints to be well conditioned in the context of some convolutions.

One way to guarantee nonnegativity in a quadratic spline function is to constrain its coefficients to be nonnegative as has been done with splines in monotone regression (Winsberg & Ramsay, 1980). However, the resulting function could still be as seriously multimodal as the function shown in Fig. 17.3. An approach which guarantees both nonnegativity and unimodality is to place inequality constraints on the slope of the function at each of its knots between and including the upper and lower bounds on x (Bloxom, 1979). Specifically, once a piece of the quadratic spline is designated to contain the mode of the distribution, a nonnegativity constraint can be placed on the slope of the spline (see the third function graphed in Fig. 17.2) at each of the knots below the mode and a nonpositivity constraint can be placed on the slope of the spline at each of the knots above the mode. The slope is then guaranteed to be nonnegative below the mode and nonpositive above the mode, because the estimate is a quadratic polynomial between each pair of knots. Once unimodality is thus guaranteed,

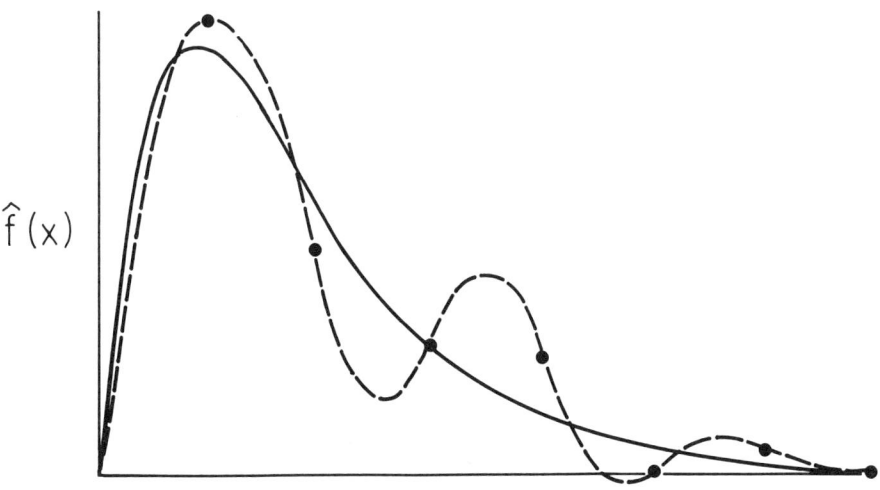

FIG. 17.3. Spline density estimate without inequality constraints.

nonnegativity of the estimate can be guaranteed by constraining the estimate to be nonnegative at the upper upper and lower bounds on x.

The use of these additional constraints produces a much smoother density estimate; Fig. 17.4 shows the result obtained from the same data used to obtain the estimate shown in Fig. 17.3. However, the smoothness is not obtained without cost. One cost is the potential loss of the estimate's sensitivity to the presence of mixtures in $f(x)$; outliers can produce nothing more conspicuous than a locally flat terrace in the tail of the estimate. Another cost is the additional requirement of estimating which piece of the spline lies over the mode of x. A third cost is that the use of inequality constraints increases uncertainty about the relative contributions of bias and variance to the imprecision of the density estimate. For example, as the number of knots becomes large, the variance of the estimate may not increase as rapidly as has been found in research (e.g., Lii & Rosenblatt, 1975) in which inequality constraints were not used. This is because only multiple terraces can now occur where negative values and multiple modes might otherwise occur, for example, in the tail.

In spite of these problems introduced by the use of the inequality constraints, such a modified spline approach merits consideration because of its attractively coherent rationale. When the density function being estimated is an unobserved component of a convolution, the approach is conceptually unified in the sense that only one kind of smoothing parameter, that is, the number of knots, needs to be chosen; this stands in contrast to the alternative of using transform methods which require a choice of two kinds of smoothing parameters, a window width and a series length (see Appendix). A possible additional advantage of the spline approach is that, if the smoothing parameter has a larger than optimal value, the

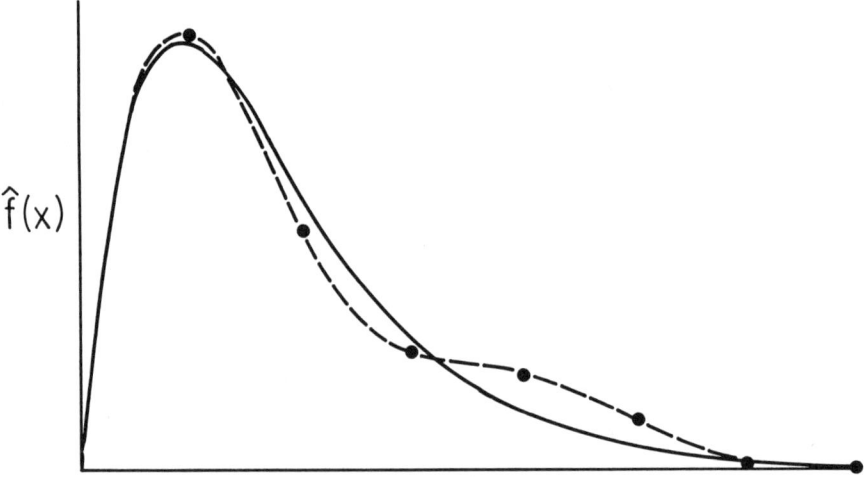

FIG. 17.4. Spline density estimate with inequality constraints.

17. PROBLEMS IN ESTIMATING RESPONSE TIME DISTRIBUTIONS

resulting loss of precision may not be large because of what may be a variance-dampening effect of the inequality constraints; it is not clear how such protection might be obtained for nonoptimal values of the smoothing parameters in the transform methods.

Fitting the Density Estimator to the Data. In addition to selecting a type of function to map response times onto a density estimator and using that function to deal with response time contamination, it is necessary to select a criterion to be optimized when choosing parameters for the estimator. A criterion which is fairly commonly used with a variety of approaches (Tapia & Thompson, 1978) is the likelihood, $L = \prod_i \hat{f}(T_i)$, or, alternatively, the log likelihood, $\ln L = \sum_i \ln \hat{f}(T_i)$, of the data. This seems like a natural criterion to use here because of the close connection between the function being estimated and the function being optimized. Furthermore, when constraints are placed on the density estimate (e.g., on a spline function) and when these constraints form penalty functions which are added to the log likelihood, the resulting criterion, called the penalized log likelihood, is made even more attractive because of its Bayesian interpretation. In that interpretation, the product of exponential functions of the penalty functions is assumed to be proportional to the prior joint distribution of the parameters of the density estimator. If that product is multiplied by the likelihood of the data, the result is a function which is proportional to the posterior joint distribution of the parameters. The logarithm of that resulting function is what is being optimized (Tapia & Thompson, 1978).

One type of constraint used to form a penalty function is an equality, for example, $\phi = 1 - \int_{-\infty}^{+\infty} \hat{f}(t)\, dx = 0$, the use of which constrains $\hat{f}(t)$ to integrate to one over the range of t. Such a constraint can be used to define an appropriate penalty function, for example, $-\phi^2/r$ (for some small r), to be added to the log likelihood of the data.

Another type of constraint used to form a penalty function is an inequality, for example, $\theta = -\hat{f}'s(t) < 0$; if this constraint is placed on the slope of a spline density estimate at each knot above the designated mode, it eliminates the possible occurrence of additional modes above the designated mode. Such a constraint can be used to define an appropriate penalty function, for example, $r \ln \theta$ (for some small r), to be added to the log likelihood of the data.

Optimizing the penalized log likelihood is a procedure which can easily be extended to the case in which a model contains more than one density function. For example, where the density function of interest is an unobserved component of a convolution and where density estimates for the observed component and convolution can be obtained in closed form, one can optimize the joint log likelihood,

$$\ln L = \sum_i^{n_1} \ln \hat{g}(Y_i) + \sum_j^{n_2} \ln h(U_j)$$

with penalty functions being added to the log likelihood to incorporate constraints which are placed on any of the density estimates. The next section of this chapter illustrates the use of this approach.

Althernatives to the method of maximum penalized likelihood do not have the attractive feature of conceptually unifying the criterion being optimized, the functions being estimated and the constraints placed on the functions being estimated. However, the potential use of some alternative approaches should at least be mentioned, because those approaches can be computationally more efficient than the maximum likelihood approach. The computational problem is that the use of inequality constraints may require a rather extensive iterative search of the space of admissible density estimates to find that estimate which optimizes the criterion. Where this involves repeated computation of the criterion, the search can be much more rapid with methods which use criteria other than the log likelihood function, especially when large sample sizes are employed.

For example, a class of optimization criteria which can be computed relatively rapidly is one defined in terms of the weighted squared discrepancies between a vector of n points on the estimate of the cumulative distribution function, $\hat{F}(T)$, and a vector of the corresponding points on the sample cumulative step function, say, $F^*(T)$. This function is

$$[F^*(T) - \hat{F}(T)]' \, D \, [F^*(T) - \hat{F}(T)]$$

where D is a square matrix of a priori weights. If the elements of $\hat{F}(T)$ are linear functions of parameters to be estimated, as is the case when the density estimate is a quadratic spline, the optimization criterion can be written as a sum of small-order bilinear and quadratic forms. Then, the time needed to iteratively compute the criterion can be shown to be independent of the length of the vectors $F^*(T)$ and $\hat{F}(T)$, that is, to be independent of the sample size.

A Small Simulation Study. The previous sections of this chapter have indicated that (a) a constrained quadratic spline function can be an appropriate estimator of a response time density function, particularly when the response time of interest is an unobserved component of a convolution, and (b) the method of maximum penalized likelihood can be an appropriate way to estimate the spline's coefficients. However, the usefulness of combining these approaches depends on the precision of the resulting estimate, particularly when sample sizes (n_1 and n_2) are as small as 100; such a sample size is not infrequently the largest one available in empirical studies of response time. The following simulation study illustrates patterns in error of estimation which may occur with such a sample size.

The design of the simulation study is illustrated in Fig. 17.5. In each replication the unobserved component's density function, $f(x)$, was one of two gamma distributions. One distribution was a standardized gamma distribution with a

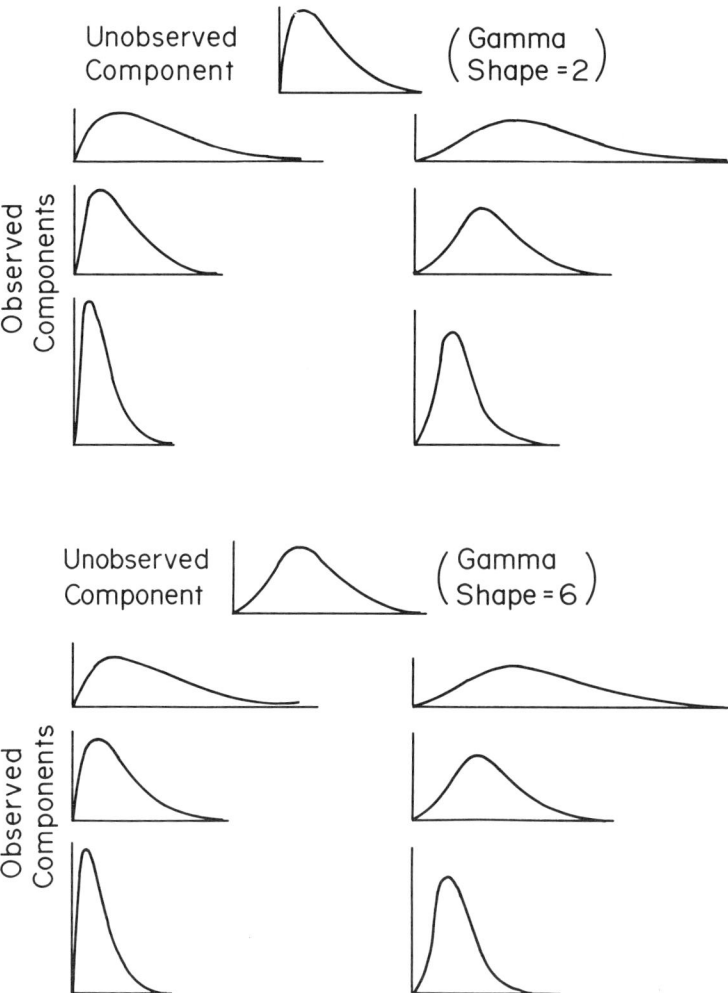

FIG. 17.5. Distributions sampled in simulation study.

shape parameter equal to 2, that is, it was the sum of two exponential components, each of which had a mean and a variance of 1. Thus, that gamma distribution was fairly skewed, with a mean and variance equal to 2. The second unobserved component's distribution was a standardized gamma distribution with a shape parameter of 6, that is, it was the sum of six exponential components, each of which had a mean and variance of 1. That distribution was much less skewed than the first one and had a mean and variance equal to 6. These two gamma distributions are illustrated at the top and at the middle, respectively, of Fig. 17.5.

For each of these two distributions of the unobserved component, the distribution of the observed component, $g(y)$, was one of six gamma distributions. Three of these distributions had a shape parameter equal to 2; three of them had a shape parameter equal to 6. For each shape parameter, the scale of y was modified such that for one of the three distributions it had the same variance as the unobserved component; for another distribution it had a variance equal to one-third of the variance of the unobserved component; and for the third distribution it had a variance equal to three times the variance of the unobserved component. The resulting six distributions of the observed component for each of the two unobserved components are illustrated in the top and bottom halves of Fig. 17.5.

For each of the 12 models just described, samples were obtained by summing exponential random variables generated by the subroutine GGUB in the IBM scientific subroutine package; random seeds were employed. Under each model, one sample of $n_1 = 100$ observations was obtained for the observed component, Y_i. Also for each model, one sample of $n_2 = 100$ observations was obtained for the convolution, $U_j = Y_j + X_j$, where Y_j was sampled independently of Y_i (although Y_j and Y_i were drawn from the same distribution); X_j was sampled from the distribution of the unobserved component.

The density estimation procedure began by letting the estimates of $f(x)$ and $g(y)$ be quadratic splines with six equally spaced knots between the upper and lower bounds on the random variables; the lower bound in each case was 0; the upper bound on y was the maximum order statistic in the sample of Y_i; the upper bound on x was initially set equal to the maximum order statistic in the sample of U_j and was adjusted downwards if the initial estimate of $f(x)$ had more than one entire piece of the spline's upper tail equal to 0. The estimate of the convolution's density function was obtained by integration of the estimates of $f(x)$ and $g(y)$. The weights of the quadratic spline functions were estimated by the method of maximum penalized likelihood. As described in the previous section of this chapter, inequality constraints were placed on the slopes of the estimates of $f(x)$ and $g(y)$ to keep the estimates nonnegative and unimodal; in each estimate, the segment containing the mode was selected to be that which optimized the penalized log likelihood function; equality constraints were placed on the estimates of $f(x)$ and $g(y)$ such that they and, therefore, the convolution's density estimate, integrated to 1 between the lower and upper bounds of the random variable; also, the slope of the upper tail of each component's density was constrained to equal 0 at the upper bound.

The algorithm for maximizing the penalized log likelihood function was a linear programming algorithm which used the type of inequality and equality penalty functions, ϕ and Θ, respectively, described in the previous section of this chapter (Mylander, Holmes, & McCormick, 1973); the scaling factor, r, of the constraints was initially large and was decreased after each optimization of the penalized likelihood, until r reached a small value specified a priori. In each

17. PROBLEMS IN ESTIMATING RESPONSE TIME DISTRIBUTIONS   317

optimization of the penalized likelihood, the Gauss-Newton procedure was used to compute step sizes. Using this method and the sample sizes just indicated, the CPU time on a DEC 1099 was between 10 and 12 minutes for each of the 12 simulations.

Figures 17.6 and 17.7 illustrate the density estimates of the unobserved component for each of the 12 simulations shown in Fig. 17.5. Figure 17.6 shows the results obtained when the unobserved component's density function was a standardized gamma distribution with a shape parameter equal to 2; the results of the six simulations are arranged in the same configuration as the distributions of the observed components shown in the upper half of Fig. 17.5. For example, the estimate illustrated in the upper left-hand section of Fig. 17.6 is that which was obtained when the observed component had a gamma shape parameter equal to 2 and a variance equal to three times the variance of the unobserved component. Fig. 17.7 shows the results obtained when the unobserved component's density function was a standardized gamma distribution with a shape parameter equal to 6; the results of the six simulations are arranged in the same configuration as the

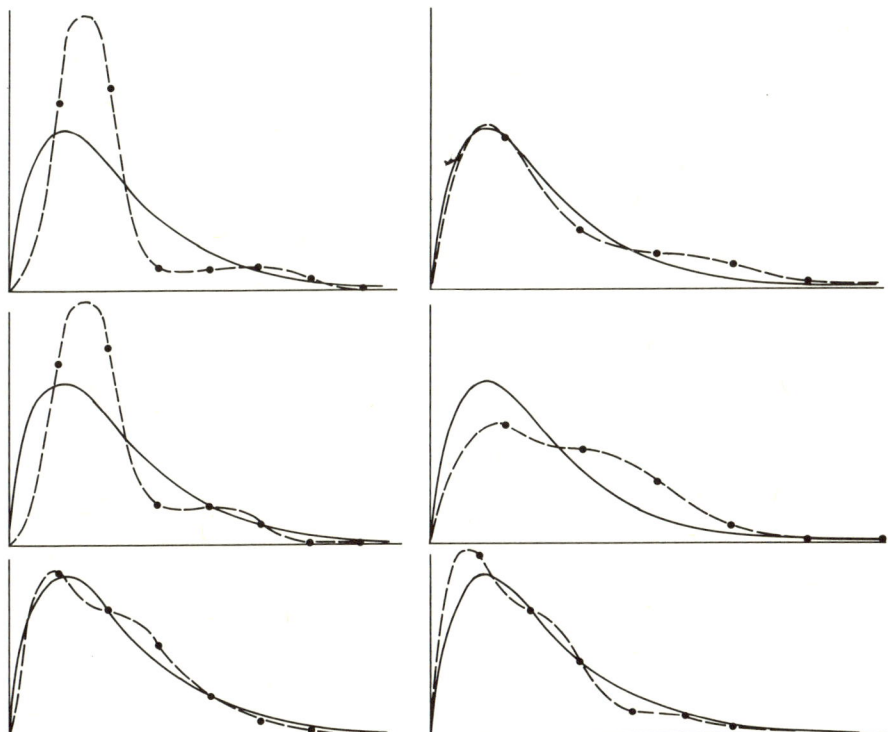

FIG. 17.6. Estimates of unobserved component's density with gamma shape = 2.

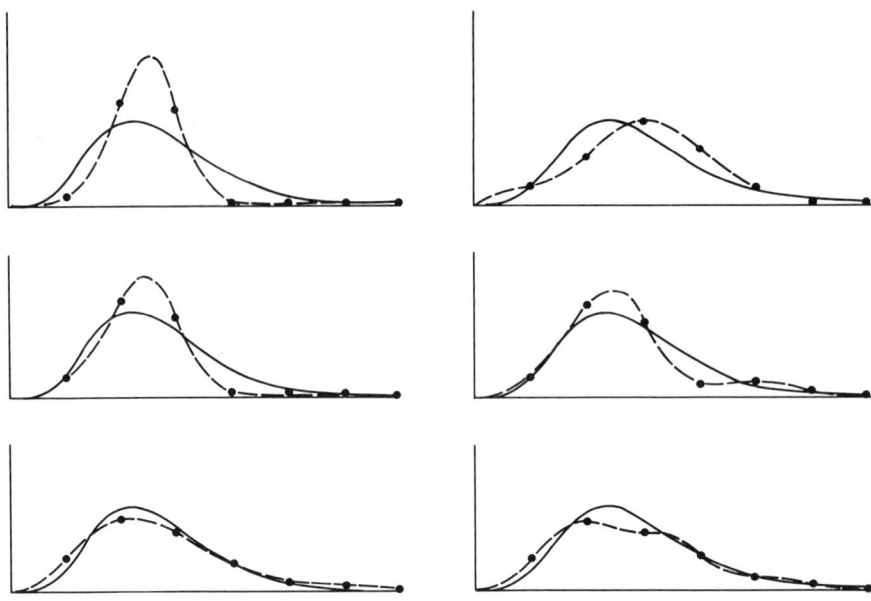

FIG. 17.7. Estimates of unobserved component's density with gamma shape = 6.

distributions of the observed components shown in the bottom of Fig. 17.5. For all graphs in Figs. 17.6 and 17.7, the density function being estimated is represented by a solid line; the estimate is represented by a broken line; the knots are shown as filled circles on the estimate.

An inspection of Figs. 17.6 and 17.7 shows the precision of the density estimates to be quite variable across models. However, one subset of the results is surprisingly good, given the sample size used for the observed component and the convolution. Specifically, where the variance of the observed component was one-third of the variance of the unobserved component (the lower pair of results in each figure), the estimate was quite frequently on or very near the true density and did not show clear evidence of bias where it departed from the true density. This is encouraging for the use of the method in psychophysical studies, because the observed component in such studies can have a variance much smaller than the variance of the convolution and, therefore, of the unobserved component. For example, in Burbeck's (1979) study of the response latency to the offset of an auditory signal, the variance of the observed component (the reaction time with a 70 dB signal) was less than one-tenth of the variance of the convolution (the response time with 20–26 dB signals against a 10 dB masking tone); this implies that the variance of the observed component was less than one-ninth of the variance of the unobserved component (the detection latency with the offset of the weaker signals). The relative size of the variance of the observed compo-

17. PROBLEMS IN ESTIMATING RESPONSE TIME DISTRIBUTIONS 319

nent was well below the relative size of the observed component's variance in the present study where at least moderately good results were found.

Another promising result of the simulation study is that the modes of the density estimates were generally close to the modes of the true density functions in almost all of the models. Unfortunately, there appears to be a positive bias in the estimated density at the mode, at least under some conditions. This problem seems most acute where the observed component was highly skewed, that is, had a gamma shape parameter equal to 2, and had a variance greater than or equal to the variance of the unobserved component.

The presence of this bias is disappointing but is also interesting because of the context in which it occurred. To see this, it is helpful to think of the problem of estimating the unobserved component's distribution as an instance of the filtering problem mentioned earlier. The unobserved component can be viewed as a signal which is partially masked by the noise of the observed component. The precision with which the signal's distribution can be recovered depends inversely on the extent to which that distribution is distorted and swamped by the observed component. It is not surprising, then, that the distortion and swamping was greatest when the distribution of the observed component was its least symmetric and had a large variance.

As was indicated earlier in this chapter, part of the motivation here for density estimation is the need to obtain an estimate of the response time hazard function. Thus, it is important to examine the precision of estimates of the hazard functions as well as the precision of the density estimates in the simulation study.

Figures 17.8 and 17.9 illustrate the estimates of the hazard functions obtained from the corresponding density estimates shown in Figs. 17.6 and 17.7. The estimate of the hazard function was obtained by

$$\hat{r}(x) = \frac{\hat{f}(x)}{1 - \hat{F}(x)}.$$

In each section of Figs. 17.8 and 17.9, the true density's hazard function is shown as a solid line and terminates at the ninth decile of the true distribution. The estimate of the hazard function in each case is indicated by a broken line which terminates at the ninth decile of the estimated distribution.

An inspection of Figs. 17.8 and 17.9 shows the precision of the estimated hazard function to be quite variable across models. However, as was the case with the density estimates, one subset of the results is surprisingly good. Specifically, when the variance of the observed component was one-third of the variance of the unobserved component *and* when the distribution of the observed component was not very skewed, that is, had a gamma shape parameter equal to 6, the estimate was on or very near the true hazard function. This too, is encouraging for the use of the method in psychophysical studies, because the observed component in such studies can have a rather symmetric distribution as well as a relatively small variance. For example, in Burbeck's (1979) study, the

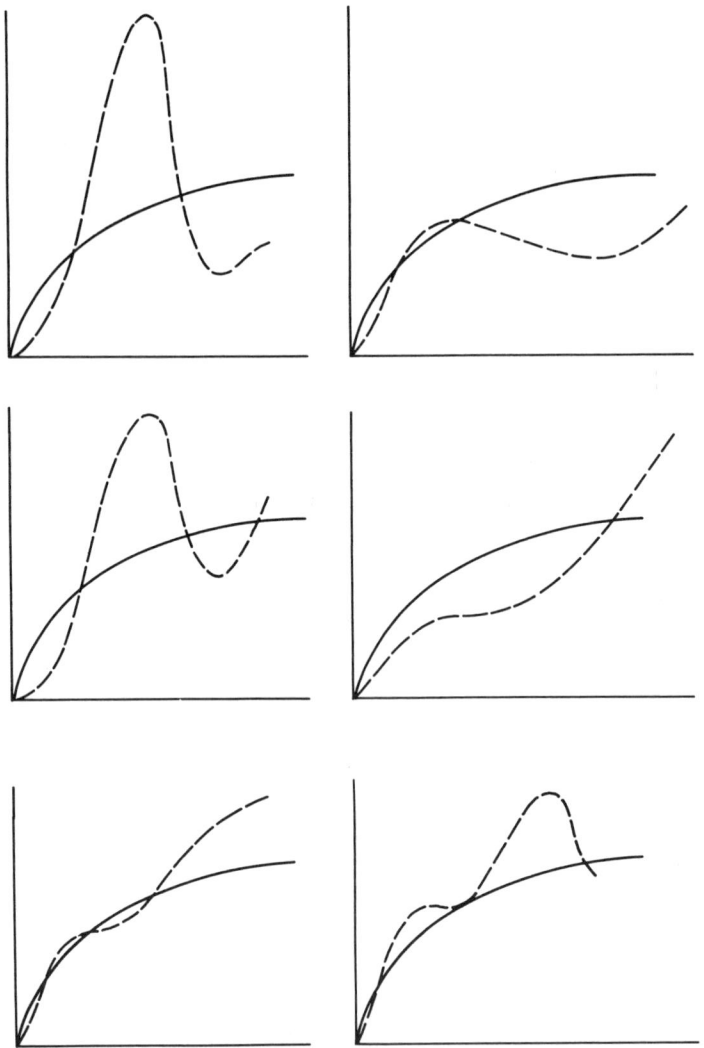

FIG. 17.8. Estimates of unobserved component's hazard function with gamma shape = 2.

reaction time distribution (with the 70 dB signal) exhibited a rather striking symmetry, probably due to reaction time being bounded below by a physical limit of about 100 milliseconds and bounded above by the subject's slowest response to change in a strong signal.

Except where the observed component had a relatively small variance and was not very skewed, the precision of the estimates of the hazard functions does not

17. PROBLEMS IN ESTIMATING RESPONSE TIME DISTRIBUTIONS   321

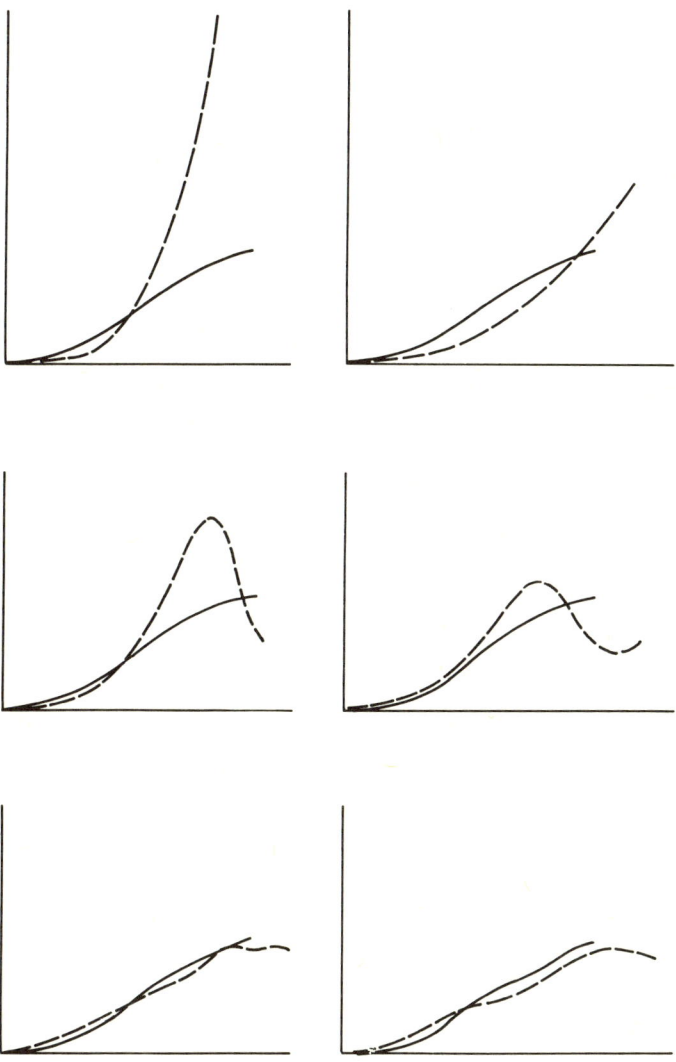

FIG. 17.9. Estimates of unobserved component's hazard function with gamma shape = 6.

seem to be very promising for the use of the present method when sample sizes are like the one used in this simulation study. Often the estimated hazard function rather strikingly over- or under-estimated the true hazard function as well as showing rather severe departures from monotonicity; this was especially pronounced in those conditions where the density estimate appeared to have a strong positive bias at the mode, that is, where the observed component had a gamma shape parameter equal to 2 and had a variance greater than or equal to the variance of the unobserved component.

DISCUSSION AND SUMMARY

In the course of discussing some problems of estimating response time distributions, this chapter has indicated how a constrained quadratic spline function might provide a useful estimate of the density function of an unobserved component of a convolution. This estimate is smooth, unimodal (but possibly terraced) and nonnegative and integrates to 1 between the lower and upper bounds of the random variable. It was also indicated how the method of maximum penalized likelihood can be employed to estimate the parameters of the spline function, as Good and Gaskins (1981) and Tapia and Thompson (1978) advocated for other kinds of density estimation. It is interesting to note that those authors eschewed the use of spline density estimates because of the complexity of obtaining such estimates or because those estimates can have negative values. This chapter illustrated how such estimates can be obtained in a straightforward way without incurring negative values.

Although the simulation suggested one context where fairly good density estimates might be obtained, the precision of the estimates cannot be evaluated at all completely at this point. This is because the simulation study provided only one estimate per model. The results are suggestive of one pattern of bias that can occur in the estimate, but they provide no evidence about the variance of the estimate. Thus, we have no evidence about the shape of a confidence region which can be placed around points on the estimate.

The pattern of apparent bias in the unobserved component's density estimate is not a surprising one when that component is viewed as a signal which is partially masked by noise provided by the observed component. The distortion of the density estimate is greatest when the noise is most skewed and variable. This intuitively plausible connection between the bias and its empirical context suggests that such bias could just as easily occur with other procedures for estimating the density of an unobserved component. For example, Kohfeld et al. (1981) obtained density estimates which were much less inflected than the ones shown in Figs. 17.6 and 17.7, but some of that smoothness could easily have been obtained at the expense of added bias at the mode.

Using the unobserved component's density to estimate the component's hazard function clearly appears to be a hazardous exercise except where there is evidence that the observed component's distribution is rather symmetric and has a variance much less than the unobserved component's variance. In other circumstances, even though the density estimate is smooth and unimodal, the hazard function's estimate can have inaccuracies in the form of severe and inappropriate departures from monotonicity. There is no apparent reason to believe that this problem would be alleviated by the use of the density estimates obtained from other procedures. The problem seems to be most pronounced here in models for which the density estimate is most biased. For reasons mentioned in the preceding paragraph, this links the difficulty more to the empirical context than to the method of estimation.

The nature of the errors in the hazard estimates suggests that, in future work, it will be important to consider placing constraints on an estimate of the unobserved component's hazard function instead of on the density estimate itself. If the density estimate were expressed in terms of its hazard function and if the hazard function were a quadratic spline, the hazard function could be constrained in a number of interesting ways, for example, to be increasing, decreasing, accelerating or decelerating; such constraints could be defined in terms of the slope of the hazard estimate at the knots of the spline. The resulting hazard estimate would have a more plausible functional form than the hazard estimates obtained in the present simulation study and may also provide density estimates which are even smoother, that is, less terraced in the tails, than the density estimates obtained here.

APPENDIX: ESTIMATING DENSITY FUNCTIONS

Before describing some commonly employed types of density estimators, it is useful to discuss three kinds of criteria of precision of density estimates: local criteria (an estimate's precision at a point of the random variable), global criteria (an estimate's precision integrated over the entire range of the random variable), and regional criteria (an estimate's precision in the neighborhood of a point on the random variable). Analytic studies have generally employed the first two of these kinds of criteria and have obtained results on the bias, $E[\hat{f}(t) - f(t)]$, and variance, $E\{\hat{f}(t) - E[\hat{f}(t)]\}^2$, of density estimates as well as on a composite of squared bias and variance. The local composite index is referred to as mean squared error at a point, $E[\hat{f}(t) - f(t)]^2$; the global composite index is referred to as the mean integrated squared error, $E\int_{-\infty}^{+\infty}[\hat{f}(t) - f(t)]^2 \, dt$. The study of these two composite indices has been emphasized, because most density estimates are biased (Rosenblatt, 1956). Accordingly, the practice of seeking a minimum variance unbiased estimator has not been followed in the study of density estimation.

Regional criteria of the precision of a density estimate are rather diverse, partly because there is not a consensus on the relevant range of the random variable. One set of indices describes the visual smoothness of a density estimate. Examples of such indices are the magnitude of the second- and third-order derivatives of the estimate at a point, the number of modes in the estimate, and the number of discontinuities in estimates of the cumulative distribution function, the density function, and the slope of the density function; small values of these indices are characteristic of a smooth density estimate. Of course, these indices measure the precision of a density estimate only if the density function being estimated is smooth. Fortunately, most commonly considered classes of density functions are visually smooth, leading many investigators to have a strong prior belief in a density's smoothness even when they do not have a strong prior belief about other features of the density. Thus, smoothness is used rather often in practice as a criterion of precision and is emphasized in the following discussion of density estimation.

A second set of indices of regional precision describes the sensitivity of a density estimate to fine structure in the density function being estimated. Examples of such indices are the estimate's bias and variance at a point, if the bias and variance are known to be increasing functions of the higher order derivatives of the density being estimated; also of interest is the covariance of the estimate at one point with the estimate at neighboring points. Small absolute values of these indices are characteristic of an estimate which follows fine structure. Of course, indices of sensitivity to fine structure measure the precision of an estimate only if the density being estimated has, or is believed to have, a fine structure, for example, multiple modes of the kind produced by mixtures.

In addition to investigating the local, global, and regional precision of density estimates, some studies have given attention to whether an estimate satisfies the definition of a density function, that is, whether it has an integral increasing from 0 to 1 over the range of the random variable and is nonnegative at all points on the random variable. However, satisfying the definition of a density function has not been valued in all investigations of density estimation. Specifically, negative values of the estimate have been tolerated where they can be attributed to sampling error, for example in the tails.

Types of Density Estimators. One of the most widely discussed density estimators is a class of kernel estimates developed by Rosenblatt (1956) and by Parzen (1962). The estimate is

$$\hat{f}(t) = \frac{1}{n} \sum_i \frac{1}{h(n)} w\left[\frac{t - T_i}{h(n)}\right]$$

where there are n observations, T_i; $h(n)$ is a positive-valued function which approaches 0 as n approaches infinity; a variety of weighting functions, $w(u)$, can provide rather precise density estimates (Silverman, 1978); if $w(u)$ is nonnegative, the estimate is everywhere nonnegative. The scaling function, $h(n)$, is sometimes termed the window width and is quite important in obtaining the optimal mean squared error at a point (Silverman, 1978; Tapia & Thompson, 1978, p. 60). It has been shown that, for any true density function, the asymptotic variance of the estimate at a point on t is a decreasing function of the window width. Also, the asymptotic squared bias of the estimate at a point on t is an increasing function of the window width. Thus, obtaining a balance between these two kinds of error of estimation requires a careful choice of the window width (Lii & Rosenblatt, 1975; Wahba, 1975, 1976).

The window width also plays an important role in the smoothness of the density estimate. Larger values provide a greater smoothing of the data, resulting in a smaller number of modes and inflections in the estimate. Correspondingly, larger values decrease the ease with which the estimate can follow the fine structure of the true density function. This problem can be alleviated somewhat if the function, $w(u)$, is band limited; for example, if $w(u)$ is non-zero only where $|u| \leq \frac{1}{2}$, then points on t which are separated by more than the window width have density estimates which are uncorrelated.

A second type of density estimator which has been widely discussed is the orthogonal series proposed by Kronmal and Tarter (1968). That estimate is

$$\hat{f}_m(t) = \sum_{i=0}^{m} \hat{a}_i v_i(t)$$

in which the $v_i(t)$ are functions whose weighted cross-products integrate to 0 over the range of the random variable, that is, $\int_{-\infty}^{+\infty} v_i(t) v_j(t) w(t) \, dt = 0$ for $i \neq j$ and where $w(t)$ is greater than 0. Specifically, Krommal and Tarter proposed that the $\hat{a}_i$ be the sample trigonometric moments and that the $v_i(t)$ be the corresponding trigonometric functions of the random variable, t; with the use of both the sine and cosine functions and with a suitable scaling of t, the series is a truncated Fourier series. On the assumption that the characteristic function of the density function being estimated is a decreasing function of its frequency, Krommal and Tarter proposed that the first m sample trigonometric moments be used. The resulting density estimate is nonnegative over most of the range of the random variable but small negative values can occur in the tails. It has been shown that the parameter m is important in expressions for bounds on the optimal mean squared error at a point and the optimal mean integrated squared error for most commonly considered density functions, with small values of m producing large squared bias and with large values of m producing a large variance of the estimate (Wahba, 1975).

The parameter m is also a smoothing parameter for this type of estimate. Lowering m filters out high frequencies and reduces the number of modes; increasing m adds to the multimodality of the estimate while increasing its ability to follow fine structure in the true density function. However, it should be noted that, unlike with the kernel estimate, moderately separated points on the density estimate cannot be assumed to be uncorrelated.

A third type of density estimator which has been rather widely discussed is a quadratic spline function (Boneva, Kendall, & Stefanov, 1971; Wahba, 1975). This estimate is $\hat{f}(t) = d/dt \, \hat{F}(t)$, where $\hat{F}(t)$ is a piece-wise cubic polynomial interpolator between points (called knots) on the sample cumulative distribution function. $\hat{F}(t), \hat{f}(t)$, and $\hat{f}'(t)$ are constrained to be continuous at the knots; in addition, various constraints are placed on those three functions at upper and lower bounds which are specified for the random variable. In analytic studies, the knots on the interpolator are either equidistant on t (Boneva et al., 1971, Lii & Rosenblatt, 1975; Rosenblatt, 1976) or placed at every k-th order statistic (Wahba, 1975). In both cases, the density estimate can easily have negative values, particularly in the tails (Lii & Rosenblatt, 1975; Tapia & Thompson, 1978). The number of knots on the interpolator or, inversely, the distance between knots, is an important contributor to the asymptotic mean squared error at a point (Lii & Rosenblatt, 1975; Rosenblatt, 1976); in addition, Wahba (1975) derived an upper bound of the optimal mean squared error at a point, in which "optimal" is defined as squared bias and variance contributing equally to that error.

The number of knots is also a smoothing parameter in the sense that it places an upper limit on the number of inflections in the density estimate. Because the spline is composed of quadratic polynomials, there can be no more inflections in the density estimate than there are knots placed between the upper and lower bounds of the random variable. Thus, decreasing the number of knots can increase the smoothness of the estimate, but this occurs at the expense of the estimate's ability to follow fine structure in the true density function. The estimate's ability to follow fine structure is also hampered by the continuity constraints on the slope of the density, because those constraints induce covariance in neighboring segments of the estimate (Lii & Rosenblatt, 1975).

In spite of extensive research on kernel, orthogonal series, and spline density estimation, there is still no evidence that one approach generally provides the most precise estimate. The asymptotic precision and bounds on the asymptotic precision of the estimators are of the same order of magnitude across approaches, provided that the smoothing parameter is optimally selected for each approach (Wahba, 1975). Unfortunately, knowledge of this fact is not very useful in practice, because the optimal value for each type of smoothing parameter depends on the functional form of the true but unknown density function. In spite of this limitation, heuristics have been developed so that each approach can provide fairly precise estimation if the density function being estimated is fairly smooth and if sample sizes are at least 50–100. The heuristics typically involve a search for a value of the smoothing parameter which results in a plausible-appearing estimate, that is, one which is not seriously multimodal and which contains no more than a few small negative values in the tails.

REFERENCES

Barlow, R. E., & Proschan, F. *Statistical theory of reliability and life testing.* New York: Holt, Rinehart & Winston, Inc., 1975.

Bloxom, B. Estimating an unobserved component of a serial response time model. *Psychometrika,* 1979, *44,* 473–484.

Boneva, L., Kendall, D., & Stefanov, I. Spline transformations: Three new diagnostic aids for the statistical data analyst (with Discussion). *Journal of the Royal Statistical Society (Series B),* 1971, *33,* 1–70.

Burbeck, S. L. *Change and level detectors inferred for simple reaction times.* Unpublished dissertation, University of California, Irvine, 1979.

de Boor, C. *A practical guide to splines.* New York: Springer-Verlag, 1978.

Good, I. J., & Gaskins, R. A. Density estimation and bump-hunting by the penalized likelihood method exemplified by scattering and meteorite data. *Journal of the American Statistical Association,* 1980, *75,* 42–56.

Green, D. M. Fourier analysis of reaction time data. *Behavioral Research Methods and Instruments,* 1971, *3,* 121–125.

Kohfeld, D. L., Santee, J. L., & Wallace, N. D. Loudness and reaction time: II. Identification of detection components at different intensities and frequencies. *Perception and Psychophysics,* 1981, *29,* 550–562.

Kronmal, R. A., & Tarter, M. E. The estimation of probability densities by Fourier series methods. *American Statistical Association Journal,* 1968, *63,* 925–952.

Lii, K. S., & Rosenblatt, M. Asymptotic behavior of a spline estimate of a density function. *Computing and Mathematics with Applications,* 1975, *1,* 223–235.

Lord, F. M., & Novick, M. R. *Statistical theories of mental test scores.* Reading, Mass.: Addison-Wesley, 1968.

Luce, R. D., & Green, D. M. A neural timing theory for response times and psychophysics of intensity. *Psychological Review,* 1972, *79,* 14–57.

McGill, W. J. Stochastic latency mechanisms. In R. D. Luce, R. R. Bush, & E. Galanter, *Handbook of mathematical psychology* (Vol. 1). New York: John Wiley & Sons, Inc., 1963.

Mylander, W. C., Holmes, R. L., & McCormick, G. P. *A guide to SUMT-version 4: The computer program implementing the sequential unconstrained minimization technique for nonlinear programming* (Paper RAC–P–63). McLean, Va.: Research Analysis Corporation, 1973.

Parzen, E. On estimation of a probability density function and mode. *Annals of Mathematical Statistics,* 1962, *33,* 1065–1076.

Rice, J., & Rosenblatt, M. Estimation of the log survivor function and hazard functions. *Sankhya (Series A),* 1976, *38,* 60–78.

Rosenblatt, M. Remarks on some non-parametric estimates of a density function. *Annals of Mathematical Statistics,* 1956, *27,* 832–837.

Rosenblatt, M. Asymptotics and representation of cubic splines. *Journal of Approximation Theory,* 1976, *17,* 332–343.

Schumaker, L. L. *Spline functions: Basic theory.* New York: Wiley, 1981.

Silverman, B. W. Choosing the window width when estimating a density. *Biometrika,* 1978, *65,* 1–11.

Sternberg, S. The discovery of processing stages: Extensions of Donders' method. In W. G. Koster (Ed.) *Attention and performance II.* Amsterdam: North-Holland, 1969.

Tapia, R. A., & Thompson, J. R. *Nonparametric probability density estimation.* Baltimore: The Johns Hopkins University Press, 1978.

Tatsuoka, K. K., & Tatsuoka, M. M. *Time-score analysis in criterion-referenced tests* (Tech. rep. E–1). Urbana, Illinois: University of Illinois, Computer-based Education Research Laboratory, February, 1978.

Townsend, J. T., & Ashby, G. F. *On the stochastic modelling of elementary psychological processes.* Cambridge: Cambridge University Press, 1982.

Wahba, G. Optimal convergence properties of variable knot, kernel, and orthogonal series methods for density estimation. *The Annals of Statistics,* 1975, *3,* 15–29.

Wahba, G. Histosplines with knots which are order statistics. *Journal of the Royal Statistical Society (Series B)*, 1976, *38*, 140–151.

Winsberg, S., & Ramsay, J. O. Monotonic transformations to additivity using splines. *Biometrika*, 1980, *67*, 669–674.

18 The Ideal Type Model

Warren S. Torgerson
The Johns Hopkins University

While browsing through Webster's Unabridged Dictionary the other day I came across the word "educe" along with its forms "education" and "eductive." I remembered that Spearman had used the term long ago when he wrote about "education of relations," but I had always thought he had trouble with his spelling. I find myself now in much the same position as the young person who was so pleased to discover that he had been speaking *prose* all of his life.

According to Webster, to *educe* means "to bring into manifestation (as a form, quality, or law conceived to be present in a latent, potential, or undeveloped state)."

Now when people ask me about my field I can tell them that ever since Fred Lord was a graduate student, I have been interested mostly in psychological problems that require the development and application of *eductive* models—models whose purpose is to educe structure latent in sets of data.

Multidimensional scaling, factor analysis, and cluster analysis are the most widely known eductive methods available for aiding an investigator who is primarily concerned with discovery of an underlying structure in a given set of data. The search for structure in this sense goes well beyond the statistical criterion of obtaining a convenient and parsimonious representation that adequately reproduces the interesting properties of the original observations. In the case of factor analysis, concern is with the structure of individual differences with respect to a specified domain of variables. With multidimensional scaling, the primary objective is the use of observations on similarity to learn something about how a set of stimuli were perceived or organized by the subjects. Various cluster analysis procedures are available as alternative analytic approaches for either type of data.

A fourth approach, the ideal type model I wish to discuss today, is related in one way or another to each of these three well-known approaches. The ideal type model is a variety of multidimensional scaling in that it is concerned with the spatial representation of similarity structures. It also involves notions that are formally identical with the positive manifold, simple structure ideas of factor analysis. And, since the notion of ideal types leads to the notion of typology which leads to the idea of classification which leads one to think of clustering, ideal types and clusters can easily be confused. Non-hierarchical cluster structures can, in fact, be considered as degenerate ideal types, but the ideal type model does not imply existence of clusters in general.

In the ideal type model, the spatial location of a given stimulus point is given by its distance from each of a number of ideal types. Thus the degree of dissimilarity, that is, the distance, between a pair of stimuli depends on how close each is to the various ideals. The rationale of the ideal type model leads to representation of the stimuli as points in a multidimensional hyperspherical space, where observed dissimilarities are interpreted as angular distances in the positive orthant on the surface of a hypersphere.

Back in 1965, I used the top diagram in Fig. 18.1 as an illustrative example of the basic idea. The hypothetical stimuli were all alloys of copper, tin, and zinc. The assumption was made that the alloys were similar to the extent that they had similar compositions and that they got more different in a reasonable way as their compositions got more different. It was also assumed that copper, tin, and zinc were equally different from each other.

If one obtained measures of similarity for all pairs of alloys, and then analyzed the data using a standard nonmetric multidimensional scaling program such as KYST or TORSCA, a two-dimensional configuration would be obtained, with all stimuli lying on or within the curved triangle of the top picture. It would fit the data. The Euclidean representation of the data does, however, have unfortunate counter-intuitive properties. First, a dimensional interpretation, though parsimonious, would seem forced. One could interpret one direction easily enough— copperiness or orangeness for example. But interpretation of the remaining dimensions then taxes the imagination. A zinciness-tinniness dimension somehow lacks authority. This difficulty is typical when dimensional interpretations of ideal type structures are attempted. Second, combinations of just two ideals ought to be on a straight line between them. And all such combinations ought to be equally distant from any third ideal which is itself equally distant from the other two. A Euclidean representation can satisfy one or the other, but not both.

A representation using hyperspherical geometry eliminates these problems. The straight line is a great circle, and any points along it stay equally distant from the third ideal type. When, as in this example, the two-dimensional spherical space is imbedded in a three-dimensional Euclidean space, and an angular distance of 90 degrees (orthogonality) represents independence or lack of similarity, things begin to fall in place. In the imbedding n + 1 dimensional Euclidean

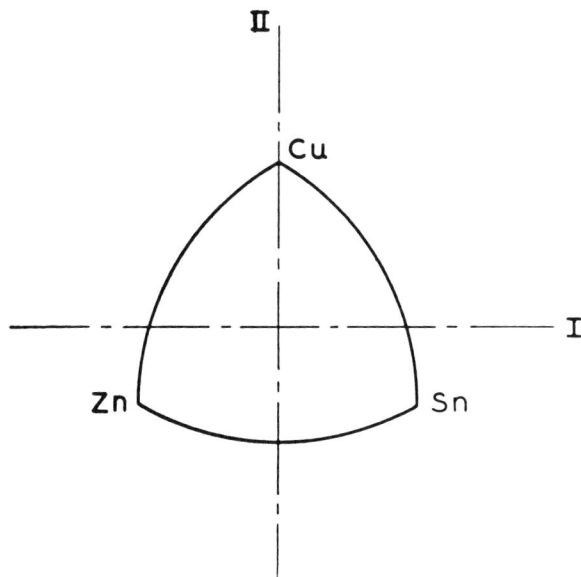

Alloys of copper, tin, and zinc. All possible alloys would lie within the curved triangle.

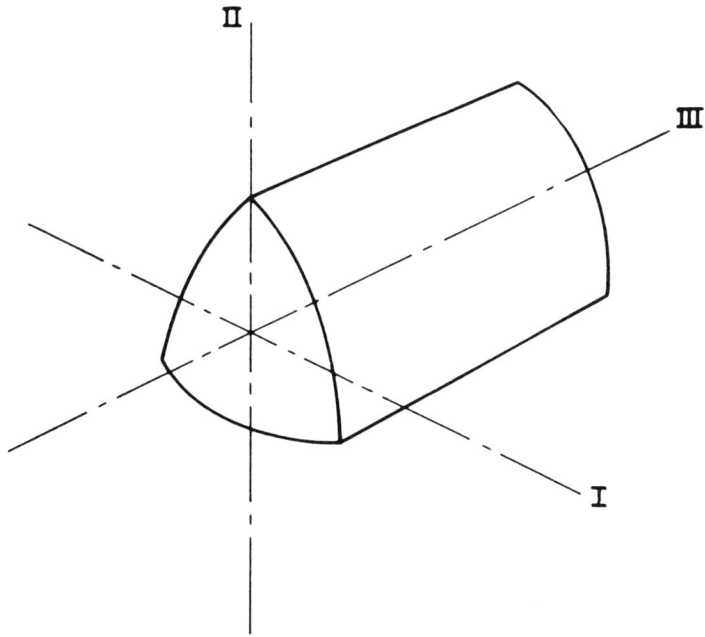

Dimensions I and II represent the three elements. Dimension III represents an independent, quantitative variable. All stimuli lie within the curved prism.

FIG. 18.1. Illustration of ideal type structures (from Torgerson, 1965, Figures 9 and 10).

space, ideal types correspond to pure factors, alloys correspond to tests that load on several factors, and, in short, we are comfortably in a world formally equivalent to Thurstone's positive manifold, simple structure.

The structure at the bottom of the Fig. 18.1 generalizes the ideal type notion to a mixed case, where similarity between stimuli depends not only upon the ideal type structure but also on variation along the usual types of quantitative dimensions. The illustration gives a Euclidean representation with all stimuli falling on or within the curved prism. It has the same shortcomings as those mentioned for the figure at the top. Once again, the shortcomings can be eliminated by using a more appropriate spatial model. Addition of quantitative Euclidean dimensions to the hyperspherical space gives us a hypercylindrical spatial model.

Dr. Timothy Satalich and I have been working together on analytical solutions for these models for the last several years. A satisfactory computer program for the hyperspherical case was developed in 1980 (Torgerson & Satalich, 1980). The much more difficult solution for the hypercylindrical model was worked out by Satalich (1981) and is described in detail in his dissertation.

For the hyperspherical model we are given only quantitative observations on dissimilarity of all pairs of n stimuli. The dissimilarity estimates are interpreted as angular distances in a hyperspherical space of unknown dimensionality. The problem is to solve for the dimensionality and the configuration of stimuli to reveal the underlying ideal type structure, if such exists. The present program, called HYP-2, is fully metric, but can be generalized easily to the nonmetric case by adding a best monotone transform subroutine and arbitrarily specifying the radius of the hypersphere (under nonmetric conditions the radius is not determined uniquely).

The analytical problem for the hypercylindrical model is more complex. The dissimilarities are interpreted as hypercylindrical distances in a mixed space of Euclidean and hyperspherical dimensions. The solution partitions the total space into two subspaces and solves for the projections of the stimuli on an arbitrary set of axes for the Euclidean subspace and the configuration of stimuli revealing the underlying ideal type structure for the hyperspherical subspace. The program, called HYPCYL, can operate in either a fully exploratory or partially confirmatory mode.

Several illustrative examples of the use of the HYP-2 and HYPCYL programs to educe an underlying ideal type structure are given below.

An Experiment on the Perceptual Organization of a Domain of Geometrical Shapes

The primary purpose of this experiment[1] was to run an empirical check on the ideal type model and to test the HYP-2 hyperspherical scaling program with real

---

[1]Carried out by T. A. Satalich

data. The stimuli, shown in Fig. 18.2, progress in small steps from a circle to a triangle, from the triangle to a square, and from the square back to the circle. According to the ideal type hypothesis, these stimuli should be on the edges of a spherical triangle with no side longer than 90 degrees, and with the vertices occupied by the circle, triangle, and square. Four additional stimuli were constructed to lie within the spherical triangle. Subjects were student volunteers from The Johns Hopkins University.

All pairs of stimuli were presented to the subjects, whose task was to rate their

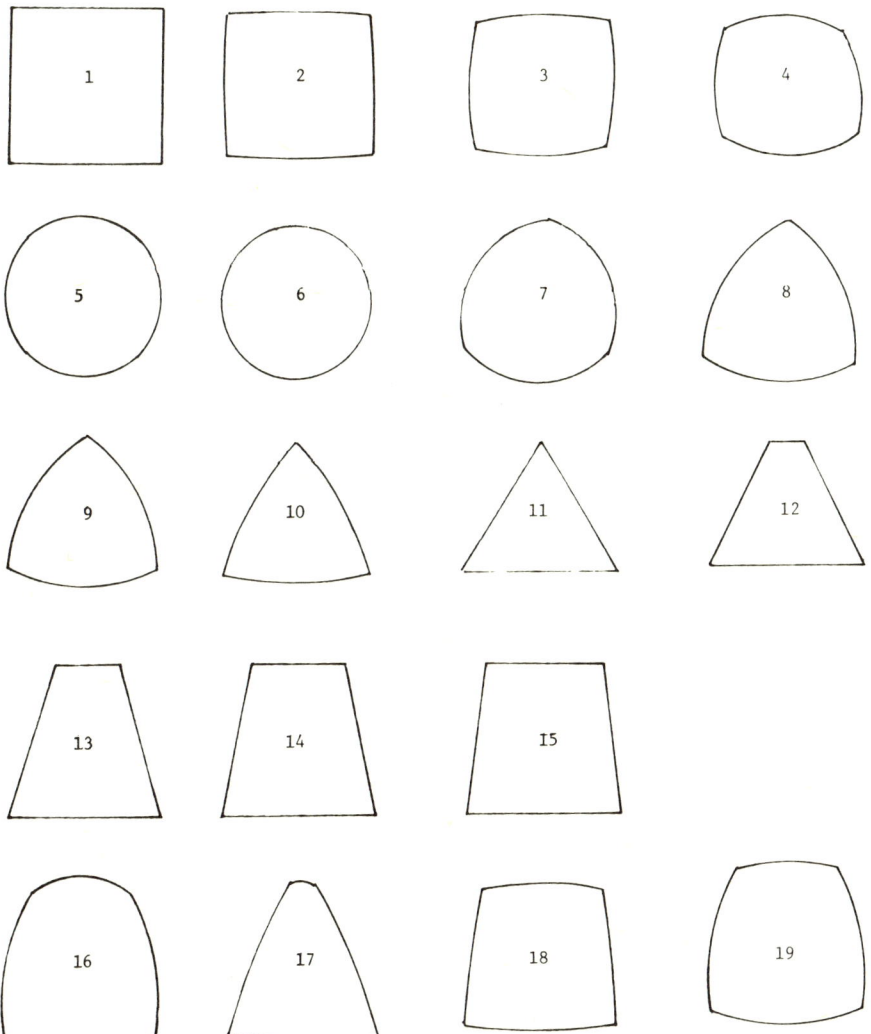

FIG. 18.2. Stimuli for the first illustrative experiment.

similarity on a scale from zero (identical) through 9 (most dissimilar). An inverse principal components analysis was carried out to reveal any important individual differences between subjects. None were found. The similarity ratings for each pair were then averaged and the resulting matrix of average similarity ratings used as input for the HYP-2 program. A three-dimensional solution (the embedding Euclidean space) was found to fit the data adequately. Figure 18.3 gives a "surface" plot of the configuration. In this type of plot the points depict the vector termini as they would appear if one looked down toward the surface of the positive orthant of the spherical subspace defined by any set of three ideal types.

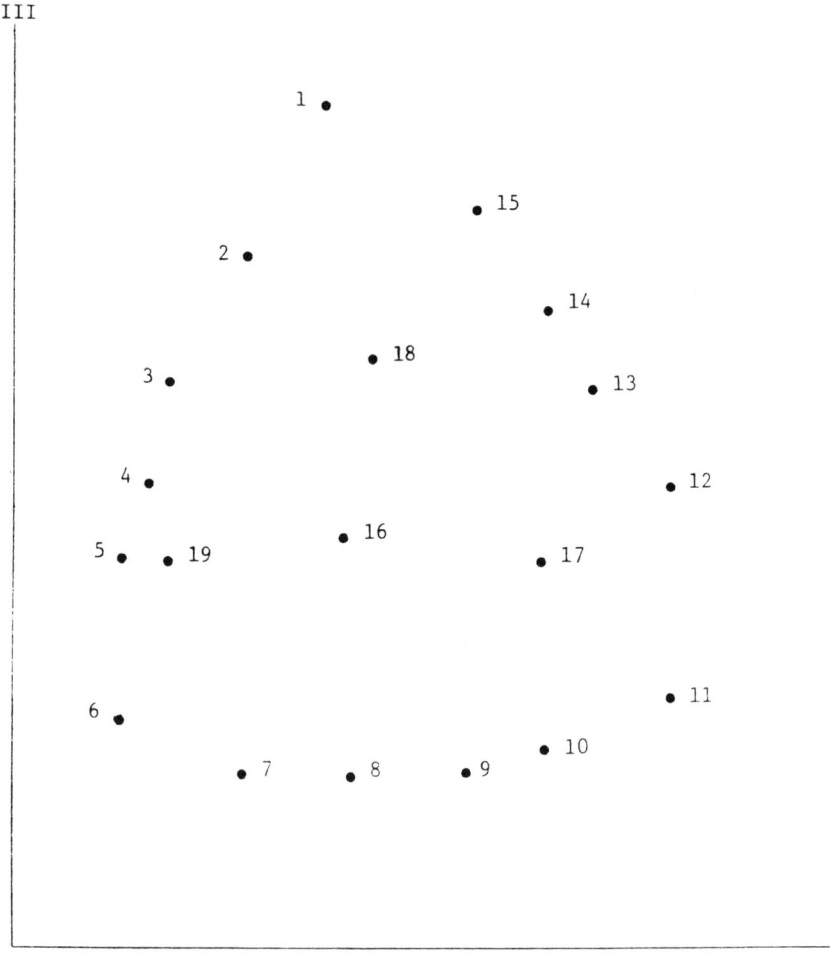

FIG. 18.3. Surface plot showing the positive manifold, simple structure of 19 geometric forms.

The second and third principal components of the projections of the stimuli into this subspace are the coordinates of the plot.

The plot shows the almost perfect positive manifold, simple structure configuration hypothesized for this domain of stimuli.

Effects of Random Error on the Recovery of Ideal-Type Structures

Random or systematic points were generated to lie on or within a right spherical triangle of a unit sphere as required by a three-ideal-type structure. Arc distances were calculated. To each distance was added a random error drawn from a normal distribution. The standard deviation of the error distribution was either 5, 10, or 20% of the root mean square true distance for the particular set of points. The analyses were carried out to provide information on two questions: (a) goodness of fit for a three-ideal-type solution as measured by stress (the 5, 10, and 20% error rates ought to yield stress values around .048, .091, and .167 respectively). Columns 2 and 9 of Table 18.1 show that stress in all cases was just about what it ought to be. (b) A check on three criteria we routinely use in deciding on dimensionality. First, the largest positive root of the residual space ought to be approximately equal to the absolute value of the largest negative root. Columns 3 and 4 of the table show the correspondence. Second, the number of residual positive roots ought to be about equal to the number of negative roots, ignoring those roots that are essentially zero. Columns 5 and 6 of the table compare the two. Third, the sum of the residual positive roots ought to be about equal to the absolute value of the sum of the negative roots. Columns 7 and 8 give the pairs of sums.

A Partial Replication of Dr. Nancy Henley's Classical Investigation on the Semantics of Animal Terms

Henley (1969) obtained category ratings of similarity for all pairs of a set of 30 animal names. A multidimensional analysis of the similarity matrix was carried out using the TORSCA program. A three-dimensional Euclidean solution was judged to give an acceptable fit to the data. Her obtained configuration is shown in Fig. 18.4. Henley did note the tendency of the animal terms to group roughly into categories, but interpreted the structure in dimensional terms. Dimension 1 was interpreted as size; Dimension 2 as mildness-ferocity, and Dimension 3 as resemblance or relatedness to man. The first dimension seemed clear, but the remaining two seemed to require the kind of forced interpretation mentioned in the preceding discussion of the alloy example. Mildness-ferocity, with lions and tigers at one end, and cows and sheep at the other, seems reasonable until one notes that animals like mouse and chipmunk lie about halfway between these extremes. In like manner, the resemblance-to-man dimension looks good at one

TABLE 18.1
Some Effects of Random Normal Error:
True Euclidean Dimensionality = 3, (Hyperspherical = 2)

1	2	3	4	5	6	7	8	9
\multicolumn{9}{c}{Random Points on Hypersphere}								
15	20	-.46	.36	5	6	-1.23	1.11	.17
15	20	-.43	.56	5	6	-1.42	1.77	.15
15	20	-.47	.34	5	5	-1.22	1.06	.14
15	20	-.54	.72	6	5	-1.79	1.76	.18
15	20	-.42	.34	5	5	-1.13	.95	.17
15	20	-.53	.44	6	6	-1.56	1.78	.18
25	20	-.63	.53	9	10	-2.74	2.66	.18
15	10	-.32	.34	5	5	- .96	.97	.10
25	10	-.43	.41	9	10	-1.83	1.96	.09
15	5	-.11	.11	4	4	- .34	.32	.04
\multicolumn{9}{c}{Systematic Points on Hypersphere}								
16	20	-.73	.74	6	6	-2.13	2.33	.17
16	10	-.39	.38	7	5	-1.35	1.22	.09
16	5	-.20	.20	5	5	- .64	.60	.04

Column
1. Number of Stimuli
2. Percent Error: Sigma Error = X Percent of Root Mean Square True Distance
3. Largest Negative Root
4. Fourth Largest Positive Root
5. Number of Negative Roots Smaller than -.05
6. Number of Positive Roots After First Three Larger than .05
7. Sum of Negative Roots
8. Sum of Positive Roots After the First Three
9. Stress

end (gorilla, chimpanzee, monkey) but would require that subjects perceive animals like chipmunks, giraffes, and camels to be more man-like than pigs or dogs. New data were obtained on the same set of animal terms using a method of multidimensional category rating.[2] Since size seemed likely to be a meaningful dimension, the HYPCYL program was used to analyze the matrix of dissimilarities. The partially confirmatory mode was used, which helps the rotation process by providing one or more input vectors as targets for the dimensional subspace. The target vector used was Torgerson's subjective rank order of size for the 30 animals.

The solution obtained for one quantitative dimension and five ideal types fits the data quite well. The correlation between the obtained quantitative dimension and the target vector was .95. Overall stress was .07. Results of the varimax

---

[2]The experiment was carried out by Elizabeth De Palma.

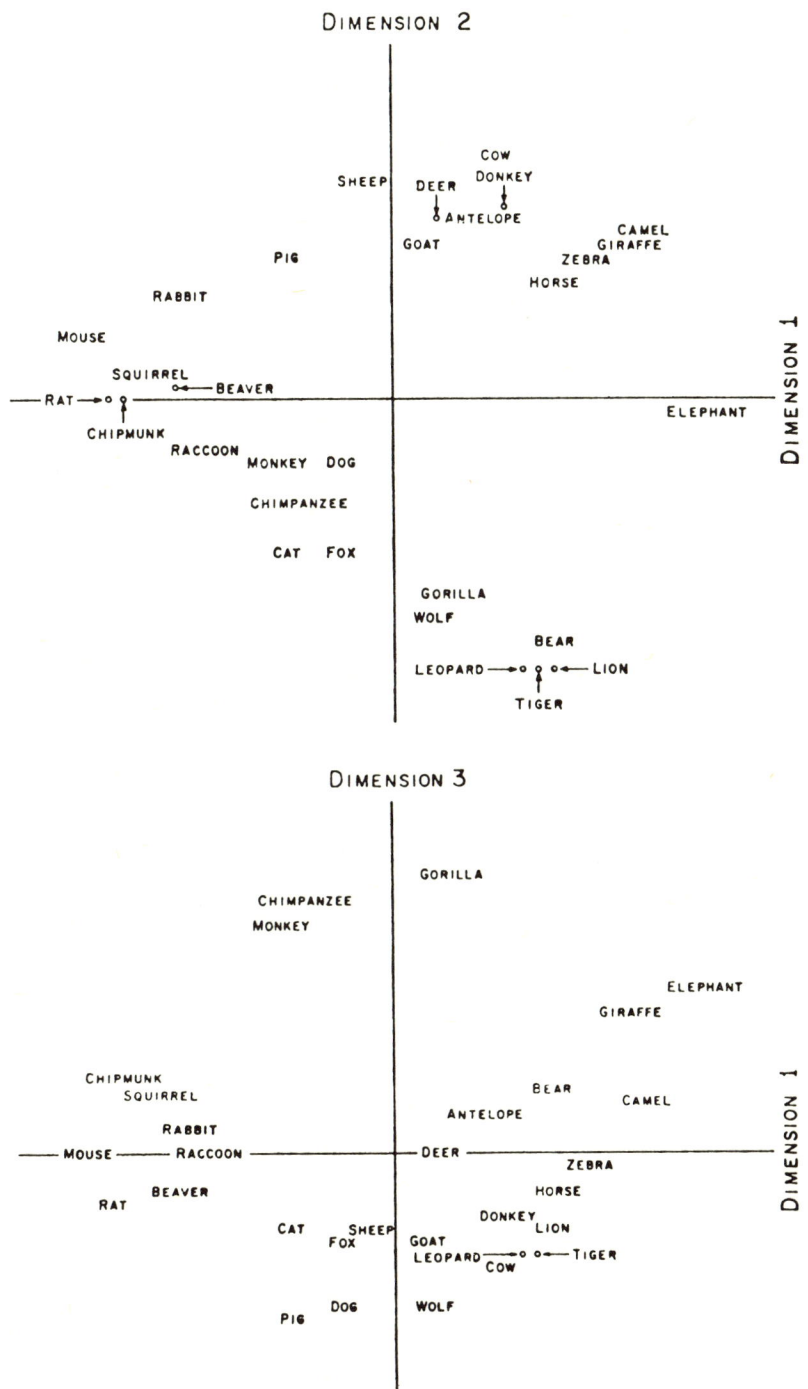

FIG. 18.4. Henley's three-dimensional solution for 30 animals (from Henley, 1979, Figures 1 and 2, 1969, Academic Press, Inc. with permission of the author and publishers).

rotation to ideal types are shown in Table 18.2. Varimax gives the factor loadings for each stimulus on each factor after rotation to orthogonal simple structure, as defined by the varimax criterion. In the present context, factors are ideal types, and loadings are the cosines of the arc distances in the hyperspherical subspace of each animal name from each ideal type. Arc distances less than $\cos^{-1} .60$ are italicized in the table. The interpretation of most of the ideal types is clear:

Ideal Types
1. a hoofed, herbivorous mammal
2. a man-like ape
3. a carnivore
4. a varmint
5. a domestic meat animal
6. a bear

Note that camel is about halfway between the prototypical ungulate and the prototypical varmint. Elephant just does not belong with this group of animal names. Although it is closest to the prototypical varmint, it is really just about in the middle of the subspace defined by the man-like ape (.45), the carnivore (.46), the varmint (.62), and the meat animal (.42). It would probably appear as its own ideal type in a solution with a hyperspherical subspace of larger dimensionality.

The Structure of Words Used to Describe the Nature of Experienced Pains

This illustrative example is one of an extensive series of studies aimed at developing a structural representation of the varieties of pain, based on the words used by patients in their attempts to describe the nature of their pain. The seventeen descriptors listed in the first column of Table 18.3 are a subset of terms compiled by Melzack and Torgerson (1971). The method of multidimensional category rating was used to obtain measures of dissimilarity between all pairs of descriptors. Subjects rated how well word X would describe a pain that was best described by word Y. The cognitive meanings of the descriptors vary both in intensity or severity and in quality of the described pain. Melzack and Torgerson's reported intensity scale values for the descriptors were used as a target vector for a one quantitative dimension, four ideal type HYPCYL analysis of the obtained dissimilarity matrix.

Again, an excellent fit to the data was obtained. The single dimension of the quantitative subspace correlated .92 with the original Melzack-Torgerson intensity values. Stress for the overall configuration was only .04. Results of the varimax rotation to ideal types are given in Table 18.3. The cosines of the arc distances of those descriptors closest to a given ideal type are italicized. The first

TABLE 18.2
Animal Names
Projections of Stimuli on Six Orthogonal Ideal Types

	1	2	3	4	5	6
Antelope	.84	.15	.39	.30	-.03	.17
Bear	.14	.47	.38	.41	.13	.66
Beaver	.29	.26	.32	.70	.24	.44
Camel	.67	.16	.24	.65	.18	-.08
Cat	.29	.20	.80	.44	.17	.08
Chimpanzee	.19	.94	.19	.19	.06	.05
Chipmunk	.37	.33	.26	.77	.17	.26
Cow	.61	.19	.19	.34	.63	.20
Deer	.83	.16	.34	.33	.00	.25
Dog	.54	.23	.60	.14	.45	.27
Donkey	.80	.18	.27	.27	.42	-.08
Elephant	.16	.43	.46	.62	.42	.16
Fox	.46	.19	.65	.32	.26	.40
Giraffe	.69	.20	.40	.57	-.00	.01
Goat	.77	.17	.16	.26	.47	.23
Gorilla	.15	.94	.24	.14	.11	.10
Horse	.82	.18	.34	.26	.35	.02
Leopard	.30	.20	.90	.22	.10	.10
Lion	.26	.23	.88	.31	.03	.05
Monkey	.19	.93	.18	.21	.10	.11
Mouse	.37	.14	.31	.83	.22	-.02
Pig	.27	.10	.16	.40	.85	.04
Rabbit	.58	.16	.34	.65	.08	.32
Raccoon	.41	.38	.42	.61	.28	.24
Rat	.32	.12	.35	.84	.25	.01
Sheep	.71	.17	.11	.39	.43	.34
Squirrel	.46	.26	.23	.73	.26	.27
Tiger	.26	.20	.89	.30	.07	.01
Wolf	.42	.19	.72	.12	.31	.41
Zebra	.81	.23	.43	.29	.15	-.06

ideal type is a bright pain, the second is a slow rhythmic temporal type of pain, the third is thermal, and the fourth characterizes an almost vibratory, perhaps arrhythmic type. No term in the study is solely descriptive of the fourth type. Flickering and quivering are fairly close, but are also rather close to both the bright and the slower temporal types; jumping is closer to the temporal; and tickling is closer to bright. A finer grained examination of the entries of Table 18.3 illustrates the meaningful *quantitative* nature of the ideal type of structure. Thus smarting, a bright type of pain, deviates toward thermal pain. And of the four primarily thermal descriptors, searing and burning describe pains with more of the brightness characteristic than the terms hot and scalding.

TABLE 18.3
Pain Descriptors
Projections of Stimuli on Four Orthogonal Ideal Types

	1	2	3	4
Flickering	.60	.62	.39	*.35*
Quivering	.57	.58	.22	*.54*
Pulsing	.26	*.94*	.21	.08
Throbbing	.15	*.97*	.18	.01
Thumping	.14	*.99*	-.03	.05
Beating	.22	*.97*	.08	-.06
Pounding	.04	*.99*	.07	.01
Jumping	.21	*.89*	-.10	*.40*
Tickling	*.86*	.26	.24	*.36*
Tingling	*.87*	.25	.33	.27
Itching	*.94*	.12	.32	-.04
Smarting	*.81*	.30	.46	-.21
Stinging	*.94*	.10	.33	-.02
Hot	.22	.06	*.97*	.00
Burning	.38	.06	*.92*	-.07
Scalding	.29	.04	*.94*	.14
Searing	.49	.19	*.84*	.11

SUMMARY COMMENTS ON IDEAL TYPE STRUCTURES

Ideal type structures have long been popular as verbal or naive conceptualizations of the way things are. The stereotypes of everyday language seem much more like ideal types than like classes or even than like typical examples of categories. The various typologies of personality theory correspond to the ideal type conceptualization rather than the discrete categories of the classification methodology. The Sheldon-Stevens somatotypes (1942), where any individual's body type can be specified by numerical ratings according to degree of ectomorphy, endomorphy, and mesomorphy, is an obvious ideal type structure. Psychiatric categories also seem functionally more like ideal types than classes. Few, if any, real patients fit a psychiatric category exactly, but instead shade off in various directions toward other categories. Much the same seems to be the case for many other medical categories. Dr. Broca probably saw the only patient whose symptoms corresponded exactly to those of Broca's aphasia.

In most of these examples, the implicit conceptual model fits the ideal type notions, but the language used is the language of classification structures. More importantly, perhaps partly because of the language, the methodology used in research is often appropriate for classes, and not especially, or maybe not even slightly, appropriate for ideal type structures. Clustering procedures only sound like they are appropriate. But rejection of clustering procedures in favor of the purely dimensional approaches of the usual multidimensional scaling or factor analysis procedures simply substitutes one wrong for another. Neither set of procedures is appropriate for an ideal type structure.

REFERENCES

Henley, N. M. A psychological study of the semantics of animal terms. *Journal of Verbal Learning and Verbal Behavior,* 1969, *8,* 176–184.

Melzack, R., & Torgerson, W. S. On the language of pain. *Anesthesiology,* 1971, *34,* 50–59.

Satalich, T. A. *Hypercylindrical multidimensional scaling.* Unpublished doctoral dissertation, The Johns Hopkins University, 1981.

Sheldon, W. H., & Stevens, S. S. *The varieties of temperament.* New York: Harper, 1942.

Torgerson, W. S. Multidimensional scaling of similarity. *Psychometrika,* 1964, 30, 379–393.

Torgerson, W. S., & Satalich, T. A. *Hyperspherical and hypercylindrical multidimensional scaling: the ideal type model.* Paper presented at the spring meeting of the Psychometric Society, Iowa City, May, 1980.

V COMMENTS ON THE MEASUREMENT OF TRAITS

One way of characterizing Fred Lord's major message to psychometrics is that test theory should shift its emphasis from estimating true scores to measuring attributes. Intrinsic to this shift as embodied in Item Response Theory is the concept of latent trait, which is some characteristic or attribute of persons, such as ability level, that accounts for individual consistencies in response to items differing in difficulty, in extent of discrimination along the attribute, and in the probability of success at low attribute values. Although latent trait is a highly generalized and abstract construct in Item Response Theory, the question arises as to the applicability of IRT and other test theory models to the variety of specific traits conceptualized in psychological theory and under the kinds of testing conditions that present-day political and social constraints require.

Anne Anastasi examines the nature of psychological traits in relation to response variance attributable to situations, to trait-situation interactions, and to transitory states of the organism. She suggests that the identification and measurement of psychological traits may require assessment of individuals across a variety of situations and transitory states; furthermore, that aggregation across such multiple items of behavior serves to cancel out specific situational and trait aspects, leaving an index of behavioral consistency at the trait level. This implies aggregation across behavioral items with common trait variance and specific situation and state variance, which appears to be compatible in principle with the emphasis on unidimensionality in Item Response Theory and other test theory models. However, Anastasi stresses that aggregation can occur in different ways and that the measurement focus might instead be on situational categories or transitory states and not just on intraindividual trait consistencies—indeed, all three types of constructs are needed for a comprehensive view of behavior.

Robert Thorndike bemoans the practical problems entailed in collecting the necessary data for test development, norming, and analysis as these problems are increasingly exacerbated by political and social constraints being imposed on test administration. It is not just that stratified probability samples are difficult to arrange, which was always the case, but that sizable samples of cooperating individuals are now more difficult to come by, especially individuals from special populations. Although Thorndike is particularly concerned that the test disclosure requirements of "truth-in-testing" legislation may ultimately degrade the quality of standardized tests, he sees a potential solution to the disclosure problem in computerized tailored testing with very large item banks, a solution that may indeed be feasible with the advent and practical application of Item Response Theory. This suggests the possibility that modern statistical theories of mental tests might also be useful in alleviating some of the other test development, norming, and analysis problems highlighted so forcefully by Thorndike.

19 Traits, States, and Situations: A Comprehensive View

Anne Anastasi
Fordham University

My contribution to this book relates not so much to the measurement of traits in terms of test theory, which has been so elegantly developed by Fred Lord, as to the psychological interpretation of trait constructs. In particular, it concerns the meaning of traits as related to—and enriched by—research on the behavioral diversities associated with temporary states and with situational specificity.

The 1980s are witnessing a broadening in our understanding of how traits are formed, developed, and manifested in the observable behavior of individuals. Several independent lines of research are contributing to this enhanced understanding. The relevant research has been conducted by investigators from widely different psychological specialties. At the outset, it was also accompanied by sharp controversy and even, in some cases, by the total rejection of trait concepts. The eventual rapprochement and the gradual abandonment of extremist positions is now leading toward a more flexible and comprehensive concept of psychological traits.

TRAITS AND SITUATIONS

The Controversy. A long-standing controversy regarding the generalizability of traits versus the situational specificity of behavior reached a peak in the late 1960s and the 1970s. Several developments in the 1960s focused attention on narrowly defined "behaviors of interest" and away from broadly defined traits. In the cognitive domain, this focus is illustrated by individualized instructional programs and criterion-referenced testing (Glaser, 1963; Maier & Hirshfeld, 1978; Panell & Laabs, 1979; Talmage, 1975) and by the diagnosis and treatment of learning disabilities (Gottlieb, Zinkus, & Bradford, 1979; Lerner, 1971; Waugh & Bush, 1971). In the noncognitive or personality domain, the strongest impetus toward behavioral specificity came from psychologists identified with social learning theory and with the general orientation characterizing behavior modification and behavior therapy (Bandura, 1969; Bandura & Walters, 1963; Goldfried & Kent, 1972; Mischel, 1968, 1969, 1973).

Criticism was directed especially toward the early view of traits as fixed, unchanging, and underlying causal entities. Few psychometricians today would argue for such a concept of traits. The scarcity of this type of "trait theorist" was eloquently characterized by Jackson and Paunonen in their chapter in the 1980 *Annual Review of Psychology*. They wrote, "Like witches of 300 years ago, there is confidence about their existence, and even possibly their sinister properties, although one is hard pressed to find one in the flesh or even meet someone who has" (p. 523). It seems to be a popular sport to fabricate a description of what psychometricians allegedly believe and then to demonstrate the obvious falsity of the belief. This is the familiar technique of setting up a straw man and then demolishing it. It is easy to find applications of this technique in current criticisms of what intelligence tests measure, of the meaning of an IQ, and of the distinction between aptitude and achievement tests, to name a few examples. The psychometric barn is littered with a superabundance of loose straw!

Turning to the other side of the controversy, we find that situational specificity is much more characteristic of personality traits than it is of abilities. For example, a person may be quite sociable and outgoing at the office but shy and reserved at social gatherings. Or a student who cheats on examinations may be scrupulously honest in money matters. An extensive body of empirical evidence has been assembled by social learning theorists (Mischel, 1968; Peterson, 1968) showing that individuals exhibit considerable situational specificity in many nonintellective dimensions, such as aggression, social conformity, dependency, rigidity, honesty, and attitudes toward authority.

Part of the explanation for the higher cross-situational consistency of cognitive than of noncognitive functions may be found in the greater standardization of the individual's reactional biography in the intellectual than in the personality domain (Anastasi, 1948, 1970). The formal school curriculum, for example, contributes to the development of broadly applicable cognitive skills in the verbal and numerical areas. Personality development, in contrast, occurs under far less uniform conditions. In the personality domain, moreover, the same response may lead to social consequences that are positively reinforcing in one situation and negatively reinforcing in another. The individual may thus learn to respond in quite different ways in different contexts.

It is also noteworthy that factor-analytic studies of animals have yielded factors in which cognitive and noncognitive aspects of behavior are not sharply differentiated (Anastasi, 1948, 1970). Even when the variables analyzed are derived from performance on typical learning tasks, such as mazes, discrimination apparatus, and problem-solving situations, one finds such factors as docility, wildness-timidity, and impulsiveness or activity. This intertwining of aptitude and emotional factors may also have an experiential origin. Unlike the schoolchildren or college students of the usual human factor-analytic research, animals have not been exposed to that classic dichotomy between curricular and extracurricular experiences, between standardized intellectual development and unstandardized emotional development.

Impact on Test Development and Assessment Procedures. With regard to testing methodology, concern with situational variance is most clearly evident among investigators who identify with social learning theory (Endler & Hunt, 1966, 1968, 1969; Goldfried & D'Zurilla, 1969; Kjerulff & Wiggins, 1976), although it is also apparent in the work of others (Frederiksen, 1972). Special instruments were developed to assess the behavior of individuals in different types of situations. Analysis of the results showed the extent to which behavior variance depended upon persons, situations, and the interaction between the two.

This approach to behavioral assessment can be illustrated by an investigation dealing with the way graduate students cope with stressful situations (Kjerulff & Wiggins, 1976). Through a series of systematic procedural steps, the investigators assembled brief verbal descriptions of 26 stressful situations encountered by graduate students, with special reference to those situations that might adversely affect their remaining in graduate school. Respondents then rated each of the 26 situations on a 7-point scale to indicate how they would feel if they were in that situation. Some of the rating scales concerned the degree to which the student would feel angry with others, angry with self, or responsible for the situation. Other scales involved the degree to which the student would feel anxious, rejected, depressed, or discouraged. There were also questions designed to assess the individual's professional self-concept.

The basic data in this study involved three different modes: persons, situations, and types of response. Using multimode factor analysis (Levin, 1965; Tucker, 1964, 1966, 1972), the investigators were able to identify major factors in situations (e.g., academic failure, interpersonal problems), in responses (e.g., anger at self versus others, general anxiety), and in persons. The person mode sorted students into two types. One type included those who desired professional respect, who rated themselves high in competence, and who planned to be doing research of major importance. The other type comprised those who tended to rate themselves at the opposite pole in these characteristics. In addition, multimode factor analysis provides a core matrix which integrates the three modes and permits their joint interpretation. For example, students who rated themselves as less competent professionally tended to feel anger at themselves for academic failure and anger at others for interpersonal problems; they felt extremely anxious when facing academic problems, but not at all anxious in stressful situations for which there was no clear source of blame, such as losing subjects in an experiment.

Two other ways of dealing with the role of situational context in behavioral assessment are noteworthy. One involves the development of tests that assess the manifestations of a trait within a specified class of situations. This can be illustrated by test anxiety inventories (Morris, Davis, & Hutchings, 1981; Sarason, 1980; Spielberger, 1980). Persons high in test anxiety tend to perceive evaluative situations as personally threatening. Besides a total score indicative of anxiety proneness in test situations, such inventories may provide subscores on two major components identified through factor analysis, namely worry and emotionality. The general instructions may also be modified to define the anxiety-provoking situations even more specifically by asking students to respond, for example, with reference to mathematics tests or essay tests.

Another approach has been designated as interactional assessment (McReynolds, 1979). This term refers to the joint assessment of the person and the environment in which he or she must function. Attention focuses on how a particular individual will respond within specific situations. Although the general interactional model has been recognized for some time, only limited progress has been made toward the development of appropriate assessment procedures. McReynolds (1979) has described six possible approaches that meet the needs of interactional assessment. They range widely in the fullness and objectivity with which persons and situations are measured. An example is the systematic assessment of the person through traditional tests and other familiar techniques in combination with the informal observation of relevant environments, as in visiting the foster homes to which a child may be assigned. At the other end of the range is the direct observation of actual behavior samples of persons-in-situations. A practical compromise utilizes simulated behavior samples of persons-in-situations, as in role-playing techniques.

TRAITS AND STATES

Another major way to categorize behavior involves the differentiation between traits and states. In contrast to situational variance, state variance represents systematic changes in the condition of the organism over time periods of moderate duration. Such changes reflect principally the effects of intervening experiences occurring either in the normal course of everyday life or through planned interventions. If the situational context in which the individual is assessed differs appreciably in the different testing sessions, then state and situational differences are confounded. In that case, the response differences reflect both the effect of the immediate situation and the effect of intervening experiences. In actual assessment operations, however, interest centers on one type of effect, and conditions are controlled so as to minimize the other. For instance, we can obtain a measure of test anxiety, which is situationally defined behavior, before and after the respondents have undergone a therapeutic intervention (Morris, Davis, & Hutchings, 1981).

The distinction between trait assessment and state assessment is clearly exemplified in the State-Trait Anxiety Inventory developed by Spielberger and his co-workers (Speilberger, Gorsuch, & Lushene, 1970; Spielberger, Vagg, Barker, Donham, & Westberry, 1980). In the construction of this instrument, state anxiety (A-State) was defined as a transitory emotional condition characterized by subjective feelings of tension and apprehension. Such states vary in intensity and fluctuate over time. A-State is measured in this inventory by 20 short descriptive statements which respondents answer in reference to how they feel *at the moment* (e.g., I feel calm; I am jittery). The answers are recorded by indicating the intensity of the feeling (not at all, somewhat, moderately so, very much so).

In contrast, trait anxiety (A-Trait) refers to relatively stable anxiety proneness, that is, the individual's tendency to respond to situations perceived as threatening with elevated A-State intensity. Respondents are instructed to indicate how they *generally* feel by marking the frequency with which each of 20 statements applies to them (almost never, sometimes, often, almost always). Examples of the statements are "I am inclined to take things hard," "I am a steady person." Only three identical items appear in the state and trait forms of the inventory.

Conceptually, A-Trait is identified with a set of constructs described as acquired behavioral dispositions. These constructs "involve residues of past experience and predispose an individual *both* to view the world in a particular way and to manifest 'object consistent' response tendencies" (Spielberger et al., 1970, p. 3). Persons high in A-Trait tend to exhibit A-State elevations more often than do persons low in A-Trait, because they react to a wider range of situations as threatening or dangerous. Whether or not A-State increases in a given situation depends upon the extent to which the individual perceives the situation as threatening or dangerous on the basis of his or her past experience.

The development of this state-trait inventory illustrates some special points of test construction. Internal consistency reliability was about equally high (in the .80s and .90s) for A-Trait and A-State forms. Retest reliability was in the high .70s for A-Trait but much lower, as would be expected, for A-State. Retests over intervals of 20 and 104 days yielded A-State correlations ranging from .27 to .54. Retests within one hour, following the introduction of experimental conditions designed to raise or lower stress levels, yielded still lower correlations. What such low correlations indicate is an interaction between persons and situational stress. Although the group means reflected the anticipated differences in A-State following experimental manipulations, the effects varied sufficiently among individuals to result in low test-retest correlations.

The construct validity of both A-State and A-Trait forms was demonstrated in various ways, including item selection, evaluation of items and total scores, and subsequent research by both test authors and independent investigators. In successive revisions, items were selected on the basis of item-test correlations and item correlations with external criteria. For the A-Trait, items and total scores yielded high correlations with other self-report anxiety inventories, and they yielded a pattern of correlations with other personality tests that was generally consistent with expectation. Validity data were also obtained by comparing the mean A-Trait scores of various contrasted groups. For the A-State form, both items and total scores were evaluated principally against experimental variables designed to raise or lower anxiety states, such as taking a final course examination or a difficult intelligence test, seeing a film depicting accidents in a woodworking shop, or undergoing a 10-minute period of relaxation training.

The state-trait differentiation was applied by Spielberger and his associates (1980) in two other, more recently developed inventories, one designed to assess anger and the other providing separate scales for anxiety, anger, and curiosity. Other investigators had for some time been developing instruments to assess what they variously termed "affects," "feelings," "moods," "states," or "mood states." Several were designed for use in clinical work, as in evaluating the effects of different types of therapy. A number were developed for use in particular research projects. A few have been published for more general uses (e.g., Curran & Cattell, 1976; Lubin, 1967; McNair & Lorr, 1981; McNair, Lorr, & Droppleman, 1971; Zuckerman & Lubin, 1960–1967). The specific states covered include anxiety, depression, hostility, fatigue, and confusion, among others.

Most of these inventories measure only states, the specified time ranging from "this moment," through "now—today," to "the past week including today." At least one inventory (Zuckerman & Lubin, 1960–1967) employs the same items with different instructional sets to assess both trait and state for anxiety, depression, and hostility. A difficulty with this procedure is that the items may not represent the best selection for either purpose. In fact, in this case, the criteria for item selection were more appropriate for trait measurement for two of the scales and more appropriate for state measurement for the third. The available instruments for assessing states, either with or without parallel trait measures, vary widely in methodological sophistication and in psychometric quality. While most are still at the research stage, however, they are of interest in focusing attention on both the theoretical and practical value of the state-trait distinction.

Still another approach to the problem of trait consistency and behavioral diversity is provided by the motivational theory formulated by John Atkinson (1981) and tested through computer simulation. Representing behavior as a stream of activity rather than a series of discrete incidents, Atkinson and his coworkers were able to reconcile enduring individual differences in personality traits (such as achievement drive) with changing behavior over short time periods. Essentially, the explanation can be found in the changing motivational state of the organism, which reflects the waxing and waning of the relative strengths of different behavior tendencies. When a particular tendency becomes dominant among simultaneously aroused competing tendencies, it is expressed in appropriate behavior. This expression of a tendency in activity reduces the strength of that tendency, whereupon another tendency rises to a dominant position and leads to other behavior. Working with a model of a TAT-type procedure for assessing the achievement motive, Atkinson was able to show that it is possible to obtain high construct validity of total scores (as high as .90) when internal consistency is very low (as low as .07). He argued that the individual does not respond to each TAT card independently, but rather responds through a continuous stream of behavior. The proportion of time the examinee spends describing, for example, achievement-motivated activities in response to different cards is a function of the cumulative effect of responding to successive cards and the differential incentives for achievement and other competing motives in the particular cards.

The examples cited thus far to illustrate both situational and state variance in behavior have been drawn predominantly from the noncognitive domain. As was suggested at the outset, such variation is likely to be more conspicuous in personality characteristics than in aptitudes, and this difference is consistent with an experiential interpretation. It should be noted, however, that mood changes and situationally contingent feelings may significantly affect both learning and task performance in cognitive areas. There has been an increasing amount of research on this relation, with some suggestive results. The evidence indicates, for example, that emotionally toned material tends to be recalled better than does neutral material (Zajonc, 1980), and that more is learned in a mood of elation than in a mood of depression (Hettena & Ballif, 1981).

TRAIT CONCEPTS REEXAMINED

Both the theoretical discussions and the research on traits-versus-situations and traits-versus-states have undoubtedly enriched our understanding of the many conditions that determine individual behavior. Concurrently, there has been a growing consensus among the adherents of contrasting views. This rapprochement was especially evident in a number of well-balanced and thoughtful discussions of the problem published in the 1970s (D. J. Bem & Allen, 1974; D. J. Bem & Funder, 1978; Bowers, 1973; Endler & Magnusson, 1976; Epstein, 1979, 1980; Hogan, DeSoto, & Solano, 1977; Mischel, 1977, 1979). Several noteworthy points emerged from these discussions. When random samples of persons and situations are investigated, individual differences contribute more to total behavior variance than do situational differences. Interaction between persons and situations contributes as much as do individual differences, or slightly more. To identify broad personality traits, we need to measure individuals across many situations and aggregate the results (Epstein, 1980). Whether we aggregate items, tests, or criterion measures, the combining serves to cancel out specific situational aspects, leaving an index of behavioral consistency at the trait level (Green, 1978).

The degree of behavioral specificity among situations itself varies from person to person. In this connection, Mischel (1979) refers to individual differences in the discriminativeness of social behavior. Persons differ in the extent to which they alter their behavior to meet the demands of each situation. In this respect, moderate inconsistency indicates effective and adaptive flexibility, while excessive consistency indicates maladaptive rigidity. It might be added that such situational variability is implied in the concept of psychological androgyny (S. L. Bem, 1974, 1981; Spence & Helmreich, 1978). As currently used in sex-role inventories, the term "androgyny" characterizes an individual who manifests the favorable traits stereotypically associated with both men and women. This combination can be illustrated by a person who rates high in *both* assertiveness and compassion, or in *both* competence and emotional expressiveness. Thus, it has been argued that the androgynous person is better able to adapt to varying situational demands than is the more traditionally sex-typed person.

From another angle, the particular situations across which behavior is consistent may vary among persons. Intersituational consistency is influenced by the way individuals perceive and categorize situations (Mischel & Peake, 1982). And such grouping of situations in turn depends on the individual's goals and on his or her prior experience with similar situations. This conception of behavior consistencies derives from the early idiographic approach to personality assessment formulated by Gordon Allport (1937) and by George Kelly (1955, 1963), among others (see Landfield & Leitner, 1980).

Situations themselves also differ in the behavioral constraints they impose. Thus, we could predict with a high level of confidence that readers will remain silent in a library and that motorists will stop at a red light. Similarly, most persons—whatever their trait structure—are likely to swim at the beach and to read in the library. Nevertheless, certain individuals may spend their time reading while at the beach, and others may spend all too much time daydreaming about swimming while in the library.

While contributing to our understanding of individual behavior, the proponents of situational specificity have come to recognize the need for trait categories, for both theoretical and practical reasons. If an individual's behavior exhibited no significant consistencies across situations or across transitory states, both science and society would be in a state of chaos. To meet different assessment needs, behavioral observations can be aggregated in different ways and with appropriate degrees of generality or specificity (Mischel & Peake, 1982). The focus may be on intraindividual consistencies, on situational categories of broad or narrow scope. or on transitory states. All three types of classification are needed for a comprehensive view of behavior.

Meanwhile, trait theorists for their part had been moving away from the extreme views of traits as rigidly fixed, predetermined, universal, causal entities. Research on the modifiability of traits and on the role of cultural and experiential conditions in trait formation has been progressing apace (Anastasi, 1948; 1970; 1982, Chs. 12, 13; Carroll, 1966; Ferguson, 1954, 1956; Humphreys, 1962, 1970; Khan, 1970, 1972; Reinert, 1970). Of particular interest are the various efforts to link motivation and cognition in trait development. Performance on an aptitude test, as well as in school, on the job, or in any other context is influenced by the individual's achievement drive, persistence, value system, freedom from handicapping emotional problems, and other characteristics traditionally classified under the heading of "personality."

There is increasing recognition of the role of students' motivation in school learning (Bloom, 1976, Ch. 4; Nichols, 1979). The individual's interests, attitudes, and self-concept as a school learner influence his or her openness to a learning task, the desire to learn it well, the attention given to it, and the time actively devoted to the task. And there is evidence that these individual reactions are significantly related to educational achievement.

Even more important is the cumulative effect of motivational characteristics on the direction and extent of the individual's intellectual development. This relationship has been explored very fully in the comprehensive schema formulated by John Atkinson and his associates (Atkinson, 1974; Atkinson & Birch, 1978, Ch. 4; Atkinson, O'Malley, & Lens, 1976). The relation is reciprocal. Not only do personality characteristics affect intellectual development, but intellectual level also affects personality development. The success an individual attains in the development and use of his or her aptitudes is bound to influence that person's emotional adjustment, interpersonal relations, and self-concept. In the self-concept, we can see most clearly the mutual influence of aptitudes and personality traits. The child's achievement in school, on the playground, and in other situations helps to shape that child's self-concept. And this self-concept at any one stage influences subsequent performance, in a continuing spiral.

Traditionally, cognition has been the concern of psychometricians and learning theorists, while feelings and motivation have been the concern of social psychologists and personality theorists. This is an artificial and unrealistic separation that has impoverished the study of how traits are formed and of the way heredity and environment contribute to their development (Hayes, 1962; Scarr, 1981). There are now encouraging indications of emerging linkages among diverse areas of investigation. Such advances should expand and strengthen our understanding of behavior.

REFERENCES

Allport, G. W. *Personality: A psychological interpretation.* New York: Holt, 1937.
Anastasi, A. The nature of psychological "traits." *Psychological Review,* 1948, *55,* 127–138.

Anastasi, A. On the formation of psychological traits. *American Psychologist*, 1970, *25*, 899–910.
Anastasi, A. *Psychological testing* (5th ed.). New York: Macmillan, 1982.
Atkinson, J. W. Motivational determinants of intellective performance and cumulative achievement. In J. W. Atkinson & J. O. Raynor, *Motivation and achievement*. Washington, D.C.: Winston, 1974.
Atkinson, J. W. Studying personality in the context of an advanced motivational psychology. *American Psychologist*, 1981, *36*, 117–128.
Atkinson, J. W., & Birch, D. *An introduction to motivation* (2nd ed.). New York: Van Nostrand, 1978.
Atkinson, J. W., O'Malley, P. M., & Lens, W. Motivation and ability: Interactive psychological determinants of intellective performance, educational achievement, and each other. In W. H. Sewell, R. M. Hauser, & D. L. Featherman (Eds.), *Schooling and achievement in American society*. New York: Academic Press, 1976.
Bandura, A. *Principles of behavior modification*. New York: Holt, Rinehart & Winston, 1969.
Bandura, A., & Walters, R. H. *Social learning and personality development*. New York: Holt, Rinehart & Winston, 1963.
Bem, D. J., & Allen, A. On predicting some of the people some of the time: The search for cross-situational consistencies in behavior. *Psychological Review*, 1974, *81*, 506–520.
Bem, D. J., & Funder, D. C. Predicting more of the people more of the time: Assessing the personality of situations. *Psychological Review*, 1978, *85*, 485–501.
Bem, S. L. The measurement of psychological androgyny. *Journal of Consulting and Clinical Psychology*, 1974, *42*, 155–162.
Bem, S. L. *Manual for the Bem Sex-Role Inventory*. Palo Alto, Calif.: Consulting Psychologists Press, 1981.
Bloom, B. S. *Human characteristics and school learning*. New York: McGraw-Hill, 1976.
Bowers, K. Situationism in psychology: An analysis and a critique. *Psychological Review*, 1973, *80*, 307–336.
Carroll, J. B. Factors of verbal achievement. In A. Anastasi (Ed.), *Testing problems in perspective*. Washington, D.C.: American Council on Education, 1966.
Curran, J. P., & Cattell, R. B. *Eight State Questionnaire (8SQ)*. Champaign, Ill.: Institute for Personality and Ability Testing, 1976.
Endler, N. S., & Hunt, J. McV. Sources of behavioral variance as measured by the S-R Inventory of Anxiousness. *Psychological Bulletin*, 1966, *65*, 336–346.
Endler, N. S., & Hunt, J. McV. S-R inventories of hostility and comparisons of the proportions of variance from persons, responses, and situations for hostility and anxiousness. *Journal of Personality and Social Psychology*, 1968, *9*, 309–315.
Endler, N. S., & Hunt, J. McV. Generalizability of contributions from sources of variance in the S-R inventories of anxiousness. *Journal of Personality*, 1969, *37*, 1–24.
Endler, N. S., & Magnusson, D. Toward an interactional psychology of personality. *Psychological Bulletin*, 1976, *83*, 956–974.
Epstein, S. The stability of behavior: I. On predicting most of the people much of the time. *Journal of Personality and Social Psychology*, 1979, *37*, 1097–1121.
Epstein, S. The stability of behavior: II. Implications for psychological research. *American Psychologist*, 1980, *35*, 790–806.
Ferguson, G. A. On learning and human ability. *Canadian Journal of Psychology*, 1954, *8*, 95–112.
Ferguson, G. A. On transfer and the abilities of man. *Canadian Journal of Psychology*, 1956, *10*, 121–131.
Frederiksen, N. Toward a taxonomy of situations. *American Psychologist*, 1972, *27*, 114–123.
Glaser, R. Instructional technology and the measurement of learning outcomes. *American Psychologist*, 1963, *18*, 519–522.
Goldfried, M. R., & D'Zurilla, T. J. A behavioral-analytic model for assessing competence. In C.

D. Spielberger (Ed.), *Current topics in clinical psychology* (Vol. 1). New York: Academic Press, 1969.

Goldfried, M. R., & Kent, R. N. Traditional versus behavioral personality assessment: A comparison of methodological and theoretical assumptions. *Psychological Bulletin*, 1972, *77*, 409–420.

Gottlieb, M. I., Zinkus, P. W., & Bradford, L. J. (Eds.). *Current issues in developmental pediatrics: The learning-disabled child*. New York: Grune & Stratton, 1979.

Green, B. F., Jr. In defense of measurement. *American Psychologist*, 1978, *33*, 664–670.

Hayes, K. J. Genes, drives, and intellect. *Psychological Reports*, 1962, *10*, 299–342.

Hettena, C. M., & Ballif, B. L. Effects of moods on learning. *Journal of Educational Psychology*, 1981, *73*, 505–508.

Hogan, R., DeSoto, C. B., & Solano, C. Traits, tests, and personality research. *American Psychologist*, 1977, *32*, 255–264.

Humphreys, L. G. The organization of human abilities. *American Psychologist*, 1962, *17*, 475–483.

Humphreys, L. G. A skeptical look at the factor pure test. In C. Lunneborg (Ed.), *Current problems and techniques in multivariate psychology*. Seattle: University of Washington, 1970.

Jackson, D. N., & Paunonen, S. V. Personality structure and assessment. *Annual Review of Psychology*, 1980, *31*, 503–551.

Kelly, G. A. *The psychology of personal constructs*. New York: Norton, 1955.

Kelly, G. A. *A theory of personality*. New York: Norton, 1963.

Khan, S. B. Development of mental abilities: An investigation of the "differentiation hypothesis." *Canadian Journal of Psychology*, 1970, *24*, 199–205.

Khan, S. B. Learning and the development of verbal ability. *American Educational Research Journal*, 1972, *9*, 607–614.

Kjerulff, K., & Wiggins, N. H. Graduate student styles for coping with stressful situations. *Journal of Educational Psychology*, 1976, *68*, 247–254.

Landfield, A. W., & Leitner, L. M. (Eds.). *Personal construct psychology: Psychotherapy and personality*. New York: Wiley, 1980.

Lerner, J. W. *Children with learning disabilities: Theories, diagnosis, and teaching strategies*. Boston: Houghton Mifflin, 1971.

Levin, J. Three mode factor analysis. *Psychological Bulletin*, 1965, *64*, 442–452.

Lubin, B. *Depression Adjective Check List*. San Diego, Calif.: Educational and Industrial Testing Service, 1967.

Maier, M. H., & Hirshfeld, S. F. *Criterion-referenced job proficiency testing: A large scale application* (Research Report 1193). Alexandria, Va.: U.S. Army Research Institute for the Behavioral and Social Sciences, February 1978.

McNair, D., & Lorr, M. *Profile of Mood States—Bi-polar Form (POMS-BI)*. San Diego, Calif.: Educational and Industrial Testing Service, 1981.

McNair, D. M., Lorr, M., & Droppleman, L. F. *Profile of Mood States (POMS)*. San Diego, Calif.: Educational and Industrial Testing Service, 1971.

McReynolds, P. The case for interactional assessment. *Behavioral Assessment*, 1979, *1*, 237–247.

Mischel, W. *Personality and assessment*. New York: Wiley, 1968.

Mischel, W. Continuity and change in personality. *American Psychologist*, 1969, *24*, 1012–1018.

Mischel, W. Toward a cognitive social learning reconceptualization of personality. *Psychological Review*, 1973, *80*, 252–283.

Mischel, W. On the future of personality measurement. *American Psychologist*, 1977, *32*, 246–254.

Mischel, W. On the interface of cognition and personality: Beyond the person-situation debate. *American Psychologist*, 1979, *34*, 740–754.

Mischel, W., & Peake, P. K. Beyond déjà vu in the search for cross-situational consistency. *Psychological Review*, 1982, *89*, 730–755.

Morris, L. W., Davis, M. A., & Hutchings, C. H. Cognitive and emotional components of anxiety:

Literature review and a revised worry-emotionality scale. *Journal of Educational Psychology,* 1981, *73,* 541–555.

Nichols, J. G. Quality and equality in intellectual development: The role of motivation in education. *American Psychologist,* 1979, *34,* 1071–1084.

Panell, R. C., & Laabs, G. J. Construction of a criterion-referenced, diagnostic test for an individualized instruction program. *Journal of Applied Psychology,* 1979, *64,* 255–261.

Peterson, D. *The clinical study of social behavior.* New York: Appleton-Century-Crofts, 1968.

Reinert, G. Comparative factor analytic studies of intelligence throughout the human life-span. In L. R. Goulet & P. T. Baltes (Eds.), *Life-span developmental psychology: Research and theory.* New York: Academic Press, 1970.

Sarason, I. G. (Ed.). *Test anxiety: Theory, research, and applications.* Hillsdale, N.J.: Lawrence Erlbaum Associates, 1980.

Scarr, S. *On the development of competence and the indeterminate boundaries between cognition and motivation: A genotype-environment correlation theory.* Invited address presented at the meeting of the Eastern Psychological Association, New York, April, 1981.

Spence, J. T., & Helmreich, R. L. *Masculinity and femininity: Their psychological dimensions, correlates, and antecedents.* Austin: University of Texas Press, 1978.

Spielberger, C. D. *Test Anxiety Inventory: Preliminary professional manual.* Palo Alto, Calif: Consulting Psychologists Press, 1980.

Spielberger, C. D. and associates. *Preliminary manual for the State-Trait Anger Scale* (STAS). Center for Research in Community Psychology, University of South Florida, Tampa, Florida, August 1980.

Speilberger, C. D., Gorsuch, R. L., & Lushene, R. E. *STAI manual for the State-Trait Anxiety Inventory.* Palo Alto, Calif.: Consulting Psychologists Press, 1970.

Spielberger, C. D., Vagg, P. R., Barker, L. R., Donham, G. W., & Westberry, L. G. The factor structure of the State-Trait Anxiety Inventory. In I. G. Sarason & C. D. Spielberger (Eds.), *Stress and anxiety,* (Vol. 7). New York: Hemisphere, 1980.

Talmage, H. (Ed.). *Systems of individualized education.* Berkeley, Calif.: McCutchan, 1975.

Tucker, L. R. The extension of factor analysis to three-dimensional matrices. In N. Frederiksen (Ed.), *Contributions to mathematical psychology.* New York: Holt, Rinehart & Winston, 1964.

Tucker, L. R. Some mathematical notes on three-mode factor analysis. *Psychometrika,* 1966, *31,* 279–311.

Tucker, L. R. Relations between multidimensional scaling and three-mode factor analysis. *Psychometrika,* 1972, *37,* 3–27.

Waugh, K. W., & Bush, W. J. *Diagnosing learning disorders.* Columbus, Ohio: Merrill, 1971.

Zajonc, R. B. Feeling and thinking: Preferences need no inferences. *American Psychologist,* 1980, *35,* 151–175.

Zuckerman, M., & Lubin, B. *Multiple Affect Adjective Check List.* San Diego, Calif.: Educational and Industrial Testing Service, 1960–1967.

20 How Can We Practice What We Preach?

Robert L. Thorndike
Teachers College, Columbia University

In the 30 years since Fred Lord earned his doctorate in psychology from Princeton University, we have witnessed solid progress in the elaboration of mathematical models for conceptualizing the nature of psychological tests and in the sharpening of methodologies for analyzing test data. These scholarly and theoretical advances will, I am sure, be fully developed and debated by others at this conference. Yet severe limitations have been imposed on the application of these advances to the practical task of developing tests as a result of a number of social and political developments during this same period. As my contribution to this gathering, I have elected to identify some of these limiting developments and to comment on their impact on the endeavors of the practical test developer.

I would speak first of what I have sensed in some academic quarters as a generalized hostility to all tests and testing. This hostility seems to have two broad facets: On the one hand, I see an egalitarianism that is prone to deny the existence of individual differences in potential for academic achievement and that considers tests to be pernicious and somehow "undemocratic." On the other hand, I see an escapism that tends to reject all attempts to appraise the effectiveness of schools in producing learning among their pupils as an invasion of the teacher's personal domain. There are other more specific concerns that I will consider shortly, but I believe that this general and diffuse hostility has made it more and more difficult for test developers to approach schools and obtain their cooperation in collecting the data that are crucial for the development of effective tests. This applies equally to the opportunity for pretesting items to evaluate which of them can most appropriately be included in a new test and to participation in the administration of final test forms in order to compile normative data and the other statistics needed for test interpretation.

Item pretesting in a school setting is, of course, an imposition that provides no immediate or obvious return to the cooperating school. In spite of this and the generalized hostility, among an author's or publisher's friends in the school testing community it is usually possible to find someone who will arrange for a modest amount of testing time with some type of student population. The really sticky problem arises when one tries to obtain an adequate sample of special populations—for example, ethnic minority students. Concern for test "fairness," which will be discussed in more detail later, generates pressure to try out new items in special populations to enable us to compute discrimination and, especially, difficulty indices separately for subgroups of special interest. But if the comparative statistics are to have enough precision to be of practical value in identifying "unfair" items, it is as important to have a sizeable sample from each special group as from the general population. The standard error of measurement based on a small sample from a special group will contribute disproportionately to the standard error of the difference and thus will render uninterpretable any observed between-group differences. Adequate minority and other subgroup samples are often hard to come by.

Where a test is widely used as an administrative requirement, as in a number of ETS programs, and a section of research materials can be incorporated in an operational administration, this problem of adequate subgroup sampling is relatively less acute. But for small-scale testing programs—or for those tests, for example, that are developed outside of large nationally administered admissions programs or military programs—the problem of obtaining access to the number and types of examinees needed for test development work can become quite severe.

This leads us to the problem of test norms. Of course, norms are not a problem in the case of large-scale admissions programs such as the College Board SAT where no reference is made to a population other than those individuals who take the test. Rather, a major problem in this instance is one of equating successive test forms so as to maintain a stable score scale over time. But, the publisher of tests for sale to school districts or individual users is under both economic and legislative pressure to produce norms for various special populations and at fairly frequent intervals.

Twenty-five years ago it seemed to me reasonable to undertake the design of a stratified probability sample of schools for the norming of a new test form and to anticipate that the design could be maintained to a reasonable approximation in the actual administration. The discrepancies between the design and the data collected often seemed sufficiently minor so that they could be compensated for by a modest range of differential weights applied to different cells in the design. Currently, I question whether this is still the case. The proportion of refusals, for one reason or another, among school systems approached for help in norming now tends to be so high that any probability sampling is severely vitiated and, as we have seen, certain cells in the sampling design seem particularly hard to fill.

Moreover, the school districts willing to participate in the norming of new forms of a test series tend to be disproportionately the users of that series—with whatever bias that may introduce.

It now seems that we will once again be thrown back on a "quota sample"—a sample of convenience likely to depart in numerous and often unknown ways from the population that we hope to represent. We *may* still be able to do a shrewd job of judging the ways in which the obtained sample deviates from the intended population and of adjusting for the judged differences—but there can be no guarantee that we have been successful and there is little basis for determining the precision or the bias in the adjusted distributions.

For individually administered tests, some type of quota sampling has almost always been used for normative purposes. A possible exception is the 1972 renorming of the Stanford–Binet in which group IQ test scores were used as the basis for a stratified sample. Typically, a multidimensional grid is created and applied to each appropriate group, for example, by age and sex. The dimensions of the grid frequently include geographical region, ethnicity, and two or three demographic characteristics of the parents. Test examiners for the norming are instructed to locate (according to design rules) and test a specified number of cases from each cell of the grid. Such demographic variables as parental occupation or educational level are at the heart of the matter. The accuracy with which these variables are assessed and the extent to which systematic bias is eliminated in choosing individuals for each cell of the stratified design determine the soundness of the norms.

In contrast, it has hardly seemed practical to gather dependable demographic information for the many thousand individuals needed for establishing group-administered test norms and so demographic information about schools and communities has been used instead. However, a problem exists in that much of the publicly available demographic data refers to political rather than educational units and data on schools is frequently out of date. Although it is usually possible to describe some gross demographic variables such as enrollment percentage by ethnic group, it is often difficult to check the extent to which a given school or subsample of schools is representative of the particular school system as a whole. In any event, it seems highly unlikely that either pupils or school administrators will be able or willing to provide accurate detailed demographic information about individuals in the sample to an outside testing agency.

These problems of test development and sampling are compounded by the requirement of "informed consent" on the part of the parent or examinee before a test can be given. Informed consent first became a requirement by Public Health Service funded research involving human subjects and very quickly was required for any federally funded study. The purpose was to protect participants from possible physical and psychic injury and from unreasonable invasion of privacy. Informed consent has subsequently been extended, in some school systems, so as to protect the school administration from parental backlash. The intent of the regulation was generally benign, and in some situations the need was real—though one may perhaps be permitted to question the damage that might result from participation in normative or research administrations of scholastic ability and achievement tests. However, one primary side effect of this regulation has been to introduce additional and sometimes undetermined biases into research and normative testing results. Though I must confess that I have made no careful search for them, I am not aware of any systematic studies carried out to determine the nature and extent of possible sampling bias introduced as a result of the informed consent requirement. Intuitively, one suspects that parents who believe that their child would not do well on the test exercises would be most likely to refuse permission for testing. But it is possible that refusal is based more on attitudes and temperament than on expectations of poor test performance. The point is that we just don't know what kind of biases the regulation may be generating.

Superimposed on the design and sampling concerns just addressed, a quite different set of practical and psychometric problems are introduced by pressures that test exercises be "fair" to members of all major subgroups with which a test may be used. In any event, one encounters real problems in defining what is meant by a "fair" item and one faces serious practical difficulties in obtaining the evidence of fairness called for by one's definition.

There are two quite different and perhaps supplementary approaches to the identification and elimination or avoidance of unfair items—one editorial and one statistical. The editorial approach focuses on the identification and revision or exclusion of items that would appear offensive or stereotypic to any group of examinees. As was discussed at a recent ETS conference, major test developers and publishers have prepared guidelines for item writers and test reviewers that are designed to minimize the occurrence of such content.

Such internal preventive maintenance may be augmented by the appointment of external review panels to provide a further check to eliminate possibly offensive test content or phrasing. For this function, a panel constituted of members of the various subgroups in question appears to have a type of "face validity." The problem here is to know how large a panel must be before its pooled judgment reliably represents the viewpoints sought. Another major function of an external review panel is to identify those items that are unfair from a performance point of view, that is, items on which the reference group will show an actual performance deficit relative to the majority group or other special population groups. I suspect that panel judges can usefully serve this function for occasional items, especially those in which a different language background provides a different set of meanings for English words. However, I question whether a panel either from the Federal bench or from the Association of Black Psychologists generally would have a very good batting average in identifying those test items that were particularly difficult (or particularly easy) for minority group members.

Given that one is able to reach agreement on the criteria that qualify a person for inclusion on the panel of competent item evaluators, one then faces the very real logistic problem of recruiting a panel of judges who meet the specifications. Furthermore, one faces the technical problems of specifying the form in which the panel members are to respond and the problem of combining their judgments meaningfully to arrive at a guide for action. Does one require a majority or some fraction of dissatisfied judges or does one reject every item to which any judge objects on any grounds? At least, the external panel approach will probably identify a certain number of items that are likely to be offensive to members of the groups represented by the judges, and this is not to be disparaged as an outcome. How much correspondence there is between predicted unfairness and actual deficit performance by the subgroup of concern is, I believe, largely unexplored.

Following the other major approach to identifying unfair items, statistical evidence of unfairness may be sought in actual performance data from special groups in question. In this case we face both the question of defining what constitutes unfairness and the practical problem of collecting data adequate to answer the question as we have posed it.

Few persons who work with tests would assert that the simple existence of performance differences between groups implies unfairness in a test qua test. The observation that elementary school girls tend to do better than their male counterparts on tests of reading, while the reverse holds true for tests of science knowledge is not an indictment of the two types of tests, but rather a statement of the situation that exists throughout much of the world as it is constituted today. So the cue for unfairness in an item must be sought in evidence that the particular item is peculiarly difficult (or easy) for some group, that it behaves in a significantly different way from typical items in its universe of items. Over the past decade, an assortment of indices have been proposed that are designed to estimate the degree of this peculiarity and whether it meets standards of statistical significance.

In general these are procedures for partialing out overall ability level in the function that the test is measuring and seeing whether there is a significant residual difference for the specific item. A few such "significant" differences will usually be found in any large set of items, sometimes penalizing and sometimes favoring the special group. But one is left with the uncomfortable concern as to which of the allegedly "significant" values—in each direction—are the 5% of cases that by pure chance are "significant at the .05 level."

But even if one has reached an intellectually satisfying definition of significant peculiarity for an item, one still faces the practical problem of getting the necessary data on the items of a set so that the definition can be applied. It has been my experience recently that although school people are vociferous in their demand that test exercises be tried out with minority group members, they tend to be far from enthusiastic about providing the types and sizes of samples from which estimates of bias might be dependably obtained.

A further practical issue arises when one asks which special groups should be singled out for studies to identify item bias. Is one expected to provide evidence on an adequate sample of black pupils? Of Hispanics? Of native Americans? Of orientals? Of males and females separately? Of low-, middle-, and high-socioeconomic levels? Of urban and rural children? Where is the ending?

A still different pressure has been felt in recent years from the so-called "truth-in-testing" legislation. Already in New York and California, producers of admissions tests that are used programmatically are required to file copies of the test booklets and keys and to release to any one who has taken the test that person's answer sheet together with the test items and key. Though test developers may feel that public concerns about the accuracy of a test result are somewhat paranoid, a certain number of widely publicized instances of error in an item's key or a reported score indicate that the concerns do have some basis in reality. Test developers *do* occasionally miskey an item and, though a single item may have a very minor effect upon an individual's standing on the test, such an event can have disastrous impact on the test's reputation. More seriously for the individual, machine scoring and computerized record keeping are not infallible and gross errors may occasionally occur—as they did in the past when tests were scored and recorded by hand. So there is a real case to be made for letting the examinee or parent check the test key or the scoring of the answer sheet—both as an evidence of good will and to permit catching the rare gross error. But, whatever gains are generated by this procedure are achieved only at considerable cost. The cost is partly monetary, but perhaps more seriously, in the quality of the instrument that is produced.

The primary impact of "truth-in-testing" legislation is on "secure" tests that are not available for general distribution and use. The major implication of the release of test questions, scoring keys, and answer sheets to examinees—aside from the clerical expense involved in doing so—is that test forms can be used only once and new test forms must continuously be developed. This is not as great a problem in very large volume admissions testing programs like the College Board SATs that have historically used a given form only for a limited number of administrations over a specified number of years in any case. Where hundreds of thousands are tested, the very considerable cost of preparing a new form can be spread over so many examinees that the added test development cost per examinee is bearable. But there have been a number of smaller and more specialized admissions testing programs for which this has not been the case. For these programs, if test exercises are to be pretested with samples of adequate size and diversity, the burden of preparing new forms may become overpowering. Then, either the cost per examinee must become prohibitive or the quality of the product must be down graded—by reduction in item review, item tryout, and other refining procedures that have been developed over the years to guarantee quality in a testing instrument.

Perhaps the solution to the truth-in-testing problem lies in computerized testing with a very large item bank and selection for each examinee of a tailored set of items from the pool. The prospect of item banking and computerized adaptive tailored testing becomes feasible given a means of characterizing items as with the IRT parameters generated by Fred Lord's work. One wonders how legislators and legal beagles would respond to a situation in which no two examinees took the same test!

I have spoken thus far of tests that are being developed in testing agencies where there is some sophistication about the process of test development and an attempt to carry through a reasonably complete sequence of blue printing, item writing, item review and editing, administration and analysis of preliminary sets of items, selection of items for inclusion in the light of the pretest results, and norming and analysis of the resulting test. It is important to realize that for much testing upon which selection or licensing decisions are made this still does not happen. Test exercises may be written by persons whose competence lies primarily in some substantive field and who have had little or no training or experience in item-writing skills. Substantive and/or editorial review may be limited. Time pressures and requirements of test security may preclude pretesting of items before they are included in the test. And setting of standards of acceptable performance may be arbitrary and possibly capricious. There are many persons making tests today for whom the developments of the past 30 years—nay, the past 50 years—are unknown or unheeded. We must work to bring these testing agencies up to our best standards while at the same time we battle to keep social pressures from degrading our own products.

Author Index

Numbers in *italics* indicate pages with bibliographic information.

A

ACER Intermediate Test D, 98, *100*
Agunwamba, C. C., 239, 241, *252*
Ahlawat, K. S., 201, *213*, 258, 280, *281*
Aitkin, M., 112, *114*, 121, 123, *138*, 147, *157*
Allen, A., 351, *354*
Allport, G. W., 352, *353*
Anastasi, A., 346, 353, *353*, *354*
Anastasio, E. J., 6, *24*, 42, *50*
Andersen, E. B., 113, *114*, 118, 120, 122, 123, 124, 125, 126, *137*, 146, 147, 150, *157*
Anderson, J. E., 82, *101*
Anderson, S. B., 4, *24*, 42, *49*
Anderson, T. W., 118, *137*, 207, *212*, 247, *252*
Appelbaum, M. I., 42, 47, *49*, 81, 100, *101*
Ashby, G. F., 303, 309, *327*
Atkinson, J. W., 350, 353, *354*

B

Bailey, J. P., Jr., 258, *281*
Baker, F. B., 118, *137*

Ball, S., 4, *24*
Ballif, B. L., 351, *355*
Baltes, P. B., 81, 84, 91, *101*, 103, *115*
Bandura, A., 346, *354*
Barker, L. R., 349, 350, *356*
Barlow, R. E., 304, *326*
Bayley, N., 81, *101*
Beatty, J., 251, *253*
Begun, J., 57, *65*
Bem, D. J., 351, *354*
Bem, S. L., 352, *354*
Bentler, P. M., 117, *137*, 238, 239, 240, 241, 242, 243, 244, 245, 246, 247, 248, 249, 251, *252*, *253*
Berk, R. A., 28, 37, *39*
Bickel, P. I., 42, *49*
Binet, A., 69, *80*
Birch, D., 353, *354*
Birnbaum, A., 69, 71, *80*, 118, 121, *137*, 160, *181*
Bloom, B. S., 353, *354*
Bloxom, B., 310, 311, *327*
Blumenthal, S., 126, *138*
Blyth, C. R., 42, *50*
Bock, R. D., 69, 71, *80*, 104, 105, 106, 108, 111, 112, *114*, *115*, 121, 122, 123, *137*, *138*, 147, *157*, 160, *181*, 216, *234*

AUTHOR INDEX

Boneva, L., 325, 326, *327*
Bowers, K., 351, *354*
Box, G. E., 48, *50*
Bradford, L. J., 346, *355*
Breland, H. M., 33, 36, 37, *39*
Brennan, R. L., 290, *300*
Brillinger, D. R., 114, *115*
Brown, L., 120, *138*
Browne, M. W., 190, *196*, 238, 247, 248, 251, *252*, *253*
Burbeck, S. L., 309, 310, 318, 319, *327*
Burdick, D. S., 47, *50*
Burr, E. J., 203, *213*
Burt, C., 258, *281*
Bush, W. J., 346, *356*

C

Cain, G. C., 39, *39*, 42, 46, *50*
Callender, J. C., 239, *252*
Campbell, D. T., 46, *50*
Carlson, J. E., 47, *50*
Carroll, J. B., 215, *234*, 258, 259, 262, 266, 267, 278, 280, *281*, 289, *299*, 353, *354*
Cartwright, B., 47, *53*
Cattell, R. B., 239, *252*, 258, *281*, 350, *354*
Changas, P. S., 179, *182*
Chen, J. J., 48, *52*
Christoffersson, A., 216, *234*, 235
Chung, Kai-Lai, 42, *50*
Clark, C., 241, *252*
Cliff, N., 287, 290, 291, 293, 295, *299*
Cochran, W. G., 42, *50*, *52*
Cook, L. L., 118, *138*
Cohen, J., 42, 47, *50*, *52*
Cohen, M. R., 42, *50*
Cole, N. S., 48, *52*
Comrey, A. L., 249, *252*, 258, *281*
Cook, T. D., 46, *50*
Cooley, T. F., 28, 37, *39*
Coombs, C. H., 287, *299*
Cramer, E. M., 42, 47, *49*, *51*
Cronbach, L. J., 33, 35, *39*
Curran, J. P., 350, *354*

D

Davis, M. A., 348, *355*
Dawes, R., 289, *299*
Day, N. E., 113, *115*
de Boor, C., 308, *327*

De Finetti, B., 46, *50*
Della Riccia, G., 242, 243, *252*
Dempster, A. P., 105, 108, *115*, 147, *157*
Denny, J. L., 120, *138*
De Soto, C. B., 351, *355*
Dijkstra, T. K., 248, *252*
Dingman, H. F., 215, *234*
Donham, G. W., 349, 350, *356*
Drasgow, F., 294, *299*
Droppleman, L. F., 350, *355*
Drösler, J., 88, *101*
Ducamp, A., 296, *300*
D'Zurilla, T. J., 347, *355*

E

Eels, K., 250, *253*
Eignor, D. R., 118, *138*
Elashoff, J. D., 42, 46, *50*
Elderton, W. P., 168, 174, *181*
Elston, R. C., 105, *115*
Endler, N. S., 347, 351, *354*
Engen, T., 260, *281*
Epstein, S., 351, 352, *354*
Erlebacher, A., 46, *50*
Etezadi-Amoli, J., 197, 208, 212, *212*
Evans, F. R., 28, *39*
Evans, S. H., 6, *24*, 42, *50*

F

Falmagne, J. C., 296, *300*
Fearn, T., 105, *115*
Feller, W., 140, *157*
Fellner, H., 141, *157*
Ferguson, G. A., 215, *234*, 353, *354*
Festinger, L., 286, *300*
Fischer, G. H., 69, *80*, 124, 125, *138*
Fisher, R. A., 46, *50*
Fleiss, J. L., 42, *50*
Frederiksen, N., 347, *354*
Funder, D. C., 351, *354*

G

Gabriel, R., 57, *65*
Gaebelein, J., 47, *50*
Games, P. A., 4, *24*, 42, *50*
Gandet, H., 42, 46, *51*
Gardner, M., 42, 47, *50*
Gaskins, R. A., 322, *327*

Gaylord, R. H., 215, *235*
Geiselman, R. E., 251, *253*
Gibbons, R. D., 112, *115*
Gilford, J. A., 118, *138*
Glaser, R., 345, *354*
Gocka, E. F., 47, *50*
Goldberger, A. S., 28, *39*, 42, *50*
Goldfried, M. R., 346, 347, *354*, *355*
Good, I. J., 322, *327*
Goodenough, W. H., 286, *300*
Goodman, L., 118, 138, 286, 290, 293, *300*
Gorsuch, R. L., 258, *281*, 349, *356*
Gottlieb, M. I., 346, *355*
Gourlay, N., 215, *234*, 258, 259, *281*
Green, B. F., 71, *80*, 226, *234*, 286, *300*, 352, *355*
Green, D. M., 309, 310, *327*
Grizzle, J. E., 105, *115*
Guertin, W. H., 258, *281*
Guilford, J. P., 215, *234*, 257, 258, 259, 268, 269, 278, *281*
Guttman, L., 82, *101*, 204, *212*, 215, 222, *234*, 239, 243, 252, 260, *281*, 286, 288, *300*

H

Haberman, S. J., 118, *138*, 147, *157*
Hägglund, G., 185, 187, 188, 189, 193, *196*
Hakstian, A. R., 239, *252*
Hambleton, R. K., 118, *138*
Hamer, R. M., 48, *52*
Hammel, E. A., 42, *49*
Hand, D. J., 42, *50*
Harman, H. H., 258, *281*
Harnisch, D. L., 287, 290, 294, *300*
Harter, H. L., 64, *65*
Harville, D. A., 105, 108, *115*
Hayes, K. J., 353, *355*
Heckman, J. J., 28, 39, *39*, 42, *50*
Helmreich, R. L., 352, *356*
Henley, N. M., 335, 337, *341*
Henry, N. W., 118, *138*
Herr, D. G., 47, *50*
Hettena, C. M., 351, *355*
Hindley, C. B., 81, 100, *101*
Hirshfeld, S. F., 345, *355*
Hocking, R. R., 47, *52*
Hogan, R., 351, *355*
Hogarty, P. S., 81, 100, *101*
Holland, P. W., 4, 8, *24*

Holmes, R. L., 316, *327*
Holzinger, K., 193, *196*
Horst, P., 292, 293, *300*
Humphreys, L. G., 82, *101*, 353, *355*
Hunt, J. McV., 347, *354*
Hutchings, C. H., 348, *355*

I

IMSLIB, 147, *157*

J

Jackson, D. N., 346, *355*
Jackson, J., 286, 295, *300*
Jackson, P. H., 48, *50*, *52*, 239, 241, 244, 252, *253*
James, W., 105, *115*
Jennrich, R. I., 185, *196*
Jensen, A. R., 82, *101*, 258, *281*
Joe, G. W., 47, *50*
John, E., 258, *281*
Johnson, N. L., 140, *157*, 168, 174, *181*
Jones, L. V., 42, *51*
Jöreskog, K. G., 28, 29, 30, 32, 39, *40*, 82, *101*, 117, *138*, 185, 186, 187, 188, 189, 190, 191, *196*, 238, 252

K

Kalbfleisch, J. D., 114, *115*
Kalton, G., 42, *51*
Kane, M. T., 290, *300*
Keats, J. A., 91, 97, 98, *101*
Kelley, T. L., 106, *115*
Kelly, G. A., 352, *355*
Kendall, D., 325, 326, *327*
Kendall, M. G., 165, *181*, 247, *252*
Kendall, P. L., 42, *51*
Kent, R. N., 346, *355*
Keren, G., 47, *51*
Kestelman, H., 204, *212*
Khan, S. B., 353, *355*
Kim, J-O., 258, *281*
Kjerulff, K., 347, *355*
Klebelsberg, D., 152, *157*
Knol, D. L., 248, *253*
Kohfeld, D. L., 309, 310, 322, *327*
Kotz, S., 140, *157*
Kristof, W., 238, *252*
Kronmal, R. A., 325, *327*

Kruskal, W. B., 290, 293, *300*
Kuder, G. F., 292, *300*
Kuhn, H. W., 245, *252*
Kurata, M., 287, 291, 294, 295, *300*

L

Laabs, G. J., 345, *356*
Laird, N. M., 108, *115*, 147, *157*
Landfield, A. W., 352, *355*
Lawley, D. N., 118, *138*, 185, 193, *196*, 216, *235*
Lazersfeld, P. F., 42, 46, *51*, 118, *138*
Ledermann, W., 242, *252*
Leitner, L. M., 352, *355*
Lens, W., 353, *354*
Lerner, J. W., 346, *355*
Levin, J., 347, *355*
Levine, M., 161, *181*, 294, *299*
Lewis, C., 47, 48, *51*, *52*, 238, 239, *253*
Lewis, D., 269, *281*
Libby, D. L., 48, *52*
Lieberman, M., 69, *80*, 108, *115*, 123, *138*, 216, *234*
Lii, K. S., 308, 312, 325, 326, *327*
Lindley, D. V., 4, *24*, 42, 45, 46, 48, *51*, 105, *115*
Lingoes, J. C., 287, *300*
Linn, R. L., 33, 37, *39*, *40*, 42, *51*, 287, 290, 294, *300*
Livingston, P. S., 168, 174, *182*
Loevinger, J. A., 285, 286, 291, *300*
Lord, F. M., 3, 4, 9, 11, 13, 14, 15, 17, *24*, 27, 33, *40*, 42, 45, 46, 47, *51*, 69, 71, *80*, 81, *101*, 118, 121, *138*, 139, 155, *158*, 160, 161, *181*, 185, *196*, 201, 212, 216, *235*, 238, 247, 249, *253*, 259, 262, *281*, 283, *300*, 303, 309, *327*
Lorr, M., 350, *355*
Lubin, B., 350, *355*, *356*
Luce, R. D., 309, *327*
Lushene, R. E., 349, *356*

M

Madansky, A., 118, *138*, 185, 186, *196*
Madsen, M., 113, *114*, 126, *137*
Magnusson, D., 351, *354*
Maier, M. H., 345, *355*
Marx, M. H., 82, 89, *101*
Masters, G. N., 125, *138*

Maxwell, A. E., 193, *196*
Maxwell, S. E., 42, *51*
Mc Call, R. B., 81, 100, *101*
Mc Cormick, G. P., 316, *327*
Mc Donald, R. P., 197, 198, 199, 201, 202, 203, 205, 206, 208, 209, 210, 211, 212, *212*, *213*, 258, 280, *281*
Mc Gill, W. J., 140, *158*, 304, *327*
Mc Nair, D., 350, *355*
Mc Reynolds, P., 348, *355*
Meehl, P. E., 42, 46, 47, *51*
Meeker, M., 250, *253*
Melzack, R., 338, *341*
Miller, R. G., 55, 56, *65*
Mischel, W., 346, 351, 352, *355*
Mislevy, R. J., 71, *80*, 112, 113, *115*
Mokken, R. J., 291, 293, *300*
Morris, L. W., 348, *355*
Moses, L. E., 42, *51*
Mosier, C. I., 259, *281*
Mueller, C. W., 258, *281*
Muirhead, R. J., 248, *253*
Mulaik, S. A., 258, *281*
Murphy, R. T., 4, *24*
Muthen, B., 28, 29, 30, 32, 39, *40*, 216, *235*
Mylander, W. C., 316, *327*

N

Nagel, E., 42, *50*,
Nesselroade, J. R., 81, 84, 91, *101*, 103, *115*
Nichols, J. G., 353, *356*
Novick, M. R., 4, *24*, 27, *40*, 42, 43, 45, 46, 47, 48, *50*, *51*, *52*, 81, *101*, 118, *138*, 160, 161, *181*, 238, 239, 249, *253*, 303, 309, *327*

O

O'Connell, J. W., 42, *49*
O'Fallon, W. M., 47, *50*
Olsen, R., 28, *40*
O'Malley, P. M., 353, *354*
O'Neill, B. V., 47, *50*
Osburn, H. G., 239, *252*
Overall, J. E., 47, *52*
Owen, C. F., 81, 100, *101*

P

Panell, R. C., 345, *356*
Parzen, E., 324, *327*

Paunonen, S. V., 346, *355*
Peake, P. K., 352, *355*
Pearson, K., 27, *40*
Perdsom, B., 42, 46, *51*
Peritz, E., 57, *65*
Petersen, N. S., 47, *52*
Peterson, D., 346, *356*
Piaget, J., 82, 86, *101*
Powers, D. E., 37, 38, *40*
Powers, W. T., 83, 85, *101*
Pratt, J. W., 108, *115*
Preisler, H. K., 114, *115*
Proctor, C. H., 287, *300*
Proschan, F., 304, *326*

R

Ramsay, J. O., 311, *328*
Ramsey, P. H., 57, 60, 61, 63, *65*
Rao, C. R., 94, *101*, 126, *138*, 189, 190, *196*
Rasch, G., 69, *80*, 118, 122, 127, *138*, 141, 147, *158*, 160, *181*
Rawlings, R. R., Jr., 47, *52*
Ray, S. C., 28, 37, *39*
Reilly, R. R., 33, *40*, 42, *52*
Reinert, G., 353, *356*
Reventlow, I., 141, *158*
Reynolds, C. R., 33, *40*
Reynolds, T. J., 295, *299*
Rice, J., 305, 310, *327*
Richardson, M. W., 292, *300*
Robbins, H., 113, *115*
Robinson, S. M., 185, *196*
Rogers, W. T., 239, *252*
Rosen, A., 42, 46, 47, *51*
Rosenbaum, P. R., 23, *24*
Rosenberg, B., 105, *115*
Rosenblatt, M., 305, 308, 310, 312, 323, 325, 326, *327*
Rubin, D. B., 4, 6, 8, 22, 23, *24*, *25*, 42, *52*, 105, 108, *115*, 147, *157*
Rubin, J., 207, *212*
Rummel, R. J., 258, *281*
Ryan, T. A., 56, *65*

S

Saetveit, J. G., 269, *281*
Saltz, E., 286, *301*
Samejima, F., 69, *80*, 160, 161, 162, 164, 165, 168, 169, 170, 171, 172, 173, 174, 175, 177, 179, *181*, *182*
Sanathanan, L., 126, *138*
Santee, J. L., 309, 310, 322, *327*
Sarason, I. G., 348, *356*
Satalich, T. A., 332, *341*
Sato, T., 285, 287, 290, 291, 294, 295, *300*
Scarr, S., 353, *356*
Schaeffer, G. A., 33, 35, *39*
Scheiblechner, H., 139, 142, 145, 146, 155, *158*
Schuhfried, G., 152, *158*
Schumaker, L. L., 308, *327*
Seashore, C. E., 258, 259, 268, 269, *281*
Shapiro, A., 242, 243, 246, 247, 248, *253*
Shapiro, L., 242, 243, *252*
Sheldon, W. H., 340, *341*
Silverman, B. W., 324, *327*
Simon, H. A., 42, *52*
Simpson, E. H., 42, 43, *52*
Skeels, H. M., 97, 100, *101*
Skodak, M., 97, 100, *101*
Smith, A. F. M., 48, *51*, 105, *115*
Smith, I. L., 47, *52*
Snedecor, G. W., 42, *52*
Snijders, T. A. B., 242, 243, 244, 246, *253*
Solano, C., 351, *355*
Solmon, L. C., 42, *52*
Somers, R. H., 289, *301*
Sörbom, D., 117, *138*, 190, *196*, 238, *252*
Speed, F. M., 47, *52*
Spence, J. T., 352, *356*
Spiegel, D. K., 47, *52*
Spielberger, C. D., 348, 349, 350, *356*
Stanley, J. C., 46, *50*
Stefanov, I., 325, 326, *327*
Stein, C., 105, *115*
Sternberg, S., 303, 309, *327*
Stevens, S. S., 90, *101*, 340, *341*
Stone, M. H., 125, *138*
Stuart, A., 165, *181*, 247, *252*
Swaminathan, H., 118, *138*
Swinford, F., 193, *196*

T

Talmage, H., 345, *356*
Tapia, R. A., 304, 313, 322, 324, 326, *327*
Tarter, M. E., 325, *327*
Tatsuoka, K., 287, 290, *301*, 303, *327*
Tatsuoka, M., 287, 290, *301*, 303, *327*

ten Berge, J. M. F., 242, 243, 244, 246, *253*
Thayer, D. T., 48, *50, 52*
Thissen, D., 111, *115*
Thompson, J. R., 304, 313, 322, 324, 326, *327*
Thurstone, L. L., 90, 93, 99, *101*
Tiao, G., 48, *50*
Timm, N. H., 47, *50*
Tjur, T., 126, *138*
Torgerson, W. S., 331, 332, 338, *341*
Townsend, J. T., 303, 309, *327*
Tsutakawa, R. K., 105, 108, *115*
Tucker, A. W., 245, *252*
Tucker, L. R, 160, *182,* 216, 220, *235,* 346, 347, *356*

U

Urry, V. W., 69, *80*

V

Vagg, P. R., 349, 350, *356*
Van der Flier, H., 290, *301*
von Békésy, G., 260, *281*

W

Wagner, C. H., 42, *52*
Wahba, G., 325, 326, *327, 328*
Walker, D. A., 260, *281*
Wallace, N. D., 309, 310, 322, *327*
Walters, R. H., 346, *354*
Wang, M., 48, *51*
Warner, W. L., 250, *253*
Waugh, K. W., 346, *356*

Wechsler, D., 251, *253*
Weeks, D. G., 117, *137*
Weinreich, M., 135, *138*
Weiss, D. J., 69, *80,* 259, *282*
Welsch, R. E., 56, *65*
Werts, C. E., 33, *40,* 42, *51*
Westberry, L. G., 349, 350, *356*
Wherry, R. J., 215, *235*
White, B. W., 286, *301*
Wickelgren, W. A., 83, 89, 90, *101*
Wiggins, N. H., 347, *355*
Wiley, D. E., 42, *52*
Willingham, W. W., 42, *53*
Winkler, W., 152, *158*
Winsberg, S., 311, *328*
Wold, H., 42, *53*
Wolf, G., 47, *53*
Wolins, L., 42, *53*
Woodhouse, B., 244, *253*
Woodward, J. A., 239, 241, 242, 243, 244, 245, 246, 247, 248, 249, 251, *252, 253*
Woodworth, G. E., 48, *53*
Wottawa, H., 141, *158*
Wright, B. D., 69, *80,* 125, *138*
Wu, C., 108, *115*

XYZ

Yule, G. U., 42, *53*
Zajonc, R. B., 351, *356*
Zegers, F. E., 242, 243, 244, 246, 248, *253*
Zeisel, H., 42, 46, *53*
Zellner, A., 106, *115*
Zinkus, P. W., 346, *355*
Zuckerman, M., 350, *356*
Zuschlag, B., 152, *158*

Subject Index

A

Ability distribution, 288
Ability measures, 81
Activity stream, motivational theory, 350–351
Adaptive flexibility, 352
Adaptive testing, 69
Additive concatenation, parameters, 142–144, 155–157
Adverse impact, 43
Affect
 cognitive development, 353
 cognitive performance, 351, 353
All-pairs power, 61
Analysis of covariance, 3, 4, 14, 18, 23, 24
Androgyny, psychological, 352
Any-pair power, 61
Anxiety measures, 348, 349–350
Armed Services Vocational Aptitude Battery (ASVAB), 69, 71
Assumptions, 19
 testable, 19
 untestable, 19
Asymptotic standard errors, 191
Average causal effect, 22

B

Basic function, 166
Basic parameters, 142, 153–154
Bayesian approach, 114
 interpretation, 313
 method, 104
Best monotone transform subroutine, 332
Bias, 321
Bias studies, 33
Binary data, 216–225, 232, 280, 299
Binary fit function, 222–225
Bivariate P.D.F. approach, 176–177
Bock's multinomial model, 160, 162

C

Categorical data, 117
Causal effect, 8, 19
Causal inference, 3, 4, 11, 19
Causal statements, 18
Caution index, 290, 294
Chance consistency, 287
Characteristic functions, 310
Chi-square, 211
Cholesky decomposition, 110
Clark algorithm, 112
Classification methodology, 340
Classification structures, 340
Cluster analysis, 329, 330
Clustering procedure, 340
Cognitive development, 81, 82, 88, 98
 model, 86

SUBJECT INDEX

Cognitive growth, 81, 82, 94, 100
  curve, 84, 89
  ideographic approach, 82
  negative exponential representation, 90
  nomothetic approach, 82
Cognitive meaning, 338
College Board SAT, 358, 362
Common factor, 220, 226, 227, 229, 232
  loadings, 206
  model, 225, 227
  scores, 220, 222
Common factor analysis
  non-parametric, 212
Completely randomized experiment, 19
Computer simulation activity stream, 350, 351
Computer terminals, 70
Computerized adaptive testing (CAT), 69, 71, 77, 79
Computerized testing, 363
Concomitant variable, 5, 7
Conditional maximum likelihood (CML) estimation, 123, 126, 135, 142, 145, 147–148, 150
Conditional moment, 170
Conditional P.D.F. approach, 177
  proportioned sum procedure, 177, 178
  simple sum procedure, 177, 178
  weighted sum procedure, 177
Conditional probability, 46
Conditional suppression, 100
Confidence intervals, 55
Confident inequalities, 55
Confirmatory analysis, 197
Confirmatory methods, 206–212
Conjugate direction method, 208
Consumer complaint behavior, 135
Contingency table, 117
Control group mean, 8, 20
Controlled causal studies, 7
Controlled randomization, 5
Convolution, decision time, 309
  unobserved component, 314
Correlations, different difficulties, 257–280
Covariance adjusted difference, 12
Covariance structures, 198–201, 203, 211
Covariates, 7, 21, 22
Cumulative normal distribution function, 201
  model, 210
Curvilinear manifold, 204

D

Day's method, 113
Decay factor, 83
Demographic variables, 43, 359
Density estimates, 317–325
  kernel, 324
  orthogonal series, 325
Depression-rating data, 129
Derived score, 95
Descriptive inference, 19
Descriptive studies, 7, 23
Design matrix, 142
Development of ability, 85
Deviation I.Q., 81, 99
Dichotomous data, 285, 294
Dichotomous response level, 160, 166, 173
  normal ogive model, 166
Difficulty factors, 201, 212, 225
Difficulty influences, correlations and factor analysis, 257–280
Dimensional analysis, 89
Dimensional balance, 89
Dimensionless constant, 85, 89
Discrete item response
  bivariate P.D.F. approach, 176, 177
  conditional P.D.F. approach, 177–180
  latent trait, 173, 174
  normal approximation method, 169–173
  operating characteristic, 169–173
Discrete response level, 160
Distal stimulus, 85
Distribution
  estimate, 303
  gamma, 304
  hazard function, 304
  moments, 203–205
  non-parametric density, 306
  response time, 303
  rotation, 205
  truncated normal, 304
Dominance relation, 287, 296
Ducamp-Falmagne consistency, 296
Dynamic consistency principle, 83, 89–94

E

Educative models, 329
  cluster analysis, 329
  factor analysis, 329
  multidimensional scaling, 329

Elementary symmetric function, 124
EM algorithm, 108
Empirical Bayesian methods, 48, 113
Environment equation, 85
Equidistant weights, 131
Errors-in-variables model, 187
Estimated operating characteristic, 169, 170
Euclidean representation, data, 330
   three-dimensional solution, 335
Exchangeable prior distributions, 48
Exchangeability, 46
Expected A Posteriori (EAP) estimator, 107, 111
Experimental manipulation, 5
Exploratory methods, 203–206
   devices, 197, 211
Exploratory nonlinear common-factor analysis, 203–205
Exponential family type distribution, 120
Exponential growth curve, 84, 90
   negative, 89, 94
Exponential latency model, 139–147
Exponential power distribution, 48

F

Factor analysis, 185, 216, 257–280, 329, 330, 341
   animal behavior, 346–347
   minimum trace, 242
   model, 186, 216, 220
   multimode, 347
   nonlinear, 197
Factor score, 22, 225–227
   distribution, 212
   loadings, 225, 229
   uniqueness, 226
Fairness, 360
Fisher model, 48
Fourier transforms, 310

G

Gain score, 11
Gamma distribution, 304, 314
Gauss-Hermite quadratures, 110
Gauss-Newton procedure, 317
General nonlinear common factor model, 198, 202, 206
Goodman-Krushal coefficient, 290, 293
Goodness of fit, 124

Graded response level, 160
   heterogeneous, 160, 161
   homogeneous, 160
   logistic model, 162
   normal ogive model, 162, 171
Greatest lower bound to reliability, 237, 239
   algorithm, 245
   coefficient, 248
   variance of coefficient, 247
Group curves, 89, 91, 94, 96
Guessing, 257
Guttman scales, 202, 216, 227, 283–301
   consistency, 293
   evaluation of consistency, 286
   original index, 286
   reproducibility, 286
Guttman's principal components of scalability, 215, 216

H

Harmonic analysis, 201, 203
Hazard functions, 319
   estimates, 319
Henley animal names, 335
Hermite-Tchebycheff orthonormal polynomial series, 201, 202
Heteroscedastic variances, 210
Homogeneity of test, 280
Homoscedastic, 199, 207
Hyperbolic formulation, 89
Hyperbolic growth curve, 88, 91, 95–97
Hyperbolic relationship, 84
Hypercylindrical spacial model (HYPCYL), 332, 336
   analysis, 338
Hyperspherical geometry, 330
   case, 332
Hypothetical construct, 159

I

Ideal type model, 329–340
   quantitative nature, 339
Independent variable, 6
Indeterminate components, 204
Indices
   consistency, 292
   homogeneity, 291
   inter-item agreement, 292
   KR-18, 293, 299

Indices (*continued*)
KR-20, 292, 299
parallel form, 292–294, 299
Individual differences, 82, 83, 94, 99, 100, 104, 329, 357
Individualized testing, 69
Inequality constraints, 311
Information functions, 161–165
Informed consent requirement, 359, 360
Instrumental variables estimator, 188
Intelligence tests, 69
Inverse principal components analysis, 334
IRT parameters, 363
Item banks, 363
Item bias, 362
Item characteristic curve, 283
Item characteristic function, 160, 173, 180, 210
  approach, 216
  estimated, 179
  logistic, 220
Item information functions, 72
Item parameters, 173
  bias, 147, 150
  consistency, 147
  difficulty, 172
  discrimination, 172
  normalization, 147, 150, 154
Item pretest, 358
Item response category, 170
Item response curve, 71
  (see also, item characteristic curve)
Item response information
  function, 162, 163
  square root, 164, 165
Item response theory (IRT), 69, 74, 159, 201, 210, 212, 283, 299
Item review, 362
Item scores, 199
Interactional assessment, 348

J,K

Joint maximum likelihood estimation, 145–147, 150
Kelley estimator, 107
Kendall's tau, 287, 299
  coefficient, 287
  Somer version, 289
Kernel estimate, 324
Kurtosis, 227
KYST scaling program, 330

L

Laplace series transforms, 310
Latent ability, 100
Latent growth curve, 84, 88, 89, 100
Latent space, 160
Latent structure model, 118
Latent trait, 81, 88, 179, 197–211, 216
  (see also, item response theory)
  conditional moments, 173–175
  distributions, 174, 260–262
  joint distributions, 267, 268
  maximum likelihood estimate, 169
  theory, 69, 159, 160
Lazarsfeld latent distance model, 202
Likelihood equation, 162
Likelihood function, 162
Likelihood ratio criterion, 207
Linear common factor model, 199, 209, 211, 212
Linear exponential model (LEM), 142, 153
Linear factor analysis, 211, 212
Linear latent variable model, 237
Linear regression, 31
  random, 108
Local independence principle, 161, 198, 206
Log likelihood, 217, 225, 227, 229, 313
Logistic model, 160, 162, 201
  functions, 210, 212, 260
Logistic transformation, 71
Longitudinal data, 81, 82, 108
  ability measures, 81
  simplex structure, 82
  trend analysis, 81
Longitudinal designs, 103
Longitudinal research, 103
Loop gain, 85, 86
Lord's paradox, 13, 17
Loss function, 210
  maximum determinant, 210
  MINRES, 207
  ordinary least squares, 206

M

Manifest data, 285
Marginal maximum likelihood (MML), 108, 112, 113, 147, 190
Maximum A Posteriori (MAP) estimator, 107, 111
Maximum likelihood estimate, 165–181, 203, 207

SUBJECT INDEX 375

asymptotic property, 165
conditional distribution, 165, 166
latent trait, 169, 173–175
Maximum likelihood solution, 225
   criterion, 222
Maximum penalized likelihood, 314
Maximum subrange procedure, 55–65
McNemar's test, 112
Mean integrated squared error, 323
Mean square error, 321
Measurement of change, 103
Measurement of difference, 82
Mental age, 90, 93, 96, 99
Method of moments, 168, 176
Microcomputers, 70
Micro-processor testing system, 152
Model components, 200, 203, 204
Model scores, 220, 227
Model-testing procedure (M-T), 57
Monotone regression, 311
   function, 212
Monte Carlo method, 165, 170
   integration, 112
Multidimensional category rating, 338
Multidimensional scaling, 329, 330, 341
Multinomial response model, 160
Multiple-choice test item, 160
   models, 161
Multiple-factor linear model, 201
Multivariate analogue of reliability, 106
Multivariate categorical data, 117
Multivariate central limit theorem, 204
Multivariate normality, 212

N

Natural language, 18
N.C.I. index, 290
Negative exponential, 87–89
   distribution, 140
   form, 94
Negative feedback system, 86, 88
Newman-Keuls procedure, 56
Newton method, 146
Newton-Raphson procedure, 126
   algorithm, 146
Nominal response level, 160
Nonlinear models, 205, 208, 210, 212
   common factor, 210, 211, 212
Nonlinear multivariate regression equation, 198
Nonlinear structures, 205

Nonorthogonal experimental designs, 47
Non-parametric density estimation, 306
Nontailored data, 288
Normal approach method, 175
Normal approximation method, 169–173
   bivariate P.D.F. approach, 175
Normal ogive model, 160, 162, 166, 171, 173, 201, 202, 210, 212
Normalization, 142

O

Observed binary response, 287
Operating characteristic
   density, 160
   discrete item response, 164
   information function, 163
   item response, 163
   normal ogive model, 171
   response pattern, 163
Orderly partitions, 59
Orthogonal series, density estimator, 325
Orthogonal simple structure, 338
Orthonormal component, 203, 211
Orthonormal functions, 204
Orthonormal polynomials, 204, 205
   fourth moment, 205
Outcome variable, 5, 6

P

Pairwise multiple comparisons, 55, 57
Panel designs, 103
Parallel form indices, 292, 299
Parallel regressions, 22
Parameter estimation, 141, 145–147
Parameters, individual differences, 90
Partially confirmatory mode, 336
Pearson correlation, 287, 292
Pearson type distribution, 174
   criterion, 174
   distribution, 174
   system method, 174
Penalized log likelihood, 313
Penalty functions, 313
Peritz procedure, 57
Person-by-item matrix, 287
Person characteristic function, 260
Personality theory, 340
Personality traits versus cognitive traits, 346
Phi coefficients of correlation, 215, 216, 225
Piaget conservations, 86

Pitch discrimination ability, 268
Point-biserial correlation, 290, 294
Polychotomous model, 121
Polynomial models, 197, 203
  pairwise interactions, 208, 212
  regression, 206
  series, 202, 205
Pooled judgment, 360
Potthoff-Roy procedure, 104
Power test, 70
Predictive bias, 33
  overprediction, 33
Predictive validity, 27
Prescribed polynomials, 205, 212
Prior distributions, 49
PROTEAN program, 205
Proximal stimulus, 85, 87

Q

Quadratic spline, 306, 325
Quality index, 290
Quantal hypothesis, 260
Quartimax method, 205
Quota sample, 359

R

Random error, 335
Random guessing principle, 160
Randomization, 19, 20, 22, 43
Rasch model, 113, 117, 123–125, 160
Ratio I.Q., 95, 96, 97, 99
Reading age, 95, 99
Reading speed, 141
Regression coefficients, 199
Regression equations, 35
Regression functions, 199, 200, 206, 210
Relevant subpopulation, 46
Reliability
  coefficients, 237
  composite, 237, 238
Reproducibility index, 286, 287
Residual covariance, 207
  matrix, 198, 211
Response pattern, 161
  information function, 162
  operating characteristic, 161
Response time, 139–157
Robust model distributions, 49
Robustness, 179
Role of mathematics, 18

S

Sample analogues, 205
Sample covariance matrix, 199
Sample free, 145
Sample surveys, 103
Sampling, 359
  bias, 360
Scalefreeness, 188
Scalogram analysis, 288
Scedastic variance, 262–265
Seashore Sense of Pitch Test, 268–280
"Secure" tests, 362
Selectable population, 29
Selected samples, 27
Selection bias, 38
Selection effects, 27
Selection process, 37–39
Sheldon-Stevens somatotypes, 340
Significant difference, items, 361
Simplex matrix, 280
Simplex model, 88
Simpson's paradox, 43
Simulation, 147–151
Simulation study, 314
Simultaneous inference, 55
Single-factor cubic model, 201
Situational categories, individual differences, 352
Situational specificity, 345, 346
  assessment procedures, 347
  individual differences, 352
  personality traits, 346
Situational variance versus individual variance, 351–352
Skewness, 227
Smoothness, 323
Social learning theory, 346–348
  behavioral assessment, 347–348
Special populations, 358
Speed test, 140
Spline function, 212
Stagewise development, 87
Standard error of measurement, 358
  asymptotic, 191
Standard score, 94, 95, 100
Stanford-Binet I.Q. test, 359
State anxiety, 349
State-trait anxiety inventory, 349–350
States versus traits, 348–350
Statistical lower bound, 249
Statistical Theories of Mental Test Scores, 42

SUBJECT INDEX 377

Stochastic models, 283
Stratified probability sample, 358
Strictly linear model, 199, 201, 202
Strictly nonlinear models, 199–212
Strongly ignorable treatment assignment, 23
Studentized range statistic, 55
Sufficient statistics, 141–144, 155–156
Suppression ratio, 100
System equation, 85

T

Tailored testing, 69, 72, 287
  data, 291
  efficiency, 71
  implied orders, 298
Technical item parameters, 153
Test anxiety inventories, 348
Test bias, 321
Test development, 359
Test fairness, 358
Test information function, 163, 167
  square root, 164, 168, 174
Test interpretation, 357
Test items
  binary, 166
  graded, 166
  operating characteristics, 169
  unknown, 169
Test norms, 358, 359
Test security, 70
Test unidimensionality, 293
Tetrachoric correlations, 215, 225, 293
Theory construction, 81
Three-factor linear model, 201
Three-ideal-type structure, 335
Three-parameter logistic model, 160
Thurstone's positive manifold, 332
Time-dependent process, 83
Topastic variance, 266
Torgerson, subjective rank order, 336
TORSCA scaling program, 330, 335
Trait anxiety, 349–350
Trait categories
  comprehensive view, 351–353
  diversity of classification, 352
  need, 352
Traits, 351–353
  behavioral diversity, 350
  early view, 346
  generalizability, 345
  modifiability, 353
  popular misconceptions, 346
  versus situations, 345–348
  versus states, 348–351
Treatment group mean, 8, 20
True scores, 283, 299
Truncated normal distribution, 304
"Truth-in-testing" legislation, 362
Two-common factor solution, 227
Two-parameter Beta method, 175
Two-set ordinal data, 287
Two-stage least squares estimator, 189

U

Uncontrolled causal studies, 7, 8
Underprivileged students, 14
Unfair test items, 361
Unidimensional latent space, 160
Unique factors, 216, 217, 232
  scores, 220, 222, 225, 226
Unique maximum condition, 162, 169
Unselected populations, 31
Unweighted least squares, 190
Utilities, 49

V, W, Y

van der Flier index, 290
Varimax rotation, 338
Vienna Determination Apparatus, 152
Walker-Guttman function, 260
Weakly parallel tests, 169
Weighted least-squares estimate, 203
Wide-sense linear models, 199–212
Wide-sense linear regression theory, 208
Yule model, 48